Lecture Notes in Computer Science

Commenced Publication in 1973
Founding and Former Series Editors:
Gerhard Goos, Juris Hartmanis, and Jan van Leeuwen

Norbert Fuhr   Mounia Lalmas
Saadia Malik   Gabriella Kazai (Eds.)

Advances in XML Information Retrieval and Evaluation

4th International Workshop of the Initiative
for the Evaluation of XML Retrieval, INEX 2005
Dagstuhl Castle, Germany, November 28-30, 2005
Revised Selected Papers

 Springer

Volume Editors

Norbert Fuhr
Saadia Malik
University of Duisburg-Essen
Faculty of Engineering Sciences, Information Systems
Lotharstr. 65, 47048 Duisburg, Germany
E-mail: {fuhr,malik}@is.informatik.uni-duisburg.de

Mounia Lalmas
Gabriella Kazai
Queen Mary University of London
Department of Computer Science
Mile End Road, London E1 4NS, UK
E-mail: {mounia,gabs}@dcs.qmul.ac.uk

Library of Congress Control Number: 2006927241

CR Subject Classification (1998): H.3, H.4, H.2

LNCS Sublibrary: SL 3 – Information Systems and Application, incl. Internet/Web
and HCI

ISSN   0302-9743
ISBN-10   3-540-34962-6 Springer Berlin Heidelberg New York
ISBN-13   978-3-540-34962-4 Springer Berlin Heidelberg New York

Springer is a part of Springer Science+Business Media

springer.com

© Springer-Verlag Berlin Heidelberg 2006
Printed in Germany

Typesetting: Camera-ready by author, data conversion by Scientific Publishing Services, Chennai, India
Printed on acid-free paper   SPIN: 11766278   06/3142   5 4 3 2 1 0

Preface

Content-oriented XML retrieval has been receiving increasing interest due to the widespread use of eXtensible Markup Language (XML), which is becoming a standard document format on the Web, in digital libraries, and publishing. By exploiting the enriched source of syntactic and semantic information that XML markup provides, XML information retrieval (IR) systems aim to implement a more focused retrieval strategy and return document components, so-called XML elements – instead of complete documents – in response to a user query. This focused retrieval approach is of particular benefit for collections containing long documents or documents covering a wide variety of topics (e.g., books, user manuals, legal documents, etc.), where users' effort to locate relevant content can be reduced by directing them to the most relevant parts of the documents. Implementing this, more focused, retrieval paradigm means that an XML IR system needs not only to find relevant information in the XML documents, but it also has to determine the appropriate level of granularity to be returned to the user. In addition, the relevance of a retrieved component may be dependent on meeting both content and structural query conditions.

Evaluating the effectiveness of XML retrieval systems, hence, requires a test collection where relevance assessments are provided according to a relevance criterion, which takes into account the imposed structural aspects. In 2002, the INitiative for the Evaluation of XML Retrieval (INEX) started to address these issues. The aim of the INEX initiative is to establish an infrastructure and provide means, in the form of a large XML test collection and appropriate scoring methods, for the evaluation of content-oriented XML retrieval systems. Now, in its fourth year, INEX is an established evaluation forum for XML IR, with over 50 participating organizations worldwide.

2005 was an exciting year for INEX, and brought with it many changes and new aspects to the evaluation. Several new tracks and tasks, a new relevance assessment procedure and new evaluation measures were introduced. In total, seven research tracks were included in INEX 2005, which studied different aspects of XML information access: Ad-hoc retrieval, Interactive, Relevance Feedback, Heterogeneous, Natural Language Processing, and two new tracks for 2005, Multimedia and Document Mining.

The INEX 2005 workshop, held at Schloss Dagstuhl (Germany), November 28–30, 2005, brought together researchers in the field of XML retrieval, who participated in the INEX 2005 evaluation campaign. Participants were able to present and discuss their approach to XML retrieval and evaluation. These proceedings contain revised papers describing work carried out during INEX 2005 in the various tracks.

INEX is funded by the DELOS Network of Excellence on Digital Libraries, to which we are very thankful. We would also like to thank the IEEE Computer

Society and the Lonely Planet for providing us the data sets, which were used to build two of the XML collections used in INEX 2005. We gratefully thank the organizers of the various tasks and tracks who did a superb job, their work is greatly appreciated. Finally, special thanks go to the participating organizations and people for their contributions.

March 2005

Norbert Fuhr
Mounia Lalmas
Saadia Malik
Gabriella Kazai

Organization

Project Leaders

Norbert Fuhr   University of Duisburg-Essen
Mounia Lalmas   Queen Mary, University of London

Contact Persons

Saadia Malik   University of Duisburg-Essen
Zoltan Szlavik   Queen Mary, University of London

Topic Format Specification

Börkur Sigurbjörnsson   University of Amsterdam
Andrew Trotman   University of Otago

Online Relevance Assessment Tool

Benjamin Piwowarski   Universidad de Chile

Evaluation Measures

Gabriella Kazai   Queen Mary, University of London
Arjen P. de Vries   CWI
Paul Ogilvie   Carnegie Mellon University
Benjamin Piwowarski   Universidad de Chile

Relevance Feedback Task

Yosi Mass   IBM Research Lab
Carolyn J. Crouch   University of Minnesota Duluth

Natural Language Processing Task

Shlomo Geva   Queensland University of Technology
Alan Woodley   Queensland University of Technology

Heterogeneous Collection Track

Ray Larson   University of California, Berkeley

Interactive Track

Birger Larsen   Royal School of LIS
Anastasios Tombros   Queen Mary, University of London
Saadia Malik   University of Duisburg-Essen

Document Mining Track

Ludovic Denoyer   Laboratoire d'Informatique de Paris 6
Patrick Gallinari   Laboratoire d'Informatique de Paris 6
Anne-Marie Vercoustre   INRIA

XML Multimedia Track

Roelof van Zwol   Utrecht University
Gabriella Kazai   Queen Mary, University of London
Mounia Lalmas   Queen Mary, University of London

Table of Contents

Methodology

Overview of INEX 2005
Saadia Malik, Gabriella Kazai, Mounia Lalmas, Norbert Fuhr 1

INEX 2005 Evaluation Measures
Gabriella Kazai, Mounia Lalmas 16

EPRUM Metrics and INEX 2005
Benjamin Piwowarski 30

HiXEval: Highlighting XML Retrieval Evaluation
Jovan Pehcevski, James A. Thom 43

The Interpretation of CAS
Andrew Trotman, Mounia Lalmas 58

Multiple Tracks

TIJAH Scratches INEX 2005: Vague Element Selection, Image Search,
Overlap, and Relevance Feedback
*Vojkan Mihajlović, Georgina Ramírez, Thijs Westerveld,
Djoerd Hiemstra, Henk Ernst Blok, Arjen P. de Vries* 72

XFIRM at INEX 2005: Ad-Hoc and Relevance Feedback Tracks
Karen Sauvagnat, Lobna Hlaoua, Mohand Boughanem 88

Ad-Hoc Track

The Effect of Structured Queries and Selective Indexing on XML
Retrieval
Börkur Sigurbjörnsson, Jaap Kamps 104

Searching XML Documents – Preliminary Work
Marcus Hassler, Abdelhamid Bouchachia 119

Query Evaluation with Structural Indices
Paavo Arvola, Jaana Kekäläinen, Marko Junkkari 134

B^3-SDR and Effective Use of Structural Hints
  Roelof van Zwol 146

Field-Weighted XML Retrieval Based on BM25
  Wei Lu, Stephen Robertson, Andrew MacFarlane 161

XML Retrieval Based on Direct Contribution of Query Components
  Gilles Hubert 172

Using the INEX Environment as a Test Bed for Various User Models
for XML Retrieval
  Yosi Mass, Matan Mandelbrod 187

The University of Kaiserslautern at INEX 2005
  Philipp Dopichaj 196

Parameter Estimation for a Simple Hierarchical Generative Model for
XML Retrieval
  Paul Ogilvie, Jamie Callan 211

Probabilistic Retrieval, Component Fusion and Blind Feedback for
XML Retrieval
  Ray R. Larson 225

GPX – Gardens Point XML IR at INEX 2005
  Shlomo Geva 240

Implementation of a High-Speed and High-Precision XML Information
Retrieval System on Relational Databases
  Kei Fujimoto, Toshiyuki Shimizu, Norimasa Terada,
  Kenji Hatano, Yu Suzuki, Toshiyuki Amagasa, Hiroko Kinutani,
  Masatoshi Yoshikawa 254

The Dynamic Retrieval of XML Elements
  Carolyn J. Crouch, Sudip Khanna, Poorva Potnis,
  Nagendra Doddapaneni 268

TopX and XXL at INEX 2005
  Martin Theobald, Ralf Schenkel, Gerhard Weikum 282

When a Few Highly Relevant Answers Are Enough
  Miro Lehtonen 296

RMIT University at INEX 2005: Ad Hoc Track
  Jovan Pehcevski, James A. Thom, S.M.M. Tahaghoghi 306

SIRIUS: A Lightweight XML Indexing and Approximate Search System
at INEX 2005

Eugen Popovici, Gildas Ménier, Pierre-François Marteau 321

Machine Learning Ranking and INEX'05

Jean-Noël Vittaut, Patrick Gallinari 336

Relevance Feedback Track

Relevance Feedback for Structural Query Expansion

Ralf Schenkel, Martin Theobald 344

Natural Language Query Track

NLPX at INEX 2005

Alan Woodley, Shlomo Geva 358

From Natural Language to NEXI, an Interface for INEX 2005 Queries

Xavier Tannier 373

Heterogeneous Track

Processing Heterogeneous Collections in XML Information Retrieval

*Maria Izabel Menezes Azevedo, Klérisson Vinícius Ribeiro Paixão,
Diego Vinícius Castro Pereira* 388

Interactive Track

The Interactive Track at INEX 2005

Birger Larsen, Saadia Malik, Anastasios Tombros 398

What Do Users Think of an XML Element Retrieval System?

Jaap Kamps, Börkur Sigurbjörnsson 411

Users Interaction with the Hierarchically Structured Presentation in
XML Document Retrieval

Heesop Kim, Heejung Son 422

Document Mining Track

XML Documents Clustering by Structures

Richi Nayak, Sumei Xu 432

A Flexible Structured-Based Representation for XML Document Mining
Anne-Marie Vercoustre, Mounir Fegas, Saba Gul,
Yves Lechevallier 443

Sequential Pattern Mining for Structure-Based XML Document
Classification
Calin Garboni, Florent Masseglia, Brigitte Trousse 458

Transforming XML Trees for Efficient Classification and Clustering
Laurent Candillier, Isabelle Tellier, Fabien Torre 469

Clustering XML Documents Using Self-organizing Maps for Structures
M. Hagenbuchner, A. Sperduti, A.C. Tsoi, F. Trentini,
F. Scarselli, M. Gori 481

Multimedia Track

INEX 2005 Multimedia Track
Roelof van Zwol, Gabriella Kazai, Mounia Lalmas 497

Integrating Text Retrieval and Image Retrieval in XML Document
Searching
D. Tjondronegoro, J. Zhang, J. Gu, A. Nguyen, S. Geva 511

Combining Image and Structured Text Retrieval
D.N.F. Awang Iskandar, Jovan Pehcevski, James A. Thom,
S.M.M. Tahaghoghi 525

Multimedia Strategies for B^3-SDR, Based on Principal Component
Analysis
Roelof van Zwol 540

Author Index 555

Overview of INEX 2005

Saadia Malik[1], Gabriella Kazai[2], Mounia Lalmas[2], and Norbert Fuhr[1]

[1] Information Systems, University of Duisburg-Essen, Duisburg, Germany
{malik, fuhr}@is.informatik.uni-duisburg.de
[2] Department of Computer Science, Queen Mary, University of London, London, UK
{gabs, mounia}@dcs.qmul.ac.uk

Abstract. Since 2002, INEX has been working towards the goal of establishing an infrastructure, in the form of a large XML test collection and appropriate scoring methods, for the evaluation of content-oriented XML retrieval systems. This paper provides an overview of the work carried out as part of INEX 2005.

1 Introduction

The INitiative for the Evaluation of XML retrieval (INEX) has, since 2002, been working towards the goal of establishing an infrastructure, in the form of a large XML test collection and appropriate scoring methods, for the evaluation of content-oriented XML retrieval systems. As a result of a collaborative effort, during the course of 2005, the INEX test collection has been further extended with an additional 4 712 new scientific articles from publications of the IEEE Computer Society, 87 new topics, and relevance judgements for 63 of these topics. Using the constructed test collection and the developed set of measures, the retrieval effectiveness of the participating organisations were evaluated and their results compared.

2005 has brought with it a lot of changes and new aspects to the evaluation. Several new tracks and tasks, a new relevance assessment procedure and new evaluation measures [2] were introduced. This paper presents an overview of these aspects and describes the work carried out as part of INEX 2005.

Section 2 gives a brief summary of this year's participants. Section 3 provides an overview of the expanded test collection. Section 4 outlines the retrieval tasks in the main ad-hoc track. Section 5 briefly reports on the submission runs for the ad hoc retrieval tasks. Section 6 describes the relevance assessment phase. The different measures used to evaluate retrieval performance are described in a separate paper [2]. Section 7 provides a short description of the tracks of INEX 2005. The paper wraps up with conclusions and outlook to INEX 2006.

2 Participating Organizations

In response to the call for participation, issued in March 2005, 35 old and 12 new organizations registered. However throughout the year a number of groups dropped out due to resource requirements, while 11 further groups joined the initiative. The final 41 active groups along with their participation details are summarised in Table 1.

N. Fuhr et al. (Eds.): INEX 2005, LNCS 3977, pp. 1–15, 2006.

Table 1. List of active INEX 2005 participants

Organisations	Submitted topics	Assessed topics	Submitted runs
Max-Planck-Institut für Informatik	1	4	10
Royal School of LIS	5	2	0
University of California, Berkeley	2	2	20
University of Granada	4	2	0
University of Amsterdam	4	2	18
University of Otago	6	2	0
Queen Mary, University of London	0	2	0
University of Toronto	5	2	0
Utrecht University	6	2	16
City University London and Microsoft Research Cambridge	5	2	6
University of Kaiserslautern	3	2	14
IRIT	5	2	26
RMIT University	6	2	26
École Nationale Supérieure des Mines de Saint-Etienne	6	2	0
Queensland University of Technology	4	2	28
Universtity of Klagenfurt (ISYS)	0	2	3
University of Tampere	4	2	17
Carnegie Mellon University	3	2	4
University of Illinois at Urbana-Champaign	7	2	0
IBM Haifa Research Lab	6	2	26
University of Minnesota Duluth	8	2	24
Universidade Estadual de Montes Claros	4	2	8
The Hebrew University of Jeru	6	2	14
UCLA	6	2	2
University of Udine	0	2	0
VALORIA Lab, University of South-Brittany	0	2	0
Nagoya University	6	2	0
Laboratoire d'Informatique de Paris 6 (LIP6)	4	2	17
University of Waterloo	2	2	7
Kyungpook National University	0	2	9
University of Helsinki	0	2	7
Cirquid Project (CWI and University of Twente)	6	2	16
Universität Duisburg-Essen	1	1	0
Oslo University College	2	2	5
Universidad de Chile	0	1	0
Organizations participating only in the XML document mining track			
INRIA			
Charles de Gaulle University			
University of Wolongong			
Organization participating only in the interactive track			
Rutgers University			

3   The Test Collection

Test collections, as traditionally used in the information retrieval (IR), consist of three parts: a set of documents, a set of information needs called topics and a set of relevance assessments listing the relevant documents for each topic. Although a test collection for XML IR consists of the same three parts, each component is rather different from its traditional IR counterpart.

Table 2. New additions to the IEEE collection in INEX 2005

id	Publication title	Year	Size (Mb)	No. of articles
an	IEEE Annals of the History of Computing	2002-2004	5.1	118
cg	IEEE Computer Graphics and Applications	2002-2004	7.6	220
co	Computer	2002-2004	14.8	664
cs	Computing in Science & Engineering	2002-2004	6.4	219
ds	IEEE Distributed Systems Online	2004	0.6	39
dt	IEEE Design & Test of Computers	2002-2004	6.1	263
ex	IEEE Intelligent Systems	2002-2004	8.2	240
ic	IEEE Internet Computing	2002-2004	7.0	264
it	IT Professional	2002-2004	3.4	142
mi	IEEE Micro	2002-2004	5.2	195
mu	IEEE Multimedia	2002-2004	4.6	161
pc	IEEE Pervasive Computing	2002-2004	5.1	160
so	IEEE Software	2002-2004	7.6	341
sp	IEEE Security & Privacy	2003-2004	4.4	179
tb	IEEE Transactions On Computational Biology & Bioinformatics	2004	0.8	12
tc	IEEE Transactions on Computers	2002-2004	27.5	319
td	IEEE Transactions on Parallel & Distributed Systems	2002-2004	23.2	235
tg	IEEE Transactions on Visualization and Computer Graphics	2002-2004	9.2	109
tk	IEEE Transactions on Knowledge and Data Engineering	2002-2004	26.9	255
tm	IEEE Transactions On Mobile Computing	2002-2004	6.5	79
tp	IEEE Transactions on Pattern Analysis and Machine Intelligence	2002-2004	28.9	350
tq	IEEE Transactions On Dependable and Secure Computing	2002-2004	1.1	12
ts	IEEE Transactions of Software Engineering	2002-2004	18.4	192
	Total new XML content added in INEX 2005 (incl. volume files):		228.6	4 768

In IR test collections, documents are considered units of unstructured text, queries are generally treated as bags of terms or phrases, and relevance assessments provide judgments whether a document as a whole is relevant to a query or not. XML documents, on the other hand, organize their content into smaller, nested structural elements. Each of these elements in the document's hierarchy, along with the document itself (the root of the hierarchy), represents a retrievable unit. In addition, with the use of XML query languages, users of an XML IR system can express their information need as a combination of content and structural conditions, e.g. users can restrict their search to specific structural elements within the collection. Consequently the relevance assessments for an XML collection must also consider the structural nature of the documents and provide assessments at different levels of the document hierarchy. These three components of the INEX test collection are described in the next sections.

3.1 Documents

This year the collection of documents that forms the INEX ad-hoc test collection has been extended with further publications donated by the IEEE Computer Society. The additional new resources are summarised in table 2. A total of 4 712 new articles (excluding the 56 new volume.xml files) from the period of 2002-2004 have been added to the previous collection of 12 107 articles, giving a total of 16 819 articles. This meant that the INEX ad-hoc test collection grew by 228Mb in size to a total of 764Mb.

3.2 Topics

As in previous years, INEX 2005 distinguished two basic types of topics: Content-Only (CO) and Content-And-Structure (CAS) topics. These topic types reflect two types of users with varying levels of knowledge about the structure of the searched collection. The first type simulates ignorant users, who either do not have any knowledge of the document structure or who choose not to use such knowledge. This profile is likely to fit most users searching XML digital libraries. The latter type of user aims to make use of any insight about the document structure that they may possess. They may then use this knowledge as a precision enhancing device in trying to make the information need more concrete. This user type is more likely to fit librarians.

Building on these basic types, INEX 2005, defined and investigated various extensions and interpretations of topic types.

Content-Only + Structure (CO+S). In an effort to investigate the usefulness of structural hints, the Content-Only (CO) topics, as used in previous years of INEX, were extended into so-called Content-Only + Structure (CO+S) topics. The aim was that the use of these topics enabled the comparison of a system's performance across two retrieval scenarios (on the same topic): when structural hints are taken into account (+S) and when these hints are ignored (CO).

As in previous years, queries with content-only conditions (CO queries) were defined as requests that ignore the document structure and contain only content related conditions, e.g. only specify what an element should be about without specifying what that component is. The topic format of CO queries includes a topic title, description and narrative.

The extended CO+S topics in INEX 2005 included an optional field called CAS title, which is a representation of the same information need but including additional knowledge in the form of structural hints (see the discussion on Topic format in this section).

Content-And-Structure (CAS). The aim of the Content-And-Structure (CAS) topics this year was to support investigations on the different possible interpretations of structural constraint within a query, i.e. strict or vague, and the effect of this interpretation on retrieval effectiveness.

```
<inex_topic topic_id="231" query_type="CO+S" ct_no="98" >
 <title>markov chains in graph related algorithms</title>
 <castitle>
    //article//sec[about(.,+"markov chains" +algorithm +graphs)]
 </castitle>
 <description>Retrieve information about the use of markov chains
    in graph theory and in graphs-related algorithms.
 </description>
 <narrative>I have just finished my MSc. in mathematics, in the field
    of stochastic processes. My research was in a subject related to
    Markov chains. My aim is to find possible implementations of my
    knowledge in current research. I'm mainly interested in
    applications in graph theory, that is, algorithms related to
    graphs that use the theory of markov chains. I'm interested in
    at least a short specification of the nature of implementation
    (e.g. what is the exact theory used, and to which purpose),
    hence the relevant elements should be sections, paragraphs or
    even abstracts of documents, but in any case, should be part of
    the content of the document (as opposed to, say, vt, or bib).
 </narrative>
</inex_topic>
```

Fig. 1. A CO+S topic from the INEX 2005 test collection

The actual definition of CAS topics have not changed from previous years: CAS topics are topic statements that contain explicit references to the XML structure, and explicitly specify the contexts of the user's interest (e.g. target elements) and/or the contexts of certain search concepts (e.g. containment conditions). More precisely, a CAS query contains two kinds of structural constraints: where to look (i.e. the support elements), and what to return (i.e. the target elements).

What was new in INEX 2005, was the explicit nature in which structural constraints were to be interpreted by a search system. Each structural constraint could be considered as a strict (must be matched exactly) or vague (simply as hints) criterion. The former closer reflects the database-oriented view, where only records that exactly match the specified structure should be returned to the user. The latter is closer to the IR view, where users' information need is assumed to be inherently uncertain. Four combinations of vague and strict interpretations of the structural constraints are then possible, depending on how the target elements and/or the containment conditions are treated:

- VVCAS: where the structural constraints in both the target elements and the support elements are interpreted as vague.
- SVCAS: where the structural constraints in the target elements are interpreted as strict and the structural constraints in the support elements are interpreted as vague.
- VSCAS: where the structural constraints in the target elements are interpreted as vague and the structural constraints in the support elements are interpreted as strict.
- SSCAS: where the structural constraints in both the target elements and the support elements are interpreted as strict.

```
<inex_topic topic_id="269"  query_type="CAS" ct_no="117" >
 <title> </title>
 <castitle>
   //article[about(.,interconnected networks)]//p[about(.,
   Crossbar networks)]
 </castitle>
 <description>We are looking for paragraphs that talk about
   Crossbar networks from articles that talk about interconnected
   networks.
 </description>
 <narrative>With networking between processors gaining significance,
   interconnected networks has become an important concept.
   Crossbar network is one of the interconnected networks. We are
   looking for information on what crossbar networks exactly are,
   how they operate and why they are used to connect processors.
   Any article discussing interconnected networks in the context
   of crossbar networks is considered to be relevant. Articles
   talking about interconnected networks such as Omega networks
   are not considered to be relevant. This information would be
   used to prepare a presentation for a lecture on the topic, and
   hence information on crossbar networks makes an element relevant.
 </narrative>
</inex_topic>
```

Fig. 2. A CAS topic from the INEX 2005 test collection

Topic format. Both CO+S and CAS topics are made up of several parts, each representing the same information need, but for different purposes.

- **Title:** A short explanation of the information need. It serves as a summary of the content of the user's information need. A word in the title can have an optional $+$ or $-$ prefix, where $+$ is used to emphasize an important concept, and $-$ is used to denote an unwanted concept.
- **CAS Title (castitle):** A short explanation of the information need, specifying any structural requirements. The CAS title is optional in CO+S topics, but mandatory in CAS topics. Similarly to topic title, a word in the CAS title can have a $+$ or $-$ prefix. CAS titles are expressed in the query language of NEXI [5].
- **Parent:** Only used for CAS topics. Each CAS topic containing more than one about function was submitted with a set of sub-topics describing the information need of each single about clause. In order to match the sub-topics with the topic the parent had to be identified in the sub-topic.
- **Description:** a one or two sentence natural language definition of the information need.
- **Narrative:** a detailed explanation of the information need and a description of what makes a document/component relevant or not. The narrative was there to explain not only what information is being sought for, but also the context and motivation of the information need, i.e., why the information is being sought and what work task it might help to solve. The latter was required for the interactive track (see Section 7.1).

The title and the description had to be interchangeable. This was a requirement of the natural language processing track (see Section 7.4). The DTD of the topics is shown in Figure 3.

```
<!ELEMENT inex_topic
(title,castitle?,parent?,description,
  narrative)>
 <!ATTLIST inex_topic
   topic_id    CDATA   #REQUIRED
   query_type  CDATA   #REQUIRED
   ct_no       CDATA   #REQUIRED
>
<!ELEMENT title       (#PCDATA)>
<!ELEMENT castitle    (#PCDATA)>
<!ELEMENT parent      (#PCDATA)>
<!ELEMENT description (#PCDATA)>
<!ELEMENT narrative   (#PCDATA)>
```

Fig. 3. Topic DTD

Attributes of a topic are: topic_id (which in INEX 2005 ranges from 202 to 288), query_type (with possible values of "CAS" or "CO+S") and ct_no, which refers to the candidate topic number (ranging from 1 to 145[1]). Examples of both types of topics are given in Figures 1 and 2.

Topic creation. Topics were created by the participating groups. Each group was asked to submit up to 6 candidate topics (3 CO+S and 3 CAS). A detailed guideline was provided to the participants for the topic creation [7].

Four steps were identified for this process: 1) Initial Topic Statement creation, 2) Collection Exploration, 3) Topic Refinement, and 4) Topic Selection. The first three steps were performed by the participants themselves while the selection of topics was decided by the organisers.

During the first step, participants created their initial topic statement. These were treated as a user's description of his/her information need and were formed without regard to system capabilities or collection peculiarities to avoid artificial or collection biased queries. During the collection exploration phase, participants estimated the number of relevant documents/components to their candidate topics. The HyREX retrieval system [1] was made available to participants to help with this task. Participants were asked to judge the top 25 retrieved results and record for each found relevant document/component its file name and its XPath. Those topics having at least 2 relevant documents/components but less than 20 documents/components were to be submitted as candidate topics. In the topic refinement stage, the topics were finalised ensuring coherency and that each part of the topic could be used in stand-alone fashion.

---

[1] Note that, due to the withdrawal of some topics, this is not a continuous range.

Table 3. Statistics on CAS and CO+S topics on the INEX 2005 test collection

	CAS	CO+S
Number of topics	40	47
Average length of title (in words)	-	3.8
Boolean operators (and/or) in title	-	44
Prefix operators (+/-) in title	-	7
Phrases in title	-	20
Boolean operators (and/or) in castitle	5	13
Prefix operators (+/-) in castitle	2	9
Phrases in castitle	52	17
Average length of topic description (in words)	13	17
Average length of narrative (in words)	73	91

After the completion of the first three stages, topics were submitted to INEX. A total of 139 candidate topics were received, of which 87 topics (40 CO+S and 47 CAS) were selected to form the final set of topics added to the test collection. Topic selection was based on a combination of criteria such as 1) balancing the number of topics across all participants, 2) eliminating topics that were considered too ambiguous or too difficult to judge, 3) uniqueness of topics, and 4) considering their suitability to the different tracks. Table 3 shows some statistics on the final set of INEX 2005 topics.

4   Retrieval Tasks

The main retrieval task at INEX 2005 was defined as the ad-hoc retrieval of XML documents [8]. In information retrieval literature, ad-hoc retrieval is described as a simulation of how a library might be used. It involves the searching of a static set of documents using a new set of topics. While the principle is the same, the difference for INEX is that the library consists of XML documents, the queries may contain both content and structural conditions and, in response to a query, arbitrary XML elements may be retrieved from the library.

Unlike previous years, INEX 2005 distinguished several retrieval strategies, each based on different assumptions regarding a search system's output. These strategies have been explicitly investigated within the ad-hoc sub-tasks that build on the use of CO and CO+S queries. For tasks based on the use of CAS queries, systems' were assumed to follow the Thorough retrieval strategy only.

4.1   Ad-Hoc Sub-tasks Based on CO Queries

CO.Focussed: This strategy was intended for approaches concerned with the focussed retrieval of XML elements, i.e. aiming at targeting the appropriate level of granularity of relevant content that should be returned to the user for a given topic. An explicit assumption here was that a retrieval run should not contain any overlapping elements. The aim was for systems to find the most exhaustive and specific element on a path within a given document containing relevant information and return to the user only this most appropriate unit of retrieval. In the case where an XML retrieval system has estimated a parent and one if its child elements to be equally exhaustive and specific for a given topic, the parent element were to be returned. In addition, when a parent has been estimated as more exhaustive than one of its child elements, but the child element has been estimated as more specific than its parent, then the child element was to be selected. In this way, preference for specificity over exhaustivity was given.

CO.Thorough: This strategy was intended for XML retrieval approaches that do not deal with the problem of overlap when generating their output list for the evaluation, but consider this an interface and results presentation issue, which is to be resolved at a later stage, outside the scope of the evaluation. The aim here was for systems to find all relevant elements within the collection. Due to the nature of relevance in XML retrieval (e.g. if a child element is relevant, so will be its parent, although to a greater or lesser extent), an XML retrieval system that has estimated an element to be relevant may decide to return all its ancestor elements. This means that runs for this task may contain a large number of overlapping elements. It is however a challenge to rank these elements appropriately, as systems that rank highly exhaustive and specific elements before less exhaustive and specific ones were to obtain better effectiveness.

CO.FetchBrowse: This strategy was intended for XML retrieval approaches that are based on a mixture of document retrieval and element retrieval strategies. The aim of the fetch and browse retrieval strategy was to first identify relevant articles (the fetching phase), and then to identify the most exhaustive and specific elements within the fetched articles (the browsing phase). In the fetching phase, articles had to be ranked according to how exhaustive and specific they were (i.e. the most exhaustive and specific articles were to be ranked first). In the browsing phase, ranking had to be done according to how exhaustive and specific the relevant elements in the article were, compared to other elements in the same article.

4.2   Ad-Hoc Sub-tasks Based on CO+S Queries

Upon discovering that a CO query returned many irrelevant hits, a user may decide to add structural hints in order to improve precision. These structural hints were expressed in the `<castitle>` part of the CO+S topics, which was then used as the query for the CO+S sub-tasks. The aim of the CO+S sub-tasks was to specifically investigate the usefulness of the structural hints. As for the CO sub-tasks, three retrieval strategies were defined: COS.Focussed, COS.Thorough and COS.FetchBrowse.

4.3   Ad-Hoc Sub-tasks Based on CAS Queries

As described in section 3.2, different interpretations of CAS topics on the basis of target and support elements were possible, resulting in the sub-tasks of VVCAS, SVCAS, VSCAS and SSCAS. In these sub-tasks, the aim was to retrieve the most exhaustive and specific elements with respect to the topic of request, where overlap among retrieval results was allowed (Thorough strategy). An analysis of the outcome of the CAS sub-tasks can be found in a separate paper [4].

5   Submissions

During the retrieval runs, participating organisations evaluated the 87 INEX 2005 topics (40 CO+S and 47 CAS queries) against the IEEE Computer Society document collection and produced a list (or set) of document components (XML elements) as their retrieval results for each topic. The top 1500 components in a topic's retrieval results were then submitted to INEX. Table 4 summarises the submissions to the different ad-hoc tasks. For each topic, around 500 articles along with their components were pooled from all the submissions in round robin way for relevance assessment. Table 5 shows the pooling effect on the CAS and CO+S topics.

Table 4. Number of runs submitted to the different ad-hoc tasks

CO.Focussed	44	COS.Focussed	27
CO.Thorough	55	COS.Thorough	33
CO.FetchBrowse	42	COS.FetchBrowse	25
VVCAS	28	SSCAS	25
VSCAS	23	SVCAS	23

Table 5. Pooling effect for CAS and CO+S topics

	CAS topics	CO+S topics
Number of articles submitted	176 735	236 060
Number of articles in pools	23 250	20 135
Number of components submitted	812 207	1 337 214
Number of components in pools	92 905	80 019

6   Assessments

6.1   Relevance Dimensions and Scales

Relevance assessments were given according to two relevance dimensions [9]:

- **Exhaustivity (e)**, which describes the extent to which the document component discusses the topic of request.
- **Specificity (s)**, which describes the extent to which the document component focuses on the topic of request.

While the above definition of the relevance dimensions has remained unchanged since 2003, the scale that these dimensions were measured on has been revised in INEX 2005. The scale for exhaustivity was changed to 3 + 1 levels: highly exhaustive ($e = 2$), somewhat exhaustive ($e = 1$), not exhaustive ($e = 0$) and "too small" ($e =?$). The latter category of "too small" was introduced with the aim to allow assessors to label document components, which although contained relevant information were too small to sensibly reason about their level of exhaustivity[2]. Specificity was measured automatically on a continuous scale with values in $[0, 1]$, where $s = 1$ represents a fully specific component (i.e. contains only relevant information). Values of specificity were derived on the basis of what ratio of a document component has been highlighted by the assessor (see section 6.2).

We denote the relevance degree of an assessed component, given by the combined values of exhaustivity and specificity, as (e, s), where $e \in \{?, 0, 1, 2\}$ and $s \in [0, 1]$. For example, $(2, 0.72)$ denotes a highly exhaustive component, 72% of which is relevant content.

6.2   Relevance Assessments Procedure

A relevance assessment guideline explaining the relevance dimensions and how and what to assess was distributed to the participants [9]. This guide also contained the manual to the online assessment tool, developed by Benjamin Piwowarski. The tool is referred to as X-RAI (XML Retrieval Assessment Interface - see Figures 4 and 5).

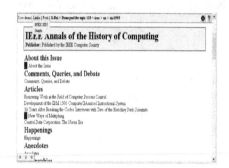
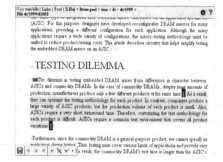

Fig. 4. X-RAI in assessment mode   **Fig. 5.** X-RAI Article view

In order to reduce assessment effort, a highlighting procedure was used in INEX 2005 leading to the following process for assessment:

- In the first pass, assessors were asked to highlight text fragments that contained only relevant information - see Figure 5.
- In the second pass, assessors judged the exhaustivity level of any elements that had highlighted parts.

As a result of this process, any elements that have been fully highlighted were automatically labeled as fully specific ($s = 1$). The main advantage of this highlighting

---

[2] The notion of "too small" has originally been employed in INEX 2002, there as a degree of coverage. It was removed from subsequent INEX evaluations as it was showed that assessors often labeled descendant components of target elements in CAS queries as "too small". Its reintroduction into the evaluation, but this time, more appropriately, as a degree of exhaustivity, was deemed necessary in order to free assessors from the burden of having to assess very small text fragments whose level of exhaustivity could not be sensibly decided.

approach was that assessors now only had to judge the exhaustivity level of the elements that have highlighted parts (in the second phase). The specificity of any other (partially highlighted) elements was calculated automatically as a function of the contained relevant and irrelevant content, and more specifically, as the ratio of relevant content to all content, measured in number of words or characters. All non-highlighted elements were automatically assumed as not exhaustive ($e = 0$).

6.3 CAS Assessments

This year there were four sets of CAS judgments, one for each of the four CAS interpretations - each derived from the same initial set of judgments. These are described in [4].

7 INEX 2005 Tracks

In addition to the main ad hoc track, six research tracks were included in INEX 2005, each studying different aspects of XML information access: Interactive, Relevance Feedback, Heterogeneous, Natural Language Processing, and two new tracks for 2005, Multimedia and Document Mining tracks.

7.1 Interactive Track

In its second year, the Interactive Track (iTrack) focused on addressing some fundamental issues of interactive XML retrieval. In addition, the track also expanded by including two additional tasks and by attracting more participating groups. A total of 11 research groups and 108 test persons participated in the three different tasks that were included in the track. Details of the track can be found in [3].

7.2 Relevance Feedback Track

The Relevance Feedback track investigated approaches for queries that also include structural hints (rather than content-only queries as in 2004). To limit the number of submissions, a subset of ad-hoc tasks were chosen for participants to test their relevance feedback algorithms. These included CO.Thorough, CO+S.Thorough and VVCAS tasks. The reported evaluation scores for each relevance feedback submission measured the relative and absolute improvement of the relevance feedback run over the original base run. Five groups submitted 15 runs for CO.Thorough task, 9 runs for COS.Thorough task and 3 runs for VVCAS task.

7.3 Heterogeneous Track

The Heterogeneous track expanded by studying new collections with different DTDs and their effect on XML IR system effectiveness. The following document collections have been made available:

- Berkeley (Library catalog entries for CS literature): 12 800 XML items
- CompuScience (Bibliographic entries from the Computer Science database of FIZ Karlsruhe): 250 987 XML items.

- bibdbpub (BibTeX converted to XML by the IS group at Univ. of Duisburg-Essen): 3 465 XML items.
- dblp (Bibliographic entries from the Digital Bibliography & Library Project in Trier): 501 101 XML items.
- hcibib (Human-Computer Interaction Resources, bibliography from www.hcibib. org): 26 402 XML items.
- qmuldcsdpub (Publications database of QMUL Department of Computer Science): 2 024 XML items.
- ZDNet (Articles and Comments) provided by ZDNet.com to the INEX evaluation: 96 351 items (4 734 Articles and 91 617 comments on those articles). This sub-collection was added in 2005.

7.4 Natural Language Processing Track

The Natural Language Processing track (NLPX) focused on whether it is possible to express topics in natural language, which is then to be used as basis for retrieval. For this year, two tasks were defined NLQ2NEXI and NLQ. NLQ2NEXI required the translation of a natural language query, provided in the element of a topic, into a formal INEX <title> query element. The NLQ task had no restrictions on the use of any NLP techniques to interpret the queries as they appeared in the <description> element of a topic. The objective was not only to compare between different NLP based systems, but to also compare the results obtained with natural language queries with the results obtained with NEXI queries by any other system in the ad hoc track. During the topic creation stage, it was ensured that the description component of the topics were equivalent in meaning to their corresponding NEXI title, so it was possible to re-use the same topics, relevance assessments and evaluation procedures as in the ad hoc track. The topic descriptions were used as input to natural language processing tools, which processed them into representations suitable for XML search engines. Three groups submitted 12 runs for CO.Focussed task, 5 runs for COS.Thorough task, 5 runs for COS.FetchBrowse and 8 runs for CAS tasks. The results showed that NLQ2NEXI task performed better than the NLQ task.

7.5 Multimedia Track

The main objective of the Multimedia track was to provide a pilot evaluation platform and forum for structured document access systems that do not only include text in the retrieval process, but also other types of media, such as images, speech, and video. Full details of the track can be found in [6].

7.6 Document Mining Track

The aim of the Document Mining track, run in collaboration with the PASCAL network of Excellence[3], was to develop machine learning methods for structured data mining and to evaluate these methods for XML document mining tasks. The track in 2005 focused on classification and clustering for XML documents. Two new collections were

---

[3] http://www.pascal-network.org/

developed: The WIPO corpus which is composed of 75 250 XML documents, and the MovieDB corpus (based on the Internet Movie Database) which consists of 9 463 XML documents.

8   Conclusion and Outlook

INEX 2005 has shown that XML retrieval is a challenging field. In addition to learning more about XML retrieval approaches, INEX 2005 has introduced several new aspects and made several changes to the evaluation methodology:

- The document collection was extended to include now 16 819 articles of the IEEE Computer Society's publications, increasing the size of the collection to a total of 764Mb (containing over 10 million XML elements). A number of new document collections were also added and used in the various tracks. For example, the multimedia track conducted experiments using the Lonely Planet WorldGuide XML collection.
- A new assessment procedure was introduced with the aim to reduce assessment effort (both with respect to cognitive load and time required).
- A range of ad-hoc retrieval tasks were investigated with the aim to address specific research questions, e.g. the impact of structure as precision enhancing device or the interpretation of structural query constraints.
- In addition to the ad-hoc retrieval tasks, several retrieval strategies were studied, each based on different assumptions regarding what users would want to obtain as the outcome of a search.
- A new set of evaluation measures were employed with the aim to address problematic issues encountered with precision-recall like metrics.
- INEX 2005 run a total of 7 tracks, each studying different aspects of XML information access: Ad-hoc, Interactive, Relevance Feedback, Heterogeneous, Natural Language Processing, and two new tracks for 2005, Multimedia and Document Mining tracks.

INEX 2006 will start in March of this year. In addition to the current tracks, INEX 2006 will have two new tracks: User case studies and XML entity ranking tracks. In addition, a new test collection will be used, based on the Wikipedia project. Statistical analysis of the various measures employed are also currently ongoing; results of this will provide input for selecting which of these measures to use in 2006.

References

1. Norbert Fuhr, Norbert Gövert, and Kai Großjohann. HyREX: Hyper-media retrieval engine for XML. In *Proceedings of the 25th Annual International Conference on Research and Development in Information Retrieval*, page 449, 2002. Demonstration.
2. Gabriella Kazai and Mounia Lalmas. INEX 2005 evaluation metrics. In *Advances in XML Information Retrieval and Evaluation: Fourth Workshop of the INitiative for the Evaluation of XML Retrieval (INEX 2005), Lecture Notes in Computer Science, Vol 3977, Springer-Verlag*, 2006.

3. Birger Larsen, Saadia Malik, and Anastasios Tombros. The interactive track at INEX 2005. In *Advances in XML Information Retrieval and Evaluation: Fourth Workshop of the INitiative for the Evaluation of XML Retrieval (INEX 2005), Lecture Notes in Computer Science, Vol 3977, Springer-Verlag,* 2006.

4. Andrew Trotman and Mounia Lalmas. The Interpretation of CAS. In *Advances in XML Information Retrieval and Evaluation: Fourth Workshop of the INitiative for the Evaluation of XML Retrieval (INEX 2005), Lecture Notes in Computer Science, Vol 3977, Springer-Verlag,* 2006.

5. Andrew Trotman and Börkur Sigurbjörnsson. Narrowed extended XPATH I (NEXI). In *Advances in XML Information Retrieval, Third Workshop of the Initiative for the Evaluation of XML Retrieval (INEX 2004), Dagstuhl, Germany, December 6-8, 2004, Revised Selected Papers, Lecture Notes in Computer Science, Vol 3493,Springer-Verlag,* page 16–40, 2005.

6. Roelof van Zwol, Gabriella Kazai, and Mounia Lalmas. INEX 2005 multimedia track. In *Advances in XML Information Retrieval and Evaluation: Fourth Workshop of the INitiative for the Evaluation of XML Retrieval (INEX 2005), Lecture Notes in Computer Science, Vol 3977, Springer-Verlag,* 2006.

7. Börkur Sigurbjörnsson, Andrew Trotman, Shlomo Geva, Mounia Lalmas, Birger Larsen, and Saadia Malik INEX 2005 Guidelines for Topic Development. In *INEX 2005 Workshop Pre-Proceedings, Dagstuhl, Germany, November 28–30, 2005,* page 375–384, 2005.

8. Mounia Lalmas INEX 2005 Retrieval Task and Result Submission Specification. In INEX 2005 Workshop Pre-Proceedings, Dagstuhl, Germany, November 28–30, 2005, page 385–390, 2005.

9. Mounia Lalmas and Benjamin Piwowarski INEX 2005 Relevance Assessment Guide. In INEX 2005 Workshop Pre-Proceedings, Dagstuhl, Germany, November 28–30, 2005, page 391–400, 2005.

INEX 2005 Evaluation Measures

Gabriella Kazai and Mounia Lalmas

Queen Mary, University of London,
Mile End Road, London, UK
{gabs, mounia}@dcs.qmul.ac.uk

Abstract. This paper describes the official measures of retrieval effectiveness employed in INEX 2005: the eXtended Cumulated Gain (XCG) measures. In addition, results of correlation analysis are reported, examining the correlation between the employed quantisation functions and the different measures for the INEX 2005 ad-hoc tasks.

1 Introduction

In INEX 2005, a new set of measures, the eXtended Cumulated Gain (XCG) measures, were introduced with the aim to provide a suitable evaluation framework, where the dependency among XML document components can be taken into account. In particular, two aspects of dependency were considered: 1.) near-misses, which are document components that are structurally related to relevant components, such as a neighbouring paragraph or a container section, and 2.) overlap, which regards the situation when the same text fragment is referenced multiple times, as in the case when a paragraph and its container section are both retrieved.

The XCG measures are an extension of the Cumulated Gain based measures proposed in [2]. These measures were chosen as they have been developed specifically for graded relevance values and with the aim to allow IR systems to be credited according to the retrieved documents' degree of relevance. The motivation for the XCG measures was to extend the CG metrics for the problem of content-oriented XML IR evaluation, where the dependency of XML elements is taken into account. The extension lies partly in the way the gain value for a given document component is calculated via the definition of so-called relevance value (RV) functions, and partly in the definition of the ideal recall-bases. The former allows to consider the dependency of result elements within a system's output, while the latter regards the dependency of elements within the test collection's recall-base[1].

The new measures aim to overcome the limitations of `inex-eval`, the previous official measure of INEX. One such issue is that `inex-eval` is not well-suited to handle multiple degrees of relevance. In addition, `inex-eval` has no mechanisms for both rewarding partial scores to near-misses and to handle overlap.

---

[1] The term recall-base refers to the collection of assessments within the test collection that forms the ground-truth for the evaluation experiments.

N. Fuhr et al. (Eds.): INEX 2005, LNCS 3977, pp. 16–29, 2006.

2   Definition of an Ideal Recall-Base

As described in [6], in INEX 2005 relevance assessments were given according to two relevance dimensions: *exhaustivity* (*e*) and *specificity* (*s*). The relevance degree of an assessed component, given by the combined values of exhaustivity and specificity, is denoted as (e, s), where $e \in \{?, 0, 1, 2\}$ and $s \in [0, 1]$. The value of $e =?$ is used to denote elements judged as 'too small'. Within the evaluation, $e =?$ is equated to $e = 0$.

An important property of the exhaustivity dimension is its propagation effect, reflecting that if a component is relevant to a query, then all its ascendant elements will also be relevant. Due to this property, all nodes along a relevant path[2] are always relevant (with varying degrees of relevance), hence resulting in a recall-base comprised of sets of overlapping elements.

In order to evaluate tasks based on the Focussed retrieval strategy[3], where overlap is not allowed, it is necessary to remove overlap from the collected assessments in the recall-base. For this purpose, we define an ideal recall-base as a subset of the full recall-base, where overlap between relevant reference elements is removed so that the identified subset represents the set of ideal answers, i.e. those elements that should be returned to the user.

The selection of ideal nodes into the ideal recall-base is done through the definition of preference relations on the possible (e, s) pairs and a methodology for traversing an article's XML tree. The preference relations are given by quantisation functions, while the following methodology is adopted to traverse an XML tree and select the ideal nodes: Given any two components on a relevant path, the component with the higher quantised score is selected. In case two components' scores are equal, the one higher in the tree is chosen (i.e. parent/ascendant). The procedure is applied recursively to all overlapping pairs of components along a relevant path until one element remains. After all relevant paths have been processed, a final filtering is applied to eliminate any possible overlap among ideal components, keeping from two overlapping ideal paths the shortest one.

The use of an ideal recall-base supports the evaluation viewpoint (needed for the Focussed strategy) whereby components in the ideal recall-base *should* be retrieved, while the retrieval of near-misses *could* be rewarded as partial successes, but other systems *need not* be penalised for not retrieving such near-misses.

The following quantisation functions are used in INEX 2005: $quant_{strict}$ (Equation 1), $quant_{gen}$ (Equation 2) and $quant_{genLifted}$ (Equation 3). The strict function models a user for whom only fully specific and highly exhaustive components are considered worthy. The generalised (gen) function credits document components according to their *degree* of relevance, hence allowing to model varying levels of user satisfaction gained from not fully specific and highly exhaustive, but still relevant components or near-misses. Both $quant_{strict}$ and $quant_{gen}$ functions

---

[2] A relevant path is a path in an article file's XML tree, whose root node is the article element and whose leaf node is a relevant component (i.e. $quant(e, s) > 0$) that has no or only non-relevant descendants.

[3] CO.Focussed, COS.Focussed, CO.FetchBrowse and COS.FetchBrowse.

ignore elements assessed as 'too small', since by default these are treated as $e = 0$. In order to consider too small elements within the evaluation, the $quant_{genLifted}$ quantisation function is introduced, which adds $+1$ to lift all values of exhaustivity[4]. The effect of this in the evaluation is that it allows the scoring of too small elements as near-misses.

$$quant_{strict}(e, s) : \begin{cases} 1 & \text{if} \quad e = 2 \quad \text{and} \quad s = 1, \\ 0 & \text{otherwise.} \end{cases} \tag{1}$$

$$quant_{gen}(e, s) := e \cdot s \tag{2}$$

$$quant_{genLifted}(e, s) := (e + 1) \cdot s \tag{3}$$

3   eXtended Cumulated Gain (XCG) Measures

The XCG measures are a family of evaluation measures that are an extension of the cumulated gain (CG) based metrics of [2] and which aim to consider the dependency of XML elements (e.g. overlap and near-misses) within the evaluation. The XCG measures include the user-oriented measures of normalised extended cumulated gain ($nxCG$) and the system-oriented effort-precision/gain-recall measures (ep/gr).

3.1   Normalised xCG ($nxCG$)

We define xCG as a vector of accumulated gain. Given a ranked list of document components where the element IDs are replaced with their relevance scores, the cumulated gain at rank i, denoted as $xCG[i]$, is computed as the sum of the relevance scores up to that rank:

$$xCG[i] := \sum_{j=1}^{i} xG[j] \tag{4}$$

For each query, an ideal gain vector, xI, can be derived by filling the rank positions with the relevance scores of all documents in the recall-base (or as in the case of the Focussed strategy, with the relevance scores of all elements in the ideal recall-base) in decreasing order of their degree of relevance. The corresponding cumulated ideal gain vector is referred to as xCI.

A retrieval run's xCG vector can then be compared to this ideal ranking by plotting both the actual and ideal cumulated gain functions against the rank position. By dividing the xCG vectors of the retrieval runs by their corresponding ideal xCI vectors, we obtain the normalised xCG ($nxCG$) measure:

$$nxCG[i] := \frac{xCG[i]}{xCI[i]} \tag{5}$$

---

[4] Note that this is only applied to relevant elements of the recall-base, hence non-relevant nodes remain as $e = 0$.

For a given rank i, the value of $nxCG[i]$ reflects the relative gain the user accumulated up to that rank, compared to the gain he/she could have attained if the system would have produced the optimum best ranking. For any rank, the normalised value of 1 represents ideal performance.

Systems may be compared at various cutoff values, e.g. $nxCG[1]$ or $nxCG[500]$. In addition, we may average $nxCG[i]$ scores up to a given rank as:

$$MAnxCG[i] := \frac{\sum_{j=1}^{i} nxCG[j]}{i} \tag{6}$$

An advantage of this latter measure is that it reflects on the quality of the ranking, whereas $nxCG$ reports a set-based value, measured at a single point in the ranking.

3.2 Calculating an Element's Relevance Value

The definition of the $nxCG$ measure is based on the gain value, $xG[i]$, that a user obtains when examining a returned result component at a given rank i. In this section we detail how this gain is calculated.

We define a *relevance value (RV) function*, $r(c_i)$, as a function that returns a value in $[0, 1]$ for a component c_i in a ranked result list, representing the component's relevance or gain value to the user. The gain value will depend on the returned component's exhaustivity and specificity (i.e. its (e, s) values) as well as on how overlap and near-misses are handled. I.e. for the Focussed tasks overlap and near-misses are taken into account, whereas for the Thorough tasks the relevance value is a direct function of (e, s).

Focussed tasks. Focussed tasks are evaluated based on the assumption that returned overlapping components represent only as much gain as the amount of new relevant information they contain and that the retrieval of near-misses is considered useful to the user. The evaluation parameter that represents this setup is referred to as "overlap=on".

Overlap: Following the assumption that any already viewed components become irrelevant to the user, we define the following result-list dependent relevance value (RV) function, $rv(c_i)$:

$$rv(c_i) := \begin{cases} quant(assess(c_i)) & \text{if } c_i \text{ has not yet been seen,} \\[2ex] (1 - \alpha) \cdot quant(assess(c_i)) & \text{if } c_i \text{ has been fully seen,} \\[2ex] \alpha \cdot \dfrac{\sum_{j=1}^{m}(rv(c_j) \cdot |c_j|)}{|c_i|} & \text{if } c_i \text{ has been partially seen before.} \\ \quad + (1 - \alpha) \cdot quant(assess(c_i)) & \end{cases} \tag{7}$$

where $assess(c_i)$ is a function that returns the assessment value pair (e, s) for the i-th component in the ranking if it is given within the recall-base and $(0, 0)$ otherwise. The function $quant(\cdot)$ is a quantisation function, m is the number of c_i's child nodes and $|\cdot|$ is the length of an element (in characters or words). The $\alpha \in [0, 1]$ weighting factor reflects a user's intolerance to being returned redundant components or component-parts. The higher the α value, the less value a redundant relevant component represents to the user.

According to the above equation, for a not-yet-seen component, the component's relevance value is only dependent on the component's quantised assessment value: $quant(assess(c_i))$. For a component that has been already fully seen by the user, the component's quantised assessment value, $quant(assess(c_i))$, is weighted by $(1 - \alpha)$. For example, using $\alpha = 1$, which represents a user who does not tolerate already viewed components, we obtain an RV score of 0 for a fully seen component, reflecting that it represents no value to the user any more. Finally, if a component has been seen only in part before, then its relevance value is calculated recursively based on the relevance values of its descendant nodes, combined with its own quantised assessment value. The intolerance weighting factor of α is again used to modify the value attributed to already seen components. For example, using $\alpha = 1$ means that only not-yet-seen sub-components will be scored, while using $\alpha = 0$ will return the unmodified quantised score of the component, regardless how much of it the user has seen already.

Near-misses: To consider the retrieval of near-misses within the evaluation, we reward a partial score for the retrieval of non-ideal elements that are structurally related to ideal components. This year, only those relevant elements (as per quantisation function) of the full recall-base were considered near-misses which were not included in the ideal recall-base.

Given this set of near-misses and the ideal recall-base, the XCG measures are applied such that the ideal gain vector of a query, xI, is derived from the ideal recall-base, and the gain vectors, xG, corresponding to the system runs under evaluation are based on the full recall-base. The relevance score of a near-miss component is calculated by Equation 7.

Before the final gain value can be assigned to $xG[i]$, we apply a dependency normalisation function, which ensures that the total score for any sub-tree of an ideal node cannot exceed the maximum score achievable when the ideal node itself is retrieved. For example, an ideal node may have a large number of relevant child nodes whose total RV score may exceed that of the ideal node. The following dependency normalisation function, rv_{norm}, safeguards against this by ensuring that for any $c_j \in S, rv(c_i) + \sum^S rv(c_j) \leq rv(c_{ideal})$ holds:

$$rv_{norm}(c_i) = min(rv(c_i), rv(c_{ideal}) - \sum^S rv(c_j)) \tag{8}$$

where c_{ideal} is the ideal node that is on the same relevant path as c_i, S is the set of nodes in the ideal node's sub-tree that have already been retrieved (before c_i).

The final gain value: The final gain value of a result element in a ranked output list of an XML IR system, taking into account near-misses and overlaps, is given by the normalised relevance score of:

$$xG[i] := rv_{norm}(c_i) \tag{9}$$

where $rv_{norm}(c_i)$ is defined in Equation 8, $rv(c_i)$ is given in Equation 7.

Thorough tasks. Thorough tasks were evaluated using the full recall-base as the basis for deriving the ideal gain vectors. The evaluation parameter that represents this setup is referred to as "overlap=off".

For the Thorough tasks, systems obtain a score for returning as many of the relevant reference elements as possible, including all overlapping nodes. The gain value of a result element in a ranked output list is calculated as:

$$xG[i] := rv(c_i) := quant(assess(c_i)) \qquad (10)$$

where $assess(c_i)$ is a function that returns the assessment value pair (e, s) for the i-th component in the ranking if it is given within the recall-base and $(0, 0)$ otherwise. The function $quant(\cdot)$ is a quantisation function.

3.3 Effort-Precision and Gain-Recall: ep/gr

The cumulated gain based measures described so far provide a recall-oriented view of effectiveness at fixed rank positions. Next we want to measure the amount of effort required of the user to reach a given level of cumulated gain when scanning a given ranking compared to an ideal ranking. The horizontal line drawn at the cumulated gain value of r, shown in Figure 1, illustrates this view. Based on this, we define effort-precision ep as:

$$ep[r] := \frac{i_{ideal}}{i_{run}} \qquad (11)$$

where i_{ideal} is the rank position at which the cumulated gain of r is reached by the ideal curve and i_{run} is the rank position at which the cumulated gain of r is reached by the system run. A score of 1 reflects ideal performance, i.e. when the user needs to spend the minimum necessary effort to reach a given level of gain.

Effort-precision can be calculated at arbitrary gain-recall points, where gain-recall is calculated as the cumulated gain value divided by the total achievable cumulated gain [5]:

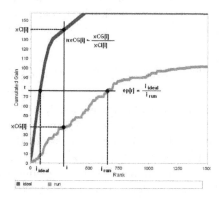

Fig. 1. Calculation of $nxCG$ and effort-precision (ep)

$$gr[i] := \frac{xCG[i]}{xCI[n]} = \frac{\sum_{j=1}^{i} xG[j]}{\sum_{j=1}^{n} xI[j]} \qquad (12)$$

where n is the total number of documents in the recall-base.

The meaning of effort-precision at a given gain-recall value is the amount of relative effort (where effort is measured in terms of number of visited ranks) that the user is required to spend when scanning a system's output ranking compared to the effort an ideal ranking would take in order to reach a given level of gain relative to the total gain that can be obtained.

This method follows the same viewpoint as standard precision/recall, where recall is the control variable and precision the dependent variable. As with precision/recall, interpolation techniques are necessary to estimate effort-precision values at non-natural gain-recall points (e.g. when calculating effort-precision at standard recall points). We adopted linear interpolation for estimating values between two natural recall points, i.e. using straight lines ($y = ax + b$).

As with standard precision/recall, the non-interpolated mean average effort-precision, denoted as *MAep*, is calculated by averaging the effort-precision values measured at natural recall-point, i.e. whenever a relevant XML element is found in the ranking. For non-retrieved relevant elements the score of 0 is used. Note that calculating *MAep* still requires interpolation over the ideal curve as natural recall points of a run may not coincide with natural recall points of the ideal ranking.

We also calculate an average over the interpolated effort-precision values at standard recall points, i.e. $[0.01, 0.02, ..., 1]$, which we refer to as *iMAep*.

Analogue to recall/precision graphs, we plot effort-precision against gain-recall and obtain a detailed summary of a system's overall performance.

3.4   The Q and R Measures

A criticism of the $nxCG$ measures is that they do not average well across topics [3] (in [8]). The reason for this is that as the total number of relevant documents differs across topics, so does the upper bound performance at fixed ranks.

A solution has been suggested in [8] in the form of the following measures. Here the explicit incorporation of the rank position in the denominator ensures that performance is calculated against an always increasing ideal value:

$$Q - measure = \frac{1}{R} \sum_{j=1}^{i} isrel(d_j) \frac{cbg(j)}{cig(j) + j} \qquad (13)$$

where R is the total number of relevant documents, d_j is the document retrieved at rank j, $isrel(\cdot)$ is a binary function that returns 1 if the document is relevant (to any degree) and 0 otherwise. The function $cbg(\cdot)$ is a so-called cumulated bonus gain function, which is defined as $cbg(i) := bg(i) + cbg(i-1)$, where $bg(i) := g(i) + 1$ if $g(i) > 0$ and $bg(i) := 0$ otherwise, and $g(i)$ is the gain value at rank i. The function $cig(\cdot)$ is the cumulated bonus gain derived for the ideal vector (analogue to $cbg(\cdot)$).

$$R - measure = \frac{cbg(R)}{cbg(R) + R} \qquad (14)$$

We employ extended versions of the above measures, adapted to XML through the definition of $g(i) := xG[i]$. We refer to these measures as Q and R.

4   Results Reported in INEX 2005

The results of the following measures were reported in INEX 2005:

- Effort-precision/gain-recall (ep/gr) graphs.
- Non-interpolated mean average effort-precision ($MAep$).
- Interpolated mean average effort-precision ($iMAep$).
- Normalised xCG ($nxCG$) graphs, plotting the $nxCG$ value obtained at $[1, 2, ..., 100]\%$ of the length of the output list, i.e. 1500.
- Normalised xCG ($nxCG$) at various fixed ranks (e.g. $nxCG[25]$).
- Mean average $nxCG$ at various fixed ranks (e.g. $MAnxCG[50]$).
- Q and R.

The official system-oriented evaluation was based on the ep/gr measures, with $MAep$ being the main overall performance indicator. The official user-oriented evaluation was based on the $nxCG[10]$, $nxCG[25]$ and $nxCG[50]$ performance indicators. All results are accessible on the INEX 2005 website[5].

5   EvalJ

All measures have been implemented within a single Java project, the EvalJ evaluation package, which can be downloaded from SourceForge.net[6]. Instruction for how to download the project are at https://sourceforge.net/cvs/?group_id=136430. Alternatively, installer files can be accessed from http://evalj.sourceforge.net/. There is a README included within EvalJ, detailing how to get going and how to run the various evaluation measures.

6   Evaluating Different Tasks

The XCG measures in EvalJ take several parameters, which define how e.g. overlap is to be handled. These parameters are read at run time from a config file. A config file, `inex2005.prop` is provided within EvalJ, containing the official parameter settings for INEX 2005. These are detailed below.

Note that the difference between the CO and COS evaluations was that the former was based on all assessed CO+S topics (29 topics), whereas the latter was evaluated using only those assessed topics that contained a $< castitle >$ element (19 topics). In this case the assessment pool IDs were given within the POOL parameter to filter the total set of assessments. The pool IDs represent the following topics: 202, 203, 205, 207, 208, 210, 212, 216, 219, 222, 223, 228, 229, 230, 232, 233, 234, 236, 239.

---

[5] http://inex.is.informatik.uni-duisburg.de/2005/
[6] https://sourceforge.net/projects/evalj/

6.1   CO.Focussed and COS.Focussed

These tasks were evaluated using the "overlap=on" option, which means that overlap and near-misses are considered within the evaluation. The ideal recall-base is generated automatically within the evaluation based on the selected quantisation function and the methodology described in section 2.

```
TASK: CO.Focussed
METRICS: nxCG, ep/gr, q
ALPHA: 1.0
OVERLAP: on
QUANT_FUNCTIONS: gen, strict, genLifted
DCV: 10, 25, 50
ASSESSMENTS_DIR: .../adhoc2005/official/CO+S/*/
QUERY_TYPE: CO+S
SUBMISSIONRUNS_DIR: .../inex2005_runs/*/

TASK: COS.Focussed
METRICS: nxCG, ep/gr, q
ALPHA: 1.0
OVERLAP: on
QUANT_FUNCTIONS: gen, strict, genLifted
DCV: 10, 25, 50
ASSESSMENTS_DIR: .../adhoc2005/official/CO+S/*/
QUERY_TYPE: CO+S
SUBMISSIONRUNS_DIR: .../inex2005_runs/*/
POOLS: 275,297,273,353,300,283,309,327,292,319,321, 325,301,315,265,361,
       364,349,279
```

6.2   CO.Thorough and COS.Thorough

These tasks were evaluated using the "overlap=off" option, which means that overlap is tolerated within the evaluation. Therefore, no ideal recall-base is generated and the gain value of a component is only a function of its exhaustivity and specificity values, regardless if it overlaps or not with a previously returned element.

```
TASK: CO.Thorough
METRICS: nxCG, ep/gr, q
ALPHA: 1.0
OVERLAP: off
QUANT_FUNCTIONS: gen, strict, genLifted
DCV: 10, 25, 50
ASSESSMENTS_DIR: .../adhoc2005/official/CO+S/*/
QUERY_TYPE: CO+S
SUBMISSIONRUNS_DIR: .../inex2005_runs/*/

TASK: COS.Thorough
METRICS: nxCG, ep/gr, q
ALPHA: 1.0
OVERLAP: off
```

```
QUANT_FUNCTIONS: gen, strict, genLifted
DCV: 10, 25, 50
ASSESSMENTS_DIR: .../adhoc2005/official/CO+S/*/
QUERY_TYPE: CO+S
SUBMISSIONRUNS_DIR: .../inex2005_runs/*/
POOLS: 275,297,273,353,300,283,309,327,292,319,321,325,301,315,265,361,
       364,349,279
```

6.3   CO.FetchBrowse and COS.FetchBrowse

The evaluation methodology for these task is different from all other tasks in that two separate evaluation scores were calculated: an article-level and an element-level score.

The article-level score regards a system's ability to find relevant documents in the first place. To obtain this score, we first filter the recall-base to contain only those article nodes that have at least one relevant element according to the chosen quantisation. E.g. for strict quantisation, only those articles are kept that contain at least one highly exhaustive and fully specific element. The ideal gain vector is obtained by sorting the filtered set by quantised score. Since articles do not overlap, the process is the same for both overlap=on and off modes. We compare the obtained ideal gain vector to the list of article nodes that is *derived* from a system run. To derive the list of articles from a run, we reduce each XML element in the run to its article root and keep from any two duplicate entries the first occurrence (e.g. from $<a1/e1, a1/e2, a2>$ we derive $<a1, a2>$).

The element-level score reflects a system's ability to locate relevant elements within an article. Each cluster of an article and its contained elements are examined individually. The order of clusters is ignored here (it was already considered at the article-level), but the order of elements within a cluster is taken into account. The recall-base for a given cluster consists of the relevant elements within the given article (as per quantisation and overlap setting), where elements are ordered in decreasing quantised value. The list of elements within a cluster of a run is then compared against the cluster's recall-base directly. The individual cluster-scores are then averaged over all clusters and then over all queries.

We only report effort-precision/gain-recall measures for the FetchBrowse tasks, as the selection of an appropriate document cutoff value for $nxCG$ is an open question (due to the small number of relevant elements within each cluster-recall-base).

FetchBrowse tasks have been evaluated both with "overlap=on" and "overlap=off" options. The "overlap=off" option evaluates systems according to the Thorough strategy assumption. The "overlap=on" option evaluates systems according to the Focussed strategy assumption.

```
TASK: CO.FetchBrowse
METRICS: ep/gr
ALPHA: 1.0
OVERLAP: on, off
QUANT_FUNCTIONS: gen, strict, genLifted
DCV: 10, 25, 50
```

```
ASSESSMENTS_DIR: .../adhoc2005/official/CO+S/*/
QUERY_TYPE: CO+S
SUBMISSIONRUNS_DIR: .../inex2005_runs/*/
```

```
TASK: COS.FetchBrowse
METRICS: ep/gr
ALPHA: 1.0
OVERLAP: on, off
QUANT_FUNCTIONS: gen, strict, genLifted
DCV: 10, 25, 50
ASSESSMENTS_DIR: .../adhoc2005/official/CO+S/*/
QUERY_TYPE: CO+S
SUBMISSIONRUNS_DIR: .../inex2005_runs/*/
POOLS: 275,297,273,353,300,283,309,327,292,319,321,325,301,315,265,361,
       364,349,279
```

6.4   SSCAS, SVCAS, VSCAS and VVCAS

These tasks are evaluated based on the Thorough task assumption, with "overlap=off".

```
TASK: SSCAS #or SVCAS, VSCAS, VVCAS
METRICS: nxCG, ep/gr, q
ALPHA: 1.0
OVERLAP: off
QUANT_FUNCTIONS: gen, strict, genLifted
DCV: 10, 25, 50
ASSESSMENTS_DIR: .../official/SSCAS/ #or .../SVCAS/, .../VSCAS/, .../VVCAS/
QUERY_TYPE: CAS
SUBMISSIONRUNS_DIR: .../inex2005_runs/*/
```

7   Correlation Analysis of Results

7.1   Correlation of XCG Measures

We examined correlation among the different XCG measures by calculating the Kendall τ correlation [1] between their resulting respective system rankings.

The correlation measure of Kendall's τ is a nonparametric measure of the agreement between two rankings. It computes the distance between two rankings as the minimum pair-wise adjacent swaps necessary to turn one ranking into the other. The distance is normalised by the number of items being ranked such that two identical rankings produce a correlation of 1 and two rankings that are a perfect inverse of each other produces a score of -1. The expected correlation of two rankings chosen at random is 0. Previous work has considered all rankings with correlations greater than 0.9 as equivalent and rankings with correlation less than 0.8 as containing noticeable differences [9].

Table 1 shows the averaged correlation values over the following ad-hoc tasks: CO.Focussed, CO.Thorough, COS.Focussed, COS.Thorough, SSCAS, SVCAS,

VSCAS, VVCAS. This means that the average correlation for each measure was calculated over 24 correlation scores: 8 tasks, each having three variants for the three quantisation functions. Although different tasks and different quantisations resulted in somewhat different correlation values amongst the different measures, the overall general trend is reflected within this table.

The low levels of correlation between the overall performance measures, e.g. *MAep*, and the fixed cutoff measures, e.g. $nxCG[25]$, show that these measures reflect different aspects of a system's performance and that systems which perform well according to one criterion may not do so well according to another. However, since *MAep*, *iMAep* and *Q* are highly correlated, it may be enough to report only one of these measures in the future. *MAnxCG* and *nxCG* at the various cutoffs also report fairly similar results, and hence the evaluation could focus just on one or two of these measures.

Table 1. Averaged correlation of the XCG measures over 8 ad-hoc sub-tasks

	MAnxCG			nxCG			MAep	iMAep	Q
	[10]	[25]	[50]	[10]	[25]	[50]			
MAnxCG[25]	0.85								
MAnxCG[50]	0.77	**0.90**							
nxCG[10]	0.83	**0.91**	0.86						
nxCG[25]	0.71	0.85	**0.92**	0.82					
nxCG[50]	0.64	0.76	0.85	0.74	0.85				
MAep	0.64	0.72	0.75	0.70	0.74	0.76			
iMAep	0.63	0.71	0.74	0.70	0.73	0.75	**0.93**		
Q	0.60	0.69	0.72	0.68	0.71	0.73	**0.93**	0.87	
R	0.58	0.66	0.69	0.65	0.69	0.71	0.83	0.78	0.85

7.2   Correlation of Quantisation Functions

Next, we examined correlation among the different quantisation functions by calculating the Kendall τ correlation between the resulting respective system rankings.

Table 2 shows the averaged correlation values over the following ad-hoc tasks: CO.Focussed, CO.Thorough, COS.Focussed, COS.Thorough, SSCAS, SVCAS, VSCAS, VVCAS. This means that the average correlation for each measure was calculated over 80 correlation scores: 8 tasks, each having each having results reported for ten measures. Although different tasks and different measures resulted in somewhat different correlation values amongst the different quantisation functions, the overall general trend is reflected within this table.

The low correlation between the strict and both versions of the generalised quantisation functions indicates that these quantisations result in very noticeable result differences among systems. It is clear that systems that perform well according to the strict quantisation may not suit a user represented by the generalised quantisation functions. On the other hand, the two generalised quantisation functions show rather similar behaviour, although their averaged correlation is still below 0.9. This suggests that 'too small' elements do have some effect on system performance. To

Table 2. Averaged correlation of the quantisation functions over 8 ad-hoc sub-tasks

	strict	gen
gen	0.56	
genLifted	0.60	0.89

reflect this, future INEX evaluations may limit the number of quantisation functions to the use of the $quant_{strict}$ and $quant_{genLifted}$ functions.

8   Conclusions

INEX 2005 introduced a new set of measures, the XCG measures, with the aim to address limitations of the previous official measure (`inex-eval`) and provide a suitable evaluation framework, where the dependency among XML document components can be taken into account.

Future work on the XCG measures will aim at 1.) exploring alternative methods for deriving ideal recall-bases, 2.) incorporating new relevance value functions that allow scoring near-misses that are not already included in the full recall-base, e.g. non-relevant sibling nodes, and 3.) investigating various discounting functions. In addition, we are aiming to conduct further studies into the measures' reliability and sensitivity, extending on previous work in [4].

Furthermore, other quantisation functions are currently also being investigated, including weighted versions of the harmonic mean function [7].

Acknowledgments

We would like to thank many participants of the INEX Workshop on Element Retrieval Methodology, Glasgow, July 2005 for their comments and suggestions, which essentially led to the use of the XCG framework at INEX 2005. We are also and especially grateful to Saadia Malik, Benjamin Piwowarski and Arjen de Vries for their invaluable help with hands-on work as well as for the many useful comments and email discussions. We thank Shlomo Geva and Jovan Pehcevski for their helpful comments and questions. Finally, many thanks to all members of the organisers mailing list for their contributions to many of the email discussions.

References

1. W. Conover. *Practical Non-Parametric Statistics, 2nd edn.* John Wiley & Sons, Inc., New York, NY, USA, 1980.
2. K. Järvelin and J. Kekäläinen. Cumulated Gain-based evaluation of IR techniques. *ACM Transactions on Information Systems (ACM TOIS)*, 20(4):422–446, 2002.
3. N. Kando, K. Kuriyama, and M. Yoshioka. Information retrieval system evaluation using multi-grade relevance judgements - discussion on averageable single-numbered measures (in japanese). Technical report, 2001.

4. G. Kazai and M. Lalmas. eXtended Cumulated Gain Measures for the Evaluation of Content-oriented XML Retrieval. *ACM Transactions on Information Systems (ACM TOIS)*, To appear.
5. J. Kekäläinen and K. Järvelin. Using graded relevance assessments in IR evaluation. *Journal of the American Society for Information Science and Technology*, 53(13):1120–1129, 2002.
6. S. Malik, G. Kazai, M. Lalmas, and N. Fuhr. Overview of inex 2005. In N. Fuhr, M. Lalmas, S. Malik, and G. Kazai, editors, *Advances in XML Information Retrieval and Evaluation: Fourth Workshop of the INitiative for the Evaluation of XML Retrieval (INEX 2005), Schloss Dagstuhl, 28-30 November 2005*, volume 3977 of *Lecture Notes in Computer Science*, pages 1–15. Springer-Verlag, 2006.
7. C. J. V. Rijsbergen. *Information Retrieval*. Butterworth-Heinemann, Newton, MA, USA, 1979. Available at http://www.dcs.glasgow.ac.uk/Keith/Preface.html.
8. T. Sakai. New performance metrics based on multigrade relevance: Their application to question answering. In *NTCIR Workshop 4 Meeting Working Notes*, June 2004.
9. E. M. Voorhees. Evaluation by highly relevant documents. In *SIGIR'01: Proceedings of the 24th annual international ACM SIGIR conference on Research and development in information retrieval*, pages 74–82, New York, NY, USA, 2001. ACM Press.

EPRUM Metrics and INEX 2005

Benjamin Piwowarski

Centre for Web Research, Universidad de Chile
bpiwowar@dcc.uchile.cl

Abstract. Standard Information Retrieval (IR) metrics are not well suited for new paradigms like XML IR in which retrievable information units are document elements. These units are neither predefined nor independent, and the elements returned by IR systems may overlap and contain near misses. Part of the problem stems from the classical hypotheses on the user behaviour that do not take into account the structural or logical context of document elements or the possibility of navigation between retrievable units. The Expected Precision Recall with User Model (EPRUM) metric is based on a more realistic user model which encompasses a large variety of user behaviours. In this paper, we present the EPRUM metric used for evaluating the official submissions of INEX 2005 and detail the settings we used. We do not present the full derivation of the EPRUM metric but we give a thorough example of its computation along with the complete set of formulas needed to compute precision at different recall values. We also discuss the implication of such a metric on several key problems of XML Information Retrieval as the notion of the ideal list and the problem of the overlap.

1 Introduction

This document describes the EPRUM metric in the context of XML Retrieval. EPRUM is a metric that aims at providing a unique and comprehensive framework for the evaluation of XML Retrieval systems[1], by defining a user model which is a two fold extension of the classical user model. First, the evaluated list can be composed of more complex objects than simple links to documents or elements – thus allowing a natural evaluation of the Fetch&Browse task. Second, the user is "allowed" to browse into the structural context of a retrieved element: For example, if a subsection is returned, the user can browse to one of its paragraph or to to its enclosing section. Overlap and near misses are naturally handled, as we define an ideal list of non overlapping elements that can only be seen once by the user (a system is rewarded when an "ideal" element is seen by the user).

EPRUM is an extension of the of precision-recall. As Generalised Recall [3] and Precision-Recall with User Modelling [4], EPRUM is based on a user and relevance probabilistic model that are the basis of the precision and recall derivations. This user model has parameters that can be tuned so that they mimic the "average" user behaviour.

The plan of this paper is as follows. In Section 2, we show how we define precision at a given recall level. This definition is an alternative to the classical definition of precision-recall (PR) and yields the standard result when the user model parameters are set to mimic the usual assumed user behaviour (the list is composed of elements

---

[1] But not limited to: the relevance model could be used in standard information retrieval and its user model could be reused in passage retrieval, web retrieval, video retrieval, etc.

N. Fuhr et al. (Eds.): INEX 2005, LNCS 3977, pp. 30–42, 2006.

and the user does not browse from a retrieved element). In Section 3, we describe the different parameters of EPRUM and present the peculiar instantiation of the user model we chose for evaluating INEX 2005 runs. In Section 4, we present the main EPRUM formulas that can be used to evaluate any system run and illustrate them with examples of evaluation for both the Focussed and the Fetch&Browse tasks. Eventually, we discuss the implication of the EPRUM user model for the notion of ideal lists and of overlap in Section 5.

A note about relevance: We distinguish between the relevance of an element (the element contains some relevant material) and the ideality of an element (the fact that the element is the unit the user wants to see, i.e. that it belongs to the "ideal recall base").

2   The EPRUM Metric

EPRUM is an extension of precision-recall: It is based on a definition whose special case is the standard precision-recall as defined in TREC [6]. Precision is defined *as the ratio of the minimum number of ranks that a user has to consult in the list returned by an ideal system and by the evaluated system,* given that the user wants to see a given amount of ideal units. At a given recall level l ($0 < l \leq 1$), precision is defined formally as:

$\text{Precision}(l) =$

$$
\mathbb{E}\left[
\begin{array}{c}
\text{Achievement indicator} \\
\text{for a recall } l
\end{array}
\times
\frac{
\begin{array}{c}
\text{Minimum number of consulted list items} \\
\text{for achieving a recall } l \text{ (over all lists)}
\end{array}
}{
\begin{array}{c}
\text{Minimum number of consulted list items} \\
\text{for achieving a recall } l \text{ (system list)}
\end{array}
}
\right]
\tag{1}
$$

It is easy to see that this is just an alternative definition of the precision at a given recall level. In classical IR, if a system retrieves $A + B$ documents, where A is the number of relevant documents and B the number of not relevant documents, then an ideal system would achieve the same recall with a list reduced to A documents. The above definition would result in a precision $\frac{A}{A+B}$ which is the exact definition of precision – the ratio of the number of relevant documents to the number of retrieved documents. The achievement indicator is used to set the precision to 0 if the recall level cannot be achieved; this is also the classical definition of precision-recall. This definition relates to the expected search length [1] and to the precision-recall as defined in [5].

The following example illustrates the definition of the EPRUM metric; let the list returned by a system be the following:

where gray nodes are ideal units while white nodes are not ideal. The standard definition of precision would assign a precision of respectively 1, 0.25 and 0 for recalls of 1, 2 and 3 (or more). With the definition we chose, we get the same values – the classical user model is deterministic in standard IR, so we can omit the mathematical expectation for now:

Recall 1. The minimum number of elements the user has to consult, over all possible lists, is 1. The value is the same for the system list and the user was able to see one element. Precision is 1.

Recall 2. The minimum number of elements the user has to consult, over all possible lists, is 2. For the evaluated system, the user will have to consult the list until d - that is, the minimum number of items that he has to consult is 4. Precision is 2/4=0.5.

Recall 3. In this case, the same process would give us a precision of 3/5 (because the user has to consult the whole list), but has the recall cannot be attained by the user, the achievement indicator is 0 and hence precision is also 0.

As shown in this example, this definition of precision-recall gives the same results as the standard definition. The interest of this formulation is that we can define and use more complex user and relevance models, and starting from the same definition, derive a generalisation of precision-recall. It is possible to prove that, using the final formula of EPRUM and setting its parameters so as to mimic the standard user behaviour in "flat" IR, we get exactly the same result as trec_eval [6].

3   What is Needed to Compute EPRUM?

EPRUM can be computed given three different sets of parameters:

1. The probability that a user *considers* an element of the corpus. This probability reflects the fact that the user clicks on a result in the list returned by a the IR system and will eventually have look at the element that is associated with the list item. In the context of XML Retrieval, we have to distinguish two cases: the Fetch&Browse task and the others. In the case of the Focussed task, we suppose that a user will *always* consider an element by clicking on its link in the returned list (this is the classical user model). In the case of the Fetch&Browse task, the user model is more complex and is described latter.

2. The probability that a user *browses* from a considered element to any neighbour element. That is, a user, when considering an element, will most probably navigate around it to its close context (i.e., in an XML document this would be the previous siblings, next siblings, ancestors, etc.). This behaviour is stochastic, that is defined by a probability, since we don't expect *all* the users to behave the same way. The probability of browsing from a considered element x to an element y could be measured, in a user experiment, by the proportion of users that would browse to y after having considered x. An element is *seen* if and only if the user browsed to it from a considered element.

3. The probability that a user finds a unit ideal. This probability is closely related to the concept of quantisation but has a well defined meaning in EPRUM: In a user experiment, its value would be the proportion of users that would find the given unit ideal if they had exactly the same information need.

Unfortunately, we still don't have enough user data to compute even an approximated user model. Nevertheless, it is possible to define simple yet realistic behaviours. In

INEX 2005, we chose user models close to the ones implied by xCG (where only elements overlapping with an ideal unit can be rewarded) which was the official INEX 2005 metric. The underlying motivation was to compare faithfully with EPRUM systems that were optimised for xCG. We defined the following user models:

1. For the consideration,

   Focussed. In the focussed task, we made the hypothesis, like in standard IR, that a user always considers an element pointed by a list item. That is, if the third list item is element x then the user will consult the element x (he will see the content of this element). At a given rank i, the probability of considering an element for the focussed task is either 0 (the element is not in the i first ranks) or 1 (the element is in the first i list elements):

   $$P(x \in C_i) = \begin{cases} 1 & \text{if } x \text{ is within the first } i \text{ elements of the list} \\ 0 & \text{otherwise} \end{cases}$$

   Fetch&Browse. An item in the list is not anymore only one element but it is rather a set of elements from the same document. We view this task as follows: The returned list, as displayed to the user, is a list of documents. When the user clicks on a document link, he is presented a document where system selected elements are highlighted and ordered – imagine that there is button that can focus on each selected element in turn. The user begins by seeing the first ranked element, then the second, etc. for a given article.

   We make the hypothesis that the probability that the user keeps on consulting the list of elements depends on the amount of irrelevant material contained in the previous consulted elements – this is somehow similar to the T2I (tolerance to irrelevance) user model [7]. That is, the probability that the user keeps on going after having consulted an element in the document directly depends on the element overlap with the ideal elements. For an element ranked j within the ith document group, the probability that the user considers it is defined as:

   $$P(x_j \in C_i) = P(x_{j-1} \in C_i)$$
   $$\times \left(k + (1-k) \times \frac{\text{size of intersection of } x_{j-1} \text{ with ideal elements}}{\text{size of the element}} \right)$$

   where $P(x_1 \in C_i) = 1$ by definition (the user always consult the first highlighted element).

   The coefficient k is the minimum probability for a user to consider the next element in the list. For INEX 2005, we empirically set k to 0.8. For example, if the three first elements, say of size 10 characters, returned for an article have no intersection with an ideal element, the probability that the user considers the second one is $0.8 + 0.2 \times 0 = 0.8$, that she considers the third one is $0.8 \times (0.8 + 0.2 \times 0) = 0.64$, etc. Note that a run that returns only elements within (or equal to) ideal targets have their probability of considering an element always equal to 1. In this case (and only in this case), the order among elements within the article doesn't change the performance of the system with respect to this instantiation of EPRUM parameters.

2. For the browsing or navigational behaviour, we chose a simple user model – the user, from a considered element, can go up or down. We call this behaviour "hierarchic": The proportion of users that navigate from an element to one of its descendant, or from an element of its ancestor, is equal to the ratio of the sizes of the elements:

$$P(x \to y) = \begin{cases} \frac{\text{size of } y}{\text{size of } x} & \text{if } y \text{ is an ancestor of } x \\ \frac{\text{size of } y}{\text{size of } x} & \text{if } x \text{ is an ancestor of } y \\ 0 & \text{otherwise} \end{cases}$$

For instance, 30 % of the users would go from a section of size 10 its enclosing paragraph of size 3. Note that more realistic user models, like the T2I one, could be used. We chose this simple model because submitted runs were optimised for the inex_eval or the XCG metrics which have an implicit user definition which is close to this hierarchic behaviour. Note also that a user always browse from a considered element x to x (it implies that the fact that x is consulted is equivalent to the fact that x is seen by the user) as $P(x \to x) = 1$.

3. The set of ideal elements was computed using the Kazai's algorithm [2] using the Exh quantisation:

$$q(x) = \begin{cases} 0 & \text{if "too small"} \\ 0 & \text{if exhaustivity is } 0 \\ 0.5 & \text{if exhaustivity is } 1 \\ 1 & \text{if exhaustivity is } 2 \end{cases}$$

This algorithm was chosen for its simplicity, and because it produces intuitively correct sets of ideal elements. Starting from the original assessments, the process is as follows. For each relevant path (*i.e.* a path from the deepest element with a non zero quantisation to the root of the document), the element with the higher quantisation within that path is added to the ideal set. In order to remove any overlap from the ideal set, elements that contain an ancestor in this set are all removed. The resulting set does not contain overlapping elements and is considered as the set of elements a user would want to see. The probability that a user – among all the user issuing the same query need – is satisfied by an element of this set is set to 0.5 (resp. 1) when its exhaustivity is 1 (resp. 2): Said otherwise, 100% of the users would be satisfied with an highly exhaustive element while only 50% of them would be satisfied with a fairly exhaustive element.

As there are two possible quantisations (0.5 and 1), we have to "average" (an example is given in the next section) the precision-recall curves with two ideal sets: The first one is composed of all the ideal elements, while the second one is composed of the highly exhaustive ideal elements only.

Note that when an element is not in this ideal set, it does not mean that a system returning this element will not be rewarded because a user can still browse to the ideal element.

4   EPRUM Formulas and Examples

We present in this section the evaluation of four lists for the Focussed (and SVCAS, VVCAS) and Fetch&Browse tasks. We used a small database where only two (or three) elements are ideal, as illustrated in Fig. 1. We first give the different formulas needed to compute EPRUM given an ideal set of elements $\mathfrak{I}$ and a particular user model instantiation.

Starting from formula (1), the precision at a given recall ℓ (ℓ is the number of ideal units the user wants to see) can be rewritten:

$$\text{Precision}(\ell) = \mathbb{E} \left[\begin{array}{c} \text{Minimum number of consulted list items} \\ \text{for achieving a recall } \ell \text{ (over all lists)} \end{array} \right] \} (E1)$$

$$\times \, \mathbb{E} \left[\frac{\begin{array}{c} \text{Achievement indicator} \\ \text{for a recall } \ell \end{array}}{\begin{array}{c} \text{Minimum number of consulted list items} \\ \text{for achieving a recall } \ell \text{ (system list)} \end{array}} \right] \} (E2)$$

It can be shown that:

$$(E1) = \sum_{\text{rank } i} i \left(P(F_i^* \geq r) - P(F_{i-1}^* \geq r) \right)$$

$$(E2) = \sum_{\text{rank } i} \frac{1}{i} \left(P(F_i \geq r) - P(F_{i-1} \geq r) \right)$$

where r is the smallest integer superior or equal to $\ell \times$ (number of ideal elements) and F_i (resp. F_i^*) is the number of ideal elements found by the user after he consulted the i first ranks of the system list (resp. the ideal list). If we consider the classical case, where an ideal element is retrieved or not at each rank, then $P(F_i \geq r)$ is either 0 or 1. In this case, it is easy to see that the expected value E1 (resp. E2) is the actual value (or inverse value) of the rank where the rth ideal element has been retrieved.

In order to compute the probability $P(F_i = r)$ needed by formulas E1 and E2, we first need to know the value of the probability $P(x \in S_i)$ that an ideal element x is seen after the user has considered ranks 1 to i. As we use the same user model as in [3], we can use a nearly identical formula:

$$P(x \in S_i) = 1 - \prod_{y} (1 - P(y \in C_i)P(y \rightarrow x)) \quad (2)$$

where $P(y \in C_i)$ and $P(y \rightarrow x)$ are given by the chosen user model instantiation. In INEX 2005, we chose two different instantiations (one for the focussed/VVCAS/SVCAS tasks and the other for the Fetch&Browse task) as described in the preceding section.

Given $P(x \in S_i)$ for any ideal element x and any rank i, it is possible [3] to compute $P(F_i = r)$ and hence $P(F_i \geq r)$:

$$P(F_i = r) = \sum_{\substack{A \subseteq \mathfrak{I} \\ |A| = r}} \prod_{x \in A} P(x \in S_i) \prod_{x \in \mathfrak{I} \setminus A} P(x \notin S_i) \quad (3)$$

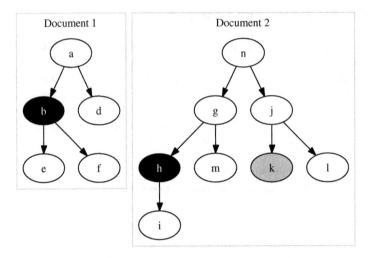

Fig. 1. The example database, composed of two documents and thirteen elements. There are three ideal elements. Two of them are highly exhaustive (b and h, with a black background) for the query while one of them is fairly exhaustive (k). The size of each element is 1 + the size of its children (in an imaginary unit: this could be for instance the number of words divided by 100): In this database, each element directly contains some text and possibly some descendants. The size of e (f, i, m, k or l) is 1, the size of b is 3, the size of a is 5, etc. The probability of navigating from an element to the other being the ratio of sizes, the probability to navigate from f to b is for instance $\frac{1}{3}$.

where $\Im$ is the set of ideal elements and the summation is taken over all the subsets A of cardinality r of the ideal set of element $\Im$. The above formula simply enumerates all the cases where *exactly* r ideal elements are seen by the user. It is possible to compute it in quadratic time with respect to the cardinality of $\Im$, or to approximate it using the normal law.

The above formulas can be used to compute the precision at any recall level. It is also possible to compute precision at a given rank but this is not described in this paper. The last important input, which was until now only evoked, is the ideal list. In the general case, it is not easy to derive an ideal list from an arbitrary user model. It can also be shown that there might not exist a unique ideal list for some user model instances, but rather a set of ideal lists – one for each recall value.

However, in the case of the user models we used in INEX 2005, the ideal lists are quite easy to generate: For the Focussed/VVCAS/SVCAS tasks, it is simply the ideal set elements ordered by exhaustivity value. For the Fetch&Browse task, the ideal list is composed of the documents ordered by decreasing sum of exhaustivity values of the ideal elements they contain. For each document, the ideal list to return is simply the set of ideal elements that that document contains.

In order to illustrate EPRUM behaviour, we now apply the different formulas with the two different user models we chose for INEX 2005.

4.1 Focussed and VVCAS, SVCAS

In order to illustrate the EPRUM metric, we use the following lists for the focussed, VVCAS and SVCAS tasks (all these tasks do not define precisely the target element, so the hierarchic behaviour makes sense):

A List b,h,k: This is the ideal list, composed of the ideal elements - with the "most" ideal first.
B List k, h, b: This is the ideal list, but ordered by increasing order of ideality.
C List f, h, k: The list **A** but with b (first element) replaced by one of its child.
D List h, f, k: The list **C**, swapping the two first elements.

We assume that the probability that the user has seen more than one ideal element *before* beginning to consult the list is 0; that is, $P(F_0 \geq r) = 0$ for $r > 0$. We then distinguish two cases:

1. If the user is satisfied with an element of exhaustivity at least 2 (75 % of the users – there is a justification that for simplicity we don't present in the paper):

   Recall 1 (level 1/2). $(E1)$ is 1; $(E2)$ is resp. 1, $\frac{1}{2}$, $1 \times (\frac{1}{3} - 0) + \frac{1}{2} \times (1 - \frac{1}{3}) = \frac{2}{3}$, and 1 for lists **A**, **B**, **C** and **D**. Precision is 1, $\frac{1}{2}$, $\frac{2}{3}$, and 1.

   Recall 2 (level 1). $(E1)$ is 2; $(E2)$ is resp. $\frac{1}{2}$, $\frac{1}{3}$, $\frac{1}{2} \times (\frac{1}{3} - 0) = \frac{1}{6}$, and $\frac{1}{6}$ for lists **A**, **B**, **C** and **D**. Precisions are 1, $\frac{2}{3}$, $\frac{1}{3}$ and $\frac{1}{3}$.

2. If the user is satisfied with an element of exhaustivity at least 1 (25 % of the users):

   Recall 1 (level 1/3). $(E1)$ is 1; $(E2)$ is resp. 1, 1, $1 \times (\frac{1}{3} - 0) + \frac{1}{2} \times (1 - \frac{1}{3}) = \frac{2}{3}$, and 1 for lists **A**, **B**, **C** and **D**. Precision is 1, 1, $\frac{2}{3}$, and 1.

   Recall 2 (level 2/3). $(E1)$ is 2; $(E2)$ is resp. $\frac{1}{2}$, $\frac{1}{2}$, $\frac{1}{2} \times (\frac{1}{3} - 0) + \frac{1}{3} \times (1 - \frac{1}{3}) = \frac{7}{18}$, and $\frac{7}{18}$ for lists **A**, **B**, **C** and **D**. Precisions are 1, 1, $\frac{7}{9}$ and $\frac{7}{9}$.

   Recall 3 (level 1). $(E1)$ is 3; $(E2)$ is resp. $\frac{1}{3}$, $\frac{1}{3}$, $\frac{1}{3} \times (\frac{1}{3} - 0) = \frac{1}{9}$, and $\frac{1}{9}$ for lists **A**, **B**, **C** and **D**. Precisions are 1, 1, $\frac{1}{3}$ and $\frac{1}{3}$.

There is a way to combine the two sets of precisions that we do not describe here but give an example instead. If a user wants to see more than two third of the ideal elements for list **B**, then for 75 % of the users this means a precision of $\frac{2}{3}$ (only highly exhaustive elements satisfy the user) and for 25 % of them this means a precision of 1: Hence the precision of $.75 \times \frac{5}{6} + .25 \times 1 = .875$. For the same list, if a user wants to see between $\frac{1}{2}$ (excluded) and $\frac{2}{3}$ (included) of the ideal elements, then for 75 % of the users that means seeing 2 ideal elements with a precision $\frac{2}{3}$, and for 25 % of the users that means seeing 2 ideal elements with a precision 1. Hence, a precision of $.75 \times \frac{2}{3} + .25 \times 1 = .75$.

   The evaluations order the runs in an order which is appropriate: **A** has the maximum score and **C** is worse than **D** (**D** and **C** have their two first list item swapped, and **D** has a fully ideal element as its top ranked element). List **B**, containing only ideal elements, is overall better than **C** and **D**.

Table 1. Evolution of the different probabilities, with respect to the different lists (A, B, C, D) for the Focussed/VVCAS/SVCAS tasks. The three columns below probability $P(x \in S_i)$ correspond respectively to the probability that element a, b, or c is seen by the user after rank i. The probability P_2 (resp. P_1) is the probability that the user found at least ... ideal elements after rank i, given that he is only satisfied with elements at least highly (resp. fairly) exhaustive.

	List (b,h,k): A								List (k,h,b): B							
	$P(x \in S_i)$			$P_2(F_i \geq)$		$P_1(F_i \geq)$			$P(x \in S_i)$			$P_2(F_i \geq)$		$P_2(F_i \geq)$		
rank	b	h	k	1	2	1	2	3	b	h	k	1	2	1	2	3
1	1	0	0	1	0	1	0	0	0	0	1	0	0	1	0	0
2	1	1	0	1	1	1	1	0	0	1	1	1	0	1	1	0
3	1	1	1	1	1	1	1	1	1	1	1	1	1	1	1	1

	List (f,h,k) C								List (b,i,k): D							
	$P(x \in S_i)$			$P_2(F_i \geq)$		$P_1(F_i \geq)$			$P(x \in S_i)$			$P_2(F_i \geq)$		$P_1(F_i \geq)$		
rank	b	h	k	1	2	1	2	3	b	h	k	1	2	1	2	3
1	$\frac{1}{3}$	0	0	$\frac{1}{3}$	0	$\frac{1}{3}$	0	0	1	0	0	1	0	1	0	0
2	$\frac{1}{3}$	1	0	1	$\frac{1}{3}$	1	$\frac{1}{3}$	0	1	$\frac{1}{3}$	0	1	$\frac{1}{3}$	1	$\frac{1}{3}$	0
3	$\frac{1}{3}$	1	1	1	$\frac{1}{3}$	1	1	$\frac{1}{3}$	1	$\frac{1}{3}$	1	1	$\frac{1}{3}$	1	1	$\frac{1}{3}$

Table 2. Precision-recall for the Focussed, VVCAS, and SVCAS tasks. The precision for the four lists and four recall intervals are shown in the four last lines. The line "correspondence" shows what is the number of ideal elements the user wants to see if, among the elements in the ideal set, (1) he considers that only elements with an exhaustivity 2 are ideal (2) he considers that elements with an exhaustivity at least 1 are ideal.

recall level	$]0, \frac{1}{3}]$	$]\frac{1}{3}, \frac{1}{2}]$	$]\frac{1}{2}, \frac{2}{3}]$	$]\frac{2}{3}, 1]$
correspondence	1,1	1,2	2,2	2,3
A	1	1	1	1
B	0.63	0.63	.75	0.88
C	0.67	0.69	0.44	0.33
D	1	0.94	0.44	0.33

4.2 Fetch and Browse

For the fetch&browse example, we illustrate EPRUM behaviour using the following lists:

A List D2[h,k] D1[b]: this is the ideal list composed of elements from two documents, D2 and D1. D2 is to be ranked before D1 because it contains more ideal elements.

B List D1[b] D2[h,k]: the ideal list in reverse order.

C List D2[i,k] D1[b]: the first document returned contains a near miss (i); as i is fully specific (contained in an ideal element), the probability that the user consults the next element (k) is 1.

D List D2[g,k] D1[b]: in this list, the first element of the first returned document is an element that overlaps partially with an ideal element; hence, the user will *consider* the element k of D2 with a probability inferior to 1. Said otherwise, some users only will continue to consult the second highlighted highlighted elements within D2. The probability that the user consults the element k in D2 is $0.8 + 0.2 \times \frac{1}{2} = 0.9$ as one half of g overlaps with the ideal element h: At the first rank (document D2) the user sees h with a probability .5, and k with a probability .9. Another thing to note, is that if h and k satisfy the user, then he sees at first rank at least one ideal element with a probability $\frac{1}{2} \times .9 + \frac{1}{2} \times .1 + \frac{1}{2} \times .9 = \frac{1.9}{2}$, the three terms of the sum being the case where (1) the user sees h and k, (2) the user sees k but not h, and (3) the user sees h but not k.

Note also that the only real difference between lists C and D is that the first element is not fully specific (because the same proportion of users will browse from element g to h and from element i to h).

Table 3. Evolution of the different probabilities, with respect to the different lists (A, B, C, D) for the Fetch&Browse task. The three columns below probability $P(x \in S_i)$ correspond respectively to the probability that element a, b, or c is seen by the user after rank i. The probability P_2 (resp. P_1) is the probability that the user found at least 2 (resp. 1) ideal elements after rank i, given that he is only satisfied with elements at least highly (resp. fairly) exhaustive.

List D2[h,k] D1[b]: A

	$P(x \in S_i)$		$P_2(F_i \geq)$		$P_1(F_i \geq)$	
rank	b h	k	1	2	1 2	3
1	0 1	1	1	0	1 1	0
2	1 1	1	1	1	1 1	1

List D1[b] D2[h,k]: B

	$P(x \in S_i)$		$P_2(F_i \geq)$		$P_2(F_i \geq)$	
rank	b h	k	1	2	1 2	3
1	1 0	0	1	0	1 0	0
2	1 1	1	1	1	1 1	1

List D2[i,k] D1[b]: C

	$P(x \in S_i)$		$P_2(F_i \geq)$		$P_1(F_i \geq)$	
rank	b h	k	1	2	1 2	3
1	0 $\frac{1}{2}$	1	$\frac{1}{2}$	0	1 $\frac{1}{2}$	0
2	1 $\frac{1}{2}$	1	1	$\frac{1}{2}$	1 1	$\frac{1}{2}$

List D2[g,k] D1[f]: D

	$P(x \in S_i)$		$P_2(F_i \geq)$		$P_1(F_i \geq)$		
rank	b h	k	1	2	1	2	3
1	0 $\frac{1}{2}$	.9	$\frac{1}{2}$	0	$\frac{1.9}{2}$	$\frac{.9}{2}$	0
2	1 $\frac{1}{2}$	.9	1	$\frac{1}{2}$	1	$\frac{1.9}{2}$	$\frac{.9}{2}$

Like in the previous Section, we distinguish two cases:

1. If the user is satisfied with an element of exhaustivity at least 2 (75% of the users – there is a justification that we don't present here):
   Recall 1 (level 1/2). ($E1$) is 1; ($E2$) is resp. 1, 1, $1 \times (\frac{1}{2} - 0) + \frac{1}{2} \times (1 - \frac{1}{2}) = \frac{3}{4}$, and $\frac{3}{4}$ for lists **A, B, C** and **D**. Precision is 1, 1, $\frac{3}{4}$, and $\frac{3}{4}$.
   Recall 2 (level 1). ($E1$) is 2; ($E2$) is resp. $\frac{1}{2}$, $\frac{1}{2}$, $\frac{1}{2} \times (\frac{1}{2} - 0) = \frac{1}{4}$, and $\frac{1}{4}$ for lists **A, B, C** and **D**. Precisions is 1, 1, $\frac{1}{2}$ and $\frac{1}{2}$.
2. If the user is satisfied with an element of exhaustivity at least 1 (25 % of the users):
   Recall 1 (level 1/3). ($E1$) is 1; ($E2$) is resp. 1, 1, 1, and $1 \times (\frac{1.9}{2} - 0) + \frac{1}{2} \times (1 - \frac{1.9}{2}) = \frac{3.9}{4}$ for lists **A, B, C** and **D**. Precision is 1, 1, 1, and $\frac{3.9}{4}$.
   Recall 2 (level 2/3). ($E1$) is 1; ($E2$) is resp. 1, $\frac{1}{2}$, $1 \times (\frac{1}{2} - 0) + \frac{1}{2} \times (1 - \frac{1}{2}) = \frac{3}{4}$, and $1 \times (\frac{.9}{2} - 0) + \frac{1}{2} \times (\frac{1.9}{2} - \frac{.9}{2}) = \frac{2.8}{4}$ for lists **A, B, C** and **D**. Precisions are 1, $\frac{1}{2}$, $\frac{3}{4}$ and $\frac{2.8}{4}$.

Recall 3 (level 1). $(E1)$ is 2; $(E2)$ is resp. $\frac{1}{2}, \frac{1}{2}, \frac{1}{2} \times (\frac{1}{2} - 0) = \frac{1}{4}$, and $\frac{1}{2} \times (\frac{9}{2} - 0) = \frac{9}{4}$ for lists **A**, **B**, **C** and **D**. Precisions are 1, 1, $\frac{1}{2}$ and $\frac{9}{2}$.

Using the same technique that in the previous section, we now combine the precisions for these two sets of users.

Table 4. Precision-recall for the list A-D (Fetch&Browse). The precision for the four lists and four recall intervals are shown. The line "correspondence" shows what is the number of ideal elements the user wants to see if, among the elements in the ideal set, (1) he considers that only elements with an exhaustivity 2 are ideal (2) he considers that elements with an exhaustivity at least 1 are ideal.

recall level	$]0, \frac{1}{3}]$	$]\frac{1}{3}, \frac{1}{2}]$	$]\frac{1}{2}, \frac{2}{3}]$	$]\frac{2}{3}, 1]$
correspondence	1,1	1,2	2,2	2,3
A	1	1	1	1
B	1	.88	.88	1
C	.81	.75	.56	.50
D	.81	.74	.55	.49

The evaluations are as expected; list **A** has the maximum score, followed by list **B** (where the two documents were swapped). Then list **C** is superior to **D**, although very close: the difference lies in the fact that a part of the users did not continue to explore the document as the first element (for list **D**) was not fully specific.

5 Implications

The EPRUM metric makes explicit the user behaviour by defining a probabilistic user model. The probabilistic model is important since in XML IR we cannot expect all the users to behave the same way in a given document. This model has two interesting implications in XML IR:

The notion of ideal list. The ideal list is used both by EPRUM and xCG metrics to compute respectively the ideal precision/recall and effort/gain curves. While in xCG the notion of ideal list and ideal set of elements are the same, this is not the case in EPRUM: The ideal set of elements is, as in xCG, the set of elements that would satisfy users with the same query need. Contrarily to xCG, the ideal list of EPRUM *is not always* the set of ideal elements and depends on the specific user model. To illustrate this point, let us take a very peculiar (and not so realistic) user model: A user *always* browses to the first and the last paragraph of a consulted section. If the set ideal elements is reduced to two paragraphs – the first and the last of a section S, then the ideal set is composed of the two paragraphs while the ideal list is reduced to the section S.

A consequence of that separation is that there might exist more than one ideal list, one for any given recall r. Let's take an example to illustrate this point: Let **a**, **b**, and **c** be three elements; **b** and **c** are ideal. The list is composed of elements in the corpus. The probability of navigating from **a** to **b** (or **c**) is 0.9. For a recall 1, an ideal list would be a simple list restricted to one of the ideal elements, **b** or **c**, with an expected length of 1. For a recall 2, an ideal list would be (**a,b,c**) because 81 % of the users would see two ideal elements after the first rank, 9 % after the second and 10 % after the third – thus implying an expected search length of 1.29 (instead of 2 with a list composed of **b** and **c**).

Overlap. The preceding example also illustrate another consequence of the EPRUM user model: Overlap might be a good property of the returned list. Let **a** be an ancestor of **b** and **c** in the previous example. As 19% of the users did not see the two elements after having consulted **a** in the list, it is necessary to return the two overlapping elements **b** and **c** so that 100% of the users eventually see all the ideal elements. This situation might arise whenever it is more interesting (in terms of expected search length) to first return one ancestor rather than each of its ideal descendants.

In INEX 2005, the chosen user model implies that there is only one ideal list (or a set of ideal lists but with the same expected search lengths for each recall value) and that the ideal list does not contain overlapping elements. However, it is interesting to underline the fact that choosing more complex user model might imply multiple ideal lists for different recall values and overlap in the ideal list. This would also be the case for the xCG metrics family if they reward near misses that are neither ancestors nor descendants of an ideal element.

6   Discussion

Most metrics used to compare the performance of semi-structured document search engines rely – sometimes implicitly – on a simplistic user behaviour: The user is supposed to consult exclusively the elements of the list returned by the engine. This user model is no more adapted to recent IR tasks like XML. In particular it does not allow considering user ability to navigate between elements, using the list as entry points to the information he seeks.

In this article, we briefly presented the EPRUM metric and showed how it was used in INEX 2005 to evaluate participant submissions. EPRUM is a generalisation of precision-recall that reduces to standard recall-precision if browsing between elements is not allowed and if element relevance is binary. It is also worth noting that EPRUM is somehow a natural extension of xCG (in particular of the new EP/GR metric) where the user and relevance model are explicit and the metric formulas derived from a theoretic user model, thus providing a consistent framework for XML IR evaluation.

Specifying explicitly the user model allows EPRUM to be set so that it measures the "average satisfaction" of users with the same query need. It is possible to set the metric's parameters so that the user model is closer to the real user behaviour in the context of XML IR when user experiments are available. We hope that such data will be available if, as discussed during the INEX 2005 workshop, topics in INEX 2006 are created using an interface that will log all the actions undertaken by the topic creator.

Further work are planned to investigate an instantiation of EPRUM parameters that would use experimental data from the INEX interactive track and to compare more thoroughly xCG and EPRUM. With respect to the latter, we expect to reach a quite high correlation when the EPRUM instantiation is as close as possible to the implied xCG models: Preliminary experiments have shown that the correlations between average precision of each topic and each system run in INEX 2005 are respectively 0.75, 0.62 and 0.78 for the Pearson, Kendall and Spearman coefficients. In order to compare the two metrics, it would be necessary to analyse the differences in detail.

EvalJ

EPRUM is implemented in the EvalJ software, along with all the other metrics of INEX. It can be downloaded from this URL:http://evalj.sourceforge.net

References

[1] W. S. Cooper. Some inconsistencies and misidentified modelling assumptions in probabilistic information retrieval. In N. J. Belkin, P. Ingwersen, and A. M. Pej, editors, *Proceedings of the 14th ACM SIGIR*, Copenhagen, Danemark, 1992. ACM Press.

[2] G. Kazai and M. Lalmas. Notes on what to measure in inex. In A. Trotman, M. Lalmas, and N. Fuhr, editors, *Proceedings of the INEX 2005 Workshop on Element Retrieval Methodology*. University of Otago, Univierisity of Glasgow, Information Retrieval Festival, 2005.

[3] B. Piwowarski and P. Gallinari. Expected ratio of relevant units: A measure for structured information retrieval. In N. Fuhr, M. Lalmas, and S. Malik, editors, *INitiative for the Evaluation of XML Retrieval (INEX). Proceedings of the Second INEX Workshop*, Dagstuhl, France, Dec. 2003.

[4] B. Piwowarski, P. Gallinari, and G. Dupret. An extension of precision-recall with user modelling (PRUM): Application to XML retrieval. submitted for publication, 2005.

[5] V. V. Raghavan, G. S. Jung, and P. Bollmann. A critical investigation of recall and precision as measures of retrieval system performance. *ACM Transactions on Information Systems*, 7(3):205–229, 1989.

[6] E. M. Voorhees. Common evaluation measures. In *The Twelfth Text Retrieval Conference (TREC 2003)*, number SP 500-255, pages 1–13. NIST, 2003.

[7] A. Vries, G. Kazai, and M. Lalmas. Tolerance to irrelevance: A user-effort oriented evaluation of retrieval systems without predefined retrieval unit. In *Proceedings of RIAO (Recherche d'Information Assistée par Ordinateur (Computer Assisted Information Retrieval)), Avignon, France*, Apr. 2004.

HiXEval: Highlighting XML Retrieval Evaluation

Jovan Pehcevski and James A. Thom

School of Computer Science and Information Technology, RMIT University
Melbourne, Australia
{jovanp, jat}@cs.rmit.edu.au

Abstract. This paper describes our proposal for an evaluation metric for XML retrieval that is solely based on the highlighted text. We support our decision of ignoring the exhaustivity dimension by undertaking a critical investigation of the two INEX 2005 relevance dimensions. We present a fine grained empirical analysis of the level of assessor agreement of the five topics double-judged at INEX 2005, and show that the agreement is higher for specificity than for exhaustivity. We use the proposed metric to evaluate the INEX 2005 runs for each retrieval strategy of the CO and CAS retrieval tasks. A correlation analysis of the rank orderings obtained by the new metric and two XCG metrics shows that the orderings are strongly correlated, which demonstrates the usefulness of the proposed metric for evaluation of XML retrieval performance.

1 Introduction

How to properly evaluate XML retrieval effectiveness is a much-debated question among the XML retrieval research community. Over the past four years INEX has been used as an arena to investigate the behaviour of a variety of evaluation metrics. However, unlike in previous years a new set of official metrics was adopted at INEX 2005, which belong to the eXtended Cumulated Gain (XCG) family of metrics [2, 4]. Two official INEX 2005 metrics are nxCG (with the nxCG[r] measure), which for a rank r measures the relative retrieval gain a user has accumulated up to that rank, compared to the gain they could have accumulated if the system had produced the optimal ranking; and ep/gr (with the MAep measure), which for a cumulated gain level measures the amount of relative effort (as the number of visited ranks) a user is required to spend compared to the effort they could have spent while inspecting an optimal ranking [3].

Since 2003, two relevance dimensions — exhaustivity and specificity — have been used in INEX to measure the extent to which an element is *relevant* to the information need expressed by an INEX topic. A highlighting assessment approach was used at INEX 2005 to gather relevance judgements for the retrieval topics [7]; here, the specificity of an element is automatically computed as the ratio of highlighted to fully contained text, while the assessor is asked to explicitly judge the exhaustivity of that element. Figure 1 shows a sample of relevance

N. Fuhr et al. (Eds.): INEX 2005, LNCS 3977, pp. 43–57, 2006.

```
<file collection="ieee" name="co/2000/r7108">
 <element path="/article[1]" E="1" size="13,556" rsize="5,494"/>
 <element path="/article[1]/bdy[1]" E="1" size="9,797" rsize="4,594"/>
 <element path="/article[1]/bdy[1]/sec[2]" E="1" size="2,064" rsize="2,064"/>
 <element path="/article[1]/bdy[1]/sec[2]/st[1]" E="?" size="30" rsize="30"/>
</file>
```

Fig. 1. A sample from the INEX 2005 CO topic 203 relevance judgements for article co/2000/r7108. For each judged element, E shows the value for exhaustivity (with possible values ?, 1 and 2), size denotes the element size (measured as total number of contained characters), while rsize shows the actual number of characters highlighted as relevant by the assessor

judgements obtained for INEX 2005 Content Only (CO) topic 203. For each judged element, E shows the exhaustivity of the element, with possible values of ? (too small), 1 (partially exhaustive), and 2 (highly exhaustive); size denotes the total number of characters contained by the element; and rsize shows the actual number of highlighted characters by the assessor.

To measure the *relevance* of an element, the official INEX 2005 metrics combine the values obtained from the two INEX relevance dimensions. For example, if the observed value for E is 1 and both values for size and rsize are the same, the element is deemed as *highly specific* but only *partially exhaustive* [7]. A quantisation function is then used to combine these two values into a number that is subsequently used to reflect the relevance of the element [3]. However, in previous work we have shown that finding the best way to combine the values from exhaustivity and specificity to reflect the relevance of an element is too difficult [8]; moreover, recent analysis by Trotman has also shown that the element level agreement between two assessors across the twelve double-judged topics at INEX 2004 is very low, suggesting that "quantization functions based on relevance levels will prove unsound" [10]. In Section 2 we revisit and validate the above claim by analysing the level of assessor agreement across the five topics that were double-judged at INEX 2005.

Another criticism of the official INEX metrics is their lack of simplicity, and their slight departure from the well-established information retrieval norms [1]. Further to this, to consider the level of overlap among retrieved elements, the XCG family of metrics use a rather ad hoc methodology in constructing the so-called *ideal recall-base* [3], where a dependency normalisation function is also used to adjust the scores of the descendents of the ideal elements. To date, critical analysis of whether the reliance on these or alternative choices has a positive or negative impact on the XML retrieval evaluation has not been provided.

We contend that the purpose of the XML retrieval task is to find elements that contain *as much relevant information as possible*, without also containing a significant amount of non-relevant information. To measure the extent to which an XML retrieval system returns relevant information, we follow an evaluation methodology that only takes into account the amount of highlighted text in a retrieved element, without considering the E value of that element. In Section 3 we introduce HiXEval (pronounced hi–ex–eval) – an Evaluation metric for XML retrieval that extends the traditional definitions of precision and recall to include the knowledge obtained from the INEX 2005 Highlighting assessment task.

We recognise that there are no absolute criteria for the choice of a metric for XML retrieval. However, we argue that HiXEval meets all the requirements needed for an unbiased XML retrieval evaluation, and show in Section 4 that, given the strong correlations of its rank orderings to the ones obtained by the XCG metrics, it can and should be used to evaluate XML retrieval effectiveness.

2 Analysis of INEX 2005 CO and VVCAS Relevance Judgements

In this section, we analyse the INEX 2005 relevance judgements obtained for the CO and Vague Content And Structure (VVCAS) topics. First, we analyse the distribution of the E?, E1, and E2 judged elements across the INEX 2005 topics. Then, we analyse the level of assessor agreement obtained from the five topics that have been double-judged at INEX 2005 (four CO, and one VVCAS).

2.1 Distribution of Relevant Elements

The INEX 2005 IEEE document collection comprises 16,820 scientific articles published between 1995–2004, with an average article length of 44,030 characters. Currently, there are 29 CO and 34 VVCAS topics that have corresponding relevance judgements available[1]. We use relevance judgements for both parent and child VVCAS topics in our analysis.

By analysing the INEX 2005 relevance judgements, we aim to discover whether the average number, size, and proportion of contained relevant information in judged elements differ depending on the *exhaustivity* value given to these elements. For example, we expect to find many relevant elements whose exhaustiveness is judged as "?", making them too small. The proportion of relevant information found in these elements (their *specificity* value) is expected to be very high, reflecting the fact that most of the contained information is relevant. Conversely, it is reasonable to expect that the distribution of other relevant elements (such as E1 or E2) is likely to differ from the distribution of the too small elements, both in terms of their average number, size, and proportion of contained relevant information.

Table 1 shows our analysis of the INEX 2005 CO and VVCAS relevance judgements. As expected, for both types of topics the assessment trends are clear: The too small (E?) elements are the most common, the smallest in size, and contain the highest proportion of relevant information. In contrast, the highly

---

[1] We use version 7.0 of the INEX 2005 ad hoc relevance judgements.

Table 1. Statistical analysis of the distribution of E? (too-small), E1, and E2 relevant elements across the INEX 2005 CO and VVCAS topics. Numbers for Size and RSize represent averages obtained from each of the 29 CO and 34 VVCAS topics, respectively. Mean average values (calculated across all topics) are shown in bold.

Value	CO			VVCAS		
	Total (elements)	Size (bytes)	RSize (%)	Total (elements)	Size (bytes)	RSize (%)
E? (too-small)						
Mean Average	**1706**	**190**	**97**	**5710**	**101**	**99**
Minimum	2	4	59	2	7	91
Maximum	14,543	1,497	100	44,628	497	100
Median	392	72	100	2,422	74	100
Standard Deviation	3,281	359	8	9,118	104	2
E1						
Mean Average	**389**	**7,508**	**60**	**439**	**9,359**	**64**
Minimum	14	497	20	8	1,738	21
Maximum	1,519	13,477	100	1,876	20,236	100
Median	251	7,177	59	365	7,835	71
Standard Deviation	378	3,379	19	415	5,156	20
E2						
Mean Average	**143**	**18,039**	**55**	**174**	**21,575**	**58**
Minimum	2	2,686	16	14	3,746	19
Maximum	1,203	45,909	100	839	55,028	94
Median	46	17,297	50	53	16,832	54
Standard Deviation	237	10,961	20	222	12,550	19

exhaustive (E2) elements are the least common, the largest in size, and contain the smallest proportion of relevant information. The partially exhaustive (E1) elements lie in between.

These statistics show that — on average, at least — the assignment of the three exhaustivity grades seems to properly reflect their initial relevance definitions [7]. However, a closer look at the too small element distribution reveals some inconsistencies in connection to the E? relevance grade. For example, Table 1 shows that the maximum average size of the too small elements is 1,497 characters, which is found for CO topic 207. On the other hand, the minimum value for the proportion of contained relevant information is 59%, found for CO topic 222. A closer inspection of the relevance judgements for these two topics reveals many cases where an article body is judged to be too small, while the whole article is judged to be either E1 or E2, despite the fact that the sizes of the article and its body are nearly the same. Given that the average size of an article in the INEX 2005 document collection is 44,030 characters, we should ask the question: How can a 40KB article body be so incomplete that it is judged to be too small?

These and similar examples suggest that assessors seem to have their own interpretations of what *too small* means; arguably, these interpretations could have an adverse effect on retrieval evaluation, especially in cases where *exhaustivity* is given a high weight by the evaluation metric.

Next, for each grade of the two INEX relevance dimensions, we undertake an analysis of the level of agreement between the two assessors of the five double-judged topics at INEX 2005, to find whether there is indeed a reason for ignoring the exhaustivity dimension during evaluation.

2.2 Level of Assessor Agreement

Four of the five topics double-judged at INEX 2005 are CO topics (numbers 209, 217, 234, and 237), while one is a VVCAS topic (number 261). As shown in Table 2, we calculated two separate assessor agreements: one at article level, and another at element level. The ∪ values represent the number of unique relevant items judged by the two assessors, while ∩ values are the number of mutually agreed relevant items. The level of assessor agreement is shown by the ∩/∪ values.

The assessor agreements shown in Table 2 are calculated for seven different cases: once for all relevant (non-zero) items, and for six other cases when relevant items belong to each of the six relevance grades of the two INEX relevance

Table 2. Overall article and element level agreement between two assessors for the five topics double-judged at INEX 2005. Agreements are calculated on all relevant (non-zero) items, and separately on items that belong to a relevance grade of an INEX relevance dimension. For an INEX 2005 topic, the value of ∪ represents the total number of unique relevant items judged by the two assessors, while ∩ shows the number of mutually agreed relevant items. The ∩/∪ values reflect the level of agreement between the two assessors. Mean average ∩/∪ values are shown in bold.

Topic (Type)	Non-zero (∪)	(∩)	(∩/∪)	E? (∩/∪)	E1 (∩/∪)	E2 (∩/∪)	S1 (∩/∪)	S2 (∩/∪)	S3 (∩/∪)
Article level									
209 (CO)	133	48	0.36	—	0.05	0.33	0.19	0.06	0.00
217 (CO)	58	19	0.33	0.00	0.10	0.17	0.00	0.00	0.19
234 (CO)	254	193	0.76	—	0.14	0.22	0.71	0.58	0.00
237 (CO)	134	25	0.19	—	0.09	0.13	0.19	—	—
261 (VV)	38	11	0.29	—	0.03	0.70	0.14	0.50	0.00
Mean	123	59	**0.39**	**0.00**	**0.08**	**0.31**	**0.25**	**0.28**	**0.05**
Element level									
209 (CO)	17,599	2,122	0.12	0.08	0.12	0.07	0.08	0.03	0.10
217 (CO)	10,441	1,911	0.18	0.17	0.01	0.06	0.00	0.01	0.18
234 (CO)	5,785	2,824	0.49	0.01	0.15	0.15	0.62	0.22	0.43
237 (CO)	1,630	220	0.13	0.02	0.10	0.11	0.14	0.05	0.09
261 (VV)	5,470	1,657	0.30	0.30	0.12	0.29	0.12	0.23	0.30
Mean	8,185	1,747	**0.24**	**0.12**	**0.10**	**0.14**	**0.19**	**0.11**	**0.22**

dimensions. Since the specificity dimension at INEX 2005 is measured on a continuous [0-1] scale, we decided to divide this scale to three equal relevance sub-scales, and to assign the marginally specific (S1) items to the (0-0.33] scale, the fairly specific (S2) items to (0.33-0.67] scale, and the highly specific (S3) items to the (0.67-1.0] scale. We have also experimented with different (three- and four-graded) variations of relevance sub-scales, and found that the choice of the sub-scale does not influence the validity of the reported results.

At article level, the assessor agreement for non-zero articles (those articles considered relevant by both assessors, irrespective of their relevance grades) varies from 0.19 on topic 237, to 0.76 on topic 234. The mean article-level agreement between the two assessors is 0.39, which is greater than the value of 0.27 reported by Trotman on the INEX 2004 topics [10], but still lower than the three values — 0.49, 0.43, and 0.42 — reported by Voorhees on the TREC-4 topics [11]. When considering article-level agreements on individual relevance grades, we observe that the highest level of agreement between the two assessors is 0.31 (on highly exhaustive E2 articles).

At element level, the assessor agreement when all the non-zero elements are considered varies from 0.12 on topic 209, to 0.49 on topic 234. The mean element-level agreement between the two assessors is 0.24, which is (again) greater than the value of 0.16 reported by Trotman on the INEX 2004 topics [10]. Unlike for the article-level agreements, the agreement between the two assessors on individual relevance grades seems to be higher for specificity rather than for exhaustivity, with the highest level of agreement (0.22) on highly specific S3 elements. We realise, however, that these values should be treated with care, since results from only five topics — the only ones known to be double-judged at INEX 2005 — are used in our analysis.

Although this analysis provides a useful insight as to how the concept of *relevance* is understood by the INEX assessors, it still does not provide enough evidence to answer the following question: Is it easier for the assessor to be consistent while highlighting relevant content, or while choosing an exhaustivity value using a three-graded relevance scale? We believe that the first activity is a series of *independent* relevant-or-not decisions, whereas the second activity additionally involves comparison with other *dependent* decisions, given that the exhaustivity value for a parent element is always equal or greater than the value of any of its children. In Table 3 we present a fine-grained analysis of the element-level agreement on each of the six relevance grades, by only considering those elements that were mutually agreed to be relevant by both assessors.

The methodology is as follows. First, we take all the judgements obtained from each assessor of the five *official* INEX 2005 topics, and then for each topic we select only those relevant (non-zero) elements that are also confirmed to be relevant by the *additional* assessor of the INEX 2005 topic. We refer to these elements as *mutually agreed* (MA) elements. Next, for both exhaustivity and specificity, we count how many of the MA elements belong to a particular relevance grade. For example, Table 3 shows that the distribution of the 2,824 MA elements

Table 3. Fine grained element level agreement between two assessors for the five topics double-judged at INEX 2005. For an INEX 2005 topic, MA represents the number of mutually agreed relevant (non-zero) elements. For a relevance grade of an INEX relevance dimension, the value of ∪ represents the number of relevant elements judged by the assessor of the official INEX 2005 topic, which are part of the mutually agreed relevant elements for that topic. The value of ∩/∪ reflects the fraction of elements confirmed to belong to the same relevance grade by the additional assessor of the INEX 2005 topic. Mean average ∩/∪ values are shown in bold.

		E?		E1		E2		S1		S2		S3	
Topic	MA	(∪)	(∩/∪)	(∪)	(∩/∪)	(∪)	(∩/∪)	(∪)	(∩/∪)	(∪)	(∩/∪)	(∪)	(∩/∪)
209	2,122	1,629	0.73	424	0.50	69	0.70	94	0.84	59	0.25	1,969	0.83
217	1,911	1,889	0.88	15	0.33	7	0.86	1	0.00	1	1.00	1,909	0.97
234	2,824	878	0.01	810	0.81	1,136	0.19	782	0.96	145	0.49	1,897	0.99
237	220	29	0.28	145	0.86	46	0.26	129	0.89	29	0.34	62	0.90
261	1,657	1,545	0.98	72	0.54	40	0.70	19	0.58	25	0.48	1,613	1.0
Mean	1,747	1,194	**0.58**	293	**0.61**	260	**0.54**	205	**0.65**	52	**0.51**	1,490	**0.94**

for topic 234 is as follows. For exhaustivity, 878 are too small, 810 are E1, and 1,136 are E2 elements. For specificity, 782 are S1 elements, 145 are S2, and 1,897 are S3 elements. Last, for each relevance grade, we calculate the proportion of MA elements that are also confirmed to belong to the same relevance grade by the additional assessor of the INEX 2005 topic. These numbers are then averaged across the five INEX topics. For example, for topic 234 the E1 relevance grade has the highest level (0.81) of MA element agreement for exhaustivity (but almost zero agreement for E?), while two relevance grades for specificity, S1 and S3, have almost perfect MA element agreement.

From the average numbers, we identify two cases where conclusions can be drawn: the case of the E? relevance grade, with the average of 1,194 MA elements, and the case of S3 relevance grade, with the average number of 1,490 MA elements. We observe that (on average) only 58% of the E? MA elements are also confirmed to be E? by the additional assessors of the INEX 2005 topics. This confirms our previous conjecture that the assessors do not agree on the exact interpretation of too small. Conversely, on average 94% of the S3 MA elements are also confirmed to be S3, indicating that assessors clearly agree on the highlighted relevant content. The agreements for the other four relevance grades (all above 50%) are more or less similar, however no conclusions can be drawn due to the relatively small average number of MA elements.

The results obtained from the analysis of the level of assessor agreement suggest that there is good reason for ignoring the exhaustivity dimension during evaluation, since it appears to be easier for the assessor to be consistent when highlighting relevant content than when choosing one of the three exhaustivity values. In the next section, we present an evaluation metric for XML retrieval that solely uses *specificity* to evaluate the XML retrieval effectiveness.

3   HiXEval — Highlighting XML Retrieval Evaluation

Our proposal for an alternative metric for XML retrieval is mainly motivated by the need to simplify the XML retrieval evaluation, as well as the need to use a metric that is conformant to the well-established evaluation measures used in traditional information retrieval. The HiXEval metric credits systems for retrieving elements that contain as much highlighted (relevant) textual information as possible, without also containing a significant amount of non-relevant information. To measure the extent to which an XML retrieval system returns relevant information, we only take into account the amount of highlighted text in a retrieved element, without considering the value of exhaustivity for that element. We propose to extend the traditional definitions of precision and recall as follows.

$$Precision = \frac{amount\ of\ relevant\ information\ retrieved}{total\ amount\ of\ information\ retrieved}$$

$$Recall = \frac{amount\ of\ relevant\ information\ retrieved}{total\ amount\ of\ relevant\ information}$$

Let $\mathbf{e}$ be an element that belongs to a ranked list of elements returned by an XML retrieval system. Three distinct scenarios are possible for this element:

1. $\mathbf{e}$ is a not-yet-seen element (NS);
2. $\mathbf{e}$ has previously been fully seen (FS), and
3. $\mathbf{e}$ is an element-part, that has been in part seen previously (PS).

Let $rsize(\mathbf{e})$ be the number of highlighted (relevant) characters. To measure the value of retrieving relevant information from $\mathbf{e}$ at rank $\mathbf{r}$, we define the relevance value function $\mathbf{rval_r}(\mathbf{e})$ as:

$$\mathbf{rval_r}(\mathbf{e}) = \begin{cases} rsize(\mathbf{e}) & \textit{if } \mathbf{e} \textit{ is } NS \\ rsize(\mathbf{e}) - \alpha \cdot rsize(\mathbf{e}) & \textit{if } \mathbf{e} \textit{ is } FS \\ rsize(\mathbf{e}) - \alpha \cdot \sum_{\mathbf{e'}} rsize(\mathbf{e'}) & \textit{if } \mathbf{e} \textit{ is } PS \end{cases}$$

where $\mathbf{e'}$ represents a previously retrieved element that at the same time is descendant of $\mathbf{e}$, which appears at rank higher than $\mathbf{r}$ (if any). The parameter α is a weighting factor that represents the importance of retrieving non-overlapping elements in the ranked list. By introducing α in the $\mathbf{rval_r}(\mathbf{e})$ function, different models of user behaviour can be represented. For example, setting α to 1 (overlap=on) models users that do not tolerate overlap, and ensures that the system will only be credited for retrieving relevant information that has not been previously retrieved by other overlapping elements. Conversely, setting α to 0 (overlap=off) models tolerant users and ensures that the system is always credited for retrieving relevant information, regardless of whether the same information has previously been retrieved.

Let $size(\mathbf{e})$ be the total number of characters contained by $\mathbf{e}$, and **Trel** the total amount of relevant information for an INEX topic (if $\alpha = 1$, then **Trel** is the number of highlighted characters across all documents; if $\alpha \in [0, 1)$, then **Trel** is the number of highlighted characters across all elements). Let $\mathbf{i}$ be an integer that reflects the rank of an element, and $\mathbf{i} \in [1, r]$.

We measure the fraction of *retrieved relevant information* as:

$$\text{P@r} = \frac{1}{\mathbf{r}} \cdot \sum_{\mathbf{i}=1}^{\mathbf{r}} \frac{\mathbf{rval_i(e)}}{size(\mathbf{e})}$$

The P@r measure ensures that, to achieve a *precision* gain at rank $\mathbf{r}$, the retrieved element $\mathbf{e}$ needs to contain *as little non-relevant information as possible*.

We measure the fraction of *relevant information retrieved* as:

$$\text{R@r} = \frac{1}{\textbf{Trel}} \cdot \sum_{\mathbf{i}=1}^{\mathbf{r}} \mathbf{rval_i(e)}$$

The R@r measure ensures that, to achieve a *recall* gain at rank $\mathbf{r}$, the retrieved element $\mathbf{e}$ needs to contain *as much relevant information as possible*.

In addition to the above measures, we also calculate values for MAP and iMAP, which represent mean average precision (calculated at natural recall levels), and interpolated mean average precision (calculated at standard 11 recall levels), respectively.

The two precision and recall values could be combined in a single value for a given rank $\mathbf{r}$ using the F-measure (the *harmonic mean*) as follows.

$$\text{F@r} = \frac{2 \cdot \text{P@r} \cdot \text{R@r}}{\text{P@r} + \text{R@r}}$$

By comparing the F@r values obtained from different systems, it would be possible to see which system is more capable of retrieving as much relevant information as possible, without also retrieving a significant amount of non-relevant information.

4 HiXEval Versus XCG in XML Retrieval Experiments

In this section, we demonstrate the usefulness of HiXEval compared to the XCG-based metrics in XML retrieval experiments. More specifically, we make direct use of the INEX evaluation methodology — its desire to order XML retrieval runs to understand which retrieval techniques work well and which do not — to find how the run orderings generated by the HiXEval measures compare to the run ordering obtained when using measures from the XCG family of metrics.

We present results for all the retrieval strategies explored in the two INEX 2005 sub-tasks (CO and CAS).[2] From the XCG family of metrics, we use nxCG and

---

[2] Results for retrieval strategies in the +S sub-task are not included, since they are similar to the results presented for the CO sub-task.

ep/gr in our experiments. The genLifted quantisation function is used with both metrics, which means that the E? elements are included during evaluation [3]. We use the rank (Spearman) correlation coefficient to measure the extent to which the rank orderings obtained from a pair of measures correlate. We choose this primarily because, with non-parametric correlation using the Spearman coefficient, there is no need to assume that data in the pairs come from normal distributions. Values of the Spearman coefficient range from +1 (perfect positive correlation), through 0 (no correlation), to -1 (perfect negative correlation). All reported values are statistically significant ($p < 0.01$).

4.1   INEX 2005 CO Sub-task

Three retrieval strategies are explored in the CO sub-task: Thorough, Focussed, and FetchBrowse [6]. We use different settings for each evaluation measure of the nxCG, ep/gr and HiXEval metrics depending on the strategy used. For example, for the Focussed strategy we use a setting which penalises runs that retrieve overlapping elements (overlap=on), whereas for the Thorough strategy a setting that ignores the overlapping retrieved elements is used (overlap=off).

Thorough Retrieval Strategy. The upper part of Table 4 shows Spearman correlation coefficients calculated from the run orderings using the 55 submitted runs for the INEX 2005 CO.Thorough retrieval strategy. We observe that each of the three nxCG measures is strongly correlated to the corresponding precision measure of HiXEval. Interestingly, there is low correlation between the three nxCG measures and their corresponding recall measures in HiXEval. The table

Table 4. Spearman correlation coefficients calculated from the run orderings obtained from pairs of evaluation measures using the 55 submitted runs for the INEX 2005 CO.Thorough (upper part) and 44 runs for the CO.Focussed (lower part) retrieval strategies. Correlation scores between an evaluation measure from the XCG family of metrics and its corresponding measure from HiXEval are shown in bold.

Metric (measure)	nxCG 10	nxCG 25	nxCG 50	ep/gr MAep	HiXEval P@10	HiXEval R@10	HiXEval P@25	HiXEval R@25	HiXEval P@50	HiXEval R@50	HiXEval MAP
CO.Thorough (overlap=off)											
nxCG (nxCG[10])	1.00	0.94	0.91	0.82	**0.96**	0.31	0.91	0.28	0.88	0.34	0.83
nxCG (nxCG[25])	0.94	1.00	0.97	0.86	0.90	0.35	**0.95**	0.33	0.94	0.39	0.85
nxCG (nxCG[50])	0.91	0.97	1.00	0.92	0.85	0.40	0.92	0.37	**0.96**	0.43	0.89
ep/gr (MAep)	0.82	0.86	0.92	1.00	0.74	0.52	0.80	0.49	0.87	0.54	**0.94**
CO.Focussed (overlap=on)											
nxCG (nxCG[10])	1.00	0.98	0.96	0.95	**0.92**	0.17	0.89	0.23	0.88	0.22	0.73
nxCG (nxCG[25])	0.98	1.00	0.98	0.96	0.90	0.17	**0.91**	0.24	0.89	0.23	0.73
nxCG (nxCG[50])	0.96	0.98	1.00	0.98	0.92	0.17	0.92	0.24	**0.93**	0.23	0.76
ep/gr (MAep)	0.95	0.96	0.98	1.00	0.91	0.18	0.92	0.25	0.93	0.24	**0.82**

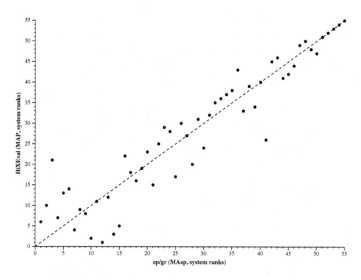

Fig. 2. Correlation between run orderings generated by MAep (ep/gr) and MAP (HiXEval) using the 55 submitted runs for the CO.Thorough retrieval strategy. The Spearman correlation coefficient is 0.94.

also shows coefficients when the measures from the nxCG and ep/gr metrics are compared with each other. The overall trend observed when pairs of these measures are compared (in terms of how well they correlate) is also observed when comparing the corresponding pairs of XCG and HiXEval measures. The Spearman coefficient shows that there is a strong correlation (0.94) between run orderings generated by MAep (ep/gr) and MAP (HiXEval) when comparing mean average precision. The graph of Fig. 2 provides a detailed overview of the observed correlation between these run orderings, showing that the biggest differences in rankings occur with the best performing systems.

The observed correlations between the corresponding measures of HiXEval and XCG (all greater than 0.9) show that similar run orderings are generated by the two metrics.

Focussed Retrieval Strategy. The lower part of Table 4 shows Spearman correlation coefficients calculated from the run orderings using the 44 submitted runs for the INEX 2005 CO.Focussed retrieval strategy. The calculated correlation numbers for the three nxCG measures and their corresponding HiXEval precision measures are again greater than 0.9, with a similar trend to that observed for the CO.Thorough strategy. However, the correlation coefficient is lower for this strategy (0.82) when comparing mean average precision. Unlike for the CO.Thorough strategy, there are strong correlations between MAep and each of the three *precision* measures of HiXEval, whereas there is almost no correlation between MAep and each of the three *recall* measures. This suggests that, for the CO.Focussed retrieval strategy, the methodology used in creating the *ideal recall-base* has an adverse effect on the overall recall, which seems to dramatically influence the run orderings obtained from MAep measure of the ep/gr metric.

Table 5. Spearman correlation coefficients calculated from the run orderings obtained from pairs of evaluation measures using the 31 correctly submitted runs for the INEX 2005 CO.FetchBrowse-Article (upper part) and CO.FetchBrowse-Element (middle and lower parts) retrieval strategies. Correlation scores between the MAep measure (ep/gr) and the MAP measure (HiXEval) are shown in bold.

Metric (measure)	ep/gr	HiXEval		
	MAep	Prec	Rec	MAP
CO.FetchBrowse-Article (overlap=off,on) ep/gr (MAep)	1.00	0.69	0.70	**0.85**
CO.FetchBrowse-Element (overlap=off) ep/gr (MAep)	1.00	0.90	0.88	**0.95**
CO.FetchBrowse-Element (overlap=on) ep/gr (MAep)	1.00	0.80	0.92	**0.67**

FetchBrowse **Retrieval Strategy.** The evaluation methodology for this retrieval strategy is different from those for the other two CO strategies in that two separate evaluation results are reported: an article-level result and an element-level result, the latter calculated by using both (off and on) overlap settings [3]. To obtain element-level results, in addition to MAP we report values obtained by the following two HiXEval measures: Prec, which measures precision at final rank for each article cluster, averaged over all clusters and then over all topics; and Rec, which measures recall at final rank for each article cluster, also averaged over all clusters and topics. To obtain article-level results with HiXEval, we used the article-derived runs along with their corresponding relevance judgements, which means that values for Prec and Rec refer to those for precision and recall at final cut-offs (1500), respectively.

Table 5 shows Spearman correlation coefficients calculated from the run orderings using the 31 correctly submitted runs for the INEX 2005 CO.FetchBrowse retrieval strategy. For article-level results, the calculated value for the Spearman coefficient between MAep and MAP is 0.85. The probable cause for this behaviour is that different methodologies are used by the two metrics to determine the preferred article answers; indeed, the ep/gr metric uses knowledge of the highest scoring element within an article to obtain the ordering of the ideal article gain vector, whereas articles are inspected on their own merit by HiXEval.

Table 5 also shows that, for element-level results, the overlap setting dramatically changes the observed level of correlation between the rank orderings of the two metrics. With overlap set to off, there is a strong correlation between the two mean average precision measures. With overlap set to on there is little correlation between MAep and MAP; however, we observe that in this case MAep is better correlated with recall (0.92) than with precision (0.80). We believe that the probable cause for this behaviour is that, unlike the case of the CO.Focussed retrieval strategy where overlap is also set to on, here the number of relevant elements that comprise the ideal recall-base for each *article cluster* is much smaller, which in turn makes it easier for runs to achieve perfect recall for a given cluster. The small correlation value between MAep and MAP, however, suggests that the two metrics could have differently implemented the mean average precision measure for this overlap setting.

4.2   CAS Sub-task

Four retrieval strategies are explored in the CAS sub-task: SSCAS, SVCAS, VSCAS, and VVCAS; these differ in the way the target and support elements of a CAS topic are interpreted [6]. We use the overlap=off setting for each evaluation measure of nxCG, ep/gr, and HiXEval.

Table 6. Spearman correlation coefficients calculated from the run orderings obtained from pairs of evaluation measures using 25 submitted runs for SSCAS, 23 runs for SVCAS and VSCAS, and 28 runs for VVCAS retrieval strategies. Correlation scores between an evaluation measure from the XCG family of metrics and its corresponding measure from HiXEval are shown in bold.

Metric (measure)	nxCG			ep/gr	HiXEval						
	10	25	50	MAep	P@10	R@10	P@25	R@25	P@50	R@50	MAP
SSCAS											
(overlap=off)											
nxCG (nxCG[10])	1.00	0.97	0.75	0.69	0.82	**0.95**	0.62	0.98	0.60	0.92	0.58
nxCG (nxCG[25])	0.97	1.00	0.84	0.66	0.81	0.94	0.69	**0.97**	0.68	0.95	0.55
nxCG (nxCG[50])	0.75	0.84	1.00	0.57	0.80	0.79	0.92	0.77	**0.91**	0.90	0.53
ep/gr (MAep)		0.69	0.66	0.57	1.00	0.74	0.64	0.64	0.62	0.66	0.70	**0.96**
SVCAS											
(overlap=off)											
nxCG (nxCG[10])	1.00	0.98	0.98	0.94	**0.98**	0.94	0.91	0.92	0.94	0.92	0.93
nxCG (nxCG[25])	0.98	1.00	0.99	0.94	0.97	0.93	**0.94**	0.93	0.96	0.94	0.93
nxCG (nxCG[50])	0.98	0.99	1.00	0.95	0.97	0.92	0.93	0.93	**0.96**	0.94	0.92
ep/gr (MAep)		0.94	0.94	0.95	1.00	0.93	0.86	0.84	0.88	0.89	0.91	**0.95**
VSCAS											
(overlap=off)											
nxCG (nxCG[10])	1.00	0.97	0.96	0.83	**0.98**	0.76	0.95	0.74	0.94	0.71	0.88
nxCG (nxCG[25])	0.97	1.00	0.99	0.86	0.96	0.73	**0.98**	0.72	0.97	0.71	0.91
nxCG (nxCG[50])	0.96	0.99	1.00	0.86	0.94	0.75	0.97	0.75	**0.97**	0.74	0.92
ep/gr (MAep)		0.83	0.86	0.86	1.00	0.81	0.59	0.88	0.64	0.86	0.63	**0.90**
VVCAS											
(overlap=off)											
nxCG (nxCG[10])	1.00	0.93	0.90	0.75	**0.96**	0.57	0.93	0.56	0.91	0.59	0.73
nxCG (nxCG[25])	0.93	1.00	0.97	0.85	0.92	0.62	**0.95**	0.65	0.98	0.67	0.84
nxCG (nxCG[50])	0.90	0.97	1.00	0.90	0.87	0.72	0.90	0.74	**0.95**	0.76	0.91
ep/gr (MAep)		0.75	0.85	0.90	1.00	0.72	0.72	0.75	0.76	0.84	0.75	**0.91**

Table 6 shows Spearman correlation coefficients calculated from the run orderings using different numbers of submitted runs for each of the four INEX 2005 CAS retrieval strategies. We observe that there is a strong correlation between the two metrics for the CAS sub-task, irrespective of the retrieval strategy used. However, the observed correlation between each of the three measures of nxCG with the two precision and recall measures of HiXEval changes depending on the way the target element is interpreted. For the two *strict* CAS retrieval strategies (SS and SV), nxCG seems to be more recall- than precision-oriented, whereas for the *vague* CAS retrieval strategies the reverse is true. We suspect that, as with CO.FetchBrowse-Element retrieval strategy, the fewer relevant elements comprising the recall-base for the two strict CAS strategies may have an impact on the evaluation methodology of the nxCG metric.

5   Conclusions and Future Work

HiXEval addresses many of the concerns that have been raised in connection with the XCG-based metrics. Its main features are simplicity, compatibility with the well-understood measures used in traditional information retrieval, ability to model different user behaviours, and most importantly, minimal reliance on subjective decisions during evaluation. Indeed, if there was broad acceptance of HiXEval, there would be no need for assessors to judge exhaustivity, as only highlighting of relevant passages would be required. This would substantially reduce the time taken to undertake the relevance judgements.

The HiXEval metric is based solely on the specificity dimension, which, as we have shown through our analysis of the level of assessor agreement of the five INEX 2005 topics, is much better interpreted by assessors than the definition of the exhaustivity dimension. Moreover, our correlation analysis of the rank orderings between HiXEval and the two XCG-based metrics has confirmed that both metrics perform broadly the same task, and thus measure the same (or similar) retrieval behaviour.

The correlation analysis has also identified the different *orientations* of the XCG-based metrics; indeed, regardless of whether the level of overlap among retrieved elements is considered or not, in the case where the number of the so-called *ideal* retrieval elements is rather small, the XCG metrics seem to be more recall- than precision-oriented. Conversely, with a sufficient number of ideal retrieval elements in the recall-base, the two metrics are clearly precision-oriented.

In the future we intend to check the reliability and stability of HiXEval and the two XCG metrics. We plan to undertake reliability tests for the HiXEval metric, similar to the ones performed for XCG and the INEX-2002 metrics [5]. To test stability, we plan to measure significance and error rates by pursuing a simplification of the methodology used by Sanderson and Zobel [9]. We also plan to further investigate the observed differences on the best performing systems.

Acknowledgements

We thank Saied Tahaghoghi and the anonymous reviewer for their comments.

References

1. D. Hiemstra and V. Mihajlovic. The Simplest Evaluation Measures for XML Information Retrieval that Could Possibly Work. In *Proceedings of the INEX 2005 Workshop on Element Retrieval Methodology*, pages 6–13, Glasgow, UK, 2005.
2. K. Jarvelin and J. Kekalainen. Cumulated gain-based evaluation of IR techniques. *ACM Transactions on Information Systems (TOIS)*, 20:422–446, 2002.
3. G. Kazai and M. Lalmas. INEX 2005 evaluation metrics. In *INEX 2005 Workshop Pre-Proceedings, Dagstuhl, Germany, November 28–30, 2005*, pages 401–406, 2005.
4. G. Kazai and M. Lalmas. Notes on what to measure in INEX. In *Proceedings of the INEX 2005 Workshop on Element Retrieval Methodology*, pages 22–38, Glasgow, UK, 2005.
5. G. Kazai, M. Lalmas, and A. P. de Vries. Reliability tests for the XCG and INEX-2002 metrics. In *Advances in XML Information Retrieval: Third International Workshop of the Initiative for the Evaluation of XML Retrieval, INEX 2004, Dagstuhl Castle, Germany, December 6-8, 2004, Revised Selected Papers*, volume 3493 of *LNCS*, pages 60–72, May 2005.
6. M. Lalmas. INEX 2005 retrieval task and result submission specification. In *INEX 2005 Workshop Pre-Proceedings, Dagstuhl, Germany, November 28–30, 2005*, pages 385–390, 2005.
7. M. Lalmas and B. Piwowarski. Inex 2005 relevance assessment guide. In *INEX 2005 Workshop Pre-Proceedings, Dagstuhl, Germany, November 28–30, 2005*, pages 391–400, 2005.
8. J. Pehcevski, J. A. Thom, and A.-M. Vercoustre. Users and Assessors in the Context of INEX: Are Relevance Dimensions Relevant? In *Proceedings of the INEX 2005 Workshop on Element Retrieval Methodology*, pages 47–62, Glasgow, UK, 30 July 2005.
9. M. Sanderson and J. Zobel. Information retrieval system evaluation: effort, sensitivity, and reliability. In *Proceedings of the ACM-SIGIR International Conference on Research and Development in Information Retrieval*, pages 162–169, Salvador, Brazil, 2005.
10. A. Trotman. Wanted: Element Retrieval Users. In *Proceedings of the INEX 2005 Workshop on Element Retrieval Methodology*, pages 63–69, Glasgow, UK, 2005.
11. E. M. Voorhees. Variations in relevance judgements and the measurment of retrieval effectiveness. *Information Processing & Management*, 36(5):697–716, 2000.

The Interpretation of CAS

Andrew Trotman[1] and Mounia Lalmas[2]

[1] Department of Computer Science, University of Otago, Dunedin, New Zealand
andrew@cs.otago.ac.nz
[2] Department of Computer Science, Queen Mary, University of London, London, UK
mounia@dcs.qmul.ac.uk

Abstract. There has been much debate over how to interpret the structure in queries that contain structural hints. At INEX 2003 and 2004, there were two interpretations: SCAS in which the user specified target element was interpreted strictly, and VCAS in which it was interpreted vaguely. But how many ways are there that the query could be interpreted? In the investigation at INEX 2005 (discussed herein) four different interpretations were proposed, and compared on the same queries. Those interpretations (SSCAS, SVCAS, VSCAS, and VVCAS) are the four interpretations possible by interpreting the target elements, and the support elements, either strictly or vaguely. An analysis of the submitted runs shows that those that share an interpretation of the target element correlate - that is, the previous decision to divide CAS into the SCAS and VCAS (as done at INEX 2003 and 2004) was sound. The analysis is supported by the fact that the best performing VSCAS run was submitted to the VVCAS task and the best performing SVCAS run was submitted to the SSCAS task.

1 Introduction

Does including a structural hint in a query make a precision difference and if so how should we interpret it? At INEX 2005 the *ad hoc* track has been investigating this question. Two experiments were conducted, the CO+S experiment, and the CAS experiment.

In the CO+S experiment the participants were asked to submit topics with content only (CO) queries containing just search terms, and optionally an additional structured (+S) query specified in the NEXI [10] query language. Given these two different interpretations of the same information need it is possible to compare the precision of queries containing structural hints to those that do not *for the same information need*. The details of the CO+S experiment are beyond the scope of this paper.

In a separate experiment participants were asked to submit topics containing queries that contain content and structure (CAS) constraints specified in NEXI [10]. These topics were used to determine how the structural hints, necessarily present in a CAS topic, should be interpreted by a search engine. The two extreme views are the database view that all structural constraints must be

N. Fuhr et al. (Eds.): INEX 2005, LNCS 3977, pp. 58–71, 2006.

upheld, and the information retrieval view that satisfying the information need is more important than following the structural constraints of the query.

This contribution discusses the mechanics of the CAS experiment from the topic submission process, the document collection, through to the evaluation methods. The different tasks are compared using Pearson's product moment correlation coefficient showing that there were essentially only two tasks, those that in previous years have gone by the name VCAS and SCAS. Further analysis shows that of the tasks SSCAS is the easiest and VVCAS the hardest.

2   CAS Queries

Laboratory experiments in information retrieval following the Cranfield methodology (described by Voorhees [12]) require a document collection, a series of queries (known as topics), and a series of judgments (decisions as to which documents are relevant to which topics). In element retrieval this same process is followed - except with respect to a document element rather than a whole document.

Content and structure queries differ from content only queries in so far as they contain structural hints. Two types of structural hints are present, those that specify where to look (support elements) and those that specify what to return to the user (target elements). In INEX topic 258

```
//article[about(.,intellectual property)]//sec[about(., copyright law)]
```

the search engine is being asked to identify documents about intellectual property and from those extract sections about copyright law. The target element is //article//sec (extract //article//sec elements). The support elements are //article (with support from //article about intellectual property) and //article//sec (and support from //article//sec about copyright law). Full details of the syntax of CAS queries is given by Trotman and Sigurbjörnsson [10]. The applicability of this language to XML evaluation in the context of INEX is also discussed by Trotman and Sigurbjörnsson [11].

2.1   Query Complexity

The simplest CAS queries contain only a single structural constraint. Topic 270,

```
//article//sec[about( ., introduction information retrieval)]
```

asks for //article//sec elements about "introduction information retrieval". A more complex (multiple clause) query can be decomposed into a series of single constraint (single clause) queries (or child queries). Topic 258,

```
//article[about(.,intellectual property)]//sec[about(., copyright law)]
```

could be written as a series of single constraint queries, each of which must be satisfied. In this case it is decomposed into topic 259,

```
//article[about(.,intellectual property)]
```

and topic 281,

```
//article//sec[about(., copyright law)]
```

if both hold true of a document then the (parent) query is true of that document - and the target element constraints can be considered. The same decomposition property holds true for all multiple constraint CAS topics (so long as the target element is preserved) - it is inherent in the distributive nature of the query language.

Having separate parent and children topics makes it possible to look at different interpretations of the same topic. As a topic is judged according to the narrative the judgments are by definition vague. Strict conformance of these judgments to the target element can be generated using a simple filter. This is the approach taken at INEX 2003 and 2004 for the so-called SCAS and VCAS tasks. But what about the sub-clauses of these topics? Should they be interpreted strictly or vaguely? With the judgments for the child topics, vague and strict conformance to these can also be determined. With the combination of child and parent judgments it is possible to look at many different interpretations of the same topic.

2.2 Topic Format

INEX captures not only the query, but also the information need of the user. These are stored together in XML. Methods not dissimilar to this have been used at TREC [2] and INEX [1] for many years. As an example, INEX topic 258 contains several parts all discussing the same information need:

```
<?xml version="1.0" encoding="ISO-8859-1"?>
<!DOCTYPE inex_topic SYSTEM "topic.dtd">
<inex_topic topic_id="258"  query_type="CAS" ct_no="72">
<InitialTopicStatement>
I have to give a computer science lesson on intellectual property
and I'm looking for information or examples on copyright law to
illustrate it. As I'm looking for something which is specific, I
don't think I can find a whole article about it. I'm consequently
looking for section elements.
</InitialTopicStatement>
<castitle>
//article[about(.,intellectual property)]//sec[about(., copyright law)]
</castitle>
<description>
Return sections about copyright law (information or examples) in an
article about intellectual property.
</description>
<narrative>
I have to give a computer science lesson on intellectual property,
and I'm looking for information or examples on copyright law to
```

illustrate it. More precisely, I'd like to have information about
authors rights and how to protect your creation. As I'm looking for
something which is specific, I don't think I can find a whole
article about it. I'm consequently looking for section elements.
Information or examples can concern copyright on software,
multimedia or operating systems. Copyright on literary work can help
but only for examples. Information concerning domain names and
trademarks is not relevant.
</narrative>
</inex_topic>

- <**InitialTopicStatement**> a description of why the user has chosen to use a search engine, and what it is that the user hopes to achieve.
- <**castitle**> the CAS query specified in the NEXI language [10].
- <**description**> a natural language expression of the information need using the same terms as are found in the <**castitle**>. This element is used by the natural language track at INEX [13].
- <**narrative**> a description of the information need and what makes a result relevant. When judgments are made they are made against this description so it is important that it precisely describes the difference between relevant and irrelevant results. For experiments that additionally take into account the context of a query (such as the interactive track [8]), the purpose for which the information is needed (the work-task) is also given in the narrative.

Both the parent query and the child queries are stored in this way - but an additional element, the <**parent**> element, is present in child topics. This element stores the castitle of the child's parent. This method of linking children to parents was chosen over using identifiers as it was considered less likely to be prone to human input error.

2.3   Query Interpretation

A contentious point about CAS queries is the interpretation. The strict view is that the structural hints are constraints and the search engine should follow them to ensure returning elements that satisfy the user. The vague view is that the structural hints are hints and can be down-played so long as a returned element is relevant in the mind of the user (it satisfies the information need).

A single clause query might be interpreted strictly, or vaguely - that is the constraint might be followed or can be ignored. If, for example, a user asks for an article abstract about "information retrieval", then perhaps an article introduction might just as well satisfy the need - or perhaps not.

With multiple clause queries, there are many possible interpretations. In the CAS experiment at INEX 2005, the strict and vague interpretations are applied to both the target element, and the support elements. This gives four interpretations written XYCAS where X is the target element and Y is the support element, and either X or Y can be S for strict or V for vague. Those interpretations are:

- **VVCAS:** The target element constraint is vague and the support element constraints are vague. This is the information retrieval view of the topic.
- **SVCAS:** The target element constraint is strict, but the support element constraints are vague.
- **VSCAS:** The target element constraint is vague, but the support element constraints are followed strictly.
- **SSCAS:** Both the target element constraint and the support element constraint are followed strictly. This is the database view.

3   Document Collection

The document collection used in the experiments was the INEX IEEE document collection version 1.8. This collection contains 16,819 documents taken from IEEE transactions and magazines published between 1995 and 2004. The total size of the source XML is 705MB. This is the latest version of the INEX collection at publication date.

4   Data Acquisition

This section discusses the acquisition of the queries from the participants and the verification that they are representative of previous years. It also discusses the acquisition of the judgments and the construction of the different judgment sets.

4.1   Query Acquisition

The document collection was distributed to the participating organizations. They were then each asked to submit one CAS topic along with any associated single clause child-topics (should they exist). These topics then went through a selection process in which queries were parsed for syntactic correctness, semantic correctness, consistency, and validated against their child topics. A total of 17 queries passed this selection process.

The breakdown of CAS topic complexity (excluding child-topics) for each of INEX 2003, 2004, and 2005 is given in Table 1. From visual inspection it can be seen that the breakdown in 2005 is representative of previous years, most queries contain two clauses with approximately the same number of three and one clause topics. In 2005 there were no topics with more than 3 clauses.

Table 1. A Breakdown of the complexity of INEX 2005 CAS topics shows that they are representative of previous years

Clauses	1	2	3	4+
2003	7 (23%)	12 (40%)	6 (20%)	5 (17%)
2004	4 (12%)	22 (65%)	4 (12%)	4 (12%)
2005	3 (18%)	12 (71%)	2 (12%)	0 (00%)

Table 2. The 17 topics and the topic numbers of their children

Parent	Children	Parent	Children	Parent	Children
244	245, 246	258	259, 281	270	
247	248, 249, 276	260		275	274, 273
250	251, 252	261	262, 263	280	277, 278, 279
253	254, 255	264	282, 283	284	266, 285
256	272, 271	265	267, 268	288	242, 243
257		269	286, 287		

4.2   Child Topics

Each topic and child topic was given a unique identifier (stored in the topic_id attribute of the inex_topic tag). Table 2 shows which topics are parent topics and which topics are their children. Topic 258, for example, has topics 259 and 281 as children whereas topic 260 is a single clause query and has no children.

It may appear at the onset that these child topics can be used as part of the evaluation giving a total of 47 topics. This, however, is not the case. The guidelines for topic development [7] identifies that for evaluation purposes queries must be diverse, independent, and representative. Using both the parent and the children topics for computing performance violates the independence requirement - and weights evaluation in favor of longer topics (which have more children).

Using just the child topics, and discarding the parents, violates the requirement that topics are representative. In Table 1, the breakdown of topics from previous years is shown. Most topics have two clauses, whereas child topics (by definition) have only one. The children, without their parents, are not representative.

4.3   Judgment Acquisition

The topics and child-topics were distributed to the participants. Each participating group was invited to submit up to two runs for each CAS task. At least one was required for VVCAS. A run consisted of at most 1,500 ranked results for each parent and child topic. There were no restrictions on which part of the topic was used to generate the query - participants were permitted to use the narrative, or description, or castitle if they so chose.

These results were then pooled in a similar manner to that used at TREC (and shown to be robust there by Zobel [15]). The details of the INEX pooling method are give by Piwowarski and Lalmas [6] and a discussion of the robustness is provided by Woodley and Geva [14].

The pool identifies which documents and elements the search engines considered relevant to the query. Using a graphical interface (the 2005 version of X-Rai [5, 6]) to the document collection, the original author of the query (where possible) was asked to identify which elements of which documents in the judgment pool were, in fact, relevant to the information need. Assessors first highlighted relevant passages from the text, and then they assigned relevance values to all elements in this region on a three points scale: highly exhaustive, partly exhaustive, or too small. This assessment was performed for the parent topics in isolation of the child topics - and not necessarily by the same assessor.

As a topic may contain many different interpretations of the information need (for example the description and the castitle) all judgments were made with reference to the description contained in the topic narrative.

4.4   CAS Relevance Assessments

In a separate experiment the consistency of the judgments is being measured across multiple assessors. This is done by asking two or more judges to assess the same topic, without knowledge of the other's decisions. Of the CAS topics, those listed in Table 3 were multiple-judged.

The consequence of this multiple assessment process is that there is no single set of relevance assessments. Inline with INEX 2004, the assessments are divided into two groups: set-a, and set-b (see Pehcevski *et al.* [4] and Trotman [9] for a discussion of the 2004 results of this experiment). The INEX 2005 assignment was made based on proportion of completion at the date the first relevance assessments were released. Those judgments that, from visual inspection, appeared most complete were assigned to set-a, while the other was assigned to set-b. In this way set-a, the set used to generate the official results, was most complete and therefore most reliable.

Internal to X-Rai (the online assessment tool), each assessment of each topic by each judge is given an internal identifier - the pool id. Table 3 also shows which pool ids were assigned to which judgment set.

Table 3. Topics assessed by more than one assessor. Listed for each set against each topic is the pool-id of the assessments.

	Pool	
Topic	Set-a (official)	Set-b (other)
261	350	362
244	354	358
250	356	369
258	289	360

4.5   CAS Relevance Sets

From set-a, four sets of judgments were generated, one for each of the four CAS interpretations - each derived from the same initial set of judgments.

- **VVCAS:** The assessments as done by the assessors (against the narrative). These assessments are unmodified from those collected by INEX from the assessor.

- **SVCAS:** Those VVCAS judgments that strictly satisfy the target element constraint. This set of judgments was computed by taking the VVCAS judgments and removing all judgments that did not satisfy the target element constraint. This was done by a simple matching process. All those elements that were, indeed, the target element were included and those that were not were removed. Topic 260 is an exception. In this case the target element is specified as //bdy//*. To satisfy this constraint all descendants of //bdy (excluding //bdy) are considered to strictly comply.
- **VSCAS:** A relevant element is not required to satisfy the target constraint, however the document must satisfy all other constraints specified in the query. That is, for a multiple clause topic, an element is relevant only if it comes from a document in which the child-topics are strictly adhered to. In all except two topics, given the conjuncton of documents relevant to the child topics, this is any relevant element from the VVCAS set that comes from this conjunction. In one exception (topic 247), this conjunction is replaced with a disjunction. In the other exception (topic 250) there are (presently) no judgments as the assessment task has not been completed.
- **SSCAS:** Those VSCAS judgments that satisfy the target element constraint. These are computed from the VSCAS judgments in the same way that SVCAS judgments are computed from VVCAS judgments - strict conformance to the target element.

The guidelines for topic development [7] identify groups of tags that are equivalent. For example, for historic paper publishing reasons the sec, ss1, ss2 and ss3 tags are all used to identify sections of documents in the collection. The strict conformance to a given structural constraint occurs with reference to the equivalence list - //article//bdy//ss1 strictly conforms to //article//sec.

These relevance sets are considered to be the full recall base for each interpretations of CAS. Different metrics and quantizatons functions could further reduce the relevance sets. For example, in the case of struct quantization only those elements that conform to the interpretation of CAS and further conform to the interpretation of strict are considered relevant.

5 Measurement

The official metric used to report the performance of a system at INEX 2005 is MAep, the mean average nxCG rank at 1500 elements. This measure is described by Kazai and Lalmas [3]. The results (produced using xcgeval) for the INEX 2005 CAS task are available from INEX. There were 99 runs submitted to the CAS tasks, of which 25 were SSCAS, 23 SVCAS, 23 VSCAS, and 28 VVCAS[1].

Of the 17 topics used for evaluation (the parent topics of Table 2) judgments currently exist for only 10 topics - at the time of writing the assessment task had not been completed for the other 7 topics. Of those 10 topics, only 7 have any elements that strictly conform to their child topic structural constraint. The comparison of systems herein is based only on these topics.

---

[1] Submissons version 1 and judgments version 7 are used throughout.

Table 4. Number of relevant elements for each topic using generalised quantization

Topic	SSCAS	SVCAS	VSCAS	VVCAS
253	0	23	0	156
256	492	724	1431	2101
257	96	96	711	711
260	5159	5159	5264	5264
261	0	59	0	4437
264	6	40	155	1272
265	0	40	0	211
270	35	35	850	850
275	111	183	12870	16965
284	2	111	326	14265

Table 5. Number of relevant elements for each topic using strict quantization

Topic	SSCAS	SVCAS	VSCAS	VVCAS
253	0	0	0	11
256	139	162	198	228
257	0	0	0	0
260	66	66	66	66
261	0	0	0	2
264	0	0	12	44
265	0	0	0	1
270	1	1	2	2
275	18	22	330	424
284	0	5	4	196

In Table 4 and Table 5 the number of relevant elements for each topic of each task is shown. The judgments for strict quantization are highly sparse - for the SSCAS task, there are only 4 topics with highly specific and highly exhaustive judgments. It does not seem reasonable to draw any conclusions from only 4 topics so the remainder of this analysis applies to only the generalized quantization of results.

By taking all runs submitted to any CAS task and correlating the performance on one task to the performance on another (say, VVCAS with SSCAS), it is possible to see if a search engine designed for one interpretation also performs well on other interpretations (and therefore if there is any material difference in the tasks). That is, if a search engine is designed to answer in one way but the user expects results in another, does it matter? Taking all the CAS runs (including the "unofficial" runs) the IBM Haifa Research Lab run VVCAS_no_phrase_no_tags submitted to the VVCAS task performs best using the VVCAS judgments (with a MAep score of 0.1314), but if the user need included a strict interpretation of the topic (it was evaluated using the SSCAS judgments) then it is at position 50 with a score of 0.0681.

By comparing the performance of runs submitted to each task it is possible to determine if one task is inherently easier, or harder, than the others. With a harder task there is more room for improvement - further investigation into this task might result in improvements all-round.

5.1 Do the Judgment Sets Correlate?

Table 6 shows the Pearson's product moment correlation coefficient computed for all runs when scored at each task. Scores close to 1 show a positive correlation, those close to -1 a negative correlation and those at 0 show no correlation.

It is clear from the table that VVCAS and VSCAS are strongly correlated. A search strategy that performs well at one task performs well at the other. SSCAS and SVCAS, both with a strict interpretation of the target element are less strongly correlated. There is little correlation between a strict interpretation of the target element and a vague interpretation of the target element (SVCAS and VSCAS, for example).

Figure 1 shows this correlation for the vague target element tasks. There is a cluster of best-scoring runs at the top-right of the graph. They are runs that have performed well at both VVCAS and VSCAS. These four runs are those from IBM Haifa Research Lab. Although different runs perform best on the

Table 6. Pearson's product moment correlation coefficient between each CAS task

	SSCAS	SVCAS	VSCAS	VVCAS
SSCAS	1.0000	0.8934	0.4033	0.3803
SVCAS	0.8934	1.0000	0.3409	0.3768
VSCAS	0.4033	0.3409	1.0000	0.9611
VVCAS	0.3803	0.3768	0.9611	1.0000

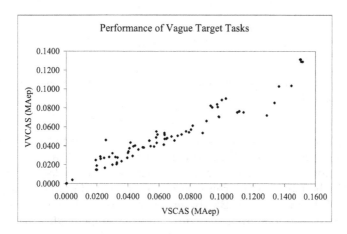

Fig. 1. Plot of performance of all submitted runs using VVCAS and VSCAS shows a strong correlation of one to the other

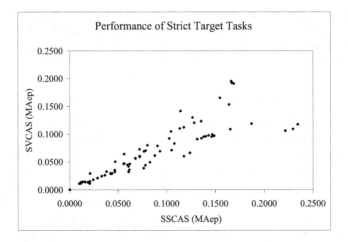

Fig. 2. Plot of performance of all submitted runs using SVCAS and SSCAS shows a strong correlation of one to the other

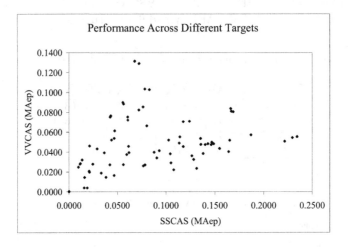

Fig. 3. Plot of performance of all submitted runs using VVCAS and SSCAS shows little correlation of one to the other

VVCAS and VSCAS task, both "best" runs were submitted to the VVCAS task - providing further evidence of the correlation of the two tasks.

Figure 2 shows the same for the strict target element tasks. The cluster is not seen. The best performing run measuring on the SVCAS task was submitted to the SSCAS task (again IBM Haifa Research Lab). These same runs were only bettered by the four from the University of Tampere when measured for the SSCAS task. Although Tampere produced runs that performed well at the

SSCAS task and not at the SVCAS task, IBM Haifa Research Lab produced runs that performed well at both tasks. Again further evidence of the correlation of the two tasks.

Figure 3 shows the performance of SSCAS against VVCAS. It is clear from this figure that those runs that perform well at one task do not perform well at the other. It appears, from visual inspection, that they are average performers at each other's tasks.

5.2   Tasks Complexity

For each task the performance (MAep) of each of the top performaing 21 runs submitted to that task was computed. This number was chosen because different numbers of runs were submitted to each task, and for all tasks there were at least 21 runs with a non-zero score. Table 7 presents the performance of the best run, the mean computed over all runs submitted to the task, and the worst run submited to each task. It can be seen that the best performing run was submitted to the SSCAS task, and for that task the average run performs better that the average run from other tasks. From this we deduce that the SSCAS task is easier than the other tasks. This task may be easiest because the required structural constraints are specified explicitly in the query and the search engine can use this as a filter to remove known non-relevant elements from the result list.

Normally it is invalid to measure the performance of two different search engines by measuring the performance of one on one collecion and the second on a second collection (or set of topics, or judgments). In this experiment the document collection and topics are fixed, the judgments are derived from a single common source, and mean performance across several search engines is compared. We believe this comparison is sound.

Table 7. Mean performance of top 21 runs from each task

	SSCAS	SVCAS	VSCAS	VVCAS
Mean	0.1285	0.0832	0.0628	0.0690
Std Dev	0.0510	0.0484	0.0439	0.0310
Best	0.2343	0.1922	0.1508	0.1314
Worst	0.0381	0.0292	0.0039	0.0208

6   Conclusions

The Pearson's correlation shows that there are only two different interpretations of the query, those with a strict interpretation of the target element and those with a vague interpretation of the target element (the database and the information retrieval views). It is possible to ignore the interpretation of the child elements and concentrate on only the target elements. In previous years, INEX has made a distinction between strict and vague conformance to the target element, but has disregarded conformance to child constraints (the so-called SCAS and VCAS tasks). This finding suggests the experiments of previous years did, indeed, make the correct distinction. Checking child constraints does not appear worthwhile for content-oriented XML retrieval.

The vague task has proven more difficult than the strict task. Strict conformance to the target element can be computed as a filter of a vague run - from those vague elements, remove all that do not conform to the target element constraint. The vague interpretation of CAS is a better place to concentrate research effort.

If the CAS task continues in future years, a single set of topics, without the child topics is all that is necessary for evaluation and participants should concentrate on the vague interpretation of topics.

References

1. Fuhr, N., Gövert, N., Kazai, G., and Lalmas, M. (2002). INEX: Initiative for the evaluation of XML retrieval. In *Proceedings of the ACM SIGIR 2000 Workshop on XML and Information Retrieval*.

2. Harman, D. (1993). Overview of the first TREC conference. In *Proceedings of the 16th ACM SIGIR Conference on Information Retrieval*, (pp. 36-47).

3. Kazai, G., and Lalmas, M. (2006). INEX 2005 evaluation metrics. In *Advances in XML Information Retrieval and Evaluation: Fourth Workshop of the INitiative for the Evaluation of XML Retrieval (INEX 2005), Lecture Notes in Computer Science, Vol 3977, Springer-Verlag*.

4. Pehcevski, J., Thom, J. A., and Vercoustre, A.-M. (2005). Users and assessors in the context of INEX: Are relevance dimensions relevant? In *Proceedings of the INEX 2005 Workshop on Element Retrieval Methodology, Second Edition*, (pp. 47-62).

5. Piwowarski, B., and Lalmas, M. (2004). Interface pour l'évaluation de systèmes de recherche sur des documents XML. In *Proceedings of the Premiere COnference en Recherche d'Information et Applications (CORIA'04)*.

6. Piwowarski, B., and Lalmas, M. (2004). Providing consistent and exhaustive relevance assessments for XML retrieval evaluation. In *Proceedings of the 13th ACM conference on Information and knowledge management*, (pp. 361-370).

7. Sigurbjörnsson, B., Trotman, A., Geva, S., Lalmas, M., Larsen, B., and Malik, S. (2005). INEX 2005 guidelines for topic development. In *Proceedings of INEX 2005*.

8. Tombros, A., Larsen, B., and Malik, S. (2004). The interactive track at INEX 2004. In *Proceedings of INEX 2004*, (pp. 410-423).

9. Trotman, A. (2005). Wanted: Element retrieval users. In *Proceedings of the INEX 2005 Workshop on Element Retrieval Methodology, Second Edition*, (pp. 63-69).

10. Trotman, A., and Sigurbjörnsson, B. (2004). Narrowed Extended XPath I (NEXI). In *Proceedings of INEX 2004*, (pp. 16-40).

11. Trotman, A., and Sigurbjörnsson, B. (2004). NEXI, now and next. In *Proceedings of INEX 2004*, (pp. 41-53).

12. Voorhees, E. M. (2001). The philosophy of information retrieval evaluation. In *Proceedings of the The Second Workshop of the Cross-Language Evaluation Forum on Evaluation of Cross-Language Information Retrieval Systems*, (pp. 355-370).

13. Woodley, A., and Geva, S. (2004). NLPX at INEX 2004. In *Proceedings of INEX 2004*, (pp. 382-394).
14. Woodley, A., and Geva, S. (2005). Fine tuning INEX. In *Proceedings of the INEX 2005 Workshop on Element Retrieval Methodology, Second Edition*, (pp. 70-79).
15. Zobel, J. (1998). How reliable are the results of large-scale information retrieval experiments? In *Proceedings of the 21st ACM SIGIR Conference on Information Retrieval*, (pp. 307-314).

TIJAH Scratches INEX 2005: Vague Element Selection, Image Search, Overlap, and Relevance Feedback[*]

Vojkan Mihajlović[1], Georgina Ramírez[2], Thijs Westerveld[2], Djoerd Hiemstra[1], Henk Ernst Blok[1], and Arjen P. de Vries[2]

[1] University of Twente,
P.O. Box 217, 7500 AE Enschede, The Netherlands
{v.mihajlovic, d.hiemstra, h.e.blok}@utwente.nl
[2] Centre for Mathematics and Computer Science,
P.O. Box 94079, 1090 GB Amsterdam, The Netherlands
{georgina, thijs, arjen}@cwi.nl

Abstract. Retrieving information from heterogeneous data sources in a flexible manner and within a single (database) framework is still a challenge. In this paper we present several extensions of our prototype database system TIJAH developed for structured retrieval. The extensions are aimed at modeling vague selection of XML elements and image retrieval. All three levels (conceptual, logical, and physical) of the TIJAH system are enhanced to support the extensions. Additionally, we analyze different ways of removing overlap and explain how structural information can be used for relevance feedback.

1 Introduction

In this paper we discuss our participation at INEX 2005 with TIJAH, a three-level database system for structured information retrieval. The TIJAH system [12, 13, 15] is developed as a transparent XML-IR database system consisting of conceptual, logical, and physical levels. TIJAH was originally developed to handle queries with the strict selection of XML elements, specified in the NEXI query language [18] and to reason about textual information. This year we extended it in three directions: toward handling vague specification of XML elements in the query (similar to [5]), toward supporting retrieval from heterogeneous domains (images and videos), following the guidelines from multimedia retrieval database systems [3], and toward supporting different approaches to remove overlap. Moreover, we continue with the relevance feedback experiments [16] using the TIJAH system.

The first point that we want to address in this paper is handling imprecise specification of elements in the XML search. Similarly to users giving a number of terms as hints for searching within a document, XML elements specified

---

[*] The research described in this paper is funded by NWO grant number 612.061.210.

N. Fuhr et al. (Eds.): INEX 2005, LNCS 3977, pp. 72–87, 2006.
© Springer-Verlag Berlin Heidelberg 2006

within the query need not be considered as a strict requirement but as a hint for structural search. Therefore, when formulating a query the user can state that the search (support) element or answer (target) element should be treated as a hint or as a constraint in the retrieval process. To support vague search we introduced *vague element selection* as a concept in our TIJAH system.

On the other hand, to cope with the heterogeneous data sources (text and images) each level of the TIJAH system is extended with new features that can express *image search*. Image search is handled in the same framework as text search: At the conceptual level where NEXI query language is extended for query by example image search, and at logical level where new operators are introduced in the Score Region Algebra (SRA) [13]. However, due to different nature of the domain data, images are stored and handled in a different manner than textual XML data at the physical level.

We also present our approaches for removing overlap and for relevance feedback. To remove overlapping elements from the result set (for the user not to see the same information twice), we define a *utility* function that intends to capture the amount of *useful* information each element contains. Once we know the *utility* value of each node, we remove overlap by returning the most *useful* node in each path. Our relevance feedback approach uses the structural characteristics of the relevant elements to update the priors in a language modeling framework.

The paper is organized as follows. The following section explains the extensions introduced in the TIJAH system to model vague XML element specification. Section 3 details our approach for image retrieval. The overlap and relevance feedback approaches are discussed in Section 4 and 5 respectively. We wrap-up the paper with the results from the experiments performed for each track and its sub-tasks in Section 6 and with conclusions and future directions in Section 7.

2   Vague Node Selection

This section details the motivation and the implementation of vague selection of nodes in our three-level database framework. We explain the extensions on each level aimed for vague search on elements.

2.1   Vague Element Node Selection in NEXI

Instead of extending our conceptual parser for rewriting content-and-structure (CAS) and content-only plus structure (COS) queries into SV, VS, and VV CAS and COS queries (SSCAS and SSCOS are equal to CAS and COS in our case), where prefix 'S' denotes strict and 'V' vague specification of target and support elements, we decided to extend the NEXI grammar with one extra symbol '∼'. The 'tilde' symbol is used in front of the element name in the query specification, denoting that the element name does not have to be strictly matched in the query evaluation. We support this decision by arguing that the user should be responsible for stating his confidence in the knowledge of the hierarchical organization of the data he is querying, or whether he is certain or not what the element name is in which he wants to search for information.

Since we decided to extend the NEXI syntax with the vague selection we had to manually rewrite the queries for each CAS and COS scenario except the SSCAS and SSCOS. For example, the (SS)CAS query 225:

```
//article[about(.//fm//atl, "digital libraries")]
                //sec[about(.,"information retrieval")]
```
is rewritten into three variants:

- SVCAS: `//article[about(.//~fm//~atl, "digital libraries")]`
  `                //sec[about(.,"information retrieval")]`
- VSCAS: `//article[about(.//fm//atl, "digital libraries")]`
  `                //~sec[about(.,"information retrieval")]`
- VVCAS: `//article[about(.//~fm//~atl, "digital libraries")]`
  `                //~sec[about(.,"information retrieval")]`

We decided not to consider the 'article' element as a vague element in case it is not the target element or it is not the element in which the *about* search should be performed, as in these cases the 'article' element just serves as a focusing element for deeper search in the XML tree.

Vague element selection can be treated similarly as a query expansion on terms in traditional IR. For example, if a user searches for the term 'conclusion', he might also be satisfied with terms 'decision', 'determination', 'termination', or 'ending' in the answer. In structured documents, if a user asks for 'car' elements, he would probably not mind getting 'auto' or 'vehicle' elements as an answer. The problem of element name matching is studied in the research area of schema matching and numerous techniques exist that try to resolve this problem (see [4] for survey). However, we decided to simplify the vague element name search task and use the results from INEX 2004 assessments to find the expanded element names. We define the list of expanded element names based on the list of element names assessed as relevant in INEX 2004 assessments process. The lists that we exploit in this paper, termed *element name expansion lists* are the following[1]:

- One manual set of lists with the default score 0.55, based on 2004 experiments (for the complete lists see [14]). For example, sec expansion list looks like: {sec, abs, fm, vt, p, article, bdy, bm, app}. The lists are formed out of highly exhaustive elements in the assessments list and by making the lists symmetric in terms of adding the most useful IEEE collection element names, such as sec,p,abs,..., to the expanded name list of other element names that are in the particular expanded element name list. For example, since for the abs element name, the kwd element name is in its expanded list, abs is added to the kwd expansion list.
- One set of lists automatically generated out of assessments with marginal, fair, or high exhaustivity and specificity. The default score is based on a number of relevant elements of that specific name, normalized by a total number of relevant elements, for all distinct target elements. For example, if 5 out of 50 elements assessed as relevant for sec answer element in the 2004 assessments set are p elements than the default score for p elements is 0.1.

---

[1] A more exhaustive set of expansion lists can be found in [14].

2.2   A Complex Selection Operator for Vague Node Selection

The logical level is based on Score Region Algebra – SRA [13]. The SRA data model consists of a set of regions, each defined by its start (s), end (e), type (t), name (n), and score (p). The operators in SRA are selection operators $(\sigma_{n=name,t=type}(R), \sigma_{\diamond num}(R), R_1 \sqsupset R_2$, and $R_1 \sqsubset R_2)$, score computation operator $(R_1 \sqsupset_p R_2)$, score combination operators $(R_1 \sqcap_p R_2$ and $R_1 \sqcup_p R_2)$, and score propagation operators $(R_1 \blacktriangleright R_2$ and $R_1 \blacktriangleleft R_2)$. Retrieval models are transparently implemented using abstract functions for score computation $(f_\sqsupset)$, combination $(\otimes$ and $\oplus)$, and propagation $(\blacktriangleright$ and $\blacktriangleleft)$ [13].

The vague node selection at the conceptual level (NEXI) is translated into complex vague node selection operator at the logical level. The operator is defined in SRA as a union of all XML element regions that match the names of the 'expanded name regions' within the element name expansion list. By default all 'expanded regions' are down-weighted by a predefined factor. The definition of the operator is as follows:

$$\sigma_{n=name,t=type}^{expansion(class)}(R_1) := \{(r_1.s, r_1.e, r_1.n, r_1.t, r.p) \mid r_1 \in R_1 \ \land \ r_1.t = type$$

$$\land \ (r_1.n, r.p) \in expansion(class, name)\} \tag{1}$$

Here $expansion(class)$ is a set that contains all the expansions for all the region names in one expansion class, where expansion list for each region $name$ is:

$$expansion(class, name) := \{(ex\_n_1, ex\_w_1), (ex\_n_2, ex\_w_2), ..., (ex\_n_n, ex\_w_n)\}$$

Here ex_n_i is an expanded element name and ex_w_i is a real number in the range $[0, 1]$ denoting the down-weight factor. The operator $\sigma_{n=name,t=node}^{expansion(class)}(R_1)$ assigns name (ex_n) and score (ex_w) values to the region name (n) and score (p) based on the name and score values in the expansion list $expansion(class, name)$.

For the vague selection we use the fusion of equivalence classes [11] (eq_class) and our manual and automatic INEX 2004 expansion element name lists. This is done in such way that every expanded element name in these lists that has the equivalent name in the eq_class $name$ part is also expanded with the eq_class equivalent names for $name$. This expansions are termed $manual55$ for manual run and mm for the automatic one. Therefore, the eq_class selection on section elements can be expressed as $\sigma_{n='sec',t=node}^{expansion(eq\_class)}(R)$, and vague node selection $(\sim\textsf{sec})$, using manual expansion list, can be transformed into the next SRA operation $\sigma_{n='sec',t=node}^{expansion(manual55)}(R)$. In such a way we can transparently define the set of expanded nodes and their respective weights and use them for vague node selection in a vague element name selection retrieval scenarios.

2.3   The Implementation of the Vague Selection Operator

At the physical level, since we are working with the known INEX IEEE data collection, and as we used static INEX equivalence element name list and expansion element name lists based on INEX 2004 assessments, we decided to replicate the lists and store them as tables at the physical level, i.e., in MonetDB [1]. Thus, we have three tables with *(entity_name, expansion_name, expansion_weight)* for *manual*55, *mm*, and *eq_class* lists. The complex selection operator is then implemented as an additional MIL function (MIL stands for MonetDB Interpreter Language and is used to implement operators in TIJAH [15]) that uses data from these tables.

For example, the vague *name* selection operator on region table R and the 'expansion regions' table S for the *manual*55 element names in the expansion list, in relational algebra can be defined as:

$$\pi_{r.s, r.e, r.n, r.t, s.weight}(\sigma_{s.n=name}(S) \bowtie_{s.n=r.n} (\sigma_{r.t=node}(R)))$$

Retrieval Models. We based the instantiation of retrieval models on the best models used for flat-file information retrieval, as well as XML retrieval: language models [7], the Okapi/Inquery model [2, 17], and Garden Point XML (GPX) [6]. For the relevance score computation we used language modeling in most of the cases (Equation 2) and Okapi and GPX in some of them (details of these models can be found in [13]). We used sum for upwards ($f_\blacktriangleright(r_1, R_2)$) and downwards ($f_\blacktriangleleft(r_1, R_2)$) score propagation (Equation 3). Abstract score combination operators $\otimes$ and $\oplus$ are implemented both as simple sum, or as product and sum, except in the case of the GPX model where the instantiation is given in Equation 4. In Equations 2 to 4: $r_1 \prec r_2 \equiv r_1.s > r_2.s \wedge r_1.e < r_2.e$, $size(r) = r.e - r.s - 1$, and *Root* is the collection root region.

$$f_\lnot^{LM}(r_1, R_2) = p_1 \cdot (\lambda \frac{\sum_{r_2 \in R_2 | r_2 \prec r_1} p_2}{size(r_1)} + (1 - \lambda) \frac{|R_2|}{size(Root)}) \tag{2}$$

$$f_\blacktriangleright(r_1, R_2) = p_1 \cdot \sum_{r_2 \in R_2 | r_1 \prec r_2} p_2 \ , \qquad f_\blacktriangleleft(r_1, R_2) = p_1 \cdot \sum_{r_2 \in R_2 | r_2 \prec r_1} p_2 \tag{3}$$

$$p_1 \otimes p_2 = p_1 \oplus p_2 = \begin{cases} p_1 + p_2 & \text{if } p_1 = 0 \vee p_2 = 0 \\ A \cdot (p_1 + p_2) \text{ otherwise} \end{cases} \tag{4}$$

3   Image Similarity Search

To enable search on multimedia collection (provided by Lonely Planet) we also introduced extensions to the TIJAH system defined along three levels of our prototype DB. Also, we extended the NEXI syntax with an extra token 'src:' that defines the location of the source image with which the destination image should be matched. Therefore, in multimedia query 11:

```
//destination[about(.//image, fruit vegetables src:/images/BN2787_4.jpg)]
    //point_of_interest[about(., food fruit vegetable market)]
```

the first *about* contains a request for image similarity search. The destination image that need to be matched is `images/BN2787_4.jpg`. In the preprocessing step, the 'src:' part of the *about* is transformed into *about_image* and its relative path given in the NEXI 'src:' specification is resolved into the path to the location where the data for image matching is stored. The image about command is then forwarded to the logical level.

3.1 Image Search in SRA

To express image search in SRA we extended the SRA operator set with the additional operators σ^i and $\sqsupset_p^i$. The σ^i operator has similar definition as basic score region algebra operator $\sigma_{n=name,t=type}(R)$, except that the score p is now computed by a call to an external function f^i. The function f^i uses information extracted from the sample image and the image that should be selected and it computes the score of an image region based on similarity between the sample image and the selected image:

$$\sigma_{n=name}^{i\approx sample}(R_1) := \{(r_1.s, r_1.e, r_1.n, r_1.t, f^i(r_2.n, sample) \mid r_1 \in R_1 \ \wedge \ \exists r_2 \in C$$

$$\wedge \ r_2 \prec r_1 \ \wedge \ r_2.t = attr\_val \ \wedge \ r_1.t = attr \ \wedge \ r_1.n = name\} \qquad (5)$$

Here *sample* is the location of the sample image data specified with the 'src:' statement in the NEXI query, resolved in the preprocessing step, C is a set of all regions in the database, *attr* is the attribute node, and *attr_val* is value of the attribute *attr*.

The operator $\sqsupset_p^i$ is defined in the same way as $\sqsupset_p$ operator (for the exact definition see [13]), except that it allows computing score of a region containing images with the usage of different scoring formula than for terms (e.g., given in Equation 2). Therefore, the *about_image* in the multimedia query 1 is transformed into the next SRA expression:

$$\sigma_{n='image',t=node}(C) \ \sqsupset_p^i \ \sigma_{n=file\_name}^{i\approx 'BN2787\_4.jpg'}(C)$$

3.2 Implementation of Image Search

At indexing time, we estimated a generative probabilistic model of each of the images in the collection (see below); the model parameters are stored in separate tables in the database. In addition, we constructed a table that links the image identifiers to the corresponding nodes in the collection tree. The image selection operator is implemented as a new MIL function that computes the similarity between each collection image model and the example image.

Retrieval Model. Similarity between example images and collection images is estimated using Gaussian mixture models (GMM). To this end, each of the images in the collections ($\omega(n_i)$) is modeled as mixtures of Gaussians with a fixed number of components K:

$$P(\boldsymbol{x}|\omega(n_i)) = \sum_{k=1}^{N_K} P(K_{i,k}) \, \mathcal{G}(\boldsymbol{x}, \boldsymbol{\mu}_{i,k}, \boldsymbol{\Sigma}_{i,k}), \qquad (6)$$

where N_K is the number of components in the mixture model, $K_{i,k}$ is component k of class model $\omega(n_i)$ and $\mathcal{G}(\boldsymbol{x}, \boldsymbol{\mu}, \boldsymbol{\Sigma})$ is the Gaussian density with mean vector $\boldsymbol{\mu}$ and covariance matrix $\boldsymbol{\Sigma}$. The score of an image node given an example image from a query, is determined by the likelihood that the corresponding model generates the feature vectors ($\mathcal{X} = \{x_1, x_2, \dots, x_n\}$) representing the example image. Like in the LM case for text, we interpolate with a background model based on collection statistics:

$$f^i(n_i, sample) = \prod_{x \in \mathcal{X}_{sample}} [\lambda \cdot P(x|\omega(n_i)) + (1 - \lambda) \cdot P(x)] \qquad (7)$$

The feature space of the vectors x is based on the DCT coefficients[2] obtained from 8x8 pixel blocks. For details of the feature vectors and the GMMs, see [19]. Equation 7 is used for similarity computation in the image selection operator $\sigma_{n=name}^{i \approx sample}(R_1)$. In image containment ($R1 \sqsupset_p^i R2$) the result score is computed as a product of scores of the region in the left and region in the right operand.

4   Overlap Removal

In an XML retrieval setting, to identify the most appropriate elements to return to the user is not an easy problem. IR systems have difficult task to find out which are the most exhaustive and specific elements in the tree and return only these to the user, producing result lists without overlapping elements. So far, most of the approaches presented to remove overlap consist of post-filtering the ranked lists in one way or another. Basically, by selecting the highest scored element from each of the paths.

This would be a good strategy if the retrieval model would consider, when ranking, not only the estimated relevance of the XML element itself but also its *usefulness* compared to other elements in the same path. However, since most retrieval models rank elements independently, it is not always the case that the highest scored element is the most appropriate unit to return to the user. Therefore, the strategies to remove overlap that rely too much in the retrieval model scores are not always the most effective (see Section 6.1).

In the approach presented in this paper, we define an *utility* function that intends to capture the amount of *useful* information each element contains. This function is equivalent to giving an *utility* prior to the retrieval model scores. Our goal is to help the retrieval model to give a better estimation of the *usefulness* of each node and, in consequence, gain effectiveness when removing overlap.

To model the *usefulness* of a node, three important aspects need to be considered: (1) the relevance score estimated by the retrieval model, (2) the size of the element, and (3) the amount of irrelevant information it contains. For example, if a highly relevant element is very small, the amount of *useful* information it carries is also small. Whereas if a not so high scored element is longer, the amount of *useful* information that the user will read is larger. Thus, the decision of which elements are most *useful* should be related not only to the retrieval model scores but also to its length. That is why length normalization techniques are also used in XML Retrieval [9]. Similarly, whether to return a certain element or to return some of its children should be decided according to the amount of *irrelevant* information the user will have to read if the parent is returned.

---

[2] Discrete Cosine Transform, captures both color and texture information.

To implement these ideas, we define an *utility* function that estimates the *usefulness* of a node as the product of the amount of relevant information that element contains, the element's score, and its length. Formally, for each of the XML nodes (E), the *utility* value is estimated as:

$$U(E) = (1 - \frac{\sum_{i \in nrch(E)} size(i)}{size(E)}) \cdot P(E) \cdot size(E) \tag{8}$$

Where $P(E)$ is the estimated relevance score given by the retrieval model and $nrch(E)$ is the set of non relevant children of E. Those children in which the *amount of relevant information* (estimated as the product of the element's length and score, $P(E) * size(E)$) is lower than a threshold (*quality* threshold). This utility function is equivalent to giving a length prior to the elements, but instead of using the whole element's length as prior, we try to estimate the size of the relevant information contained in it.

5   Relevance Feedback

The main idea of any relevance feedback strategy is to use the knowledge of relevant items to retrieve more relevant items. So far, research has concentrated on using content-related information from the known relevant elements. However, for XML retrieval the structural characteristics of the relevant elements might also play an important role. Following the lines of what we started last year [15], we investigate the potential of the structural information for this type of task and analyze if retrieving structurally similar elements improves retrieval effectiveness.

5.1   Structural Information in Relevant Elements

We study two different aspects of the structure of documents that can help the retrieval system to discriminate between relevant and non relevant elements. Namely, the containing journal of an element (the journal where that element belongs to) and the element type. Table 1 shows the number of different journals and element types judged relevant per topic. If we compare these numbers to the total number of different journals (24) and different element types (187) contained in the new collection, we can see that the knowledge of which journals and element types are relevant for each of the topics is a very important piece of information that can help retrieval systems to perform a better search.

One way to use the knowledge of which structural characteristics are relevant for a certain topic is to increase the a priori belief in relevance of the elements that have the same structural characteristics. In this way, we use the information of which relevant journals and element types are found in the top 20, to calculate priors and increase the a priori belief in relevance of the elements that are contained in that journal or that are from that specific element type.

Table 1. Number of different journals and element types judged relevant per topic. Statistics taken from relevance assessments 2005 version 2. Average over 28 CO topics. All degrees of relevance are taken into account.

Type info.	Avg.	Median	Max	Min
Relevant journals	7.9	8	16	2
Relevant element types	34.4	34.5	73	9

5.2 Updating Priors in a Language Modeling Framework

For our baseline experiments, we used statistical language models (see Section 2.3). Using Bayes' rule and assuming independence between query terms, the probability of an element E given a query Q can be estimated as the product of the probability of generating the query terms q_i from the element's language model and the prior probability of the element:

$$P(E|Q) \propto \prod_{q_i \in Q} P(q_i|E)P(E) \tag{9}$$

Typically, little prior knowledge about the probability of an element is available and either uniform priors are used, or $P(E)$ is taken to be related to the element's length (i.e.,long elements are assumed to be more likely to contain relevant information) (cf. [9]). However, once we have some information about relevant elements, for example from a user's relevance judgments, we can use this information to update the priors. From the judgments, we can discover the characteristics of relevant elements and update the priors in such a way that elements with similar characteristics are favored[3].

Therefore, once we get information about the structural characteristics of the relevant elements for a given topic, we define the priors for the journals and element types and use them to retrieve structurally similar elements. However, since in the top 20 we may not have seen all relevant journals or element types, there is the risk of assigning a prior equal to zero to element types or journals that do actually contain relevant information. To avoid this effect of relying too much on what is seen in the top 20, we interpolate $P(x(E)|rel)$ with the general probability of seeing elements from $x(E)$. Thus the prior becomes:

$$P_x(E) = \frac{\alpha P(x(E)|rel) + (1 - \alpha)P(x(E))}{P(x(E))}, \tag{10}$$

where $x(E)$ identifies the journal (element type) to which E belongs, $P(x(E)|rel)$ is estimated as the fraction of relevant items belonging to the journal (element type) and $P(x(E))$ is the fraction of elements in the collection that belongs to that journal (element type).

---

[3] Strictly speaking $P(E)$ can no longer be called a prior, since it depends on the topic at hand.

6   Experiments

Among numerous tracks and scenarios specified for INEX 2005, we participated in the following: all CO and CAS ad-hoc track sub-tasks, multimedia track, interactive track, and relevance feedback track. Below, after introducing the metrics reported in the paper, we will explain in detail our approaches for each of these (sub)tasks.

Metrics. The official INEX metrics for 2005 ad-hoc and relevance feedback track are based on extended Cumulative Gain (xCG) metrics [10]. The official metrics are: normalized xCG (nxCG), effort-precision/gain-recall (ep/gr), and extended Q and R[4]. The evaluation can be done either with the generalized or with the strict quantization. In this paper we report the evaluation results obtained with nxCG (also denoted as CG in Table 4) at various recall points: 10, 25, and 50 and mean average ep/gr. For multimedia track we report mean average precision (MAP) values.

Note that for any document cut-off value, say 10, it can be shown that, if strict quantization is used (or any other binary quantization), and overlap is not taken into account, and the total number of relevant elements is bigger than 10, then nXCG at 10 and precision at 10 give exactly the same results. However, if the number of relevant elements is smaller than 10 for some topics, then this might have a big impact on the measured performance.

For instance, IBM Haifa's run "SSCAS_no_phrase_no_plus" and Max Planck Institute's (MPI) run "MPII_TopX_SSCAS" have the same average precision at 10 over 4 topics with relevant elements: 0.225 for both runs (over topic 256, 260, 270 and 275). That is, on average 22.5% of the elements inspected in the top 10 is highly exhaustive and specific. However, for one of these 4 SSCAS topics (topic 270), only 1 relevant document is known. Because of this, the nXCG at 10 over the 4 topics is twice as high for MPI (0.450), which found the document in its top 10, as it is for IBM (0.225), which did not find it in its top 10. Apparently, a 100% gain in nXCG does not have to say much about the actual percentage of relevant items seen by the user. Precision at x is less sensitive to the total number of known relevant elements than XCG at x, and therefore defining the ideal recall base as needed for XCG is not really an issue for precision [8].

6.1   Ad-Hoc Track: CO Queries

Thorough. The aim of the *Thorough* retrieval strategy is to find all highly exhaustive and specific elements. Thus, to find all relevant information regardless of overlapping results. This year we submitted only two runs with the aim of using them as baseline runs for the other tasks and sub-tasks. Description and results for these two runs are given in Table 2. Although under the strict quantization there are not big differences between the two runs, under the generalized, one of the runs ($\lambda = 0.4$) outperforms the other considerably. We used this run as baseline for the rest of the CO experiments.

---

[4] http://inex.is.informatik.uni-duisburg.de/2005/inex-2005-metricsv6.pdf

Table 2. CO.Thorough experiments with strict (^{S}) and generalized (^{G}) quantization

Run id	Description	nXCG[10]	nXCG[25]	nXCG[50]	ep/gr
LMs_04_lp^S	LMs, $\lambda = 0.4$, lp	0.0923	0.0885	0.1020	0.0511
CO_LMs_trm_085^S	LMs, $\lambda = 0.85$, lp	0.0923	0.0855	0.0859	0.0490
LMs_04_lp^G	LMs, $\lambda = 0.4$, lp	0.2480	0.2433	0.2213	0.0795
CO_LMs_trm_085^G	**LMs, $\lambda = 0.85$, lp**	0.2161	0.1856	0.1839	0.0596

Focused. The aim of the *Focused* retrieval strategy is to find the most exhaustive and specific element in a path. Once the element is identified and returned, none of the remaining elements in the path should be returned. In other words, the result list should not contain overlapping elements. In our experiments for this task, we investigate the differences in terms of effectiveness between different approaches to remove overlap and evaluate the approach presented in Section 4.

To compare approaches, we implemented two already known ways of removing overlap: namely, the *naive* and the *common* approach. The *naive* approach filters out from the result list everything except one specific type of element (assuming that there is no overlap between elements of the same type). The *common* approach is implemented as follows: first, we select the highest scored element from the result list and remove its ancestors and descendants, then we take the second highest scored element and remove its ancestors and descendants, and we continue recursively until all elements from the result list have been either selected or removed. To evaluate our approach we use different *quality* thresholds. We observe that although there are no significant differences between the performance of the runs under the generalized quantization, under the strict one, the best improvements are achieved when the threshold is not very high, i.e., when elements are less punished for having irrelevant information. We only report the results of the best run overall with the threshold defined as the score

Table 3. CO.Focussed experiments with strict (^{S}) and generalized (^{G}) quantization

Approach	nXCG[10]	nXCG[25]	nXCG[50]	ep/gr
Naive: select articles^S	0.0115	0.0154	0.0192	0.0116
Naive: select sections^S	0.0308	0.0417	0.0404	0.0136
Naive: select paragraphs^S	**0.1209**	**0.1538**	**0.1630**	**0.0654**
Common^S	0.0978	0.0927	0.1082	0.0509
Utility^S	0.1016	0.1373	0.1498	0.0561
Naive: select articles^G	0.1582	0.1226	0.1024	0.0443
Naive: select sections^G	0.1857	0.1753	0.1519	0.0588
Naive: select paragraphs^G	**0.2310**	**0.2197**	**0.2105**	**0.0764**
Common^G	0.2193	0.1909	0.1892	0.0728
Utility^G	0.2127	0.1919	0.1977	0.0742

of the element at position 375 (1500/4) in the original result list. Note that the score of this element is usually very small and many of the elements exceed this threshold. The results of all these runs are shown in Table 3.

For all measures and quantizations, the approach that performs the best is the one that retrieves only paragraphs. In general, for the *naive* approach, and as expected for a *focused* retrieval task, the longer the element, the worse the performance. However, it is somehow surprising that the retrieval of sections, which is also a rather focused unit, is not performing well. The *common* approach performs well but under the strict quantization is still far from the best run. This might be because our baseline contains a length prior that rewards longer elements. Therefore, when removing overlap, the longer elements, which probably are not the most exhaustive and specific on the path, are selected. Comparing the scores of the approach presented in this paper to the ones of the *common* run, we see that under the strict quantization the re-ranking of the scores using the *utility* function does improve performance considerably (in terms of precision at high recall levels). That means that the utility function does help the retrieval model to make a better estimation of the most *useful* elements in the paths. Unfortunately, in all runs our approach is outperformed by the naive approach of selecting paragraphs. A possible cause of this could be that our approach rewards longer elements too much, but further analysis need to be done to test this an other hypothesis.

6.2   Ad-Hoc Track: CAS and COS.Thorough Experiments

In our experiments with queries that use structure we aimed at comparing vague node selection approaches for all four query types (SS, SV, VS, and VV CAS and COS) with two query rewriting techniques that we used previous years for INEX [12, 15]. These rewriting techniques treat structural constrains as strict but mix the terms in different about clauses. In the first rewriting approach (rw I), all terms that are in different *about* clauses in the same predicate expression, and are not at the top level (i.e., not in about(., term) expression), are added to an extra top-level *about* clause in the same predicate expression. The second approach (rw II), is an extension of the first one, where not only the terms from non top-level *abouts* are added to the new *about*, but also all the terms from the other predicate, if there exists any, are added to the top-level *about* in each predicate.

We report the results using only VVCAS and COS.Thorough assessments as we wanted to test the approaches on the same assessments set. We present only the results using generalized quantization as the results using strict quantization lead to the same conclusions (see extensive set of experiments in [14]). The runs given in bold are the best ones for each series of experiments. In the first set of experiments we test how much we can improve the effectiveness when using rewriting techniques. The first three rows in Table 4 show that rewriting techniques help; e.g., the rw II shows overall better scores, especially for early precision as can be seen in CAS runs, and it also has higher MAP values.

Table 4. INEX 2005 CAS and COS.Thorough experiments with different vague scenarios and rewriting techniques evaluated using nxCG at different recall points and ep/gr with generalized quantization

Exp. class	CAS				COS.Thorough			
	CG[10]	CG[25]	CG[50]	MAP	CG[10]	CG[25]	CG[50]	MAP
eq_class	0.2799	0.2851	0.2644	0.05033	0.2677	0.2258	0.1787	0.03205
rw I	0.2687	0.2834	0.2645	0.04670	0.2715	0.2430	0.1894	0.03323
rw II	**0.3030**	**0.2977**	**0.2679**	**0.05476**	**0.2872**	**0.2467**	**0.1898**	**0.03409**
mm(sv)	0.2865	**0.2882**	**0.2626**	0.05219	0.2772	0.2333	0.1951	0.03657
man55(sv)	**0.3066**	0.2853	0.2419	0.05291	0.2727	0.2349	0.1972	0.03650
mm(vs)	0.2672	0.2658	0.2524	0.06749	0.2827	0.2499	0.2042	0.04283
man55(vs)	0.2316	0.2417	0.2391	0.06720	0.2751	0.2410	0.2060	0.04587
mm(vv)	0.2811	0.2728	0.2529	0.07062	**0.2912**	0.2580	0.2258	0.06060
man55(vv)	0.2545	0.2553	0.2428	**0.07296**	0.2851	**0.2585**	**0.2315**	**0.06872**
mm(vv)^{rwI}	0.2734	0.2641	**0.2603**	0.05899	0.2929	0.2686	0.2262	0.06168
man55(vv)^{rwI}	0.2427	0.2691	0.2469	0.06872	**0.3040**	0.2676	**0.2395**	**0.07168**
mm(vv)^{rwII}	**0.3092**	0.2815	0.2366	0.05760	0.2873	0.2492	0.2168	0.05878
man55(vv)^{rwII}	0.3005	**0.2943**	0.2556	**0.06896**	0.2956	**0.2688**	0.2262	0.06891

In the second set of experiments we replace the strict queries with the vague ones. The improvements are significant and they can go up to more than 100% (e.g., for the MAP in COS "man55(vv)" run). Clearly, vague element selection has higher MAP values than rewriting techniques, but in all CAS experiments it has lower precision at low recall points. This can indicate that rewriting techniques might be used as a precision tool, while vague element selection can be considered as a recall tool. Looking at different vague scenarios, namely SV, VS, and VV, and except for some early precision scores, VV runs seem to have the best performance. Therefore, "mm(vv)" and "man55(vv)" runs are used in combination with rewriting techniques for further experiments.

The third set of experiments confirms our assumption about the rewriting techniques as a precision and vague element search as a recall enhancement tool. As can be seen in Table 4 in most of the cases the combination of rw I and rw II rewriting techniques and manual and automatic vague element search improves early precision. However, not in all cases we managed to keep the MAP values, especially for the rw II combinations as can be seen in CAS runs.

6.3   Multimedia Track: Image Queries

An important goal of our multimedia extension was to showcase and test the flexibility and extendibility of the SRA approach. In addition, we tested if using visual similarity can contribute to better results. To this end, we compared the multimedia queries discussed in Section 3 to similar queries with all image similarity clauses (`src:`) removed. The results of these two approaches using three different models for text search is given in Table 5. There exist differences

Table 5. Results for MM track

LM	MAP	Okapi	MAP	GPX	MAP
text only	0.2751	text only	0.2110	text only	0.2567
multimedia	0.2600	multimedia	0.2133	multimedia	0.2627

between the models, but we did not find any improvement using visual similarity, in fact the best run uses only textual language models and is significantly better than its multimedia counterpart. We believe this is partially due to the nature of the collection and topics, but more research is needed to investigate if and how visual information can help to improve retrieval results in this collection.

6.4   Relevance Feedback Track

To analyze the effects of using structural information in the relevance feedback process as described in Section 5, we designed two main experiments. The first one varies the values for α in Equation 10 to analyze the effects of assigning different importance to the structural information found in the top 20. The values used are: 0.75, 0.5 and 0.25. This experiment is done on top of the baseline used in the rest of experiments, namely: CO_LMs_04_lp. The second experiment aims to identify which of the two types of structural information provides better improvement to the overall effectiveness of the IR system. Therefore, we fix the value of α in Equation 10 to 0.5 and analyze the gain obtained when using journal priors, element priors, and both priors at the same time. This experiment is done on top of one of our runs for the COS.Thorough task that uses the VVCAS approach explained in Section 2.

Since the official results show that very little gain is obtain for any of the runs, we do not report the numbers here. However, we observe that the journal prior seem to slightly improve recall and that there is no significant differences in performance when using different α's. The element prior seems to deteriorate the retrieval scores. We believe that this prior would perform much better when combined with a content-oriented query expansion, but further analysis and experiments need to be done in order to test this hypothesis.

7   Conclusions and Future Work

Throughout the paper we show that the TIJAH database system is flexible enough to incorporate advanced search techniques, such as vague element selection and relevance feedback, and search on heterogeneous data sources, such as a combination of images and text. For vague search, query rewriting techniques seem to be more suitable for obtaining higher precision at low recall points, while vague element selection is more suitable for higher average precision. Their combination however can boost the early precision, but it can also have negative influence on mean average precision. The simple image search model shows no improvements when combined with text search model. The approach presented to re-rank retrieval scores using an *utility* function seems to improve effectiveness when removing overlap. Unfortunately, this method does not outperform the simple approach of selecting the paragraph elements. Using only the structural characteristics of the elements in a relevance feedback process does not help retrieval performance in our case.

We plan to continue the experimental evaluation of different scenarios for search in structured documents: (1) the focused search using different *utility* functions to improve the effectiveness of overlap removal, (2) the vague element search with different assignment of non-uniform down-weighting factors and its combination with rewriting techniques, (3) the usage of structural relevance feedback in combination with content-oriented query expansion, and (4) the image search for improving retrieval results.

Acknowledgments

We would like to thank Roberto Cornacchia at CWI, Amsterdam, for providing the visual similarity code and for pre-processing the Lonely Planet images.

References

1. P. Boncz. *Monet: a Next Generation Database Kernel for Query Intensive Applications*. PhD thesis, CWI, 2002.
2. J. P. Callan, W. B. Croft, and S. M. Harding. The INQUERY Retrieval System. In *Proceedings of the 3rd DEXA Conference*, 1992.
3. A.P. de Vries. *Content and Multimedia Database Management Systems*. PhD thesis, University of Twente, Twente, The Netherlands, 1999.
4. A. Doan and A.Y. Halevy. Semantic Integration Research in the Database Community. *AI Magazine*, 26:83–94, 2005.
5. N. Fuhr and K. Großjohann. XIRQL: An XML Query Language Based on Information Retrieval Concepts. *ACM TOIS*, 22(2):313–356, 2004.
6. S. Geva. GPX - Gardens Point XML Information Retrieval at INEX 2004. In N. Fuhr, M. Lalmas, and S. Malik, editors, *Proceedings of the 3rd INEX Workshop*, volume 3493 of *Lecture Notes in Computer Science*, pages 276–291, 2005.
7. D. Hiemstra. *Using Language Models for Information Retrieval*. PhD thesis, University of Twente, Twente, The Netherlands, 2001.
8. D. Hiemstra and V. Mihajlović. The Simplest Evaluation Measures for XML Information Retrieval that Could Possibly Work. In *Proceedings of the INEX 2005 Workshop on Element Retrieval Methodology*, 2005.
9. J. Kamps, M. de Rijke, and B. Sigurbjörnsson. Length Normalization in XML Retrieval. In *Proceedings of the 27th ACM SIGIR Conference*, pages 80–87, 2004.
10. G. Kazai, M. Lalmas, and A.P. de Vries. The Overlap Problem in Content-oriented XML Retrieval Evaluation. In *Proceedings of the 27th ACM SIGIR Conference*, 2004.
11. G. Kazai, M. Lalmas, and S. Malik. INEX'03 Guidelines for Topic Developments. In *Proceedings of the 2nd INEX Workshop*, ERCIM Workshop Proceedings, 2004.

12. J. List, V. Mihajlović, A. de Vries, G. Ramirez, and D. Hiemstra. The TIJAH XML-IR System at INEX 2003. In *Proceedings of the 2nd INEX Workshop*, ERCIM Workshop Proceedings, 2004.

13. V. Mihajlović, H.E. Blok, D. Hiemstra, and P.M.G. Apers. Score Region Algebra: Building a Transparend XML-IR Database. In *Proceedings of the ACM CIKM Conference*, 2005.

14. V. Mihajlović, D. Hiemstra, and H. E. Blok. Vague Element Selection and Query Rewriting for XML Retrieval. In *Proceedings of the 6th Dutch-Belgian Information Retrieval Workshop*, 2006.

15. V. Mihajlović, G. Ramírez, A.P. de Vries, D. Hiemstra, and H.E. Blok. TIJAH at INEX 2004: Modeling Phrases and Relevance Feedback. In *Proceedings of the 3rd INEX Workshop*, volume 3493 of *Lecture Notes in Computer Science*, pages 276–291, 2005.

16. G. Ramírez, T. Westerveld, and A.P. de Vries. Structural Features in Content Oriented XML Retrieval. In *Proceedings of the ACM CIKM Conference*, 2005.

17. S. E. Robertson and S. Walker. Some Simple Effective Approximations to the 2-Poisson Model for Probabilistic Weighted Retrieval. In *Proceedings of the 17th ACM SIGIR Conference*, 1994.

18. A. Trotman and R. A. O'Keefe. The Simplest Query Language That Could Possibly Work. In N. Fuhr, M. Lalmas, and S. Malik, editors, *Proceedings of the 2nd INEX Workshop*, ERCIM Publications, 2004.

19. T. Westerveld. *Using generative probabilistic models for multimedia retrieval*. Ph.d. thesis, University of Twente, Enschede, The Netherlands, November 2004.

XFIRM at INEX 2005: Ad-Hoc and Relevance Feedback Tracks

Karen Sauvagnat, Lobna Hlaoua, and Mohand Boughanem

IRIT-SIG,
118 route de Narbonne, F-31 062 Toulouse Cedex 4, France

Abstract. This paper describes experiments carried out with the XFIRM system in the INEX 2005 framework. The XFIRM system uses a relevance propagation method to answer CO and CAS queries. Runs were submitted to the ad-hoc and relevance feedback tracks.

1 Introduction

The approach we used for our participation at INEX 2005 is based on the XFIRM system [6], and uses a relevance propagation method. The XFIRM system was adapted for submitting runs to the ad-hoc track (for CO, CO+S, and CAS tasks) and the relevance feedback track.

2 Experimental Setup

2.1 XFIRM Data Model

The XFIRM system is based on a relevance propagation method. We use a generic data model that allows the implementation of many IR models and the processing of heterogeneous collection. We consider that a structured document sd_i is a tree, composed of leaf nodes ln_{ij} and attributes a_{ij} and simple nodes n_{ij} (all nodes that are not leaf nodes or attributes).

Structured document: $sd_i = (\{n_{ij}\}, \{ln_{ij}\}, \{a_{ij}\})$

In order to easily browse the document tree and to quickly find ancestors-descendants relationships, the model uses a representation of nodes and attributes based on the Xpath Accelerator approach [2].

All leaf nodes are indexed, because even the smallest leaf nodes can be relevant or can give information on the relevance of their ancestors. Intuitively, *title* or *subtitle* nodes are not informative, but if a query term occurs in those nodes, such information can be useful for evaluating the relevance of the ancestor node. Such an approach has other advantages: the index process can be done automatically, without any human intervention and the system will be so able to handle heterogeneous collections automatically; and secondly, even the most specific query concerning the document structure will be processed, since all the document structure is stored.

N. Fuhr et al. (Eds.): INEX 2005, LNCS 3977, pp. 88–103, 2006.

During query processing, relevance values are assigned to leaf nodes and relevance score of inner nodes are then computed dynamically, thanks to a propagation of leaf nodes score through the document tree. An ordered list of subtrees is then returned to the user.

2.2 Evaluation of Leaf Nodes Scores

Whatever the considered type of queries, a first step in query processing is to evaluate the relevance value of leaf nodes ln according to the query. Let $q = t_1, \ldots, t_n$ be this query. Relevance values are computed thanks to a similarity function $RSV_m(q, ln)$, where m is an IR model.

$$RSV_m(q, ln) = \sum_{i=1}^{n} w_i^q * w_i^{ln} \tag{1}$$

Where w_i^q and w_i^{ln} are respectively the weights of term i in query q and leaf node ln.

According to previous experiments [8], we choose to use the following term weighting scheme, which aims at reflecting the importance of terms in leaf nodes, but also in whole documents:

$$w_i^q = tf_i^q \qquad w_i^{ln} = tf_i^{ln} * idf_i * ief_i \tag{2}$$

Where tf_i^q and tf_i^{ln} are respectively the frequency of term i in query q and leaf node ln, $idf_i = log(|D|/(|di|+1)) + 1$, with $|D|$ the total number of documents in the collection, and $|di|$ the number of documents containing i, and ief_i is the inverse element frequency of term i, i.e. $log(|N|/|nf_i|+1) + 1$, where $|nf_i|$ is the number of leaf nodes containing i and $|N|$ is the total number of leaf nodes in the collection.

Inner nodes relevance values are evaluated thanks to one or more propagation functions, which depend on the searching task. Such propagation functions are described in the following sections.

3 CO Task

3.1 Inner Nodes Relevance Values Evaluation

In our model, each node in the document tree is assigned a relevance value which is function of the relevance values of the leaf nodes it contains. We believe that terms that occur close to the root of a given subtree are more significant for the root element that ones on deeper levels of the subtrees. It seems therefore that the larger the distance of a node from its ancestor is, the less it contributes to the relevance of its ancestor. This affirmation is modelled in our propagation formula by the use of the $dist(n, ln_k)$ parameter. $dist(n, ln_k)$ is the distance between node n and leaf node ln_k in the document tree, i.e. the number of arcs that are necessary to join n and ln_k.

It is also intuitive that the more a node contains relevant leaf nodes, the more it is relevant. We then introduce in the propagation function the $|L_n^r|$ parameter, which is the number of leaf nodes being descendant of n and having a non-zero relevance value (according to equation 1).

A relevance propagation function using these parameters has been tested in the INEX 2004 framework [6]. In the 2005 evaluation campaign, we propose to add two parameters:

- We propose to increase small nodes importance during propagation. Indeed, we think that authors of documents use small nodes to highlight impor-tant informations. These nodes can therefore give precious indications on the relevance of their ancestors. In our propagation function, this intuition corresponds to the $\beta(ln_k)$ parameter.
- We introduce the ρ parameter, inspired from work presented in [3], which allows the introduction of document relevance in inner nodes relevance eval-uation. The idea behind context is: an element in a relevant document should be better ranked than an identical element in a non-relevant document.

The relevance value r_n of a node n is therefore computed according the following formula:

$$r_n = \rho * |L_n^r|. \sum_{ln_k \in L_n} \alpha^{dist(n,ln_k)-1} * \beta(ln_k) * RSV(q, ln_k)$$

$$+(1-\rho) * |L^r|. \sum_{ln_k \in L} \alpha^{dist(root,ln_k)-1} * \beta(ln_k) * RSV(q, ln_k)$$

$$= \rho * |L_n^r|. \sum_{ln_k \in L_n} \alpha^{dist(n,ln_k)-1} * \beta(ln_k) * RSV(q, ln_k)$$

$$+(1-\rho) * r_{root} \qquad (3)$$

where ln_k are leaf nodes being descendant of n and L_n is the set of leaf nodes being descendant of n. r_{root} is the relevance score of the root element, i.e. the relevance score of the whole document, evaluated with equation 3 with $\rho = 1$. $\beta(ln_k)$ is evaluated as follows:

$$\beta(ln_k) = \begin{cases} l_k/\Delta l \ if \ dist(n, ln_k) = 1 \ and \ l_k < \Delta l \\ log(\Delta l/l_k) \ if \ dist(n, ln_k) > 1 \ and \ l_k < \Delta l \\ 1 \ else \end{cases} \qquad (4)$$

with l_k the length of node ln_k and Δl the average length of leaf nodes in the collection. If a node is smaller than the average length of leaf nodes, its role in the propagation function is emphasized.

3.2 Runs

CO.Thorough strategy. For the CO.Thorough task, all nodes having a non-zero relevance value are returned by the XFIRM system. We experimented using various values of $\rho \in [0..1]$.

CO.Focussed strategy. In order to reduce/remove nodes overlap, we use two different algorithms:

1. For each relevant path, we keep the most relevant node in the path (around 20% of nodes overlap still remains)
2. For each relevant path, we keep the most relevant node in the path. The results set is then parsed again one time, to eliminate any possible overlap among ideal components.

CO.FetchAndBrowse strategy. In this task, elements are first ranked by the relevance of the document they belong to, and then by their own relevance. We use the following algorithm:

1. relevance values are computed for each document in the collection;
2. relevance values are computed for each node of the collection;
3. documents are ranked by decreasing order of relevance;
4. for each document, elements they contain are ranked by decreasing order of relevance and are returned to users.

Document relevance is computed with the Mercure system [1]. Previous experiments [5] have shown that for a fetch and browse strategy, results are better when evaluting document relevance with the Mercure system (which was developed for this purpose) than with our relevance propagation method (which aims at find elements instead of documents).

3.3   Results

All results described in this paper use the inex1.8 version of the collection, which is the official 2005 collection. However, due to a misunderstanding, our official submissions were obtained with the inex1.6 version of the collection. For information, official submissions are mentioned in italic characters and are followed by the '*' symbol.

Table 1. CO.Thorough strategy. Quantisation: Generalised.

	nxCG[10]	nxCG[25]	nxCG[50]	ep/gr - MAP	Q	R
$\rho = 1$	0,1684	0,168	0,1772	0,0562	0,1100	0,2231
$\rho = 0.9$ *	0,15 *	0,156 *	0,174 *	0,043 *	0,085 *	0,188 *
$\rho = 0.9$	0,1712	0,1696	0,1786	0,0577	0,1089	0,2179
$\rho = 0.8$	0,1634	0,1845	0,1859	0,0569	0,1057	0,2138
$\rho = 0.7$	0,1727	0,2006	0,1883	0,0569	0,1044	0,2110
$\rho = 0.6$	0,1713	0,2058	0,1928	0,0565	0,1031	0,2078
$\rho = 0.5$	0,1762	0,2036	0,1894	0,0561	0,1019	0,2051
$\rho = 0.4$	0,1802	0,2075	0,1897	0,0557	0,1009	0,2040
$\rho = 0.3$	0,1931	0,2116	0,188	0,0555	0,1001	0,2020
$\rho = 0.2$	0,2049	0,2126	0,1857	0,0553	0,0996	0,2010
$\rho = 0.1$	0,2083	0,2144	0,1868	0,0548	0,0986	0,2011
$\rho = 0$	0,2384	0,2126	0,1862	0,0542	0,0976	0,1981

Table 2. CO.Thorough strategy. Quantisation: Strict.

	nxCG[10]	nxCG[25]	nxCG[50]	ep/gr - MAP	Q	R
$\rho = 1$	0,012	0,0299	0,0464	0,0009	0,0012	0,0208
$\rho = 0.9$ *	0,011 *	0,025 *	0,047 *	0,001 *	0,001 *	0,021 *
$\rho = 0.9$	0,012	0,0258	0,0462	0,0012	0,0015	0,0216
$\rho = 0.8$	0,008	0,0329	0,0475	0,0014	0,0016	0,0213
$\rho = 0.7$	0,008	0,0425	0,0514	0,0015	0,0017	0,0216
$\rho = 0.6$	0,008	0,0505	0,0522	0,0016	0,0018	0,0218
$\rho = 0.5$	0,012	0,0569	0,0546	0,0017	0,0019	0,0209
$\rho = 0.4$	0,016	0,0585	0,0555	0,0017	0,0019	0,0206
$\rho = 0.3$	0,024	0,0617	0,0555	0,0017	0,0020	0,0199
$\rho = 0.2$	0,036	0,0633	0,0555	0,0018	0,0020	0,0199
$\rho = 0.1$	0,044	0,0633	0,0563	0,0019	0,0021	0,0199
$\rho = 0$	0,0684	0,0636	0,0579	0,0019	0,0021	0,0194

Table 3. CO.Focussed strategy. Quantisation: Generalised.

		nxCG[10]	nxCG[25]	nxCG[50]	ep/gr - MAP	Q	R
	$\rho = 1$	0,1202	0,1214	0,1279	0,0393	0,0798	0,1543
	$\rho = 0.9$	0,112	0,1073	0,0941	0,0260	0,0609	0,1249
Algorithm 1	$\rho = 0.8$	0,1146	0,106	0,093	0,0256	0,06042	0,1208
	...	...	...	...	...	...	...
	$\rho = 0.1$	0,1042	0,094	0,0852	0,0231	0,0577	0,1177
	$\rho = 0$	0,0951	0,0901	0,078	0,0235	0,0607	0,1172
	$\rho = 1$ *	0,119 *	0,122 *	0,119 *	0,030 *	0,060 *	0,132 *
	$\rho = 1$	0,1364	0,1445	0,1453	0,0396	0,0748	0,1579
	$\rho = 0.9$*	0.104 *	0.104 *	0.089 *	0.022 *	0.052 *	0.106 *
	$\rho = 0.9$	0,1299	0,1171	0,1021	0,0276	0,0624	0,1271
Algorithm 2	$\rho = 0.8$	0,1235	0,1144	0,0988	0,0271	0,0622	0,1258
	...	...	...	...	...	...	...
	$\rho = 0.1$	0,1131	0,1033	0,092	0,0256	0,0613	0,1197
	$\rho = 0$	0,0951	0,0901	0,078	0,0235	0,0607	0,1172

CO.THOROUGH strategy. Tables 1 and 2 show the results obtained with different values of ρ.

Best results are obtained with small values of ρ, especially for the strict quantisation function. This seems to show that root relevance (i.e. document relevance) has a high impact on elements relevance.

CO.FOCUSSED strategy. Tables 3 and 4 show the results obtained with different values of ρ.

Algorithm 2 (results without any nodes overlap) allows to obtain better results than algorithm 1 for all metrics. As opposed to results obtained for the

Table 4. CO.Focussed strategy. Quantisation: Strict.

		nxCG[10]	nxCG[25]	nxCG[50]	ep/gr - MAP	Q	R
	$\rho = 1$	0,012	0,016	0,0336	0,0024	0,0034	0,0051
	$\rho = 0.9$	0,014	0,0156	0,0188	0,0030	0,0038	0,0015
Algorithm 1	$\rho = 0.8$	0,014	0,0156	0,0196	0,0031	0,0039	0,0011
	...	...	...	...	...	...	...
	$\rho = 0.1$	0,004	0,0056	0,0128	0,0011	0,0016	0,0008
	$\rho = 0$	0	0,004	0,012	0,0009	0,0015	0
	$\rho = 1$ *	0,011 *	0,006 *	0,025 *	0,002 *	0,003 *	0,004 *
	$\rho = 1$	0,016	0,0112	0,0296	0,0034	0,0046	0,0066
	$\rho = 0.9$*	0.014 *	0.020 *	0.028 *	0.004 *	0.004 *	0.002 *
	$\rho = 0.9$	0,014	0,0172	0,0204	0,0031	0,0039	0,0018
Algorithm 2	$\rho = 0.8$	0,014	0,0172	0,0236	0,0031	0,0039	0,0011
	...	...	...	...	...	...	...
	$\rho = 0.1$	0,004	0,0072	0,0176	0,0013	0,0019	0,0011
	$\rho = 0$	0	0,004	0,012	0,0009	0,0015	0

Table 5. CO.FetchBrowse strategy. ep/gr - MAP-Element metric.

	Generalised	Strict
$\rho = 1$	0,1167	0,0063
$\rho = 0.9$ *	0,108 *	0,006 *
$\rho = 0.9$	0,1229	0,0068
	...	...
$\rho = 0.1$	0,1183	0,0065
$\rho = 0$	0,0731	0,0042

CO. Thorough strategy, document relevance seems to have no impact on element relevance (best results were obtained with $\rho = 1$).

CO.FETCHBROWSE strategy.   Results obtained with the CO.FetchBrowse strategy are described in table 5. Results are good compared to other participants, since we were ranked in the top 5 for both quantisation functions. Moreover results are substantially better for the MAP metric than those obtained for the CO.Thorough strategy (see tables 1 and 2). We observe for example up to 113% increase for the generalised quantisation function with $\rho = 0.9$.

4   CAS Task

4.1   Inner Nodes Relevance Value Evaluation

The evaluation of a CAS query is carried out as follows:

1. INEX (NEXI) queries are translated into XFIRM queries

2. XFIRM queries are decomposed into sub-queries SQ and elementary sub-queries ESQ, which are of the form: $ESQ = tg[q]$, where tg is a tag name, i.e. a structure constraint, and $q = t_1, ..., t_n$ is a content constraint composed of simple keywords terms.
3. Relevance values are then evaluated between leaf nodes and the content conditions of elementary sub-queries
4. Relevance values are propagated in the document tree to answer to the structure conditions of elementary sub-queries
5. Sub-queries are processed thanks to the results of elementary sub-queries
6. Original queries are evaluated thanks to upwards and downwards propagation of the relevance weights

Step 3 is processed thanks to formula 1. In step 4, the relevance value r_n of a node n to an elementary subquery $ESQ = tg[q]$ is computed according the following formula:

$$r_n = \begin{cases} \sum_{ln_k \in L_n} \alpha^{dist(n,ln_k)-1} * RSV(q, ln_k) \ if \ n \ \in construct(tg) \\ 0 \ else \end{cases} \quad (5)$$

where the $construct(tg)$ function allows the creation of set composed of nodes having tg as tag name, and $RSV(q, ln_k)$ is evaluated during step 2 with formula 1. The $construct(tg)$ function uses a *Dictionnary* Index, which provides for a given tag tg the tags that are considered as equivalent. For example, a *title* node can be considered as equivalent to a *sub-title* node. This index is built manually. More details about CAS queries processing are can be found in [7].

4.2   Runs

In order to answer the different searching tasks, we used different Dictionnary indexes:

– The DICT index is composed of equivalencies given in the INEX guidelines. For example, *ss1*, *ss2* and *ss3* nodes are considered as equivalent to *sec* nodes.
– The ExtendedDICT is composed of very extended equivalencies. For example, *sec*, *ss1*, *ss2* and *ss3* nodes are equivalent to both *p* and *bdy* nodes.

SSCAS strategy. We use the DICT index and results are filtered in order to answer strictly to constraints on the target element and support elements.

VVCAS strategy. We use the EXtendedDICT index, and no filter is applied on results.

SVCAS strategy. We use the DICT index. No filter is applied on results: they match the structure constraint on the target element in a strict way (since the DICT index is used), and their relevance score is eventually increased by the relevance score of results of subqueries on support elements.

VSCAS strategy. We use the DICT index on support elements and the ExtendedDICT on target elements.

4.3 Results

Results for all strategies are showed in tables 6, 7, 8 and 9. We are in the top 10 for almost all metrics.

Results are especially good for the SVCAS strategy, which is not really surprising. Our original model processes CAS queries with a SVCAS strategy: relevance score of target elements are eventually increased by score of results of subqueries on support elements [7]. Relevance propagation seems consequently to be a very good solution for processing CAS queries with a SVCAS strategy.

Table 6. SSCAS strategy

		nxCG[10]	nxCG[25]	nxCG[50]	ep/gr - MAP	Q	R
Generalised	*DICT* *	*0,329* *	*0,397* *	*0,374* *	*0,105* *	*0,157* *	*0,258* *
	DICT	0.2861	0.2722	0.338	0.109	0.178	0.246
Strict	*DICT* *	*0,325* *	*0,31* *	*0,32* *	*0,016* *	*0,02* *	*0,121* *
	DICT	0.35	0.329	0.338	0.0166	0.021	0.1169

Table 7. VVCAS strategy

		nxCG[10]	nxCG[25]	nxCG[50]	ep/gr - MAP	Q	R
Generalised	*ExtendedDICT* *	*0,29* *	*0,258* *	*0,246* *	*0,061* *	*0,101* *	*0,206* *
	ExtendedDICT	0.3047	0.2727	0.2487	0.0687	0.115	0.219
Strict	*ExtendedDICT* *	*0,067* *	*0,076* *	*0,136* *	*0,005* *	*0,006* *	*0,044* *
	ExtendedDICT	0.0885	0.0756	0.1244	0.0054	0.0059	0.0468

Table 8. SVCAS strategy

		nxCG[10]	nxCG[25]	nxCG[50]	ep/gr - MAP	Q	R
Generalised	*DICT* *	*0,303* *	*0,272* *	*0,276* *	*0,105* *	*0,181* *	*0,301* *
	DICT	0.2645	0.2758	0.2916	0.1378	0.2318	0.330
Strict	*DICT* *	*0,42* *	*0,408* *	*0,416* *	*0,017* *	*0,02* *	*0,1* *
	DICT	0.44	0.4571	0.4662	0.017	0.022	0.11

Table 9. VSCAS strategy

		nxCG[10]	nxCG[25]	nxCG[50]	ep/gr - MAP	Q	R
Generalised	*DICT+ExtendedDICT* *	*0,194* *	*0,21* *	*0,207* *	*0,07* *	*0,119* *	*0,218* *
	DICT+ExtendedDICT	0.237	0.2346	0.2292	0.047	0.069	0.159
Strict	*DICT+ExtendedDICT* *	*0*	*0,007* *	*0,023* *	*0,007* *	*0,008* *	*0,07* *
	DICT+ExtendedDICT	0.1667	0.15	0.15	0.006	0.007	0.05

5   CO+S Task

5.1   Inner Nodes Relevance Value Evaluation

In the CO+S task, queries are processed as in the CAS task. Nodes relevance values are evaluated using equation 5.

5.2   Runs

+S.THOROUGH strategy and +S.FOCUSSED strategy.   We either use the DICT or ExtendedDICT dictionnary index, since the aim of the task is to investigate the usefulness of the structural hints.

+S.FETCHBROWSE strategy. We follow the same algorithm as the one used for the CO.FETCHBROWSE strategy.

5.3   Results and Comparison to the CO Task

+S.THOROUGH strategy.   Results are not as good as those obtained without structural hints (see table 1 and 2 for comparison).

+S.FOCUSSED strategy. As opposed to results obtained for the +S.THOROUGH strategy, results here are better than those obtained without using structural hints (see tables 3 and 4 for comparison).

+S.FETCHBROWSE strategy.   As for the +S.THOROUGH strategy, results obtained without using structural hints are better than those obtained for the CO.FETCHBRWOSE strategy (see table 5 for comparison).

Table 10. COS.Thorough strategy. Quantisation: Generalised.

	nxCG[10]	nxCG[25]	nxCG[50]	ep/gr - MAP	Q	R
DICT *	0,172 *	0,147 *	0,123 *	0,016 *	0,03 *	0,089 *
DICT	0,1759	0,162	0,1422	0,0192	0,0369	0,1022
*ExtendedDICT**	0,169 *	0,191 *	0,187 *	0,045 *	0,088 *	0,001 *
ExtendedDICT	0,1787	0,2037	0,206	0,0569	0,1086	0,2166

Table 11. COS.Thorough strategy. Quantisation: Strict.

	nxCG[10]	nxCG[25]	nxCG[50]	ep/gr - MAP	Q	R
DICT *	0,024 *	0,037 *	0,047 *	0 *	0 *	0,008 *
DICT	0,0242	0,0321	0,0362	0,0003	0,0004	0,0062
*ExtendedDICT**	0,027 *	0,042 *	0,056 *	0,001 *	0,001 *	0,019 *
ExtendedDICT	0,0308	0,0434	0,0532	0,0012	0,0014	0,0210

Table 12. COS.Focussed strategy. Quantisation: Generalised.

	nxCG[10]	nxCG[25]	nxCG[50]	ep/gr - MAP	Q	R
DICT	0,1567	0,1362	0,121	0,0458	0,1046	0,1783
*ExtendedDICT**	*0,144 **	*0,128 **	*0,127 **	*0,031 **	*0,069 **	*0,143 **
ExtendedDICT	0.1586	0.1497	0.1428	0.0410	0.0855	0.1674

Table 13. COS.Focussed strategy. Quantisation: Strict.

	nxCG[10]	nxCG[25]	nxCG[50]	ep/gr - MAP	Q	R
DICT	0,0231	0,0308	0,0345	0,0096	0,01183	0,0166
*ExtendedDICT**	*0,009 **	*0,009 **	*0,025 **	*0,002 **	*0,004 **	*0,004 **
ExtendedDICT	0.0154	0.0163	0.0571	0.0032	0.0046	0.0086

Table 14. +S.FetchBrowse strategy. ep/gr - MAP-Element metric.

	Generalised	Strict
*DICT **	*0,111 **	*0,015 **
DICT	0.0155	0,0008
*ExtendedDICT **	*0.0747 **	*0,005 **
ExtendedDICT	0,072	0.0058

6 Relevance Feedback Track

For the RF track, we used three different algorithms that are described below.

6.1 Structure-Oriented Relevance Feedback

Our goal in what we call structure-oriented RF is to enrich the initial query by adding structural constraints. Our approach consists in refining the initial query by extracting from the set of judged elements the structure that could contain the information needed by the user. The idea behind structure-oriented RF is therefore to find for each query, the *appropriate generic structure* which is the generic structure shared by the greatest amount of relevant elements.
The generative structure is extracted as follows. Let:

- E^r be the set of relevant elements,
- e_i be an element $\in E^r$,
- e_i be characterized by a path p_i and a score w_i initialized at the begining of algorithm (and set to 1 for the experiments presented here). p_i is only composed of tag names. For example: $/article/bdy/sec$.
- CS be a set of Common Structures, obtained as result.

For each $(e_i, e_j)_{i \neq j} \in E^r \times E^r$, we apply the SCA algorithm, which allows to retrieve the smallest common ancestor of e_i and e_j. The path of this smallest common ancestor is then added to the set of common structures CS. The SCA algorithm is processed for each pair of E^r elements. The SCA algorithm is described below:

$SCA(e_i, e_j)$
Begin
If $p_i.first = p_j.first$, then
    if $p_i.last = p_j.last$, then if $\exists e_p(p_p, w_p) \in CS/p_p = p_i$
                                                  then $w_p \leftarrow w_p + w_j$
                              else $w_i \leftarrow w_i + w_j$
                              $CS \leftarrow sp_i$
    else
    if $head(p_j) \neq null$, then $p'_j \leftarrow head(p_j)$
                                      $w'_j \leftarrow w_j/2$
                                      $SCA(e_i(p_i, w_i), e'_j(p'_j, w'_j))$
                                      else $SCA(e_j, e_i)$
End

$p.last$ is the last tag of the path p and $head(p)$ is a function allowing to reduce the path p, i.e. to remove the last tag of the path. For example, $head(/article/bdy/section) = /article/bdy$. In our approach, we choose to only compare the $p.last$ tags of elements, since we are looking for component types (i.e. tags) instead of complete paths.

In order to express the new (CAS) query, we then extract the top ranked structure according w_i in the CS set. This structure will be either used as it is in the new query; this form is called **complex form=p** or simplified in a simple tag form called **simple form=p.last**. Original query terms are then added to the structural constraint.

Example for a given query, we consider three elements e_1, e_2 and e_3 judged relevant having the following corresponding paths (we consider a path as a structure):
$p_1=$ /article/bdy/sec/ss1, $p_2=$ /article/bdy/sec/ss1/ss2 and $p_3=$ /article/bdy. Initial scores $w_1=w_2=w_3 = 1$ are assigned to structures p_1, p_2 and p_3 (see table 15). Let CS be the set of Common Structures in which we add the generative structure. At the begining of the algorithm, CS is empty.
The first step of generative structure extraction consists in:

- checking if the two structures have the same root: $(article)$.
- comparing the last tags of p_1 structure and p_2 structure: $p_1.last = ss1$ and $p_2.last = ss2$.

Table 15. The Input of extraction generative structure

Relevant element	Path	Score
$e_1(p_1, w_1)$	$p_1 = $ /article/bdy/sec/ss1	$w_1=1$
$e_2(p_2, w_2)$	$p_2 = $ /article/bdy/sec/ss1/ss2	$w_2=1$
$e_3(p_3, w_3)$	$p_3 = $ /article/bdy	$w_3=1$

- As the tags are different ($ss1 \neq ss2$), we move to high level of p_2 structure p_2' ($p_2' = head(p_2) = /article/bdy/sec/ss1$) . p_2''s score is $w_2' = w_2/2$.
- $p_2'.last = ss1 = p_1.last$. So, the p_1 structure will be added to CS with $w_1 + w_2/2 = 1 + 1/2$ score.

The second step corresponds to matching of the two stuctures $p_1 = /article/bdy/sec/ss1$ and $p_3 = /article/bdy$:

- matching in $p_1 \longrightarrow p_3$ direction gives empty result.
- We match them in inverse direction ($p_3 \longrightarrow p_1$). The Common Structure is retrieved after 2 iterations ($(head(head(p_1))).last = bdy = p_3.last$).
  $\Rightarrow$ The score of p_1 is divided by 2^2 and the structure $p_3 = /article/bdy$ is added in the SC set with $w_3 + w_1/4 = 1 + 1/4$ score.

In the third step, we proceed in matching p_2 and p_3. The same process as above is applied. The Common Structure is extracted when applying three iterations. The w_2 score is divided by $2^3 = 1/8$.
We notice that p_3 structure is already in the CS set. So, we increment its score by adding $w_2/8$.

The most generative structure is the one with the highest score in CS (see table 16).

Table 16. The Ouput of extraction generative structure: the CS set

Structure	Score
/article/bdy/sec/ss1	$1 + 1/2 = 1.5$
/article/bdy	$1 + 1/4 + 1/8 = 1.375$

We select in this example **/article/bdy/sec/ss1**.
Let Q be an initial CO query: Q= "Information Retrieval". The new CAS query is reformulated as follow:

- Structure-Oriented RF in its simple form: *"ss1[about(., "Information Retrieval")]"*.
- Structure-Oriented RF in its complex form: *"//article/bdy/sec/ ss1[about(., "Information Retrieval ")]"*.

Let Q' be a structred query (COS or VVCAS): Q'="*article[about(., "Information Retrieval")]*". The new query is:

- Structure-Oriented RF: *"article[about(., "Information Retrieval")] OR ss1[about(.,"Infomation Retrieval")]"*.

6.2 Content-Oriented Relevance Feedback

Our Content-Oriented Relevance Feedback approach is based on the Rocchio' algorithm [4]. Our aim is to extract the most expressive terms from relevant elements. The content-oriented RF processes as follows :

- We consider the set of relevant elements (E^r) : $E^r = e_1^r, e_2^r, ..., e_k^r, ...e_m^r$,
- A relevant element e_k^r is composed of a set of leaf nodes(ln_j) : $e_k^r = ln_1^k, ..., ln_j^k, .ln_n^k$
- A leaf node ln_j^k is a sequence of terms: $ln_j = \{t_{ij}\}$.

Each term is assigned a score according to the following formula:

$$score(t_{ij}, ln_j^k) = \frac{tf_i^j}{size(ln_j)} \qquad (6)$$

Where tf_i^j is the frequency of term t_i in leaf node ln_j^k and $size(ln_j)$ is the number of terms in ln_j.

We then compute the score of terms for each relevant element. For each term, we sum its scores in different leaf nodes.

$$score(t_i, e_k^r) = \sum_{ln_j \in e_k^r} score(t_i, ln_j) \qquad (7)$$

As a result, we obtain a set of expressive words for each element judged as relevant. Best terms are selected according to the following formula:

$$score(t_i) = \sum_{e_k^r \in E^r} score(t_i, e_k^r) \qquad (8)$$

The new query is finally composed of terms ranked in the top k according to formula 8, that are added to the original query terms.

6.3   Content-and-Structure-Oriented Relevance Feedback

In this approach, we propose to combine the structure-oriented Relevance Feedback method and the content-oriented Relevance Feedback described above. The new query (CAS) is composed of the most appropriate generic stucture (complex or simple form) and of terms ranked in the top k according to formula 8, that are added to the original query terms.

6.4   Runs and Results

Relative Improvement *(RI)* and Absolute Improvement *(AI)* according *MAnxCG[50]*, *MAnxCG[1500]* and *MAep* measures using strict and generalized quantizations are used to evaluate our runs.

Due to a misunderstanding, official results use inex1.6 version of the collection. They are presented in table 17, applying the Content and Structure-Oriented approach.

The results differ w.r.t the query types (if we consider MAep measure, CO: very negative improvement, CO+S important improvement and VVCAS negative improvement). Such observations are not enough to conclude. We therefore tested the three approches presented above for all 3 CO. Thorough, COS. Thorough and VVCAS task using the inex1.8 version of the collection.

Table 17. Official Result of Content and Structure-Oriented RF

	MAnxCG[50] strict	MAnxCG[50] gen	MAnxCG [1500] strict	MAnxCG [1500] gen	MAep strict	MAep gen
AI-VVCAS-RF	-0.0397	-0.0813	0.0437	-0.0251	-0.0020	-0.0008
RI-VVCAS-RF	-0.5231	-0.3135	0.1975	-0.1007	-0.0795	-0.0142
AI-COS-RF	-0.0014	-0.0176	0.0168	0.078	0.0001	0.0202
RI-COS-RF	-0.1728	-0.1371	0.1502	0.6933	0.0421	1.8222
AI-CO-RF	-0.0169	-0.0597	-0.1679	-0.1494	-0.0072	-0.0324
RI-CO-RF	-0.6576	-0.3703	-0.723	-0.551	-0.7217	-0.7860

Impact of Structure-Oriented RF. According to table 18, we notice that the Structure-Oriented approach has a positive impact in case of COS queries (RI gen(MAep =1,6708, MAnxCG@1500=0.808)). This confirms our hypothesis : *adding structural constraints leads to refining query.* This hypothesis is however not proved in case of CO and VVCAS queries and we notice that results obtained by adding a complex form are worse than those using a simple form. We can explain the negative impact in CO case by the fact that the user prefers more than one element type. In the case of VVCAS queries, the reformulation query using the *OR* operator may not be appropriate.

Table 18. Impact of Structure-Oriented RF

	MAnxCG [1500] strict	MAnxCG [1500] gen	MAep strict	MAep gen
AI-VVCAS-RF	-0.0929	-0.0748	0.0000	-0.0124
RI-VVCAS-RF	-0.4200	-0.2914	-0.0063	-0.1810
AI-COS-RF	0.0449	0.0941	0.0005	0.0208
RI-COS-RF	0.3630	0.8394	1.5790	1.0821
AI-CO-RF (simple form)	-0.0822	-0.0999	-0.0007	-0.0189
RI-CO-RF(simple form)	-0.3540	-0.3685	-0.5391	-0.3397
AI-CO-RF (complex form)	-0.1653	-0.1792	-0.0011	-0.0348
RI-CO-RF(complex form)	-0.7119	-0.6610	-0.9014	-0.6240

Impact of Content-Oriented RF. We have evaluated the adding of the 10 top terms to initial queries. According to table 19, we notice a positive improvement in case of CO+S queries (generalized quantization) and in case of VVCAS (strict and generalized quantizations). These observations confirm the results obtained in classical IR. We do not observe improvement in case of CO queries. Therefore, it is necessary to look for other methods to extract and extend unstructured queries.

Impact of Content and Structure-Oriented RF. According to above observations, the combined RF seems efficient in case of CO+S and VVCAS task. Indeed, table 20 shows that the relative improvement in generalized quantization

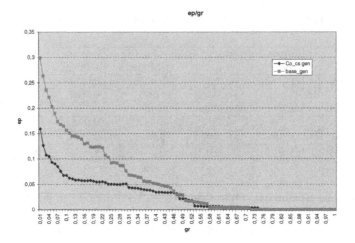

Fig. 1. Comparaison of the base run and of the Structure Oriented RF approach in case of CO queries

Table 19. Impact of Content-Oriented RF

	MAnxCG [1500] strict	MAnxCG [1500] gen	MAep strict	MAep gen
AI-VVCAS-RF	0.222	0.0095	0.0004	0.0022
RI-VVCAS-RF	0.1004	0.0370	0.0698	0.0321
AI-COS-RF	-0.0143	0.0515	0.0001	0.0103
RI-COS-RF	-0.1156	0.4594	0.01568	0.5343
AI-CO-RF	-0.1218	-0.1201	-0.0007	-0.0333
RI-CO-RF	-0.5245	-0.4430	-0.5787	-0.5977

Table 20. Impact of Content and Structure-Oriented RF

	MAnxCG [1500] strict	MAnxCG [1500] gen	MAep strict	MAep gen
AI-VVCAS-RF	0.0228	0.0082	0.0005	0.0031
RI-VVCAS-RF	0.01031	0.0319	0.0985	0.0451
AI-COS-RF	-0.0132	0.0535	0.0001	0.0107
RI-COS-RF	-0.1067	0.4773	0.4588	0.5537
AI-CO-RF	-0.1960	-0.1812	-0.0010	-0.0415
RI-CO-RF	-0.7736	-0.7451	-0.8441	-0.6684

is more than 50% in the case of CO+S queries and 7% in the case of VVCAS queries. These results confirm the classical IR results and the generative structure effectiveness to refine structured queries. Results are still negative in the case of CO queries.

Discussion. We compared different approaches according to each query type. We notice that improvements obtained by Content and Structure Oriented RF are more important in case of VVCAS query type. The Structure-Oriented RF approach is the most effective according to CO+S queries (in generalized quantization). In ep/gr curve of CO queries (figure 1), we notice that Structure-Oriented RF are effective according the precision effort values where (gr$\in$ [0.5,0.53], [0.59,0.68] and [0.73,0.75]). RF is consequently partially benefic for CO queries. We will look for methods extending these intervals in our future works.

References

1. M. Boughanem, T. Dkaki, J. Mothe, and C. Soule-Dupuy. Mercure at TREC-7. In *Proceedings of TREC-7*, 1998.
2. T. Grust. Accelerating XPath location steps. In *Proceedings of the 2002 ACM SIGMOD International Conference on Management of Data, Madison, Wisconsin, USA*, pages 109–120, 2002.
3. Y. Mass and M. Mandelbrod. Component ranking and automatic query refinement for XML retrieval. In *Proceedings of INEX 2004, Springer*, pages 73–84, 2005.
4. J. Rocchio. *Relevance feedback in information retrieval*. Prentice Hall Inc., Englewood Cliffs, NJ, 1971.
5. K. Sauvagnat. *Modle flexible pour la recherche d'information dans des corpus de documents semi-structurs*. PhD thesis, Toulouse : Universit Paul Sabatier, 2005.
6. K. Sauvagnat and M. Boughanem. Using a relevance propagation method for adhoc and heterogeneous tracks at inex 2004. In *Proceedings of INEX 2004, Springer - LNCS - , Dagstuhl, Germany*, pages 337–348, March 2004.
7. K. Sauvagnat, M. Boughanem, and C. Chrisment. Using relevance propagation for processing content-and-structure queries. *Information Systems, special issue on SPIRE 04, to appear*, 2006.
8. K. Sauvagnat, L. Hlaoua, and M. Boughanem. Xml retrieval: What about using contextual relevance ? In *Proceedings of SAC 2006, Dijon, to appear*, 2006.

The Effect of Structured Queries and Selective Indexing on XML Retrieval

Börkur Sigurbjörnsson[1] and Jaap Kamps[1,2]

[1] ISLA, Faculty of Science, University of Amsterdam
[2] Archives and Information Studies, Faculty of Humanities, University of Amsterdam

Abstract. We describe the University of Amsterdam's participation in the INEX 2005 ad hoc track, covering the *Thorough, Focused*, and *Fetch-Browse* tasks and their structured (*+S*) counterparts. Our research questions for this round of INEX were threefold. Our first and main research question was to investigate the contribution of structural constraints to improved retrieval performance. Our main results were that the two types of structural constraints have different effects. Constraining the target of result elements gives improvements in terms of early precision. Constraining the context of result elements improves mean average precision. Our second research question was to experiment with selective indexing strategies based on either the length of elements, the tag-name of elements considered relevant in earlier INEX years, or simply by indexing all sections or articles. Our experiments show that disregarding 80–90% of the total number of elements does not decrease retrieval performance. Third, we considered the automatic creation of structured queries using blind feedback. Here, our results are inconclusive, mainly due to few queries used and lack of comparison to traditional blind feedback.

1 Introduction

In this paper we describe the University of Amsterdam's participation in the INEX 2005 adhoc track. The three research questions we addressed in this year's round of INEX were to explore the contribution of structured constraints, to try to make our system more efficient by reducing the size of our index, and to construct structured queries as a form of query expansion. These research questions built on experiences obtained in our previous INEX participations.

In previous years we created our runs based on an index of all overlapping XML elements [11, 12]. Our main technical objective this year was to experiment with different methods of creating a more selective index. The aim was to create a more efficient retrieval system without sacrificing retrieval effectiveness. We measured the effect of several different index reduction schemes. In the *Focused* task we looked at two simple non-overlapping indexes: section index and article index. As a baseline we used a run from our overlapping element index, where overlap was removed in a list based manner. Both the section run and the article run performed considerably worse than the baseline. In the *Thorough* task we

N. Fuhr et al. (Eds.): INEX 2005, LNCS 3977, pp. 104–118, 2006.

looked at two reductions of our full overlapping element index: one based on element length and another based on past relevance assessments. Our main finding was that even with a 80–90% reduction in the number of indexing units, we do not see a reduction in retrieval effectiveness.

In our experiments with structured queries in previous years, we found that structural constraints lead to improvements in early precision. This year we wanted to explore whether different types of structural constraints contribute differently to this gain. We measured the effect of different aspects of structural constraints. The $CO+S$ tasks provide an excellent framework for these experiments. We compared four runs using different structural aspects. First of all, we had a baseline where no structural constraints were used. We had two runs which used a single aspect of the structured queries: either by restricting the type of target element, or by restricting the context of target element. Finally, we had a run which used both aspects of structured queries. Our main finding is that the target constraints are useful for improving early precision. On the other hand, the context constraints are more useful for mean average precision.

Some of the topics in the $CO+S$ task were only formulated using a content only query, but had no content and structure formulation. For these queries we attempted to create a structured query automatically using blind relevance feedback. As with so many blind feedback experiments, our results are inconclusive, partly due to a limited number of queries used.

Finally, we also looked at the the new *FetchBrowse* task, for which we considered the simple clustering of our *Focused* runs. That is, for the *FetchBrowse* task we re-ordered our *Focused* runs such that results from the same document appear at consecutive positions in the ranking. Our results for this task are inconclusive, mainly because it is not clear how to evaluate this task.

The remainder of the paper is organized as follows. In Section 2 we introduce our retrieval framework: indexing, query processing, and retrieval. We describe our runs in Section 3. In Section 4 we present and discuss our results. We review related work in Section 5. Finally, we provide some more discussion and conclusions in Section 6.

2   Retrieval System

2.1   Indexing

For effective and efficient XML retrieval indexing plays an important role. Any element can, in theory, be retrieved. It has been shown, however, that not all elements are equally likely to be appreciated as satisfactory answers to an information need [5]. In particular, retrieval of the very many, very small elements is not likely to be rewarded by users. Furthermore, users (and hence metrics) may be willing to partially reward near misses. This prompted us to investigate whether we could reduce our indexing size, both in terms of retrievable units and storage size, without harming our retrieval effectiveness.

Element Indexes. For retrieving elements we built four indexes.

- *Overlapping element index* We built the "traditional" overlapping element index in the same way as we have done in the previous years (see further [11, 12]).
- *Length based index*: Very short elements are not likely to be regarded as relevant. We analyzed the average length of elements bearing different tag-names. We then indexed only element types having an average length above a certain threshold. For INEX 2005 we set the threshold to be 25 terms. The term count was applied before stop-words were removed. The choice of threshold value was not based on rigorous empirical analysis; hence, thresholding is a subject for future work.
- *Qrel based index*: Elements with certain tag-names are more likely than others to be regarded as relevant. We analyzed the INEX 2003 and 2004 assessments and looked at which elements were assessed more frequently than other. We indexed only elements that had appeared relatively frequently in previous assessment sets (i.e., they should constitute at least 2% of the total assessments). As a result, we indexed only 8 element types: `article`, `bdy`, `sec`, `ss1`, `ss2`, `p`, `ip1`, and `fig`.
- *Section index*: Retrieval of non-overlapping elements is a hot topic in XML retrieval. We wanted to investigate how simple one can make non-overlapping retrieval. We built an index based on non-overlapping passages, where the passage boundaries are determined by the structure. We decided to go for a simple solution. We indexed only section elements (`<sec>`). We believed that this simple strategy would be effective, despite (or perhaps even due to) the fact that the sections do not provide a full coverage of the collection.

Article Indexes. For retrieving articles we built two indexes.

- *Article index*: the "normal" article index
- *Fielded index*: An article index containing both content and a selection of fields. This index was used for processing context restrictions for the structured queries. The fields were chosen based on INEX 2003 and 2004 structured queries. For our INEX 2005 experiments we used: `abs`, `fm//au`, `fm//atl`, `kwd`, `st`, `bb//au`, `bb//atl`, and `ip1`. Those fields were the ones most frequently used in the INEX 2003 and INEX 2004 content-and-structure queries.

For all indexes, stop-words were removed, but no morphological normalization such as stemming was applied. Table 1 shows some statistics of the different indexes.

2.2   Query Pre-processing

Recall that the fielded article index only contains the most common query constraints. More precisely, our system handles two types of constraints: target constraints and context constraints. The context constraints we support are a

Table 1. Properties of the the different indexes. *Unit* stands for the number of retrievable units. *Storage* stands for the size occupied in physical storage. *Query time* stands for the time needed to retrieve 200 retrieval units from the index for each of the INEX 2003-2005 CO topics. All retrieval times are relative to the maximum retrieval time.

Index	Units	Storage	Query time
Element index	10,629,617	1.9G	1.00
Length based	1,502,277	1.3G	0.81
Qrel based	1,581,031	1.1G	0.66
Sections	96,600	223M	0.14
Articles	16,819	204M	0.08
Query fields	16,819	275M	–

kind of 'meta-data' constraints on the article. We support 8 types of context constraints. In terms of end-to-end usage, one can think of this as an advanced query interface where the user can add query terms to the following meta-data fields:

- *Abstract*: Article's abstract (abs).
- *Article author*: Authors of the article (fm//au).
- *Article title*: Title of the article (fm//atl).
- *Article keywords*: Keywords manually assigned to the article (kwd).
- *Section title*: Section title (st).
- *Referenced author*: Author name in the bibliography (bb//au).
- *Referenced title*: Article title in the bibliography (bb//atl).
- *Initial paragraph*: First paragraph of a section (ip1).

We pre-processed the <castitle> queries such that they matched our indexing scheme. We processed the <castitle> constraints in different ways, depending on their format. *First*, for the the <castitle> constraints that match our fielded article index, we only need to rewrite the query such that it fits our indexing scheme. For example, the query:

```
//article[about(.//abs, ipv6)]//sec[about(., ipv6 deployment)
or about(., ipv6 support)]
```

becomes

```
abs:ipv6 ipv6 deployment ipv6 support.
```

Second, for the constraints that only partly match our indexing scheme, we need to do additional processing, i.e.,

```
//*[about(.//au, moldovan) and about(., semantic networks)]
```

becomes

```
fm//au:moldovan bb//au:moldovan semantic networks,
```

Table 2. Frequency of different context constraints in the castitle queries. *Query freq.* refers to how many queries contained the constraint. *Total freq.* refers to how often the constraint was used in total. *Match* refers to how the constraint matches our indexing scheme.

Context constraint	Query freq.	Total freq.	Match
//*//au	1	1	partial
//*//p	1	1	
//sec//fig	1	1	
//article//atl	1	2	partial
//article//abs	3	3	full
//article//kwd	1	1	full
//article//bdy	3	4	
//article//sec	1	1	
//article//bb	1	1	
//article//bdy//sec	1	1	
//article//sec//p	2	2	

since our index makes a distinction between article authors and referenced authors. *Third*, for <castitle> constraints that do not fit our index, we simply extract the query terms. i.e.,

```
//article[about(.//bdy, synthesizers) and about(.//bdy, music)]
```

becomes

```
synthesizers music.
```

For the 28 INEX 2005 <castitle> queries, 11 had context constraints that did not match our scheme and 2 had context constraints that did partially match our scheme. Table 2 shows the frequency of different context constraints in the query set. Out of 11 types of constraints we only support 4. Of the 7 constraint types that we do not support 5 have the element names p, sec, and bdy as their deepest context. We believe that the usefulness of these constraints is limited since almost all text is contained within such a context. The remaining two constraint types (using bb and fig) it might have been useful to be able to handle.

2.3 Automatically Generating Structured Queries

For queries without a <castitle>, we added structured query fields using pseudo relevance feedback on the fielded article index [10]. We calculated the top 20 feedback terms and we added up to n fielded terms where n is the length of the original query. For example, the query

```
computer assisted composing music notes midi
```

becomes

```
bb//atl:music bb//atl:musical st:music ip1:musical ip1:music
fm//au:university computer assisted composing music notes midi.
```

2.4   Retrieval

For all our runs we used a multinomial language model [4]. We use the same mixture model implementation as we used in INEX 2004 [12]. We assume query terms to be independent, and rank elements according to:

$$P(e|q) \propto P(e) \cdot \prod_{i=1}^{k} P(t_i|e), \tag{1}$$

where q is a query made out of the terms $t_1, \ldots, t_k$. We estimate the element language model by taking a linear interpolation of three language models:

$$P(t_i|e) = \lambda_e \cdot P_{mle}(t_i|e) + \lambda_d \cdot P_{mle}(t_i|d) + (1 - \lambda_e - \lambda_d) \cdot P_{mle}(t_i), \tag{2}$$

where $P_{mle}(\cdot|e)$ is a language model for element e; $P_{mle}(\cdot|d)$ is a language model for document d; and $P_{mle}(\cdot)$ is a language model of the collection. The parameters λ_e and λ_d are interpolation factors (smoothing parameters). Finally, we assign a prior probability to an element e relative to its length in the following manner:

$$P(e) = \frac{|e|}{\sum_e |e|}, \tag{3}$$

where $|e|$ is the size of an element e. For a more thorough description of our retrieval approach we refer to [12].

We handled the structured queries slightly differently. For each structured query, e.g.

```
//*[about(.//au, moldovan) and about(., semantic networks)]
```

we have a *fielded version*, e.g.

```
fm//au:moldovan bb//au:moldovan semantic networks,
```

and a *content-only* version, e.g.

```
moldovan semantic networks.
```

We used the *fielded version* to create an article run using the fielded article index. We used the *content-only* version to create an element run using an element index. We created a new element run by re-ranking the existing element run using the scores from the article run, i.e., each element is assigned the score of its containing article. Finally, we combined the two element runs using the combination method combSUM [2].

3   Runs

Our retrieval model has two smoothing parameters, λ_e for the element model and λ_d for the document or article model, and the remaining weight $(1 - \lambda_e - \lambda_d)$ will be put on the collection model. These parameters determine the amount of smoothing and optimal values, especially in the case of XML retrieval, depend on the statistics provided by the index. We are using widely different indexes, varying from an index containing all individual elements or subtrees to indexes containing only the article or section elements, it is non-trivial to compare these settings over different indexes. Hence, we typically fix the parameters at values corresponding to traditional adhoc document retrieval, with 0.85 of the weight on the collection model. The exception here are the *Focused* element index runs, where we put more weight on the element and document model based on pre-submission experiments.

3.1   Content-Only Runs

CO.Focused. In our focused task we experimented with two different ways of choosing focused elements to retrieve: first, based on the hierarchical segmentation of the collection, and second, based on a linear segmentation of the collection. We also wanted to compare these two approaches with a non-focused baseline, namely a document retrieval system. We submitted three runs:

- *F-Articles* (UAmsCOFocArticle). A baseline run created using our article index. We used a $\lambda = 0.15$ and a normal length prior.
- *F-Elements* (UAmsCOFocElements). A run created using a mixture model of the overlapping element index and the article index. We set $\lambda_e = 0.4$ and $\lambda_d = 0.4$. No length prior was used for this run. Overlap was removed in a list-based fashion, i.e., we traversed the list from the most relevant to the least relevant and threw out elements overlapping with an element appearing previously in the list.
- *F-Sections* (UAmsCOFocSections). A run created using a mixture model of the section index and the article index. We set $\lambda_e = 0.05$ and $\lambda_d = 0.1$. A normal length prior was used.

CO.Thorough. The main research question was to see if we could get away with indexing only a relatively small number of elements. In our runs we compared three element indexes. The "normal" element index, the qrel-based element selection and the length-based element selection. We submitted three runs:

- *T-Elements* (UAmsCOTElementIndex). A run using a mixture model of the full element index and the article index. We set $\lambda_e = 0.05$, $\lambda_d = 0.1$, and used a normal length prior.
- *T-Qrel* (UAmsCOTQrelbasedIndex). A run using a mixture model of the qrel-based element index and the article index. We set $\lambda_e = 0.05$, $\lambda_d = 0.1$, and used a normal length prior.
- *T-Length* (UAmsCOTLengthbasedIndex). A run using a mixture model of the length-based element index and the article index. We set $\lambda_e = 0.05$, $\lambda_d = 0.1$, and used a normal length prior.

CO.FetchBrowse. For the fetch and browse we mirrored the focused task submissions, but clustered the results so that elements within the same article appear together in the ranked list.

- *FB-Articles* (UAmsCOFBArticle) This run was exactly the same as the article run we submitted for the focused task.
- *FB-Elements* (UAmsCOFBElements) We took the focused element run and reordered the results in such a way that elements from the same document are clustered together. The document clusters are ordered by the highest scoring element within each document. We returned a maximum of 10 most relevant elements from each article.
- *FB-Sections* (UAmsCOFBSections) We took the focused section run and reordered the result set in such a way that the elements from the same document are clustered together. The document clusters are ordered by the highest scoring section within each document.

3.2   Content-Only with Structure Runs

For the CO+S task we experimented with three ways of using structural constraints.

Target-only. For queries that have a CAS title we only return elements which satisfy the target constraint of the CAS title. For queries asking for sections, we accepted the equivalent tags as listed in the topic development guidelines. NB! We used the terms in the title field of the queries because we want a direct comparison to CO runs. Retrieval was performed using a mixture model using the overlapping element index and the normal document index.

Context-only. We retrieved elements as described in Section 2.4.

Target and Context. We retrieved elements as described in Section 2.4. Additionally we filtered out elements that did not match the target constraint.

+S.Focused

- *F-Target* (UAmsCOpSFocStrictTarget). A run created using a mixture model of the overlapping element index and the article index. We set $\lambda_e = 0.4$ and $\lambda_d = 0.4$. No length prior was used for this run. Target restriction was implemented for queries that had one. Overlap was removed in a list-based fashion
- *F-Context* (UAmsCOpSFocConstr). We applied the context-only approach, described above, on the focused CO element run (UAmsCOFocElements).
- *F-ContTarg* (UAmsCOpSFocConstrStrTarg). We applied the context-only approach on the strict on target run (UAmsCOpSFocStrictTarget).

+S.Thorough

- *T-Target* (UAmsCOpSTStrictTarget). A run created using a mixture model of the overlapping element index and the article index. We set $\lambda_e = 0.05$ and $\lambda_d = 0.1$. We applied a normal length prior. Target constraints were respected for queries that had one.

- *T-Context* (UAmsCOpSTConstr). We applied the context-only approach, described above, on the thorough CO element run (UAmsCOTElementIndex).
- *T-ContTarg* (UAmsCOpSTConstrStrTarg). We applied the context-only approach on the strict on target run (UAmsCOpSTStrictTarget).

+S.FetchBrowse

- *FB-Target* (UAmsCOpSFBStrictTarget). We reordered the focused strict on target run (UAmsCOpSFocStrictTarget) such that results from the same article were clustered together. Only the 10 most relevant elements were considered for each article.
- *FB-Context* (UAmsCOpSFBConstr). We reordered the focused run using constraints (UAmsCOpSFocConstr) such that results from the same article are clustered together. Only the 10 most relevant elements were considered for each article.
- *FB-ContTarg* (UAmsCOpSFBConstrStrTarg). We reordered the focused run using constraints and strict targets (UAmsCOpSFocConstrStrTarg) such that results from the same article are clustered together. Only the 10 most relevant elements were considered for each article.

4   Results

In this section we will present and discuss our results. The results are based on version 7 of the INEX 2005 assessments. The results were generated using version 1.0.3 of EvalJ. We will report our results using a limited number of metrics, compared to the plethora of metrics available as part of EvalJ. We will use two MAP-like metrics: MAnxCG@1500 (called MAnxCG from now on), and ep/gr (MAep). Three early-precision metrics will be used: nxCG@5, nxCG@10, and R-measure. Our assumption is that these metrics provide a representative subset of all the available metrics. We will report results using the generalized quantization. The INEX organizers have labeled the nxCG measures as the "the official" measures for user-oriented tasks and ep/gr measures as "the official" for system-oriented tasks.

We will report results in 4 subsections. First, we will look at index reduction experiments. Next, we will look at effects of manually adding structural constrains. Then, we will look at the effects of automatically created structural constraints. Finally, we will present our results for the FetchBrowse task.

4.1   Index Reduction

For the INEX reduction we will look at two tasks: CO.Focused and CO. Thorough. For the CO.Focused task we compare a general element index to two reduced indices, section index and article index. For the CO.Thorough task we compare the same general element index to two reduced indices, length-based reduction and qrel-based reduction.

Table 3. *CO.Focused* runs, using *generalized* quantization and overlap *on*

	MAP-like precision				Early precision					
	MAnxCG		ep/gr (MAep)		nxCG@5		nxCG@10		R-measure	
F-Elements	0.262	–	0.068	–	0.202	–	0.194	–	0.155	–
F-Sections	0.200 -24%		0.062	-8.8%	0.174 -14%		0.150 -23%		0.211 36%	
F-Article	0.096 -63%		0.046	-32%	0.178 -12%		0.165 -15%		0.189 22%	

Table 4. *CO.Thorough* runs, using *generalized* quantization and overlap *off*

	MAP-like precision				Early precision					
	MAnxCG		ep/gr (MAep)		nxCG@5		nxCG@10		R-measure	
T-Elements	0.301	–	0.082	–	0.266	–	0.257	–	0.262	–
T-Length	0.294 -2.3%		0.083	1.2%	0.268 0.8%		0.256 -0.4%		0.265 1.1%	
T-Qrel	0.294 -2.3%		0.086	4.9%	0.280 5.3%		0.267 3.9%		0.269 2.7%	

Results for the CO.Focused task can be seen in Table 3. We see that the full element retrieval approach improves over both index reduction methods, except in the case of R-measure.

Results for the CO.Thorough task can be seen in Table 4. There is very little difference between the three runs. This means that reducing the indexed elements from 10.6M elements to circa 1.5M (14-15%) did not affect the effectiveness of the retrieval. Table 1 shows, however, that the reduced indexes lead to improved efficiency.

4.2   Structural Constraints

In this section we will analyze the effect of adding structural constraints to queries. We will distinguish between two types of constraints: target-constraints and context-constraints. Target constraints restrict the target of the results to be of certain tag-type, e.g. "give me only sections". Context-constraints restrict the environment in which the result elements live, e.g. "give me results from articles that are authored by Moldovan".

We will report results for the CO(+S).Focused task. We will look at results for 4 runs: our 3 official CO+S.Focused runs and our CO.Focused baseline run (F-Elements). In this sub-section we will only look at the 19 (assessed) CO+S topics that had a structured version. The remaining 10 (assessed) CO+S topics will be discussed in the next sub-section.

Table 5 shows the evaluation results. First let's look at the effect of context-constraints. The context-constraint run (F-Context) performs considerably better than our CO baseline (F-Elements). The improvement is, however, negligible for the nxCG@5 and nxCG@10. Next let's look at the effect of target-constraints. We see that in terms of MAnxCG the performance of our target-constraint run (F-Target) is considerably worse than our CO baseline. In terms of nxCG@5,

Table 5. *CO(+S).Focused* runs, using *generalized* quantization and overlap *on.* Here, we evaluate only over the 19 queries having a `<castitle>`.

	MAP-like precision			Early precision					
	MAnxCG		ep/gr (MAep)		nxCG@5		nxCG@10		R-measure	
F-Elements	0.289	–	0.074	–	0.219	–	0.211	–	0.139	–
F-Context	0.326	13%	0.086	16%	0.234	7%	0.213	1%	0.166	19%
F-Target	0.226	-22%	0.077	4%	0.253	16%	0.246	17%	0.204	47%
F-ContTarg	0.241	-17%	0.092	24%	0.260	19%	0.246	17%	0.228	64%

nxCG@10, and R-measure, there is a considerable performance improvement when we constrain the target. By using both context and target constraints we gain back some of the MAP score lost by enforcing the target constraint, while maintaining our early-precision improvement.

4.3   Automatic Structural Constraints

In this section we will look at the effects of automatically generating structural constraints. We could, in principle, have generated automatic structured queries for all the CO queries. However, in practice, we only did it for the topics that did not have a `<castitile>` representation. Hence the comparison will only be done over the limited number of topics. Since we only create context-constraints we will only compare our baseline CO (F-Elements) run and our F-Context run. The F-Target is in this case equivalent to F-Elements and F-ContTarg is equivalent to F-Context.

Table 6 shows the results of the evaluation. As with so many blind-feedback experiments the results are mixed. We will not analyze these results further here. It remains as future work to evaluate the structured blind-feedback over a greater number of queries, and compare it with normal content-based blind-feedback.

Table 6. *CO(+S).Focused* runs, using *generalized* quantization and overlap *on.* Here we evaluate only over the 10 queries that do *not* have a `<castitle>`.

	MAP-like precision			Early precision					
	MAnxCG		ep/gr (MAep)		nxCG@5		nxCG@10		R-measure	
F-Elements	0.213	–	0.057	–	0.171	–	0.163	–	0.185	–
F-Context	0.230	8.0%	0.046	-19%	0.161	-5.8%	0.166	1.8%	0.155	-16%

4.4   FetchBrowse

Here we discuss our FetchBrowse results. We will evaluate the task in with respect to two different aspects. First, since our FetchBrowse runs are simply reordering of our Focused runs, we evaluate the FetchBrowse using the same metrics as the Focused task. Second, since the FetchBrowse is an extension of a

Table 7. *CO.FetchBrowse* runs, using *generalized* quantization and overlap *on*

	MAP-like precision		Early precision		
	MAnxCG	ep/gr (MAep)	nxCG@5	nxCG@10	R-measure
FB-Elements	0.263 –	0.066 –	0.162 –	0.171 –	0.160 –
FB-Sections	0.207 -21%	0.052 -21%	0.130 -20%	0.119 -30%	0.194 21%
FB-Article	0.096 -63%	0.046 -30%	0.178 10%	0.165 -3.5%	0.189 18%

Table 8. *CO.Focused* and *CO.FetchBrowse* runs, using *generalized* quantization and overlap *on*

	MAP-like precision		Early precision		
	MAnxCG	ep/gr (MAep)	nxCG@5	nxCG@10	R-measure
F-Elements	0.262 –	0.068 –	0.202 –	0.194 –	0.155 –
FB-Elements	0.263 0.4%	0.066 -2.9%	0.162 -20%	0.171 -12%	0.160 3.2%
F-Sections	0.200 –	0.062 –	0.174 –	0.150 –	0.211 –
FB-Sections	0.207 3.5%	0.052 -16%	0.130 -25%	0.119 -21%	0.194 -8.1%

Table 9. *CO.Focused* and *CO.FetchBrowse* runs, using *generalized* quantization

	MAP	P@5	P@10	R-prec
FB-Articles	0.489 0%	0.690 0%	0.648 0%	0.481 0%
FB-Elements	0.441 -10%	0.655 -5.1%	0.635 -2.0%	0.465 -3.3%
FB-Sections	0.455 -7.0%	0.648 -6.1%	0.607 -6.3%	0.483 0.4%

document retrieval task, we will massage our runs into document retrieval runs and evaluate using `trec_eval`.

Table 7 shows the results of evaluating the FetchBrowse task as a Focused task. The results are quite similar to the results for the Focused task. That is, the element run outperforms the section and article runs, except for R-measure.

Let us take a closer look at the difference between our Focused and our Fetch-Browse runs. Table 8 shows the difference between the two run-types. The results are quite similar except perhaps for nxCG@5 and nxCG@10. That is, the re-ordering we did to transform the Focused runs into FetchBrowse runs did not change our results much, when we look at the metrics for Focused.

Let us now look at the document retrieval quality of our FetchBrowse runs. Since the 'Fetch' part of the task refers to plain old document retrieval we evaluate it using the standard document retrieval metrics that come with the `trec_eval` package. We transform our runs and assessments to TREC format. An article is considered relevant in the TREC sense if it contains a relevant element. We use thus a rather lenient quantization. Results of our evaluation can be seen in Table 9. We see that the two element-based runs are worse than the article run. In terms of mean average precision, FB-Elements is even significantly worse than FB-Articles (at .95 significance level).

5   Related Work

Here we will discuss some related work. The main goal with this section is to locate our work within the INEX community.

Language-Models for XML Retrieval. A number of alternative language modeling approaches for XML retrieval have been used in INEX. Mihajlović et al. [8] use a standard multinomial language model [4] including a number of advanced features such as phrase modeling. Especially in the context of the relevance feedback task, they experimented with a range of priors, such as a length prior, an XML tag name prior, and a journal prior. Ogilvie and Callan [9] take a quite different approach. First, standard language for all text nodes are estimated. Second, language models for all elements are constructed by, bottom-up, repeatedly calculating a mixture language model of all child nodes.

Selective Indexing. Various types of selective indexing schemes have been used in INEX. Gövert et al. [3] used a predefined list of tag names. The list is compiled after careful analysis of tag name semantics. Mass et al. [7] and Clarke et al. [1] used existing relevance assessments to define the appropriate units for their index. Index reduction based on eliminating the very many very short elements has been used by many teams at INEX.

Structured constraints. In this paper we have looked at the effectiveness of strict interpretation of target constraints and compared it to a baseline where target constraints are ignored. There is quite some room in between the two approaches. Liu et. al. [6] propose a few relaxations of target constraints, both based on path similarity and content similarity.

Structured Feedback. Automatic generation of structured queries has been proposed previously by Mihajlović et al. [8]. They use true relevance feedback to expand queries with journal information and target constraints.

6   Conclusions

In this year's INEX we had three main research questions. We wanted to explore the effect of different types of structured constraints on retrieval effectiveness. We also wanted to see if we could use selective indexing to make our system more efficient without loosing retrieval effectiveness. And, third, we consider the automatic construction of structured queries using blind relevance feedback.

We showed that context-constraints and target-constraints have different effect on retrieval performance. The context constraints are helpful for improving average precision. Interpreting the target constraints in a strict manner does hurt average precision, but do give considerable improvement if we look at early precision.

For the Focused task, we compared two selective indexes to our full element index: section index and article index. Retrieving sections and articles is more efficient than retrieving from the full element index. The effectiveness of section and article retrieval is, however, inferior to retrieval from the full element index.

For the Thorough task, we experimented with two different pruning of the full overlapping element index, using element length and past qrels as pruning criteria. Neither of the pruning strategies lead to a considerably lower average performance. Both pruning strategies were, however, more efficient than the full overlapping element index.

For the FetchBrowse task, it is difficult to draw any final conclusions since it is not clear how this task should be evaluated. For the document ranking part of the FetchBrowse task, ranking documents based on their own retrieval score outperformed the document retrieval based on the highest scoring of either elements or sections.

The results of our automatic generation of structured queries are inconclusive. Further experiments are needed to verify its (in)effectiveness.

Acknowledgments

This research was supported by the Netherlands Organization for Scientific Research (NWO) under project numbers 017.001.190, 220-80-001, 264-70-050, 354-20-005, 612-13-001, 612.000.106, 612.000.207, 612.066.302, 612.069.006, 640.-001.501, and 640.002.501.

References

1. C. L. Clarke and P. L. Tilker. MultiText experiments for INEX 2004. In Fuhr et al. [?], pages 85–87.
2. E. A. Fox and J. A. Shaw. Combination of multiple searches. In *The Second Text REtrieval Conference (TREC-2)*, pages 243–252, 1994.
3. N. Gövert, M. Abolhassani, N. Fuhr, and K. Grossjohan. Content-based XML retrieval with HyRex. In N. Fuhr, N. Gövert, G. Kazai, and M. Lalmas, editors, *Proceedings of the First Workshop of the INitiative for the Evaluation of XML Retrieval (INEX 2002)*, pages 26–32. ERCIM, 2003.
4. D. Hiemstra. *Using Language Models for Information Retrieval*. PhD thesis, University of Twente, 2001.
5. J. Kamps, M. de Rijke, and B. Sigurbjörnsson. The importance of length normalization for XML retrieval. *Information Retrieval*, 8:631–654, 2005.
6. S. Liu, R. Shahinian, and W. Chu. Vague content and structure (VCAS) retrieval over document-centric XML collections. In A. Doan, F. Neven, R. McCann, and G. J. Bex, editors, *Proceedings of the Eighth International Workshop on the Web and Databases (WebDB 2005)*, pages 79–84, 2005.
7. Y. Mass and M. Mandelbrod. Retrieving the most relevant XML components. In N. Fuhr, M. Lalmas, and S. Malik, editors, *INEX 2003 Workshop Proceedings*, pages 53–58, 2004.
8. V. Mihajlović, G. Ramírez, A. P. de Vries, D. Hiemstra, and H. E. Blok. TIJAH at INEX 2004 modeling phrases and relevance feedback. In Fuhr et al. [?], pages 276–291.

9. P. Ogilvie and J. Callan. Hierarchical language models for XML component retrieval. In Fuhr et al. [?], pages 224–237.
10. J. Ponte. Language models for relevance feedback. In W. Croft, editor, *Advances in Information Retrieval*, chapter 3, pages 73–96. Kluwer Academic Publishers, Boston, 2000.
11. B. Sigurbjörnsson, J. Kamps, and M. de Rijke. An Element-Based Approch to XML Retrieval. In *INEX 2003 Workshop Proceedings*, pages 19–26, 2004.
12. B. Sigurbjörnsson, J. Kamps, and M. de Rijke. Mixture models, overlap, and structural hints in XML element retrieval. In Fuhr et al. [?], pages 196–210.

Searching XML Documents – Preliminary Work

Marcus Hassler and Abdelhamid Bouchachia

Dept. of Informatics, Alps-Adria University, Klagenfurt, Austria
marcus.hassler@uni-klu.ac.at, hamid@isys.uni-klu.ac.at

Abstract. Structured document retrieval aims at exploiting the structure together with the content of documents to improve retrieval results. Several aspects of traditional information retrieval applied on flat documents have to be reconsidered. These include in particular, document representation, storage, indexing, retrieval, and ranking. This paper outlines the architecture of our system and the adaptation of the standard vector space model to achieve focussed retrieval.

1 Introduction and Motivation

Traditionally, content-based retrieval systems rely either on the Boolean model or the vector space model (VSM) [1, 2, 3] to represent the flat structure of documents as a bag of words. Extensions of these models have been proposed, e.g., the fuzzy Boolean model and knowledge-aware models. However, all of these indexing models do ignore the organization of text and the structure of documents until recently with the advent of "queriable digital libraries".

XML documents have a standard structure defined by a DTD or XML schema. While this structure provides documents with hierarchical levels of granularity, and hence more precision can be achieved by means of focussed retrieval, it does, however, imply more requirements on the representation and retrieval mechanisms. With the new generation of retrieval systems, the two aspects, the structure and the content, have to be taken into account. To minimally achieve that in presence of nested structure like chapter-section-subsection-paragraph, the traditional information retrieval techniques, e.g., the VSM, have to be adapted to fit the context of structure-aware retrieval. To design such systems, four basic aspects are of high importance:

(a) Representation: Textual content of the hierarchically structured documents is generally restricted to the leave nodes. Hence, representation mechanisms of the inner nodes content have to be defined.
(b) Retrieval granularity: A basic question is whether the indexing/retrieval unit must be known ahead of time or is completely dynamically decided by the user or eventually by the system itself.
(c) Ranking: Related to the first two aspects, a strategy for ranking the retrieved results has to be decided.

N. Fuhr et al. (Eds.): INEX 2005, LNCS 3977, pp. 119–133, 2006.

(d) Result presentation: The way results are presented is a key issue [4, 5, 6] and has to be considered early in the design of the system as part of requirements engineering. Once ranked, the results are displayed showing their context of appearance. Further functionality enabling browsing is required.

Taking these aspects into account, we developed a retrieval system. It is fully implemented in Java and consists of three subsystems: indexing, retrieval and RMI (Remote Method Invocation) communication server as depicted in Fig. 1.

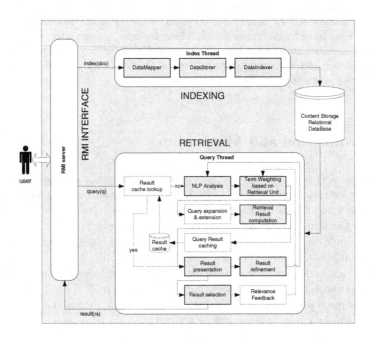

Fig. 1. Architecture of the system

The RMI server takes incoming requests for indexing and querying the system and initiates a new thread for each call. The basic motivation behind this is to achieve some degree of parallelism. The maximum number of parallel threads depends on the performance of the hardware. From the software architecture point of view, both index and query subsystem, use a pipelined pattern of processing units (Fig. 1). Dashed components describe planned extensions. For portability and tuning purposes, all subsystems are independently configurable via configuration files. During indexing, documents are transformed into our XML schema (DataMapper), stored in the database (DataStorer), and indexed for retrieval (DataIndexer). As soon as a query is sent to the system it is analyzed by a query thread. Documents in the database are matched against the query and relevant elements[1] are ranked in decreasing order.

---

[1] We use element and node interchangeable.

In this paper, we will discuss the aspects (a)–(d), but with more focus is more on the representation and the indexing/retrieval problem. First, in Sec. 2, a generic schema for document representation is presented, onto which the XML documents are mapped. Section 3 describes the underlying database model used for storing the content and the corresponding representation. The most interesting issues namely indexing and retrieval are discussed in Sec. 4 and Sec. 5 respectively. Section 7 concludes the paper.

2 Document Structure

The hierarchical structure for the content of documents is usually described by means of a set of tags (e.g. chapter, section, subsection, etc.), as shown in Fig. 2[2].

In order to represent a collection of documents having different structure, we apply an XSLT transformation to derive a common document format (schema). This step eliminates structural ambiguities and resolves semantic relativism [7].

As illustrated in Fig. 3a, we introduce a general document format (defined through XML schema) that consists of only three main elements: DOC (document), SEC (section) and FRA (fragment). The DOC element defines the root of the document. SEC is the basic structural element of a document. By recursively defining SEC (e.g., section) as either containing raw content FRAs (e.g., paragraphs) and/or made up of other SECs (e.g., subsections), the depth of nested structures is unlimited. To define smallest retrievable units for indexing and retrieval, we rely on fragments (FRAs). They stand for the leaf nodes in our document schema (see Fig. 3a). Note that if a query refers to another tag not in the set {DOC, SEC, FRAGMENT}, this latter is interpreted as SEGMENT.

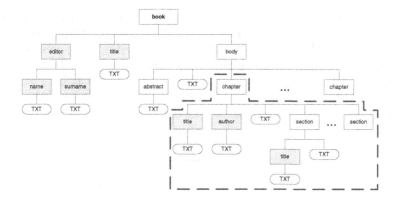

Fig. 2. Example XML document

---

[2] This example will be used throughout the paper. It is important to point out that the approach presented here is general, but we used the IEEE collection just to illustrate the processing steps of the system. In other words, the system is collection-independent and therefore portable.

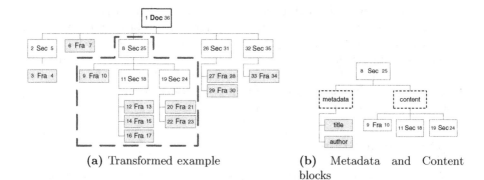

(a) Transformed example

(b) Metadata and Content blocks

Fig. 3. XML document representation

A node in an XML document is viewed as a tuple (*metadata,content*), where *metadata* refers to descriptive information of the node itself, while *content* refers to the segment's content, properly said (see Fig. 3b). Generally, the first type of nodes requires database-supported (exact) match during retrieval, while the second type is subject to partial matching (VSM).

2.1 Metadata

In addition to the content block, the metadata block of a node contains information describing that node. Examples of metadata are `author`, `year` and `keywords` for a `DOC` or the `title` for a `SEC` element. The fragment metadata block is used to describe its actual content by means of `content_type`, `language`, and possibly `title` (figures, tables).

To allow a semantic interpretation of the content of an element, a type hierarchy is proposed by Gövert [8]. An extension of the proposed type hierarchy for metadata is depicted in Fig. 4. There, types are derived from a common base element. The first level in the hierarchy (bold) corresponds to database supported data types. Further types in subsequent levels in the hierarchy have one of the basic database types as supertype (e.g., `PersonName` is a String). In addition, data types predicates for comparison are defined. This allows to process sec-

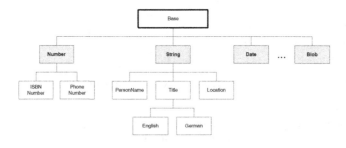

Fig. 4. Hierarchical metadata types

tion titles, phone numbers, and author names for instance. This type hierarchy is used during parsing to optimize the storage efficiently. In addition, it helps characterize the type of match required during retrieval.

2.2   Content

Generally, the content block of DOCs and SECs are defined as ordered lists of further (sub)SECs and FRAs. The content block of FRAs is defined as bytecode or empty. For indexing and retrieval purposes, content is interpreted based on its type (metadata). Defining a fragment's content as text block (paragraph) only might be too restrictive. Therefore, a fragment in our sense refers to paragraphs, enumerations, lists, figures, tables, formulas, images, sounds, videos, definitions, theorems, etc. On the other hand, a fragment (FRA) defines the smallest retrievable unit of a document. It can be understood as building block (elementary content container). However, the granular unit is application specific and can be set at wish to fit sentences as well as the whole text of a chapter.

From the structuring point of view, additional markup within a FRA's content might be needed. Our schema supports mathematical environments (using MATH) and two types of links (using LINK), internal and external links. Internal links are links within the same document, e.g., citations, figure/table references within the text and the table of contents. External links refer to external resources, including reference entries in the references section, references to email/internet addresses and file references.

While the content block in DOCs and SECs is mandatory, in FRAs it is not. This allows to include external content by its metadata only. An external source attribute within the metadata block can be used to refer to the content somewhere else (e.g., a picture file). In contrast to SEC elements, which define their own context based on their path, e.g., /DOC/SEC/SEC, fragments define a separate context. As to indexing and retrieval, a fragment in a section lies within the same context as a fragment in a chapter or subsubsection. This difference is important in the context of a dynamic term space, discussed in Sec. 5.3.

3   Storage

For efficiency purposes, we use a relational database to store the XML documents. The goal is to accelerate the access to various structural neighbors of each node in the document (descendants, ancestors, and siblings). Being a tree, an XML document can easily and unambiguously be traversed. Therefore, each node is represented by its document ID and preorder/postorder. We depart from the idea of *preorder* and *postorder* introduced in [9, 10], supporting non-recursive ancestor/descendant detection and access. Table 1 shows an excerpt of the structural information of a document representation. Likewise, we designed another for the corresponding content.

A structural entry is described by the tuple ($docID$, pre, $post$, $parentID$, $tagID$, $pathID$). The root element has $pre = 1$ and $parentID = 0$ (no parent) per definition. The attribute $tagID$ is included for fast name lookup and access.

Table 1. Structural entries

docID	pre	post	parentID	tag	path
d_1	1	36	0	Doc	/Doc
d_1	2	5	1	Sec	/Doc/Sec
d_1	3	4	2	Fra	/Doc/Sec/Fra
d_1	6	7	1	Fra	/Doc/Fra
d_1	8	25	1	Sec	/Doc/Sec
d_1	9	10	8	Fra	/Doc/Sec/Fra
d_1	11	18	8	Fra	/Doc/Sec/Sec
d_1	12	13	11	Fra	/Doc/Sec/Sec/Fra

For the sake of performance, we added the elements path (XPath without positional information) $pathID$ to circumvent recursive path generations by using the $parentID$ relation.

The content of nodes (in particular leaf nodes) is stored in a separate table, as suggested in [11]. However, the content of inner nodes can always be recovered from their descendants as will be discussed in Sec. 4. Note that some content entries do not have a corresponding representation entry (e.g. figures, tables).

To improve retrieval performance, metadata handling is completely shifted to the database. This is achieved by grouping all metadata according to its element. Instead of having multiple structural and content entries, a single row ($docID$, pre, $meta_1$, ..., $meta_n$) is used to store all metadata together. Metadata of nodes (DOC, SEC, FRA) are stored in separated but very similar tables as shown in Tab. 2 for the case of sections. The reason of supporting only a single set of SEC metadata is that all SEC elements (chapters, sections, subsections, etc.) are assumed to have quite homogenous metadata (e.g., `title`). Although this may lead to some '$NULL$' values (unavailable metadata for some elements) in the database, the whole set can be accessed by a single select statement. This simplifies and speeds up querying of metadata considerably. A global view is depicted in Fig. 5. Both, metadata and content entries, are optional. Additional types of representations (e.g. semantic concepts, figure representations, etc.) can easily be integrated.

Table 2. Metadata entries for SEC

docID	pre	title	author	...
d_1	2	Introduction	R. Smith	
d_1	8	XMl Retrieval	J. Alf	
d_1	11	Granularity	$NULL$	

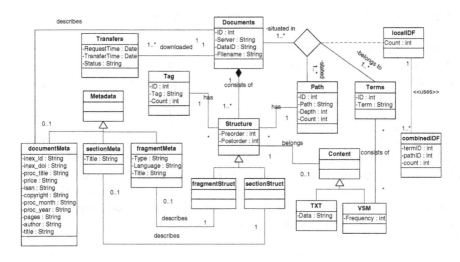

Fig. 5. Conceptual database schema

4   Indexing

To represent texts as a vector of terms and their term frequencies, our natural language processing (NLP) involves several subtasks containing tokenization, tagging, term extraction, stemming, filtering and term frequency calculation. Our implementation is based on abstract components. Taking advantage of the the modularity aspect, different implementations of the same component can be instantiated and selected during runtime. Hence, our system can easily be adapted to process documents in other languages. Our prototype also involves ready made-components like the tagger, and the stemmer.

During the indexing process, only the content of leaf nodes need to be parsed. Their representation, a term frequency vector, is stored in the database (VSM table). Consequent updates of the localIDF, combinedIDF table, and Terms table are immediately done. These update operations are also carried out during re-indexing or removal of documents.

The index of inner nodes is obtained by simply merging the index of its descendants. This is done by summing up their term frequencies. This operation is equivalent to process the concatenated contents of the descendant nodes. It is also possible to store the result of the merge operation so that no index computation is required later during the retrieval process. This reduces search time, but increases the size of the database. It is important to stress that the weight vectors are computed during retrieval using the available term frequency vectors.

We define the *context of a node* as the set of all elements having the same path (all chapters, all sections, etc.). In order to dynamically characterize both, the granularity during indexing and retrieval, we applied a propagation of term statistics (e.g. tf), in contrast to the weight propagation methodology [12]. In addition, the inverse document frequency (idf) for each node is calculated dynamically based on the node's context. Term weights are computed based on the term frequencies and the idf in this context. This allows to perform focussed retrieval on any level in the document tree. To achieve that in a given context, tf of all nodes lying at this level will require tfs of their descendants. Using term statistic propagation, the descendants' tf are simply summed up. We avoid recursive data accesses by exploiting preorder and postorder of document elements (only one SQL select statement).

As to term weighing, we use different $idf_{j,c}$s of the same term j in different contexts c. This strategy weighs the same term with the same term frequency differently depending on c (e.g. chapter vs. subsection). Clearly our approach puts more attention on the actual context during retrieval. If the unit of retrieval is defined explicitly, elements in this context are focussed and compared only among them. Representations of elements in other contexts do not influence the result.

To implement this idea, we use two tables (see Fig. 5): a table `localIDF` stores tuples of the form ($docID$, $pathID$, $termID$, n_j), where n_j refers to the number of elements containing term $termID$ in the path $pathID$ within a document $docID$. Consider the example given in Tab. 3, the first Tab. 3a indicates that the term "car" occurs twice in /DOC/SEC nodes of document d_1. To calculate the $idf_{j,c}$ of a term j in a context c, we have to define N_c and n_j. N_c is the number of nodes with $pathID = c$. N_c can simply be derived via the table holding the structural entries (see Tab. 1). n_j is given by counting the rows containing $pathID = c$ and $termID = j$. In the above example, this results in an inverse document frequency for the term "car" in the node /DOC/SEC of $idf_{car,/DOC/SEC} = \log \frac{3}{2}$. This definition of $idf_{j,c}$ leads to different idfs in different contexts.

Since Tab. 3a is quite large, we introduced a summarized shortcut-table `combinedIDF` Tab. 3b with the overall goal to reduce the time access to idf values. Same paths associated with the same terms are precalculated (e.g. term "car"). For the sake of dynamic document environments (adding, removing and re-indexing), we still need the information provided by Tab. 3a to adjust the n

Table 3. idf calculation

(a) Table `localIDF`

docID	path	term	n_j
d_1	/DOC/SEC	car	2
d_1	/DOC/SEC/SEC	mouse	1
d_2	/DOC/SEC	car	1
d_2	/DOC/SEC/SEC	dog	1
d_2	/DOC/SEC/SEC	mouse	3
d_3	/DOC/SEC	water	1
d_3	/DOC/SEC/SEC	dog	2

(b) Table `combinedIDF`

path	term	n
/DOC/SEC	car	3
/DOC/SEC	water	1
/DOC/SEC/SEC	mouse	4
/DOC/SEC/SEC	dog	3

values correctly. In addition, all N_c values, the numbers of elements with the same path, are stored in the `Path` table (see Fig. 5).

Given a particular context (e.g. `/DOC/SEC`), our indexing strategy allows on-the-fly computation of the representations associated with these nodes (considered as documents). Hence, our indexing method stores only term frequency vectors in the database; weight computation is totally executed on the fly during the retrieval process. The advantages of this methodology are:

- It behaves exactly like the traditional models at the document level.
- There is no need for empirical parameters as augmentation weights.
- Elements of smaller granularity (of lower level) do not automatically have sparser feature vectors (leading to smaller similarity), hence they define their own context. Since the number of terms is at max the total number of terms in the whole collection.
- Documents can dynamically be added, removed, and re-indexed, without impacting the weights of other representations.

5   Retrieval

This section explains the retrieval process. In particular, it describes how and which information is required by the system to answer a user query appropriately. This includes formulation of the query, setting of specific parameters, matching, filtering, and presentation of the result.

5.1   Query Formulation

The actual query input is done via an input interface which allows to enter different types of queries: `KWD` (keyword) and `NLQ` (natural language query, free text), which are translated into `INEX` queries. The `INEX` query supports NEXI-like inputs. Hence, we distinguish between metadata and content, we adapted our query parser to support both kinds of information. Similar to the `about(path,terms)` syntax, we added a construct: `meta(path,condition)`. This allows us, for example, to efficiently deal with queries like: "return all documents written by Einstein" using the command `//DOC[meta(.,author like '%Einstein%')]`.

In order to avoid long and confusing single-line queries, we use chains of INEX queries. In our opinion, this concept is also closer to the natural way of questioning, by successively refining the list of results. Each subquery result works as a strict filter, allowing only elements of the same or smaller granularity to be retrieved. This improves the performance without skipping searched elements. Furthermore, we use these chains for reweighing elements regarding to a user-defined generality factor (gf), described below. In addition to the INEX-query chains, several query parameters can be specified by the user (see Fig. 6):

- **Maximum results** $(maxRes)$: Defines the maximum number of returned results ranging from 1 to $MAXINT$.

- **Minimum similarity** ($minSim$): Defines the minimum similarity of returned results ranging from 0 to 1, truncating the list of results below a given similarity threshold.
- **Content importance** (ci): Defines the importance of the content similarity to calculate the retrieval status value (rsv). This parameter ranges from 0 (only meta similarity) to 1 (only content similarity). The final similarity is computed as $rsv = simCont * ci + simMeta * (1 - ci)$.
- **Generality factor** (gf): This parameter ($\in [0,1]$) influences the retrieval granularity. The higher the parameter, the more importance of first subqueries, computed as $sim_{new} = sim_{old} * gf + sim_{new} * (1 - gf)$.
- **Result type** (rt): Defines which kind of results we wish to obtain: thorough or focussed (see Sec. 5.6).

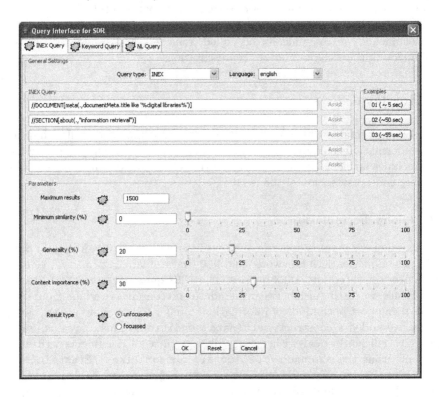

Fig. 6. Query Interface

5.2   Search and Retrieval Paths

The search path specifies which elements are to be investigated and matched against the current query. In contrast, the retrieval path specifies which elements are to be returned to the user. Generally these two path are equal, e.g. `//SEC[about(.,wine)]`. This means that the retrieval path is always the same or more general as the search path. So first relevant documents, then relevant sections within those documents, and at a last stage relevant fragments within those sections are identified. Difficulties arise when relevant ancestor elements contain smaller elements that are further specified. For instance, a query that retrieves sections containing paragraphs about a certain topic is not easy given the recursive structure that a section can have.

Our parser for NEXI-like queries implements the following strategy: if the searched element satisfies the retrieval path, only the element itself is returned. Otherwise, the closest parent satisfying the retrieval path condition is returned. In all cases, at most one element is retrieved. So a query like `//SEC[about(./FRA,global warming)]` searches all `SEC` elements at any level (retrieval paths) containing `FRA` paragraphs about "global warming" and returns the most relevant element. A more complex query is `//(DOC|SEC)[about(./SEC, anything)]`. Here only document or section elements containing sections about "anything" are to be retrieved, not the sections themselves that are about "anything".

5.3 Dynamic Term Space

In the context of structured documents, the idea of representing elements at different structural levels within the same term space has to be reconsidered. Assume a number of document sections $\mathbb{S} = \{s_1 \ldots s_n\}$ containing a set of unique terms $\mathbb{T}_s$ and a set of chapters $\mathbb{C} = \{c_1 \ldots c_m\}$ containing a set of unique terms $\mathbb{T}_c$. Note the implicit relation between term space $\mathbb{T}_s$ and term space $\mathbb{T}_c$: $\mathbb{T}_s \subseteq \mathbb{T}_c$. Let q be a query containing terms $\mathbb{T}_q$ addressing sections $\mathbb{S}$ and chapters $\mathbb{C}$. To calculate the similarity $sim(s_i, q)$ between a section and a query, both feature vectors have to be within the same term space. The same thing holds for comparing chapters and the query $sim(c_i, q)$.

Neglecting the context, sections and chapters are represented in the same (global) term space. As a consequence, the feature vectors of low level nodes become sparser and their similarities compared to nodes of higher levels drop. To overcome this problem, we adopted the concept of a "dynamic term space". In contrast to the global term space, and following the concept of context, nodes in the same context generate a term space. Using a static term space improves performance, but unfortunately decreases the similarity of low-level nodes compared with higher ones. Reducing zero weighted elements in the feature vectors leads to higher precision during the match of low-level nodes. The number of different indexing representations (different contexts) is expected to be quite limited. For instance, the mapped INEX collection does not exceed six structural levels (`/DOC/SEC/SEC/SEC/SEC/FRA`). During retrieval the term space for each context is constructed once, so retrieval performance drops insignificantly.

5.4 Result Computation

INEX queries are stated using keywords in the `about(path,`kwd_1 kwd_2 $\ldots$ kwd_n`)` syntax. This syntax allows to express several different semantics of keywords that have to be considered:

- information retrieval techniques
- +information +retrieval techniques
- information retrieval -techniques
- "information retrieval" techniques
- +"information retrieval" techniques

'+' (MUST) and '-' (CANNOT) indicate whether a term has to be or should not be present in an element. Based on this, a fast preselection is systematically done on candidate elements. Hence, index terms are stemmed, also these terms have to be for comparison.

More complex is the treatment of quoted keywords. Are the keywords books and "books" equivalent? This depends on whether "books" should occur as it is (noun in plural form), or should it be stemmed and treated so. It is obvious that quoted expressions are particulary difficult to process. Consider "red cars". The term red is an adjective, it is not included in the index. Furthermore, it is possible that in another context (e.g. "Red Cross"), it is (part of) a proper noun and, therefore, exists in the index. In our approach, we treat quoted keywords in two steps: First, we treat them as unquoted, calculating the similarity as given. Then, we apply a string matching strategy on the original text associated with the element to sort the results.

Combinations of MUST/CANNOT and quoted expressions are treated as if all terms within quotes are separately marked as MUST/CANNOT and an initial result set is computed. This result is reduced to those node containing exactly the quoted expression.

Note that the computed result consists of tuples of the form ($docID$, $preorder$, $postorder$, $simMeta$, $simCont$). $docID$ (document ID), $preorder$ and $postorder$ come directly from the database. $simMeta$ and $simCont$ are the calculated meta similarity and content similarity.

5.5   Ranking and Result Presentation

Ranking is the task by which retrieved elements are decreasingly ordered by their relevance. Therefore, we use a combination of metadata and content similarity to compute a retrieval status value rsv (see Sec. 5.1). The ranking process itself is impacted strongly by the desired granularity. Note that this granularity is either pre-specified or stated explicitly in the user query. For example, if the user specifies the document level (context), say section, the system should return only relevant sections. The similarity can be calculated using two strategies. The first strategy is to match the query against sections with content aggregated from its descendants. The second strategy, which we have considered, is to match the query against the most representative fragment of each section.

After all desired elements are matched against the user query, the combined similarity values $metaSim$ and $contSim$ are used for ranking. The results are presented to the user as a sorted list in decreasing order (see Fig. 7). The user is then able to select a particular result, enabling a display of whole document in an explorer-like view (see Fig. 8). The document structure is presented as an

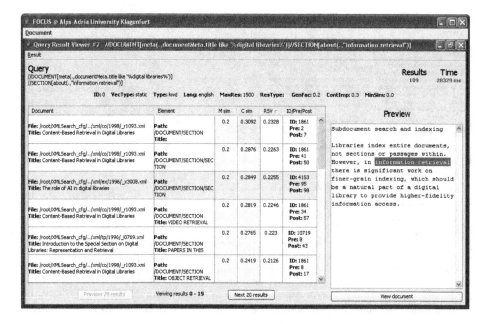

Fig. 7. Result Set

expandable tree, where the selected element is expanded and focused. Having similarity values available on the screen, the document can be efficiently browsed. Colors are used to reflect the degree of similarity of the matched elements.

5.6 Result Filtering

In INEX 2004, two kinds of retrieval strategies, thorough and focussed, were defined. *Thorough retrieval* returns all relevant elements of a document. Hence, all ancestors of a relevant element are relevant to a certain degree. This may lead to multiple result elements along the same path (e.g., a section and its contained paragraphs).

Focussed retrieval, on the other hand, aims at returning only the most relevant element along a path. Basically, it relies on two principles [13]: (a) if an element is relevant to a certain degree, so must be its parent; (b) only one node along a path of relevant elements is returned. Overlapping elements in the result set are discarded. This strategy is implemented as post filtering process to refine the result set. We rely on preorder and postorder to do this efficiently. In other words, all low-ranked ancestors and descendants are discarded. This strategy reduces the number of returned elements drastically.

5.7 Query Refinement

In most cases a final search result is achieved through iterative refinement of the query. The number of results is reduced step by step by adding new information

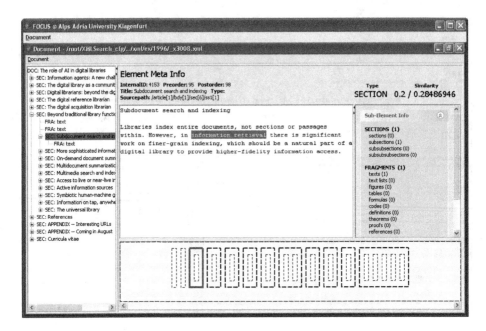

Fig. 8. Result Browser

to the query. To enable such a feature, we allow the user to include a list of preliminary results together with a query. If such a result is set within a query it acts as a strict filter during query computation.

6 Initial Experiments

In the current evaluation, we will show only some initial experiments. Indeed, only three retrieval runs were evaluated (CO and COS -both Thorough- and SSCAS). The results are shown in Tab. 4 ($nxCG$) and Tab. 5 (ep/gr). The number between parentheses in each cell indicates the rank of our system compared with the other participating systems. The results illustrate that our approach is less competitive in the case of CO and COS tasks. In contrast to that, it is ranked among the first 10 systems in the case of CAS.

Table 4. Metric: nxCG, Quantization: strict, Overlap=off

nxCG at	CO	COS	SSCAS
10	0.0115(47)	0.0000(28)	0.3250(4)
25	0.0221(42)	0.0094(24)	0.3200(7)
50	0.0416(41)	0.0118(26)	0.3489(9)

To overcome the limitations observed in the case of CO and COS tasks, further work is underway. It concerns various aspects related to document processing (e.g.

Table 5. Metric: ep/gr, Quantization: strict, Overlap=off

CO	COS	SSCAS
0.0051(45)	0.0016(30)	0.1001(5)

stop words filtering of metadata) and adjustment of the system parameters (sec. 5.1). Additional experimental work with regard to Focused tasks is to be done.

7   Conclusion

The paper described the basic tasks of an XML retrieval system. Details on the methodology are provided. An initial experimental evaluation is already, but only partly, conducted showing promising results. However, a thorough empirical work is still needed along with some additional features of the system.

References

1. Baeza-Yates, R., Ribeiro-Neto, B.: Modern Information Retrieval. Addison Wesley, ACM Press, New York, Essex, England (1999)
2. Salton, G., Lesk, M.E.: Computer evaluation of indexing and text processing. Journal of the ACM **15** (1968) 8–36
3. Salton, G.: The SMART Retrieval System - Experiments in Automatic Document Processing. Prentice Hall Inc., Englewood Cliffs, NJ (1971)
4. Grosjohann, K., Fuhr, N., Effing, D., Kriewel, S.: A user interface for XML document retrieval. In: 32. GI-Jahrestagung. Springer (2002)
5. Grosjohann, K., Fuhr, N., Effing, D., Kriewel, S.: Query formulation and result visualization for XML retrieval. In: Proceedings ACM SIGIR 2002 Workshop on XML and Information Retrieval, ACM (2002)
6. Fuhr, N., Grosjohann, K., Kriewel, S. In: A Query Language and User Interface for XML Information Retrieval. Volume 2818 of LNCS. Springer (2003) 59–75
7. Fuhr, N., Grosjohann, K.: XIRQL: A query language for information retrieval in XML documents. In: Proc. of the 24th ACM SIGIR, ACM Press (2001) 172–180
8. Gövert, N.: Bilingual information retrieval with HyREX and Internet translation services. In: Cross-Language Information Retrieval and Evaluation. Volume 2069 of LNCS. (2001) 237–244
9. Grust, T.: Accelerating XPath location steps. In: Proc. of the 2002 ACM SIGMOD, ACM Press (2002) 109–120
10. Hiemstra, D.: A database approach to content-based xml retrieval. In: INitiative for the Evaluation of XML Retrieval (INEX, Workshop), ERCIM (2003) 111–118
11. Florescu, D., Kossmann, D.: A performance evaluation of alternative mapping schemes for storing XML data in a relational database. Technical report (1999)
12. Abolhassani, M., Fuhr, N.: Applying the divergence from randomness approach for content-only search in XML documents. In: 26th European Conf. on Information Retrieval Research (ECIR), Springer Verlag (2004)
13. Kazai, G., Lalmas, M., Rölleke, T.: Focussed structured document retrieval. In: Proceedings of the 9 Retrieval (SPIRE 2002), Springer (2002) 241–247

Query Evaluation with Structural Indices

Paavo Arvola[1], Jaana Kekäläinen[2], and Marko Junkkari[1]

[1] Department of Computer Sciences, Kanslerinrinne 1,
33014 University of Tampere, Finland
junken@cs.uta.fi, paavo.arvola@uta.fi
[2] Deparment of Information Studies, Kanslerinrinne 1,
33014 University of Tampere, Finland
jaana.kekalainen@uta.fi

Abstract. This paper describes the retrieval methods of TRIX system based on structural indices utilizing the natural tree structure of XML. We show how these indices can be employed in the processing of CO as well as CAS queries, which makes it easy for variations of CAS queries to be processed. Results at INEX 2005 are discussed including the following tasks: CO.Focussed, CO.FetchBrowse, CO.Thorough and all of the CAS tasks. While creating result lists, two different overlapping models have been applied according to task. The weights of the ancestors of an element have been taken into account in re-weighting in order to get more evidence about relevance.

1 Introduction to TRIX Retrieval System

The present study comprises of retrieval experiments conducted within the INEX 2005 framework addressing the following research questions: ranking of elements of 'best size' for CO queries, query expansion, and handling of structural conditions in CAS queries. In INEX 2005 we submitted runs for the following tasks: CO.focussed, CO.thorough, CO.FetchBrowse, and all of the CAS tasks.

Next we introduce the TRIX (Tampere information retrieval and indexing of XML) approach for indexing, weighting and re-weighting. Then, Section 2 describes the processing of CAS queries and in Section 3 the results of INEX 2005 are presented and analyzed. Finally conclusions are given in Section 4. Graphical representations of our official results are given in the appendix.

1.1 Structural Indices and Basic Weighting Schema

In TRIX the management of structural aspects is based on the *structural indices* [2,4,5,8]. The idea of structural indices in the context of XML is that the topmost (root) element is indexed by $\langle 1 \rangle$ and its children by $\langle 1,1 \rangle$, $\langle 1,2 \rangle$, $\langle 1,3 \rangle$ etc. Further, the children of the element with the index $\langle 1,1 \rangle$ are labeled by $\langle 1,1,1 \rangle$, $\langle 1,1,2 \rangle$, $\langle 1,1,3 \rangle$ etc. This kind of indexing enables analyzing of the relationships among elements in a straightforward way. For example, the ancestors of the element labeled by $\langle 1,3,4,2 \rangle$ are associated with the indices $\langle 1,3,4 \rangle$, $\langle 1,3 \rangle$ and $\langle 1 \rangle$. In turn, any descendant related to the index $\langle 1,3 \rangle$ is labeled by $\langle 1,3,\xi \rangle$ where ξ is a non-empty

N. Fuhr et al. (Eds.): INEX 2005, LNCS 3977, pp. 134–145, 2006.

part of the index. In the present approach the XML documents in the collection are labeled by positive integers 1, 2, 3, etc. From the perspective of indexing this means that the documents are identified by indices $\langle 1 \rangle$, $\langle 2 \rangle$, $\langle 3 \rangle$, etc., respectively. The length of an index ξ is denoted by $len(\xi)$. For example $len(\langle 1,2,2,3 \rangle)$ is 4. *Cutting operation* $\delta_i(\xi)$ selects the subindex of the index ξ consisting of its i first integers. For example if $\xi = \langle a,b,c \rangle$ then $\delta_2(\xi) = \langle a,b \rangle$. In terms of the cutting operation the root index at hand is denoted by $\delta_1(\xi)$ whereas the index of the parent element can be denoted by $\delta_{len(\xi)-1}(\xi)$.

The retrieval system, TRIX, is developed further from the version used in the 2004 ad hoc track [3] and its basic weighting scheme for a key k is slightly simplified from the previous year:

$$
w(k, \xi) = \frac{kf_\xi}{kf_\xi + v \cdot \left((1-b) + b \cdot \dfrac{\xi f_c}{\xi f_k} \right)} \cdot \frac{log\left(\dfrac{N}{m} \right)}{log(N)}
\tag{1}
$$

where

- kf_ξ is the number of times k occurs in the ξ element,
- N is the total number of content elements in the collection,
- m is the number of content elements containing k in the collection,
- ξf_c is the number of all descendant content elements of the ξ element
- ξf_k is the number of descendant content elements of the ξ element containing k,
- v and b are constants for tuning the weighting.

This formula is utilized only for such elements where kf_ξ is greater than 0. This ensures that the ξf_c and ξf_k are equal or greater than 1, because we define that the lowermost referable element, the content element, contains itself. Otherwise the weight of an element for the key k is 0. The constants v and b allow us to affect the 'length normalization component' ($\xi f_c / \xi f_k$) or LNC and tune the typical element size in the result set. In our runs for INEX 2005 b is used for tuning, while v is set to 2. Small values of b (0-0.1) yield more large elements, whereas big values (0.8-1) yield more small elements. This is because the LNC tends to be large in small matching elements; it is likely that the smaller the ξf_k value is the bigger is the LNC. A large b value emphasizes the LNC component, whereas a small one the key frequency. While b is set to 0, the system considers the root element always to be the best one in a document, because in case of two overlapping elements have the same weight, the ancestor one is privileged. Table 1 shows the average distribution of top 100 elements in our result lists (Content only), when b is set to 0.1 and to 0.9. Testing the parameters in INEX collections has shown that value 2 for v gives a smooth overall performance and ranging b allows tuning the size of the elements in the result list. The underline overlap percentage is 0. In the table the '+' sign means all the equivalent tags. E.g. p+ means all paragraph tags: p, ip1, ip2 etc.

Table 1. The average distribution of top 100 elements, when b is set to 0.1 and to 0.9

	p+	sec+	bdy	article
b = 0.9	31.7	14.1	19.3	0.4
b = 0.1	8.8	13.1	42.2	8.6

The weighting formula yields weights scaled into the semi-closed interval (0,1]. The weighting of phrases and the operations for + and - prefixes have the same property. They are introduced in detail in [3]. A *query term* is a key or phrase with a possible prefix + or -. A CO query q is a sequence of query terms $k_1, ..., k_n$. In relevance scoring for ranking the weights of the query terms are combined by taking the average of the weights:

$$w(q,\xi) = \frac{\sum_{i=1}^{n} w(k_i,\xi)}{n} \tag{2}$$

After this basic calculation elements' weights can be re-weighted. Next we consider the used re-weighting method, called contextualization.

1.2 Contextualization

In our runs we use a method called contextualization to rank elements in more effective way in XML retrieval [1, see also 7]. Re-weighting is based on the idea of using the ancestors of an element as a context. In terms of a contextualization schema the context levels can be taken into account in different ways. Here we applied four different contextualization schemata.

1) Root (denotation: $c_{r1.5}(q, \xi)$)
2) Parent (denotation: $c_p(q, \xi)$)
3) Tower (denotation: $c_t(q, \xi)$)
4) Root + Tower (denotation: $c_{rt}(q, \xi)$)

A contextualized weight is calculated using weighted average of the basic weights of target element and its ancestor(s), if exists. Root contextualization means that the contextualized weight of an element is a combination of the weight of an element and its root. In our runs the root is weighted by the value 1.5. This is calculated as follows:

$$c_{r1.5}(q, \xi) = \frac{w(q,\xi) + 1.5 * w(q,\delta_1(\xi))}{2.5} \tag{3}$$

Parent contextualization for an element is an average of the weights of the element and its parent.

$$c_p(q, \xi) = \frac{w(q,\xi) + w(q,\delta_{len(\xi)-1}(\xi))}{2} \tag{4}$$

Tower contextualization is an average of the weights of an element and all its ancestors.

$$c_t(q, \xi) = \frac{\sum_{i=1}^{len(\xi)} w(q,\delta_i(\xi))}{len(\xi)} \tag{5}$$

So called Root + Tower contextualizaton means the plain tower contextualization with root multiplied by two. This can be seen as a combination of parent and root contextualizations.

$$c_{rt}(q, \xi) = \frac{w(q,\delta_1(\xi)) + \sum_{i=1}^{len(\xi)} w(q,\delta_i(\xi))}{len(\xi)+1} \tag{6}$$

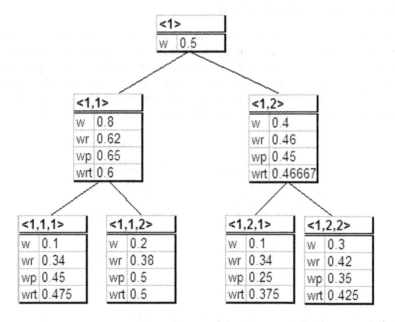

Fig. 1. A tree presentation of an XML document illustrating different contextualization schemata

In Figure 1 the effects of the present contextualization schemata are illustrated. The basic weights are only sample values. In it, XML tree with elements assigned initial weights (w) and contextualized weights: Root (wr), Parent (wp) and Root + Tower (wrt) is given. For instance, element with index $\langle 1,1,2 \rangle$ has an basic weight of 0.2. Parent contextualization means an average weight of $\langle 1,1,2 \rangle$ and $\langle 1,1 \rangle$. Root is the weighted average of $\langle 1,1,2 \rangle$ and $\langle 1 \rangle$ where the weight of $\langle 1 \rangle$ has been multiplied by 1.5. Root + Tower is the weighted average of weights of $\langle 1 \rangle$, $\langle 1,1 \rangle$ and $\langle 1,1,2 \rangle$, where the weight of $\langle 1 \rangle$ has been calculated twice.

In [1] we have discovered that a root element carries the best evidence related to the topics and assessments of INEX 2004. However, contextualizing the root only has an effect on the order of elements in the result list, and it does not change the order of elements within a document. Generally, if we contextualize the weights of elements x and y with the weight of their ancestor z, the order of x and y will not change in the result list. Further, the mutual order of x, y and z will not change if no re-weighting (i.e. contextualization) method is applied to element z. The root element (article) possesses no context in our approach. Hence in the CO.FetchBrowse task, where documents have to be ordered first, the Root contextualization will not have an effect on the rankings of other elements. However, within a document there are still several other context levels, and by utilizing those levels, it is possible to re-rank elements within a document. This finding has been utilized in the CO.FetchBrowse task.

1.3 Handling the Overlap in Results

In Figure 2 two overlap models, which our system supports, are illustrated. First, an element to be returned is marked with a letter P. On the left side there is a situation where all overlapping elements are excluded from the result list, even if their weight would be sufficient, but smaller than P. In other words, P has higher score than its descendants or ancestors. The model indicates that the overlap percentage is 0. On the right side all elements can be accepted, regardless of their structural position in the document.

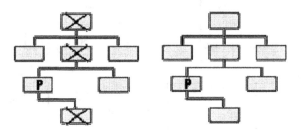

Fig. 2. Two overlap models

We have used the former (left) model in the CO.Focussed and CO.FetchBrowse tasks and the latter (right) model in the CO.Thorough and all of the CAS tasks. Next, we introduce the overall processing of CAS and the structural constraints involved.

2 Processing CAS-Queries

In the CAS queries an element may have constraints concerning itself, its ancestors or descendants. These constraints may be only structural, or structural with content. For instance in query

//A[about(.,x)]//B[about(.//C,y)]

B is the structural constraint of a target element itself. A is a structural constraint of a target element's ancestor, and is C target element's descendants. All of these structural constraints have also content constraints, namely x or y. So, to be selected to a result list, an element must fulfil these constraints. The processing of CAS queries can be divided into four steps:

- First step: Generate a tree according to the target element's content constraint, and weight elements, which fulfil the target element's structural constraint.
- Second step: Discard all the target elements which do not fulfil the structural ancestor and descendant constraints. Due to the nature of hierarchical data, ancestors are always about the same issue as their descendants, i.e. they share the descendants' keys. So the content constraints of descendant elements are taken into account here as well.
- Third step: Generate trees according to each ancestor element's content constraint. Discard elements, where the structural descendant and ancestor content constraint are not fulfilled, i.e. corresponding elements do not exist in any sub tree.
- Fourth step: Collect the indices of elements left in the third step fulfilling the ancestor structural constraint, and discard all of the target elements, which do not have such indices among ancestor elements.

To clarify this, processing of a CAS query can be demonstrated with a sufficiently complex example.

A query:

//article[about(.//abs, logic programming)]//bdy//sec[about(.//p, prolog)]

breaks down into following parts:

- an element with structural constraint **sec** is the target element with content constraint *prolog*
- **p** is a structural descendant constraint of the target element with the same content constraint as **sec** : *prolog*
- **article** is a structural ancestor constraint of the target element with a content constraint *logic programming*
- **abs** is a structural descendant constraint of **article** with the same content constraint *logic programming*
- **bdy** is a structural ancestor constraint of the target element without any content constraints

In the first step, shown in Figure 3, we form a tree of elements with non-zero weights according to the query *prolog*. In other words all the elements with zero weights are discarded from an XML tree structure.

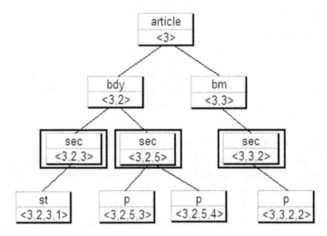

Fig. 3. A tree presentation of a sample XML document having only elements with a weight greater than 0 according to the query *prolog*

In the second step (Figure 4), we exclude target element $\langle 3,3,2 \rangle$, because the structural ancestor constraint **bdy** is not fulfilled. Element $\langle 3,2,3 \rangle$ is also to be excluded, because the descendant constraint **p** is not fulfilled.

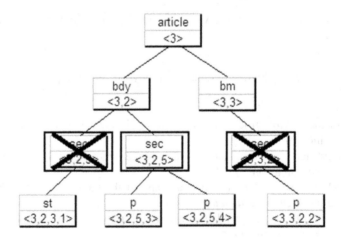

Fig. 4. A tree presentation of a sample XML document having only elements with a weight greater than 0 according to the query *prolog*, where target elements not fulfilling the constraints are excluded

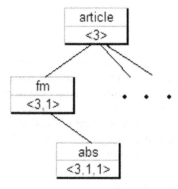

Fig. 5. A tree presentation of a sample XML document having only elements with a weight greater than 0 according to the query logic programming

In the third step we form a tree with non-zero weights according to the query *logic programming*, as seen in Figure 5.

In the tree, there is an **abs** element as a descendant of **article**, so both of the structural and content constraints are fulfilled. Hence, we take the index of the article: ⟨3⟩, and see that the index belongs to a descendant of the remaining target element ⟨3,2,5⟩. So, this and only this element is to be returned from this document.

2.1 Taking Vagueness into Account in CAS

In the current evaluations there are four different kinds of interpretations for structural constraints for processing NEXI, in our approach the structural constraints are interpreted strictly. However for SVCAS, VSCAS and VVCAS the query has been modified. Our system handles vague interpretation so that the corresponding element names have been ignored. In NEXI language this can be implemented by replacing the names with a star. Thus we have modified CAS queries as follows:

The initial CAS query (and SSCAS):
//A[about(.,x)]//B[about(.,y)]

SVCAS:
//*[about(.,x)]//B[about(.,y)]

VSCAS:
//A[about(.,x)]//*[about(.,y)]

VVCAS would then logically correspond to:
//*[about(.,x)]//*[about(.,y)]

For simplification we have processed VVCAS like a CO query. In the present example VVCAS corresponds to the query: //*[about(.,x y)].

3 Results

3.1 CAS Runs

In the content and structure queries, only elements which fulfil the constraints are accepted to the results. The ranking of the elements has been done according to the target element's textual content. Besides the target element, other content constraints have been taken into account as a full match constraint without any weighting. This full match content constraint within a structural constraint has been interpreted in disjunctive way. It means, that only one occurrence of any of the keys in a sub query is sufficient enough to fulfil the condition. For instance in the query

//A[about(.,x y z)]//B[about(.//C,w)]

for B to be returned, it is sufficient that the A element includes only one of the keys x, y or z. Naturally the B element should be about w, and also have a descendant C about w. This approach, the CAS processing with structural indices and the TRIX matching methods lead to fairly good results with the generalized quantization in all of the CAS tasks and especially in the SSCAS task (see Figure 6 in Appendix). Also the CO-style run in the VVCAS task (Figure 9) worked out fairly well.

There was a slight error in our submissions of results. Accidentally we sent runs intended for SVCAS for VSCAS, and vice versa. Figures 7 and 8 show the situation, where the "*should have been*"-runs are the thick upper ones in the nXCG curves. The overload of elements of wrong type led to a quite rotten score in SVCAS. Surprisingly, despite the error, VSCAS results proved to be quite satisfactory. Especially, according to the early precision of our runs, the ranking was as high as 3rd and 4th in the generalized quantization and 3rd and 8th in the strict quantization of the nXCG metrics. However, in general the right interpretation of both of those tasks leads to a substantial improvement of effectiveness (see Figures 7 and 8).

3.2 CO Runs

In the CO runs we have used Root+Tower contextualization (Tampere_..._tower), and Root contextualization (Tampere_..._root). In addition we have applied a query expansion method from Robertson [6], taking 5 or 10 expansion words from 7 top documents from the first result set (Corresponding runs: Tampere_exp5_b09_root, Tampere_exp10_b01_root). Figure 10 shows the slight improvement of the expanded run compared with a similar run without any expansion.

Because of the prevention of overlapping elements, promoting large elements may not be wise in the focussed task. That is because if a large element is returned, then every descendant is excluded from the results. However, in thorough task promoting large elements is not that risky. Hence, we used small b values for the thorough and large values for the focussed runs. Favouring small elements might have caused another kind of problem, though. In the relevance assessments many of the paragraph sized elements are marked as too small. That leads to a situation, where a whole relevant branch is paralyzed, when a too small leaf element is returned.

In the topic 229 there is a spelling error "latent semantic anlysis", which in our system would lead to a poor score. To minimize the error rate and also to improve recall, we have opened the phrases in all of the queries. For instance, query *"latent semantic anlysis"* would become *"latent semantic anlysis" latent semantic anlysis*. A manual correction of the mistake improves overall performance by 1-2 percentage depending on the task. These features and also the effect of the contextualization improve recall and scores in the generalized quantization, although the early precision suffers slightly (see Figures 10 and 11). A run without contextualization improves the early precision from 0,1657 to 0,2401 in CO.Focussed task with generalized quantization (nxCG@10). Accordingly the ep/gr value improves slightly as well.

4 Conclusions

This paper presents our experiments and results at INEX 2005. The results for the CO task show that Root contextualization is not generally better than Root + Tower, except for the early precision. In general, our approach is in many runs quite recall oriented, and we also do better in the generalized than strict quantization. Therefore, improving top precision in all tasks and quantizations remains as one of our primary goals.

This was the first time we participated in (strict) CAS task. The analyzing power of structural indices enables a straightforward processing of CAS queries. In addition, results in INEX 2005 give a good baseline for future development.

References

1. Arvola, P., Junkkari, M., and Kekäläinen, J.: Generalized Contextualization Method for XML Information Retrieval. In Proceedings of ACM Fourteenth Conference on Information and Knowledge Management (CIKM'2005), (2005) 20-27.
2. Junkkari, M.: PSE: An object-oriented representation for modeling and managing part-of relationships. Journal of Intelligent Information Systems, 25(2), (2005) 131-157.
3. Kekäläinen, J., Junkkari, M., Arvola, P., and Aalto, T.: TRIX 2004: Struggling with the overlap. In Advances in XML Information Retrieval: Third International Workshop of the Initiative for the Evaluation of XML Retrieval, INEX 2004. LNCS 3493. Springer, Heidelberg, (2005) 127-139.
4. Knuth, D.: Fundamental Algorithms: The Art of Computer Programming. Vol. 1, Addison Wesley, (1968).
5. Niemi, T.: A Seven-Tuple Representation for Hierarchical Data Structures. Information Systems, 8(3), (1983) 151-157.
6. Robertson, S.E. and Walker, S.: Okapi/Keenbow at TREC-8, Proc. NIST Special Publication 500-246: The Eighth Text Retrieval Conference Text (TREC), (1999) 151-162.
7. Sigurbjörnsson, B., Kamps J., and de Rijke, M.: An Element-Based Approach to XML Retrieval. In INEX 2003 Workshop Proceedings (2003) 19-26.
8. Tatarinov, I., Viglas, S., Beyer, K.S. Shanmugasundaram, J., Shekita, E.J., and Zhang C.: Storing and Querying Ordered XML Using a Relational Database System. In Proceedings of the 2002 ACM SIGMOD International Conference on Management of Data, (2002) 204-215.

Appendix

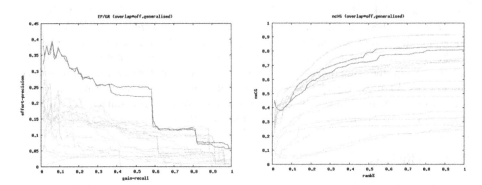

Fig. 6. SSCAS: The EP/GR and nXCG curves of the generalized quantization

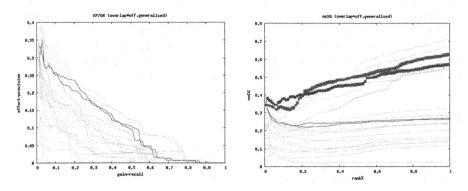

Fig. 7. VSCAS: The EP/GR and nXCG curves of the generalized quantization

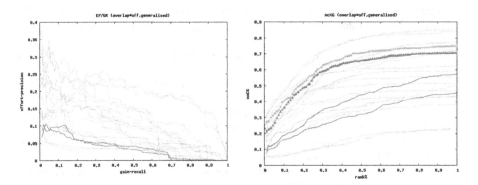

Fig. 8. SVCAS: The EP/GR and nXCG curves of the generalized quantization

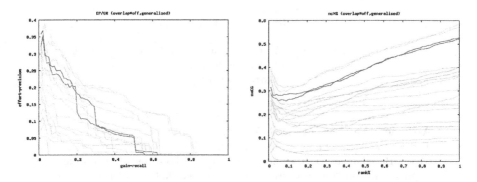

Fig. 9. VVCAS: The EP/GR and nXCG curves of the generalized quantization

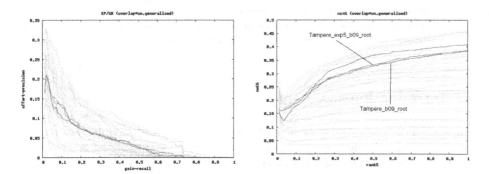

Fig. 10. CO.Focussed: The EP/GR and nXCG curves of the generalized quantization

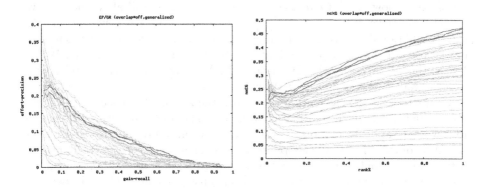

Fig. 11. CO.Thorough: The EP/GR and nXCG curves of the generalized quantization

B^3-SDR and Effective Use of Structural Hints

Roelof van Zwol

Utrecht University, Centre for Content and Knowledge Engineering,
Utrecht, The Netherlands
roelof@cs.uu.nl

Abstract. The focus in this article is on the use of structural hints to increase the retrieval performance of models for structured document retrieval. Based on an effective model for structured document retrieval for 'content only' queries, two extensions are defined that allow the retrieval model to include structural hints provided by the user into the retrieval process. The underlying hypothesis states that if the user is capable of providing structural clues, besides the content-based criteria of his/her information need, the retrieval performance can be increased. To test this hypothesis the two extensions are evaluated using a selection of the retrieval tasks defined for the INEX 2005 Ad-hoc track.

1 Introduction

Structured document retrieval, also referred to as XML retrieval, focusses on the retrieval of (XML) document fragments, rather than complete documents. By exploiting the structure of a document a user no longer has to read/scan entire articles, but is pointed directly towards the relevant sections of the article that match the user's information need.

A user can simply express his information need using a combination of search terms, also known as a *Content-Only* (CO) query. This will allow the retrieval model to retrieve literally any document fragment. Alternatively, the user can specify additional structural constraints that limit the retrieval model to retrieve only those document fragments that satisfy the structural constraints. Within INEX, the INitiative for the Evaluation of XML retrieval [1], this is referred to as a *Content-and-Structure* (CAS) query.

Characteristic for information retrieval is the notion of relevance of retrieved information for a given information need. In the case of structured document retrieval relevant information can be excluded from the results, if a strict interpretation of the structural constraints is used. This is not necessarily a problem, if the user is confident that the requested information is to be found within the specified section. Otherwise, the structural constraints should merely be interpreted as structural *hints* by the underlying retrieval model.

This distinction in interpretation of the structural constraints is reflected in the various retrieval tasks set for the INEX 2005 Ad-hoc track[2]. Besides the CO-based tasks, a number of CO+S and VVCAS tasks have been defined, where

N. Fuhr et al. (Eds.): INEX 2005, LNCS 3977, pp. 146–160, 2006.
© Springer-Verlag Berlin Heidelberg 2006

the user model is based on a vague interpretation of the structural constraints. In addition, a so called SSCAS task is defined, where the structural constraints of the user information need should be interpreted strictly.

The objective in this article is to study the effect of structural hints on the retrieval performance. Three cases can therefore be distinguished: 1) The user information need contains no structural clues about where to find the relevant information in the document; 2) The user information need contains structural hints of where to find the relevant information, but the user is not fully confident about these structural constraints; 3) The user is fully confident about where the relevant information is captured in the document, and the structural constraints should be strictly interpreted.

The underlying hypothesis used for the research presented in this article states that *the effectiveness of the retrieval model can be increased, if structural hints are provided by the user.* For this purpose, the GPX retrieval model for XML retrieval [3] is adopted by the B^3-SDR system as the basic retrieval model. This relatively simple, yet effective, model performs very well on the CO tasks defined for INEX. But, the model has no build-in mechanism to actively reward the structural hints defined for the topics that are used in the CO+S and VVCAS tasks.

Two extensions have been defined that use the structural clues to drive the retrieval process. The first extension rewards document fragments that (partly) fulfil the structural requirements of the information need, causing them to appear higher in the ranking. For example, if the user expects that the requested information is found in the abstract of an article, then the relevance score of a document fragment is increased, if its path contains the requested elements. The second extension penalises those document fragments that contain *excessive* elements in their path. In this case the relevance score of a document fragment decreases, if its path contains additional elements that are not specified in the information need. For instance, if only a paragraph of an abstract is returned while the entire abstract was requested, the relevance score of this particular fragment is lowered.

The effect of the extensions on the retrieval performance is evaluated using the 'thorough' tasks defined for the INEX 2005 Ad-hoc track, e.g. the CO.Thorough, CO+S.Thorough, VVCAS and SSCAS tasks. The objective of these tasks is to retrieve all highly exhaustive and specific XML elements. Comparison of the results for the different tasks, should provide new insights in the effectiveness of structural hints on the retrieval performance.

1.1 Organisation

In Section 2 the basic model for structured document retrieval is discussed. The extensions to the model that include the structural hints into the retrieval process are defined in Section 3. The evaluation results are then discussed in Section 4. Finally, the conclusions and future work are presented in Section 5.

2   Basic Model for Structured Document Retrieval

Many, if not all, of the retrieval models used for structured document retrieval are based on existing text retrieval strategies. The retrieval model that was introduced by [3], and integrated in the B^3-SDR system is primarily based on an inverted file [4] structure commonly used for text retrieval.

2.1   Data Structure

In Example 1, a fragment of the inverted file is given that is created when indexing the XML-based *Docbook* [5] version of this article. Each entry of the inverted file consists of the quadruple: *term, document, path, position*. Two pre-processing operations [6], lexical cleaning and stop-word removal, are used to produce the inverted file. Stemming is used as an optional post-processing step.

Example 1. Fragment of inverted file.

term	document	path	position
many	a007.xml	/article[1]/section[2]/para[1]	1
retrieval	a007.xml	/article[1]/section[2]/para[1]	7
models	a007.xml	/article[1]/section[2]/para[1]	8
structured	a007.xml	/article[1]/section[2]/para[1]	11
document	a007.xml	/article[1]/section[2]/para[1]	12
retrieval	a007.xml	/article[1]/section[2]/para[1]	13
...			

The B^3-SDR system uses Monet [7], a binary relation DBMS, to store and query the inverted file structure. Due to the many elements that exist within an XML document, the size of the inverted file will grow rapidly.

To maintain a reasonable system performance, the inverted file structure is normalised according to the schema presented in Figure 1. The table NodeInfo stores information about each XML element, which can be uniquely referenced by its *nodeId*. Besides the *nodeId*, a reference to its parent (*parentNode*), the name of the element (*nodeName*), and the name of the document (*document*) and the unique path to the node (*path*) within the document is stored for each XML element.

The table TermLeaveWeight is sorted on the term name and contains the attributes: *termWeight, nodeId,* and *position*. *TermWeight* and *nodeId* are used to connect the relevance weight of a term found within a specific node. The attribute *position*[] contains an array of term positions within a node for a particular term. This is used to detect term phrases, which are specified in the information request.

To speed up the query process a termindex is maintained. For each term, specified in the information request a slice is taken from the table termLeaveWeight that starts at position *startPos* and ends at *endPos*. This can be considered a 'dynamic' horizontal fragmentation of the inverted file. When stemming is used, a query term is stemmed first, and the *stem* attribute is used to select stemmed terms that match the query term.

NodeInfo				
nodeId	parentNode	nodeName	document	path

TermLeaveWeight		
termWeight	nodeId	position[]

TermIndex			
term	stem	startPos	endPos

Fig. 1. Optimised (relational) database schema of the inverted file structure

2.2   Retrieval Model

During the post-processing step, a term weight t_w is calculated for each unique term within a leave node, using the following formula:

$$t_w = \frac{t_i}{f_i}, \tag{1}$$

with:

- t_i: the number of occurrences of term i in XML leave node.
- f_i: the number of occurrences of term i in the entire XML document collection.

CO queries. When a content-only (CO) query is processed, the first step is to calculate the relevance weights for each of the leave nodes. The relevance weight L of a leave node is calculated as:

$$L = F_t^{n-1} \sum_{i=1}^{n} t_{w_i}, \tag{2}$$

with:

- t_{w_i}: the relevance weight of term i for an XML leave node.
- n: the number of unique query terms, that occur within an XML leave node.
- F_t: a term factor used to scale up leave elements with multiple distinct terms.

The formula of Equation 2 sums over the term weights that are found within a leave node, and multiplies that with the term factor (F_t) to the power of the number of terms that are found in the node. The effect is that leave nodes containing more relevant query terms will appear higher in the ranking. According to heuristic experiments carried out by [3] best retrieval performance is achieved with a term factor F_t of 5.

The next step involves calculating the relevance scores N_{CO} of the ancestor nodes, given the set of retrieved leave nodes. The (final) relevance weight N_{CO} of an arbitrary node is calculated with the formula:

$$N_{CO} = D(m) \sum_{i=1}^{m} L_i, \tag{3}$$

with m being the number of child elements L, with $L_i > 0$; and decay function $D(m)$ defined as:

$$D(m) = \begin{cases} D_{single} & \text{if } m = 1, \\ D_{multiple} & \text{if } m > 1. \end{cases} \quad (4)$$

The decay function $D(m)$ regulates the relevance weights inherited from the child nodes. If a node X has only one child with $L_i > 0$, then the relevance of node X is lower than of its child node. In other words, its better to return the child node, since the child node will have a higher specificity. If there are more than one children of node X, for which $L_i > 0$, node X is likely to be more exhaustive than its children, which should be rewarded. Without such a decay function, e.g. with D_{single} and $D_{multiple}$ set to 1, elements close to the document root will always be judges more relevant than its child nodes, which is counter intuitive. Usable values for D_{single} and $D_{multiple}$ are within the range $< 0, 1]$. According to [3] suitable values for D_{single} and $D_{multiple}$ are 0.49, and 0.99, respectively.

CAS queries. A bit more complex is the procedure followed to produce a ranking for NEXI CAS queries. A CAS query always contains one or two filters [8]. E.g. a filter is specified with the square brackets ([...]) and can contain one or more about-clauses that define the content-based search criteria of the information need. Furthermore, the CAS query has to end with a filter, limiting the possible forms of a CAS query to: C[D] or A[B]C[D]. Consider the following example CAS query:

```
//article[about(., "retrieval model") and about(.//title, structured
document retrieval)]//para[about(., XML retrieval)]
```

This CAS query contains two filters and is of form A[B]C[D]. This query can be split in two queries: a support query (A[B]), and a request query (AC[D]). Applying this to the example would give:

Support query:

```
//article[about(., "retrieval model") and about(.//title, structured
document retrieval)]
```

Request query:

```
//article//para[about(., XML retrieval)]
```

The request query defines the desired element of retrieval, in this case a paragraph, discussing 'XML retrieval', while the support query specifies additional constraints of the information need.

When a strict interpretation of the structural constraints is used to obtain a ranking, the following procedure is followed for both the support and request query:

1. Evaluation of the about-clauses: An initial ranking is produce for each about-clause, as if it is a CO query.
2. Filtering the initial rankings: Each ranking is filtered to match the path conditions specified in the about-clause, e.g for one of the about-clauses in the example this will be: //article//title.

3. Projection of the relevance score values (rsv): In strict mode, only article elements should be returned by the system for the support query. Therefore the rsv values in the ranking for an about-clause, are transposed to match the article element.
4. Combinatory logic is used to combine different the rankings within a filter.
5. Finally, a min-max normalisation step is used to scale the rsv values to fit the $[0, 1]$ range.

Two sets of rankings remain, one for the support query and one for the request query. Only those nodes of the request query are returned that have a matching ancestor in the support query.

When using a vague interpretation of the structural constraints, instead of a strict interpretation, the ranking is simply extended with each of the intermediate results not yet contained in the ranking. As a result, the structural *hints* are ignored.

3 Using the Structural Hints

The two extensions to the retrieval model presented in this section aim at integrating the structural hints, when processing a CAS query in the vague interpretation mode. The path factor extension rewards those nodes that (partially) match the path conditions of the query. The request penalty factor is used to penalise those nodes that contain excessive elements not specified in the query in their path.

3.1 The Path Factor Extension

Applying the path factor extension to a (ranked) list of nodes, will push those nodes to the top of the list that (partially) match the path elements specified in the (support or request) query. It is expected that the top of the ranking will then contain highly relevant XML elements that also satisfy all the structural criteria of the information need, followed by highly relevant elements that only partially (or not) match the structural criteria. The path factor extension corrects the relevance score that is computed for a node using the following formula:

$$N_{VCAS+F_p} = F_p{}^e N_{CO} \tag{5}$$

with:

- N_{CO}: the relevance score of an XML node, based on the content-only part of an about-clause.
- e: the number of path elements that match the path conditions of the query.
- F_p: A path factor used to reward nodes that satisfy structural constraints $(< 1, \infty])$.

This straightforward manipulation of the ranking increases the relevance scores of those XML nodes that satisfy the structural criteria of the information need.

Let the path factor F_p for example be set to 4, then the relevance score of a node that has two matching (ancestor) elements in its path, will be increased by a factor 16. It is hard to predict what would be suitable values for F_p, since this also depends on the confidence of the user in the appropriateness of the structural hints. In Section 4, the results are presented for different values of F_p, and their influence on the retrieval performance.

3.2   The Request Penalty Factor

The request penalty factor will decrease relevance scores of those nodes that contain excessive elements in their path, which are not specified in the query. Contrary to the path factor extension, the request penalty factor can only be used to re-rank the final set of results of a query, i.e. the result set that is obtained after merging the intermediate results of the (optional) support query with the request query. For ease of notation, the relevance score of a node, contained in this set is referred to as N_{VCAS}. The relevance score N_{VCAS+F_r}, after applying the request penalty factor, is then calculated as:

$$N_{VCAS+F_r} = F_r{}^{p-e} N_{VCAS} \qquad (6)$$

with:

- N_{VCAS}: the relevance score of the XML node.
- p: the path length of the XML node.
- e: the number of path elements that match the structural constraints of the query.
- F_r: a request penalty, used to penalise for excessive path elements ($< 0, 1]$).

It is expected that the request penalty factor decreases the relevance scores of the 'too small' elements that are particularly found near the leaves of the XML tree structure, i.e. titles of sections, or pieces of text that an author wants to emphasise on. Such elements are too small to be judged relevant, outside their surrounding context [2]. Although the retrieval of too small XML elements can be considered a usability issue that can be solved at the interface, applying the penalty factor can also be an effective apparatus to allow the user to directly manipulate the ranking, and filter small elements from the top of the ranking.

4   Evaluation

The evaluation of the retrieval model, and in particular the evaluation of the extensions for using structural hints, will focus on the *thorough* tasks that are defined for INEX 2005. The aim of the *thorough* retrieval strategy is to retrieve all highly exhaustive and specific elements[9]. Within this task, it is allowed to return overlapping elements. If a child element is relevant, then so will be the ancestor(s) of that element to a greater of lesser extent. Overlap is not considered an issue within this task, as it should be dealt with at the user interface, upon presenting the results.

In the subsections below the results are presented for the following tasks: *CO.Thorough, CO+S.Thorough, VVCAS*, and *SSCAS*. The user model defined for the CO.Thorough task assumes that the user information need does not contain any structural hints, and therefore allows for the evaluation of (the configuration of) the basic retrieval model. The extensions of the model that incorporate structural hints into the retrieval process are evaluated in the CO+S.Thorough and VVCAS tasks. These tasks take the structural hints defined in the information request into account, using a vague interpretation. Finally, the SSCAS task allows for the evaluation of retrieval strategies, based on a user model that uses a strict interpretation of the structural constraints defined in the information request.

4.1 Metrics

A number of official metrics are defined for the evaluation of retrieval strategies within INEX[10]. In this article a sub-set of these metrics is used. For each task, a summary of the results is given where for each run the following metrics are reported: *iMAep, nxCG[10],nxCG[50],nxCG[100]*,and *nxCG[1500]*.

The *iMAep*, short for interpolated Mean Average effort-precision, is calculated as the average of effort-precision values at the standard gain-recall points. The *nxCG[i]* values, normalised extended Cumulated Gain for a given rank i, reflect the relative gain the user accumulated up to that rank, compared to the gain he/she could have attained if the system would have produced the optimum best ranking.

For each of these metrics both overlap and quantisation can be differentiated. Overlap, as discussed before is allowed for the Thorough tasks (overlap=off). The quantisation function has two modes: strict and general. If the evaluation is performed with the quantisation function in strict mode, an element is considered relevant (1) for a given information need, if it contains *highly* exhaustive and *highly* specific information. If the evaluation is run with the quantisation function in general mode, an element is relevant $(exh * spec)$, if it contains any degree of exhaustive and specific information. A more detailed description of the metrics can be found in [10].

Since the objective of the thorough tasks is to retrieve all highly exhaustive and specific elements, only the results based on the strict quantisation function are reported here. In general, the comparison of the results with the generalised quantisation function showed that the results are (1) almost similar, but (2) more discriminative when using the strict quantisation function.

4.2 Task: CO.Thorough

For a CO.Thorough run, four parameters need to be set. The following notation is used to identify a particular run for the CO task: co[*stem*, F_t, D_{single}, $D_{multiple}$], where *stem* is a boolean value indicating the use of stemming, F_t refers to the value used for the term factor, and the $D_{multiple}$ and D_{single} refer to the multiplication factors used by the decay function $D(m)$.

The evaluation of the basic retrieval model can be split in two steps, using the CO.Thorough task. The first step is to examine the effect of the term factor on the retrieval performance. In Table 1.a the summary statistics are given, when using a term factor of 1, 3, 5, 10, and 20. Figure 2.a shows the performance of the different runs using the nxCG measures at different (%) positions in the ranking. It reveals that the performance stabilises for larger values of F_t (5,10, 20). Without the term factor, e.g. $F_t = 1$, the model has the lowest performance. To evaluate the optimal configuration of the other parameters of the model, a term factor F_t of 5 is used. The performance is near optimal, and using larger values of F_t would increase the differences between rsv values and reduce the (visible) effects of the structural extensions to the basic model.

When comparing runs co[0,5,.49,.99] and co[1,5,.49,.99], it becomes clear that stemming is not a useful feature to increase the effectivity of the retrieval performance. Therefore, stemming will not be used in the remainder of the experiment.

Table 1. Task: CO.Thorough - summary statistics

Task id	iMAep	nxCG[10]	nxCG[50]	nxCG[100]	nxCG[1500]
co[0,1,.49,.99]	0.0088	0.004	0.0622	0.114	0.3371
co[0,3,.49,.99]	0.0145	0.0324	0.0892	0.1695	0.4154
co[0,5,.49,.99]	0.0153	0.0337	0.1513	0.1909	0.4149
co[0,10,.49,.99]	**0.0162**	**0.0422**	**0.1597**	**0.1924**	**0.4194**
co[0,20,.49,.99]	0.0159	0.0422	0.1586	0.19	0.4129
co[1,5,.49,.99]	0.0059	0.0124	0.0561	0.0746	0.3031

(a) Variation in term factor values

Task id	iMAep	nxCG[10]	nxCG[50]	nxCG[100]	nxCG[1500]
co[0,5,.25,1.0]	0.0187	0.0462	0.1473	0.1799	0.4444
co[0,5,.49,.99]	0.0153	0.0337	0.1513	0.1909	0.4149
co[0,5,.79,.99]	0.0137	0.028	0.1392	0.1888	0.4073
co[0,5,.99,.99]	0.0129	0.032	0.0927	0.1856	0.4009
co[0,5,.99,.49]	**0.0269**	**0.0884**	**0.1638**	**0.1996**	**0.4519**
co[0,5,1.0,1.0]	0.0149	0.028	0.0911	0.1742	0.4026
co[0,5,2.0,1.0]	0.0059	0.02	0.0254	0.0884	0.3185
co[0,5,10.0,20.0]	0.0005	0	0.008	0.008	0.0708

(b) Variation in decay values

The second step in the evaluation of the basic model focusses on different values for decay function $D(m)$, for which the results are presented in Table 1.b and Figure 2.b. Natural values for D_{single} and $D_{multiple}$ are in the range of $< 0, 1]$, but the results also show the performance for runs with $D(m)$ values higher than one. Using such values will cause the model to position those XML elements in the top of the ranking, that are close to the document root. As can be expected, the effectivity will drop, because the *specificity* of (large) XML elements is usually low. For the runs that are within the pre-defined range little variation is observed. Interesting to see is that a small increase in effectivity is gained at the top of the ranking for values of $D(m)$ with $Dsingle > Dmultiple$,

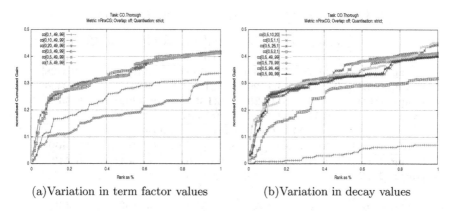

(a)Variation in term factor values   (b)Variation in decay values

Fig. 2. Task: CO.Thorough

i.e. such as is the case for run co[0,5,.99,.49]. This behaviour requires further investigation, and can currently not be explained. With the $D(m)$ values set to: $D_{single} = .49$ and $D_{multiple} = .99$ the most fluent increase in effectivity is achieved. Therefore this setting of $D(m)$ is used for the evaluation of the other features of the retrieval model.

Based on the observations for the CO.Thorough task, the following setting of the basic model is used for the evaluation of the CO+S.Thorough, VVCAS, and SSCAS tasks: co[0,5,.49,.99].

4.3   Task: CO+S.Thorough

The objective of the CO+S.Thorough run is to evaluate the retrieval of highly exhaustive and specific elements that contain relevant content. Structural hints are used in addition to the content-oriented information need.

To uniquely identify a run for the CO+S.Thorough and VVCAS and SSCAS tasks, the following notation is used: vague$[F_p, F_r]$. F_p represents the path factor value that is used for the run, while F_r refers to the request penalty factor. Whenever one the the values is set to 1, the corresponding extension is disabled. the prefix *vague* is used to denote that the run interprets the structural aspects of the information need as a hint (vague), while the prefix *strict* is used to identify runs that were constructed using a strict interpretation.

This task is therefore suitable to evaluate the effect of the structural extensions on the retrieval performance. The results of the evaluation for the path factor extension are given in Table 2.a and Figure 3.a. When observing the results for the variation in path factor values, it becomes clear that the path factor extension has a positive effect on the retrieval performance. In particular it improves the effectiveness at the lower recall levels. The strict run is also plotted here to illustrate the difference in performance, when the structural aspects of the information need should be interpreted strictly. From this behaviour it can be concluded that it is useful to specify structural hints to improve the retrieval

Table 2. Task: CO+S.Thorough - summary statistics

Task id	iMAep	nxCG[10]	nxCG[50]	nxCG[100]	nxCG[1500]
strict[]	0.0038	0.0065	0.0312	0.0261	0.0646
vague[1,1]	0.0091	0.0235	0.0716	0.1067	0.3428
vague[5,1]	0.0143	0.0529	0.1204	0.2153	0.3496
vague[10,1]	0.0149	**0.0529**	**0.1351**	**0.2202**	**0.3526**
vague[20,1]	**0.0151**	0.0529	0.1351	0.2164	0.3524

(a) Variation in path factor values

Task id	iMAep	nxCG[10]	nxCG[50]	nxCG[100]	nxCG[1500]
vague[1,1]	0.0091	0.0235	**0.0716**	**0.1067**	**0.3428**
vague[1,.25]	0.0054	0.0235	0.0159	0.0218	0.2972
vague[1,.5]	**0.0211**	**0.0712**	0.059	0.0952	0.3206
vague[5,1]	0.0143	0.0529	**0.1204**	**0.2153**	**0.3496**
vague[5,.25]	0.0062	0.0235	0.0454	0.0512	0.2964
vague[5,.5]	**0.0436**	**0.0712**	0.0982	0.1687	0.3238

(b) Variation in request penalty factor values

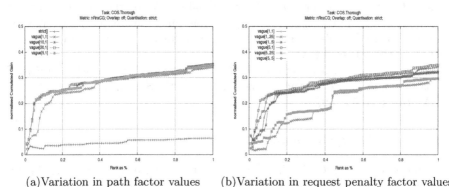

(a) Variation in path factor values   (b) Variation in request penalty factor values

Fig. 3. Task: CO+S.Thorough

performance, especially if the user is not fully confident about what kind of information he/she is looking for.

The results for the request penalty factor extension are less positive, as shown in Table 2.b and Figure 3.b. When studying the vague[5,*] runs in Figure 3.b it becomes clear that the combination of the two extensions is not resulting in a visible increase in retrieval performance. While the iMAep values suggests that the effectivity doubles when $F_r = .5$. However, choosing smaller values for F_r will cause the performance to drop significantly. Observing the vague[1,*] runs shows similar behaviour for the nxCG-plots, and even larger differences for the iMAep values. Most likely, the iMAep is sensitive for a good performance at the top of the ranking, see for comparison nxCG[10] scores of the vague[*,.5] runs. Without the path factor extension activated, these differences are even larger.

4.4   Tasks: VVCAS and SSCAS

To objective of the VVCAS and SSCAS tasks is almost similar to the CO+S.Thorough task. However, in the CAS tasks it is specified explicitly where to look for relevant information (support query), and what to return (request query)[2]. Either one of these conditions can be executed using a strict or vague interpretation, hence four different sub-tasks can be defined. Here the focus is on the VVCAS and the SSCAS tasks, where the support and request queries are both interpreted vaguely and strict, respectively.

Task: VVCAS In Table 3.a and Figure 4.a the results are presented for the VVCAS task, when only the path factor extension is used. From the figure, it becomes clear that the runs with a $F_p > 4$ perform equally well, while the iMAep values suggest that higher values of F_p (10, 20) are more effective. This is inline with the behaviour as observed for the path factor extension in the CO+S.Thorough task.

One of the observations for a request penalty factor of 0.5 in the CO+S.Thorough task was that according to the iMAep and nxCG[<50] measures a small increase in effectiveness is gained. The results presented in Table 3.b and Figure 4.b contradict this observation for the VVCAS task. Further increasing the request penalty factor (0.8 and 0.9) shows that little or no additional gain is achieved, according to the iMAep measure.

Task: SSCAS Within the SSCAS task the user model is adjusted to examine the retrieval performance of the system when the user is fully confident in the structural requirements of his/her information need. In effect, the assessment pool is adjusted to fit only the elements specified in the query. With respect to the structural extensions defined in this article, it is useful to examine the behaviour of the runs when the user has indeed a 'strict' information need, but the retrieval model treats the structural requirements as hints.

Table 3. Task: VVCAS - summary statistics

Task id	iMAep	nxCG[10]	nxCG[50]	nxCG[100]	nxCG[1500]
strict[]	0.0197	0.1111	0.1222	0.1173	0.1613
vague[1,1]	0.0232	0.1444	0.1276	0.1294	0.5535
vague[5,1]	0.0334	0.1889	0.1571	0.1931	0.5815
vague[10,1]	0.036	0.2111	0.1615	0.1975	**0.5883**
vague[20,1]	**0.0366**	**0.2111**	**0.1637**	**0.1998**	0.5881

(a) Variation in path factor values

Task id	iMAep	nxCG[10]	nxCG[50]	nxCG[100]	nxCG[1500]
vague[1,1]	0.0232	**0.1444**	**0.1276**	0.1294	0.5535
vague[1,.5]	0.0164	0.0667	0.0384	0.05	0.3701
vague[1,.8]	**0.0248**	0.0889	0.0882	0.0909	0.5585
vague[1,.9]	0.0223	0.0667	0.0793	**0.1408**	**0.5597**

(b) Variation in request penalty factor values

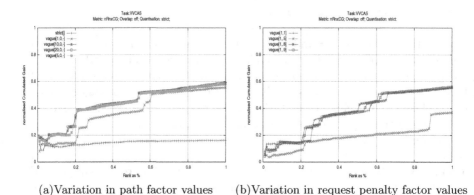

(a)Variation in path factor values   (b)Variation in request penalty factor values

Fig. 4. Task: VVCAS

Table 4. Task: SSCAS - summary statistics

Task id	iMAep	nxCG[10]	nxCG[50]	nxCG[100]	nxCG[1500]
strict[]	**0.091**	**0.175**	**0.4194**	**0.4423**	**0.7028**
vague[1,1]	0.025	0.025	0.0689	0.0716	0.5951
vague[5,1]	0.047	0.1	0.1128	0.3456	0.622
vague[10,1]	0.054	0.15	0.1228	0.3557	0.6372
vague[20,1]	0.057	0.15	0.1278	0.3607	0.6408

(a) Variation in path factor values

Task id	iMAep	nxCG[10]	nxCG[50]	nxCG[100]	nxCG[1500]
vague[1,1]	0.025	0.025	0.0689	0.0716	**0.5951**
vague[1,.5]	**0.026**	**0.1**	0.045	0.0592	0.3132
vague[1,.8]	0.025	0.025	**0.0789**	0.0805	0.567
vague[1,.9]	0.024	0	0.0639	**0.0956**	0.5872

(b) Variation in request penalty factor values

Table 4 and Figure 5 presents the results of the same runs as used for the VVCAS task, but now based on the restrictions of the SSCAS task.

Focussing on the path factor extension again (Table 4.a and Figure 5.a) it is clear that the strict run is now most effective. However, the results also show that the retrieval performance increases for the vague runs, when the path factor extension is enabled. This is only possible, when the support and request elements of the retrieved document fragments exactly match the structural constraints of the query. From this behaviour it can be concluded that the path factor extension successfully re-ranks the results, obeying the structural hints specified by the user.

Table 4.b and Figure 5.b show the results of the request penalty extension for the SSCAS task. It reveals no new information, but confirms the earlier inconsistent observations. It therefore must be concluded that the request penalty factor extension has no significant and consistent contribution to the effectiveness of the retrieval performance.

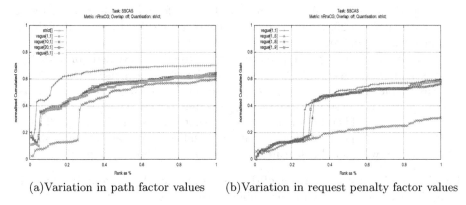

(a) Variation in path factor values   (b) Variation in request penalty factor values

Fig. 5. Task: SSCAS

5   Conclusions

The research presented in this article contributes to one of the focal areas of the INEX 2005 Ad-hoc track: *Can structural hints be used effectively*. In other words, can structural clues about where to find relevant information in the document be used to increase the retrieval performance. To answer this question, three types of user models are distinguished, that vary over the interpretation of the structural conditions of the information need: ignore, vague, and strict. These user models are implemented in the different tasks set for the Ad-hoc track, and correspond with the CO, CO+S/VVCAS, and SSCAS tasks respectively.

To investigate this, a model for structured document retrieval is adopted that was first introduced by [3]. This basic model is especially effective for the CO and SSCAS tasks, but lacks a mechanism to rewards the structural hints when a vague interpretation is used. Therefore two extensions are introduced that take the structural hints into account. The path factor extension rewards nodes that contain elements in their path, which are also specified in the query. The request penalty extension is used to penalise nodes, when excessive elements are contained in the path, which are not defined in the query.

The following can be concluded based on the results presented in this article:

- Comparing the best performing runs, discussed in Section 4, for the different tasks shows that the runs can easily compete with the top ranked runs, reported for the official runs. Note that the official runs submitted for the B^3-SDR system suffered from a serious sorting bug, and had to be discarded.
- The results for the CO.Thorough task revealed that the co[0,5,.49,.99] has reasonable performance and is a good candidate for comparing the different user models. Best performance, however is reported for the co[0,5,.99,.49] run.
- The CO+S and VVCAS tasks allowed for the evaluation of the extensions that incorporate the structural hints into the retrieval process. Comparing the various runs, clearly revealed a significant increase in effectiveness, when

the path factor extension was enabled. Best performance was obtained with a path factor of 20. Additional experiments are needed to find out if this is the optimal configuration.

- Evaluation of the request penalty factor extension, revealed contradicting observations: Based on the CO+S.Thorough task, an increase in performance was visible when a request penalty factor of .5 is used, however a decrease in effectivity is observed when using the same request penalty factor for the VVCAS task. Therefore, it is concluded that this extension is not effective from a system point of view. Additional studies and future research should determine whether this feature is useful from a usability perspective.

Finally, based on the comparison of the results for the VVCAS and SSCAS task, if can be concluded that structural hints have a positive effect on the retrieval performance regardless of the interpretation mode that is used.

References

1. Fuhr, N., Lalmas, M., Malik, S., Szlávik, Z., eds.: Advances in XML Information Retrieval. Volume 3493 of Lecture Notes in Computer Science. Springer (2005)
2. Trotman, A., Lalmas, M.: The interpretation of cas. In: INEX 2005 Workshop Pre-proceedings, Schloss Dagstuhl, Germany (2005) 40 – 53
3. Geva, S.: GPX - Gardens Point XML Information Retrieval at INEX 2004. In: Advances in XML Information Retrieval. Volume 3493. Springer, Schloss Dagstuhl, Germany (2005) 211 – 223
4. Blumer, A., Blumer, J., Haussler, D., McConnell, R., Ehrenfeucht, A.: Complete inverted files for efficient text retrieval and analysis. Journal of the ACM **34**(3) (1987) 578 – 595
5. Walsh, N., Muellner, L.: DocBook: The Definitive Guide. O'Reilly (1999)
6. Baeza-Yates, R.A., Ribeiro-Neto, B.: Modern Information Retrieval. Addison-Wesley Longman Publishing Co., Inc., Boston, MA, USA (1999)
7. Zukowski, M., Boncz, P.A., Nes, N., Heman, S.: MonetDB/X100 - A DBMS In The CPU Cache. IEEE Data Engineering Bulletin **28**(2) (2005) 17 – 22
8. Trotman, A., Sigurbjörnsson, B.: Narrowed Extended XPath I (NEXI). In: Advances in XML Information Retrieval. Volume 3493. Springer, Schloss Dagstuhl, Germany (2005) 16 – 40
9. Lalmas, M.: INEX 2005 retrieval task and result submission specification. In: INEX 2005 Workshop Pre-proceedings, Schloss Dagstuhl, Germany (2005) 385 – 390
10. Kazai, G., Lalmas, M.: Inex 2005 evaluation metrics. In: INEX 2005 Workshop Pre-proceedings, Schloss Dagstuhl, Germany (2005) 401 – 406

Field-Weighted XML Retrieval Based on BM25

Wei Lu[1], Stephen Robertson[2], and Andrew MacFarlane[3]

[1] Center for Studies of Information Resources
School of Information Management
Wuhan University, China
sa713@soi.city.ac.uk
[2] Microsoft Research
Cambridge, U.K
ser@microsoft.com
[3] Centre for Interactive Systems Research
Department of Information Science
City University London
andym@soi.city.ac.uk

Abstract. This is the first year for the Centre for Interactive Systems Research participation of INEX. Based on a newly developed XML indexing and retrieval system on Okapi, we extend Robertson's field-weighted BM25F for document retrieval to element level retrieval function BM25E. In this paper, we introduce this new function and our experimental method in detail, and then show how we tuned weights for our selected fields by using INEX 2004 topics and assessments. Based on the tuned models we submitted our runs for CO.Thorough, CO.FetchBrowse, the methods we propose show real promise. Existing problems and future work are also discussed.

1 Introduction

Being an important data exchange and information storage standard, XML is now widely used, especially for scientific data repositories, Digital Libraries and on the Web. Many sophisticated systems [1, 2, 3, 4, 5] and retrieval models [6, 7, 8, 9, 10] for XML documents have been proposed.

XML documents often contain sub-fields (elements), e.g. INEX collections from IEEE contain fields such as title, abs, bdy, bm, st etc. Practitioners have found it beneficial to exploit the document's internal structure to improve retrieval performance [11]. Researchers have looked at various techniques in order to investigate this problem. Wilkinson [12] and Ogilvie et al [13] have proposed and tested different ways to weight and combine the scores obtained on different fields of a document; Kraaij et al [14] propose a flexible algorithm based on language models but have not implemented it; and Myaeng et al [15] combine terms found in different document representations using Bayesian inference networks. Robertson et al [11] give a more detailed review of this area in their paper.

In practice, many systems use a linear combination of the scores obtained from scoring every field due to the complexity of the ranking algorithms deployed.

N. Fuhr et al. (Eds.): INEX 2005, LNCS 3977, pp. 161–171, 2006.

Robertson et al [11] discuss the dangers of linear combination in detail and propose an alternative solution, the linear combination of term frequencies based on BM25 (BM25F will be used in the rest of the paper instead of "field-weighted models based on BM25"), to extend standard ranking functions to multiple weighted fields. Their experiment based on two existing collection Reuters vol. I collection and the 2002 TREC Web-Track crawl of the .gov for document level retrieval shows that the method was beneficial. Some related work using Okapi, BM25 or field combination in INEX 2004 is documented in [16, 17, 18, 19, 20].

In this paper, we extend this method further to element level XML retrieval based on INEX 05 collections. In section 2, we discuss in detail the field-weighted models. Section 3 further illustrates the experiment of this method on INEX 05 and Evaluation results are reported in section 4. A conclusion and further work to be undertaken are described at the end.

2   BM25F Model

In this section we describe the BM25F model in detail. We first introduce the models for document level weighting in section 2.1. And then we further discuss the implementation of the model to XML element level retrieval.

2.1   BM25F for Document Level Weighting

BM25F is the field-weighted version of BM25. It is derived from Robertson et al [11] for document level retrieval. For ad-hoc retrieval, and ignoring any repetition of terms in the query, BM25 can be simplified to [11]:

$$w_j(d,C) = \frac{(k_1 +1)tf_j}{k_1((1-b)+b\dfrac{dl}{avdl}+tf_j)} \log \frac{N - df_j + 0.5}{df_j + 0.5} \tag{1}$$

where C denotes the document collection, tf_j is the term frequency of the jth term in document d, df_j is the document frequency of term j, dl is the document length, $avdl$ is the average document length across the collection, and k_1 and b are tuning parameters.

Then the document score is obtained by term weights of terms matching the query q:

$$W(d,q,c) = \sum_j w_j(d,c) \cdot q_j \tag{2}$$

BM25F is based on a linear weighted combination of term frequencies across fields. It can be defined as follows:

$$wf_j(d,C) = \frac{(k_1' +1)tf_j'}{k_1'((1-b)+b\dfrac{dl'}{avdl'})+tf_j'} \log \frac{N - df_j + 0.5}{df_j - 0.5} \tag{3}$$

where tf'_j denotes the weighted term frequency of the jth term in d, dl' is the weighted document length, $avdl'$ is the weighted average document length across the collection, k'_1 is the weighted free parameter.

Suppose we have nF fields $f = 1, \ldots, nF$. In a given document d, term j has frequency $tf_{d,j,f}$ in field f. There are various ways of defining the length of fields or documents, but the simplest way is to use the number of indexed terms (tokens). This means that the length of the field in this document is

$$dl_f = \sum_{j \in V} tf_{d,j,f}$$

where V is the vocabulary, i.e. all indexed terms.

With no field weighting, the term frequency of t in the whole document is

$$tf_{d,j} = \sum_f tf_{d,j,f}$$
$$dl = \sum_f dl_f = \sum_f \sum_j tf_{d,j,f} = \sum_j tf_{d,j}$$

and the document length is

Average document length is

$$avdl = \frac{1}{N} \sum dl$$

With field weights W_f, these are modified as follows:

$$tf'_{d,j} = \sum_f W_f tf_{d,j,f}$$

$$dl' = \sum_f W_f dl_f = \sum_f \sum_j W_f tf_{d,j,f} = \sum_j tf'_{d,j}$$

$$avdl' = \frac{1}{N} \sum dl'$$

and

$$k'_1 = k_1 \frac{atf_{weighted}}{atf_{unweighted}} = k_1 \frac{avdl'}{avdl}$$

where atf is the average term frequency.

Function (3) is used for document weighting. However XML retrieval requires not only document level but also element level retrieval. This means an algorithm for element weighting is required. In section 2.2, we further discuss the field-weighted weighting function for element level retrieval (BM25E) derived from function (3).

2.2 Proposed Model BM25E for Element Weighting

From function (3), we can see that linear combination of weighted field frequencies is used instead of original term frequency in specified document. We hypothesize that this method could also be applied to element retrieval. Our basic view is that an element is to be treated like a document, except that it may inherit information from other elements in the document. Thus each element has (in addition to its own text, which is treated as one field) extra fields consisting of text inherited from other elements. The details of our idea are as follows:

Suppose we have nE elements $e = 1, \ldots, nE$ in given collection C. Term j has frequency $tf_{e,j}$ in element e. el_e is the element length and $avel$ is the average element length. Then we simply extend BM25 to element retrieval as follows:

$$w_j(e,d,C) = \frac{(k_1 + 1)tf_{e,j}}{k_1((1-b)+b\frac{el_e}{avel})+tf_{e,j}} \log \frac{N - df_j + 0.5}{df_j + 0.5} \qquad (4)$$

Accordingly, Function BM25E would be,

$$wf_j(e,d,C) = \frac{(k_1' + 1)tf_{e,j}'}{k_1'((1-b)+b\frac{el_e'}{avel'})+tf_{e,j}'} \log \frac{N - df_j + 0.5}{df_j + 0.5} \qquad (5)$$

where $tf_{e,j}'$ denotes the weighted term frequency of jth term in e, el_e' is the weighted element length, $avel'$ is the weighted average element length across the collection, k_1' is the weighted free parameter. Similar to those parameters in section 2.1, given an element weights W_f to element $f (f \in e)$ which contributes to a given element e's score,

$$tf_{e,j}' = \sum_f W_f tf_{f,j}$$

$$el_e' = \sum_f W_f el_f = \sum_f \sum_j W_f tf_{f,j} = \sum_{f,j} tf_{f,j}'$$

$$avel' = \frac{1}{M} \sum_e el_e'$$

and

$$k_1' = k_1 \frac{atf_{weighted}}{atf_{unweighted}} = k_1 \frac{avel'}{avel}$$

where M is the total number of element in collection C.

Equation (5) says that if we have some fields (elements) which are to contribute to the score of the element for retrieval, then we should include them by means of a linear combination of term frequencies, weighted by a set of field weights, following the method devised for BM25F. Theoretically, f could be any element in collection C. In fact, if all elements in a document d contribute to a given element in this document, then we come back to BM25F (3). If all W_f equal 1, then the weighting function is equivalent to BM25 (1).

What we need to say is that this statement does not in any way define the implementation, but merely the principle of how elements are to be treated. Detail implementation of our experiment is further discussed in section 3.

3   Experiment of BM25E on INEX 2005

In this section, the INEX collection and its structure will be introduced. We will then describe the assumptions we used for our experiments. Finally, our experiment environment and procedures are introduced.

3.1 Data Sets

There are two datasets have been used for our experiment: INEX 1.4 and INEX 1.7. Both of these two collections are from IEEE Computer Society publications.

Inex 1.4: This data set is the INEX collection for 2004 which contains 12107 arti cles of IEEE Computer Society publications from 1995 to 2002.

Inex 1.6: This data set is the INEX collection for 2005 which contains 16819 arti cles of IEEE Computer Society publications from 1995 to 2004.

More details of these collections can be found in table 1.

Table 1. Figures of INEX collections

Data sets	INEX 1.4	INEX 1.6
Size of Data(MB)	494	705
# of elements	8,239,873	11,411,135
# of attributes	2,204,688	4,669,699
# of Articles	12,107	16,819
Avg. Path Level	8	8

3.2 Data Structures

The tags shown in Table 2 are the tags used in the INEX collections, which seem to be appropriate for retrieval. Many different tags are used in the documents, but some of them are clearly presentational in nature rather than structural, and often also include very small segments of text.

Table 2. INEX selected tags and its meaning

Content Name	Tags
article title	atl
article abstract	abs
body text	bdy
section	sec, ss1, ss2, ss3
section title	st
paragraph	ilrj, ip1, ip2, ip3, ip4, ip5, item-none, p, p1, p2, p3
bibliography	bib
appendix	bm

As discussed in [11], W_f needs to be tuned for each selected field which contributes to the document's weight in BM25F. The same method should also be used for BM25E. Although in theory, every context element would contribute to given element e, in practice, there are more than about ten-million elements in each INEX collection and it is very difficult to tune every element's W_f. The problem then lies in what elements should be chosen for optimisation.

Robertson et al [11] chose title as the tuned field. In this experiment, considering the data structures of INEX, we choose **atl, abs** and **st** as the tuned elements. We believe that title and abstract in some extent reflect the content of an article, and section title in some extent tells us the section and its sub-elements' content. We believe these elements could contribute to the weight of relevant elements. This issue will be discussed in more detail in section 3.3.

3.3 Some Assumptions for BM25E on INEX 2005

Due to the costs of implementation and some other factors such as time limitations, we declare our assumptions for the experiments on the elements which should be inherited for other retrievable ones and the ways to compute $avel'$ and k'_1. They are as follows:

Assumption 1: elements in one document do not have an effect on elements in other documents. Elements except **atl, abs** and **st** also don't have an effect on other elements which are not their ancestors in the same document.

Assumption 2: Elements **atl** and **abs** contribute to the weight of elements **bdy, bm** and their child elements. Elements **st** contributes to the weight of the section it belongs to, and also of the section's child elements and article element. All **st** elements have the same W_f without considering the level they belong to.

Assumption 3: Due to the complexity of computing $avel'$ and k'_1, we substitute the article level values $avdl'$ and k'_1.

Assumption 1 is simple and easy to understand. In Assumption 2, the question may lie in that what role element **st** plays in the relevant section's other parent elements except article element. Assumption 3 is based on a guess that this replacement of parameters would not have too great an effect on the results. These issues will be tackled in further research.

3.4 Experiment Environment and Procedures

This is the first year for the CISR to take part in INEX. We largely conduct our work on Okapi in a Linux environment (using Red Hat 9). Okapi was designed as a traditional document retrieval system, and not to deal with XML data. We have therefore done significant development work for both XML indexing and element level XML retrieval in order to participate in INEX.

Our experimental procedure is as follows: firstly, we tune W_f for selected elements **atl**, **abs** and **st**; secondly, we use Okapi's Basic Search System (BSS) to get a document result set; and finally we use a newly designed XML element weighting and displaying interface to get our final submissions required by INEX, among which, selected W_f parameters are used to get optimized runs. We should also state that only **article**, **abs**, **bdy**, **bm**, **section** and **paragraph** elements are considered as potential relevant elements for our final runs in our experiment. This may lose some relevant elements, but some small irrelevant elements are filtered at the same time. In the next section, we report our evaluation result for INEX 05.

4 Evaluation

In order to examine the new data structures and algorithms building for our INEX experiments, we used INEX 04 ad-hoc topics and assessment to tune W_f for **atl**, **abs** and **st** on document level by using the average precision score (we did not evaluate using the INEX methodology at the element level). All the text of the element that is not included in {**atl**, **abs**, **st**} is given a fixed weight of 1. Our method shows that tuning W_f for these selected elements contributes to an improvement in retrieval performance on the INEX 04 collection. Trotman et al [21] used a genetic algorithm to learn parameter values for structural elements, with a range of 0 to 1. We however use a combinatorial method on a given set of parameters using a range of 1 to 3000. The tuning values for W_f are all integers in our experiment. We first tuned W_f {**atl**, **abs**, **st**} from {1, 1, 1} to {10, 10, 10} using increments of 1. Result shows that the values of {10, 3, 10} for W_f get the highest average precision score. The best tuning results were obtained when the tuning values for **atl** and **st** are both 10 and tuning values for **abs** are all between 3 to 6, we therefore investigated the tuning scope for **atl** and **st**. We then tried to tune W_f {**atl**, **abs**, **st**} from {1, 1, 1} to {50, 10, 50} in increments of 1. The results shows that a higher value for **atl** yielded better results, the best scope for **st** is from 12 to 25, while the best scope for **abs** was about the same for the first set of tuning experiments conducted. We conducted some further tuning experiments with a larger scope for **atl** and the ranges for **abs** and **st** set to between 1~10 and 10~30 respectively. In these experiments we tuned **atl** from 1 to 300 using increments of 10 and then used increments of 50 for **atl**, to a maximum value of 3000. We believed that there was no point in investigating larger values. The best average precision score was recorded when the tuned value for **atl** is around 2400. Finally, we tuned **atl** from 2100 to 2700 in increments of 1 in order to obtain the best optimized results. Our experiment shows when using the values of 2356, 4 and 22 for W_f in elements **atl**, **abs** and **st** respectively we obtained the highest performance for article

Table 3. Tuned results for INEX 04 on document level

W_f {atl, abs, st}	Avg precision
2356, 4, 22	0.143698
2416, 5, 22	0.143678
2668, 5, 25	0.143435
10, 4, 9	0.129819
1, 1, 1	0.124023

level retrieval on INEX 04 data. We are a little surprised that the best-tuned value for **atl** is so high. The implication is that the selected elements, particularly **atl** and **st** contributed much to the document level XML retrieval in the INEX collection. See table 3 for some of our tuned result for INEX 04.

Due to the time and resource limitations, we only submitted runs for CO.Thorough and CO.FetchBrowse. Based on these tuning experiments and considering the difference between document level retrieval and element level retrieval, and also being concerned that tuned W_f values for **atl** and **st** would be too high, we choose 3 sets of tuning constants of values for W_f {atl, abs, st}, namely {2356, 4, 22}, {1000, 4, 22} and {15, 4, 8}, for submitting CO.Thorough runs; and chose another 3 sets of tuning constants of values for W_f {atl, abs, st}, namely {1000, 4, 22}, {300, 4, 18} and {98, 4, 13}, for submitting CO.FetchBrowse runs.

Though we tuned W_f in document level, we are still pleased to see that our official runs for CO.Thorough rank at the top of the total 55 official runs, especially for "Metric: nxCG(25), Quantization: strict, Overlap=off", our 3 runs ranks 1st, 2nd and 36th respectively; for "Metric: nxCG(50), Quantization: strict, Overlap=off", our 3 runs ranks 1st, 2nd and 16th respectively; and for "Metric: ep-gr, Quantization: strict,Overlap=off", our 3 runs ranks 7th, 12th and 27th respectively. Fig. 1 and Fig. 2 show our official result for strict CO.Thorough metrics. We also tried to use metric nxCG to compare our 3 official runs for CO.Thorough with the non field-weighted run whose W_f\{ atl, abs, st } is {0, 0, 0}(As we've mentioned above, all the text of the element that is not included in {atl,abs,st} is given a fixed weight of 1. The values {0,0,0} here just mean these 3 chosen fields have no effect on other elements except their ancestors and themselves. For their ancestors and themselves, non weighted tf are still considered). Result shows that the non field-weighted run ranks last while the former two runs rank top.

The experiment shows that the first two sets of tuning constants, W_f {1000, 4, 22} and W_f {2356, 4, 22}, ranks better than the third groups W_f (15, 4, 8). The evidence is that **atl** and **st** does contribute to retrieval performance and it also implies that combining field-weighted term frequencies of selected elements is a beneficial method. Tuning constant set W_f\{1000, 4, 22} rank first for Metric "nxCG(25 and 50), Quantization: strict, Overlap=off" also suggests that it may be better if W_f is tuned on element level. This behavior may also be caused by the difference of the topics and data sets between INEX 2004 and INEX 2005. It is worth doing a further set of tuning experiments on the INEX 2005 topics and data sets.

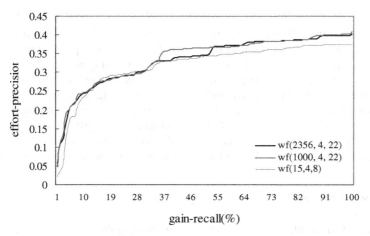

Fig. 1. Metric nxCG, Quantization: strict,Overlap=off

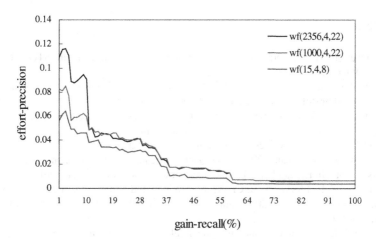

Fig. 2. Metric ep-gr, Quantization: strict,Overlap=off

Results also show that our method performs better for models which consider only fully specific and highly exhaustive components than those models which considering varying levels of relevant components. The reason may be because the selection of elements we chose to submit for our experiments. We intend to investigate this issue further.

5 Conclusion

We extend document level field-weighted retrieval function BM25F to element level retrieval function BM25E. We have applied this method to INEX 2005 CO XML retrieval and results show that our method is beneficial.

However there are still some limitations in our element level retrieval function. Firstly, values for *avdl'* and k'_1 are used at the article level, not element level. The creation of a practical algorithm to generate values for tuning parameters at the element level is a challenging task. Secondly, parameter tuning is undertaken at document level by using average precision method, not on element level by using INEX official metrics. It should be noted that the element **st** has the same weight at different levels, and further experiments need to be undertaken to investigate this problem. Thirdly, we only submit runs for CO.Thorough and CO.FetchBrowse tasks, so more tasks need to be done to test our method. And also our system for XML element retrieval needs to be upgraded. We will investigate these problems in further research.

Acknowledgements

Thanks to China Scholarship Council (CSC) for funding the visit of the first author to City University, London in order to conduct this research.

References

[1] A. Deutsch, M. Fernandez, D. Suciu. Storing semistructured data with STORED. In Proc. SIGMOD, 1999.
[2] J. Harding, Q. Li, B. Moon. XISS/R: XML Indexing and Storage System Using RDBMS. In Proceedings of the 29th VLDB Conference, 2003
[3] Software AG. Tamino XML database. http://www.softwareag.com/tamino/.
[4] XYZFind. XML Database. http://www.xyzfind.com.
[5] HYREX. http://ls6-www.cs.uni-dortmund.de/ir/projects/hyrex/.
[6] N. Fuhr, K. Großjohann. XIRQL: A Query Language for Information Retrieval in XML Documents. In Research and Development in Information Retrieval, 2001.
[7] J. E. Wolff, H. Florke, A. B. Cremers. Searching and Browsing Collections of Structural Information. In Proc. IEEE Forum on Research and Technology Advances in Digital Libraries, 2000.
[8] T. Schlieder, H. Meuss. Querying and Ranking XML Documents. Special Topic Issue Journal American Society for Informations Systems on XML and Information Retrieval, 2002.
[9] T. Schlieder. Similarity Search in XML Data using Cost-Based Query Transformations. In Proc. 4th Intern. Workshop on the Web and Databases, 2001.
[10] A. Theobald, G. Weikum. The Index-Based XXL Search Engine for Querying XML Data with Relevance Ranking. In Proc. 8th Internation Conf. on Extending Database Technology, 2002.
[11] S. Robertson, H. Zaragoza, M. Taylor. Simple BM25 Extension to Multiple Weighted Fields. CIKM'04, 2004.
[12] R. Wilkinson. Effective retrieval of structured documents. In Research and Development in Information Retrieval, 1994.
[13] P. Ogilvie, J. Callan. Combining document representations for known item search. In Proceedings of the 26th Annual International ACM SIGIR Conference on Research and Development in Information Retrieval (SIGIR 2003), 2003.

[14] W. Kraaij, T. Westerveld, D. Hiemstra. The importance of prior probabilities for entry page search. In Proceedings of the 25th Annual International ACM SIGIR Conference on Research and Development in Information Retrieval, 2002.

[15] S.Myaeng, D. Jang, M. Kim, Z. Zhoo. A flexible model for retrieval of SGML documents. In Proceedings of the 21st Annual International ACM SIGIR Conference on Research and Development in Information Retrieval,1998.

[16] L. A. Clarke, L. Tilker. MultiText Experiments for INEX 2004. INEX 2004 Proceedings, 2004.

[17] J. Vittaut, B. Piwowarski, Patrick Gallinari. An algebra for Structured Queries in Bayesian Networks. In INEX 2004 Workshop Proceedings, 2004.

[18] J. Kekäläinen, M. Junkkari, P. Arvola. TRIX 2004 – struggling with the overlap. In INEX 2004 Workshop Proceedings, 2004.

[19] R. Larson. Cheshire II at INEX '04: Fusion and Feedback for the Adhoc and Heterogeneous Tracks. In INEX 2004 Workshop Proceedings, 2004.

[20] P. Ogilvie, J. Callan. Hierarchical Language Models for XML Component Retrieval. In INEX 2004 Workshop Proceedings, 2004.

[21] A. Trotman. Choosing document structure weights. Information Processing & Management, 41(2), 243-264.

XML Retrieval Based on Direct Contribution of Query Components

Gilles Hubert

IRIT/SIG-EVI, 118 route de Narbonne, F-31062 Toulouse cedex 9
hubert@irit.fr

Abstract. This paper describes the retrieval approach proposed by the SIG/EVI group of the IRIT research centre at INEX'2005. This XML approach is based on direct contribution of the components constituting an information need. This paper focuses on the method evolutions since previous participation to INEX. It describes the official experiments done for each subtasks with the corresponding results and additional unofficial experiments.

1 Introduction

Due to the growing use of XML (eXtensible Markup Language) to describe documents, a growing number of systems intend to provide solutions to retrieve relevant components among XML documents. These systems are mostly evolutions of either database systems [3] or Information Retrieval (IR) systems. Among IR-based systems two main categories of proposals can be distinguished: systems based on a probabilistic model [7][12] and systems based on the vector space model [2][5]. XML retrieval needs to take into account both content and structural aspects.

In this context of various proposals, a framework such as INEX is useful. On one hand, it offers testbeds and evaluation methods that allow comparing different systems according to common criteria. On the other hand, it allows participants to try to estimate a global effectiveness of their system and to determine the contexts adapted to their system.

Among the systems that participated to INEX previous year and that obtained globally good results there are approaches based on the vector space model [8] or close principles [4][6], probabilistic methods [1][13][10][11] and database systems [9]. [8] presents an approach based on the vector space model using multiple indexes, using a document ranking method with document pivot normalization and including a possible automatic query refinement. [4] proposes an approach using inverted lists for terms stored in a database and based on different scoring formulas for leaf elements and branch elements. Our method [6] is based on direct contribution of query components. The main principles of the method are recalled in this paper. This method obtained better results for CAS (Content and Structure) topics. [1] experimented a method based on the Okapi BM25 measure only on the CO (Content Only) topics. [11] uses a multinomial language model with smoothing and associated to documents

N. Fuhr et al. (Eds.): INEX 2005, LNCS 3977, pp. 172–186, 2006.

indexes at different levels (article, element). [10] proposes a hierarchical language model to represent XML documents as trees and where a model is estimated for each XML component using linear interpolation of the component content, its children's models and its parent model. The approach proposed in [13] represents hierarchies of documents as bayesian networks and computes recursively scores from network root to leaves. [9] describes an extended version of the TIJAH system that follows a three-level database architecture and that has been extended to handle phrase modelling and to support structural relevance feedback.

In this paper, we present an IR method using principles close to approaches based on the vector space model. However, this approach is based on direct contribution of each component of the query and particularly on the presence of each term constituting the query. The paper focuses on the method evolutions done since the previous participation to INEX last year.

In the remainder of this paper a short presentation of the main ideas on which relies the retrieval method is done in Section 2. Section 3 presents how contributions of query components are mapped into scoring principles. Section 4 details the submitted runs and the obtained results. Finally, an analysis of the experiments and an introduction of future works that ensue from it are given in Section 5.

2 Participation Objectives

Participating to INEX this year has multiple objectives:
- a first interest was to evaluate the benefit of evolutions brought to the method since last participation. Evolutions intervene in the definition of the function computing the score of an XML element and the score propagation principle through the hierarchical structure of a document,
- in addition, different new subtasks corresponding to different retrieval strategies that could interest a user have been defined in INEX 2005. The experiments carried out in this context can help us to determine the strategies for which our method seems to be a possible response,
- finally, it was interesting to estimate the influence of changes introduced in the INEX 2005 framework regarding metrics and the assessment process.

3 Method Principles

The IR method described in this paper is based on principles close to approaches based on the vector space model. Document and query representations are comparable to vectors. However, the correspondence between documents and query is not estimated using a "classical" similarity measure. The method presented is based on direct contribution of each query term appearing in an XML element. The contribution can be modulated according to other components of the query such as structural constraints. A principle of score propagation completes the method with regard to the hierarchical structure of XML documents.

3.1 Representation of INEX Elements

From the document point of view, documents are represented as sets of n-tuples (XPath, term, occ) where XPath is the location of the node containing the term from the root of an XML document and occ is the number of occurrences of the term in the textual content of the node. For each XML component, concepts are extracted automatically. Concept extraction involves notably stop word removal and optionally other processes such as stemming using for example the Porter's algorithm. For INEX 2005 experiments all XML tags have been taken into account.

Example of index representation of documents:

```
...
an/1995/a1006/article[1]/bdy[1]/sec[2]/ss1[6]/p[3]   call         1
an/1995/a1006/article[1]/bdy[1]/sec[3]/p[8]          conference   1
an/1995/a1006/article[1]/bdy[1]/sec[3]/p[8]          papers       1
an/1995/a1006/article[1]/bdy[1]/sec[4]/p[10]         workshop     1
an/1995/a1006/article[1]/bdy[1]/sec[4]/p[11]         call         1
...
```

From the topic point of view, according to the INEX 2005 requirements, we used only the title part for CO topics and castitle part for CO+S and CAS topics. However our method can use the other parts constituting CO and CAS topics. For both topic types, stop words are removed and optionally terms can be stemmed. Topics are represented as pairs (target contraint, set of content indications). A content indication is a triplet (term, occurrences, preference, location constraint). Target constraints and location constraints can be restrictive XPaths for CAS and CO+S topics or wildcards (i.e. matching all elements) notably for CO topics.

Example of index representation of topics:

```
...
papers        1      0      .
workshop      1      0      .
conference    1      0      .
...
```

3.2 Scoring Function

The scoring function is defined as a combination of three values. The scoring function can be globally defined as follows:

$$Score(T, E) = \left(\sum_{\forall t \in T} f(t, E) \cdot g(t, T) \right) \cdot p(T, E)$$

where

> T is the topic
>
> t is a term representing the topic T
>
> E is an XML element
>
> $f(t,E)$ This factor measures the importance of the term t in the XML element E.
>
> $g(t,E)$ This factor measures the importance of the term t in the topic representation T.
>
> $p(T,E)$ This factor measures the global presence of the topic T in the XML element E.

On one hand, the function is defined as an addition of contributions of the concepts constituting a query. This principle allows giving relevance to elements dealing about either only one concept or several concepts. The addition tends to promote elements containing several concepts. However, depending on the different chosen functions an element dealing strongly about one concept can be evaluated higher than an element dealing lightly about many concepts.

On the other hand, the function estimates globally the relevancy of an element according to a query.

The function f that measures the importance of a term in an XML element is based on the number of occurrences of the term in the element or on the relative presence of the term regarding all the occurrences of query terms appearing in the element. This function can be defined as follows:

$$f(t,E) = \frac{Occ(t,E)}{Occ(T,E)^{\alpha}}$$

where

> t is a term representing the topic T
>
> E is an XML element
>
> $\alpha \in (0,1)$
>
> $Occ(t,E)$ Number of occurrences of the term t in the element E.
>
> $Occ(T,E)$ Total number of occurrences of all the query terms in the element E

The function g that measures the importance of a term in a topic representation is based on the frequency of the term in the topic. The frequency can be moderated by the number of XML elements containing the term. The function can also use the rank of the term according to the number of elements containing this term and regarding the numbers of elements containing the other query terms.

This function is defined as follows:

$$g(t,T) = \frac{Occ(t,T)}{Size(T)} \cdot \frac{IndRnk(t)^2}{NbElts(t)}$$

where

$Occ(t,T)$ Number of occurrences of the term t in the topic T.

Size(T)   Size of the topic T i.e. total of occurrences of all the terms representing T.

NbElts(t)   Number of elements containing the term t

IndRnk(t)   Rank of the term t according to the number of elements containing each term of the topic.

This function increases the contributions of terms appearing in few XML elements through the factor NbElts(t) and IndRnk(t).

The function p that measures the global presence of a topic in an XML element is based on the number of terms describing the topic and that appear in the element. This function is defined as follows:

$$p(T,E) = \varphi^{\left(\frac{NbT(T,E)}{NbT(T)}\right)}$$

where

T is the topic

E is an XML element

φ is a real, $\varphi \geq 0.0$

NbT(T,E)   Number of terms describing the topic T and that appear in the XML element E.

NbT(T)   Number of terms describing the topic T.

When φ is set to 1.0 the function p has no effect on the final score. The value of φ determines the influence of the function g on the final score. The influence increases with the value of φ. Using a function power intends to clearly distinguish the elements containing a lot of terms describing the topic and the elements containing few terms of the topic.

Additional notions complete the scoring function: the notion of coverage and prefix coefficients. The coverage is a threshold corresponding to the percentage minimum of topic terms that have to appear in an element to select it. It aims at ensure that only documents in which the topic is represented enough will be selected for this topic. Prefix coefficients intend to increase or reduce term contributions according to sign '+' and '-' associated to terms in the query. These notions and their integration in the scoring function are detailed in [6].

3.3 Score Propagation According to XML Structure

The hierarchical structure of XML has to be taken into account. The hypothesis on which is based our method is that an element containing a component selected as relevant is also relevant. Our approach takes into account this hypothesis propagating the score of an element to the elements it composes. The score propagated to the composed elements is decreased applying a reducing factor. The propagation principle is the following:

$$\forall\, E_a \text{ ancestor of } E \quad and \quad d(E_a, E)\cdot\alpha < 1$$

$$Score(E_a,T) = Score(E_a,T)+(1-2\cdot\lambda\cdot\left(\frac{d(E_a,E)}{d(E_a,E)+d(E_R,E)}\right)^2)\cdot Score(E,T)$$

where

λ is a constant coefficient real ≥ 0.0 and E, E_a, E_R are XML elements

$d(E_a,E)$ is the distance between E_a and E in the XPath associated to E (e.g. in the XPath /article/bdy/s/ss1/p the distance between p and bdy is equal to 3 i.e. d(bdy,p)=3)

$d(E_R,E)$ is the distance between the root E_R and E in the XPath associated to E

This process tends to consider an element having a relevant descendant less relevant than its descendant element. However, an ancestor having several relevant descendants can obtain a score greater than one of its descendants. Using the above function, the score propagated to near ascendants is slightly reduced while it is more strongly reduced for the distant ascendants. The coefficient λ allows varying the score contribution of an element in its ancestors. When $\lambda=0.0$ the score of an element is totally propagated towards its ancestors.

The following figure illustrates the score propagation principle with $\lambda=0.5$:

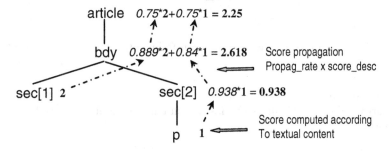

Fig. 1. Score propagation principle

3.4 Structural Constraints

Two types of structural constraints can be used to define to INEX CAS topics:
- constraints on content that is to say XPath of elements which are expected to contain searched concepts (e.g. about(.//p,'+XML +"information retrieval"),
- constraints on the granularity of elements expected as result (e.g //article[....]).

Structural constraints on content are taken into account adding a coefficient varying the contribution given by a query term. If the XML element does not verify the constraint associated to the term, the contribution given by the term is reduced. The coefficient intervenes in the function f that measures the importance of a term in an XML element (cf section 3.2) as follows:

$$f(t,E) = \beta \cdot \frac{Occ(t,E)}{Occ(T,E)^{\alpha}}$$

where

if E does not verify the structural constraint defined on t   then $0.0 < \beta < 1.0$

else $\beta = 1.0$

This principle constitutes a first solution. However, only XML elements with textual content that verify the constraints on content are affected and by propagation the elements containing them. This could be a limitation to fully respond to CAS tasks with strict verification of content constraints notably the task SSCAS. This principle should be extended to take into account XML elements without textual content and that verify the constraints on content but composed of components containing query terms and not verifying the associated constraints.

In addition, structural constraints on the granularity of elements expected as result are handled adding a coefficient varying the global score computed for an XML element according to content. If the XML element does not verify the constraint on result granularity associated to the query, the score computed is reduced. The coefficient intervenes in the scoring function as follows:

$$Score(T,E) = \gamma \cdot \left(\sum_{\forall t \in T} f(t,E) \cdot g(t,T) \right) \cdot p(T,E)$$

where

if E does not verify the structural constraint defined on T then $0.0 \leq \gamma < 1.0$

else $\gamma = 1.0$

This solution allows attaching variable importance to structural constraints on result granularity. When $\gamma = 0.0$ the structural constraints on result are strictly taken into account.

4 Experiments

At least one run based on our XML retrieval method was submitted to INEX 2005 for each subtask. For the subtasks, CO.Thorough, CO.FetchBrowse, COS.Focussed two runs were submitted.

Our experiments aim at evaluating the effectiveness of the evolution given to the scoring function, the adaptation of the method regarding the different tasks (Thorough, Focussed, Fetch and Browse, SSCAS, VVCAS, ...), the new metrics and the evolution of assessment process.

4.1 Experiment Setup

One run for all the subtasks except the subtasks Focussed uses the following scoring function:

$$Score(T,E) = \left(\sum_{\forall t \in T} Occ(t,E) \cdot \frac{Occ(t,T)}{Size(T)} \cdot \frac{IndRnk(t)^2}{NbElts(t)} \right) \cdot 400^{\left(\frac{NbT(T,E)}{NbT(T)} \right)}$$

The runs based on this function are named using the following principle: V2005T<subtask_name> e.g. V2005TCO.Thorough.

Additional runs for the subtasks CO.Thorough, CO.FetchBrowse and COS.Focussed use a scoring function with a function f that measures the importance of a term in an XML element slightly different i.e.:

$$Score(T,E) = \left(\sum_{\forall t \in T} \frac{Occ(t,E)}{Occ(T,E)} \cdot \frac{Occ(t,T)}{Size(T)} \cdot \frac{IndRnk(t)^2}{NbElts(t)} \right) \cdot 400^{\left(\frac{NbT(T,E)}{NbT(T)} \right)}$$

The runs based on this function are named using the following principle: V2005Tf<subtask_name> e.g. V2005TfCO.Thorough.

For all submitted runs the parameters of the scoring method were the same. The coefficient used to propagate a component score through the hierarchical structure of the XML document was fixed to 0.1. The coverage threshold was fixed to 35% (i.e. more than a third of terms describing the topic must appear in the text to keep the XML component). The coefficients applied to take into account the signs '+' and '-' were fixed to respectively +5.0 or -5.0 to increase or reduce 5 times the contribution of wanted respectively unwanted terms.

The values of the parameters are those which gave the best results during a training phase done with INEX 2003 and INEX 2004 CO topics using the INEX 2004 official metrics.

4.1.1 Subtasks Focussed
The runs submitted for the subtasks Focussed use scoring functions without function p effect ($\varphi=1.0$) i.e. without factor measuring the global presence of the topic in the XML element, as follows:

$$Score(T,E) = \sum_{\forall t \in T} f(t,E) \cdot g(t,T)$$

No propagation of score is done to have result without overlapping as requested for the subtask Focussed.

4.1.2 Subtasks CO+S and CAS

For all the subtasks CO+S and CAS the castitle part of topic definition has been used to define queries.

The coefficient taking into account structural constraints on content was fixed to 0.5 (i.e. the contribution of a query term is divided by 2 when the element does not verify the structural constraint associated to the term) for all the subtasks. Since the actual solution implemented in our method cannot fully take into account the structural constraints, we decided to handle them as vague even for XSCAS subtasks.

The coefficient taking into account structural constraints on result granularity was fixed to:

- 0.5 (i.e. the scores of elements not verifying the structural predicates are divided by 2) when expecting vague verification of the constraints i.e. VVCAS and VSCAS,

- 0.0 (i.e. the scores of elements not verifying the structural predicates are reset to zero) when expecting strict verification of the constraints i.e. SSCAS and SVCAS,

The value 0.5 of the two coefficients was fixed arbitrarily.

4.2 Official Results

Results of the runs for CO subtasks are detailed in the following tables. Only the results of the run that obtained the best results for each subtask are presented.

Table 1. Best results for the CO subtask Focussed

	Run	V2005TCO.Focussed					
	Quantisation	strict		generalised		generalisedLifted	
	overlap=on	precision	rank	precision	rank	precision	rank
Metric	nxCG@10	0.1266	5/44	0.1848	19/44	0.2217	17/44
	nxCG@25	0.0997	8/44	0.1735	17/44	0.1991	15/44
	nxCG@50	0.1176	9/44	0.1566	21/44	0.1761	18/44
	ep/gr (MAP)	0.0332	10/44	0.0477	24/44	0.0650	20/44

Table 2. Best results for the CO subtask Thorough

	Run	V2005TCO.Thorough					
	Quantisation	strict		generalised		generalisedLifted	
	overlap=off	precision	rank	precision	rank	precision	rank
Metric	nxCG@10	0.0231	35/55	0.1927	30/55	0.2044	34/55
	nxCG@25	0.0606	24/55	0.206	24/55	0.2124	32/55
	nxCG@50	0.1298	3/55	0.1893	29/55	0.1887	35/55
	ep/gr (MAP)	0.0129	31/55	0.0490	29/55	0.0244	31/55

Table 3. Best results for the CO subtask Fetch and Browse

	Run	V2005TfCO.FetchBrowse					
	Quantisation	strict		generalised		generalisedLifted	
Metric	overlap=on	MAP	rank	MAP	rank	MAP	rank
	ep/gr {element}	0.0077	22/40	0.0724	16/40	0.0632	18/40
	ep/gr {article}	0.1298	27/42	0.0900	28/42	0.1044	28/42
	overlap=off	MAP	rank	MAP	rank	MAP	rank
	ep/gr {element}	0.0139	12/40	0.0541	11/40	0.0362	11/40
	ep/gr {article}	0.1317	28/42	0.1295	29/42	0.1351	28/42

Table 4. Best results for the CO+S subtask Focussed

	Run	V2005TfCOS.Focussed					
	Quantisation	strict		generalised		generalisedLifted	
Metric	overlap=on	precision	rank	precision	rank	precision	rank
	nxCG@10	0.0378	13/27	0.1087	21/27	0.1275	19/27
	nxCG@25	0.0562	11/27	0.1174	19/27	0.1323	18/27
	nxCG@50	0.0521	14/27	0.1204	18/27	0.1313	15/27
	ep/gr (MAP)	0.0145	11/27	0.0516	16/27	0.0635	15/27

Table 5. Best results for the CO+S subtask Thorough

	Run	V2005TCOS.Thorough					
	Quantisation	strict		generalised		generalisedLifted	
Metric	overlap=off	precision	rank	precision	rank	precision	rank
	nxCG@10	0.0059	24/33	0.1997	23/33	0.2024	23/33
	nxCG@25	0.0089	25/33	0.1492	23/33	0.1538	23/33
	nxCG@50	0.0083	28/33	0.1294	22/33	0.1313	22/33
	ep/gr (MAP)	0.0049	23/33	0.0417	17/33	0.0271	19/33

Table 6. Best results for the CO+S subtask Fetch and Browse

	Run	V2005TCOS.FetchBrowse					
	Quantisation	strict		generalised		generalisedLifted	
Metric	overlap=on	MAP	rank	MAP	rank	MAP	rank
	ep/gr {element}	0.0034	12/25	0.0472	16/25	0.04342	15/25
	ep/gr {article}	0.1364	14/25	0.1068	15/25	0.1194	15/25
	overlap=off	MAP	rank	MAP	rank	MAP	rank
	ep/gr {element}	0.0081	9/25	0.0401	9/25	0.0292	9/25
	ep/gr {article}	0.1364	14/25	0.1265	15/25	0.1305	15/25

Our method seems to be globally more efficient for the subtasks Focussed than for the subtasks Thorough notably for strict quantisation. For the CO.Focussed subtask, nxCG metric and strict quantisation, the results are better for ranking up to 100. For the Thorough subtasks the results are on average slightly better for generalised quantisation than for strict quantisation.

For the Fetch and Browse subtasks results show better effectiveness at the element level than at the article level. Results are slightly better for generalised quantisations than for strict quantisation except for CO+S topics.

The difference of effectiveness regarding quantisations (strict vs generalised) between FetchBrowse and Thorough subtasks on one hand and Focussed subtasks on the other hand can be related to the use of a different configuration of the method for Focussed subtasks.

For CAS topics, results of the runs are detailed in the following tables:

Table 7. Results for the CAS subtask SSCAS

	Run	V2005TSSCAS					
	Quantisation	strict		generalised		generalisedLifted	
	overlap=off	precision	rank	precision	rank	precision	rank
Metric	nxCG@10	0.1250	11/25	0.3643	4/25	0.3719	4/25
	nxCG@25	0.1500	13/25	0.4816	1/25	0.4936	1/25
	nxCG@50	0.4078	2/25	0.5192	1/25	0.5233	1/25
	ep/gr (MAP)	0.0504	18/25	0.1219	13/25	0.1013	14/25

Table 8. Results for the CAS subtask SVCAS

	Run	V2005TSVCAS					
	Quantisation	strict		generalised		generalisedLifted	
	overlap=off	precision	rank	precision	rank	precision	rank
Metric	nxCG@10	0.1800	4/23	0.3240	2/23	0.3259	2/23
	nxCG@25	0.2400	7/23	0.3357	3/23	0.3420	1/23
	nxCG@50	0.4422	3/23	0.3799	1/23	0.3788	1/23
	ep/gr (MAP)	0.0938	4/23	0.1233	3/23	0.1107	4/23

Table 9. Results for the CAS subtask VSCAS

	Run	V2005TVSCAS					
	Quantisation	strict		generalised		generalisedLifted	
	overlap=off	precision	rank	precision	rank	precision	rank
Metric	nxCG@10	0.0333	17/23	0.2427	9/23	0.2460	10/23
	nxCG@25	0.0600	12/23	0.2435	9/23	0.2440	10/23
	nxCG@50	0.0567	13/23	0.2436	9/23	0.2392	10/23
	ep/gr (MAP)	0.0287	12/23	0.0908	5/23	0.0191	12/23

Table 10. Results for the CAS subtask VVCAS

	Run	V2005TVVCAS					
	Quantisation	strict		generalised		generalisedLifted	
	overlap=off	precision	rank	precision	rank	precision	rank
Metric	nxCG@10	0.1000	12/28	0.2480	14/28	0.2500	16/23
	nxCG@25	0.1267	11/28	0.2544	9/28	0.2581	14/23
	nxCG@50	0.1162	10/28	0.2373	9/28	0.2408	13/23
	ep/gr (MAP)	0.0379	10/28	0.0804	7/28	0.0176	15/23

The results for CAS subtasks are globally good particularly for generalised quantisation. Considering that CAS runs are based on the same scoring function than Thorough and FetchBrowse runs for CO topics it is not surprising to have the same behaviour regarding the quantisations (i.e. better for generalised quantisation). The results are globally better for subtask not verifying strictly structural constraints on content (i.e. SVCAS and VVCAS). This can be related to the fact that our method cannot fully handle constraints on content at the moment.

4.3 Additional Results

Our official experiments were not performed on the last version of the INEX collection. This could have penalised our official evaluations. To verify this possibility, new unofficial experiments have been done using the last version of the collection with the

Table 11. Results of additional run for the CO subtask Focussed

	Run	unofficialV2005TCO.Focussed					
	Quantisation	strict		generalised		generalisedLifted	
	overlap=on	precision	rank	precision	rank	precision	rank
Metric	nxCG@10	0.1115 *(-12%)*	7/44 *(-2)*	0.1791 *(+3%)*	19/44 *(.)*	0.2253 *(+2%)*	17/44 *(.)*
	nxCG@25	0.1136 *(+14%)*	6/44 *(+2)*	0.1838 *(+6%)*	15/44 *(+2)*	0.2200 *(+10%)*	10/44 *(+5)*
	nxCG@50	0.1136 *(-3%)*	12/44 *(-3)*	0.1702 *(+9%)*	16/44 *(+5)*	0.1982 *(+13%)*	11/44 *(+7)*
	ep/gr (MAP)	0.0399 *(+20%)*	9/44 *(+1)*	0.0616 *(+29%)*	20/44 *(+4)*	0.0841 *(+29%)*	13/44 *(+7)*

Table 12. Results of additional run for the CO subtask Thorough

	Run	unofficialV2005TCO.Thorough					
	Quantisation	strict		generalised		generalisedLifted	
	overlap=on	precision	rank	precision	rank	precision	rank
Metric	nxCG@10	0.0346 *(+50%)*	25/55 *(-2)*	0.2064 *(+7%)*	26/55 *(+4)*	0.2196 *(+6%)*	28/55 *(+6)*
	nxCG@25	0.0425 *(-30%)*	29/55 *(+2)*	0.1980 *(-4%)*	27/55 *(-3)*	0.2092 *(-2%)*	36/55 *(-4)*
	nxCG@50	0.1391 *(+7%)*	3/55 *(-3)*	0.1889 *(-0%)*	29/55 *(.)*	0.1893 *(-0%)*	35/55 *(.)*
	ep/gr (MAP)	0.0168 *(+30%)*	28/55 *(+1)*	0.0566 *(+16%)*	24/55 *(+5)*	0.0288 *(+18%)*	28/55 *(+3)*

Table 13. Results of additional run for the CAS subtask SSCAS

	Run	unofficialV2005TSSCAS					
	Quantisation	strict		generalised		generalisedLifted	
	overlap=on	precision	rank	precision	rank	precision	rank
Metric	nxCG@10	0.1500 *(+20%)*	9/25 *(+2)*	0.3942 *(+8%)*	4/28 *(+7)*	0.4157 *(+12%)*	3/25 *(+1)*
	nxCG@25	0.1778 *(+19%)*	11/25 *(+2)*	0.4821 *(+0%)*	1/28 *(+3)*	0.4936 *(+0%)*	1/25 *(.)*
	nxCG@50	0.2056 *(-50%)*	11/25 *(-9)*	0.5152 *(-1%)*	1/28 *(+2)*	0.5269 *(+1%)*	1/25 *(.)*
	ep/gr (MAP)	0.0648 *(+29%)*	14/25 *(+4)*	0.1289 *(+5%)*	12/28 *(+2)*	0.1096 *(+8%)*	14/25 *(.)*

Table 14. Results of additional run for the CAS subtask VSCAS

	Run	unofficialV2005TVSCAS					
	Quantisation	strict		generalised		generalisedLifted	
	overlap=on	precision	rank	precision	rank	precision	rank
Metric	nxCG@10	0.1000 *(+200%)*	7/23 *(+5)*	0.2862 *(+18%)*	7/23 *(+2)*	0.3046 *(+24%)*	8/23 *(+2)*
	nxCG@25	0.0600 *(+0%)*	12/23 *(.)*	0.2712 *(+11%)*	6/23 *(+3)*	0.2803 *(+15%)*	8/23 *(+2)*
	nxCG@50	0.0700 *(+23%)*	13/23 *(+1)*	0.2730 *(+12%)*	4/23 *(+5)*	0.2689 *(+12%)*	6/23 *(+4)*
	ep/gr (MAP)	0.0386 *(+34%)*	7/23 *(+7)*	0.1057 *(+16%)*	5/23 *(.)*	0.0247 *(+29%)*	8/23 *(+4)*

Table 15. Results of additional run for the CAS subtask VVCAS

	Run	unofficialV2005TVVCAS					
	Quantisation	strict		generalised		generalisedLifted	
	overlap=on	precision	rank	precision	rank	precision	rank
Metric	nxCG@10	0.1444 *(+44%)*	7/28 *(+5)*	0.2921 *(+18%)*	7/28 *(+7)*	0.3047 *(+22%)*	11/28 *(+5)*
	nxCG@25	0.1267 *(+0%)*	11/28 *(.)*	0.2751 *(+8%)*	6/28 *(+3)*	0.2820 *(+9%)*	6/28 *(+8)*
	nxCG@50	0.1228 *(+6%)*	9/28 *(+1)*	0.2587 *(+9%)*	7/28 *(+2)*	0.2651 *(+10%)*	8/28 *(+5)*
	ep/gr (MAP)	0.0597 *(+58%)*	3/28 *(+7)*	0.0962 *(+20%)*	5/28 *(+2)*	0.0230 *(+31%)*	12/28 *(+3)*

same configurations of the method used for our official runs. These experiments have shown improvements of the results notably regarding the metric ep/gr.

For example, the following tables show modified results for the new unofficial results (and the difference with the corresponding official results) with the best improvements for CO subtasks and for CAS subtasks:

5 Discussion and Future Works

A first analysis of the experiments performed and the obtained results shows that:

- the chosen functions and parameters for the scoring method seem to be globally adapted to the actual INEX framework. However, the results obtained for the subtasks Thorough show that our method handle overlap not well enough to fully respond to this kind of search. A future work will consist in evolving the method to integrate overlap handling according to different strategies.

- the solutions used to extend our method to handle structural constraints seem to be adequate. However, structural constraints on content are not fully handled by our method at present. To complete the method to handle structural constraints completely is another next step.
- other experiments have to be done to determine the method configurations adapted to each subtask. Furthermore, analyses must be carried out to determine queries processed well by our method and those leading to weaker results. This would enable to evolve the method to better respond to this last type of queries.

Acknowledgments

Research outlined in this paper is part of the project WS-Talk "WS-Talk: Web services communicating in the language of their user community" that is supported by the Sixth Framework Programme of the European Community (2002-2006), COOP-CT-2004 006026.

References

[1] Clarke C. L. A., Tilker P. L., MultiText Experiments for INEX 2004, Advances in XML Information Retrieval, LNCS 3493, 3rd International Workshop INEX, 2004, p. 85 – 87.

[2] Crouch C. J., Apte S., Bapat H., An Approach to Structured Retrieval Based on the Extended Vector Model, Proceedings of the 2nd INEX Workshop, Dagstuhl, Germany, 2003, p. 89-93.

[3] Fuhr N., Großjohann K., XIRQL: An XML query language based on information retrieval concepts. ACM Transactions on Information Systems (TOIS), vol. 22, Issue 2, 2004, p. 313-356.

[4] Geva S., GPX – Gardens Point XML Information Retrieval at INEX 2004, Advances in XML Information Retrieval, LNCS 3493, 3rd International Workshop INEX, 2004, p. 211 – 223.

[5] Grabs T., H.-J. Schek H.-J., Generating Vector Spaces On-the-fly for Flexible XML Retrieval, ACM SIGIR Workshop on XML and Information Retrieval, Tampere, 2002, p. 4-13.

[6] Hubert G., A voting method for XML retrieval, Advances in XML Information Retrieval, LNCS 3493, 3rd International Workshop INEX, 2004, p. 183-195.

[7] Larson R. R., Cheshire II at INEX'03: Component and Algorithm Fusion for XML Retrieval, Proceedings of the 2nd INEX Workshop, Dagstuhl, Germany, 2003, p. 38-45.

[8] Mass Y., Mandelbrod M., Component Ranking and Automatic Query Refinement for XML Retrieval, Advances in XML Information Retrieval, LNCS 3493, 3rd International Workshop INEX, 2004, p. 73 – 84.

[9] Mihajlović V., Ramírez G., de Vries A. P., Hiemstra D., Blok H. E., TIJAH at INEX 2004 Modeling Phrases and Relevance Feedback, Advances in XML Information Retrieval, LNCS 3493, 3rd International Workshop INEX, 2004, p. 276 – 291.

[10] Ogilvie P., Callan J., Hierarchical Language Models for XML Component Retrieval, Advances in XML Information Retrieval, LNCS 3493, 3rd International Workshop INEX, 2004, p. 224 – 237.

[11] Sigurbjörnsson B., Kamps J., de Rijke M., Mixture Models, Overlap, and Structural Hints in XML Element Retrieval, Advances in XML Information Retrieval, LNCS 3493, 3rd International Workshop INEX, 2004, p. 196-210.

[12] Trotman, A., O'Keefe, R. A.: Identifying and Ranking Relevant Document Elements, Proceedings of the 2nd INEX Workshop, Dagstuhl, Germany, 2003, 149-154.

[13] Vittaut J.-N., Piwowarski B., Gallinari P., An Algebra for Structured Queries in Bayesian Networks, Lecture Advances in XML Information Retrieval, LNCS 3493, 3rd International Workshop INEX, 2004, p. 100 – 112.

Using the INEX Environment as a Test Bed for Various User Models for XML Retrieval

Yosi Mass and Matan Mandelbrod

IBM Haifa Research Lab
Haifa 31905, Israel
{yosimass, matan}@il.ibm.com

Abstract. While in previous INEX workshops, XML retrieval tasks were divided roughly to CO (Content Only) and CAS (Content and Structure) tasks, the focus this year was to further refine those tasks so as to experiment with different user behaviors for viewing returned results. In particular interest is the new "Focussed" task that permits a single element along each path, thus solving the problem of XML result overlapping that we experimented in previous INEX workshops. In this paper we describe an algorithm for the new "Focussed" task as well as our algorithms and approaches for the other tasks.

1 Introduction

The challenge in XML retrieval is to return the most relevant components that satisfy the query concepts. While in previous INEX workshops XML retrieval was divided roughly to CO (Content Only) task and CAS (Content and Structure) task, the focus this year was to further refine those tasks so as to measure different user behaviors.

Specifically, the CO task was divided to three sub-tasks - CO.Thorough which aims at returning all relevant components, CO.Focussed which aims at returning a single element along any path and the CO.FetchBrowse which is targeted toward browsing model where the full document is browsed first and then its components. To test the importance of structure in queries, each CO query was reformulated with structural hints resulting in CO+S (Content Only plus Structure) topics. Similar to the CO task, three CO+S sub tasks were defined, namely – CO+S.Thorough, CO+S.Focussed and CO+S.FetchBrowse. Finally the CAS task was divided to four sub tasks checking combinations of Strict vs. Vagueness in target elements (elements to be returned) and in the rest of the query structure elements.

The common challenge in all those ten sub tasks (three CO, three CO+S & four CAS) is the retrieval of the most "relevant" XML components that satisfy the user needs. The main problem is that classical IR ranking methods that consider term frequency and document frequency statistics does not perform well at the component level due to component nesting in XML.

In previous INEX workshops we described a component ranking algorithm [5,6] that solved the component nesting problem by running each query against different indices where each index contains elements of the same type. The algorithm performed quite well in previous INEX workshops but its output had a high percentage

N. Fuhr et al. (Eds.): INEX 2005, LNCS 3977, pp. 187–195, 2006.

of overlapping elements. This is a viable solution for the CO.Thorough task but not for the CO.focussed task that requires a single element along each path.

In this paper we describe an algorithm for the new "Focussed" task and we also show how we applied the component ranking algorithm to the various CO, CO+S and CAS tasks.

The rest of the paper is organized as follows: In section 2 we brief the component ranking algorithm and show how it was used for the three CO runs. In section 3 we describe the CO+S runs and their results and we discuss our findings on the importance of structure in XML queries. Then in section 4 we describe our CAS approach and report results. We conclude in section 5 with summary and some conclusions.

2   CO Runs

The building block for all our CO runs was the component ranking algorithm [5,6] that we introduced in previous INEX workshops. The idea is to build different indices for the most informative component types where each index contains elements of the same type. The indices we used this year where {article, abs, bdy, sec, ss1, ss2 and p+ ip1}.

The component ranking algorithm is described in Fig 1 below. Given a query Q, we run the query in parallel on each index (step 1) and then apply an Automatic Query Refinement (AQR) phase (step 2) on each result set. The AQR algorithm we used is a Lexical Affinity (LA) Refinement algorithm, which is fully described in [2, 6]. Then in step 3, the scores of elements in each result set are normalized to $score(Q,Q)$ which as described in details in [6], normalizes scores from the different indices to the same range so that they can be compared. In step 4 we apply a document pivot scaling where scores of elements from each index are scaled by the score of their parent article. Finally all the results sets are merged into a single result set of all element types.

> For each index i
> 1.   Compute the result set R_i of running Q on index i
> 2.   Apply AQR algorithm on R_i
> 3.   Normalize scores in R_i to [0,1] by normalizing to $score(Q,Q)$
> 4.   Scale each score by its containing article score from R_0
>
> Merge all R_i's to a single result set R composed of all components sorted by their score

Fig. 1. Component ranking algorithm

We submitted 3 runs for each CO sub task experimenting combinations of using phrases vs. ignoring phrases (i.e. treating their words as simple words) and using '+' vs. ignoring '+' on words. In general the submission that ignored phrases and ignored '+' outperformed other runs. We detail below our approach for each CO sub task.

2.1 CO.Thorough

This is the traditional CO task as was used in previous INEX workshops. We used the base component ranking algorithm as depicted in Fig 1. Our runs were ranked 1st in the ep/gr generalized metric and quite high in the various nxCG metrics.

2.2 CO.Focussed

A valid CO.Focussed run as defined in [4] should have only one element along any path namely no overlapping elements are allowed. To satisfy this requirement we first perform a regular CO.Thorough run and then filter out the overlaps. The filtering is done in two stages.

In the first filtering stage we try to identify 'clusters' of highly ranked results in the XML tree and pick the most relevant element from each cluster. We refer to this stage as "smart filtering". At the end of this stage some overlaps may still be left so we perform a second brute-force filtering stage to eliminate any such overlapping elements. The two filtering stages are described below.

Smart Filtering

In the smart filtering stage we take the result set of the CO.Thorough run and group all elements by their containing article. For each such group we construct a result tree with nodes that correspond to the result components and edges that represent the ancestor-descendant relationship of the components in the original XML article. We keep for each node its assigned run score and the total number of its descendant in the original article.[1]

To tolerate variations in result scores we smooth the scores by some *ScoreThreshold* parameter as follows: For each node N_1 in the result tree and for each of its descendant nodes N we define

$$\text{diff}_{N1}(N) = |\text{score}(N_1) - \text{score}(N)| / \text{score}(N_1)$$

Using this diff_{N1} function we define for each node N1, three disjoint subsets, EQ_{N1} LT_{N1} and GT_{N1} on N_1's descendants as follows-

- $EQ_{N1} = \{N \ / \ \text{diff}_{N1}(N) \leq ScoreThreshold\}$
- $LT_{N1} = \{N \ / \ \text{diff}_{N1}(N) > ScoreThreshold \text{ and } \text{score}(N_1) < \text{score}(N)\}$
- $GT_{N1} = \{N \ / \ \text{diff}_{N1}(N) > ScoreThreshold \text{ and } \text{score}(N_1) > \text{score}(N)\}$

For ease of presentation we say that $N_1 = N_2$ if $N_2 \ \chi \ EQ_{N1}$, $N_1 < N_2$ if $N_2 \ \chi \ LT_{N1}$ and $N_1 > N_2$ if $N2 \ \chi \ GT_{N1}$.

In our runs we used *ScoreThreshold* = 0.4 though later experiments have shown that using a differentiable set of *ScoreThreshold* values for different components yields better results, but for simplicity we ignore this issue throughout the paper.

---

[1] This number is extracted as part of the indexing procedure, and is stored in the index.

The algorithm processes the result tree bottom up and at each level diagnoses the correlation between the currently examined node (N_1) and its descendents. An example of such intermediate tree after score comparison is depicted in Fig 2. The color of each node represents its relation to the root node N_1, where black > gray > white so for example, in Fig 2 below $N_1 < N_2$.

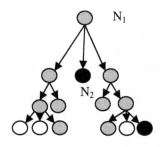

Fig. 2. Result tree

For each node N_1 we define $Good(N_1) = \{N / N$ is descendant of N_1 and $N_1 = N\}$ namely the group of all N_1's descendants with score equal to N_1 under the above EQ_{N1} definition. The algorithm distinguishes between three main cases-

1. There is some descendant node N_2 with $N_1 < N_2$. (See Fig 2). This means that N_2 is substantially more relevant than N_1 thus we remove N_1 from the result tree.

2. There is no descendant node N under N_1 such that $N_1 < N$ but there is some direct child node N_2 such that most of $Good(N_1)$ nodes are concentrated under N_2 (see Fig 3 below). If we find such node N_2 we remove N_1 from the result tree. The rational is that in this case most of N_1 score is contributed to the sub tree under N_2 so we prefer to take N_2 along this path.

   This can be measured by checking if

   $$|Good(N_2)|/|Good(N_1)| > ConcentratedThreshold$$

   for some configured *ConcentratedThreshold*. In our runs we used *ConcentratedThreshold* = 0.4.

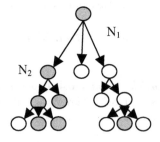

Fig. 3. Concentrated child

3. None of the previous 2 cases holds, but there is a sufficiently large number of good results, that are evenly distributed below N_1 as depicted in Fig 4 below. This can be measured by checking if

$$|Good(N_1)|/|Descendant(N_1)| > DescendantTreshhold$$

where $|Descendant(N_1)|$ is number of all descendants of N_1 in the original XML document, as kept in the index. In our runs we used *Descendant-Treshhold* = 0.25. This means that a relatively significant part of N_1 is relevant and is not concentrated under a single child so we remove all the descendants from the result tree and keep only N_1.

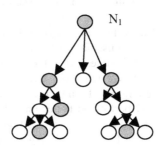

Fig. 4. Evenly distributed results

In all other cases (namely, no significant large node N_2 under N_1 and no node N_2 where most good results are concentrated and not enough good results under N1) no decision is taken, thus at the end of this stage overlapping elements may still be present in the tree. This is handled in a second brute-force filtering stage as described below.

Brute-Force Filtering
In the second filtering stage we perform a brute-force rescan of the result tree (after applying the modifications of the first stage) from bottom up. At each Node N_1 we compare score(N_1) to the score of all its descendants. If score(N_1) is bigger we take N_1 and remove all its descendants. Otherwise we remove N_1 from the result set.

Note that the second stage could be performed even without the first stage and return a valid Focussed run. We submitted one run with both stages and the second run with only the second stage. As expected, the run with both stages performed better. For example, in the ep/gr, generalized metric it was ranked 1st with MAP 0.968 while our second run got MAP 0.0909.

2.3 Fetch and Browse

In this task we first run a regular CO.Thorough run. We then pick the article elements by their score and for each article we group its returned elements ranked by their assigned score. We use <rank> instead of <rsv> for this submission because by this ordering elements scores as expressed by <rsv> are not sorted anymore. Our runs were ranked among the top 10 but not as the best ones so we still need to investigate this task.

3   CO+S Runs

The aim of the CO+S task was to investigate the usefulness of structural hints. For all three sub tasks (CO+S.Thorough, CO+S.Focussed & CO+S.FetchBrowse) we applied our Vague CAS approach (as will be shown in section 4 below) on the topic's <castitle>.

The results of most participants show that in general the CO runs performed better than the CO+S runs. Our own submissions have shown improvements for CO+S in the thorough runs only. For example, with the ep/gr generalized metric, our CO+S.Thorough run got MAP 0.0925 while our CO.Thorough run got MAP 0.0896. It should be noted that both were ranked 1st in their corresponding metric.

In the Focussed runs our CO performed better than the CO+S in all metrics. For example, with the ep/gr generalised metric, our CO.Focussed run got MAP 0.0968 while our CO+S.Focussed run got MAP 0.0809. Again both were ranked 1st in their corresponding metric.

In light of these results, we might conclude that structural hints are useful only when used as a real filter and not when used in a broader vague interpretation as defined by the CO+S task.

4   CAS Runs

Similar to previous years, the CAS topics were given by an XPath[7] expression extended with the *about* predicate that is interpreted in a broad vague semantics. XPath defines the last element in the path as a *target element* while all other query elements can be referenced as *support elements*. While in previous years the CAS task was sub classified into Vague (VCAS) and Strict (SCAS) sub tasks, an attempt was made this year to separate the vagueness of the target element from the vagueness of the support elements. Thus a combination of four sub tasks was defined :

- VVCAS – Both target and support are vague
- SSCAS – Both target and support are strict
- SVCAS – Target is strict and support is vague
- VSCAS – Target is vague and support is strict.

We decided to use the traditional SCAS and VCAS runs considering only the Vagueness of the target element in each CAS task. Therefore we submitted the four INEX tasks according to the following mapping –

INEX task	Our submission
VVCAS	VCAS
SSCAS	SCAS
SVCAS	SCAS
VSCAS	VCAS

Similar to previous INEX years we translated the CAS queries from XPath to XML Fragments [1, 3]. The difference between SCAS and VCAS runs was achieved along two dimensions: *synonym expansion* and *structural enforcement* as described below.

Synonym Expansion

Synonym expansion is a mechanism to define equivalent tags. In VCAS runs we used all the considered elements (except the article and the abs) as synonyms to each other namely {bdy, sec, ss1, ss2, p, ip1, bdy}. In SCAS runs we used two separate synonym groups: {bdy, sec, ss1, ss2} and {p, ip1}. This means that for example if <sec> is defined as a target element then in a VCAS runs <p> elements will be also returned but not in a SCAS runs.

Structural Enforcement

One of the nice features of XML Fragments[1, 3] is that it allows defining a plus ('+') prefixing both on content and/or on structure.

For example topic 244 –

//article[about (.//fm, "query optimization")]//sec[about (., "join query optimization")]

Is translated to XML Fragments[1, 3] as

```
<article>
   +<fm>query optimization</fm>
   +<sec>join query optimization</sec>
</article>
```

A '+' on a tag means that the tree below the tag is mandatory. So in the above example a result (<sec>) is returned only if it's containing article has both the <fm> constraint and the <sec> constraint. The default semantics in XML fragments is 'or' so removing the '+' as in

```
<article>
   <fm>query optimization</fm>
   <sec>join query optimization</sec>
</article>
```

will return <sec> even if the containing article does not have the <fm> constraint.

An article complying with the <fm> constraint will be ranked higher though, thus increasing the <sec>'s score via the pivot mechanism due to the Pivot scale as defined in step 4 of the component ranking algorithm from Fig 1.

For each of the VCAS and SCAS runs we submitted one run with '+' on the structure and a second run without '+' on structures. In both runs we treated phrases as simple words and we ignored plus on content

In the sequel we show our performance on the four CAS tasks and it can be clearly seen that having the '+' on structure performs better on the SCAS runs while removing the '+' from structure performs better on the VCAS runs.

4.1 VVCAS Results

Both our runs (with and without '+' on structure) were ranked top in the nxCG and the ep/gr in the generalized metric. Still the run which ignored the plus on structure preformed clearly better. This makes sense since it allows more vagueness in the structure.

4.2 SSCAS Results

Both our runs were at the top ten and there was no clear preference to the one with the plus on structure or to the other one.

4.3 VSCAS Results

Both our runs won top results (1st and 2nd) on both nxCG and ep/gr metrics but with no clear distinctions which of the two is better.

4.4 SVCAS Results

Again both runs won top results in most of the metrics where in most cases the run which treat structure strictly was better in most cases. This makes sense for SCAS since it assumes more strictness in the structure.

5 Discussion and Summary

We described a new algorithm for the "Focussed" run and we showed our approach and algorithms for the rest CO, CO+S and CAS tasks. Our main findings are that our component ranking algorithms performed quite well and our runs in all ten tasks were ranked at top places mostly in the ep/gr generalised metric. We found out that ignoring phrase boundaries and ignoring '+' on content give best results. Regarding structural hints for CO runs we found out that they helped in the Thorough task but disturbed in the Focussed task. The conclusion might be that structural hints are valuable only when used as a real filter, and not when used merely as recommendations as defined by the CO+S tasks. For CAS runs we found out that the separation of strict/vagueness in target element vs. rest of the elements was artificial. Another conclusion is that XML Fragments [1,3] enables another level of strict/vagueness through the '+' on structure.

Acknowledgment

We would like to thank the INEX organizers for the assessment tool and for the EvalJ tool they have supplied.

References

1. A.Z. Broder, Y. Maarek, M.Mandelbrod and Y. Mass. Using XML to Query XML – From Theory to Practice. In *Proceedings of RIAO'04, Avignon France*, Apr. 2004.
2. D. Carmel, E. Farchi, Y. Petruschka, A. Soffer. Automatic Query Refinement using Lexical Affinities with Maximal Information Gain. In *Proceedings of the 25th Annual International ACM SIGIR Conference on Research and Development in Information Retrieval*, 2002.
3. D. Carmel, Y. Maarek, M. Mandelbrod, Y. Mass, A. Soffer. Searching XML Documents via XML Fragments. In *Proceedings of the 26th Annual International ACM SIGIR Conference on Research and Development in Information Retrieval*, Toronto, Canada, Aug. 2003
4. Mounia Lalmas. INEX 2005 Retrieval Task and Result Submission Specification. In *INEX 2005 Workshop Pre-Proceedings*, Dagstuhl, Germany, November 28–30, 2005, page 385–390, 2005.
5. Y. Mass, M. Mandelbrod. Retrieving the most relevant XML Component, In *Proceedings of the Second Workshop of the Initiative for The Evaluation of XML Retrieval (INEX)*, 15-17 December 2003, Schloss Dagstuhl, Germany, page 53-58, 2003.
6. Y. Mass, M. Mandelbrod. Component Ranking and Automatic Query Refinement for XML Retrieval, *INEX 2004, Lecture Notes in Computer Science, Springer-Verlag GmbH Volume 3493*, page 73-84, 2005.
7. XPath – XML Path Language (XPath) 2.0, http://www.w3.org/TR/xpath20/

The University of Kaiserslautern at INEX 2005

Philipp Dopichaj

University of Kaiserslautern, Gottlieb-Daimler-Str.
67663 Kaiserslautern, Germany
dopichaj@informatik.uni-kl.de

Abstract. Digital libraries offer convenient access to large volumes of text, but finding the information that is relevant for a given information need is hard. The workshops of the Initiative for the Evaluation of XML retrieval (INEX) provide a forum for testing the effectiveness of retrieval strategies. In this paper, we present the two strategies used by the University of Kaiserslautern at INEX 2005: The first method uses background knowledge about the document schema (element relationships) to support queries with structural constraints. The second method exploits structural patterns in the retrieval results to find the appropriate results among overlapping elements. In the evaluation of the official results from the workshop, we find that element relationships does not improve retrieval quality for the test collection, but that patterns can lead to improved early precision.

1 Introduction

The Initiative for the Evaluation of XML Retrieval (INEX)[1] provides a testbed for comparing the effectiveness of content-based XML retrieval systems. The University of Kaiserslautern actively participated in the INEX workshop for the first time in 2005. Our retrieval approach is based on standard vector-space retrieval on the elements, enhanced with XML-specific additions (element relationship and context patterns).

Element relationship aims at better supporting queries with vague structural hints. It uses background knowledge of the document schema to allow matching of similar element types for increased recall. *Context patterns* address the choice of a suitable result granularity, one of the central problems of element retrieval: Due to the tree structure of XML documents, retrieval results can overlap, so the search engine needs to decide which of the overlapping results are more suitable to answering the query. Context patterns are based on the observation that the structural properties of retrieval results, like length and position, provide valuable hints about the importance of the retrieved elements.

---

[1] see http://inex.is.informatik.uni-duisburg.de/

N. Fuhr et al. (Eds.): INEX 2005, LNCS 3977, pp. 196–210, 2006.

Our paper is structured as follows: We first present a brief description of our baseline retrieval system in Section 2 and then proceed to explain our improvements in Section 3. Finally, we discuss the performance of our baseline and enhanced results as evaluated in the INEX workshop in Section 4.

2   Baseline Search Engine

The basic structure of our retrieval system is simple [2]: We use the Apache Lucene information retrieval engine[2] as the basis and add XML retrieval functionality. Instead of storing only the complete articles from the document collection in the index, we store each element's textual contents as a (Lucene) document, enriched with some metadata (most notably, the enclosing XML document and the XPath within that document); see Fig. 1 for an example.

⟨sec⟩Hello, ⟨b⟩world!⟨/b⟩
How ⟨i⟩are⟨/i⟩ you?
⟨/sec⟩

XPath	Indexed contents
/sec[1]	Hello, world! How are you?
/sec[1]/b[1]	world!
/sec[1]/i[1]	are

Fig. 1. Source document and corresponding indexed documents as seen by Lucene

Directly searching this index using Lucene would lead to bad results—overlap is not taken into account at all, and many elements on their own are useless because they are too small—, so we need to postprocess the Lucene results. We regard the results from different input documents as independent, so we can postprocess the results from each document separately (even concurrently). Overlapping results from the same document are arranged in a tree that mirrors the structure of the original XML document; this enables us to examine the relationships between the elements. Thus, retrieval is executed in these five steps (the enhancements from Section 3 are applied in step 3):

Operation	Output
1. Process query and send it to Lucene	Raw retrieval results (fragments)
2. Rearrange retrieval results	One result tree per document
3. Postprocess the result trees	One result tree per document
4. Merge the results	Flat list of results
5. Adjust scores of short elements	Flat list of results

2.1   Handling Short Results

Our baseline search engine gives rise to an anomaly that is normally not of concern in traditional information retrieval: At the lowest levels in the XML

---

[2] see http://lucene.apache.org

documents, the elements' textual contents are very short, so they may even be identical to the query. In the vector space model, documents that are identical to the query are considered perfect matches with a maximum similarity, but they are clearly useless to the searcher. Even discounting "obviously" too short elements, length plays an important role for perceived relevance: Kamps at al. [4] observed that the length of the retrieved elements is closely related to the assessed relevance. Although they found that simply discarding short results is not optimal, we decided to perform score adjustment based on element length alone, because this provides for a reasonable improvement in retrieval quality with little overhead.

Instead of just removing the very short results (we still need them in the index for our pattern-based approach), we adjust the score based on the word count. If the score is changed to zero, this is effectively the same as discarding the results, but more fine-grained control is possible: The border between "too short to return" and "long enough" is not clear-cut, but gradual. Thus, we multiply each element's score by a factor that solely depends on the element's length. In addition to reducing the score of very short elements (shorter than about 10 to 20 lines of text), we also reduce the scores of extremely long elements (longer than a typical article). We do this because we consider returning very long elements not useful in element retrieval, where it is the aim to return the shortest fragments that answer the user's query. Given l as the length of an element in words, each element's score is multiplied by $f(l)$, where

$$f(l) = \begin{cases} \sigma(l, 0.1, 75) & : & l \leq 200 \\ \sigma(l, 0.001, 10000) & : & l > 200 \end{cases}$$

and σ is the sigmoid function shifted s to the right and scaled by d:

$$\sigma(l, d, s) = \left(1 + e^{d \cdot -(l-s)}\right)^{-1}$$

In effect, results that are about 100 to 6 000 words long are hardly affected, and results shorter than 50 or longer than 13 000 words have their score reduced to (almost) zero. Fig. 2 shows a plot of this function.

2.2   Query Processing

The queries in the INEX topics are formulated in NEXI, an XML query language derived from XPath with additional information retrieval functions [7]. For content-only (CO) queries, we support the full semantics of NEXI with the following modifications:

- We discard query terms with the "-" qualifier (instead of asserting that they do not occur in the retrieved elements).
- Query terms prefixed with "+" are assigned a higher weight (instead of asserting that they occur in the retrieved elements).
- The modifiers "and" and "or" are ignored.

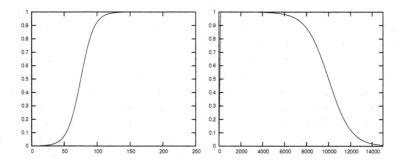

Fig. 2. Handling short results. In the left figure, we see that we reduce the scores of very short elements, and in the right figure, we see that we also punish extremely long elements.

For content-and-structure (CAS) queries, only the last tag name in paths is used for searching (for example, given `//article//fm//atl`, we prefer all `atl` elements, not only those contained in `//article//fm`). Furthermore, we consider the structural parts of the query only as hints for the best elements to retrieve. For this reason, we only submitted runs to the VVCAS task, where structural constraints for both the target and support elements are interpreted as vague.

3   Enhancements to the Baseline Search Engine

The search engine we described in the previous section provides the basis for the implementation of our new approaches. On top of it, we implemented two different enhancements that are executed as a postprocessing step; they are mostly orthogonal, so they can be applied in any combination.

3.1   Element Relationship

Many XML schemas for document authoring specify tags for semantic markup. DocBook, for example, has a `filename` tag that is used to specify that the contained text designates a file name. This markup is useful, in particular for CAS queries, because it enables the searcher to more exactly specify what he wants to retrieve. When we examined real-world documents, we realized that this markup is often not used correctly (possibly because of the author's laziness, possibly because no tag exactly matching the author's intention exists), or that there are several tags for closely related concepts. We had the idea to create a graph for allowing near misses of the markup specified in structural queries, the *element relationship graph* (ERG) [1, 2]. This inexactness obviously means that strict CAS queries (as implemented in the SSCAS, SVCAS, and VSCAS tasks) cannot be supported; we only support the VVCAS task, where both the target and support elements that are specified in the query are considered as hints only.

The ERG contains the tag names from the document schema as leaves and places them in a semi-hierarchical graph that captures semantic relations between the tag names. Each category is assigned a coherence value in the range zero to one that denotes to what degree the contained tag names are similar; this information is used for similarity calculation, see below for an example.

The approach is not well suited to visual markup that only denotes how the marked-up text should look, instead of what the semantics are. Unfortunately, the collection of IEEE magazine articles that is used for INEX uses only visual markup for the body of the text (the front matter and the bibliography are more structured, but they are rarely the target of queries); we tried to construct an ERG for this data anyway to see how well element relationship can cope with situations it was not designed for.

We based our ERG on the information available in `xmlarticle.dtd`, the main part of the collection's document type definition (DTD). In addition to the purely syntactic information used by the XML parser, the DTD also contains consistently formatted comments that indicate a two-level hierarchical structure, as we can see in Fig. 3(a). We wrote a script to convert this DTD to an ERG, assigning a coherence of 0.5 to all second-level headings and of 0.2 to the first-level headings; Fig. 3(b) shows the result of the conversion. Obviously, the higher-level categories do not correspond to tag names in the collection. These abstractions could be useful for improving the search interface (as O'Keefe [6] stated, users are unlikely to remember hundreds of tag names, so a simplified "query DTD" should be used instead of the collection DTD).

We also modeled the tags described as equivalent in the NEXI description [7], for example, the various types of sections, by including them in the ERG with a coherence of 1.

Only the last tag name from each path in the NEXI query is taken as the category to search in (as described in Section 2.2). If a retrieval result is embedded in an element with that tag name, its score is taken as is, otherwise we go upwards in the ERG and try to match any tag name from the same category, reducing the score by multiplying it with the corresponding coherence. For example, if we search in `hdr`, but a match is in a `hdr1` element, we halve the original score because we needed to generalize to a second-level category.

For more details about applying element relationship, see our previous work on this topic [1, 2].

3.2 Context Patterns

Exploiting element relationships is only feasible if the schema of the document collection are fixed and the administrator is willing and able to create an element relationship graph. If this is not the case, one needs schema-independent methods to improve retrieval results. Fortunately, there are several telltale signs what the role of a given element in a text is, without having to examine the tag name.

```
⟨!-- ============ --⟩
⟨!-- FRONT MATTER --⟩
⟨!-- ============ --⟩

⟨!ELEMENT fm (hdr?, (edinfo|au|tig|pubfm|abs|edintro|kwd|fig|figw)*)⟩

⟨!-- ++++++ --⟩
⟨!-- HEADER --⟩
⟨!-- ++++++ --⟩

⟨!ELEMENT hdr (fig?, hdr1, hdr2)⟩

⟨!ELEMENT hdr1 (#PCDATA|crt|obi|pdt|pp|ti)*⟩
⟨!ELEMENT hdr2 (#PCDATA|crt|obi|pdt|pp|ti)*⟩
```

(a) Excerpt from `xmlarticle.dtd`. The comments indicate the semantic structure of the elements.

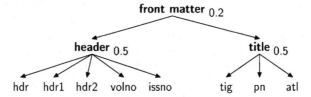

(b) The ERG for the DTD excerpt. The numbers denote the coherence values.

Fig. 3. Construction of the element relationship graph

We can achieve this by looking at *result contexts* of the retrieved nodes. For each non-leaf node, the result context consists of this node and its children, and the following data is stored for each node:

- The retrieval score of the node,
- the length of the node (in words), and
- the position of the node in the parent node.

This information can be visualized in two dimensions, one for the lengths and positions of the text fragments and the other for the score. Fig. 4 shows an example XML fragment and how it can be visualized. The horizontal position of the left-hand side of each rectangle denotes the starting position in the text of the parent element, and its width corresponds to the length of the text it contains (this implies that the parent element occupies the width of the diagram). The parent element (in the Fig. 4, the root element `/sec[1]`) is the reference for the scale of the horizontal axis.

When we examined context graphs of some trial retrieval results, we realized that we could often determine what elements were section titles or inline elements, without referring to the original XML documents. Based on this observation, we defined a set of *context patterns* for formalizing the recognition of certain structures. A pattern looks like, "if the first child in the context is short

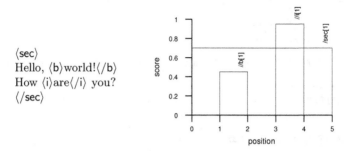

⟨sec⟩
Hello, ⟨b⟩world!⟨/b⟩
How ⟨i⟩are⟨/i⟩ you?
⟨/sec⟩

Fig. 4. XML text and corresponding context diagram. The horizontal axis denotes the positions and lengths of the text fragments, and the vertical axis shows the score (in this case random numbers).

and the parent is long, the first child is a title" (see Fig. 5 for an example). This is too vague for Boolean logic, but fuzzy logic is perfectly suitable for this task. Fuzzy logic enables us to assign degrees of membership for the features, instead of Boolean values [5]. For example, a fragment containing only one word is definitely short, and a fragment containing 5000 words is definitely not short, but what about one containing 20 words? With fuzzy logic, we do not need to make a firm decision, but we can say that this fragment is short to a degree of (for example) 50 %. Similarly, the Boolean operators like *and*, *or*, and *not* can be expressed in terms of these degrees.

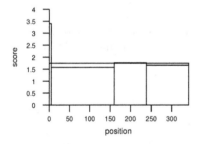

Fig. 5. Example context graph for the title pattern. The short peak at the left is the section title.

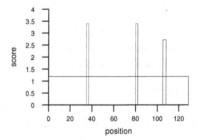

Fig. 6. An example for the inline pattern. The peaks are italicized one- or two-word phrases.

The patterns alone do not change the retrieval results in any way, so we need to take actions for modifying the relevant scores. For a match in a title, an appropriate action is to increase the parent's score (because the match indicates that the corresponding section is highly relevant) and decrease the first child's score (because the title itself contains too little information to be of any use).

We defined and examined several patterns; apart from the title pattern mentioned above, the inline pattern proved to be the most worthwhile, whereas the other patterns had no noticeable effect on the retrieval quality. It is based on the assumption that single words or short phrases directly contained in any markup denote some form of emphasis (in the IEEE collection, very short marked-up elements are typically embedded in b or i elements, denoting bold and italics). If the author of the text decided to apply such emphasizing markup to phrases, this is often an indication that the surrounding element is especially relevant for queries mentioning the phrases. Therefore, if many of an element's children are very short and have high scores, we increase the element's score. Fig. 6 shows an example of an occurrence of this pattern.

4 Evaluation

One important aspect of INEX is the comparison of XML search engines. In this section, we will describe what runs we submitted, examine the official results and present some post-INEX improvements of our methods.

4.1 Submitted Runs

We only participated in some of the subtasks of the ad-hoc task. For each of the CO and CO+S tasks, both focused and thorough, we submitted three runs:

1. *Basic,* which applied both element relationship and length-based score correction to the Lucene results (this was our baseline).
2. *Pattern,* which applied element relationship, length-based score correction and context patterns.
3. *Pattern-NoERG,* which applied length-based score correction and context patterns.

For the runs based on element relationship, we searched for the query terms in the category *Emphasis*, which contains inline elements for printing in bold or italics. As we shall later see, the selection of runs turned out to be a bad choice, since element relationship actually downgraded the retrieval quality of our systems for the content-only (CO) tasks. Because of this, we have no baseline for our best-performing run in the official results. For completeness, we generated this missing run (*Basic-NoERG*) in order to compare it to *Pattern-NoERG*.

Our system does not support any type of strict CAS queries, as the element-relationship approach was designed with vague structural matching in mind, so we did not submit any runs to the VSCAS, SVCAS, and SSCAS subtasks. For the VVCAS subtask, where only two runs per organization were permitted, we included only *Pattern* and *Pattern-NoERG*. The *Pattern-NoERG* run still rewards exact matches of the specified target elements, but all non-exact matches are considered equally bad (that is, their score is multiplied by 0.1).

For the focused subtasks, we used our thorough results and applied some postprocessing to each result tree: We repeatedly add the result with the highest RSV to the retrieval result and remove all overlapping results.

4.2   Official Results

This year's INEX workshop offered a plethora of retrieval tasks and evaluation metrics because there are different views on what constitutes a good retrieval result; therefore, it is difficult to make clear statements. Nevertheless, the following points are fairly clear (see Fig. 11, 12, and 13 in the appendix):

- Our system is more competitive with generalized quantization; with strict quantization, our ranks drop significantly.
- As expected, our results are better at high precision levels: For the top-ranked results up to roughly the 30th place, we fare well compared to the competition, but after this point, our result quality is only average.
- Only for the top-ranked results, the pattern-based approach is better than the corresponding baseline; as we later found out, this is due to undesirable interactions of several context patterns (see the next section for details).
- Employing element relationships did not lead to noticeable improvements for VVCAS (all our VVCAS runs are very close to one another), and actually degraded retrieval quality for the CO runs. Although the schema of the IEEE document collection that is used for INEX is not well-suited to our approach, we expected a better outcome, so we will need to investigate the cause.

The U form of the curves for generalized quantization is due to the fact that the ideal recall base for the vast majority of topics is much smaller than the 1 500 results that are the scale for the x axis. This leads to the ideal run increasing monotonically until all relevant results are retrieved. After this point, it will remain constant at this level.

A real run aiming at improving early precision will probably have a high number of relevant results at the very beginning, followed by a lower, more or less constant rate of relevant results. This leads to a steep decline in the beginning, up to the point where the ideal run runs out of results, where a low, constant increase starts.

4.3   Post-INEX Evaluation of Context Patterns

The counter intuitive results for our pattern-based runs—better than the baseline at low cut-off points, significantly worse at higher cut-off points—prompted us to perform further analysis. The original implementation that was used for the runs submitted to INEX evaluated several patterns without properly isolating them, so we re-implemented that short after the deadline has passed. An evaluation of this new implementation based on the INEX assessments reveals that this does indeed appear to be the cause for the bad quality at higher cut-off values (see Fig. 7).

We also evaluated the effect of the patterns we had used for the INEX submissions and found that only two of them have any noticeable effect on retrieval quality, the title pattern and the inline pattern described in Section 3.2.

Another interesting observation is that applying the two patterns in combination leads to worse results than applying the title pattern alone for the

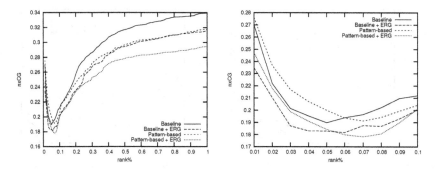

Fig. 7. Comparison of the submitted runs and a pattern run with bug fixes (task CO.Focused)

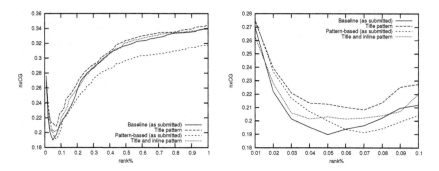

Fig. 8. Post-INEX evaluation of inline and title versus only the title pattern (without element relationship, task CO.Focused)

top-ranked documents (it does improve results for the lower ranks), as we can see in Fig. 8.

Obviously, a lot more research is needed on the context patterns, but the initial results are promising.

4.4 The Impact of Structural Hints in the Queries

Most of the CO topics (19 out of 29) also featured a CAS query in addition to the CO query. This query should be aimed at the same information need, but specify additional structural constraints that the topic author deemed useful for improving retrieval performance. As we can see in Fig. 9, CO+S definitely helps if we use element relationship (at least for the lower cutoffs up to about 20 % of the result list). In this case, using element relationship leads to a small but consistent improvement.

This comparison should not be overrated, however, since several of the CAS queries did more than just add structural constraints that are impossible to express in pure CO queries. The worst example is the topic where we achieved

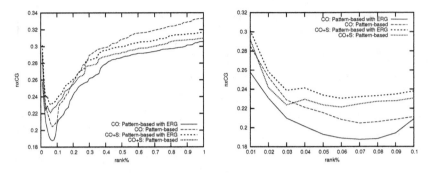

Fig. 9. Comparison of CO and CO+S (Focused, nxCG, generalized). The thick lines are the CO+S results.

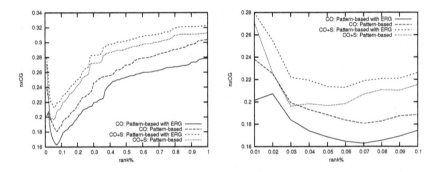

Fig. 10. Comparison of CO and CO+S, omitting questionable queries (Focused, nxCG, generalized). The thick lines are the CO+S results.

the greatest improvement with CO+S; the CAS query misspelled a word that was spelled correctly in the CO query, but apparently made irrelevant results turn up high in the list.

We observed the following shortcomings in the CO+S topics:

Inclusion of phrases in only one of the queries. Phrases are equally well supported in CO and CAS queries. Topics 205, 207.

Different keywords. (This does not include the addition of constraints that can only be expressed in CAS) Topics 222, 234, 233.

Changed modifiers. Topic 230.

Spelling in CAS query is even worse than in CO query. Topic 222.

These shortcomings can lead to differences not caused only by the inclusion of structural constraints, so we performed another comparison with these six topics omitted. Fig. 10 shows that this leads to a clear separation of the CO and CO+S curves, as well as an improvement when using element relationship. This appears to imply that structural hints help our retrieval system at least for focused searches.

5   Conclusions

As we have seen, the runs applying element relationships failed badly for the CO tasks and did not produce a consistent improvement even for the VVCAS and CO+S runs; this can in part be explained by the mismatch of the type of markup expected by this method and the markup supplied by the document collection.

Context patterns showed more promising results, but we still need to investigate why the quality of our retrieval results declines more rapidly than those of the other participants.

References

1. Philipp Dopichaj. Element relationship: Exploiting inline markup for better XML retrieval. In Gottfried Vossen, Frank Leymann, Peter C. Lockemann, and Wolffried Stucky, editors, *Datenbanksysteme in Business, Technologie und Web, 11. Fachtagung des GI-Fachbereichs "Datenbanken und Informationssysteme" (DBIS), Karlsruhe, 2.-4. März 2005*, volume 65 of *LNI*, pages 285–294. GI, 2005.
2. Benedikt Eger. Entwurf und Implementierung einer XML-Volltext-Suchmaschine. Master's thesis, University of Kaiserslautern, 2005.
3. Norbert Fuhr, Mounia Lalmas, Saadia Malik, and Zoltán Szlávik, editors. *Advances in XML Information Retrieval: Third International Workshop of the Initiative for the Evaluation of XML Retrieval, INEX 2004, Dagstuhl Castle, Germany, December 6–8, 2004*. Springer, 2005.
4. Jaap Kamps, Maarten de Rijke, and Börkur Sigurbjörnsson. The importance of length normalization for XML retrieval. *Information Retrieval*, 8(4):631–654, 2005.
5. Zbigniew Michalewicz and David B. Fogel. *How to Solve It: Modern Heuristics*, chapter 13, pages 367–388. Springer, 2nd edition, 2004.
6. Richard A. O'Keefe. If INEX is the answer, what is the question? In Fuhr et al. [3].
7. Andrew Trotman and Börkur Sigurbjörnsson. Narrowed extended XPath I (NEXI). In Fuhr et al. [3].

A   Official INEX Results

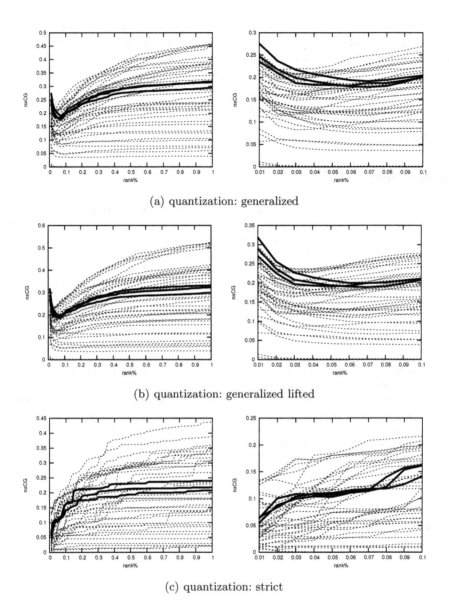

(a) quantization: generalized

(b) quantization: generalized lifted

(c) quantization: strict

Fig. 11. Official results for CO.Focused, metric nxCG. The left graphs show the whole range of cutoffs whereas the right graphs show the results up to 1 % cutoff.

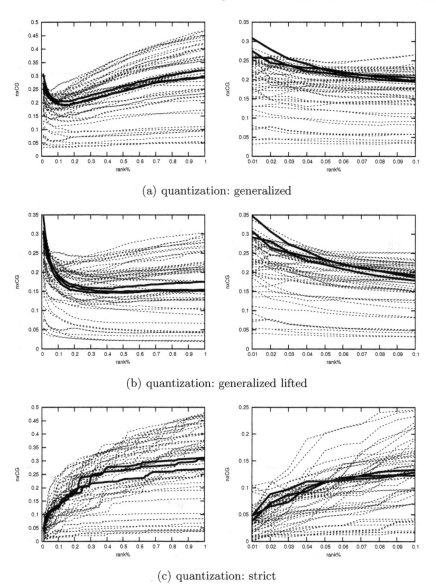

(a) quantization: generalized

(b) quantization: generalized lifted

(c) quantization: strict

Fig. 12. Official results for CO.Thorough, metric nxCG.

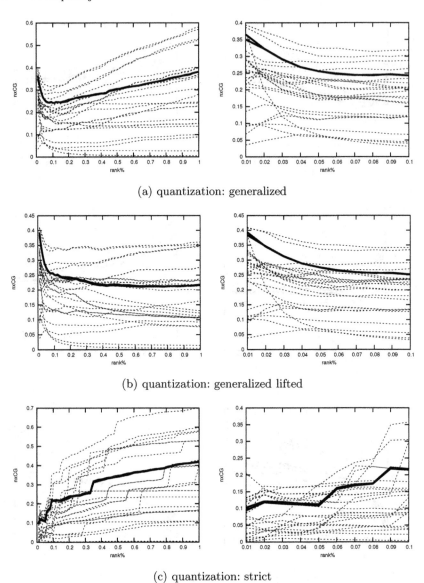

(a) quantization: generalized

(b) quantization: generalized lifted

(c) quantization: strict

Fig. 13. Official results for VVCAS, metric nxCG

Parameter Estimation for a Simple Hierarchical Generative Model for XML Retrieval

Paul Ogilvie and Jamie Callan

Language Technologies Institute, School of Computer Science,
Carnegie Mellon University
pto@lti.cs.cmu.edu, callan@lti.cs.cmu.edu

Abstract. This paper explores the possibility of using a modified Expectation-Maximization algorithm to estimate parameters for a simple hierarchical generative model for XML retrieval. The generative model for an XML element is estimated by linearly interpolating statistical language models estimated from the text of the element, the parent element, the document element, and its children elements. We heuristically modify EM to allow the incorporation of negative examples, then attempt to maximize the likelihood of the relevant components while minimizing the likelihood of non-relevant components found in training data. The technique for incorporation of negative examples provide an effective algorithm to estimate the parameters in the linear combination mentioned. Some experiments are presented on the CO.Thorough task that support these claims.

1 Introduction

In previous work [1][2][3], we proposed using hierarchical language models for ranking XML document components for retrieval. However, we left the problem of estimating parameters as future work. In this work, we present a parameter estimation method for a simplified version of the hierarchical language models.

In this work we construct a language model for each element in the document. We linearly interpolate the parent's unsmoothed language model, each child's unsmoothed language model, the document's unsmoothed language model, and the collection language model. This simplification allows us to formulate the parameter estimation problem simply so that we can apply the Generalized Expectation Maximization algorithm [4].

However, we observed that this approach places the most weight on the document language model, which results in very poor retrieval performance. We heuristically modify the likelihood we wish to maximize by including negative examples. These negative examples are non-relevant elements that come from documents that contain relevant elements. While our inclusion of negative examples ad-hoc, we have found it to work well in practice.

The next section describes the model in detail, and Section 3 presents the Generalized Expectation Maximization (GEM) algorithm for the model. Section 4 presents our adaptation of the GEM algorithm to include negative examples. We present experimental methodology and describe our system in Section 5. Section 6

N. Fuhr et al. (Eds.): INEX 2005, LNCS 3977, pp. 211–224, 2006.

contains our experiments with using the GEM algorithm on CO.Thorough task, and conclusions and discussion is contained in Section 7.

2   Model

We rank elements by estimating the probability that the language model estimated for the element generated the query. We use simple unigram language models, which are multinomial probability distributions over words in the vocabulary. That is, a language model μ specifies $P(w|\mu)$. Document elements are then ordered by $P(Q|\mu_e) = \prod_{i=1}^{|Q|} P(q_i|\mu_e)$ where μ_e is the language model estimated for a particular element e.

In order to estimate the language model μ_e, we note that we would like to incorporate evidence from the document, its parent, and its children. With that in mind, we estimate μ_e as a linear combination of several language models [1] :

$$
\begin{aligned}
P(w|\mu_e) = {} & \lambda_P P\left(w\,|\theta_{P(e)}\right) \\
& + \lambda_D P\left(w\,|\theta_{d(e)}\right) \\
& + \lambda_C P(w|\theta_C) \\
& + \lambda_O \frac{|s(e)|}{|s(e)|+\sum_{j'\in c(i)} \alpha_{t(j')}|j'|} P\left(w\,|\lambda_{s(e)}\right) \\
& + \lambda_O \sum_{j\in c(e)} \frac{\alpha_{t(j')}|j|}{|s(e)|+\sum_{j'\in c(i)} \alpha_{t(j')}|j'|} P(w\,|\lambda_j)
\end{aligned}
\tag{3}
$$

where θ_x refers to a language model estimated for x, $P(x)$ refers to the parent of x, $d(x)$ refers to the document containing x, $s(x)$ refers to the element x (self), $c(x)$ returns a list containing the children of x, $t(x)$ refers to the element type of the element x (such as bdy or sec), and C refers to the entire collection. We choose to set the λ parameters in the interpolation to be constant across

---

[1] Unfortunately, due to a bug in our system we did not rank elements by $P(Q|\mu_e)$. In our official submissions, we ranked by

$$
\begin{aligned}
& P\left(Q\,|\theta'_{P(e)}\right)^{\lambda_P} \times P\left(Q\,|\theta'_{d(e)}\right)^{\lambda_D} \\
& \times P\left(Q\,|\theta'_{s(e)}\right)^{\lambda_O \frac{|s(i)|}{|s(i)|+\sum_{j'\in c(i)} \alpha_{t(j')}|j'|}} \\
& \times \prod_{j\in c(e)} P\left(Q\,|\theta'_j\right)^{\lambda_O \sum_{j\in c(e)} \frac{\alpha_{t(j')}|j|}{|s(e)|+\sum_{j'\in c(i)} \alpha_{t(j')}|j'|}}
\end{aligned}
\tag{1}
$$

where

$$
P\left(w\,|\theta'_x\right) = (1-\lambda_C)P(w\,|\theta_x) + \lambda_C P(w\,|\theta_C)
\tag{2}
$$

This model does allow relative weighting of the different structural elements of messages in the thread. However, it does not have the intended effect of combining evidence at the word level; it only combines query level evidence. This model corresponds to the linear weighted combination of log probabilities, which we investigated in [5]. We will refer to ranking by $P(Q|\theta_e)$ as the mixture method and Equation 1 as the post query combination approach.

Rather than discuss our official submissions in Section 6, we will present experiments using the corrected $P(Q|\theta_e)$.

all elements in the collection to reduce the number of parameters we must estimate. The α parameters allow us to provide additional weight to the children of elements, where the weight is dependent on the type of the child element. Note that we also multiply alpha by the length of the element, which results in an assumption that the extra value of a child element is dependent on both the type and length of the child.

In this work, we will take θ_x to be the Maximum Likelihood Estimate from the text contained in x, which is given by:

$$P\left(w\,|\theta_x\right) = \frac{\text{count of } w \text{ in text of } x}{\text{length in words of text of } x} \tag{4}$$

Note that this is different than our previous work. In our previous work, we excluded the text of the child's elements when performing hierarchical smoothing. In this model we include that text. This allows a more clear and consistent parameter estimation scheme. The α_t parameters represent the *additional* value of a word in elements of type t. Additionally, we do not recursively smooth the elements. This is a limiting factor in current work that simplifies the parameter estimation process.

We also apply a linear length prior [6] to our rankings. That is, we multiply $P\left(Q\,|\theta_e\right)$ by $length\left(e\right)$ to obtain the retrieval status values used in our rankings.

3   Parameter Estimation Using EM

This section describes how we estimate parameters for ranking results by $P\left(Q\,|\theta_e\right)$. Suppose there are M language models in the collection, which we will denote

$$\theta_1, \theta_2, \ldots, \theta_M.$$

Suppose that we are given some queries and rankable elements that are relevant to these queries. We will treat words in these queries as observations of sampled terms drawn from the relevant elements:

$$\mathbf{x} = \left(x_1, x_2, \ldots, x_N\right),$$

where we denote the relevant elements as

$$\mu_1, \mu_2, \ldots, \mu_N.$$

Note that there may be repeated query terms and elements in these lists; this is not an issue in the estimation process.

Let us now assume that the μ elements are linear interpolations of the elements, giving:

$$P\left(x\,|\mu_i\right) = \sum_{j=1}^{M} \lambda_{ij} P\left(x\,|\theta_j\right). \tag{5}$$

This results in a model where we do not know the $\Lambda = \left(\lambda_{11}, \ldots, \lambda_{NM}\right)$ parameters.

We would like to maximize the probability of $P\left(\mathbf{x}\,|\mu\right)$. In order to reduce the number of parameters we must estimate in this model, we will assume that each μ_i is estimated from using a small number of elements we willcall the *family* of i. In relation to the model presented before, the $family$ of i will be child elements, the collection element, its parent element, its document element and the element itself:

$$family\,(i) = \left(\theta_1, \theta_{document(i)}, \theta_{parent(i)}, \theta_{self(i)}\right) \cup_{k \in children(i)} (\theta_k)$$

or using the first letter as an abbreviation for the $document$, $parent$, $self$ and $children$ functions:

$$family\,(i) = \left(\theta_1, \theta_{d(i)}, \theta_{p(i)}, \theta_{s(i)}\right) \cup_{k \in c(i)} (\theta_k). \tag{6}$$

where θ_1 is the special collection model used for smoothing. As a reminder, θ_1 is estimated using the maximum likelihood estimate using the entire text of the document collection. Given the $family$ of element i, we can rewrite Equation 5 as

$$P\,(x\,|\mu_i) = \sum_{j \in f(i)} \lambda_{ij} P\,(x\,|\theta_j), \tag{7}$$

greatly reducing the number of parameters we must estimate. Note that we also place the constraints

$$\lambda_{ij} \geq 0, \quad \sum_{j \in f(i)} \lambda_{ij} = 1 \tag{8}$$

upon the Λ parameters.

However, there are still many cases where we must estimate λ parameters for texts and we have no training data, as the $\mathbf{x}$ vector is very small in comparison to the total number of rankable texts in the corpus. We must make further assumptions to reduce the parameter space. Given our understanding of the XML retrieval domain, we will assume constant parameters across all models for the combination with the $collection$, $document$ and $parent$ elements. For the $children$ elements, we will assume that the weight placed should be a simple function of the $t = type$ of the child element and its length. Under these assumptions:

$$\lambda_{ij} = \begin{cases} \lambda_C & \text{if } j = 1, \\[2mm] \lambda_D & \text{if } j = d\,(i), \\[2mm] \lambda_P & \text{if } j = p\,(i), \\[2mm] \lambda_O \dfrac{|j|}{|s(i)| + \sum_{j' c(i)} \alpha_{t(j')}|j'|} & \text{if } j = s\,(i), \\[4mm] \lambda_O \dfrac{e^{\beta t(j)}|j|}{|s(i)| + \sum_{j' c(i)} \alpha_{t(j')}|j'|} & \text{if } j \in c\,(i), \\[4mm] 0 & \text{otherwise.} \end{cases} \tag{9}$$

where the $type$ function returns a value in $(1, 2, \ldots, T)$. This now greatly reduces the number of parameters we must estimate to $T + 4$. In addition to the constraints in Equation 8, we place this additional constraint:

$$\lambda_C + \lambda_D + \lambda_P + \lambda_O = 1 \tag{10}$$

Given Equation 9, we can rewrite Equation 7 using the parameters we must estimate:

$$P\left(x\,|\mu_i\right) = \lambda_C P\left(x\,|\theta_1\right) + \lambda_D P\left(x\,|\theta_{d(i)}\right) + \lambda_P P\left(x\,|\theta_{p(i)}\right)$$

$$+ \lambda_O \left(\begin{array}{l} \dfrac{|i|}{|i| + \sum_{j\in c(i)}\alpha_{t(j)}|j|} P\left(x\,|\theta_{s(i)}\right) + \\[2ex] \sum_{j\in c(i)} \dfrac{\alpha_{t(j)}|j|}{|i| + \sum_{j\in c(i)}\alpha_{t(j)}|j|} P\left(x\,|\theta_j\right) \end{array} \right) \tag{11}$$

We would like to maximize the likelihood of the observed data, which is

$$\mathcal{L}\left(\Lambda\,|\mathcal{X}\right) = P\left(\mathbf{x}\,|\mu\right) = \prod_{i=1}^{N} P\left(x_i\,|\mu_i\right) = \prod_{i=1}^{N}\sum_{j=1}^{M}\lambda_{ij} P\left(x_i\,|\theta_j\right) \tag{12}$$

Unfortunately, the summation within the product makes it difficult to differentiate, so we must use an alternative approach to maximizing the likelihood. We choose to use the Expectation-Maximization method to optimizing the likelihood. Given our formulation of the problem, we can derive the following update rules for our Λ and α_k parameter estimates:

$$\lambda_C^{[t]} = \tfrac{1}{N}\sum_{i=1}^{N} P\left(y=1\,|x_i, \Lambda^{[t-1]}\right)$$

$$\lambda_D^{[t]} = \tfrac{1}{N}\sum_{i=1}^{N} P\left(y=d(i)\,|x_i, \Lambda^{[t-1]}\right)$$

$$\lambda_P^{[t]} = \tfrac{1}{N}\sum_{i=1}^{N} P\left(y=p(i)\,|x_i, \Lambda^{[t-1]}\right) \tag{13}$$

$$\lambda_O^{[t]} = \tfrac{1}{N}\sum_{i=1}^{N}\sum_{j\in(s(i))\cup c(i)} P\left(y=j\,|x_i, \Lambda^{[t-1]}\right)$$

$$\alpha_k^{[t]} = \log\left(\alpha_k^{[t-1]}\right) - \dfrac{\frac{\partial}{\partial\log(\alpha_k)}Q(\Lambda,\Lambda^g)\Big|_{\alpha_k=\alpha_k^{[t-1]}}}{\frac{\partial^2}{\partial\log(\alpha_k^2)}Q(\Lambda,\Lambda^g)\Big|_{\alpha_k=\alpha_k^{[t-1]}}}$$

where

$$\frac{\partial}{\partial\alpha_k}Q\left(\Lambda,\Lambda^g\right)\Big|_{\alpha_k=\alpha_k^g} = \alpha_k^g\sum_{i:j\in c(i),t(j)=k}\frac{-a_{ik}f_{ik} + \frac{b_{ik}h_{ik}}{\alpha_k^g}}{b_{ik} + \alpha_k^g a_{ik}}$$

$$\frac{\partial^2}{\partial\alpha_k^2}Q\left(\Lambda,\Lambda^g\right)\Big|_{\alpha_k=\alpha_k^g} = \alpha_k^g\left(\begin{array}{l} \frac{\partial}{\partial\alpha_k}Q\left(\Lambda,\Lambda^g\right)\Big|_{\alpha_k=\alpha_k^g} + \\[2ex] \alpha_k^g\sum_{i:j\in c(i),t(j)=k}\dfrac{a_{ik}^2 f_{ik} - \frac{b_{ik}^2 h_{ik}}{\alpha_k^{g2}}}{\left(b_{ik} + \alpha_k^g a_{ik}\right)^2} \end{array} \right)$$

$$a_{ik} = \sum_{j' \in c(i), t(j')=k} |j'|$$

$$b_{ik} = |s(i)| + \sum_{j' \in c(i), t(j') \neq k} \log \left(\alpha_{t(j')} \right) |j'|$$

$$f_{ik} = P(y = s(i) | x_i, \Lambda^g) + \sum_{j \in c(i), t(j) \neq k} P(y = j | x_i, \Lambda^g) \tag{14}$$

$$h_{ik} = \sum_{j \in c(i), t(j)=k} P(y = j | x_i, \Lambda^g)$$

$$P(y = j | x_i, \Lambda^g) = \frac{\lambda_{ij}^g P(x_i | \theta_j)}{\sum_{j' \in family(i)} \lambda_{ij'}^g P(x_i | \theta_{j'})}$$

Equations 13-14 give us update rules that we can use to find locally optimal parameters on some training data. As the derivation of these equations makes heavy use of calculus, it is provided in the Appendix for completeness. The following section generalizes this technique heuristically to allow consideration of non-relevant examples in training.

4   Incorporating Negative Examples

While the above presentation of EM to learn parameters attempts to maximize the likelihood of training examples, doing so using only relevant elements results in very poor parameter estimation. This is a direct result of the fact that optimizing the likelihood of relevant elements may also increase the likelihood of elements that are not relevant. In our own experiments, using only relevant elements during training will result in most of the weight being placed in λ_D. We feel this may be a side effect of the bias-variance problem in estimation. The document language model has more bias than the language models estimated from the elements, but the variance is lower as the sample sizes are larger for documents than for elements. When combining the language models during smoothing, the document language models tend to have a higher likelihood of generating the query terms due to this lower variance.

In order to combat these effects, we also include negative examples in our training data. However, we do not wish to optimize the likelihood of the negative examples. We would prefer to maximize the likelihood that the language models estimated for the non-relevant elements *do not* generate the query terms. To model this one might include for each non-relevant element and query term an example where we use $(1 - P(x|\theta_j))$ in place of $P(x|\theta_j)$. Note that this is not quite the same as what we one might wish to optimize, as:

$$1 - P(Q|\mu_i) \neq \prod_{l=1}^{|Q|} (1 - P(q_l|\mu_i)) \tag{15}$$

However, this is a useful and effective approximation that requires only the above substitution for negative examples. A complication in learning using the inclusion of negative examples given above is that $P(x|\mu_i)$ tends to be very small in relation to $1 - P(x|\mu_i)$. That means that when maximizing the log likelihood, a small improvement of a positive example may outweigh a large degradation in performance in a negative example.

To accommodate for that effect, we weight the negative probabilities by raising them to a large power. For a negative example, we replace

$$P(x|\theta_j) \tag{16}$$

with

$$(1 - P(x|\theta_j))^{\nu\delta} \tag{17}$$

where ν is a user chosen parameter that specifies how much emphasis the negative examples have relative to the positive examples and δ is chosen so that the average probability of a term given the relevant examples is equal to the average probability of a term given the non-relevant examples when $\nu = 1$:

$$\delta = \frac{\log\left(\frac{1}{|positive|}\sum_{positive} P(x_i|\mu_i)\right)}{\log\left(\frac{1}{|negative|}\sum_{negative} P(x_i|\mu_i)\right)} \tag{18}$$

This approach for the incorporation of non-relevant elements is ad-hoc but effective, as we will see in the next section.

5   Experimental Methodology

We use a locally modified version of the Indri search engine of the Lemur toolkit [7] that supports the hierarchical shrinkage. The hierarchical shrinkage support will be made available in a December release. Release of the parameter estimation code is scheduled for a later release as the estimation methods are still in flux. We indexed the INEX collection using the InQuery stopword list and the Krovetz stemmer. To process queries we removed all quotes from the query (thus ignoring phrasal constraints) and all terms with a minus in front.

We will focus on the CO.Thorough task and present results using the strict and generalized quantizations for nxCG[10], nxCG[25], nxCG[50], and MAP of ep/gr to facilitate comparison to the official results presented at INEX.

6   Experiments

In this section we present experiments on the CO.Thorough task. We will disregard our official submissions as they were run with the desired model and they were not run on the entire corpus. We had some problems with using the system that prevented us from indexing the entire corpus which have since been resolved.

We trained our parameters using the INEX 1.8 corpus and CO topics 162-201. Using the INEX 2004 relevance assessments, we took one non-relevant document element as a negative example for each relevant element as a positive example. Elements were considered relevant if and only if they were highly exhaustive and highly specific. The non-relevant examples were taken from the same documents as the relevant examples. Ten iterations were used for the EM algorithm. α_k values were updated only for cases where there were at least ten examples for type k in the update rule.

Table 1 shows the a sample of the parameters the EM algorithm learned on the training topics. As ν increases, the weight on the collection language model (λ_C) decreases while the weight in the parent (λ_P) slightly increases and λ_O, the weight on the element and its children, noticeably increases.

With regards to the α parameters, the element type length-proportional weights on children, a few parameters start with relatively low values and increase rapidly as ν increases. Table 1 shows a few examples of this behavior. However, most parameters that are learned are very close to zero across all values of ν. Note that we only trained these parameters for element types where at least ten highly-specific highly-exhaustive components had a child element of that type.

There seems to be some undesirable variation in the parameters, as we can see with the α value for the p type. This may be a side effect of the algorithm being trained on relatively few examples for some types, but this should not be the case for the p tag. However, as it only really matters what the value is relative to the other tags at the same level, perhaps this variance is not an issue.

Table 1. Some parameters learned from training data. As ν increases, λ_C decreases and λ_O increases. Some α parameters seem fairly stable, such as that of the footnote type. Others increase greatly with larger ν while some seem somewhat erratic (e.g. p).

	λ				α				
ν	(C)ol	(D)oc	(P)ar	O-self	st	p	sub	footnote	ss1
1.0	0.475	0.222	0.035	0.268	0.38	0.23	0.00	0.28	0.50
2.0	0.385	0.212	0.037	0.365	1.07	0.00	0.22	2.49	0.37
3.0	0.342	0.210	0.040	0.408	22.75	9.77	7.77	2.22	1.75
4.0	0.321	0.210	0.041	0.428	189.28	0.00	9.42	1.83	6.01
5.0	0.309	0.213	0.043	0.435	48623.30	0.61	146.46	1.65	13289.10

Table 2 shows the effects of using the learned parameters for the CO task on the training topics 162-201. Note that we use the new INEX-2.2 corpus, so these results are not directly comparable to previous results on these topics. As there are many documents that in the INEX-2.2 corpus that were not available for assessment for the topics, one should regard the evaluation numbers as a suboptimal estimate of performance. Nevertheless, we are mostly interested in the relative performance of the parameters learned for different values of ν, and the values in Table 2 should be adequate for that purpose.

In Table 2 we see that setting $\nu = 1$ yields the most consistently good results for both quantizations. There also seems to be some variation in the columns that does not follow a nice curve. This is an undesirable property which could be a result of variance in the learning algorithm, a sign of instability in the evaluation metrics, or a symptom of too few topics to get a reliable point estimate given the topic variance of the system.

Table 2. Results of varying the negative weight ν on the CO task using training topics 162-201. Values in bold font indicate the largest value for a measure.

| | Strict | | | | Generalized | | | |
| | nxCG | | | MAP | nxCG | | | MAP |
ν	10	25	50	ep/gr	10	25	50	ep/gr
1.0	0.0704	0.0880	**0.1307**	**0.0034**	**0.2946**	**0.2950**	**0.2944**	**0.0852**
1.5	0.0593	**0.0906**	0.1266	0.0032	0.2938	0.2803	0.2710	0.0753
2.0	0.0593	0.0766	0.1237	0.0032	0.2899	0.2878	0.2816	0.0791
2.5	0.0704	0.0832	0.1226	0.0032	0.2922	0.2760	0.2637	0.0716
3.0	0.0704	0.0876	0.1210	0.0031	0.2911	0.2671	0.2536	0.0667
3.5	0.0704	0.0837	0.1218	0.0031	0.2920	0.2649	0.2490	0.0640
4.0	0.0593	0.0820	0.1197	0.0028	0.2903	0.2695	0.2447	0.0612
4.5	**0.0741**	0.0835	0.1219	0.0026	0.2857	0.2554	0.2383	0.0561
5.0	0.0630	0.0732	0.1087	0.0025	0.2791	0.2464	0.2256	0.0520

Table 3 shows the performance of the learned parameters on this year's CO.Thorough task. Performance for the generalized quantization peaks at $\nu = 2$ and around $\nu = 4$ for the strict quantization. This is quite a bit different from our observations on the training data. We would like to investigate this behavior in more detail. This could simply be the result of a training topic set that is too small or not representative enough. An alternative cause for difference is the change in the assessment methodology this year, which could result in assessors behaving giving different scores.

Table 3. Results of varying the negative weight ν on the CO.Thorough task using test topics 202-241. Values in bold font indicate the largest value for a measure.

| | Strict | | | | Generalized | | | |
| | nxCG | | | MAP | nxCG | | | MAP |
ν	10	25	50	ep/gr	10	25	50	ep/gr
1.0	0.0200	0.0639	0.1051	0.0021	0.2225	0.2298	0.2286	0.0854
1.5	0.0440	0.0623	0.0911	0.0022	0.2207	0.2218	0.2197	0.0801
2.0	0.0440	0.0639	0.1006	0.0022	**0.2464**	**0.2421**	**0.2340**	**0.0882**
2.5	0.0440	0.0655	0.1127	0.0026	0.2200	0.2215	0.2224	0.0813
3.0	0.0440	0.0712	0.1184	0.0027	0.2164	0.2221	0.2167	0.0771
3.5	0.0400	0.0744	0.1192	0.0022	0.2131	0.2189	0.2149	0.0717
4.0	**0.0691**	**0.0747**	**0.1225**	0.0028	0.2445	0.2248	0.2172	0.0751
4.5	0.0651	0.0715	0.1131	**0.0029**	0.2301	0.2144	0.2126	0.0701
5.0	0.0651	0.0731	0.1116	**0.0029**	0.2326	0.2183	0.2089	0.0682

If we had submitted the system optimized to the training data ($\nu = 1$), then our results would have been in the top 10 official submissions for the strict quantization nxCG@50 metric and the generalized quantization MAP ep/gr metric. Supposing we had worked out our kinks in training (whether they be a result of the algorithm or the assessments) and we had selected the runs with $\nu = 2, 4$ for evaluation, then we would have had a run performing in thetop 10 official submissions for the strict quantization nxCG@10,50 and MAP ep/gr metrics and for the generalized quantization nxCG@25,50 and MAP ep/gr metrics.

7   Conclusions

We have derived a Generalized Expectation Maximization algorithm to learn the parameters of a simple hierarchical language modeling system for the ranking and retrieval of XML elements. We showed a way to effectively incorporate non-relevant elements during training.

We investigated the interaction of the relative weight on the negative training examples ν and retrieval effectiveness on the CO.Thorough task. Experimental evidence suggests that the optimal ν parameter may depend on the quantization function used in evaluation. However, we have not done a full investigation of the choice of positive and negative examples during training. In training, we relied only on elements that were highly exhaustive and highly specific. This assumption is essentially the assumption of the strict quantization function. We have not done experiments where we use elements deemed relevant by the generalized quantization function. While we leave this to future work, we recognize this may change the optimal choice of ν for optimizing performance for measures using the generalized quantization function.

Our incorporation of negative examples is ad-hoc. As future work, we plan to simulate replication of negative examples rather than directly modifying the probabilities of the language models we are combining. This is a minor change to the algorithm and will not change the maximum likelihood derivation presented in Section 3, but it will be more technically sound than the current incorporation of negative evidence presented in Section 4. We would also like to consider the possibility of performing the negative evidence at the query level, rather than negating probabilities at the level of query terms.

For these experiments, we worked with a simplified hierarchical model. Our previous work [1][2][3] presented a hierarchical model where elements were smoothed recursively up and down the element containment tree for a document. This work was a much simplified version where the smoothing was not recursive, but addressed the question of parameter estimation. We would like to adapt the training algorithm to model recursive smoothing and learn parameters with that optimize the likelihood under that condition.

Up to this point we have discussed only flat text queries. We would like to adapt this approach to work with structured queries to learn approaches to weight elements of the query. For example, we may learn that satisfaction of a phrasal constraint should receive higher weight than a constraint on the document structure.

Acknowledgments

This research was sponsored by National Science Foundation (NSF) grant no. CCR-0122581. The views and conclusions contained in this document are those of the author and should not be interpreted as representing the official policies, either expressed or implicit, of the NSF or the US government.

References

1. Ogilvie, P., Callan, J.: Language models and structured document retrieval. In: Proceedings of the First Workshop of the INitiative for the Evaluation of XML Retrieval (INEX). (2003)
2. Ogilvie, P., Callan, J.P.: Using language models for flat text queries in xml retrieval. In: Proc. of the Second Annual Workshop of the Initiative for the Evaluation of XML retrieval (INEX), Dagstuhl, Germany (2003)
3. Ogilvie, P., Callan, J.: Hierarchical language models for xml component retrieval. In: Advances in XML Information Retrieval: Third International Workshop of the Initiative for the Evaluation of XML Retrieval, INEX 2004, Springer-Verlag (2005) 224–237
4. Neal, R., Hinton, G.E.: A view of the em algorithm that justifies incremental, sparse, and other variants. (1998)
5. Ogilvie, P., Callan, J.P.: Combining document representations for known-item search. In: Proc. of the 26th annual int. ACM SIGIR conf. on Research and development in informaion retrieval (SIGIR-03), New York, ACM Press (2003) 143–150
6. Kamps, J., de Rijke, M., Sigurbjörnsson, B.: Length normalization in xml retrieval. In: Proceedings of the Twenty-Seventh Annual International ACM SIGIR Conference on Research and Development in Information Retrieval. (2004) 80–87
7. http://lemurproject.org/: (The lemur toolkit for language modeling and information retrieval)

Appendix: EM Derivation

Suppose we were given additional information $\mathcal{Y} = (y_1, \ldots, y_N)$ which specify that the θ_{y_i} distribution generated the x_i query term. Given knowledge of $\mathbf{y}$, the likelihood becomes

$$\mathcal{L}\left(\Lambda \,|\, \mathcal{X}, \mathcal{Y}\right) = \prod_{i=1}^{N} \lambda_{iy_i} P\left(x_i \,|\, \theta_{y_i}\right) \tag{19}$$

and the log-likelihood of the data is then

$$\log \mathcal{L}\left(\Lambda \,|\, \mathcal{X}, \mathcal{Y}\right) = \sum_{i=1}^{N} \log\left(\lambda_{iy_i} P\left(x_i \,|\, \theta_{y_i}\right)\right) \tag{20}$$

The problem is now that we do not know the values of $\mathcal{Y}$. However, we may treat it as a random vector and apply Expectation-Maximization.

Suppose we have a guess at the Λ parameters we shall call Λ^g. Using Λ^g we can compute $P\left(x_i \,|\, \mu_j^g\right)$. Applying Bayes rule, we calculate

$$P\left(y_i \,|\, x_i, \Lambda^g\right) = \frac{\lambda_{iy_i}^g P\left(x_i \,|\, \theta_{y_i}\right)}{P\left(x_i \,|\, \Lambda^g\right)} = \frac{\lambda_{iy_i}^g P\left(x_i \,|\, \theta_{y_i}\right)}{\sum_{j=1}^{M} \lambda_{ij}^g P\left(x_i \,|\, \theta_j\right)} = \frac{\lambda_{iy_i}^g P\left(x_i \,|\, \theta_{y_i}\right)}{\sum_{j \in family(i)} \lambda_{ij}^g P\left(x_i \,|\, \theta_j\right)} \tag{21}$$

and

$$P(\mathbf{y} \,|\, \mathcal{X}, \Lambda^g) = \prod_{i=1}^{N} P(y_i \,|\, x_i, \Lambda^g) \qquad (22)$$

where $\mathbf{y} = (y_1, y_2, \dots, y_N)$ is an independently drawn value of the random vector. We may now estimate the expectation of Λ given Λ^g:

$$
\begin{aligned}
Q(\Lambda, \Lambda^g) &= \sum_{\mathbf{y} \in \Upsilon} \log\left(\mathcal{L}(\Lambda \,|\, \mathcal{X}, \mathbf{y})\right) P(\mathbf{y} \,|\, \mathcal{X}, \Lambda^g) \\
&= \sum_{l=1}^{M} \sum_{i=1}^{N} \log\left(\lambda_{il} P(x_i \,|\, \theta_l)\right) P(l \,|\, x_i, \Lambda^g)
\end{aligned}
\qquad (23)
$$

At this point we observe that to maximize this equation, we take the partial derivative of $Q(\Lambda, \Lambda^g)$ with respect to each of the Λ parameters.

When we maximize λ_C, we also introduce the Lagrange multiplier ϕ with the constraint that $\lambda_C + \lambda_D + \lambda_P + \lambda_O = 1$ and solve the following equation:

$$\frac{\partial}{\partial \lambda_C}\left[\sum_{l=1}^{M} \sum_{i=1}^{N} \log\left(\lambda_{il} P(x_i \,|\, \theta_l)\right) P(l \,|\, x_i, \Lambda^g) + \phi\left(\lambda_C + \lambda_D + \lambda_P + \lambda_O - 1\right)\right] = 0$$

$$\frac{\partial}{\partial \lambda_C}\left[\begin{array}{l} \sum_{i=1}^{N} \log(\lambda_C) P(y = 1 \,|\, x_i, \Lambda^g) + \phi\lambda_C \\ +\text{some constants with respect to } \lambda_C \end{array}\right] = 0$$

$$\frac{1}{\lambda_C} \sum_{i=1}^{N} P(y = 1 \,|\, x_i, \Lambda^g) + \phi = 0 \qquad (24)$$

The inclusion of the Lagrangian multiplier is a common calculus technique which allows us to enforce the constraint that the *lambda* parameters sum to one. Similarly, to maximize λ_D, λ_P, and λ_O, we use

$$\frac{1}{\lambda_D} \sum_{i=1}^{N} P(y = d(i) \,|\, x_i, \Lambda^g) + \phi = 0$$

$$\frac{1}{\lambda_P} \sum_{i=1}^{N} P(y = p(i) \,|\, x_i, \Lambda^g) + \phi = 0 \qquad (25)$$

$$\frac{1}{\lambda_O} \sum_{i=1}^{N} \sum_{j \in (s(i)) \cup c(i)} P(y = j \,|\, x_i, \Lambda^g) + \phi = 0$$

By summing these equations we get $\phi = -N$. We can then obtain the following update rules:

$$
\begin{aligned}
\lambda_C^{[t]} &= \tfrac{1}{N} \sum_{i=1}^{N} P\left(y = 1 \,\middle|\, x_i, \Lambda^{[t-1]}\right) \\[4pt]
\lambda_D^{[t]} &= \tfrac{1}{N} \sum_{i=1}^{N} P\left(y = d(i) \,\middle|\, x_i, \Lambda^{[t-1]}\right) \\[4pt]
\lambda_P^{[t]} &= \tfrac{1}{N} \sum_{i=1}^{N} P\left(y = p(i) \,\middle|\, x_i, \Lambda^{[t-1]}\right) \\[4pt]
\lambda_O^{[t]} &= \tfrac{1}{N} \sum_{i=1}^{N} \sum_{j \in (s(i)) \cup c(i)} P\left(y = j \,\middle|\, x_i, \Lambda^{[t-1]}\right)
\end{aligned}
\qquad (26)
$$

Let us continue to the α_k parameters. In order to enforce the desired constraint that each α_k be positive, we substitute α_k with $\exp(\beta_k) = e^{\beta_k}$ (we use e as a shorthand for the exponential function). We will also define a few formulas to simplify our derivations:

$$a_{ik} = \sum_{j' \in c(i), t(j') = k} |j'|$$

$$b_{ik} = |s(i)| + \sum_{j' \in c(i), t(j') \neq k} \beta_{t(j')} |j'|$$

$$f_{ik} = P(y = s(i) | x_i, \Lambda^g) + \sum_{j \in c(i), t(j) \neq k} P(y = j | x_i, \Lambda^g)$$

$$h_{ik} = \sum_{j \in c(i), t(j) = k} P(y = j | x_i, \Lambda^g)$$

(27)

To find our update rule for β_k, we take the partial derivative of the likelihood with respect to β_k and solve for β_k.

$$\frac{\partial}{\partial \beta_k} \left[\sum_{i : j \in c(i), t(j) = k} \left[\begin{array}{l} \log\left(\frac{|s(i)|}{b_{ik} + e^{\beta_k} a_{ik}}\right) P(y = s(i) | x_i, \Lambda^g) \\ + \sum_{j \in c(i), t(j) = k} \log\left(\frac{e^{\beta_k} |j|}{b_{ik} + e^{\beta_k} a_{ik}}\right) P(y = j | x_i, \Lambda^g) \\ + \sum_{j \in c(i), t(j) \neq k} \log\left(\frac{e^{\beta_{t(j)}} |j|}{b_{ik} + e^{\beta_k} a_{ik}}\right) P(y = j | x_i, \Lambda^g) \end{array} \right] \right. $$
$$\left. + \text{some constants with respect to } \beta_k \right] = 0$$

(28)

We first take the chain rule, resulting in the multiplier β_k, then take the partial derivative of the summation with respect to β_k.

$$e^{\beta_k} \sum_{i : j \in c(i), t(j) = k} \left[\begin{array}{l} \frac{-a_{ik}}{b_{ik} + \beta_k a_{ik}} P(y = s(i) | x_i, \Lambda^g) \\ + \sum_{j \in c(i), t(j) = k} \frac{b_{ik}}{e^{\beta_k}(b_{ik} + e^{\beta_k} a_{ik})} P(y = j | x_i, \Lambda^g) \\ + \sum_{j \in c(i), t(j) \neq k} \frac{-a_{ik}}{b_{ik} + e^{\beta_k} a_{ik}} P(y = j | x_i, \Lambda^g) \end{array} \right] = 0$$

(29)

$$\beta_k \sum_{i : j \in c(i), t(j) = k} \frac{-a_{ik} f_{ik} + \frac{b_{ik} h_{ik}}{e^{\beta_k}}}{b_{ik} + e^{\beta_k} a_{ik}} = 0$$

(30)

Since we cannot solve directly solve this equation for β_k, we will use a linear approximation around the point β_k^g (Newton-Raphson method):

$$\frac{\partial}{\partial \beta_k} Q(\Lambda, \Lambda^g) \approx \frac{\partial}{\partial \beta_k} Q(\Lambda, \Lambda^g)_{\beta_k = \beta_k^g} + (\beta_k - \beta_k^g) \frac{\partial^2}{\partial \beta_k^2} Q(\Lambda, \Lambda^g)_{\beta_k = \beta_k^g}$$

(31)

Since we set $\frac{\partial}{\partial \beta_k} Q\left(\Lambda, \Lambda^g\right) = 0$,

$$\beta_k \approx \beta_k^g - \frac{\frac{\partial}{\partial \beta_k} Q\left(\Lambda, \Lambda^g\right)_{\beta_k=\beta_k^g}}{\frac{\partial^2}{\partial \beta_k^2} Q\left(\Lambda, \Lambda^g\right)_{\beta_k=\beta_k^g}} \tag{32}$$

where

$$\frac{\partial}{\partial \beta_k} Q\left(\Lambda, \Lambda^g\right)_{\beta_k=\beta_k^g} = e^{\beta_k^g} \sum_{i:j\in c(i),t(j)=k} \frac{-a_{ik}f_{ik} + \frac{b_{ik}h_{ik}}{e^{\beta_k^g}}}{b_{ik} + e^{\beta_k^g} a_{ik}} \tag{33}$$

and

$$\frac{\partial^2}{\partial \beta_k^2} Q\left(\Lambda, \Lambda^g\right)_{\beta_k=\beta_k^g} = e^{\beta_k^g} \left(\begin{array}{l} \frac{\partial}{\partial \beta_k} Q\left(\Lambda, \Lambda^g\right)_{\beta_k=\beta_k^g} + \\[2mm] e^{\beta_k^g} \sum_{i:j\in c(i),t(j)=k} \frac{a_{ik}^2 f_{ik} - \frac{b_{ik}^2 h_{ik}}{e^{\beta_k^g\,2}}}{\left(b_{ik} + e^{\beta_k^g} a_{ik}\right)^2} \end{array} \right) \tag{34}$$

Thus, we will have the following update rule for our β_k parameter estimates:

$$\beta_k^{[t]} = \beta_k^{[t-1]} - \frac{\frac{\partial}{\partial \beta_k} Q\left(\Lambda, \Lambda^g\right)_{\beta_k=\beta_k^{[t-1]}}}{\frac{\partial^2}{\partial \beta_k^2} Q\left(\Lambda, \Lambda^g\right)_{\beta_k=\beta_k^{[t-1]}}} \tag{35}$$

Probabilistic Retrieval, Component Fusion and Blind Feedback for XML Retrieval

Ray R. Larson

School of Information Management and Systems,
University of California, Berkeley
Berkeley, California, USA, 94720-4600
ray@sims.berkeley.edu

Abstract. This paper describes the retrieval approaches used by UC Berkeley in our official submissions for the various Adhoc tasks. As in previous INEX evaluations, the main technique we are testing is the fusion of multiple probabilistic searches against different XML components using different probabilistic retrieval algorithms. In addition this year we began to use a different fusion/combination method from previous years. This year we also continued to use re-estimated Logistic Regression (LR) parameters for different components of the IEEE document collection, estimated using relevance judgements from the INEX 2003 evaluation. All of our runs were fully automatic with no manual editing or interactive submission of queries, and all used only the title elements of the INEX topics.

1   Introduction

When analyzing the results of the 2004 INEX evaluation we discovered a number of interesting approaches to XML retrieval that we had not previously explored. In particular we were struck by the work of Mass and Mandelbrod[13] adjusting the weights of component-level search results using the weights of document-level matching for the same documents. This seemed to have a natural affinity for the fusion approaches that we had already tried[11]. We ran a large number of experiments using the INEX 2004 relevance data and various combinations of components and weights for our version of the "pivot" value. In addition, we participated this year in CLEF and the GeoCLEF evaluations, where we were able to analyze the differences in performance between our fusion approaches and the alternative version of the Berkeley Logistic regression algorithm that has been used there for a number of years (See [3]) The best performing of those approaches (according to the incomplete analysis using the new evaluation methods for INEX that we were able to do in the short period between the end of CLEF and the submission date for INEX) were used in this year's various INEX adhoc tasks with no modification. This is the first time that we have used blind feedback and the "TREC2" version of Logistic regression in addition to using the re-estimated parameters for the "TREC3" model based on the relevance judgements from INEX 2003.

N. Fuhr et al. (Eds.): INEX 2005, LNCS 3977, pp. 225–239, 2006.

In this paper we will first discuss the algorithms and fusion operators used in our official INEX 2005 adhoc runs. Then we will look at how these algorithms and operators were used in the various submissions for the adhoc track, and finally we will examine the results and discuss possible problems in implementation, and directions for future research.

2   The Retrieval Algorithms and Fusion Operators

This year we did not use the Okapi BM-25 algorithm in our official INEX adhoc runs. Instead we used a new approach to combining and weighting the elements using only Logistic regression-based algorithms for retrieval.

In the remainder of this section we will describe the Logistic Regression algorithms that were used for the evaluation as well as the blind relevance feedback method used in combination with the TREC2 algorithm. In addition we will discuss the methods used to combine the results of searches of different XML components in the collections. The algorithms and combination methods are implemented as part of the Cheshire II XML/SGML search engine [10, 11, 9] which also supports a number of other algorithms for distributed search and operators for merging result lists from ranked or Boolean sub-queries.

2.1   TREC3 Logistic Regression Algorithm

The basic form and variables of the *Logistic Regression* (LR) algorithm used was originally developed by Cooper, et al. [6]. It provided good full-text retrieval performance in the TREC ad hoc task and in TREC interactive tasks [8] and for distributed IR [9]. As originally formulated, the LR model of probabilistic IR attempts to estimate the probability of relevance for each document based on a set of statistics about a document collection and a set of queries in combination with a set of weighting coefficients for those statistics. The statistics to be used and the values of the coefficients are obtained from regression analysis of a sample of a collection (or similar test collection) for some set of queries where relevance and non-relevance has been determined. More formally, given a particular query and a particular document in a collection $P(R \mid Q, D)$ is calculated and the documents or components are presented to the user ranked in order of decreasing values of that probability. To avoid invalid probability values, the usual calculation of $P(R \mid Q, D)$ uses the "log odds" of relevance given a set of S statistics, s_i, derived from the query and database, such that:

$$\log O(R \mid Q, D) = b_0 + \sum_{i=1}^{S} b_i s_i \tag{1}$$

where b_0 is the intercept term and the b_i are the coefficients obtained from the regression analysis of the sample collection and relevance judgements. The final ranking is determined by the conversion of the log odds form to probabilities:

$$P(R \mid Q, D) = \frac{e^{\log O(R|Q,D)}}{1 + e^{\log O(R|Q,D)}} \tag{2}$$

Based on the structure of XML documents as a tree of XML elements, we define a "document component" as an XML subtree that may include zero or more subordinate XML elements or subtrees with text as the leaf nodes of the tree. For example, in the XML Document Type Definition (DTD) for the INEX test collection defines an article (marked by XML tag $<article>$) that contains front matter ($<fm>$), a body ($<bdy>$) and optional back matter ($<bm>$). The front matter ($<fm>$), in turn, can contain a header $<hdr>$ and may include editor information ($<edinfo>$), author information ($<au>$), a title group ($<tig>$), abstract ($<abs>$) and other elements. A title group can contain elements including article title ($<atl>$) the page range for the article ($<pn>$), and these in turn may contain other elements, down to the level of individual formatted words or characters. Thus, a component might be defined using any of these tagged elements. However, *not all possible components are likely to be useful* in content-oriented retrieval (e.g., tags indicating that a word in the title should be in italic type, or the page number range) therefore we defined the retrievable components selectively, including document sections and paragraphs from the article body, and bibliography entries from the back matter (see Table 3).

Naturally, a full XML document may also be considered a "document component". As discussed below, the indexing and retrieval methods used in this research take into account a selected set of document components for generating the statistics used in the search process and for extraction of the parts of a document to be returned in response to a query. Because we are dealing with not only full documents, but also document components (such as sections and paragraphs or similar structures) derived from the documents, we will use C to represent document components in place of D. Therefore, the full equation describing the LR algorithm used in these experiments is:

$$\log O(R \mid Q, C) =$$

$$b_0 + \left(b_1 \cdot \left(\frac{1}{|Q_c|} \sum_{j=1}^{|Q_c|} \log qtf_j \right) \right)$$

$$+ \left(b_2 \cdot \sqrt{|Q|} \right)$$

$$+ \left(b_3 \cdot \left(\frac{1}{|Q_c|} \sum_{j=1}^{|Q_c|} \log tf_j \right) \right) \tag{3}$$

$$+ \left(b_4 \cdot \sqrt{cl} \right)$$

$$+ \left(b_5 \cdot \left(\frac{1}{|Q_c|} \sum_{j=1}^{|Q_c|} \log \frac{N - n_{t_j}}{n_{t_j}} \right) \right)$$

$$+ \left(b_6 \cdot \log |Q_d| \right)$$

Where:

Q is a query containing terms T,

$|Q|$ is the total number of terms in Q,
$|Q_c|$ is the number of terms in Q that also occur in the document component,
tf_j is the frequency of the jth term in a specific document component,
qtf_j is the frequency of the jth term in Q,
n_{t_j} is the number of components (of a given type) containing the jth term,
cl is the document component length measured in bytes.
N is the number of components of a given type in the collection.
b_i are the coefficients obtained though the regression analysis.

This equation, used in estimating the probability of relevance in this research, is essentially the same as that used in [5]. The b_i coefficients in the original version of this algorithm were estimated using relevance judgements and statistics from the TREC/TIPSTER test collection. In INEX 2005 we did not use the original or "Base" version, but instead used a version where the coeffients for each of the major document components were estimated separately and combined through component fusion. The coefficients for the Base version were $b_0 = -3.70$, $b_1 = 1.269$, $b_2 = -0.310$, $b_3 = 0.679$, $b_4 = -0.0674$, $b_5 = 0.223$ and $b_6 = 2.01$. The re-estimated coefficients were derived from the Logistic regression analysis using the INEX 2003 relevance assessments. In fact, separate formulae were derived for each of the major components of the INEX XML document structure, providing a different formula for each major component of the collection. These formulae were used in all the TREC3 LR runs submitted for the INEX 2005 adhoc tasks, The components and coefficients for each of b_i in formula 4 are shown in table 1.

Table 1. Re-Estimated Coefficients for The TREC3 Logistic Regression Model

Index	b_0	b_1	b_2	b_3	b_4	b_5	b_6
Base	-3.70	1.269	-0.310	0.679	-0.0674	0.223	2.01
topic	-7.758	5.670	-3.427	1.787	-0.030	1.952	5.880
topicshort	-6.364	2.739	-1.443	1.228	-0.020	1.280	3.837
abstract	-5.892	2.318	-1.364	0.860	-0.013	1.052	3.600
alltitles	-5.243	2.319	-1.361	1.415	-0.037	1.180	3.696
sec_words	-6.392	2.125	-1.648	1.106	-0.075	1.174	3.632
para_words	-8.632	1.258	-1.654	1.485	-0.084	1.143	4.004

2.2   TREC2 Logistic Regression Algorithm

We also implemented a version of the LR algorithm that has been used very successfully in Cross-Language IR by Berkeley researchers for a number of years[3]. This algorithm, originally developed by Cooper et al. [4] for TREC2 is:

$$\log O(R|C,Q) = \log \frac{p(R|C,Q)}{1 - p(R|C,Q)} = \log \frac{p(R|C,Q)}{p(\overline{R}|C,Q)}$$

$$= c_0 + c_1 * \frac{1}{\sqrt{|Q_c|} + 1} \sum_{i=1}^{|Q_c|} \frac{qtf_i}{ql + 35}$$

$$+ c_2 * \frac{1}{\sqrt{|Q_c|} + 1} \sum_{i=1}^{|Q_c|} \log \frac{tf_i}{cl + 80}$$

$$- c_3 * \frac{1}{\sqrt{|Q_c|} + 1} \sum_{i=1}^{|Q_c|} \log \frac{ctf_i}{N_t}$$

$$+ c_4 * |Q_c|$$

where C denotes a document component and Q a query, R is a relevance variable,

$p(R|C,Q)$ is the probability that document component C is relevant to query Q,

$p(\overline{R}|C,Q)$ the probability that document component C is not relevant to query Q, which is 1.0 - $p(R|C,Q)$

$|Q_c|$ is the number of matching terms between a document component and a query,

qtf_i is the within-query frequency of the ith matching term,

tf_i is the within-document frequency of the ith matching term,

ctf_i is the occurrence frequency in a collection of the ith matching term,

ql is query length (i.e., number of terms in a query like $|Q|$ for non-feedback situations),

cl is component length (i.e., number of terms in a component), and

N_t is collection length (i.e., number of terms in a test collection).

c_k are the k coefficients obtained though the regression analysis.

If stopwords are removed from indexing, then ql, cl, and N_t are the query length, document length, and collection length, respectively. If the query terms are re-weighted (in feedback, for example), then qtf_i is no longer the original term frequency, but the new weight, and ql is the sum of the new weight values for the query terms. Note that, unlike the document and collection lengths, query length is the "optimized" relative frequency without first taking the log over the matching terms.

The coefficients were determined by fitting the logistic regression model specified in $\log O(R|C,Q)$ to TREC training data using a statistical software package. The coefficients, c_k, used for our official runs are the same as those described by Chen[1]. These were: $c_0 = -3.51$, $c_1 = 37.4$, $c_2 = 0.330$, $c_3 = 0.1937$ and $c_4 = 0.0929$. Further details on the TREC2 version of the Logistic Regression algorithm may be found in Cooper et al. [4].

2.3   Blind Relevance Feedback

It is well known that blind (also called pseudo) relevance feedback can substantially improve retrieval effectiveness in tasks such as TREC and CLEF. (See for example the papers of the groups who participated in the Ad Hoc tasks in TREC-7 (Voorhees and Harman 1998)[16] and TREC-8 (Voorhees and Harman 1999)[17].)

Blind relevance feedback is typically performed in two stages. First, an initial search using the original queries is performed, after which a number of terms are selected from the top-ranked documents (which are presumed to be relevant). The selected terms are weighted and then merged with the initial query to formulate a new query. Finally the reweighted and expanded query is run against the same collection to produce a final ranked list of documents. It was a simple extension to adapt these document-level algorithms to document components for INEX.

The TREC2 algorithm has been been combined with a blind feedback method developed by Aitao Chen for cross-language retrieval in CLEF. Chen[2] presents a technique for incorporating blind relevance feedback into the logistic regression-based document ranking framework. Several factors are important in using blind relevance feedback. These are: determining the number of top ranked documents that will be presumed relevant and from which new terms will be extracted, how to rank the selected terms and determining the number of terms that should be selected, how to assign weights to the selected terms. Many techniques have been used for deciding the number of terms to be selected, the number of top-ranked documents from which to extract terms, and ranking the terms. Harman [7] provides a survey of relevance feedback techniques that have been used.

Lacking comparable data from previous years, we adopted some rather arbitrary parameters for these options for INEX 2005. We used top 10 ranked components for the initial search of each component type, and enhanced and reweighted the query terms using term relevance weights derived from well-known Robertson and Sparck Jones[14] relevance weights, as described by Chen and Gey[3]. The top 10 terms that occurred in the (presumed) relevant top 10 documents, that were not already in the query were added for the feedback search.

2.4 Result Combination Operators

As we have reported previously, the Cheshire II system used in this evaluation provides a number of operators to combine the intermediate results of a search from different components or indexes. With these operators we have available an entire spectrum of combination methods ranging from strict Boolean operations to fuzzy Boolean and normalized score combinations for probabilistic and Boolean results. These operators are the means available for performing fusion operations between the results for different retrieval algorithms and the search results from different different components of a document. We will only describe one of these operators here, because it was the only type used in the evaluation reported in this paper.

The MERGE_CMBZ operator is based on the "CombMNZ" fusion algorithm developed by Shaw and Fox [15] and used by Lee [12]. In our version we take the normalized scores, but then further enhance scores for components appearing in both lists (doubling them) and penalize normalized scores appearing low in a single result list, while using the unmodified normalized score for higher ranking items in a single list.

A new addition for this year was a merge/reweighting operator based on the "Pivot" method described by Mass and Mandelbrod[13]. In our case the new probability of relevance for a component is a weighted combination of the initial estimate probability of relevance for the component and the probability of relevance for the entire article for the same query terms. Formally this is:

$$P(R \mid Q, C_{new}) = (X * P(R \mid Q, C_{comp})) + ((1 - X) * P(R \mid Q, C_{art})) \quad (4)$$

Where X is a pivot value between 0 and 1, and $P(R \mid Q, C_{new})$, $P(R \mid Q, C_{comp})$ and $P(R \mid Q, C_{art})$ are the new weight, the original component weight, and article weight for a given query. Although we found that a pivot value of 0.54 was most effective for INEX04 data and measures, we adopted the "neutral" pivot value of 0.5 for all of our 2005 adhoc runs, given the uncertainties of how this approach would fare with the new metrics and tasks.

3   INEX 2005 Adhoc Approach

Our approach for the INEX 2005 adhoc tasks was a bit different from the methods used in previous INEX 2003 and INEX 2004 evaluations. This section will describe the indexing process and indexes used, and also discuss the scripts used for search processing. The basic database was the expanded IEEE collection. We will summarize the indexing process and the indexes used in the adhoc tasks for reference in the discussion.

3.1   Indexing the INEX 2005 Database

All indexing in the Cheshire II system is controlled by an XML/SGML Configuration file which describes the database to be created. This configuration file is subsequently used in search processing to control the mapping of search command index names (or Z39.50 numeric attributes representing particular types of bibliographic data) to the physical index files used and also to associated component indexes with particular components and documents. This configuration file also includes the index-specific definitions for the Logistic Regression coefficients (when not defined, these default to the "Base" coefficients shown in Table 1).

Table 2 lists the document-level (/article) indexes created for the INEX database and the document elements from which the contents of those indexes were extracted. These indexes (with the addition of the are the same as those used last year. The *abstract, alltitles, keywords, title, topic* and *topicshort* indexes support proximity indexes (i.e., term location), supporting phrase searching.

As noted above the Cheshire system permits parts of the document subtree to be treated as separate documents with their own separate indexes. Tables 3 & 4 describe the XML components created for INEX and the component-level indexes that were created for them.

Table 3 shows the components and the path used to define them. The first, COMP_SECTION, component consists of each identified section or subsection (<sec> ... </sec>) in all of the documents, permitting each individual section and subsection of a article to be retrieved separately. Similarly, each of the COMP_BIB, COMP_PARAS, and COMP_FIG components, respectively,

Table 2. Cheshire Article-Level Indexes for INEX

Name	Description	Contents	Vector?
docno	Digital Object ID	//doi	No
pauthor	Author Names	//fm/au/snm //fm/au/fnm	No
title	Article Title	//fm/tig/atl	No

topic	Content Words	//fm/tig/atl
		 //abs
		 //bdy
		 //bibl/bb/atl
		 //app
			Yes

topicshort	Content Words 2	//fm/tig/atl
		 //abs
		 //kwd
		 //st
			Yes

date	Date of Publication	//hdr2/yr	No
journal	Journal Title	//hdr1/ti	No
kwd	Article Keywords	//kwd	No
abstract	Article Abstract	//abs	Yes
author_seq	Author Seq.	//fm/au @sequence	No
bib_author _fnm	Bib Author Forename	//bb/au/fnm	No
bib_author _snm	Bib Author Surname	//bb/au/snm	No
fig	Figure Contents	//fig	No
ack	Acknowledgements	//ack	No
alltitles	All Title Elements	//atl, //st	Yes
affil	Author Affiliations	//fm/aff	No
fno	IEEE Article ID	//fno	No

treat each bibliographic reference (<bb> ... </bb>), paragraph (with all of the alternative paragraph elements shown in Table 3), and figure (<fig> ... </fig>) as individual documents that can be retrieved separately from the entire document.

Table 4 describes the XML component indexes created for the components described in Table 3. These indexes make individual sections (COMP_SECTION) of the INEX documents retrievable by their titles, or by any terms occurring in the section. These are also proximity indexes, so phrase searching is supported within the indexes. Bibliographic references in the articles (COMP_BIB) are made accessible by the author names, titles, and publication date of the individual bibliographic entry, with proximity searching supported for bibliography titles. Individual paragraphs (COMP_PARAS) are searchable by any of the terms in the paragraph, also with proximity searching. Individual figures (COMP_FIG) are indexed by their captions, and vitae (COMP_VITAE) are indexed by keywords within the text, with proximity support.

Table 3. Cheshire Components for INEX

Name	Description	Contents
COMP_SECTION	Sections	//sec //ss1 //ss2 //ss3
COMP_BIB	Bib Entries	//bib/bibl/bb

COMP_PARAS	Paragraphs	//ilrj|//ip1|//ip2|
		//ip3|//ip4|//ip5|
		//item-none|//p|
		//p1|//p2|//p3|
		//tmath|//tf

COMP_FIG	Figures	//fig
COMP_VITAE	Vitae	//vt

Table 4. Cheshire Component Indexes for INEX †Includes all subelements of paragraph elements

Component or Index Name	Description	Contents	Vector?
COMP_SECTION			
sec_title	Section Title	//sec/st	Yes
sec_words	Section Words	//sec	Yes
COMP_BIB			
bib_author	Bib. Author	//au	No
bib_title	Bib. Title	//atl	Yes
bib_date	Bib. Date	//pdt/yr	No
COMP_PARAS			
para_words	Paragraph Words	*†	Yes
COMP_FIG			
fig_caption	Figure Caption	//fgc	No
COMP_VITAE			
vitae_words	Words from Vitae	//vt	No

Almost all of these indexes and components were used during Berkeley's search evaluation runs of the 2005 INEX topics. The official submitted runs and scripts used in INEX are described in the next section.

3.2   INEX 2005 Official Adhoc Runs

Berkeley submitted a total of 20 retrieval runs for the INEX 2005 adhoc tasks, these included 3 for each of the CO and CO+S Focussed and Thorough tasks, two each for CO and COS FetchBrowse tasks and one run each for the VVCAS, VSCAS, SVCAS and SSCAS tasks. This section briefly describes the individual runs and general approach taken in creating the queries submitted against the INEX database and the scripts used to prepare the search results for submission. The following sections briefly describe Berkeley's INEX 2005 runs. Note that all of the runs used only the "title" or "castitle" elements of the INEX 2005 topics in searching.

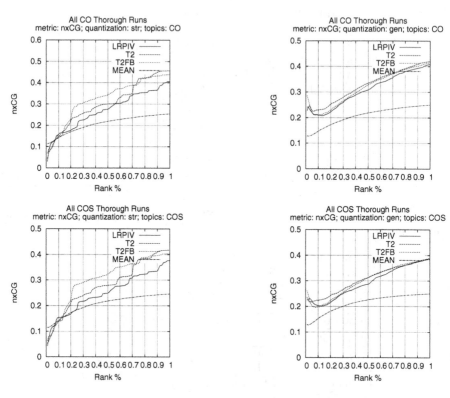

Fig. 1. Berkeley THOROUGH Runs – Strict (left) and Generalized (right) Quantization

3.3   CO and CO+S Runs

Essentially the same basic component retrieval runs were used with different post-retrieval processing for the Thorough, Focussed, and FetchBrowse tasks. Our primary focus was on the Thorough task, since that was most similiar to our most effective runs from previous INEX evaluations. The three runs for each of the CO and CO+S Thorough and Focussed tasks were:

LRPIV: Runs containing this term in their names used the TREC3 algorithm as described above for all retrieval ranking. The basic results were the combination of searches on each of the component types described in Table 3 using the TREC3 algorithm with component scores scaled using document level scores using the Pivot method described above with a pivot value of 0.5.

T2: Runs containing this term in the name used the TREC2 algorithm in place of the TREC3 algorithm, but were otherwise the same.

T2FB: Runs containing this term in the name used the TREC2 algorithm with Blind Feedback as described above, but otherwise were the same as "T2" runs.

The primary tasks that we focussed on were the CO.Thorough and CO+S. Thorough tasks. For these tasks some automatic expansion of items in the XPath to the root of the document was used. The same data was used for the CO.Thorough and CO+S.Thorough tasks, but post-processing restricted results to (approximately) those matching the structural constraints of the "castitle" for the CO+S task. Figure 1 shows the thorough tasks. In the graphs shown in Figure 1 a line giving the means for each data point over all submitted runs for the task are also shown. As Figure 1 shows, the results for all of our runs in these tasks exceeded the average for all systems.

For the CO and COS Focussed tasks, post-processing kept only the highest ranking non-overlapping elements from the unexpanded version of results. As the very poor results for the Focussed runs show, this trimming of the results was overly harsh, and eliminated many of the relevant items in the initial set. (In fact, the results for the focussed tasks were so bad that we are conducting a complete analysis of where the post-retrieval processing caused them to fail). Figure 2 shows the results of our runs for these tasks, in all cases these runs were considerably below the mean for all runs in these tasks, and in most cases includes the worst performing run overall for the task. For the strict quantization (first column of Figure 2) the TREC2 algorithm with blind feedback at least

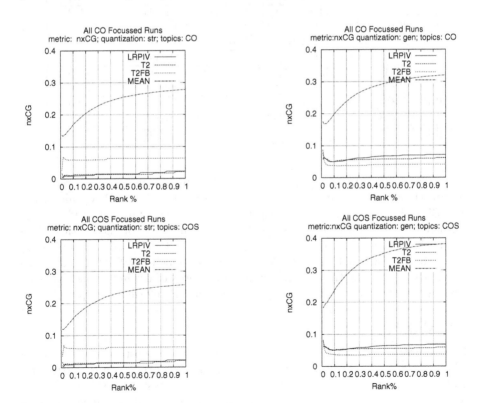

Fig. 2. Berkeley FOCUSSED Runs – Strict (left) and Generalized (right) Quantization

performed better than our other two runs. However for generalized quantization (second column of Figure 2) the TREC2 with blind feedback run is the worst performing run.

The summary average MAnxCG@10 results for the runs discussed above are shown in Table 5 for both generalized and strict quantizations. In Table 5 the tasks are shown in column 2, and the run names indicate the algorithm used (i.e., LRPIV is the TREC3 algorithm, T2 is the TREC2 algorithm and T2FB is the TREC2 algorithm with blind feedback).

Table 5. Berkeley Adhoc Runs, Tasks, and Results

Run Name	Task	MAnxCG@10 Q=gen	MAnxCG@10 Q=strict
CO_PIV50_LRPIV_FOC	CO.Focussed	0.0518	0.0038
CO_PIV50_T2_FOC	CO.Focussed	0.0692	0.0115
CO_T2FB_PIV50_NOV	CO.Focussed	0.0510	0.0132
CO_PIV50_LRPIV_FOC_COS	COS.Focussed	0.0637	0.0000
CO_PIV50_T2_FOC_COS	COS.Focussed	0.0818	0.0118
COS_T2FB_PIV50_NOV	COS.Focussed	0.0731	0.0378
CO_PIV50_LRPIV_EXP_THR	CO.Thorough	0.2170	0.0231
CO_PIV50_T2_EXP_THR	CO.Thorough	0.2324	0.0462
CO_T2FB_PIV50_THR	CO.Thorough	0.2820	0.0746
CO_PIV50_LRPIV_COSTHR	COS.Thorough	0.2289	0.0471
CO_PIV50_T2_COSTHR	COS.Thorough	0.2494	0.0588
COS_T2FB_PIV50_ALL_EXP	COS.Thorough	0.2289	0.0529
LRPIV_SSCAS	SSCAS	0.2039	0.1250
LRPIV_SVCAS	SVCAS	0.2061	0.1000
LRPIV_VSCAS	VSCAS	0.2205	0.1167
LRPIV_VVCAS	VVCAS	0.1997	0.0778

Unlike our attempt at INEX 2004 to use a simple form of "blind feedback" that used only the kwd element of the documents, use of the TREC2 algorithm and Blind Feedback with terms selected by relevance values, showed a fairly consistent improvement over the TREC2 algorithm alone, or the TREC3 algorithm alone. This was the case for Berkeley runs in CLEF and it was pleasing to see that it was equally applicable in INEX. We hope to do further analysis to attempt to determine the optimal number of records to use in feedback and the optimal number of additional terms to include in the reformulated query).

3.4   CAS Runs

Our approach to the 4 CAS tasks was to run them almost identically to the method used in INEX 2004, with a few additional constraints on the structural matching criteria. Only a single run for each of CAS tasks was submitted, and all of the runs used just the TREC3 ranking algorithm. (Given the effectiveness shown by the T2FB for the CO tasks, we now wish that we had submitted runs

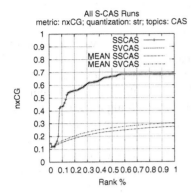
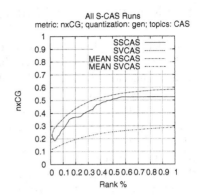

Fig. 3. Berkeley SSCAS and SVCAS Runs – Strict (left) and Generalized (right) Quantization

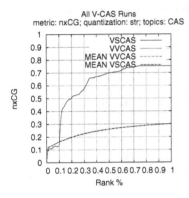
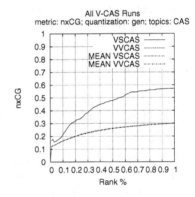

Fig. 4. Berkeley VVCAS and VSCAS Runs – Strict (left) and Generalized (right) Quantization

using that combination for consideration as well). Overall, the Berkeley CAS runs performed above average among the other submissions, with the SVCAS and VSCAS runs faring best among our CAS submissions. Figures 3 and 4 show our results for the "V-" and "S" tasks respectively, each figure also includes the overall average results for all runs for these tasks. Note that there was virtually no difference between the results obtained for our SSCAS and SVCAS runs, and similarly no difference between the results for our VVCAS and VSCAS runs (hence in Figures 3 and 4 the lines for our runs overlay each other. Our runs were well above average for all CAS tasks except for the SSCAS task, where we fell below the mean.

3.5   FetchBrowse Runs

We were informed that all of our FetchBrowse runs were rejected due to a sorting problem that incorrectly interleaved a few entries from separate documents in one topic. Therefore we have no official results for the FetchBrowse task.

4   Conclusions and Future Directions

Considerable further analysis needs to be done to digest the vast number of variables, metrics and tasks introduced in this year's INEX and to make sense of their implications for future adaptations of our system. Overall, however, we have been pleased to discover that the TREC2 with Blind Feedback method seems to work consistently better for INEX tasks than the TREC3 algorithm alone. We hope to further examine these results and to conduct further experiments to see whether combinations (fusion) of these algorithms will be more or less effective than the base algorithms alone. We also plan to do a more detailed analysis of the post-processing steps used this year to discover if some of the poorer results were simply the result of post-processing errors.

One approach to improving the combination of multiple components with collection level results (as done in the "pivot" method describe above would be to use regression analysis to determine an optimal pivot coefficient for the different components of the existing INEX database, where the dependent variable is the relevance of the component.

References

1. A. Chen. Multilingual information retrieval using english and chinese queries. In C. Peters, M. Braschler, J. Gonzalo, and M. Kluck, editors, *Evaluation of Cross-Language Information Retrieval Systems: Second Workshop of the Cross-Language Evaluation Forum, CLEF-2001, Darmstadt, Germany, September 2001*, pages 44–58. Springer Computer Scinece Series LNCS 2406, 2002.
2. A. Chen. *Cross-Language Retrieval Experiments at CLEF 2002*, pages 28–48. Springer (LNCS #2785), 2003.
3. A. Chen and F. C. Gey. Multilingual information retrieval using machine translation, relevance feedback and decompounding. *Information Retrieval*, 7:149–182, 2004.
4. W. S. Cooper, A. Chen, and F. C. Gey. Full Text Retrieval based on Probabilistic Equations with Coefficients fitted by Logistic Regression. In *Text REtrieval Conference (TREC-2)*, pages 57–66, 1994.
5. W. S. Cooper, F. C. Gey, and A. Chen. Full text retrieval based on a probabilistic equation with coefficients fitted by logistic regression. In D. K. Harman, editor, *The Second Text Retrieval Conference (TREC-2) (NIST Special Publication 500-215)*, pages 57–66, Gaithersburg, MD, 1994. National Institute of Standards and Technology.
6. W. S. Cooper, F. C. Gey, and D. P. Dabney. Probabilistic retrieval based on staged logistic regression. In *15th Annual International ACM SIGIR Conference on Research and Development in Information Retrieval, Copenhagen, Denmark, June 21-24*, pages 198–210, New York, 1992. ACM.
7. D. Harman. Relevance feedback and other query modification techniques. In W. Frakes and R. Baeza-Yates, editors, *Information Retrieval: Data Structures & Algorithms*, pages 241–263. Prentice Hall, 1992.
8. R. R. Larson. TREC interactive with cheshire II. *Information Processing and Management*, 37:485–505, 2001.

9. R. R. Larson. A logistic regression approach to distributed IR. In *SIGIR 2002: Proceedings of the 25th Annual International ACM SIGIR Conference on Research and Development in Information Retrieval, August 11-15, 2002, Tampere, Finland*, pages 399–400. ACM, 2002.

10. R. R. Larson. Cheshire ii at inex '04: Fusion and feedback for the adhoc and heterogeneous tracks. In *Advances in XML Information Retrieval: Third International Workshop of the Initiative for the Evaluation of XML Retrieval, INEX2004*, pages 322–336. Springer (LNCS #3493), 2005.

11. R. R. Larson. A fusion approach to XML structured document retrieval. *Information Retrieval*, 8:601–629, 2005.

12. J. H. Lee. Analyses of multiple evidence combination. In *SIGIR '97: Proceedings of the 20th Annual International ACM SIGIR Conference on Research and Development in Information Retrieval, July 27-31, 1997, Philadelphia*, pages 267–276. ACM, 1997.

13. Y. Mass and M. Mandelbrod. Component ranking and automatic query refinement for xml retrieval. In *Advances in XML Information Retrieval: Third International Workshop of the Initiative for the Evaluation of XML Retrieval, INEX2004*, pages 73–84. Springer (LNCS #3493), 2005.

14. S. E. Robertson and K. S. Jones. Relevance weighting of search terms. *Journal of the American Society for Information Science*, pages 129–146, May–June 1976.

15. J. A. Shaw and E. A. Fox. Combination of multiple searches. In *Proceedings of the 2nd Text REtrieval Conference (TREC-2), National Institute of Standards and Technology Special Publication 500-215*, pages 243–252, 1994.

16. E. Voorhees and D. Harman, editors. *The Seventh Text Retrieval Conference (TREC-7)*. NIST, 1998.

17. E. Voorhees and D. Harman, editors. *The Eighth Text Retrieval Conference (TREC-8)*. NIST, 1999.

GPX – Gardens Point XML IR at INEX 2005

Shlomo Geva

Centre for Information Technology Innovation
Faculty of Information Technology
Queensland University of Technology, Queensland 4001 Australia
s.geva@qut.edu.au

Abstract. The INEX 2005 evaluation consisted of numerous tasks that required different approaches. In this paper we described the approach that we adopted to satisfy the requirements of all the tasks, CAS and CO, in Thorough, Focused, and Fetch Browse mode, using the same underlying system The retrieval approach is based on the construction of a collection sub-tree, consisting of all nodes that contain one or more of the search terms. Nodes containing search terms are then assigned a score using a TF_IDF variant, scores are propagated upwards in the document XML tree, and finally all XML elements are ranked. We present results that demonstrate that the approach is versatile and produces consistently good performance across all INEX 2005 tasks.

Keywords: XML Information Retrieval, XML Search Engine, Inverted Files, XML-IR, Focused retrieval.

1 Introduction

The widespread use of Extensible Markup Language (XML) documents in digital libraries has lead to development of information retrieval (IR) methods specifically designed for XML collections [5,6]. XML is rapidly becoming the accepted standard for storage, communication, and exchange of information. Most information in typical XML documents is expressed in free form texts. INEX investigates the idea of using the specifics of XML retrieval to allow users to address content and structural needs. Like in traditional information retrieval, the user need is loosely defined and answers to queries are typically ranked lists of relevant elements. Like in database querying, structure is of importance and a simple list of keywords may not be sufficient to define a query. Most traditional IR systems are limited to whole document retrieval; however, since XML documents separate content and structure, XML-IR systems are able to retrieve the relevant portions of documents. Users interacting with XML-IR system could be interested in highly relevant and highly precise material below the document level. XML-IR systems are built on top of traditional IR and are thus typically more complex than their traditional counterparts, and many challenges remain unsolved. These issues were specifically addressed by the series of INEX workshops from 2002 to 2005, with marked improvement in performance of most systems [5,6].

Since all text IR systems base retrieval on keywords, if we ignore query expansion for a moment, one would expect that all systems would be able to identify the same candidate set of documents in response to a query when given the same set of keywords. Often it is possible to identify many tens of thousands of XML elements with

N. Fuhr et al. (Eds.): INEX 2005, LNCS 3977, pp.240–253, 2006.

a given set of keywords. The key difference between systems is in the all important ranking of candidate documents. We identify five important problems to solve in performing IR on an XML collection:

1. Adequate selection of elements that satisfy the keywords constraints.
2. Adequate selection of elements that satisfy the structural constraints.
3. The assignment of scores to nodes with matching keywords/structures.
4. The propagation of scores to antecedent or descendant elements.
5. The selection of ranked lists of results for specific tasks.

Steps 1 and 5 are common to ordinary text collection IR systems. Steps 2 to 4 are additional steps that are required in the context of XML oriented IR, and all systems participating at INEX have implemented them one way or another. Unlike in traditional IR, rather than identify relevant documents, the XML IR system is required to select and score elements at different levels of granularity.

This paper presents a system that provides a simple yet very effective and robust approach to the selection and ranking problem, and provides an effective and efficient design. A fully inverted index includes the exact location in the collection of each instance in which each term occurs. Of course such cross-reference listings predate computers. Typically in an inverted list for a term, the term locations would be stored as pairs {document-id, term-position}. Often index compression is applied to the inverted lists which can be highly compressible[7]. We chose to invert the XML collection by XPath – the location of each term is identified by an absolute XPath expression. With that simple conceptual representation of a single index (the XPath inverted list) we are able to address all the problems that are presented by the INEX 2005 set of ad-hoc tasks, without ever having to consult the collection itself.

In the remainder of this article we discuss our system implementation, the approach taken to the new INEX tasks (FetchBrowse and Focused Retrieval), and then present and discuss the evaluation results. The GPX search engine had not changed much since 2004, but a description is included here for the sake of completeness.

2 XML Document Inversion

The entire collection is inverted in one pass and inverted lists are stored in a Microsoft Access database. It should be noted that the actual storage structure is an implementation dependent issue that does not impact on the algorithms that are described here for performing XML IR. It can be implemented as a database or with conventional files, or it may even be a memory resident structure. The only requirement is that given a term, the system is able to (efficiently) return the inverted list for that term.

In our scheme each term in an XML document is identified by 3 elements. File path, absolute XPath context, and term position within the XPath context. The file path identifies documents in the collection; for instance:

C:/INEX/ex/2001/x0321.xml

The absolute XPath expression identifies a leaf XML element within the document, relative to the file's root element:

/article[1]/bdy[1]/sec[5]/p[3]

Finally, term position identifies the ordinal position of the term within the XPath context.

In principle at least, a single table can hold the entire cross reference listing of the collection (our inverted index). Table 1 contains the Xpath column of several rows in the inverted list that correspond to a particular term.

Table 1. XPath table content example

Context XPath
article[1]/bdy[1]/sec[6]/p[6]/ref[1]
article[1]/bdy[1]/sec[6]/p[6]/ref[1]
article[1]/bm[1]/bib[1]/bibl[1]/bb[13]/pp[1]
article[1]/bm[1]/bib[1]/bibl[1]/bb[14]/pdt[1]/day[1]
article[1]/bm[1]/bib[1]/bibl[1]/bb[14]/pp[1]
article[1]/bm[1]/bib[1]/bibl[1]/bb[15]
article[1]/bm[1]/bib[1]/bibl[1]/bb[15]
article[1]/bm[1]/bib[1]/bibl[1]/bb[15]/ti[1]
article[1]/bm[1]/bib[1]/bibl[1]/bb[15]/obi[1]

The structure of the database used to store the inverted lists is depicted in Figure 1. It consists of 4 tables. The **Terms** table is the starting point of a query on a given term. Two columns in this table are indexed - The **Term** column and the **Term_Stem** column. The **Term_Stem** column holds the Porter stem of the original term. The **List_Position** is a foreign key from the **Terms** table into the **List** Table. It identifies the starting position in the inverted list for the corresponding term. The **List_Length** is the number of list entries corresponding to that term. The **List** table is (transparently) sorted by Term so that the inverted list for any given term is contiguous.

A search proceeds as follows. Given a search term we obtain a starting position within the List table. We then retrieve the specified number of entries by reading sequentially. The inverted list thus obtained is *Joined* (SQL) with the **Document** and **Context** tables to obtain the complete inverted list for the term.

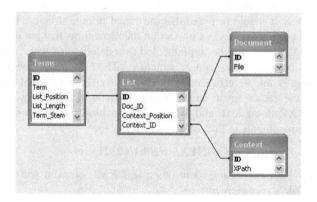

Fig. 1. Schema for XML Inverted File

3 Query Interpretation

INEX provides a test collection of over 16,000 IEEE journal articles, a set of queries and a set of evaluation metrics. Two types of queries were used at INEX 2005: CO and CAS. Content Only (CO) queries ignore document structure and only contain content stipulations. In contrast Content and Structure queries (COS,VVCAS, SVCAS, VSCAS, SSCAS) explicitly express both content and structural requirements. Both CO and CAS queries (with the exception of SSCAS) are expected to return appropriately sized relevant elements – not just whole documents, and all queries are loosely interpreted with respect to structural and keyword constraints – the overriding goal is to satisfy the user's information need rather than the strict query formulation. SSCAS queries require strict adherence to the query's structural constraints. Figures 2 and 3 are examples of both query types.

The *description, title,* and *castitle* elements express the user's information needs. The *description* expresses the user's need in natural language. The *title* expresses the user's information need as a list of keywords/phrases. The *castitle* is a formal XPath-like expression using NEXI – the formal INEX query specification language [3].

```
<inex_topic topic_id="XX" query_type="CO">
<title>
   "multi layer perceptron" "radial basis
functions" comparison
   </title>
   <description>
   The relationship and comparisons between
radial basis functions and multi layer per-
ceptrons
   </description>
   </inex_topic>
```

Fig. 2. CO Query

```
<inex_topic                    topic_id="XX"
query_type="CAS">
   <castitle>
   //article[about(.,information    re-
trieval)]//sec[about(.,compression)]
   </castitle>
   <description>
   Find sections about compression in
articles about information retrieval.
   </description>
   </inex_topic>
```

Fig. 3. CAS Query

The syntax of NEXI is similar to XPath, however, NEXI only uses XPath's descendant axis step, and extends XPath by incorporating an 'about' clause to provide an IR-like query. NEXI's syntax is **//A[about(//B,C)]** where **A** is the context path, **B** is the relative path and **C** is the content requirement. Conceptually each **'about'** clause in a NEXI query represents an individual information request. So conceptually the query

//A[about(//B,C)]//X[about(//Y,Z)]

contains two requests:

//A[about(//B,C)]
and
//A//X[about(//Y,Z)].

However, in NEXI only elements matching the leaf (i.e. rightmost) **'about'** clause, the second request here, are flagged as of direct interest to the user. We refer to these requests and elements as 'return requests' and 'return elements'. Elements that match the other **'about'** clauses, the first request here, are used to support the return elements in ranking. We refer to these requests and elements as 'support requests' and 'support elements'. It should be noted that under vague interpretation of structural constraints it is often acceptable to return elements whose XPath signature does not strictly conform to the query specification. The structural constraints are regarded as retrieval hints, much in the same way that keywords are regarded as retrieval hints.

4 Processing NEXI Queries

A NEXI query may consist of multiple sub-queries that can be evaluated in isolation, before being considered together to determine the final results list. Our evaluation of complex NEXI expressions is based on parsing and evaluation of the sub-queries. Each sub-query produces a result-tree consisting of all the elements that contain at least one of the keyword in the query (or a synonym, or any other term deemed relevant through term expansion), and are in the right context – where structural constraints are taken into consideration too. For instance, in CAS queries the strict constraints eliminate nodes that are not of the specified type. Each node in the result tree contains the necessary information to allow the computation of a score, using a variation of TF-IDF [2,7]. After the result-tree is constructed, a traversal of the result-tree generates the score for each node, from leaves to root. The results from all sub-trees, corresponding to the query, are finally combined (as described in the next section) to produce a single result tree. These results are then organized as a list and sorted according to the task on hand, with the top N results returned (N=1500 for the ad-hoc track). We generate Thorough, Focused, and Fetch-Browse results from the same result tree in a post processing step. In fact, the result tree is our approximation of the full recall base of scoring elements. Different ordered sub-sets for the various tasks are derived from it.

5 Element Scoring Scheme

Elements are ranked according to a relevance score. In our scheme leaf and branch elements need to be treated differently. Data in the INEX collection usually occurs at leaf elements, and thus, our inverted list mostly stores information about leaf elements. A leaf element is considered candidate for retrieval if it contains at least one query term. A branch node is candidate for retrieval if it contains a relevant child element. Once an element (either leaf or branch) is deemed to be a candidate for retrieval its relevance score is calculated. A heuristically derived formula (Equation 1) is used to calculate the relevance score of leaf elements. The same equation is used for both return and support elements. The score is determined from query terms contained in the element. It penalizes elements with frequently occurring query terms (frequent in the collection), and it rewards elements with more unique query terms within a result element. (Note that the same calculation also applies to nodes with text that are not leaves, but in the INEX collection only leaves contain text).

Equation 1: Calculation of a Leaf Element's Relevance Score

$$L = K^{n-1} \sum_{i=1}^{n} \frac{t_i}{f_i} \tag{1}$$

Here n is the count of unique query terms contained within the leaf element, K is a small integer (we used $K=5$). The term K^{n-1} scales up the score of elements having multiple distinct query terms. The system is not sensitive to the value of K – we experimented with $K=5$ to 25 with little difference in results. The sum is over all terms where t_i is the frequency of the ith query term in the leaf element and f_i is the frequency of the ith query term in the collection. This sum rewards the repeat occurrence of query terms, but uncommon terms contribute more than common terms. We found this variation to work much better than TF-IDF alone because it gives much greater weight to nodes that contain more unique search terms, overriding the impact of the inverse document frequency on common terms – but only when they occur in a preferable context, i.e. with other search terms.

Once the relevance scores of leaf elements have been calculated, they can be used to calculate the relevance score of branch elements. A naïve solution would be to just sum the relevance scores of each branch's relevant children. However, this would ultimately result in root (i.e. article) elements accumulating at the top of the ranked list, a scenario that offers no advantage over document-level retrieval. Furthermore, the specificity of nodes in the XML tree typically decreases as we move up the tree – article is less specific than a section which is less specific than a paragraph. Therefore, the relevance score of leaf elements should be somehow decreased while being propagated up the XML tree. On the other hand, when a node has multiple scoring descendants, its exhaustivity (coverage of the topic) usually increases. To account for this, a heuristically derived formula (Equation 2) is used to calculate the scores of intermediate branch elements.

Equation 2: Calculation of a Branch Element Relevance Score

$$R = D(n) \sum_{i=1}^{n} L_i \tag{2}$$

Where:

> n = the number of children elements
> $D(n) = 0.49$ if n = 1
>   0.99   Otherwise
> L_i = the relevance score of the ith child element

The value of the decay factor D depends on the number of relevant children that the branch has. If the branch has one relevant child then the decay constant is 0.49. A branch with only one relevant child will be ranked lower than its child. If the branch has multiple relevant children the decay factor is 0.99. A branch with many relevant children will be ranked higher than its descendants. Thus, a section with a single relevant paragraph would be judged less relevant than the paragraph itself, but a section with several relevant paragraphs will be ranked higher than any of the paragraphs.

Having computed scores for all result and support elements, the scores of support elements are added to the scores of the corresponding result elements that they support. For instance, consider the query:

$$//A[about(.//B,C)]//X[about(.//Y,Z)]$$

The score of a support element matching **//A** will be added to all result elements Matching **//A//X** but only if the specific element **A** is the ancestor of the specific elements **X** (same file, same absolute Xpath up to and including **A**).

Finally, the results consist of an entire recall tree for the query where each node is individually scored. At that point the score of each article (document root) node is added to the result of each node in that same article – thereby boosting the scores of all elements that belong to an article with many other scoring elements.

When a NEXI expression contains multiple filters the system constructs a result-tree for each of the filters. After the score of each node in each trees is determined, the scores of support elements (i.e. elements that satisfy a support filter in the NEXI expression) are added, to boost the scores of the corresponding return elements. In this manner, everything else being equal, elements with support tend to be ranked higher than elements without support.

6 Treatment of CAS Variants

The INEX ad-hoc track aimed to answer some questions with respect to the utility of the various filters of a NEXI expression. Four different sub-tasks were defined: **VVCAS, VSCAS, SVCAS,** and **SSCAS.** The GPX search engine starts with construction of a collection sub-tree using inverted lists of term posting. The SVCAS, VSCAS, and SSCAS variants require some strict structural interpretation of a result filter, the support filter/s, or both, respectively. The VVCAS variant requires loose structural interpretation of all filters.

To enforce structural constraints, filtering of result or support elements is performed on the final results. But for all the CAS variants, including VVCAS, inverted lists are filtered with the structural constraint of the *about* clause when the term posting lists are accessed. This is a very important distinction between CO and CAS. Even though CAS processing may apply vague interpretation to structural constraints,

we still start the search only with those nodes that comply with the structural constraint. The constraints are lifted only when result nodes are selected for return. This
is best explained by the following example. Consider the query -

//A[about(//B,C)]

The path filter **//A//B** is always applied to elements that contain the term C. The
about clause structural constraint **//A//B** is taken as a strong clue for retrieval and so
we only look inside elements that are on a path **//A//B**. However strict result elements
for this query must comply with the path **//A**. Here we can interpret the constraint
vaguely and return any element type that we may deem appropriate. For instance, we
may return a section where a paragraph was specified.

In our implementation in 2005 our vague structural constraint interpretation was to
ignore the structural constraint altogether. This may not have been the wisest choice,
and our CAS results were not quite as good as the CO/COS results.

Following the initial filtering all CAS variants are processed identically as described in the previous section . All CAS variants at INEX2005 were processed as
Thorough runs meaning that all relevant XML elements were returned, ignoring overlap. This is supported naturally by the system because the collection sub-tree that the
search engine constructs contains the entire recall base – as identified by the system.
Results are extracted, sorted, and the top N results returned.

7 Treatment of CO Variants

The *CO* and *COS* tasks were designed to study queries having structural constraints,
in comparison with the same queries without such constraints. The CO and COS queries were used to generate results for three different user models – Thorough, Focused, and Fetch Browse. Thorough retrieval is a system oriented task that requires
the complete recall base (or rather, the top N ranked results). Focused retrieval is a
user oriented task and requires the return of elements of just the right granularity, and
without overlap (supporting fast browsing through most relevant results in no particular order). Fetch Browse retrieval is a user oriented task that requires the return of
ranked documents and the complete ranked recall base within those documents (supporting a user browsing in document rank order with identified relevant components).

The *CO* and *COS* queries only differ in the complexity of the NEXI expression,
where a *CO* query can be expressed as a search over the entire article element. Therefore our system did not treat *CO* topic any differently to *COS* topics.

CO.Thorough retrieval was performed as for the *CAS* tasks and requires no further
discussion. The Focused retrieval task and Fetch-Browse retrieval task started with
the Thorough results recall base (i.e. The complete Thorough results tree.)

In Focused retrieval mode the system extracted from each path, leading from article to leaf, the highest ranking node. In this manner the resulting set of candidate
results contained no overlap. The results were then sorted by element score. This approach matches the notion of having a "best element on a path" which Focused
retrieval evaluation is closely related to.

In Fetch Browse retrieval we sorted the result by article score and then by element
score within, as required for this task. Section 5 describes how an element's score is

ﺽ

derived, and that of course applies to article nodes too. The article score is not necessarily correlated with the highest scoring leaf nodes; rather, it is higher for articles that contain many scoring elements. For Fetch Browse retrieval this article scoring approach is a good match with the user model that is measured by Fetch-Browse Element metric.

The only significant free parameters in all the retrieval runs were the score propagation decay constants in the construction of the thorough recall base for CAS variants and for CO.Thorough. The Focused and Fetch-Browse result sets were generated in a straight forward manner by filtering and sorting the Thorough results. We did experiment with various cut-off levels for stop words – we found no significant drop in recall-precision when we dropped all terms that occurred less frequently than 75,000 times in the collection. However, this is not a general result and will of course depend on the collection on hand and the search terms – quite clearly it is possible for all search terms to be highly frequent.

8 Results

The results that the system was able to achieve were rather good in all tasks. In this section we describe the results for each of the tasks. The official nxCG MAep score is used to report system performance over all topics. The specific details of the nxCG metric can be found in [8] and elsewhere in this publication and we skip the discussion of the details.

We summarized all the results in Tables 2 and 3. We recorded the overall rank of the best submission from QUT in each of the tasks in which it had participated. We also recorded in parenthesis the QUT position when we only consider the best submission from each participant.

The values that were obtained for nxCG@10, nxCG@25, and nxCG@50 were also pleasing, and in many instances the QUT submission was ranked 1st. The full set of

Table 2. System rank summary (Focused, Thorough, XXCAS)

Task	Strict MAep	Gen MAep	GenLifted Maep
CO Focused	4 (2)	2 (2)	1 (1)
CO Thorough	5 (3)	7 (4)	4 (3)
COS Focused	1 (1)	1 (1)	1 (1)
COS Thorough	3 (2)	1 (1)	2 (2)
VVCAS	5 (3)	8 (5)	5 (3)
VSCAS	3 (2)	3 (2)	3 (2)
SVCAS	7 (4)	8 (5)	8 (5)
SSCAS	10 (7)	7 ()4	8 (5)

official figures is included elsewhere in this publication and the reader is invited to inspect the performance of the QUT submission in the respective tables.

Table 3 contains a summary of overall performance in the Fetch-Browse task. Here the performance is good across the tasks, with the only exception being the CO Fetch-Browse Article measure. The reason for this difference lies in the metric. The Fetch-Browse Article metric measures the ability of a system to pick the articles with the highest scoring elements. This requires a different article ordering strategy to that which we used. Our strategy was to order articles by overall scores of elements within rather than by the best scoring elements. We conjecture that even in this task it would be possible to improve the score of our system with a change to the strategy – all our submissions were sorted by article score, however, the metric rewards articles with higher scoring elements more than articles with more scoring elements. By sorting with more emphasis on higher scoring elements it would be possible to push articles with higher scoring elements up the ranked list. We did not test this conjecture and it is left for future work.

Table 3. System rank summary (Fetch-Browse)

Task	Strict MAep	Gen MAep	GenLifted Maep
COS Fetch-Browse Element (overlap on)	1 (1)	1 (1)	1 (1)
COS Fetch-Browse Element (overlap off)	1 (1)	1 (1)	1 (1)
COS Fetch-Browse Article (overlap off & on)	5 (3)	4 (3)	6 (4)
CO Fetch-Browse Element (overlap on)	9 (5)	3 (3)	2 (2)
CO Fetch-Browse Element (overlap off)	3 (3)	2 (2)	1 (1)
CO Fetch-Browse Article (overlap off & on)	**22** (10)	16 **(7)**	15 (6)

The results of the CO and COS runs are of particular interest because they allow us to judge the effectiveness of the structural constraints in retrieval. We found that in all metrics and all tasks our COS runs always scored better in MAep values than the CO runs. It should be noted however that with the strict metric at low recall (below 0.05, or 75 elements) the CO runs seem to perform equally well and sometimes even better than the COS runs. This is an interesting finding because in applications where users are not interested in browsing past the first couple screens there seems to be little if any benefit in using structural constraints – at least with our system and with the collection on hand. This result cannot be taken as indicative in the general case without more extensive and rigorous testing over a more diverse document collections.

9   High Precision vs High Recall

It became clear in our experiments, before INEX 2005 (with 2004 data), and after, that retrieval for high precision and retrieval for high recall, require completely different system setting – at least with GPX. We were able to obtain much higher precision at lower recall than in the official INEX submissions, but at the cost of lower MAep values. To demonstrate this we compare a run designed for high precision with our best official retrieval run in the COS.Focussed task (ranked 3rd, 1st, 2nd overall respectively, with strict, gen, genLifted metrics). We produced new results with the same system, but we chose to reduce $D(n)$ in equation 2 to 0.01 in order to maximize the number of scoring leaves at the top of the list. This is not a good strategy for high MAep values, but we get more highly scoring elements up front. Unfortunately this also pushes up the rank many irrelevant elements. In the Thorough retrieval strategy this means that we get significantly less overlap and the MAep is usually lower. Figures 2,3,4 depict the ep-gr plots for the two submissions, the best of the QUT official runs and the unofficial high-precision run, with all 3 metrics.

The improvement is most dramatic in the case of the strict quantization. In this case the MAep of the high precision run is 0.034 while that of the official run is 0.026. With the gen and genLifted quatization the high precision run is more precise up to about 75-90 results, but after that it drops sharply and the MAep is 0.079 for the gen quantization – lower than the official run at 0.096, and the MAep for the genLifted run is 0.059 – lower than the official run at 0.069. So it is clear that in order to succeed at both high-precision and high-recall is is necessary to use different parameter settings.

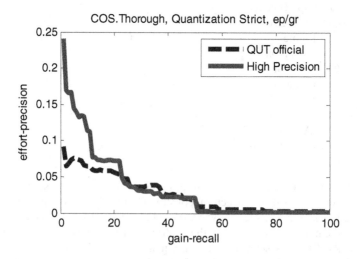

Fig. 2. High precision retrieval, strict quantization

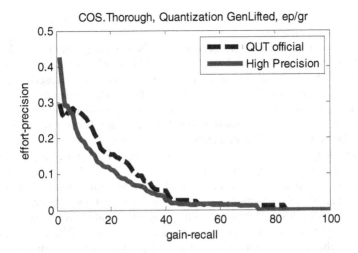

Fig. 3. High precision retrieval, gen quantization

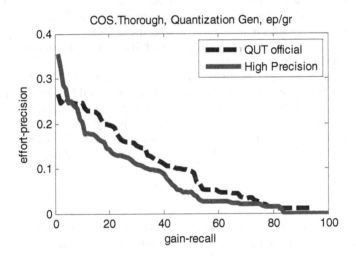

Fig. 4. High precision retrieval, genLifted quantization

The goals may well be competing and there is a trade-off. It would be useful to separate and study the high-precision task from the high-recall task. Users who never want to browse past the first couple of result pages would prefer the high precision results, while users who look for a needle in a hay stack may well be prepared to sift through long and more exhaustive lists, even if at the cost of lower precision up front.

10 Discussion

The MAep results that we were able to obtain are very pleasing for two main reasons: we have used a single system that was built to exploit the natural structure and properties of the XML tree. The system is robust and performed well on all tasks and with all official metrics.

In the Focused retrieval task it became clear from both qualitative analysis and from experimentation with 2004 data, that it would be advantageous to select elements slightly higher in the tree than the leaves – on account of increased exhaustivity – but not too high since specificity tends to drop. We could control the bias towards the leaves or the internal nodes by increasing or decreasing the decay factor for score propagation (equation 2). By choosing smaller values for $D(n)$ we were able to increase the relative scores of leaf elements. In the Thorough submission on the other hand, by increasing the value of $D(n)$ we were able to extract more scoring elements from the ancestors of highly scoring leaf elements.

While the system performs well in retrieval, there are a few issues that still need addressing. The INEX collection is inverted in about 2 hours on Pentium 4 PC, 1.8GHz clock, 1GB RAM. This is not particularly slow, and in fact most participants do not even report the indexing times (not since 2002). Since INEX 2005 we were able to reduce the indexing time to 45 minutes, by porting the software from C# to Java, and moving the database from MS Access to an industrial strength DBMS (Derby), but the program is still process bound rather than I/O bound. It would probably be possible to reduce the indexing time further, by moving to lower level programming, by index compression, and by avoiding the DBMS altogether, but the wisdom of doing that is questionable given the extensibility features and industrial acceptance of the DBMS mature technology.

Retrieval speed is perhaps not quite satisfactory. Evaluation of all 40 CO queries took just under 20 minutes. With the move to a more advanced DBMS we were able to reduce that since INEX 2005 to about 7 minutes, but even that is a bit slow for industrial strength applications with real time response. It might be interesting to study in the context of INEX how efficient systems are by comparison. Perhaps a task with a restricted response time (say, under 3 seconds) is worthwhile studying.

11 Conclusion

We have presented an approach to XML retrieval that is based on a fully inverted file structure and the construction of an exhaustive XML subtree – representing an extensive recall base (approximating the full recall base), from which we derive results for the various ad-hoc tasks in a straight forward manner. We implemented the Xpath inverted file system system with a conventional database back end (MS Access) and have used simple, yet very effective heuristic algorithms to compute relevance scores of individual nodes. The contribution to this year's INEX evaluation was in adjusting the system to handle the new tasks (FetchBrowse and Focused) and evaluating the system against the new tasks and topics. We have used the natural structure of the XML tree to compute scores for all nodes in the recall base. The system performed very well in all tasks, very often ranked 1st, 2nd, or 3rd, and rarely ranked outside the top 10 by the official nxCG MAep measure. The system shows consistently good performance across a wide range of tasks and with very few, minimal, and intuitive free parameters that can drive it towards High-Recall or High-Precision, towards Thorough, or towards Focused retrieval, with Strict or with Vague interpretation of structural constraints. We further demonstrated that, at least with the GPX system, it is possible to obtain higher precision at low recall points, or trade off precision at low recall points for higher overall recall.

References

1. S. Geva, "GPX at INEX 2004", *Advances in XML Information Retrieval. Third Workshop of the INitiative for the Evaluation of XML Retrieval,* INEX 2004, Schloss Dagstuhl, 6-8 December 2004. Lecture Notes in Computer Science LNCS 3493, **2005**. Editors N. Fuhr, M. Lalmas, S. Malik and Z. Szlavik
2. R. K. Belew, Finding Out About, Cambridge University Press, ISBN 0-521-63028-2 (hb)
3. A. Trotman and B. Sigurbjörnsson, *Narrowed Extended XPath I (NEXI),* http://www.cs.otago.ac.nz/postgrads/andrew/2004-4.pdf, 2004. Editors N. Fuhr, N Govert, G Kazai, M. Lalmas, ERCIM-030W03.
4. . J. Van Rijsbergen, R. J., Information Retrieval, Butterworths, Second Edition, 1979.
5. *Proceedings of the First Workshop of the Initiative for the Evaluation of XML Retrieval (INEX),* December 9-11 2002, Schloss Dagstuhl,
6. *Advances in XML Information Retrieval. Third Workshop of the INitiative for the Evaluation of XML Retrieval,* INEX 2004, Schloss Dagstuhl, 6-8 December 2004. Lecture Notes in Computer Science LNCS 3493, **2005**. Editors N. Fuhr, M. Lalmas, S. Malik and Z. Szlavik
7. I. H. Witten, A. Moffat, T.C. Bell, *Managing Gigabytes: compressing and indexing documents and images,* 2nd ed., Morgan Kaufman Publishers, ISBN 1-55860-570-3
8. G. Kazai, M Lalmas, A. P. De Vries, *The overlap problem in content-oriented XML retrieval evaluation* Annual ACM Conference on Research and Development in Information Retrieval Proceedings of the 27th annual international ACM SIGIR conference on Research and development in information retrieval Pages: 72 – 79, 2004, ISBN:1-58113-881-4

Implementation of a High-Speed and High-Precision XML Information Retrieval System on Relational Databases

Kei Fujimoto[1], Toshiyuki Shimizu[1], Norimasa Terada[1],
Kenji Hatano[2], Yu Suzuki[3], Toshiyuki Amagasa[4],
Hiroko Kinutani[5], and Masatoshi Yoshikawa[1]

[1] Graduate School of Information Science,
Nagoya University
Furocho, Chikusa, Nagoya 464-8601, Japan
{fujimoto, shimizu, terada}@dl.itc.nagoya-u.ac.jp,
yosikawa@is.nagoya-u.ac.jp
[2] Graduate School of Information Science,
Nara Institute of Science and Technology
8916-5 Takayama, Ikoma 630-0192, Japan
hatano@is.naist.jp
[3] College of Information Science and Technology,
Ritsumeikan University
1-1-1 Noji-Higashi, Kusatsu 525-8577, Japan
suzuki@ics.ritsumei.ac.jp
[4] Graduate School of Systems and Information Engineering,
University of Tsukuba
1-1-1 Tennodai, Tsukuba 305-8573, Japan
amagasa@cs.tsukuba.ac.jp
[5] Information Media and Education Square, Ochanomizu University
2-1-1 Ohtsuka, Bunkyo 112-8610, Japan
kinutani@edu.cc.ocha.ac.jp

Abstract. This paper describes an XML information retrieval system that we have developed. It is based on a vector space model, and implemented on top of XRel, a relational XML database system that has been developed in our research group. When a query is processed, a large number of fragments are retrieved, because a single XML document usually contains many XML fragments. Keeping all XML fragments degrades retrieval precision and increases query processing time, because some XML fragments are not appropriate as a query target. In existing methods, retrieval targets are manually selected by human experts when an XML collection is stored in the system. Such manual selection is not feasible when many kinds of XML documents are stored in the system. To cope with the problem we propose a method for automatically selecting document-centric fragments by introducing three measurements, namely, period ratio, number of different words, and empirical rules. By deleting inappropriate data-centric fragments from results of keyword query, we can improve the accuracy and performance of our system. Through performance evaluations, we confirmed the improvement of retrieval precision and query processing speed.

N. Fuhr et al. (Eds.): INEX 2005, LNCS 3977, pp. 254–267, 2006.

1   Introduction

XML (Extensible Markup Language) is a standard markup language to describe the structure and semantics of documents and data. There are two kinds of XML documents. One is data-centric XML documents, such as supply chain management data and scientific experiment data. The other is document-centric XML documents, such as scientific publications and web data. When querying data-centric XML documents, XML query languages, such as XPath and XQuery, are considered to be appropriate in the sense that the intended query results can be specifically specified by users. On the other hand, when we think about document-centric XML documents, application of information retrieval (IR) techniques is considered to be more appropriate, because query results can be chosen in terms of users' criteria, such as similarity.

In this study, we develop an IR-system for the CO sub task on top of relational XML database. Specifically, we try to enhance our XML database system, XRel [4], by integrating a keyword-retrieval function. XRel retrieves XML documents using off-the-shelf relational database systems. We introduce a novel mechanism for storing word-vectors in XRel. It enables the system to rank the results according to the similarity between the query and the vectors.

An important observation is that an XML document may consist of several portions that have different characteristics. More precisely, portions that have relatively regular structure and contain non-numerical values as well as short text, and portions that have relatively irregular structure and mainly contain text. The former is called "data-centric fragments," and the latter "document-centric fragments." For example, fragments, such as title and author can be considered as data-centric fragments. On the other hand, fragments, such as chapters, sections and paragraph, are considered to be document-centric fragments.

When XML documents are retrieved, large amount of fragments are retrieved, because a single XML document has many XML fragments. The conservation of the vector elements of all XML fragments degrades retrieval precision and also increases query processing time. In existing methods, document-centric fragments that is appropriate for retrieval targets are manually determined, and the cost of establishing systems is very high. Therefore, in this paper, we propose a method for selecting document-centric fragments by deleting data-centric fragments that are not appropriate for retrieval targets. In our method, appropriate XML fragments for keyword search are automatically determined by the statistics of XML fragments, simplifying the design of the XML document retrieval system. In our previous method in INEX 2004 [7], we used only the number of different words as statistics. In addition, we introduce period ratio and empirical rules. Based on our INEX 2004 paper, in that we described how to implement XRel, we implement XRel and period ratio, number of different words, and empirical rules. In our INEX 2004 paper, we described how to implement XRel. In this paper, we imeplement XRel and evaluate the performances in terms of retrieval precision and query processing speed.

The rest of this paper is organized as follows. Section 2 describes related work. We explain our XML information retrieval system based on a vector space model in Section 3, and the method of selecting document-centric fragments in Section 4. Section 5 shows an example of applying and evalating the method. Section 6 concludes this paper and discusses future work.

2   Related Work

As described in Section 1, there are two types of XML documents: document-centric and data-centric. In the retrieval of XML documents, data-centric XML documents were targeted at first, and retrieval by database approach using XML query languages such as XQuery [2] and XPath [3] was a main focus. However, as document-centric XML documents advance, XML fragments cannot be effectively retrieved by a database approach. In such a background, the application of information retrieval technology, especially by using keywords, is required to retrieve XML fragments. An XML document retrieval that applies such technology has been studied [7].

Hayashi et al. [8] considered that a ranking function that is based on document structure and content was important. By generating indices after setting the XML fragments as retrieval targets, they retrieved XML documents by weighted keywords with structural information. Amer-Yahia et al. added an information retrieval function to XQuery, an XML query language being standardized now, and proposed TeXQuery [9] and FlexPath [10] that efficiently retrieves XML documents.

3   XML Information Retrieval System

In this section, we explain an XML document retrieval system based on a vector space model and its implementation.

3.1   XRel

In XRel, XML documents are stored into four relations that have fixed relational schemas. The relational schemas are independent of the logical structure of documents. Therefore, changes in the logical structure do not affect the relational schemas. Each element in XML documents is managed by labels and paths from the root node to the node.

When querying XML documents using keywords, keywords are translated into SQLs based on the relational schemas. An outline of the query processing interface of the XRel architecture is shown in Figure 1. The management of XML documents in relational databases is hidden from users and applications. When a query is issued by a user or an application, it is automatically translated into the corresponding SQL in the system.

The following schemas are defined to store XML documents into a relational database:

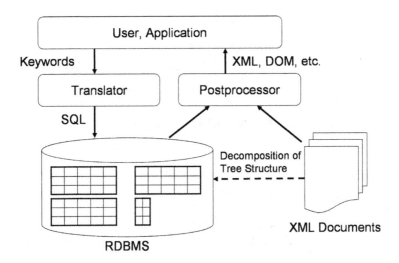

Fig. 1. Outline of query processing interface of XRel architecture

```
Element (documentID, nodeID, pathID, start, end)
     key is (documentID, nodeID)
Attribute (documentID, nodeID, pathID, start, end, value)
     key is (documentID, nodeID)
Text (documentID, nodeID, pathID, start, end, value)
     key is (documentID, nodeID)
Path (pathID, pathexp)
     key is (pathID)
```

"Element," "Attribute," "Text," and "Path" are relations to store element nodes, attribute nodes, text nodes, and all paths from the root node to a node in XML documents, respectively. The following describes the attributes of the above schemas:

```
documentID   Identifier to identify XML documents
nodeID       Serial number to identify each node
pathID       Identifier to identify paths in XML documents
sibling      Sibling Dewey Order assigned to nodes
start        Byte position of start tags
end          Byte position of end tags
value        Attribute value in Attribute relation, and
             content of element node in Text relation
pathexp      Path expressions appearing in all XML documents
```

We give an example of storing an XML document into relations. Figure 3 shows the tree structure of the XML document shown in Figure 2. The relations storing the XML documents shown in Figure 3 are shown in Table 1.

```
⟨a b="Attr"⟩
    ⟨c⟩Text 1⟨/c⟩
    ⟨c⟩Text 2⟨/c⟩
⟨/a⟩
```

Fig. 2. An XML document

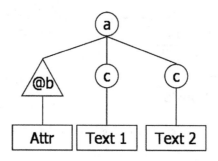

Fig. 3. An XML tree structure

Table 1. Storing XML document

Element

documentID	nodeID	pathID	start	end
1	1	1	1	47
1	3	3	15	28
1	4	3	31	44

Attribute

documentID	nodeID	pathID	start	end	value
1	2	2	4	11	Attr

Path

pathID	pathexp
1	#/a
2	#/a#/@b
3	#/a#/c

Text

documentID	nodeID	pathID	start	end	value
1	3	3	18	23	Text 1
1	4	3	34	39	Text 2

3.2   Implementation of Vector Space Model Based on XRel

XRel retrieves XML documents by keywords by implementing a vector space model based on relational databases. The following schema is defined to store each document vector of XML fragments in relational databases.

```
Token(documentID, nodeID, token, tfipf)
    key is (documentID, nodeID, token)
```

"Token" has the following four attributes:

```
documentID   Identifier to identify XML documents
nodeID       Serial number to identifiy each node
token        Each token appearing in XML fragments
tfipf        The weight of token
             Only nonzero vector element is stored
```

TF-IPF, used as token weight, is the product of TF (Term Frequency) and IPF (Inverse Path Frequency) [5]. IPF is the criterion for token specificity that takes document structure into consideration. IDF (Inverse Document Frequency) which is widely used in IR domain, expresses term specificity in a document set. IPF expresses term specificity in a set of XML fragments that have identical paths. Let N_p denote the total number of XML fragments on a path p, and let $df_p(t)$ denote the number of XML fragments that has the token t on the path p. IPF is calculated by the following expression:

$$ipf_p(t) = \log \frac{N_p}{df_p(t)} + 1.$$

3.3 Query Translation

In this section, we explain query translation. Queried keywords "keyword 1, keyword 2, ..., keyword n" are translated into the following SQL.

```
SELECT * FROM (
  SELECT t.documentID, t.nodeID, e.start, e,end, SUM(t.tfipf) score
  FROM   Token t, Element e
  WHERE  t.documentID = e.documentID
  AND    t.nodeID = e.nodeID
  AND    t.token in ('keyword 1', 'keyword 2', ..., 'keyword n')
  GROUP BY t.documentID, t.nodeID, e.start, e.end ) r
ORDER BY r.score DESC
```

The summation of the TF-IPF values of "keyword 1, keyword 2, ..., keyword n" is calculated in each XML fragment, and XML fragments are then ranked by using the summation of TF-IPF. The similarity between a query vector and a vector of an XML fragment is calculated by the inner product of two vectors. The summation of TF-IPF is the inner product of the query vector and the vectors of XML fragments. The query vector follows a boolean model.

4   Method of Selecting Document-Centric Fragments

When retrieving XML documents, the number of XML fragments is enormous. Such an enormous amount of data degrades retrieval precision and increases query processing time. To cope with this problem, we introduce a method that automatically determines appropriate fragments for the answers of keyword search from the statistics of fragments.

In structured documents, each fragment has either a data-centric or document-centric property. For example, in academic papers, titles and author fragments are data-centric. On the other hand, chapters, sections, and paragraph fragments are document-centric. Keyword retrieval is effective for retrieving document-centric fragments. So, only document-centric fragments are appropriate for keyword search.

We describe a method for selecting, from the full set of XML fragments, a set of fragments that should be considered as retrieval targets. The selection is realized by deleting the fragments that are considered inappropriate as retrieval targets (hereinafter "unnecessary fragments"). The selection is based on the statistics of the fragments. Deletion is executed in the following three steps:

1. Deleting unnecessary fragments by period ratio at the schema level.
2. Deleting unnecessary fragments by the number of different words at the instance level.
3. Deleting unnecessary fragments by empirical rules.

Deleting unnecessary fragments is expected to improve data size, query processing speed, and retrieval precision. The details of each step are as follows.

4.1 Deletion by Period Ratio

Generally speaking, texts end with ".", "?", or "!", so XML fragments that end with ".", "?", or "!" are assessed as document-centric fragments. However, some document-centric fragments do not end with ".", "?", or "!", and some data-centric fragments do end with ".", "?", or "!" at the instance level. So for each fragment set that has the same tag name, if the fragment set a has high probability of ending with ".", "?", or "!", the fragments that belong to the set are labeled document-centric.

Let D_t denote the number of fragments whose tag names are t. For leaf node t, let N_t denote the number of fragments that end with ".", "?", or "!", if t is an internal node, the number of fragments that have more than one document-centric leaf node. Period ratio is calculated as follows:

$$r_t = \frac{N_t}{D_t}.$$

Fragment sets that have low period ratio are data-centric, and thus they are deleted from retrieval targets. Concretely speaking, the corresponding rows are deleted from the "Element" and "Token" tables. The threshold for deletion is determined from the statistics of the fragment set.

4.2 Deletion by Number of Different Words

Some data-centric fragments remain in the fragment set even after filtering by period ratio, especially fragments that have a middle period ratio. So each fragment is judged whether it is data-centric at the instance level.

To this end, the number of different words that each fragment includes is used. Fragment sets that have a low number of different words are assessed as data-centric fragments, so they are deleted as retrieval targets. Concretely speaking, the corresponding rows are deleted from the "Element" and "Token" tables. The threshold for deletion is determined from the statistics of the fragment set.

4.3   Deletion by Empirical Rules

After the above processing, document-centric fragments remain mainly. However, some document-centric fragments are still inappropriate for retrieval targets. For example, if an item of a table has sentences, the item is a data-centric fragment. However, the item is inappropriate for retrieval result presentation. The table should present with the sentences that mention the table.

Then such document-centric fragments are deleted by empirical rules. The concept of stop word in the information retrieval domain was extended to the concept of 'stop path'. Such paths are deleted from the "Path" table, the fragments on the paths are deleted from the "Element" table, and the tokens that belong to the fragments are deleted from the "Token" table.

5   Experiments

This section describes examples of applying the method to the INEX test collection.

5.1   Application of Method to INEX-1.9

This section describes applications of the method to the INEX-1.9 test collection. The method includes three steps of deletion: by period ratio, by number of different words, and by empirical rules.

Executing Deletion by Period Ratio. We calculated the period ratio of the INEX-1.9 test collection. Figure 4 shows the transition of the period ratio of each fragment in decreasing period-ratio order. Each point in the plot shows a single fragment and its period ratio.

The fragments in Figure 4 were divided into three groups. The first was document-centric fragments whose period ratio is from 0.8 to 1. The second was data-centric fragments whose period ratio is from 0 to 0.2. The third was intermediate fragments whose period ratio is from 0.2 to 0.8.

Document-centric and intermediate fragments were kept, and data-centric fragments were deleted. The threshold of the period ratio for deletion was 0.21. The number of fragments decreased from about 16 million to about 4.4 million by applying this method.

Executing Deletion by Number of Different Words. We calculated the number of different words of fragments that escaped deletion by period ratio. Figure 5 shows the relation between the number of different words and the

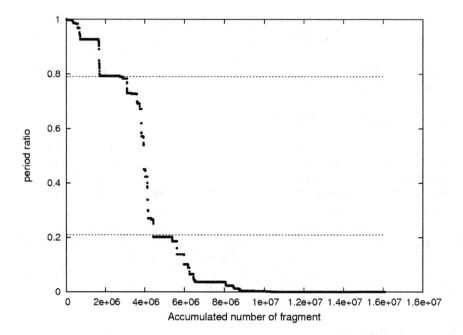

Fig. 4. Transition of period ratio

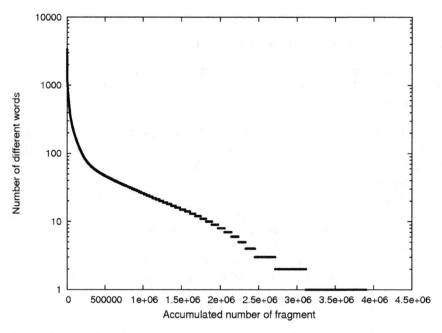

Fig. 5. Relation between number of different words and fragments that have the same number of different words

number of fragments that have the same number of different words. Each point in the plot shows a single fragment and its number of different words.

The fragments in Figure 5 were divided into three groups. The first was the large majority of fragments that have a few different words. The second was a small number of fragments that have many different words.

The large majority of fragments that have a few different words was deleted. The threshold of the number of different words for deletion was 30. The number of fragments decreased from about 4.4 million to about 0.85 million by applying this method.

Executing Deletion by an Empirical Rule. In the fragment set, from which data-centric ones were deleted by period ratio and the number of different words, we performed deletion of the fragments of tables, figures, and mathematical expressions and its descendants. The number of fragments decreased from about 0.85 million to about 0.84 million by applying this method. The number of fragments decreased from about 16 million to about 0.84 million by executing the above three steps.

5.2   Performance Evaluation

We evaluate the effectiveness of the proposed method in terms of retrieval precision and query processing speed. In this experiment, we used INEX-1.9 for the test collection and CO.Thorough sub task for performance evaluation. The experimental setup was as follows. CPU: Intel Xeon 3.8 GHz (Dual); Memory: 4096 MB; OS: Asianux 1.0; DBMS: Oracle 10g Release 1.

Evaluation of Retrieval Precision. We compared the full fragment set with the reduced fragment set in terms of retrieval precision for the top 1500 results of XML fragments. We use PR-Generalized of EvalJ metrics. Figure 6 shows the comparison of retrieval precision.

We can observe the retention of large numbers of inappropariate fragments for keyword search targets degrade retrieval precision. On the other hand, the retrieval precision of the reduced fragment set improves, especially at low recall levels. It proves that the appropriate fragments for keyword search target are selected by applying our method.

Evaluation of Query Processing Time. We compared the full fragment set with the reduced fragment set in terms of query processing time. Clustered index is created on "token" attribute of "Token" table. Figure 7 shows the comparison of the elapsed time of the topic 202 to the topic 221. Figure 8 shows the comparison of the elapsed time of the topic 222 to the topic 241. The average elapsed time of the full fragment set is about 171 seconds, while the average elapsed time of the reduced fragment set is about 17.1 seconds.

Query processing time for the reduced fragment set was shorter than the time for the full fragment set in all 40 CO queries. Query processing time has been improved up to about sixty times. We confirmed that decreasing of retrieval-targeted fragments made query processing more efficient.

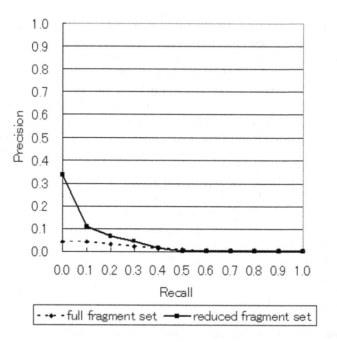

Fig. 6. Comparisons of retrieval precision

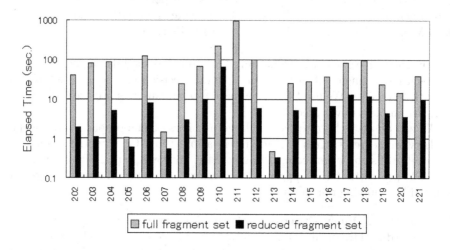

Fig. 7. Comparison of elapsed time of the topic 202 to the topic 221

Deletion Ratio. The above experiments confirm that this method is effective for the improvement of retrieval precision and query processing speed. However, some answer fragments might be deleted by this method. We counted the number of deleted fragments included in all answer fragments and calculated the ratio of deleted fragments in all answer fragments. We call it the deletion ratio. Deletion ratio D is calculated as follows:

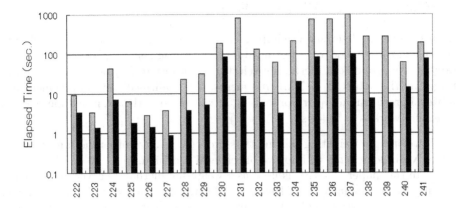

Fig. 8. Comparison of elapsed time of the topic 222 to the topic 241

Table 2. Deletion Ratio

Document ID	Exhaustivity 2	1	2&1	Document ID	Exhaustivity 2	1	2&1
202	0.000	0.214	0.077	222	0.450	0.154	0.284
203	0.000	0.144	0.140	223	0.094	0.080	0.084
205	N/A	0.215	0.215	227	0.022	0.067	0.059
206	0.133	0.347	0.262	228	0.000	0.340	0.328
207	0.600	0.326	0.441	229	0.000	0.078	0.067
208	0.070	0.199	0.185	230	0.091	0.036	0.048
209	0.000	0.053	0.048	232	0.744	0.450	0.575
210	0.047	0.171	0.153	233	0.150	0.231	0.196
212	0.000	0.813	0.705	234	0.224	0.718	0.483
213	0.000	0.262	0.234	235	0.090	0.199	0.160
216	0.060	0.129	0.109	236	0.029	0.278	0.263
217	0.000	0.048	0.037	237	0.010	0.269	0.246
218	0.000	0.253	0.252	239	0.105	0.042	0.050
219	0.000	0.132	0.121	241	0.339	0.278	0.324
221	0.049	0.316	0.186	Total	0.215	0.348	0.314

$$D = \frac{\texttt{deleted answer fragments}}{\texttt{all answer fragments}}.$$

Table 2 shows the deletion ratio of INEX-1.9. We find many fragments whose exhaustivity is 2 are deleted especially in the topics 207, 222, 232, 233, and 241. In these documents, the exhausitivity of data-centric fragments, such as italic and item of list is 2. In our method, we considered that such fragments are not exhaustive and should be deleted from retrieval targets.

6   Conclusion and Future Work

In this paper, we described the implementation of an XML information retrieval system and a method of selecting appropriate fragments for keyword search targets. We proposed a method of selecting appropriate fragments for retrieval target by the statistics of XML fragments. We confirmed the improvement of retrieval precision and query processing speed by using the proposed method.

Future work is as follows.

- Developing a weighting scheme that proactively introduces the information of XML documents to improve of retrieval precision.

  In this paper, TF-IPF is used as a weighting method. TF values are normalized by document size. Hence, the TF value of the tokens in data-centric fragments becomes high. A weighting method that proactively introduces the information of XML documents is needed to solve this problem.
- Developing a ranking method and an efficient query processing method when queries from users include paths in XML documents.

  In this paper, we supposed a case where users do not have the knowledge about document structure. In this case, we can assume queries are given by keywords. So, data-centric fragments were deleted from retrieval target by taking the features of keyword search into consideration. However, some data-centric fragments are used as selection conditions. The XPath query "/article[title="A Study on XML Document Retrieval and its Application System"]" is such an example. When selection conditions include paths, a ranking method and an efficient query processing method need to be developed.

References

1. W3C. Extensible Markup Language (XML). 1996-2003.
   http://www.w3.org/XML/
2. W3C. XQuery 1.0: An XML Query Language. 2004.
   http://www.w3.org/TR/xquery/
3. W3C. XML Path Language (XPath) Version 1.0. 1999.
   http://www.w3.org/TR/xpath/
4. Masatoshi Yoshikawa, Toshiyuki Amagasa, Takeyuki Shimura and Shunsuke Uemura: XRel: A Path-Base Approach to Strage and Retrieval of XML Documents Using Relational Database, ACM Transactions on Internet Technology, Vol.1, No.1, pp.110-141 (2001).
5. Torsten Grabs, Hans-Jorg Schek: ETH Zurich at INEX: Flexible Information Retrieval from XML with PowerDB-XML, INEX Workshop 2002, pp.141-148 (2002).
6. INitiative for the Evaluation of XML Retrieval (INEX) 2005.
   http://inex.is.informatik.uni-duisburg.de/2005/
7. Kenji Hatano, Hiroko Kinutani, Toshiyuki Amagasa, Yasuhiro Mori, Masatoshi Yoshikawa and Shunsuke Uemura: Analyzing the Properties of XML Fragments decomposed from the INEX Document Collection, Advances in XML Information Retrieval, Lecture Notes in Computer Science, Volume 3493, pp.168-182, Springer-Verlag, May 2005.

8. Yoshihiko Hayashi, Junji Tomita and Genichiro Kikui: Searching Text-rich XML Documents with Relevance Ranking, http://www.haifa.il.ibm.com /sigir00-xml/final-papers/Hayashi/hayashi.html, In ACM SIGIR 2000 Workshop on XML and Information Retrieval (2000).
9. Sihem Amer-Yahia, Chavdar Botev and Jayavel Shanmugasundaram: TeXQuery: A Full-Text SEarch Extension to XQuery, Proc. of 13th International World Wide Web Conference, ACM Press, pp. 538-594 (2004).
10. Sihem Amer-Yahia, Laks V. S. Lakshmanan and Shashank Pandit: FleXPath: Flexible Structure and Full-Text Querying for XML, Proc. of the 2003 ACM SIGMOD International Conference on MAnagement of Data, ACM Press, pp. 83-94 (2004).

The Dynamic Retrieval of XML Elements

Carolyn J. Crouch, Sudip Khanna, Poorva Potnis, and Nagendra Doddapaneni

Department of Computer Science
University of Minnesota Duluth
Duluth, MN 55812
(218) 726-7607
ccrouch@d.umn.edu

Abstract. This paper describes the current state of our system for structured retrieval. The system itself is based on an extension of the vector space model initially proposed by Fox [5]. The basic functions are performed using the Smart experimental retrieval system [10]. The major advance in our system this year is the incorporation of a facility for the dynamic retrieval of elements, which we refer to as flexible retrieval. This approach allows the system to return a rank-ordered list of elements based on a single indexing of the collection at the paragraph level. *Lnu* term weights [12,13] are generated dynamically along with the elements themselves, thus eliminating the need for propagation. Experimental results using this technique on INEX 2006 data show that it can produce results competitive with those produced by retrieval on an all-element index of the collection (and in fact produces virtually identical results for the new Fetch-and-Browse task). Early relevance feedback results are also reported.

1 Introduction

Our goal when we began our work with INEX in 2002 was to assess the utility of Salton's vector space model [11] in its extended form for XML retrieval. Familiarity with Smart [10] and faith in its capabilities led us to believe that this approach was promising if particular problems such as flexible retrieval (i.e., retrieval of elements at the desired degree of granularity) and ranking issues could be resolved. During the past year, our research has centered on an approach for the dynamic retrieval of elements which we believe provides a viable solution to both these problems.

For those interested in the background and evolution of our system, discussions are available in our earlier workshop papers [1-3]. This paper focuses on our method of flexible retrieval, which is performed dynamically at retrieval time. It returns a rank-ordered list of elements to the user. An overview of results with respect to INEX 2005 tasks is presented, comparing dynamic element retrieval with retrieval against an all all-element index of the collection. In particular, the two methods produce virtually identical results under both ep/gr and ep/gr-a when applied to the INEX Fetch-and-Browse task.

Our method of flexible retrieval is based on a single indexing of the collection at the paragraph level. (Collection statistics as required for *Lnu-ltu* term weighting are

N. Fuhr et al. (Eds.): INEX 2005, LNCS 3977, pp. 268–281, 2006.
© Springer-Verlag Berlin Heidelberg 2006

also used, but these are available from an examination of the collection as a whole and once calculated can be applied to any collection with similar characteristics.) It uses an extension of the basic vector space model proposed by Fox [5] to represent the various components of the structured document. This extension allows the incorporation of objective identifiers such as author name and date of publication with content identifiers in the representation of the document. Similarity between extended vectors is calculated as a linear combination of the similarities of the corresponding subvectors.

Flexible retrieval in this system takes place after an initial retrieval. Given a query and a paragraph indexing of the collection, we retrieve a rank-ordered list of paragraphs. Paragraphs that correlate highly with the query are used to identify documents of interest to the query (i.e., those containing potentially relevant elements). Once such a document is identified, a bottom-up representation of the document tree is generated. *Lnu* term weights are generated for the element vectors at each level in the tree. The element vectors are correlated with the *ltu*-weighted query vector used for the initial retrieval and a rank-ordered list of elements is produced.

Before formulating our 2005 experiments, we first experimented with 2004 data (where relevance judgments were available) by using both extended vector and body-only retrieval and comparing the results to those produced by corresponding retrievals against an all-element indexing of the collection. Subvector weighting was also examined. Experiments on the 2004 INEX data set indicated that extended vector retrieval substantially outperformed body-only retrieval, so our 2005 results are based on extended vector retrieval using the same subvector weights. Although we participated in a number of the 2005 tasks, our interest centers on CO processing (with respect to both the Thorough and Focused tasks) and Fetch-and-Browse. Another interest is how flexible retrieval performs with respect to what may reasonably be considered an upper bound on performance, i.e., retrieval against the all element index.

In INEX 2005 we are using, for the first time, a system which retrieves elements dynamically in an effective manner and then returns a rank-ordered list to the user. Experimental results demonstrate the successful utilization of this approach for structured retrieval.

2   Background

This section presents a brief overview of the models and term weighting method upon which our system is based—i.e., the vector space model, the extended vector space model, and *Lnu-ltu* term weighting (which is particularly applicable to element retrieval).

A basic model in information retrieval is the vector space model [11], wherein documents and queries are represented as weighted term vectors. The weight assigned to a term is indicative of the contribution of that term to the meaning of the document. The similarity between vectors (e.g., document and query) is represented by the mathematical similarity of the corresponding term vectors.

In 1983, Fox [5] proposed an extension of the vector space model—the extended vector space model—to allow for the incorporation of objective identifiers with content identifiers in the representation of a document. An extended vector can include different classes of information about a document, such as author name, date of publication, etc., along with content terms. In this model, a document vector consists of a set of subvectors, where each subvector represents a different class of information. Our current representation of an XML document/query consists of 18 subvectors (*abs, ack, article_au_fnm, article_au_snm, atl, au_aff, bdy, bibl_atl, bibl_au_fnm, bibl_au_snm,, bibl_ti, ed_aff, ed_intro, kwd, pub_yr, reviewer_name, ti, vt*) as defined in INEX guidelines. These subvectors represent the major properties of the document or article—those most likely to be of interest with respect to retrieval. Of the 18, eight are subjective, that is, contain content-bearing terms: *abs, ack, atl, bdy, bibl_atl, bibl_ti, ed_intro, kwd* (abstract, acknowledgements, article title, body, title of article cited in the bibliography, title of publication containing this article [i.e., journal title], editorial introduction, and keywords, respectively). Similarity between extended vectors is calculated as a linear combination of the similarities of the corresponding subjective subvectors. (The objective subvectors are currently used in our system only as filters on the result set returned by CAS queries. That is, when a ranked set of elements is retrieved in response to a query, the objective subvectors are used as filters to guarantee that only elements meeting the specified criteria are returned to the user.)

Use of the extended vector model for document retrieval normally raises the question of how to select coefficients for combining subvector similarities. This requires some experimentation. Early (2003 and 2004) experiments identified the following subjective subvectors as being useful for retrieval: *abs, atl, bdy, bibl_atl, kwd*. Similar experiments examined subvector weighting. Parameters producing the best results were applied to our 2005 experiments. (See Section 4 for more detail.)

Another issue of interest is the weighting of terms within subjective subvectors. Earlier experiments indicated that the best results were achieved with respect to both article and paragraph indexings when *Lnu.ltu* term weighting [13] was used. Our 2005 results are based on the use of *Lnu* term weighting for the elements. *Lnu* term weights are defined below:

$$\frac{(1+\log(term\_frequency)) \div (1+\log(average\_term\_frequency))}{(1-slope)+slope \times ((number\_unique\_terms) \div pivot)}$$

where *tf* represents term frequency, slope is an empirically determined constant, and pivot is the average number of unique terms per document, calculated across the entire collection.

3 System Description

Our system handles the processing of XML text as follows:

3.1 Parsing

The documents are parsed using a simple XML parser available on the web.

3.2   Translation to Extended Vector Format

The documents and queries are translated into Smart format and indexed by Smart as extended vectors. We selected the paragraph as our basic indexing unit in the early stages. Thus a typical vector in this system (based on our paragraph indexing) consists of a set of subjective and objective subvectors with a paragraph in the *bdy* subvector. (Other indexing units were later added to include section titles, tables, figure captions, abstracts, and lists.) *Lnu* term weighting is applied to all subjective subvectors.

3.3   Initial Retrieval

Retrieval takes place by running the topics against the paragraph indexing of the collection using Smart. The topics used in the initial retrieval may be simple (i.e., body-only) or extended vector queries. A simple query consists of search terms distributed only in the *bdy* subvector, whereas in the extended vector case the search terms are distributed across the subjective subvectors. In either case, the result is a list of *elements* (paragraphs) ordered by decreasing similarity to the query. Consider all the elements in this list with a non-zero correlation with the query. Each such element represents a terminal node (e.g., paragraph) in the body of a document with some relationship to the query.

3.4   Flexible Retrieval

A basic requirement of INEX retrieval is that the system must return components of documents or elements (i.e., abstract, paragraphs, sub-sections, sections, bodies, articles, figure titles, section titles, and introductory paragraphs) to the user rather than just the document itself. The object is to return the most relevant [highly exhaustive and specific] element(s) in response to a query. A good flexible system should return a mixture of document components (elements) to the user. These elements should be returned in rank order. The method to determine rank should incorporate both exhaustivity and specificity.

Our flexible retrieval module, Flex, is designed as follows. It takes as input a list of elements (i.e., paragraphs), rank-ordered by similarity to the query as determined by Smart in the initial retrieval stage. Each such element represents a leaf of a tree; each tree represents an article in the document collection.

Consider Figure 1, which represents the tree structure of a typical XML article. The root of the tree is the article itself, whereas the leaf nodes are the paragraphs. Flexible retrieval should return relevant document components (e.g., <sec>, <ss1>, <ss2>, <p>, <bdy>, <article>) as shown in Figure 1. In order to determine which elements of a tree to return, the system must (1) build the tree, and (2) assign a value to each non-terminal node in the tree by correlating the query with that element. (The value in this case represents a function of exhaustivity and specificity.) Elements are then returned to the user in rank order.

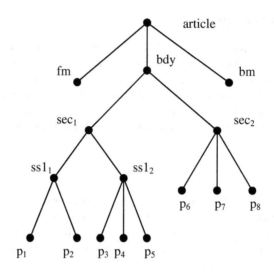

Fig. 1. Tree Structure of a Typical XML Document

Flex takes a bottom-up approach. All leaf elements having non-zero correlations with query Q have already been assigned similarity values by Smart. Consider the set of n (say 1000) top-ranked elements associated with Q. Trees are constructed for all articles with leaves in this set. To construct a tree, information about its structure and its terminal nodes must be known. Information about the structure of the tree is available as a by-product of the initial parsing of the documents. Information about its terminal nodes is found in the paragraph indexing of the collection.

The process is straight-forward. Suppose for example in Figure 1 that p_1, p_2, and p_7 were retrieved as leaf elements of the same tree. Flex would then build the tree represented in Figure 1. Each leaf is represented by a term-frequency weighted vector. Each element vector (parent) is generated by merging the terms which appear in its children and updating the frequency of each term. This process continues until the body element (*bdy*) is generated. (See [7] for details.)

A significant problem in element retrieval is the return of a rank-ordered list. Often this problem is dealt with by propagating weights from one level of the tree to another. It is difficult to know how to do this well. Our approach allows us to generate element term weights directly. *Lnu* term weights for a particular element vector are based on information available within the vector itself along with collection-dependent values of slope and pivot. The method is designed to account for differences in the length of vectors by reducing the difference between the probability of relevance and the probability of retrieval. Details of *Lnu-ltu* term weighting can be found in [12,13]; suffice it to say that once values of slope and pivot are determined at the element level, each element can be *Lnu*-weighted and correlated with the *ltu*-weighted query to produce a rank value for the element.

One problem remains with this approach. Consider the formula for the *ltu* term weighting of the query, given below.

$$(1 + \log(term\_frequency)) \times \log(N \div n_k)$$

$$(1 - slope) + slope \times ((number\_unique\_terms) \div pivot)$$

This formula is dependent on both N (the collection size) and n_k (the number of elements that contain the term). This information is not available in the local environment. N can be estimated but n_k is generally available only through an element indexing of the collection. Our conjecture was that using the original, *ltu*-weighted query (the one used in the initial Smart retrieval to collect the paragraphs) and correlating it with the *Lnu*-weighted element vectors would produce a rank-ordered list of elements superior to any ranking we could produce through weight propagation and accurate enough to produce useful results. (More recent efforts are directed at producing values for these parameters [n_k in particular] reflective of the element environment, but the results reported in this paper are based on use of the original, *ltu*-weighted query.)

For each query, after a rank-ordered list of elements is produced for each tree, the lists are merged, and the top 1500 are reported for INEX evaluation.

4 Experiments

In the following sections, we describe the experiments performed with respect to the ad-hoc task (CO, Fetch and Browse and CAS processing) and the relevance feedback task. In all cases, we use only the topic title as search words in query construction. Term weighting is *Lnu.ltu* (using the paragraph *ltu*-weighted query as described above for Flex operations); the similarity measure used is inner product. All indexing is done only at the paragraph (basic indexing unit) level unless otherwise specified.

Parameters of particular interest with respect to extended vector retrieval are the values assigned to each of the subvectors during the retrieval process (i.e., the subvector weights). Based on earlier experiments [7], subvector weights of 0 were applied to all subvectors with the exception of the three which were found to be of particular interest with respect to retrieval, namely, *bdy* (the body subvector, representing a paragraph, subsection, section, or body element), *atl* (the article title), and *abs* (the abstract). Based again on [7], subvector weights of 3, 2, and 1, respectively, were assigned to these subvectors. The parameter of most interest with respect to flexible retrieval is n, the number of paragraphs input to Flex. The value of n is set to 1000 for all runs.

4.1 Using CO Topics

Our 2005 CO experiments are designed to examine the performance of two different approaches to element retrieval. Our primary interest this year lies in determining how our flexible retrieval method—dynamic element retrieval—compares to a corresponding retrieval against an all-element index of the collection. In 2004 [3], we ran experiments to determine whether extended vector or body-only retrieval produced the better result. Since extended vector retrieval always produced a better result, all of our 2005 runs are based on the use of extended vectors. In this paper, we compare the results of [extended vector] flexible retrieval to those produced by [extended vector] conventional retrieval against an all-element index of the collection. We also examine flexible retrieval results wherein small elements—i.e., elements with sizes ranging from 10 to 50 terms—are filtered or removed from consideration in the retrieval process. Results indicate little noticeable improvement resulting from this process but scores are reported.

Experimental runs for the CO task consist of the following: Three basic runs were produced for every subtask—flexible retrieval, flexible retrieval with small elements removed (filtered paragraphs), and retrieval on the all-element index. The CO subtasks (Thorough, Focused, and Fetch-and-Browse [strict, generalized]) are reported for the official metrics (nXCG and ep/gr) and also under inex-eval for Thorough as a general indicator of relative performance over the window of 1500. Detailed information is shown in Tables 1-4; a more global view is given by the corresponding figures which appear in the Appendix.

The CO Thorough subtask aims at returning all relevant elements, whereas the Focused subtask seeks to return only the most relevant element along a path. These subtasks are implemented in our runs as indicated above via either flexible retrieval or a search of the all-element index. A brief overview of the new Fetch-and-Browse subtask is in order here. This task is implemented by performing two independent searches of the document collection. One is a normal retrieval against an article index of the collection, which produces a rank-ordered set of documents (set 1). The other is either a flexible retrieval on the paragraph index (for the Flex runs) or a retrieval on the all-element index to produce a set of rank-ordered elements (set 2). In Fetch-and-Browse, we take the first document in set 1 and collect in order from set 2 the elements which belong to this document. We then continue this process until 1500 elements are collected and reported.

As can be seen from Table 1, our all-element results were quite good in the early stages, falling into the average range at rank 100. Under inex-eval (as seen in Table 2), the all-element results were excellent, with strict better than generalized. (Further analysis is needed to examine the differences produced by the metrics.)

Table 1. CO Thorough results (nXCG and ep/gr)

Metric	All-element				Flex				Flex_Par_Filtered			
	Strict		Generalized		Strict		Generalized		Strict		Generalized	
nXCG	P	R	P	R	P	R	P	R	P	R	P	R
@1	0.039	10/55	0.267	14/55	0.039	10/55	0.289	7/55	0.039	10/55	0.289	7/55
@5	0.046	9/55	0.264	11/55	0.031	20/55	0.213	25/55	0.031	20/55	0.213	25/55
@10	0.075	6/55	0.280	3/55	0.023	36/55	0.201	27/55	0.023	36/55	0.202	26/55
@25	0.085	9/55	0.239	10/55	0.041	30/55	0.193	31/55	0.041	30/55	0.194	29/55
@50	0.103	11/25	0.223	16/55	0.058	34/55	0.190	27/55	0.057	34/55	0.191	28/55
@100	0.111	25/55	0.202	21/55	0.063	37/55	0.174	32/55	0.063	38/55	0.172	33/55
@500	0.218	29/55	0.219	26/55	0.200	31/55	0.214	30/55	0.195	32/55	0.211	31/55
@1500	0.338	26/55	0.325	21/55	0.271	31/55	0.323	23/55	0.267	33/55	0.325	22/55
ep/gr	0.025	9/55	0.059	22/55	0.022	15/55	0.060	19/55	0.022	16/55	0.061	21/55

Table 2. CO Thorough results (inex-eval)

	All-element				Flex				Flex_Par_Filtered			
Metric	Strict		Generalized		Strict		Generalized		Strict		Generalized	
inex eval	P	R	P	R	P	R	P	R	P	R	P	R
@1	0.148	3/55	0.336	15/55	0.148	3/55	0.371	7/55	0.148	3/55	0.371	7/55
@5	0.104	3/55	0.331	7/55	0.067	22/55	0.264	23/55	0.067	22/55	0.264	23/55
@10	0.111	2/55	0.332	3/55	0.048	35/55	0.240	25/55	0.048	35/55	0.240	25/55
@20	0.081	2/55	0.270	9/55	0.054	29/55	0.216	27/55	0.054	29/55	0.216	28/55
@100	0.053	1/55	0.176	12/55	0.037	21/55	0.152	28/55	0.037	22/55	0.150	31/55
@200	0.040	1/55	0.138	13/55	0.033	9/55	0.125	24/55	0.033	11/55	0.124	26/55
@1500	0.011	10/55	0.050	11/55	0.010	16/55	0.049	13/55	0.010	18/55	0.048	16/55

Table 3. CO Focused results (nXCG and ep/gr)

	All-element				Flex				Flex_Par_Filtered			
Metric	Strict		Generalized		Strict		Generalized		Strict		Generalized	
nXCG	P	R	P	R	P	R	P	R	P	R	P	R
@1	0.077	8/44	0.209	23/44	0.000	29/44	0.151	31/44	0.000	29/44	0.151	31/44
@5	0.063	11/44	0.185	20/44	0.023	26/44	0.143	33/44	0.023	26/44	0.143	33/44
@10	0.058	15/44	0.163	25/44	0.023	31/44	0.156	28/44	0.023	31/44	0.156	27/44
@25	0.077	14/44	0.153	23/44	0.026	33/44	0.142	25/44	0.026	33/44	0.145	24/44
@50	0.090	19/44	0.154	22/44	0.029	32/44	0.129	26/44	0.029	32/44	0.132	24/44
@100	0.121	17/44	0.172	21/44	0.053	31/44	0.117	30/44	0.053	31/44	0.120	29/44
@500	0.204	16/44	0.270	17/44	0.066	34/44	0.150	32/44	0.074	33/44	0.155	31/44
@1500	0.310	10/44	0.367	12/44	0.070	34/44	0.158	32/44	0.086	33/44	0.170	31/44
ep/gr	0.022	15/44	0.066	19/44	0.049	26/44	0.049	26/44	0.005	34/44	0.050	25/44

Table 4. CO Fetch-and-Browse results (ep/gr and ep/gr-a)

	All-element				Flex				Flex_Par_Filtered			
Met-ric	Strict		Generalized		Strict		Generalized		Strict		Generalized	
ep/gr	0.003	11/63	0.044	11/63	0.002	15/63	0.040	14/63	0.002	16/63	0.048	9/63
ep/gr-a	0.107	3/63	0.190	21/63	0.110	2/63	0.178	23/63	0.110	4/63	0.185	22/63

Focused results (Table 3) are not as good. Fetch-and-Browse results were fairly good under ep/gr, falling just out of the top 10 for the all-element results, which were followed closely by the Flex runs (Table 4). Our ep/gr-a (strict) results were excellent for both the flexible and the all-element runs. (In fact, virtually identical Fetch-and-Browse results were produced by the all-element and flexible methods.)

4.2 Using CAS Topics

We process CAS topics in much the same fashion as CO topics, with some important exceptions. During pre-processing of the CAS queries, the subjective and objective portions of the query and the element to be returned (e.g., abstract, section, paragraph) are identified.

Depending on its syntax, a CAS query can be divided into parts, which can be divided into subparts depending on the number of search fields. CAS preprocessing splits the query into the required number of parts, each of which is processed as a separate Smart query. For example, suppose the query specifies that a search term is to be searched for in field 1. If the field to be searched is an objective subvector, the search term is distributed in that subvector. If the search field specifies a specific subjective subvector, the search term is distributed in that subvector. Otherwise the search takes place in the paragraph subvector. The result in this last case is a set of elements returned by the Smart search which is used as input to Flex. Flex produces a ranked set of elements as the final output of this small search. After all subsearches associated with the query are complete, the final result set is produced (i.e., the original query is resolved). A ranking procedure, dependent upon the type of subtask, is applied. Lastly, a filter is applied to the element set, so that the SVCAS and SSCAS subtasks return only the type of elements sought. See [4] for more details.

As Tables 5 and 6 show, other than VSCAS in early ranks, our CAS results are at best undistinguished. The cause may lie in our post-processing element ranking procedure, which is applied to the sets of elements retrieved by the individual child queries, along with our current method of element ranking. (All of these runs exhibit no overlap.) More analysis is needed with respect to these results.

Table 5. SCAS and SVCAS results (nXCG and ep/gr)

Metric	SSCAS				SVCAS			
	Strict		Generalized		Strict		Generalized	
nXCG	P	R	P	R	P	R	P	R
@1	0.000	8/25	0.045	17/25	0.000	7/23	0.172	7/23
@5	0.050	19/25	0.163	18/25	0.000	16/23	0.207	8/23
@10	0.100	18/25	0.165	19/25	0.040	18/23	0.171	11/23
@25	0.092	18/25	0.140	19/25	0.072	18/23	0.187	11/23
@50	0.116	18/25	0.132	20/25	0.100	11/23	0.218	12/23
@100	0.120	20/25	0.128	20/25	0.113	14/23	0.258	12/23
@500	0.394	17/25	0.262	21/25	0.456	13/23	0.483	11/23
@1500	0.432	17/25	0.277	21/25	0.525	14/23	0.514	12/23
ep/gr	0.006	22/25	0.033	22/25	0.016	8/23	0.069	12/23

Table 6. VSCAS and VVCAS results (nXCG and ep/gr)

	VSCAS				VVCAS			
Metric	Strict		Generalized		Strict		Generalized	
nXCG	P	R	P	R	P	R	P	R
@1	0.167	2/24	0.355	1/24	0.000	8/28	0.301	9/28
@5	0.033	12/24	0.262	7/24	0.000	22/28	0.205	19/28
@10	0.067	11/24	0.264	8/24	0.011	21/28	0.202	18/28
@25	0.800	9/24	0.203	13/24	0.031	20/28	0.208	17/28
@50	0.100	9/24	0.183	13/24	0.038	20/28	0.188	16/28
@100	0.088	13/24	0.154	14/24	0.430	22/28	0.183	13/28
@500	0.161	13/24	0.149	13/24	0.172	16/28	0.247	10/28
@1500	0.272	13/24	0.201	13/24	0.427	8/28	0.359	12/28
ep/gr	0.005	15/24	0.032	14/24	0.005	15/28	0.054	13/28

4.3 2005 Ad-Hoc Results

Our initial approach to flexible retrieval [3] used a primitive ranking scheme which favored the return of smaller elements. Yet as Kamps, *et. al.* [6] show, in 2003 the probability of relevance increased with element length. Our current method of flexible retrieval produces a much more diverse element set. When applying our current version of Flex to the 2004 INEX collection, we were able to produce a better result in terms of average precision than that achieved by retrieval against the all-element index [7]. With the 2005 collection, Flex produces virtually identical results for Fetch-and-Browse and generally lower results for the other CO subtasks. A more accurate ranking produced by a more accurate weighting of the query vectors at the element level will reduce the discrepancy. (That is, the ranking of elements can certainly be improved by a more accurate weighting of the query vector at the element level.) However, given the very large index required, the redundancy within it, and the inefficiencies of storage and search time associated with all-element retrieval, we conclude that flexible retrieval, which produces a result dynamically based on a single index, is preferred if it can produce even a comparable result.

4.4 Relevance Feedback in INEX

The importance of relevance feedback in conventional information retrieval has long been recognized. Incorporating relevance feedback techniques within the domain of structured retrieval is an interesting challenge.

Working within the constraints of our system, the first question which arises is how to translate the exhaustivity and specificity values associated with each INEX element into an appropriate measure of relevance in our system. Conventional retrieval views relevance assessment as binary. In INEX, we have a range of values for exhaustivity and a corresponding set of values for specificity. There are many possibilities to consider when mapping these values to relevance. These early experiments recognize as relevant those elements with positive values of e and are based on an initial retrieval against the all-element index of the collection.

Evaluation is given for CO topics in terms of *P@20* (precision after the retrieval of 20 elements) performed on the residual collection. The number of terms used for expansion of the query, n, varies from 25 to 500, as seen. The number of elements assessed for relevance is 20. We have used Rocchio's algorithm [9], with α and β ranging from 1 to 5, respectively, and γ set to 0. A subset of the results are shown in Table 7.

Table 7 shows that the best results are obtained for this data set when α= 4, β = 1 and n = 300, which produces a 20 percent improvement in *P@20* over the base case. This result is very similar to that produced when the same experiment was run on the 2004 data set, which produced a best case improvement of 18 percent at α= 3, β = 1 and n = 500 [8]. These results indicate that it is possible to improve retrieval results substantially using relevance feedback at the element level. (Overlap is not considered in these results.)

Table 7. Relevance feedback results: P@20 for CO topics vs. base case (0.4034)

α	β	25	50	100	300	500
				n		
3	4	0.4155	0.4379	0.4431	0.4362	0.4397
		3.0%	8.6%	9.8%	8.1%	9.0%
3	5	0.4155	0.4362	0.4480	0.4362	0.4397
		3.0%	8.1%	11.1%	8.1%	9.0%
4	1	0.4276	0.4517	0.4672	0.4862	0.4776
		6.0%	12.0%	15.8%	20.5%	18.4%
4	3	0.4207	0.4328	0.4603	0.4500	0.4448
		4.3%	7.3%	14.1%	11.6%	10.3%
4	5	0.4155	0.4379	0.4431	0.4379	0.4379
		3.0%	8.6%	9.8%	8.6%	8.6%

5   Conclusions

Our current system has achieved one important goal—it is able to retrieve elements dynamically and return a rank-ordered list of elements to the user in response to a query. It requires only a single indexing of the collection at the paragraph level rather than multiple indexings, which are expensive to produce and maintain. The term weights generated along with the elements are exact *Lnu* weights. The order in which the elements are returned to the user is an approximation—but we believe a good approximation—of that produced by an equivalent retrieval against the all-element index. Our current work in this regard centers on producing a better estimate of n_k in the *ltu* weighting of query terms (as seen in the formula in Section 3.4). A value of n_k that more closely reflects its value at each element level will produce a more accurate ranking of elements to return to the user—one more closely aligned with that produced by retrieval on the all-element index.

Our efforts to date have centered on dynamically retrieving the most relevant set of elements associated with a query and ranking them appropriately. (That is, we have not attempted to modify the basic retrieval process so as to raise our scores/ranks under various metrics). When we are satisfied that these goals have been achieved, we will consider ways in which the results may be improved.

References

[1] Crouch, C., Apte, S., and Bapat, H. Using the extended vector model for XML retrieval. In *Proc of the First Workshop of the Initiative for the Evaluation of XML Retrieval (INEX)*, (Schloss Dagstuhl, 2002), 99-104.

[2] Crouch, C., Apte, S. and Bapat, H. An approach to structured retrieval based on the extended vector model. In *Proc of the Second Workshop of the Initiative for the Evaluation of XML Retrieval (INEX)*, (Schloss Dagstuhl, 2003), 87-93.

[3] Crouch, C., Mahajan, A., and Bellamkonda, A. Flexible retrieval based on the vector space model. In *Advances in XML Information Retrieval*, Third International Workshop of the Initiative for the Evaluation of XML Retrieval (INEX), (Schloss Dagstuhl, 2005), 292-302.

[4] Doddapaneni, N. Effective structured query processing. M.S. Thesis, Department of Computer Science, University of Minnesota Duluth, Duluth, MN (2005). http://www.d.umn.edu/cs/thesis/doddapaneni.pdf

[5] Fox, E. A. Extending the Boolean and vector space models of information retrieval with p-norm queries and multiple concept types. Ph.D. Dissertation, Department of Computer Science, Cornell University (1983).

[6] Kamps, J., de Rijke, M., and Sigurbjornsson, B. Length normalization in XML retrieval. *In Proc of the 27th Annual International ACM SIGIR Conference* (Sheffield, England, 2004), 80-87.

[7] Khanna, S. Design and implementation of a flexible retrieval system. M. S. Thesis, Department of Computer Science, University of Minnesota Duluth, Duluth, MN (2005). http://www.d.umn.edu/cs/thesis/khanna.pdf

[8] Potnis, P. Relevance feedback in a flexible retrieval environment. M.S.Thesis, Department of Computer Science, University of Minnesota Duluth, Duluth, MN (2005). http://www.d.umn.edu/cs/thesis/potnis.pdf

[9] Rocchio, J. Relevance feedback in information retrieval. In *The Smart System— Experiments in Automatic Document Processing*, G. Salton, ed. Prentice-Hall (1971), 313-323.

[10] Salton, G., ed. *The Smart Rretrieval System—Experiments in Automatic Document Processing*. Prentice-Hall. (1971).

[11] Salton, G., Wong, A., and Yang, C. S. A vector space model for automatic indexing. *Comm. ACM* 18, 11 (1975), 613-620.

[12] Singhal, A. AT&T at TREC-6. In *The Sixth Text REtrieval Conf (TREC-6)*, NIST SP 500-240 (1998), 215-225.

[13] Singhal, A., Buckley, C., and Mitra, M. Pivoted document length normalization. In *Proc. of the 19th Annual International ACM SIGIR Conference*, (Zurich,1996), 21-29.

Appendix

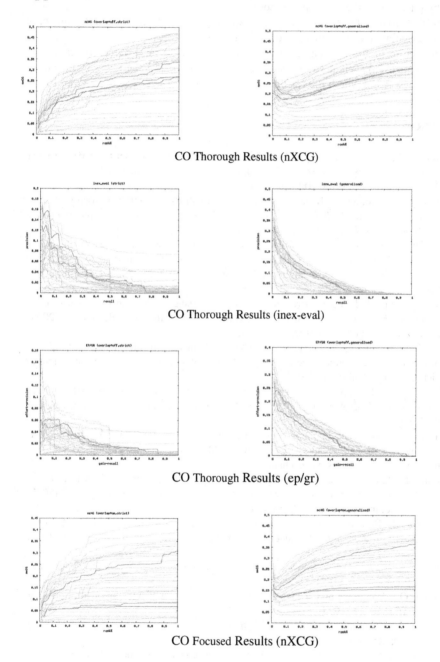

CO Thorough Results (nXCG)

CO Thorough Results (inex-eval)

CO Thorough Results (ep/gr)

CO Focused Results (nXCG)

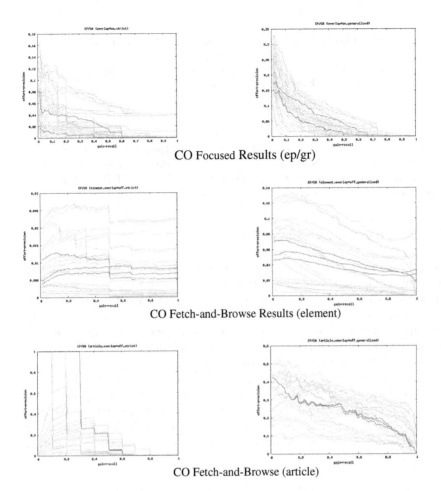

CO Focused Results (ep/gr)

CO Fetch-and-Browse Results (element)

CO Fetch-and-Browse (article)

TopX and XXL at INEX 2005

Martin Theobald, Ralf Schenkel, and Gerhard Weikum

Max-Planck-Institut für Informatik, Saarbrücken, Germany
{mtb, schenkel, weikum}@mpi-inf.mpg.de

Abstract. We participated with two different and independent search engines in this year's INEX round: The XXL Search Engine and the TopX engine. As this is the first participation for TopX, this paper focuses on the design principles, scoring, query evaluation and results of TopX. We shortly discuss the results with XXL afterwards.

1 TopX – System Overview

Our query processing methods are based on precomputed index lists that are sorted in descending order of appropriately defined scores for individual tag-term content conditions, and our algorithmic rationale for top-k queries on XML data follows that of the family of *threshold algorithms (TA)* [2, 4, 5]. In order to find the top-k matches for multidimensional queries (e.g., with multiple content and structure conditions), scoring, and ranking them, TopX scans all relevant index lists in an interleaved manner. In each scan step, when the engine sees the score for a data item in one list, it combines this score with scores for the same data item previously seen in other index lists into a *global score* using a monotonic aggregation function such as weighted summation. We perform in-memory structural joins for content-and-structure (CAS) queries using pre-/postorder labels between whole element blocks for each query condition grouped by their document ids.

1.1 Top-k Query Processing for Semistructured Data

The query processor decomposes the query into *content conditions*, each of which refers to exactly one tag-term pair, and into additional elementary tag conditions (e.g., for navigation of branching path queries), plus the path conditions that constrain the way how the matches for the tag-term pairs and elementary tag conditions have to be connected. For NEXI, we concentrate on content conditions that refer to the descendant axis, i.e., the full-text contents of elements. This way, each term is connected to its last preceding tag in the location path, in order to merge each tag-term pair into a single query condition with a corresponding list in the precomputed inverted index. Note that sequential reads are performed for these content-related tag-term-pairs, only, whereas additional structural query conditions for element paths or branching path queries are performed through a few judiciously scheduled random lookups on a separate, more compact element table.

N. Fuhr et al. (Eds.): INEX 2005, LNCS 3977, pp. 282–295, 2006.

The rationale for these distinctions is that random accesses to disk resident index structure are typically one or two orders of magnitude more expensive than sorted accesses. Note that an index list (e.g., for a single term) on a large data collection may be very long, in the order of megabytes (i.e., multiple disk tracks), and the total index size may easily exceed a several Gigabytes so that only the "hottest" fragments (i.e., prefixes of frequently needed lists) can be cached in memory. Sorted access benefits from sequential disk I/O with asynchronous prefetching and high locality in the processor's cache hierarchy; so it has much lower amortized costs than random access. Threshold algorithms with eager random accesses look up the scores for a data item in all query-relevant index lists, when they first see the data item in one list. Thus, they can immediately compute the global score of the item, and need to keep only the current top-k items with their scores in memory. Algorithms with a focus on sorted access do not eagerly look up all candidates' global scores and therefore need to maintain a candidate pool in memory, where each candidate is a partially evaluated data item d that has been seen in at least one list and may qualify for the final top-k result based on the following information (we denote the score of data item d in the i-th index list by $s(t_i, d)$, and we assume for simplicity that the score aggregation is summation):

- the set $E(d)$ of evaluated lists where d has already been seen,
- the $worstscore(d) := \sum_{i \in E(d)} s(t_i, d)$ based on the known scores $s(t_i, d)$, and
- the $bestscore(d) := worstscore(d) + \sum_{i \notin E(d)} high_i$ that d could possibly still achieve based on $worstscore(d)$ and the upper bounds $high_i$ for the scores in the yet unvisited parts of the index lists.

The algorithm terminates when the $worstscore(d)$ of the rank-k in the current top-k result, coined min-k, is at least as high as the highest $bestscore(d)$ among all remaining candidates.

1.2   Periodic Queue Maintenance and Early Candidate Pruning

All intermediate candidates that are of potential relevance for the final top-k results are collected in a hash structure (the *cache*) in main memory; this data structure has the full information about elements, *worstscores*, *bestscores*, etc. In addition, two priority queues merely containing pointers to these cache entries are maintained in memory and periodically updated. The top-k queue uses *worstscores* as priorities to organize the current top-k documents, and the candidate queue uses *bestscores* as priorities to maintain the stopping condition for threshold termination.

Results from [11] show that only a small fraction of the top candidates actually has to be kept in the candidate queue to provide a proper threshold for algorithm termination. Since TopX typically stops before having scanned all the relevant index lists completely, much less candidates than the ones that occur in the inverted lists for a query have to be kept in the cache. Both queues contain disjoint subsets of items currently in the cache. If an item's $bestscore(d)$ drops below the current min-k threshold, it is dropped from the candidate queue as well as from the cache. The queue is implemented using a Fibonacci heap, with efficient amortized lookups and maintenance.

Optionally, TopX also supports various tunable probabilistic extensions to schedule random accesses for testing both content-related and structural query conditions as well as a probabilistic form of candidate pruning, thus yielding approximate top-k results with great run time gains compared to the conservative top-k baseline and probabilistic guarantees for the result quality [11]. However, for the current INEX experiments these probabilistic extensions were not employed, because here the focus is clearly on retrieval robustness rather than cutting edge performance.

2   Data and Scoring Model

2.1   Full-Content Indexing

We consider a simplified XML data model, where idref/XLink/XPointer links are disregarded. Thus every document forms a tree of nodes, each with a *tag* and a related *content*. We treat attributes nodes as children of the corresponding element node. The content of a node is either a text string or it is empty; typically (but not necessarily) non-leaf nodes have empty content.

With each node, we can additionally associate its *full-content* which is defined as the concatenation of the text contents of all the node's descendants. Optionally, we may apply standard IR techniques such as stemming and stop word removal to those text contents. This way, we conceptually treat each element as an eligible retrieval unit (i.e., in the classic IR notion of a document) with its expanded full-content text nodes as content, with no benchmark-specific tuning or preselection of commonly retrieved tags or the use of predefined retrieval units being necessary. In the following we focus on the descendant axis (i.e., the full-content case) as the much more important case for XML IR with vague search, thus following the NEXI specification; the case for the child axis follows analogously.

```
<article
 id="conference/vldb05/theobald">
  <title>
    An efficient and versatile
    engine for TopX Search.
  </title>
  <abs>
    We present a novel engine,
    coined TopX, for ranked
    retrieval of XML documents.
  </abs>
  <sec st="Introduction">
    <par>
      Non-schematic XML data...
    </par>
  </sec>
  <sec st="Related Work">
    <par>
      Efficient evaluation of XML
      path conditions...
    </par>
  </sec>
</article>
```

Fig. 1. An XML example

Figure 1 depicts an XML example snippet and Figure 2 illustrates our logical view of that document, with expanded full-content text nodes for each element.

For example, the full term frequency (*ftf*) of the term `xml` for the root element `article` has a value of 3 which reflects that the whole article element is definitely relevant for a query containing the term `xml`, however, it might be less compact than a more specific section or paragraph which should be taken into account by the scoring model.

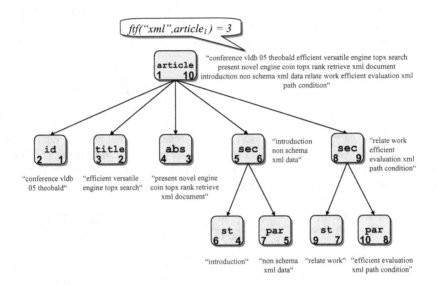

Fig. 2. Redundant full-content text nodes for elements

2.2   Content Scores

TopX provides the option to evaluate queries either in conjunctive mode or in "andish" mode. In the first case, all terms and structural conditions must be met by a result candidate, but still different matches yield different scores. In the second case, a node matches a content condition of the form $//"t_1\ t_2\ldots"$ if its content contains at least one occurrence of at least one of the terms t_1, t_2, etc. It matches the full-content condition $.//"t_1\ t_2\ \ldots"$ if its full-content contains at least one occurrence of at least one of the search terms. In the first case, the significance (e.g., derived from frequencies and element-specific corpus statistics) of a matched term influences the score and the final ranking, but – similarly to boolean XPath – documents (or subtrees) that do not contain a specified term at all or that do not strictly match all structural query conditions are dismissed.

For content scores we make use of element-specific statistics that view the content or full-content of each element node n with tag A as a bag of words:

1) the *term frequency*, $tf(t, n)$, of term t in node n, which is the number of occurrences of t in the content of n;
2) the *full-content term frequency*, $ftf(t, n)$, of term t in node n, which is the number of occurrences of t in the full-content of n;

3) the *tag frequency*, N_A, of tag A, which is the number of nodes with tag A in the entire corpus;

4) the *element frequency*, $ef_A(t)$, of term t with regard to tag A, which is the number of nodes with tag A that contain t in their full-contents in the entire corpus.

Now consider a content condition of the form A//"$t_1 \ldots t_m$", where A is a tag name and t_1 through t_m are terms that should occur in the full-contents of a subtree. Our scoring of node n with regard to condition A//"$t_1 \ldots t_m$" uses formulas of the following type:

$$score(n, A//"t_1 \ldots t_m") := \frac{\sum_{i=1}^{m} relevance_i \cdot specificity_i}{compactness(n)},$$

where $relevance_i$ reflects ftf values, $specificity_i$ is derived from N_A and $ef_A(t_i)$ values, and $compactness(n)$ considers the subtree or element size for length normalization. Note that specificity is made XML-specific by considering combined tag-term frequency statistics rather than global term statistics only. It serves to assign different weights to the individual tag-term pairs which is a common technique from probabilistic IR.

An important lesson from text IR is that the influence of the term frequency and element frequency values should be sublinearly dampened to avoid a bias for short elements with a high term frequency of a few rare terms. Likewise, the instantiation of compactness in the above formula should also use a dampened

Tag	N	avg(length)	k_1	b
article	16,808	2,903	10.5	0.75
sec	96,481	413	10.5	0.75
p	1,022,679	32	10.5	0.75
fig	109,230	13	10.5	0.75

Table 1. Element-specific parameterization of the extended BM25 model

form of element size. Highly skewed score distributions would be beneficial for candidate pruning (and fast algorithm termination), but typically at a high expense in retrieval quality. To address these considerations, we have adopted the popular and empirically usually much superior Okapi BM25 scoring model (originating in probabilistic IR for text documents [6]) to our XML setting, leading to the following scoring function:

$$score(n, A//"t_1 \ldots t_m") := \sum_{i=1}^{m} \frac{(k_1 + 1) \cdot ftf(t_i, n)}{K + ftf(t_i, n)} \cdot \log\left(\frac{N_A - ef_A(t_i) + 0.5}{ef_A(t_i) + 0.5}\right)$$

with

$$K = k_1 \left((1 - b) + b\frac{length(n)}{avg\{length(n') \mid n' \text{ with tag } A\}}\right).$$

The BM25 formula provides a dampened influence of the ftf and ef parts, as well as a compactness normalization that takes the average compactness of each element type into account. A simple hill-climbing-style parameter optimization using the 2004 INEX collection and relevance assessments yields a maximum in the MAP value for k_1 being set to 10.5, whereas the b parameter is confirmed to perform best at the default value of 0.75 provided in the literature. With regard to individual (element-specific) retrieval robustness, the above formula would also allow for a more elaborated parameter optimization for individual element types which was not considered for the current setup.

2.3   Structural Scores

For efficient testing of structural conditions we transitively expand all structural query dependencies. For example, in the query `//A//B//C[.// "t"]` an element with tag `C` (and content term `"t"`) has to be a descendant of both `A` and `B` elements. Branching path expressions can be expressed analogously. This way, the query forms a *directed acyclic graph* (DAG) with tag-term conditions as leafs, elementary tag conditions as interconnecting nodes between elements of a CAS query, and all transitively expanded descendant relations as edges. This transitive expansion of structural constraints is a key for efficient path validation and allows an *incremental testing* of path satisfiability. If `C` in the above example is not a valid descendant of `A`, we may safely prune the candidate document from the priority queue, if its $bestscore(d)$ falls below the current $min\text{-}k$ threshold without ever looking up the B condition.

In non-conjunctive (aka. "andish") retrieval, a result document (or subtree) should still satisfy most structural constraints, but we may tolerate that some tag names or path conditions are not matched. This is useful when queries are posed without much information about the possible and typical tags and paths or for vague content and structure (VCAS) search, where the structural constraints merely provide a hint on how the actual text contents should be connected. Our scoring model essentially counts the number of structural conditions (or connected tags) that are still to be satisfied by a result candidate d and assigns a small and constant score mass c for every condition that is matched. This structural score mass is combined with the content scores and aggregated with each candidate's $[worstscore(d), bestscore(d)]$ interval. In our setup we have set $c = 1$, whereas content scores were normalized to $[0, 1]$, i.e., we emphasize the structural query conditions. Note that it is still important to identify non-satisfiable structural conditions as early and efficiently as possible, because this can reduce the $bestscore(d)$ of a result candidate and make it eligible for pruning.

The overall score of a document or subtree for a content-and-structure (CAS) query is the sum of its content and structural scores. For content-only (CO) queries, i.e., mere keyword queries, the document score is the sum, over all terms, of the maximum per-term element scores within the same target element.

If TopX is configured to return entire documents as query results (e.g., for the CO/S-Fetch&Browse task), the score of a document is the maximal score of any subgraph matching a target element in the document; if otherwise the result granularity is set to elements, we may obtain multiple results according to the differently scored target elements in a document. The internal TopX query processor completely abstracts from the original query syntax (NEXI or XPath) and uses a full-fletched graph traversal to evaluate arbitrary query DAGs. Furthermore, the top-k-style nature of the engine does not require candidates to be fully evaluated at all query conditions, but merely relies on $[worstscore(d), bestscore(d)]$ bounds to determine the current top-k results and the $min\text{-}k$ threshold for algorithm termination.

3   Database Schema and Indexing

3.1   Schema

Inverted index lists are stored as database tables; Figure 3 shows the corresponding schema definitions with some example data for three tag-term pairs. The current implementation uses Oracle 10g as a backbone, mainly for easy maintenance of the required index structures, whereas the actual query processing takes place outside the database exclusively in the TopX query engine, such that the DBMS itself remains easily exchangeable. Nodes in XML documents are identified by the combination of document id (`did`) and preorder (`pre`). Navigation along all XPath axes is supported by both the `pre` and `post` attributes using the XPath accelerator technique of [3]. Additionally, the `level` information may stored to support the child-axis as well, but may be omitted for the NEXI-style descendant constraints. The actual index lists are processed by the top-k algorithm using two B^+-tree indexes that are created on this base table: one index for sorted access support in descending order of the (maxscore, did, score) attributes for each tag-term pair and another index for random access support using (did, tag, term) as key.

3.2   Inverted Block-Index

The base table contains the actual node contents indexed as one row per tag-term pair per document, together with their local scores (referring either to the simple content or the full-content scores) and their pre- and postorder numbers. For each tag-term pair, we also provide the *maximum score* among all the rows grouped by tag, term, and document id to extend the previous notion of single-line sorted accesses to a notion of *sorted block-scans*. Then TopX scans each list corresponding to the key (tag, term) in descending order of (maxscore, did, score). Each sequential block scan prefetches all tag-term pairs for the same document id in one shot and keeps them in memory for further processing which we refer to as *sorted block-scans*. Random accesses to content-related scores for a given document, tag, and term are performed through small range scans on the respective B^+ tree index using the triplet (did, tag, term) as key. Note that grouping tag-term pairs by their document ids keeps the range of the pre-/postorder-based in-memory structural joins small and efficient. All scores in the database tables are precomputed when the index tables are built.

For search conditions of the form `A[.//"t`$_1$` t`$_2$`"]` using the descendants axis, we refer to the full-content scores, based on $ftf(t_1, A)$ and $ftf(t_2, A)$ values of entire document subtrees; these are read off the precomputed base tables in a single efficient sequential disk fetch for each document until the $min\text{-}k$ threshold condition is reached and the algorithm terminates. We fully precompute and

sec[clustering]

eid	docid	score	pre	post	max-score
46	2	0.9	2	15	0.9
9	2	0.5	10	8	0.9
171	5	0.85	1	20	0.85
84	3	0.1	1	12	0.1

st[xml]

eid	docid	score	pre	post	max-score
216	17	0.9	2	15	0.9
72	3	0.8	10	8	0.8
51	2	0.5	4	12	0.5
671	31	0.4	12	23	0.4

p[evaluation]

eid	docid	score	pre	post	max-score
3	1	1.0	1	21	1.0
28	2	0.8	8	14	0.8
182	5	0.75	3	7	0.75
96	4	0.75	6	4	0.75

Fig. 3. Inverted block-index with precomputed full-content scores over tag-term pairs

materialize this inverted block index to efficiently support the NEXI-style descendant axis. With this specialized setup, parsing and indexing times for the INEX collection are about 80 minutes on an average server machine including the modified BM25 scoring model and the materialization of the inverted block-index view.

We propagate, for every term t that occurs in a node n with tag A, its local tf value "upwards" to all ancestors of n and compute the ftf values of these nodes for t. Obviously, this may create a redundancy factor that can be as high as the length of the path from n to the root. Thus, the redundant full-content indexing introduces a factor of redundancy for the textual contents that approximately corresponds to the average nesting depth of text nodes of documents in the corpus; it is our intention to trade off a moderate increase in inexpensive disk space (factor of 4-5 for INEX) for faster query response times. Note that by using tag-term pairs for the inverted index lookups, we immediately benefit from more selective, combined tag-term features and shorter index lists for the actual textual contents, whereas the hypothetical combinatorial bound of $\#tags \cdot \#terms$ rows is by far not reached.

3.3 Navigational Index

To efficiently process more complex queries, where not all content-related query conditions can be directly connected to a single preceding tag, we need an additional element-only directory to test the structural matches for tag sequences or branching path queries.

Lookups to this additional, more compact and non-redundant navigational index yield the basis for the structural scores that a candidate may achieve for each matched tag-only condition in addition to the BM25-based content scores. As an illustration of the query processing, consider the example twig query //A[.//B[.//"b"] and .//C[.//"c"]]. A candidate that contains valid matches for the two extracted tag-term pairs B:b and C:c fetched through a series of block-scans on the inverted lists for B:b and C:c, may only obtain an additional static score mass c, if there is a common A ancestor that satisfies both the content-related conditions based on their already known pre-/postorder labels. Since all structural conditions are

sec

eid	docid	pre	post
46	2	2	15
9	2	10	8
171	5	1	20
84	3	1	12

Fig. 4. Navigational index for branching path queries

defined to yield this static score mass c, the navigational index is exclusively accessed through random lookups by an additional B$^+$ tree on this table. [10] provides different approaches to judiciously schedule these random accesses for the most promising candidates according to their already known content-related scores.

3.4   Random Access Scheduling

The rationale of TopX is to postpone expensive random accesses as much as possible and perform them only for the best top-k candidates. However, it can be beneficial to test path conditions earlier, namely, in order to eliminate candidates that might not satisfy the structural query conditions but have high *worstscores* from their textual contents. Moreover, in the query model where a violated path condition leads to a score penalty, positively testing a path condition increases the *worstscore(d)* of a candidate, thus potentially improving the *min-k* threshold and leading to increased pruning subsequently. In TopX we consider random accesses at specific points only, namely, whenever the priority queue is rebuilt. At this point, we consider each candidate and decide whether we should make random accesses to test unresolved path conditions, or look up missing scores for content conditions. For this scheduling decision, we have developed two different strategies.

The first strategy, coined *MinProbe*, aims at a minimum number of random accesses by probing structural conditions for the most promising candidates, only. Since we do not perform any sorted scans for elementary tag conditions, we treat structural conditions as *expensive predicates* in the sense of [1]. We schedule random accesses only for those candidates d whose $worstscore(d) + o_j \cdot c > min\text{-}k$, where o_j is the number of untested structural query conditions for d and c is a static score mass that d earns with every satisfied structural condition.

This way, we schedule a whole batch of random lookups, if d has a sufficiently high *worstscore(d)* to get promoted to the top-k when the structural conditions can be satisfied as well. If otherwise *bestscore(d)* already drops below the current *min-k* threshold after a random lookup, we may safely prune the candidate from the queue. More sophisticated approaches may employ an analytic cost model, coined the *BenProbe* strategy in [10], in order to determine whether it is cost beneficial to explicitly lookup a candidate's remaining score in the structural and content-related query conditions.

4   Expensive Text Predicates

The use of auxiliary query hints in the form of expensive text predicates such as phrases (""), mandatory terms (+), and negation (-) can significantly improve the retrieval results of an IR system. The challenge for a top-k based query processor lies in the *efficient* implementation of these additional query constraints and their adaptation into the sorted versus random access scheduling paradigm.

4.1   Negation

The semantics of negations in a non-conjunctive, i.e. "andish", query processor is all but trivial. To cite the authors of the NEXI specification, "a user would be surprised if she encountered the negated term among the retrieval results". This leaves some space for interpretation and most commonly leads to the conclusion that the negated term should not occur in any of the top-ranked results; yet we do not want to eliminate all elements containing one of the negated terms completely, if they also contain good matches to other content-related query conditions, and we would run into the danger of loosing substantial amount of recall. Therefore the scoring of negated terms is defined to be independent of the term's actual content score. Similarly to the structural query constraints intro-duced in the previous section, an element merely accumulates some additional static score mass if it does not match the negated term. This quickly leads us back to the notion of expensive predicates and the minimal probing approach. A random lookup onto this element's tag-term offsets is scheduled, if the element gets promoted into the top-k results after a "successful" negation test, i.e., if it does not contain the negated term among its full-content text and obtains the static score for the unmatched negation. In the current setup, this static score mass was set to the same value $c = 1$ that was provided for structural query constraints.

4.2   Mandatory Terms

In contrast to term negations, the scores for mandatory query terms should still reflect the relevance of the term for a given element, i.e., the precomputed BM25-based content scores. Yet a too strict boolean interpretation of the + operator would make us run into the danger of loosing recall at the lower ranks. We therefore introduce boosting factors and a slightly modified score aggregation of the form $score(n, A//"t_1 \dots t_m") = \sum_{i=1}^{m} \beta_i + s(t_i, A)$, where $s(t_i, A)$ is the original content score, and β_i is set to 1 if the term is marked as mandatory (+) and 0 otherwise. Note that these β_i are constants at query evaluation time, and since the modified scores are taken into account for both the $worstscore(d)$ and $bestscore(d)$ bounds of all candidates, the boosting factors "naturally" enforce deeper sequential scans on the inverted index lists for the mandatory query con-ditions, typically until the final top-ranked results are discovered in those lists. Still weak matches for the remaining non-boosted query conditions may be com-pensated by a result candidate through high-scored matches in the mandatory query conditions.

4.3   Phrases and Phrase Negations

For phrase matching we store all term offsets in an auxiliary database table to-gether with the pre-/postorder labels of each term's occurrence in a document. Again, phrases are interpreted as expensive predicates and tested by random accesses to the offset table using the minimal probing approach already de-scribed for the MinProbe scheduling. The only difference now is to determine whether a candidate element may aggregate the content-related score mass for the phrase-related conditions into it's overall $worstscore(d)$ that is then used to determine its position in the top-k results. In order to keep these score aggregations monotonous in the precomputed content scores, phrase lookups are treated as binary filters, only. Similarly to the single-term negations, phrase negations are defined to yield a static score mass c for each candidate element that does not contain the negated phrase. Single-term occurrences of the negated phrase terms are allowed, though, and do not contribute to the final element score unless they are also contained in the remaining part of the query.

5   Experimental Results for TopX

5.1   CO-Thorough

For the CO-Thorough task, TopX ranks at position 22 for the nxCG[10] metric using a strict quantization with a value of 0.0379 and at rank 30 of 55 submitted runs for ep/gr with a MAep value of 0.018. We used the modified BM25 scoring model described above and also expensive text predicates to leverage phrases, negations, and mandatory terms. The very modest rank in the sensitive CO-Thorough task attests that there is still some space left for optimizations in our scoring model for the CO queries, when there is no explicit target element specified by the query ("//*"). However, there was neither any restriction given on result overlap or result granularities, nor on the expected specificity or exhaustiveness of special element types such as sections or paragraphs, such that the engine was allowed to return any type of element (also list items or even whole articles) according to their aggregated content scores. An additional simple postprocessing step based on the element granularities and overlap removal would already be expected to achieve great performance gains here. However, for the old precision/recall metrics using inex_eval with the strict quantization (INEX '04), the TopX run ranks at a significantly better position of rank 3 with a MAP value of 0.0581, which actually corresponds to the particular metric and setup for which we had been tuning the system.

5.2   COS-Fetch & Browse

The situation somewhat improves for the COS-Fetch&Browse task. Here, TopX was configured to first rank the result documents according to their highest-ranked target element and then return all target elements within the same result document, but mistakenly with the same, document-wide score instead of the elements' own scores. This bug practically rendered the element-level results useless, while the article-level evaluation is relatively promising: The TopX run without expensive predicates like phrases etc. ranks at position 10 out of 25 with a MAep of 0.1455 in the ep-gr metric for the article ranking with strict quantization. the run that exploits phrases, mandatory and negative terms was slightly worse at rank 13 with a MAep of 0.1351 for the same setting. For both runs, structure was evaluated according to a strict interpretation of the query target

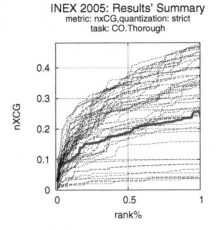

INEX 2005: Results' Summary
metric: nxCG,quantization: strict
task: CO.Thorough

Fig. 5. nxCG results for the TopX CO-Thorough run

element given which exactly matches our full-content scoring model. Here, the strict – XPath-like – interpretation of the query target element in combination with our full-content scoring model that treats each target element itself as a mini-document shows its benefits and naturally avoids overlap, since we return exactly the element type that is specified in the query and therefore seem to match the result granularity expected by a human user in a much better way.

5.3 SSCAS

Finally, the SSCAS task perfectly matches our strict interpretation of the target element with the precomputed full-content scores and no overlap being allowed. The two submitted TopX runs rank at position 1 and 2 out of 25 submitted runs for both the strict nxCG[10] metric (with a value of 0.45 for both runs) and the strict ep/gr metric (with MAep values of 0.1334 for the run that considers expensive predicates and 0.1199 for the run without them). Although this strict evaluation might be less challenging from an IR point-of-view, this task offers most opportunities to improve the efficiency of a structure-aware retrieval system, because the strict notion of all structural query components like target and support elements drastically reduces the amount of result candidates per document and, hence, across the corpus. Clever precomputation of the main query building blocks, namely tag-term pairs with their full-content scores, and index structures for efficient sorted and random access on whole element blocks grouped by document ids allows for decent run times of a true graph-based query engine that lies in the order of efficient text IR systems. Here, TopX can greatly accelerate query run times and achieve interactive response times at a remarkable result quality. Similar experiments provided in [10] yield average response times for typical INEX (CO and CAS) queries in between 0.1 and 0.7 seconds for the top 10-20 and still an average run time of about 20 seconds for the top 1,500

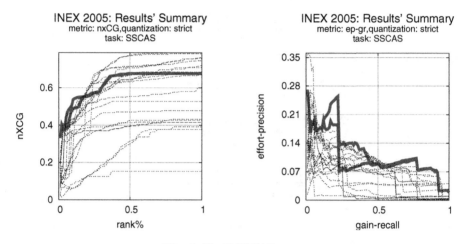

Fig. 6. TopX SSCAS runs

results as demanded by INEX (which is of course not exactly nice to handle for a top-k engine).

6   Experiments with XXL

The XXL Search Engine [7, 8, 9] was among the first XML search engines that supported content-and-structure queries with an IR-like scoring for content conditions. Focussing on aspects of semantic similarity conditions for tags and contents using ontologies, it applies an out-of-the-box text retrieval engine, namely Oracle's text engine, to evaluate content subqueries. Details of its architecture can be found in [8].

6.1   CO-Thorough

The CO.Thorough run basically represents the performance of the underlying text search engine. XXL automatically converted CO topics into corresponding Oracle text queries, using conjunctive combination of terms, enabling phrases, and applying some other simple heuristics that gave reasonable results with INEX 2003 and 2004. Surprisingly, this year's performance was not really convincing, with a rank 39 of 55 with inex_eval and the strict quantization (MAP 0.016), with similar results for the other metrics.

6.2   SSCAS

The results for the SSCAS run, where XXL has a higher influence on the outcome than with keyword-only topics, were much better. XXL is almost consistently among the top 10 for nxCG with the generalized quantization, with a peak rank of 2 for nxCG[25], and only slightly worse for strict quantization. For inex_eval, we achieved rank 11 with a MAP of 0.075. XXL has been especially built for this kind of strict structural match. The results are even better when taking the poor performance of the content-only run into account.

6.3 SVCAS and VVCAS

For the SSCAS run, XXL was configured to return a result only if it had a corresponding match (i.e., an element) for each subcondition of the query. For the SVCAS run, we relaxed this requirement and allowed results as soon as they had a match for the target subcondition, i.e., the subcondition whose result is returned as result of the query. This simple, 'andish'-like evaluation did surprisingly well, with top-15 ranks in most metrics.

For the VVCAS run, we additionally changed the tag of the target subcondition to the wildcard '*', accepting any element as result as long as it matches the associated content condition. However, this kind of relaxation turned out to be too coarse, so the results were quite poor with all metrics.

References

1. K.-C. Chang and S.-W. Hwang. Minimal probing: supporting expensive predicates for top-k queries. In *SIGMOD 2002*, pages 346–357, 2002.
2. R. Fagin, A. Lotem, and M. Naor. Optimal aggregation algorithms for middleware. *J. Comput. Syst. Sci.*, 66(4):614–656, 2003.
3. T. Grust. Accelerating XPath location steps. In *SIGMOD 2002*, pages 109–120, 2002.
4. U. Güntzer, W.-T. Balke, and W. Kießling. Optimizing multi-feature queries for image databases. In *VLDB 2000*, pages 419–428, 2000.
5. S. Nepal and M. V. Ramakrishna. Query processing issues in image (multimedia) databases. In *ICDE 1999*, pages 22–29, 1999.
6. S. E. Robertson and S. Walker. Some simple effective approximations to the 2-poisson model for probabilistic weighted retrieval. In *SIGIR*, pages 232–241, 1994.
7. R. Schenkel, A. Theobald, and G. Weikum. XXL @ INEX 2003. In *INEX 2003 Workshop Proceedings*, pages 59–68, 2004.
8. R. Schenkel, A. Theobald, and G. Weikum. Semantic similarity search on semistructured data with the XXL search engine. *Information Retrieval*, 8(4):521–545, December 2005.
9. A. Theobald and G. Weikum. Adding Relevance to XML. In *WebDB 2000*, pages 105–124, 2000.
10. M. Theobald, R. Schenkel, and G. Weikum. An efficient and versatile query engine for TopX search. In *VLDB 2005*, pages 625–636, 2005.
11. M. Theobald, G. Weikum, and R. Schenkel. Top-k query evaluation with probabilistic guarantees. In *VLDB 2004*, pages 648–659, 2004.

When a Few Highly Relevant Answers Are Enough

Miro Lehtonen

Department of Computer Science
P.O. Box 68 (Gustaf Hällströmin katu 2b)
FI–00014 University of Helsinki
Finland
Miro.Lehtonen@cs.Helsinki.FI

Abstract. Our XML retrieval system EXTIRP was slightly modified from the 2004 version for the INEX 2005 project. For the first time, the system is now completely independent of the document type of the XML documents in the collection, which justifies the use of the term "heterogeneous" when describing our methodology. Nevertheless, the 2005 version of EXTIRP is still an incomplete system that does not include query expansion or dynamic determination of the answer size. The latter is seen as a serious limitation because of the XCG-based metrics which favour systems that can adjust the size of the answer according to its relevance to the query. We put our main focus on the CO.Focussed task of the adhoc track although runs were submitted for other tasks, as well. Perhaps because of the incompleteness of our system, the initial results bring out the characteristics of our system better than in earlier years. Even when partially stripped, EXTIRP is capable of ranking the most obvious highly relevant answers at the top ranks better than many other systems. The relatively high precision at the top ranks is achieved at the cost of losing the sight of the marginally relevant content, which shows in some exceptionally steep curves, and the rankings among other systems that sink from the top ranks at low recall levels towards the bottom ranks at higher levels of recall. Another fact supporting our observation is that regardless of the metric, our runs are ranked higher with the strict quantisation than with any other quantisation function.

1 Introduction

The XML retrieval system at the University of Helsinki — EXTIRP — is completely independent of the XML document types as of 2005. In practice, the information coded in element names is ignored, which in turn lets us keep the doors open for collections of heterogeneous XML documents. The choice of ignoring the names of document structures also implies that our system specialises in the Content-Only type queries where only the content of the result elements has any significance.

As our XML search engine EXTIRP [1] has not much changed from the previous year [2], it will not be described in full detail in this paper. Instead,

N. Fuhr et al. (Eds.): INEX 2005, LNCS 3977, pp. 296–305, 2006.

we take a look at one of its qualities that makes it fundamentally different from other corresponding systems. The algorithm for selecting the indexed nodes from the XML documents follows an approach that can be applied to arbitrary XML documents. Besides considering the size of each node, it also analyses the content in order to detect a sufficient amount of full-text that would make the fragment worth indexing.

The major problem in the evaluation of our methods developed for heterogeneous XML documents is that thorough testing has been performed only on a single document collection without the desired amount of heterogeneity. Consequently, EXTIRP will be evaluated among all the other systems that may be fine-tuned for the collection of IEEE journals. Once the INEX heterogeneous collection track comes with methods for quantitative evaluation, we will be able to get a wider perspective to the system performance as well as an evaluation against other "het-track" systems. Another factor making our system quite challenged is the lack of human resources, which is why we cannot fully explore the capabilities of our system.

This article is organised as follows. In Section 2, we review what the essential parts of EXTIRP are made of. Then we focus on the selection of the indexed fragments, first by looking into related research in Section 3, and second, by presenting our own approach in Section 4. The performance of EXTIRP is analysed in Section 5.

2   Background

Before building two indices — one for words, one for phrases — EXTIRP divides the document collection into disjoint fragments. The root elements of the indexed fragments are chosen with an algorithm for *full-text fragment selection* which will be presented later in this paper in more detail. The disjoint fragments are then naturally treated as traditional documents which are independent of each other. The pros include that the traditional methods for information retrieval apply, so we use the vector space model with a weighting scheme based on the tf*idf. The biggest of the cons is that the size of the indexed fragments is static, and if bigger or smaller answers are more appropriate for some query, the fragments have to be either divided further or combined into bigger fragments. Because of the previous challenges with fragment score combination [2], we have left it for future research, and for now, the size of the answers that EXTIRP returns is determined when the fragments are chosen for indexing instead of dynamically adjusting the size according how relevant the fragment is to a query.

After the composition of the fragment index has been determined, we perform certain post-processing called *fragment expansion* on the fragment content. The purpose in the process is to take advantage of the XML markup of the fragment as well as the structured nature of the source XML document before the actual indexing methods are applied to the fragment content. The fragment expansion techniques include the association of related content according to ID and IDREF type attributes as well as structural weighting based on the local relations of text and XML elements. More details including the evaluation of the methods is described in [3].

3   Related Work

In the first four years of INEX, we have seen many different approaches to indexing XML documents. The major differences are found in the ways the indexed units are defined. As the XML documents are often processed as trees, it is natural to talk about nodes instead of elements. Hence, the challenge can be called the selection of *index nodes*. One of the earliest approaches was proposed by Fuhr et al. who treat predefined sets of elements as index nodes, e.g. sec (sections), ss1, ss2 (subsections), and p (paragraphs) [4]. Approaches similar to this have two major problems, from our point of view. First, the selection is based on element names, and as such, the method does not scale to heterogeneous XML documents. Second, the elements may be nested within each other, which has to be taken into account whenever term frequencies are computed. Therefore, traditional methods where documents are assumed to be independent may not be directly applicable to a collection of overlapping index nodes.

In order to avoid the problem of defining good index nodes, some systems blindly index all nodes [5, 6]. Although the method applies to arbitrary XML documents, the overlap of the indexed elements still requires XML-specific indexing methods. The overhead in the number of indexed nodes can be optimised by setting certain cut-off values that represent the minimum size of an indexed unit. According to the experiments by Kamps et al., the cutoff values of 20, 40, 50, and 60 index terms all reduce the amount of indexed nodes while showing little difference in the actual IR performance of the system [7]. In a similar fashion, EXTIRP comes with a configurable threshold for the minimum size requirement for the indexed nodes.

Changes in the relation between a web page and a traditional document have lead to problems that have solutions similar to that of EXTIRP for full-text fragment selection. Search engines divide the web pages into fragments, which enables block-level indexing and searching [8], whereas EXTIRP divides XML documents into fragments, thus enabling fragment-level search.

4   Selection of Full-Text Fragments

In this section, we present an algorithm that determines from heterogeneous XML documents a set of XML fragments of a chosen granularity. The indexed fragments contain at least some full-text content, so that pure data fragments are not indexed for full-text search. The distinction between data and full-text is based on the *full-text likelihood* of the fragments which nicely helps us discard the unwanted data from our full-text index. As the fragments do not overlap, we assume that they can be searched as if they were independent documents, and traditional IR methods are thus applicable.

4.1   Full-Text Likelihood

Given any XML fragment, we want to be able to make a judgment about the fragment containing a sufficient amount of full-text content to be indexed. A sufficient amount of such content makes the fragment suitable for full-text search. An automatic judgment mechanism requires that we can measure the fragments on a scale where typical full-text fragments are situated at one end of the scale and typical data fragments at the other end. The important points are not at the ends of the scale, however, but in the middle where a pivot point divides the scale into ranges of full-text and data values. Indicators that return appropriate values on such a scale actually calculate the *Full-Text Likelihood* of the fragment.

A full-text indicator that has been proven successful in this algorithm is defined as the ratio of Text nodes to Element nodes (T/E) [3]. A pivot point p between data and full-text is defined as T/E = 1.00 where a fragment with a T/E value greater than 1.00 is considered a full-text fragment. The values of the T/E measure fall in the range $[0,\infty]$ so that empty elements have the value of 0, data fragments have values in the range $]0,p]$, and full-text fragments in the range $[p,\infty[$.

4.2   Parameters for the Algorithm

The granularity level of the indexed fragments is the most significant parameter for the algorithm. In a user-centred scenario, the level of granularity could be one of the user preferences which is presented verbally, e.g. paragraph, subsection, section, or article. Because the algorithm requires the parameters in a more precise form, the name of the level is interpreted in terms of limits for the size, as well as other significant factors. For example, the granularity can be verbally presented in the form

$G = G_x$, where $x \in \{paragraph, subsection, section, document\}$,

which is converted into a size range for full-text fragments, so that

$G = \{[min, max], T/E \geq 1.00\}$.

Given granularity G, we perform the division d of a document collection C into n fragments f_1, ..., f_n. The division can also be defined as a function

$d_G(C) = \{f_1, ..., f_n\}$,

where C is a set of arbitrary XML documents. According to our goal, the fragments f_1, ..., f_n must be disjoint.

4.3   Tree Traversal

As each of the divided XML documents is considered independent of the other documents, we process the collection of documents serially, one XML document at a time. Because the definitions for different kinds of full-text fragments require that we operate on document trees, the algorithm basically defines how the tree is traversed and what to do with the traversed nodes.

The nave approach is to traverse the whole tree from first to last node and test all the element nodes on the way. Besides being slow, this approach may also lead to other problems concerning nested elements because it is possible that both the parent and the child elements qualify. However, being thorough may work if overlapping and nested fragments are acceptable in the index, but otherwise, additional testing of nodes is necessary for each node that is traversed. If we optimise the tree traversal by adding conditions on branch selection we do not only make the traversal more efficient but we also have the option of restricting the output to disjoint fragments without an extra cost.

In the optimised approach, the beginning state of the division consists of an empty fragment collection $F = \emptyset$ and the current node c which is set to be the document root. The current node is first tested for size. If the size is bigger than the maximum size of the granularity, c is assigned each of the child element nodes one by one. If the size of the current node falls in the given range, the node is tested for full-text likelihood. In the case that c has too structured content so that $T/E<1.0$, c is again assigned each of the child element nodes. Otherwise, when the size of c fits the given range and when the content passes as full-text, we add c to F and move on to the next branch in the document tree. The acceptance as a full-text fragment and a size below the given range are both stopping conditions for the recursive testing of child nodes. In other words, the child nodes are tested until they contain enough full-text or until they are too small. The tree traversal is then repeated for each document in collection C. When the algorithm stops, the fragment bodies that have been added to F represent the disjoint full-text fragments that can be selected from the XML documents in the colletion.

The pseudo code for the algorithm is presented in Figure 1. The accepted size range [Gmin, Gmax] is considered a global variable more than an actual parameter by its nature, and only the current node c is passed on at each recursive function call. The algorithm can be optimised by reordering the tests, however, the optimal order is dependent on the input documents. For example, if the test for full-text likelihood (ftl(node) fails more often than the test for

```
Algorithm SelectFullText(node) {
   if size(node) > Gmax
      // Discard node (too big)
      for each child: SelectFullText(node.child);
   else if size(node) < Gmin
      // Discard node (too small)
      break;      // Skip children
   else if ftl(node) = data // Discard node as data
      for each child: SelectFullText(node.child);
   else
      accept(node);
      break;
}
```

Fig. 1. Pseudo code of the algorithm that returns a set of disjoint qualified full-text fragments from a given XML document

the fragment size, the FTL test should come before the size test assuming that they can be computed at an equal cost.

4.4   Two Runs for the CO.Focussed Task

The algorithm for fragment selection was run with two sets of parameters for our official runs in 2005. The finer granularity of fragments was defined as $G = \{[150, 7K], T/E \geq 1.00\}$. A selection of the most common paths in the index is shown in Figure 2.

The most common root element among the total of 367,009 full-text fragments seems to be p (paragraph), but a large number of whole sections (sec) and subsections (ss1) also qualified. There were a total of 611 different paths to the root of the fragments in this collection.

The granularity for the rather coarse fragment index is defined as $G = \{[250, 20K], T/E \geq 1.00\}$. As the maximum size of the fragments is 20,000 characters, we can expect to find fewer paragraphs and also fewer fragments in this index. A selection of the corresponding paths is shown in Figure 3.

The most common path leads to a section element (sec), which is not surprising considering how the size range is defined. The number of article elements might seem strange, though. Although the article elements only represent 5.3% of all the fragments, they represent nearly 40% of the total of 16,739 article elements in the collection. To summarise, the coarse index contains a total of 125,049 full-text fragments with 308 different paths to their roots. Achieving the same composition of the index is nearly impossible if we use element names as the basis for index node selection.

The two runs that we submitted for the CO.Focussed task were built by ranking the fragments for each query. The ranking system has been described in the earlier workshop papers [1, 2]. In 2005, one run was built from each index so that both runs contained fragments of a single granularity.

Freq.	Path	Common name
75193	/article/bdy/sec/p	paragraph
62899	/article/bdy/sec	section
49373	/article/bdy/sec/ss1	subsection
25776	/article/bdy/sec/ss1/	
22990	/article/bdy/sec/ip1	introductory paragraph
12486	/article/fm	front matter
10050	/article/bdy/sec/ss1/ip1	
9138	/article/bm/vt	biography
7252	/article/bdy/sec/ss1/ss2	subsection
6087	/article/bm/vt/p	
...		
1700	/article	

Fig. 2. Most common paths to selected full-text fragments with a size in the range of 150–7,000 characters

```
Freq.          Path                        Common name

54885  /article/bdy/sec                    section
 9091  /article/bdy/sec/ss1                subsection
 8225  /article/fm                         front matter
 7970  /article/bdy/sec/p                  paragraph
 6594  /article                            article
 6340  /article/bm/vt                      biography
 4074  /article/bm/vt/p
 3405  /article/bdy/sec/ip1                introductory paragraph
 3124  /article/bm                         back matter
 1681  /article/bdy/sec/ss1/p
 1381  /article/bm/ack                     acknowledgement
 1375  /article/bm/app                     appendix
 1059  /article/bdy                        article body
```

Fig. 3. Most common paths to selected full-text fragments with a size in the range of 250–20,000 characters

5   Results

Both our runs contain results that are comparable to the traditional documents: 1) the fragments do not overlap, and 2) they represent a single level of granularity. Therefore, the results can be fairly evaluated with a variety of different metrics without too many challenges specific to XML retrieval. For example, the overlap of the answers does not have to be taken into account in order to evaluate our runs as they contain no overlap. Even if the full recall-base associated with the metric contains overlapping answers, only the evaluation scores will be overly low without an actual effect on the relative system rankings.

Moreover, the size of the relevant answers plays a minimal role as the variation in the fragment sizes is not much bigger than that in traditional Information Retrieval.

All the metrics available on the official INEX website[1] as well as on the LIP6 metric website[2] agree that the run based on the smaller fragments resulted in more relevant answers to the test queries. We will thus pay more attention to the run called 'UHelCOFoc2.xml'. Figure 4 shows all the official submissions evaluated with the official INEX 2002 metric (strict quantisation). The curves demonstrate the typical behaviour of EXTIRP: The first few answers to the queries are highly relevant, but the quality of the answers rapidly deteriorates.

The observation of rapidly sinking precision cannot be explained by looking at the metric, as similar phenomenon occurs with other metrics, as well. The relative system rankings of our best run are shown in Table 1 which suggests that EXTIRP in its current setting is only good for tasks where high precision is preferred to high recall. This observation might be interesting considering

---

[1] http://inex.is.informatik.uni-duisburg.de/2005/
[2] https://inex.lip6.fr/2005/metrics/

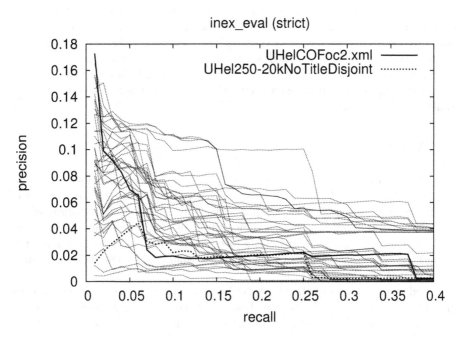

Fig. 4. EXTIRP among the top performers — when a few highly relevant answers are enough

Table 1. Relative rankings of the run 'UHelCOFoc2.xml'

Metric	@1	@5	@10	@100	@1500
ncXG (strict)	8	12	15	34	27
ncXG (generalised)	13	26	29	32	22
EPRUM (GK-SOG)	19	18	18	24	24
inex_eval (strict)	1	2	11	26	22
inex_eval (generalised)	11	19	25	31	24

applications where only few highly relevant answers are required, such as searching over slow connection and displaying results on a low-resolution display.

Although the runs submitted for the CO.Focussed task were not supposed to contain any overlapping answers, 15 out of the 44 official runs (34.1%) did, anyway. By the nature of the overlap, the fewer answers are considered, the weaker is the effect of the overlap. If we only look at the first answer to each query (precision @1), all the runs are equal in that a single answer cannot overlap with itself. The INEX 2002 metric inex_eval is known to favour overlapping relevant answers, which partly explains why other curves are less steep than those of EXTIRP.

The relative rankings reveal another feature of EXTIRP. By comparing the effect of different quantisation functions on the rankings, we see how EXTIRP is ranked higher with the strict quantisation, according to which, less than highly relevant answers are as good as irrelevant answers. This observation indicates that other systems are better at the finding the marginally relevant answers, which may be the cost of the high initial precision of our system.

Other runs were submitted for the Co.Thorough task, but due to some unfortunate bugs in the implementation, the results are not descriptive of the underlying methods.

6   Conclusion

In 2005, our primary goal was to confirm some previous observations about the characteristics of the XML retrieval system EXTIRP. Although the number of different evaluation metrics has been steadily growing, the interpretations of the results of EXTIRP has not changed much. It seems that runs consisting of nearly equi-sized answers with no overlap can be compared with the majority of metrics so that the relative rankings of the runs are similar despite the different shapes of the curves.

Based on the results of the INEX 2005 queries, we conclude that the compromised version of EXTIRP performs best when only few highly relevant answers are enough to satisfy the system requirements. Those who dream of high recall should look at different systems because even with all the additional features implemented, EXTIRP is not likely to excel in the high recall tasks. However, the relatively high precision at low recall levels has high prospects if we consider reusing the good quality. For example, query expansion is certainly one of the ways to propagate the high relevance of the answers further down the result list.

Acknowledgements

Many thanks to Antoine Doucet for his scripts and program code which he tested and made compatible with the INEX 2005 specifications.

References

1. Doucet, A., Aunimo, L., Lehtonen, M., Petit, R.: Accurate Retrieval of XML Document Fragments using EXTIRP. In: INEX 2003 Workshop Proceedings, Schloss Dagstuhl, Germany (2003) 73–80
2. Lehtonen, M.: EXTIRP 2004: Towards heterogeneity. In Fuhr, N., Lalmas, M., Malik, S., Szlávik, Z., eds.: INEX. Volume 3493 of Lecture Notes in Computer Science., Springer (2005) 372–381
3. Lehtonen, M.: Indexing Heterogeneous XML for Full-Text Search. PhD thesis, University of Helsinki (2006)
4. Fuhr, N., Großjohann, K.: XIRQL: a query language for information retrieval in XML documents. In: Proceedings of the 24th annual international ACM SIGIR conference on Research and development in information retrieval, ACM Press (2001) 172–180

5. Liu, S., Zou, Q., Chu, W.W.: Configurable indexing and ranking for XML information retrieval. In: SIGIR '04: Proceedings of the 27th annual international conference on Research and development in information retrieval, ACM Press (2004) 88–95
6. Vyas, A., Fernàndez, M., Siméon, J.: The simplest XML storage manager ever. In: Proceedings of the First International Workshop on XQuery Implementation, Experience and Perspectives <XIME-P/>. (2004) 37–42
7. Kamps, J., de Rijke, M., Sigurbjörnsson, B.: Length normalization in XML retrieval. In: SIGIR '04: Proceedings of the 27th annual international ACM SIGIR conference on Research and development in information retrieval, New York, NY, USA, ACM Press (2004) 80–87
8. Cai, D., Yu, S., Wen, J.R., Ma, W.Y.: Block-based web search. In: SIGIR '04: Proceedings of the 27th annual international ACM SIGIR conference on Research and development in information retrieval, New York, NY, USA, ACM Press (2004) 456–463

RMIT University at INEX 2005: Ad Hoc Track

Jovan Pehcevski, James A. Thom, and S.M.M. Tahaghoghi

School of Computer Science and Information Technology,
RMIT University Melbourne, Australia
{jovanp, jat, saied}@cs.rmit.edu.au

Abstract. Different scenarios of XML retrieval are analysed in the INEX 2005 ad hoc track, which reflect different query interpretations and user behaviours that may be observed during XML retrieval. The RMIT University group's participation in the INEX 2005 ad hoc track investigates these XML retrieval scenarios. Our runs follow a hybrid XML retrieval approach that combines three information retrieval models with two ways of identifying the appropriate element granularity and two XML-specific heuristics to rank the final answers. We observe different behaviours when applying our hybrid approach to the different retrieval scenarios, suggesting that the optimal retrieval parameters are highly dependent on the nature of the XML retrieval task. Importantly, we show that using structural hints in content only topics is a useful feature that leads to more precise search, but only when level of overlap among the retrieved elements is considered by the evaluation metric.

1 Introduction

Of the seven tracks at INEX 2005 — each exploring different applications of XML retrieval — our RMIT University group participated in four: ad hoc, interactive, multimedia [3], and heterogeneous. In this paper, we discuss our participation in the ad hoc track.

Two types of topics are explored in the ad hoc track: Content Only and Structure (CO+S) and Content And Structure (CAS). A CO+S topic is a request that typically ignores the document structure by only specifying plain query terms. However, there may be cases where adding structural hints to the query results in more precise search. Some CO+S topics therefore express the same information need by either ignoring or including the structural hints (we call the latter +S topics). Figure 1 shows a snippet of CO+S topic 203 that was proposed by our group, where two topic fields — title and castitle — are used to represent the two interpretations. A CAS topic is a request that contains references to the document structure and explicitly specifies the type of the returned answer elements (the target element) and the type of the contained elements of the search context (the support elements).

Within the INEX 2005 ad hoc track there are three XML retrieval sub-tasks: the CO, the +S, and the CAS sub-task, reflecting the three types of topics

N. Fuhr et al. (Eds.): INEX 2005, LNCS 3977, pp. 306–320, 2006.

used. Three retrieval strategies are explored in the CO+S sub-tasks: Focussed, Thorough, and FetchBrowse, which model different aspects of the XML retrieval task. Four retrieval strategies are explored in the CAS sub-task: SS, SV, VS, and VV, which correspond to the way target and support elements are interpreted [7].

The system we use in the ad hoc track follows a *hybrid* XML retrieval approach, combining information retrieval features from Zettair[1] (a full-text search engine) with XML-specific retrieval features from eXist[2] (a native XML database). The hybrid approach can be seen as a "fetch and browse" [2] XML retrieval approach, since full articles estimated as likely to be relevant to a query are first retrieved by Zettair (the *fetch* phase), and then the most specific elements within these articles are extracted by eXist (the *browse* phase) [9].

To calculate the similarity score of an article to a query (represented by terms that appear in the title part of an INEX topic), a similarity measure is used by Zettair. Three similarity measures are currently implemented, each based on one of the following information retrieval models: the vector-space model, the probabilistic model, and the language model. For the *fetch* phase of our hybrid system, we investigate which information retrieval model yields the best effectiveness for full article retrieval.

```
<inex_topic topic_id="203" query_type="CO+S" ct_no="5">
    <title> code signing verification </title>
    <castitle> //sec[about(., code signing verification)] </castitle>
    <description> Find documents or document components, most probably
     sections, that describe the approach of code signing and verification.
    </description>
    <narrative> I am working in a company that authenticates a wide range of
     web database applications from different software vendors. [...]
    </narrative>
</inex_topic>
```

Fig. 1. A snippet of the INEX 2005 CO+S topic 203

To identify the appropriate granularity of elements to return as answers, we use a retrieval module that utilises the structural information in the eXist list of extracted elements. For the *browse* phase of our hybrid system, we investigate which combination of the two ways of identifying element answers and the two XML-specific heuristics for ranking the answers yields the best effectiveness for element retrieval.

---

[1] http://www.seg.rmit.edu.au/zettair/

[2] http://exist-db.org/

2   Hybrid XML Retrieval

In this section, we describe the three information retrieval models implemented in Zettair, the two algorithms for identifying the CREs, and the two heuristics for ranking the CREs, all of which are used by our hybrid system.

2.1   Information Retrieval Models

The *similarity* of a document to a query, denoted as $S_{q,d}$, indicates how closely the content of the document matches that of the query. To calculate the query-document similarity, statistical information about the distribution of the query terms — within both the document and the collection as a whole — is often necessary. These term statistics are subsequently utilised by the similarity measure. Following the notation and definitions of Zobel and Moffat [14], we define the basic term statistics as:

- q, a query;
- t, a query term;
- d, a document;
- $N_{\mathcal{D}}$, the number of all the documents in the collection;
- For each term t:
  - $f_{d,t}$, the frequency of t in the document d;
  - $N_{\mathcal{D}_t}$, the number of documents containing the term t (irrespective of the term frequency in each document); and
  - $f_{q,t}$, the frequency of t in query q.
- For each document d:
  - $f_d = |d|$, the document length approximation.
- For the query q:
  - $f_q = |q|$, the query length.

We also denote the following sets:

- $\mathcal{D}$, the set of all the documents in the collection;
- $\mathcal{D}_t$, the set of documents containing term t;
- $\mathcal{T}_d$, the set of distinct terms in the document d;
- $\mathcal{T}_q$, the set of distinct terms in the query, and $\mathcal{T}_{q,d} = \mathcal{T}_q \cap \mathcal{T}_d$.

Vector-Space Model. In the vector-space model, both the document and the query are representations of n-dimensional vectors, where n is the number of distinct terms observed in the document collection. The best-known technique for computing similarity under the vector-space model is the cosine measure, where the similarity between a document and the query is computed as the cosine of the angle between their vectors.

Zettair uses pivoted cosine document length normalisation [10] to compute the query-document similarity under the vector-space model:

$$S_{q,d} = \frac{1}{W_D \times W_q} \times \sum_{t \in \mathcal{T}_{q,d}} (1 + \log_e f_{d,t}) \times \log_e \left(1 + \frac{N_{\mathcal{D}}}{N_{\mathcal{D}_t}}\right)$$

where $W_D = \left((1.0 - s) + s \times \frac{W_d}{W_{AL}} \right)$ represents the pivoted document length normalisation, and W_q is the query length representation. The parameter s represents the *slope* (we use the value of 0.25), whereas W_d and W_{AL} represent the document length (usually taken as f_d) and the average document length (over all documents in $\mathcal{D}$), respectively.

Probabilistic Model. Probabilistic models of information retrieval are based on the principle that documents should be ranked by decreasing probability of their relevance to the expressed information need. Zettair uses the Okapi BM25 probabilistic model developed by Sparck Jones et al. [11], which has proved highly successful in a wide range of experiments:

$$S_{q,d} = \sum_{t \in T_{q,d}} w_t \times \frac{(k_1 + 1)\, f_{d,t}}{K + f_{d,t}} \times \frac{(k_3 + 1)\, f_{q,t}}{k_3 + f_{q,t}}$$

where $w_t = \log_e \left(\frac{N_D - N_{D_t} + 0.5}{N_{D_t} + 0.5} \right)$ is a representation of inverse document frequency, $K = k_1 \times \left[(1 - b) + \frac{b \cdot W_d}{W_{AL}} \right]$, and k_1, b and k_3 are constants, in the range 1.2 to 1.5 (we use 1.2), 0.6 to 0.75 (we use 0.75), and 1,000 (effectively infinite), respectively. W_d and W_{AL} represent the document length and the average document length.

Language Model. Language models are probability distributions that aim to capture the statistical regularities of natural language use. In information retrieval, language modelling involves estimating the likelihood that both the document and the query could have been generated by the same language model. Zettair uses a query likelihood approach with Dirichlet smoothing [13]:

$$S_{q,d} = f_q \times \log \lambda_d + \sum_{t \in T_{q,d}} \log \left(\frac{N_D \times f_{d,t}}{\mu \times N_{D_t}} + 1 \right)$$

where μ is a smoothing parameter (we use the value of 2,000), while λ_d is calculated as: $\lambda_d = \mu / (\mu + f_d)$.

2.2   Identifying the Appropriate Element Granularity

For each INEX topic (CO, +S, or CAS), a topic translation module is first used to automatically translate the underlying information need into a Zettair query. A list of (up to) 500 `article` elements — presented in descending order of estimated likelihood of relevance — is then returned as a resulting answer list for the INEX topic[3].

To retrieve *elements* rather than full articles, a second topic translation module is used to formulate the eXist query. Depending on the topic type, either

---

[3] We retrieve (up to) 500 rather than 1,500 articles because roughly that number of articles is used to generate the pool of retrieved articles for relevance judgements.

Table 1. eXist list of matching elements for INEX 2005 CO topic 203 and article co/2000/r7108. The elements in the list are generated by using an eXist OR query.

Article	Matching element
co/2000/r7108	/article[1]/bdy[1]/sec[1]/ip1[1]
co/2000/r7108	/article[1]/bdy[1]/sec[1]/p[1]
co/2000/r7108	/article[1]/bdy[1]/sec[2]/st[1]
co/2000/r7108	/article[1]/bdy[1]/sec[2]/p[2]
co/2000/r7108	/article[1]/bdy[1]/sec[2]/p[3]
co/2000/r7108	/article[1]/bdy[1]/sec[2]/p[4]
co/2000/r7108	/article[1]/bdy[1]/sec[4]/p[1]
co/2000/r7108	/article[1]/bdy[1]/sec[6]/ip1[1]
co/2000/r7108	/article[1]/bm[1]/app[1]/p[2]
co/2000/r7108	/article[1]/bm[1]/app[1]/p[3]
co/2000/r7108	/article[1]/bm[1]/app[1]/p[4]

terms alone, or both terms and structural query constraints from the INEX topic are used to formulate the eXist query. We use the eXist OR query operator to generate the element answer list. The answer list contains (up to) 1,500 matching elements, which are taken from articles that appear *highest* in the ranked list of articles previously returned by Zettair.

Consider the eXist answer list shown in Table 1. It shows matching elements for the CO topic 203 after the eXist OR query operator is used (each matching element in the list therefore contains *one* or *more* query terms). The matching elements in the eXist answer list represent most specific (leaf) elements, and eXist correctly presents these elements in document order.

To effectively utilise the information contained in the resulting list of matching elements, we use a retrieval module capable of identifying the appropriate *granularity* of elements to return as answers, which we refer to as *Coherent Retrieval Elements* (CREs) [9]. To identify the CREs, our module first sequentially processes the list of matching elements, starting from the first element down to the last. For each pair of matching elements, their *most specific ancestor* is chosen to represent an answer element (a CRE). We denote these answer elements as oCRE elements.

The rationale behind choosing only oCRE elements as answers stems from the expectation that these elements are likely to provide better context for the contained textual information than that provided by each of their descendent leaf elements. However, it is often the case that relevance judgements for INEX topics contain very specific answer elements [4, 9]. Therefore, the problem with only presenting the oCRE elements as answers is that in most cases the matching (and thus very specific) elements are *not included* in the final answer list. To cater for this, our retrieval module supports a second, alternative algorithm for identifying the CREs. The difference from the original oCRE algorithm is that, after sequentially processing all the pairs of matching elements, those matching

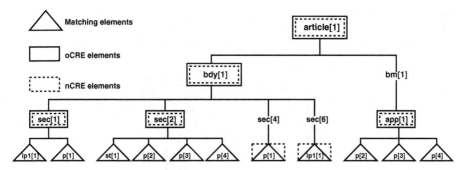

Fig. 2. Identifying appropriate element granularity: Matching, oCRE, and nCRE elements for INEX 2005 topic 203 and article `co/2000/r7108`

elements whose *immediate parents* are not identified as CREs are also included in the final list of answers. We expect these newly included matching elements to allow for more focussed retrieval. We denote these answer elements as nCRE elements.

Figure 2 shows a tree representation of the eXist list of matching elements, as previously shown in Table 1. The matching elements appear within the triangle boxes, the oCRE elements appear within the solid square boxes, while the nCRE elements appear within dashed square boxes. Once the CREs are identified, we use heuristics to *rank* and present the answer elements according to their *estimated likelihood of relevance*.

2.3 Ranking the Answer Elements

In whole document retrieval, Anh and Moffat [1] present an empirical analysis which reveals that, to maximise query effectiveness, it is very important that answer documents contain most of the query terms. To explore the validity of the above finding for XML retrieval, we consider the following ranking heuristics in our CRE module:

1. The number of distinct query terms that appear in a CRE — more distinct query term appearances (**T**) or fewer distinct query term appearances (**t**);
2. The length of the absolute path of the CRE, taken from the root element — longer path (**P**) or shorter path (**p**); and
3. The frequency of all the query terms in a CRE — more frequent (**F**) or less frequent (**f**).

Preliminary experiments using the INEX 2004 test collection show that two heuristic combinations — **TPF** and a modification of **PTF** — perform better than others in the case where more *specific* elements are target of retrieval. The two heuristic combinations can be interpreted as follows.

With **TPF**, the CREs are first sorted in a descending order according to the number of distinct query terms a CRE contains (the more distinct query terms

Table 2. Rank orderings of retrieved nCRE elements using two ranking heuristic combinations (TPF and PTF2) for article co/2000/r7108. The query used is "code signing verification", which represents the title part of the INEX 2005 topic 203.

Rank	TPF ordering	PTF2 ordering
1	/article[1]/bdy[1]/sec[2]	/article[1]/bdy[1]/sec[6]/ip1[1]
2	/article[1]/bdy[1]	/article[1]/bdy[1]/sec[2]
3	/article[1]	/article[1]/bm[1]/app[1]
4	/article[1]/bdy[1]/sec[6]/ip1[1]	/article[1]/bdy[1]/sec[1]
5	/article[1]/bm[1]/app[1]	/article[1]/bdy[1]
6	/article[1]/bdy[1]/sec[1]	/article[1]
7	/article[1]/bdy[1]/sec[4]/p[1]	/article[1]/bdy[1]/sec[4]/p[1]

it contains, the higher its rank). Next, if two CREs contain the same number of distinct query terms, the one with the longer length of its absolute path is ranked higher. Last, if the lengths of the two absolute paths are the same, the CRE with more frequent query term appearances is ranked higher than the CRE where query terms appear less frequently. The ranked list of CREs obtained by using the TPF ranking heuristic for article co/2000/r7108 and the INEX 2005 topic 203 is shown in Table 2.

The table shows that when the TPF heuristic is used, less specific CREs tend to be preferred over more specific ones. To produce more specific CREs early in the ranking, the PTF ranking heuristic could be used. With PTF, the CREs are first sorted in a descending order according to the length of the absolute path of a CRE (where the longer CRE path results in a higher rank). Next, if the lengths of the two absolute paths are the same, the CRE that contains a larger number of distinct query terms is ranked higher. Last, if it also happens that the two CREs contain the same number of distinct query terms, the CRE with more frequent query term appearances is ranked higher. However, our experiments on the INEX 2004 test collection demonstrate that the system performance degrades when using the PTF ranking heuristic, since most highly ranked (and thus very specific) elements typically contain only one query term. We therefore use a modification of this heuristic in our retrieval module to ensure that all CREs that contain exactly one query term are moved to the end of the ranked list (where ties are broken by the F heuristic). We denote this modified heuristic combination as PTF2. The ranked list of CREs obtained by using the PTF2 ranking heuristic for article co/2000/r7108 and the INEX 2005 topic 203 is also shown in Table 2.

3   Experiments and Results

In this section, we present results of experiments that evaluate the performance of our INEX 2005 runs for each retrieval strategy in both the CO+S and CAS sub-tasks. A description of each of our submitted runs is provided in Table 3.

Table 3. List of the 26 `CO+S` and `CAS` runs submitted by our RMIT University group to the INEX 2005 ad hoc track

Run ID	Topic Type	Interpretation	Similarity Measure	Answer Elements	Ranking Heuristic	Overlap Allowed
CO+S.Thorough						
nCRE-CO-PTF2	CO	CO	Okapi	nCRE	PTF2	Yes
nCRE-+S-PTF2	+S	SS	Okapi	nCRE	PTF2	Yes
nCRE-CO-TPF	CO	CO	Okapi	nCRE	TPF	Yes
nCRE-+S-TPF	+S	SS	Okapi	nCRE	TPF	Yes
oCRE-CO-PTF2	CO	CO	Okapi	oCRE	PTF2	Yes
oCRE-+S-PTF2	+S	SS	Okapi	oCRE	PTF2	Yes
CO+S.Focussed						
nCRE-CO-PTF2-NO	CO	CO	Okapi	nCRE	PTF2	No
nCRE-+S-PTF2-NO	+S	SS	Okapi	nCRE	PTF2	No
nCRE-CO-TPF-NO	CO	CO	Okapi	nCRE	TPF	No
nCRE-+S-TPF-NO	+S	SS	Okapi	nCRE	TPF	No
oCRE-CO-PTF2-NO	CO	CO	Okapi	oCRE	PTF2	No
oCRE-+S-PTF2-NO	+S	SS	Okapi	oCRE	PTF2	No
CO+S.FetchBrowse						
Okapi-CO-PTF2	CO	CO	Okapi	nCRE	PTF2	Yes
Okapi-+S-PTF2	+S	SS	Okapi	nCRE	PTF2	Yes
PCosine-CO-PTF2	CO	CO	PCosine	nCRE	PTF2	Yes
PCosine-+S-PTF2	+S	SS	PCosine	nCRE	PTF2	Yes
Dirichlet-CO-PTF2	CO	CO	Dirichlet	nCRE	PTF2	Yes
Dirichlet-+S-PTF2	+S	SS	Dirichlet	nCRE	PTF2	Yes
SSCAS						
SS-PTF2	CAS	SS	Okapi	—	PTF2	Yes
SS-TPF	CAS	SS	Okapi	—	TPF	Yes
SVCAS						
SV-PTF2	CAS	SV	Okapi	—	PTF2	Yes
SV-TPF	CAS	SV	Okapi	—	TPF	Yes
VSCAS						
nCRE-VS-PTF2	CAS	VS	Okapi	nCRE	PTF2	Yes
nCRE-VS-TPF	CAS	VS	Okapi	nCRE	TPF	Yes
VVCAS						
nCRE-VV-PTF2	CAS	VV	Okapi	nCRE	PTF2	Yes
nCRE-VV-TPF	CAS	VV	Okapi	nCRE	TPF	Yes

3.1 Evaluation Metrics

A new set of metrics is adopted in INEX 2005, which belong to the eXtended Cumulated Gain (XCG) family of metrics [6]. We use the following two official INEX 2005 metrics [5] to measure the retrieval effectiveness of our runs:

1. nxCG,with the nxCG[r] measure. The genLifted quantisation function is used with nxCG with the following values for the rank r: 10, 25, and 50. Wechoose this because with genLifted quantisation all the relevant

elements — including the so-called *too small* elements — are considered during evaluation (which is not the case with gen quantisation) [5]. The three values for the rank r are officially reported on the INEX 2005 web site.

2. ep/gr, with the MAep measure. Both strict and genLifted quantisations are used with ep/gr.

In addition to the above metrics, we also report values obtained with HiXEval: an alternative evaluation metric for XML retrieval that is solely based on the amount of highlighted relevant information for an INEX 2005 topic. The reported values are: P@r, or the proportion of relevant information to all the information retrieved at a rank r; and MAP, the mean average precision calculated at natural recall levels [8].

3.2 CO+S Sub-task

Thorough Retrieval Strategy. The evaluation results of our INEX 2005 CO+S runs for this strategy are shown in Table 4. Here, the level of overlap among retrieved elements is not considered. Several observations can be drawn from these results.

First, when comparing the two algorithms on how well they identify answer elements, results for the CO runs obtained from the three metrics show that better overall performance is achieved with the oCRE algorithm than with nCRE. This finding suggests that, for the Thorough retrieval strategy, systems capable of only retrieving contextual answers are better rewarded than systems that additionally retrieve more specific elements as answers. Second, with the nCRE algorithm for identifying answer elements, the TPF ranking heuristic — which first presents those answers that contain most of the distinct query terms, irrespective of how specific these answers are — is consistently better than the PTF2 ranking heuristic that presents more specific answers first. Finally, when comparing each

Table 4. Evaluation results of our INEX 2005 CO and +S runs for the Thorough retrieval strategy, obtained with nxCG, ep/gr, and HiXEval, using the genLifted quantisation function with nxCG. The three metrics do not consider the amount of overlap between retrieved elements (setting: off). For each evaluation measure, the best performing CO run (the first of each pair of runs) is shown in bold.

Run	nxCG [rank]			ep/gr (MAep)		HiXEval			
	10	25	50	genLifted	strict	P@10	P@25	P@50	MAP
nCRE-CO-PTF2	0.200	0.212	0.193	**0.019**	0.008	0.256	0.254	**0.216**	0.072
nCRE-+S-PTF2	0.211	0.158	0.145	0.014	0.008	0.245	0.181	0.158	0.050
nCRE-CO-TPF	0.218	0.226	0.193	**0.019**	0.009	0.262	**0.265**	**0.216**	0.073
nCRE-+S-TPF	0.224	0.166	0.1145	0.014	0.009	0.263	0.191	0.159	0.051
oCRE-CO-PTF2	**0.220**	**0.227**	**0.196**	**0.019**	**0.010**	**0.263**	0.258	0.204	**0.083**
oCRE-+S-PTF2	0.210	0.166	0.139	0.012	0.009	0.240	0.191	0.145	0.053

Table 5. Evaluation results of our INEX 2005 CO and +S runs for the Focussed retrieval strategy, obtained with nxCG, ep/gr, and HiXEval, using the genLifted quantisation function with nxCG. The three metrics do consider the amount of overlap between retrieved elements (setting: on). For each evaluation measure, the best performing CO run (the first of each pair of runs) is shown in bold.

Run	nxCG[rank]			ep/gr (MAep)		HiXEval			
	10	25	50	genLifted	strict	P@10	P@25	P@50	MAP
nCRE-CO-PTF2-NO	**0.044**	0.041	0.048	**0.012**	**0.012**	0.264	0.240	**0.191**	0.104
nCRE-+S-PTF2-NO	0.044	0.041	0.060	0.014	0.014	0.252	0.193	0.146	0.112
nCRE-CO-TPF-NO	0.040	0.041	**0.054**	0.011	0.011	0.248	0.212	0.177	0.117
nCRE-+S-TPF-NO	0.040	0.039	0.067	0.012	0.012	0.249	0.168	0.136	0.120
oCRE-CO-PTF2-NO	0.031	**0.052**	0.050	0.011	0.011	**0.298**	**0.249**	0.189	**0.118**
oCRE-+S-PTF2-NO	0.021	0.045	0.060	0.013	0.013	0.256	0.188	0.137	0.112

CO run with its corresponding +S run, the obtained results show that using structural hints from +S topics does not result in better overall performance, although runs using the nCRE algorithm seem to benefit from the structural hints at ten or fewer elements returned.

Focussed Retrieval Strategy. Table 5 shows evaluation results of our INEX 2005 CO+S runs for the Focussed retrieval strategy. Contrary to the Thorough retrieval strategy, in this case the amount of overlap between retrieved elements is considered by all the metrics. To filter overlap, we use a top-down filtering approach where elements that either contain or are contained by any element residing higher in the ranked list are removed from the resulting answer list.

When comparing our two algorithms on how well they identify answer elements, we observe that with HiXEval the oCRE algorithm overall performs better than the nCRE algorithm. However, the results obtained using MAep with both quantisations show the opposite. This suggests that the most specific elements that are retained as answers by nCRE bring additional user gain in the Focussed retrieval strategy. With the nCRE algorithm for identifying answer elements, we observe that with all but two evaluation measures the PTF2 ranking heuristic performs better than TPF.

For each of the three non-overlapping CO runs, the results obtained with ep/gr show that using structural hints from the +S topics results in increased overall retrieval performance. With HiXEval, however, this improvement is only visible when measuring the overall performance of the nCRE runs, which suggests that structural hints are not useful for runs that contain non-overlapping and *contextual* elements. The nature of the XML retrieval task, therefore, seems to influence how structural hints in the INEX +S topics should be interpreted. More precisely, using structural hints from the INEX +S topics seems to be more useful for Focussed than for the Thorough retrieval strategy.

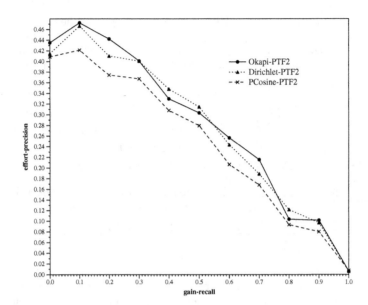

Fig. 3. Evaluation results of our INEX 2005 `CO` runs for the `FetchBrowse`-article retrieval strategy, obtained by using the `genLifted` quantisation function in the `ep/gr` INEX 2005 metric

`FetchBrowse` Retrieval Strategy. The evaluation methodology for this strategy is different than the ones that were used for the previous two strategies since two separate evaluation results are calculated: an article-level result and an element-level result [5].

By measuring the article-level results obtained from our three `FetchBrowse` runs, we aim to find which of the three information retrieval models implemented in `Zettair` yields the best performance for full article retrieval. The graph in Fig. 3 shows the results of this analysis. We observe that highest *effort-precision* at 0.3 or less *gain-recall* is achieved with the `Okapi` similarity measure, which also produces highest value for `MAep` among the three measures. Of the other two implemented measures, `Dirichlet` seems to perform better overall than `PCosine`. When compared with their corresponding `+S` runs, all the similarity measures except `Dirichlet` produce higher `MAep` values for `+S` runs than for runs that use plain text queries.

By measuring the element-level results obtained from our three `FetchBrowse` runs, we aim to investigate the extent to which each of the three information retrieval models influences the system performance for element retrieval. Table 6 shows results for the `FetchBrowse` retrieval strategy when elements are units of retrieval. The evaluation methodology implemented in the `ep/gr` metric for this strategy is explained by Kazai and Lalmas [5]. The two metrics, `ep/gr` and `HiXEval`, use both overlap settings (`on,off`). The evaluation measures used by `HiXEval` in this case are as follows: `Prec`, which measures precision at final rank for each article cluster, averaged over all clusters and then over all topics; and

Table 6. Evaluation results of our INEX 2005 `CO` and `+S` runs for the `FetchBrowse-Element` retrieval strategy. The two metrics, `ep/gr` and `HiXEval`, use both overlap settings (`on,off`). For an evaluation measure and an overlap setting, the best performing `CO` run (the first of each pair of runs) is shown in bold.

	overlap=off				overlap=on			
	ep/gr (MAep)		HiXEval		ep/gr (MAep)		HiXEval	
Run	genLifted	strict	Prec	MAP	genLifted	strict	Prec	MAP
Okapi-CO-PTF2	0.024	0.012	0.062	0.023	0.086	0.011	0.041	0.028
Okapi-+S-PTF2	0.014	0.007	0.060	0.018	0.062	0.008	0.047	0.030
PCosine-CO-PTF2	**0.025**	**0.013**	**0.066**	**0.024**	**0.090**	**0.012**	**0.043**	**0.029**
PCosine-+S-PTF2	0.014	0.008	0.063	0.019	0.065	0.009	0.048	0.030
Dirichlet-CO-PTF2	0.023	0.011	0.060	0.023	0.082	0.010	0.041	0.028
Dirichlet-+S-PTF2	0.013	0.006	0.060	0.017	0.058	0.007	0.048	0.030

`MAP`, the mean average precision (at natural recall levels) for each article cluster, averaged over all clusters and then over all topics.

Results in Table 6 show that, for `FetchBrowse` element-level retrieval, the `PCosine-CO-PTF2` run yields the highest retrieval performance among the three `CO` runs, irrespective of the metric *and* the overlap setting used. However, when the performance of each `CO` run is compared to that of its corresponding `+S` run, we observe that the overlap setting *does* have an impact on the measured comparison, but only when the `HiXEval` metric is used. When the amount of overlap between retrieved elements is not considered, the results obtained from both metrics show that the structural hints found in the `+S` topics are not useful. However, with overlap considered (setting: `on`), the results obtained from the `HiXEval` metric show that using structural hints leads to more precise search, which is reflected in increased values for both `Prec` and `MAP`. This suggests that using structural hints from the INEX `+S` topics is a useful feature in the `FetchBrowse` retrieval strategy, provided that the level of overlap among retrieved elements is considered.

3.3 CAS Sub-task

Since 2003, there has been much debate among the INEX participants over how to interpret the structure component of a CAS topic. For instance, at INEX 2003 and 2004 there were two interpretations: SCAS, which allows for a strict interpretation of the target element; and VCAS, which allows for the target element to be interpreted vaguely. However, none of these interpretations consider how the *support* elements of the CAS topic should be interpreted. Consequently, four retrieval strategies were explored in the INEX 2005 `CAS` sub-task: SS, SV, VS, and VV, which represent the four possible combinations of interpreting both the target and support elements.

Trotman and Lalmas [12] perform an extensive analysis of all the INEX 2005 runs that were submitted for the `CAS` sub-task, which reveals that those retrieval

Table 7. Evaluation results of our INEX 2005 CAS runs for the SS, SV, VS, and VV retrieval strategies, obtained with nxCG, ep/gr, and HiXEval, using the genLifted quantisation function with nxCG. The three metrics do not consider the amount of overlap between retrieved elements (setting: off). For an evaluation measure and a retrieval strategy, the best performing CAS run is shown in bold.

| Run | nxCG[rank] | | | ep/gr (MAep) | | HiXEval | | | |
	10	25	50	genLifted	strict	P@10	P@25	P@50	MAP
SSCAS									
SS-PTF2	0.288	0.339	0.360	0.070	0.044	0.184	0.138	0.117	0.055
SS-TPF	**0.316**	**0.345**	**0.368**	**0.071**	0.045	**0.208**	**0.143**	**0.124**	**0.057**
SV-PTF2	0.194	0.177	0.197	0.052	0.062	0.150	0.126	0.114	0.052
SV-TPF	0.229	0.187	0.206	0.053	**0.063**	0.185	0.134	0.121	0.055
SVCAS									
SS-PTF2	0.214	0.191	0.229	**0.065**	0.066	0.207	0.154	0.133	0.061
SS-TPF	**0.243**	**0.195**	**0.236**	**0.065**	**0.068**	**0.237**	**0.159**	**0.140**	**0.062**
SV-PTF2	0.135	0.127	0.157	0.040	0.049	0.131	0.113	0.105	0.047
SV-TPF	0.169	0.138	0.164	0.041	0.051	0.169	0.122	0.112	0.049
VSCAS									
nCRE-VS-PTF2	0.129	0.125	0.101	0.008	0.004	0.124	0.113	0.091	0.029
nCRE-VS-TPF	**0.230**	**0.144**	**0.113**	0.009	0.005	**0.210**	**0.128**	0.101	0.032
nCRE-VV-PTF2	0.098	0.108	0.100	0.011	0.006	0.097	0.100	0.092	0.046
nCRE-VV-TPF	0.198	0.127	0.112	**0.012**	**0.007**	0.183	0.114	**0.102**	**0.049**
VVCAS									
nCRE-VS-PTF2	0.164	0.171	0.142	0.006	0.005	0.204	0.187	0.153	0.042
nCRE-VS-TPF	**0.265**	**0.188**	**0.152**	0.007	0.005	0.278	0.198	0.162	0.044
nCRE-VV-PTF2	0.109	0.135	0.138	0.009	0.007	0.168	0.191	0.175	0.058
nCRE-VV-TPF	0.249	0.183	0.149	**0.010**	**0.008**	**0.286**	**0.215**	**0.186**	**0.063**

strategies that share the same interpretation of the target element correlate. In this section, we confirm their findings with our own CAS runs, by submitting the two SS runs to the SV retrieval strategy (and vice versa), and by also submitting the two VS runs to the VV retrieval strategy (and vice versa).

Table 7 presents the results of our CAS runs for each of the four retrieval strategies using measures from three evaluation metrics, where the amount of overlap between retrieved elements is not considered (overlap setting: off). For the two retrieval strategies that strictly interpret the target element (SS and SV), we observe that — regardless of the evaluation measure or metric used — the best performing run for the SS strategy, when submitted to the SV strategy, again performs best. On the other hand, we observe similar (but not the identical) behaviour for the two retrieval strategies that allow for a vague interpretation of the target element (VS and VV). More precisely, with nxCG and ep/gr the best performing run in the VS strategy also performs best when submitted to the VV strategy, whereas with HiXEval this is only true with P@50 and MAP measures.

Table 7 also shows that the performance of our CAS runs that use the TPF ranking heuristic is consistently higher than that of runs using the PTF2 heuristic, regardless of the retrieval strategy, evaluation measure, or metric used.

4   Conclusions

In this paper we have reported on our participation in the INEX 2005 ad-hoc track. We have tested three information retrieval models, two ways of identifying the appropriate element granularity, and two XML-specific ranking heuristics under different retrieval strategies in both the CO+S and CAS sub-tasks.

For the CO+S sub-task, better overall performance seems to be achieved when our retrieval module uses only contextual answer elements (oCRE), and not when most specific answer elements (nCRE) are also used. Moreover, the obtained user cumulated gain seems to be higher when the retrieval module uses the ranking heuristic which first presents those answers that contain most of the distinct query terms (TPF) than the ranking heuristic that presents more specific answers first (PTF2), although for the Focussed retrieval strategy the gain seems to be higher with PTF2. Using structural hints in the +S topics does not lead to more precise search; however, we have observed that structural hints improve both early and overall precision only for those retrieval strategies that do not allow retrieving overlapping elements. More specifically, Focussed retrieval strategy seems to benefit more from the structural hints than FetchBrowse, while there is no visible performance improvement for the Thorough retrieval strategy.

For the CAS sub-task we have observed that, regardless of the way the constraints in a CAS topic are interpreted, the TPF ranking heuristic produces consistently better performance than the PTF2 ranking heuristic. Importantly, for the CAS sub-task we have verified the previous finding by Trotman and Lalmas [12] that the structure component of an INEX CAS topic should only be interpreted in two different ways: one that allows for strict interpretation of the target element, and another that allows for its vague interpretation.

In the future, we plan to extend this work by implementing and experimenting with different combinations of information and data retrieval models in eXist to allow for more effective as well as more efficient XML retrieval.

References

1. V. N. Anh and A. Moffat. Impact transformation: Effective and efficient web retrieval. In *Proceedings of the ACM-SIGIR International Conference on Research and Development in Information Retrieval*, pages 3–10, Tampere, Finland, 2002.
2. Y. Chiaramella, P. Mulhem, and F. Fourel. A model for multimedia information retrieval. Technical report, FERMI ESPRIT BRA 8134, University of Glasgow, April 1996.
3. D.N.F. Awang Iskandar, J. Pehcevski, J. A. Thom, and S. M. M. Tahaghoghi. Combining image and structured text retrieval. In *INEX 2005 Workshop Pre-Proceedings, Dagstuhl, Germany, November 28–30, 2005*, pages 365–372, 2005.

4. K. Hatano, H. Kinutan, M. Watanabe, Y. Mori, M. Yoshikawa, and S. Uemura. Keyword-based XML fragment retrieval: Experimental evaluation based on INEX 2003 relevance assessments. In *Proceedings of the Second International Workshop of the INitiative of the Evaluation of XML Retrieval, INEX 2003, Dagstuhl Castle, Germany, December 15–17, 2003*, pages 81–88, 2004.

5. G. Kazai and M. Lalmas. INEX 2005 evaluation metrics. In *INEX 2005 Workshop Pre-Proceedings, Dagstuhl, Germany, November 28–30, 2005*, pages 401–406, 2005.

6. G. Kazai and M. Lalmas. Notes on what to measure in INEX. In *Proceedings of the INEX 2005 Workshop on Element Retrieval Methodology*, pages 22–38, Glasgow, UK, 2005.

7. M. Lalmas. INEX 2005 retrieval task and result submission specification. In *INEX 2005 Workshop Pre-Proceedings, Dagstuhl, Germany, November 28–30, 2005*, pages 385–390, 2005.

8. J. Pehcevski and J. A. Thom. HiXEval: Highlighting XML retrieval evaluation. In *INEX 2005 Workshop Pre-Proceedings, Dagstuhl, Germany, November 28–30, 2005*, pages 11–24, 2005.

9. J. Pehcevski, J. A. Thom, and A.-M. Vercoustre. Hybrid XML retrieval: Combining information retrieval and a native XML database. *Information Retrieval*, 8(4):571–600, 2005.

10. A. Singhal, C. Buckley, and M. Mitra. Pivoted document length normalization. In *Proceedings of the ACM-SIGIR International Conference on Research and Development in Information Retrieval*, pages 21–29, Zurich, Switzerland, 1996.

11. K. Sparck Jones, S. Walker, and S. E. Robertson. A probabilistic model of information retrieval: Development and comparative experiments. Parts 1 and 2. *Information Processing and Management*, 36(6):779–840, 2000.

12. A. Trotman and M. Lalmas. The Interpretation of CAS. In *INEX 2005 Workshop Pre-Proceedings, Dagstuhl, Germany, November 28–30, 2005*, pages 40–53, 2005.

13. C. Zhai and J. Lafferty. A study of smoothing methods for language models applied to information retrieval. *ACM Transactions on Information Systems*, 22(2):179–214, 2004.

14. J. Zobel and A. Moffat. Exploring the similarity space. *ACM SIGIR Forum*, 32(1):18–34, 1998.

SIRIUS: A Lightweight XML Indexing and Approximate Search System at INEX 2005

Eugen Popovici, Gildas Ménier, and Pierre-François Marteau

VALORIA Laboratory, University of South-Brittany
BP 573, 56017 Vannes Cedex, France
{Eugen.Popovici, Gildas.Menier,
Pierre-Francois.Marteau}@univ-ubs.fr

Abstract. This paper reports on SIRIUS, a lightweight indexing and search engine for XML documents. The retrieval approach implemented is document oriented. It involves an approximate matching scheme of the structure and textual content. Instead of managing the matching of whole DOM trees, SIRIUS splits the documents object model in a set of paths. In this view, the request is a path-like expression with conditions on the attribute values. In this paper, we present the main functionalities and characteristics of this XML IR system and second we relate on our experience on adapting and using it for the INEX 2005 ad-hoc retrieval task. Finally, we present and analyze the SIRIUS retrieval performance obtained during the INEX 2005 evaluation campaign and show that despite the lightweight characteristics of SIRIUS we were able to retrieve highly relevant non overlapping XML elements and obtained quite good precision at low recall values.

1 Introduction

The widespread use of XML in digital libraries, product catalogues, scientific data repositories and across the Web prompted the development of appropriate searching and browsing methods for XML documents. Approximate matching in XML provides the possibility of querying the information acquired by a system having an incomplete or imprecise knowledge about both the structure and the content of the XML documents [14, 15]. In this context, we propose and experiment with a lightweight model for indexing and querying XML documents. We develop a simple querying algebra implemented using fast approximate searching mechanisms for structure and textual content retrieval. In order to evaluate the expected benefits and drawbacks of this new kind of search functionality we propose algorithms and data structures whose principles are detailed hereinafter.

We propose specific data structures dedicated to the indexing and retrieval of information elements embedded within heterogeneous XML data bases. The indexing scheme is well suited to the characterization of various contextual searches, expressed either at a structural level or at an information content level. Search mechanisms are based on context tree matching algorithms that involve a modified Levenshtein editing distance [11] and information fusion heuristics. The implementation that is

N. Fuhr et al. (Eds.): INEX 2005, LNCS 3977, pp. 321–335, 2006.

described highlights the mixing of structured information presented as field/value instances and free text elements. Our approach is evaluated experimentally at the INEX 2005 workshop. The results are encouraging and give rise to a number of future enhancements.

The paper is organized as follows. In Section 2 we present the main functionalities and characteristics of the SIRIUS XML IR system. In Section 3 we relate on our experience on adapting and using the system in the INEX 2005 ad-hoc retrieval task. In Section 4 we present and analyze the SIRIUS retrieval evaluation results for the VVCAS, CO.Thorough, COS.Thorough, CO.Focussed and COS.Focussed tasks. Finally, in Section 5 we summarize our conclusions and propose some future work perspectives.

2 SIRIUS XML IR System

SIRIUS [6, 7] is a lightweight indexing and search engine for XML documents developed at the VALORIA laboratory of the University of South-Brittany. The retrieval approach implemented in SIRIUS is document oriented. It involves an approximate matching scheme of the structure and textual content. Instead of managing the matching of whole DOM trees, SIRIUS splits the documents object model in a set of paths. This set is indexed using optimized data structures. In this view, the request is a path-like expression with conditions on the attribute values. For instance */document(> date "1994")/chapter(= number 3)/John* is a request aiming to extract the documents (written after *94*) with the word John in the chapter number *3*. We designed a matching process that takes into account mismatched errors both on the attributes and on the xml elements. The matching process uses a weighted editing distance on XML paths: this provides an approximate matching scheme able to manage jointly the request on textual content and on document structure. The search scheme is extended by a set of Boolean and IR retrieval operators, and features a set of thesaurus rewriting rules. Recently the system was extended with a specialized set of operators for extracting, indexing and searching heterogeneous sequential and time series data embedded in heterogeneous XML documents [8].

2.1 Indexing Scheme

Each XML element in an XML document may be composed of a set of possible nested XML elements, textual pieces of information (TEXT or CDATA), unordered <attribute, value> pairs, or a mixture of such items. XML documents are generally represented as rooted, ordered, and labeled trees in which each node corresponds to an element and each edge represent a parent-child relationship.

XML Context. According to the tree structure, every node n inherits a path $p(n)$ composed with the nodes that link the root to node n. This path is an ordered sequence of XML elements potentially associated to unordered <attribute, value> pairs $A(n_i)$, that determines the XML context in which the node is occurring. A tree node n, containing textual/mixed information can be decomposed into textual sub-elements. Each string s (or word, lemma, …) of a textual sub-element is also linked to

$p(n)$. This XML context characterizes the occurrence of s within the document and can be represented as follows:

$$p(n) = <n_0, A(n_0)> <n_1, A(n_1)> \ldots <n, A(n_n)> \tag{1}$$

Index Model. The indexing process involves the creation of an enriched inverted list designed for the management of these XML contexts. For this model, the entries of the inverted lists are all the valid (i.e. *alphanumeric* terms as defined in [3]) textual sub-elements s of a tree node. For a sub-element s of a node n, four pieces of information are attached:

- a link to the URI of the document *<fileId>*,
- an index specifying the start and the end location of the node containing the sub-element within the document *<startNodeId, endNodeId>*,
- an index specifying the location of the sub-element within the document *<wordOffset>*,
- a link toward its XML context $p(n)$ *<ctxtId>*.

2.2 Searching Scheme

Most of the time, for large heterogeneous databases, one cannot assume that the user knows all of the structures – even in the very optimistic case, when all of the structural properties are known. Some straightforward approaches (such as the XPath search scheme [16]) may not be efficient in these cases. As the user cannot be aware of the complete XML structure of the data base due to its heterogeneity, efficient searching should involved exact and approximate search mechanisms.

The main structure used in XML is a tree: It seems acceptable to express a search in term of tree-like requests and approximate matching. The matching tree process involves mainly elastic matching or editing distance [9, 10]. For [9], the complexity of matching two trees T_1 and T_2 is at least $O(|T_1|.|T_2|)$ where $|T_i|$ is the number of nodes in T_i. The complexity is much higher for common subtree search [10]. This complexity is far too high to let these approaches perform well for large heterogeneous databases with documents with a high number of elements (as nodes).

We proposed [6], to focus on path matching rather than on tree matching – in a similar way with the XML fragment approach [14]. The request should be expressed as a set of path $p(r)$ that is matched with the set of sub-path $p(n)$ in the document tree. This breaks the algorithmic complexity and seems to better match the end-user needs: most of the data searches involve a node and its inherited sequence of elements rather than a full tree of elements. This 'low-level' matching only manage subpath similarity search with conditions on the elements and attributes matching. This process is used to design a more higher-level request language: a full request is a tree of low-level matching goals (as leafs) with set operators as nodes. These operators are used to merge leaf results. The whole tree is evaluated to provide a set of ranked answers. The operators are classical set operators (intersection, union, difference) or dedicated fuzzy merging processors.

Approximate Path Search. Let R be a low-level request, expressed as a path goal p^R, with conditions or constraints to be fulfilled on the attributes and attributes values. We investigate the similarity between a p^R (coding a path with constraints) and p_i^D (a root/../terminal(r) path of the tree T^D associated to an index document D) as follow:

$$\sigma(p^R, p_i^D) = 1/(1 + \delta_L(p^R, p_i^D)) \tag{2}$$

where δ_L is a dedicated editing distance (see [11]).

The search complexity is $O(l(p^R).deep(T^D).|\{p_i^D\}|)$ with $|\{p_i^D\}|$ the size of the set $\{p_i^D\}$ (i.e. the number of different paths in D, starting at the root and leading to the last element of the p^R request – terminal(r)), $l(p)$ the length of the path p and $deep(T)$ the deepest level of T. This complexity remains acceptable for this application as 99% of the XML documents have fewer than 8 levels and their average depth is 4 [13]. We designed [6] an editing pseudo-distance using a customised cost matrix to compute the match between a path p_i^D and the request path p^R. This scheme, also known as modified Levenshtein distance, computes a minimal sequence of elementary transformation to get from p_i^D to p^R. The elementary transformations are:

- **Substitution:** a node n in p_i^D is replaced by a node n' for a cost $C_{subst}(n, n')$,
- **Deletion:** a node n in p_i^D is deleted for a cost $C_{del}(n)$,
- **Insertion:** a node n is inserted in p_i^D for a cost $C_{ins}(n)$.

For a sequence $Seq(p_i^D, p^R)$ of elementary operations, the global cost $GC(Seq(p_i^D, p^R))$ is computed as the sum of the costs of elementary operations. The Wagner&Fisher algorithm [12] computes the best $Seq(p_i^D, p^R)$ (i.e. minimizes $GC()$ cost) with a complexity of $O(length(p_i^D) * length(p^R))$ as stated earlier. Let

$$\delta_L(p^R, p_i^D) = Min_k GC(Seq_k(p^R, p_i^D)). \tag{3}$$

Given p^R and p_i^D, the value for $\sigma(p^R, p_i^D)$ _ 0 when the number of mismatching nodes and attribute conditions between p^R and p_i^D increases. For a perfect match $\sigma(p^R, p_i^D) = 1$, i.e. all the elements and the conditions on attributes from the request p^R match correspondent XML elements in p_i^D.

2.3 Query Language

Complex requests are built using the low-level request p^R described above and merging operators (boolean or specialized operators). Mainly a complex request is a tree of p^R requests as leafs. Each node supports an operator performing the merging of the descendant results. Currently, the following merging operators are implemented in the system for the low-levels management:

- **or, and:** n-booleans or n-set. (**or** p^R $p^{R'}$) merges the set of solutions for p^R and $p^{R'}$. (**and** p^R $p^{R'}$) selects only the answers belonging to both answer sets.
- **without:** this operator can be used to remove solutions from a set. For instance, (**without** p^R $p^{R'}$) delivers the set of solutions for p^R _minus_ the solutions for $p^{R'}$.
- **seq:** merges some of the inverted list to provides a simple sequence management. For instance, (**seq** warning * error) express the search of a sequence of texts items.
- **same+:** should be related to the **or** operator. The **or** operator is a simple set merging operator, whereas 'same+' is a dedicated operator that takes into account

the number and the discriminating power of the retrieved terms/elements in the collection. We used a dedicated (see below) TFIDF-like function for this purpose (TFIDF stands for *Term Frequency / Inverse Document Frequency*, see [18]).

- **in:** express a contextual relation (same = the p^R have the same path, in = inside elements with the specified path),
- **in+:** add structural matching information to the set of solutions. It performs a weighted linear aggregation between the conditions on structure and the set of solutions.
- **filter:** this is a binary set operator selecting from the second set received as argument all the elements coming from document trees containing at least one relevant answer in the first set. The relevance of a returned element is computed as the arithmetic average between its relevance in the second set and the weight associated with the most relevant answer of the same document in the first set.

The system analysis a request R and produce a set of weighted results. Let $r(R) = \{ (e_i, v_i) \}$ the set of weighted results produced by the system, where e_i is a an element of the result and $v_i \in [0..1]$ a weight showing the relevance of the returned element to the request.

Let R be a complex request, or a simple (low level) p^R request. The similarity computation for a complex request involves modifications of the relevance associated with a result element and is performed recursively starting at the leafs:

$$r(\ or\ (R_0,...R_n)\ ) = \{ (e_i, v_i) \} \text{ with } v_i = \underset{k}{Max}(v_k) \text{ where } (e_i, v_k) \in \bigcup_j^n r(R_j) \ ;$$

$$r(\ and\ (R_0,...R_n)\ ) = \{ (e_i, v_i) \} \text{ with } v_i = \underset{k}{Min}(v_k) \text{ where } (e_i, v_k) \in \bigcup_j^n r(R_j) \ ;$$

$$r(\ without\ (R_0,\ R_1)\ ) = \{ (e_i, v_i) \} \text{ where } (e_i, v_i) \in r(R_0) \text{ and } (e_i, v_i) \notin r(R_1);$$

$$\text{and } (e_i, v_i^1) \in r(R_1) \ ;$$

$r(\ seq\ (M_0,...M_n)\ ) = \{ (e_i, v_i) \}$, $v_i = 1$ if $M_0..M_n$ occurs in sequence and belongs to the same context/leaf, else 0.

$r(\ in\ (path\ ,\ R_0,...R_n)) = \{ (e_i, v_i) \}$ with $v_i = Min\{ \underset{k}{Min}\ (v_k),\ \Delta(path, p(e_i))\}$ where

$(e_i, v_k) \in \bigcup_j r(R_j)$; $p(e)$ the xml context of element e ; and $\Delta(path, p(e))=1$ if

$path==p(e)$, 0 if not;

$(\ in+\ (path,\ R_0,...R_n)) = \{ (e_i, v_i) \}$ with $v_i = \beta \cdot \Delta(\ path\ ,\ p(e_i)) + (1 - \beta) \cdot \underset{k}{Min}(v_k)$

where $(e_i, v_k) \in \bigcup_j^n r(R_j)$; $\Delta\ (path, p(e)) = \sigma(path, p(e))$ the structural similarity

between the two XML contexts (section 2.2); and $\beta \in [0..1]$ a parameter used to emphasise the importance of the structural versus textual content matching ;

$r(\ same+ (R_0,...R_n)) = \{ (e_i, v_i) \}$ with $v_i = \tau \cdot \sum_k \lambda_k . v_k$ where $(e_i, v_k) \in \bigcup_j^n r(R_j)$,

λ_k is a TFIDF-like weighting factor specifying the discriminating power of a result element (e_i, v_k) in the collection : $\lambda_k = 1 - log(\ (1 + N^{D(e_i, v_k)}) / (1 + N^D)\ )$; where $N^{D(e_i, v_k)}$ is the number of documents in which (e_i, v_k) is occuring ; N^D the total number of documents in the collection ; and τ a normalization constant $\tau = 1 / \Sigma_k(\lambda_k)$;

Let e^D be a result element descendant of document D.

$r(\ filter\ (R_0,\ R_1)) = \{ (e_i^D,\ v_i) \}$ with $v_i = (v_i^1 + \underset{j}{Max}(v_j^0))/2$ where:

$\forall_D \forall_i (e_i^D, v_i^1) \in r(R_1)$ and $\forall_j (e_j^D, v_j^0) \in r(R_0)$.

3   INEX 2005 Experience

The retrieval task we are addressing at INEX 2005 is defined as the ad-hoc retrieval of XML elements. This involves the searching of a static set of documents using a new set of topics [1]. We will further present several characteristics of the test collection and of the topics used in INEX 2005 ad-hoc task. Next we will present how we tuned the SIRIUS retrieval approach for the CAS, CO and CO+S tasks.

3.1   INEX Ad-Hoc Collection

The inex-1.8 document collection contains 16819 articles taken from 24 IEEE Computer Society journals, covering the period of 1995-2004. The total size of the source files in their canonical form is about 750 MB. The collection contains 141 different tag-names composing 7948 unique XML contexts by ignoring the attributes and the attributes values. The maximum length of an index path is 20, while the average length is 8. These statistics are computed from the viewpoint of the retrieval system. That is, we use the XML tag equivalence classes (section 3.5). Also, the XML contexts associated to empty elements or containing only stop words do not count in our statistics.

3.2   INEX 2005 Topics

For the ad-hoc track of the INEX 2005 campaign a total of 40 CO and 47 CAS topics were selected by the organizers. CO (Content Only) topics contain just search terms, and optionally, an additional structured (+S) query specified in NEXI [3]. CAS queries (Fig. 1) are topic statements that contain explicit references to the XML

//article[about(.//bb, Baeza-Yates) and about(.//sec , string matching)]
//sec[about(., approximate algorithm)]

Fig. 1. CAS topic 280 expressed in NEXI language [3]

structure, and explicitly specify the contexts of the user's interest (e.g. target elements) and/or the context of certain search concepts (e.g. containment conditions).

3.3 Translating INEX 2005 Topics to SIRIUS Query Language

We use automatic transformation of the INEX 2005 topics expressed in NEXI [3] to SIRIUS [6] recursive query language.

To translate CO topics we use the *same+* (for textual content), *seq* (for strict phrase matching) and *without* (for "–" sign) operators (Section 2.3) in a straight forward way. The "+" sign and the numerical expressions are ignored.

For CAS topics, we have two cases: simple queries of the form //A[B] and complex queries of the form //A[B]//C[D]. For the simple type queries, the translation process is based on the *in+* operator (Section 2.3) (Fig. 2).

//article[about(.//bb, Baeza-Yates)	(in+ [/article/bb/] (same+ (seq Baeza Yates)))

Fig. 2. Translating CAS topic 277 to SIRIUS query language

For translating complex queries of the form //A[B]//C[D] (Fig. 3), we introduce a new *filter* operator aiming to solve element containment relationships (Section 2.3). However, for all the complex CAS and CO+S topics, the ancestor //A specified in the structural path is the *article* element. Therefore, only document *D* level containment conditions are checked in the current implementation of the operator.

```
( filter ( and ( in+  [/article/bb/]  ( same+  ( seq  Baeza Yates ) ) )
              ( in+  [/article/sec/]  ( same+  string  matching ) ) )
              ( in+  [/article/sec/]  ( same+  approximate  algorithm ) ) )
```

Fig. 3. CAS topic 280 (Fig. 1) translated to SIRIUS query language

3.4 Indexing the INEX 2005 Ad-Hoc Collection

The collection is pre-processed by removing the *volume.xml* files and transforming all the XML documents in their canonical form[1]. At indexing time, the least significant words are eliminated using a stop list. The terms are stemmed using the Porter algorithm [17]. We index only *ALPHANUMERIC* words as defined in [3] (like *iso-8601*). We did not index numbers, the attributes, the attributes values, and empty XML elements. This allowed important performance gains both in indexing and querying time as well as disk space savings. The index model (section 2.1) was implemented using BTrees structures from Berkeley DB[2] library. The indexing time on a PIV 2.4GH processor with 1.5GB of RAM for the inex-1.8 IEEE collection in its

---

[1] Canonical XML Processor, http://www.elcel.com/products/xmlcanon.html .
[2] http://www.sleepycat.com/

canonical form (~750MB) was about 60 min and showed a quasi linear evolution. The index size is about 1.28 times the size of the initial collection.

3.5 Structure Approximate Match for INEX

Structural Equivalence Classes. We create structural equivalence classes for the tags defined as interchangeable in a request: *Paragraphs, Sections, Lists*, and *Headings* in conformance with [4].

Weighting Scheme for Modelling Ancestor-Descendant Relationships. NEXI language [3] specifies a path through the XML tree as a sequence of nodes. Furthermore, the only relationship allowed between nodes in a path is the descendant relation. Therefore the XML path expressed in the request is interpreted as a *subsequence* of an indexed path, where a subsequence need not consist of contiguous nodes.

This is not suited for the weighting scheme allowing (slight) mismatch errors between the structural query and the indexed XML paths implemented in SIRIUS [6]. The ancestor-descendant relationship is penalized by the SIRIUS weighting scheme relative to a parent-child relationship. Therefore we relax the weights of the path editing distance in order to allow node deletions in the indexed paths without any penalty $C_{del}(n)=0$. To illustrate this mechanism we show in Fig. 4 the distances between the path requested in topic 277 (Fig. 2) searching works citing Baeza-Yates and several indexed path retrieved by SIRIUS using the new weighting scheme.

δ_L (/**article**/bm/bib/bibl/**bb**/au/snm,	//**article**//**bb**)	= 0
δ_L (/**article**/bm/app/bib/bibl/**bb**/au/snm,	//**article**//**bb**)	= 0
δ_L (/**article**/fm/au/snm,	// **article**//bb)	= 1

Fig. 4. Example of distances between the indexed path p_i^D and the request path p^R

In the first two cases the request path p^R is a subsequence of the retrieved paths p_i^D and therefore the editing distance is 0 independently of the length of the two index paths. In the last case, (Baeza-Yates beeing the author of the article), the editing distance is 1 highlighting the mismatch of the requested *bb* node from the indexed path.

The weighting scheme relates to an end user having precise but incomplete information about the xml tags of the indexed collection and about their ancestor-descendant relationships. It takes into account the order of occurrence of the matched nodes and the number of nodes with no matching in the request. It heavily penalizes any mismatch relatively to the information provided by the user but it is forgiving with mismatches/extra information extracted from the indexed paths.

4   SIRIUS Experiments

In all the submitted runs we use the same basic retrieval approach, namely: i) the xml elements directly containing the research terms are considered as independent and the only valid units of retrieval; ii) IDF-like weighting for the leaf nodes containing the researched terms using the *same+* operator; iii) modified editing distance on XML paths for matching the structural constraints (*in+* operator), and iv) weighted linear aggregation for content and structure matching scores.

Strict Sequence Matching Runs. We used a strict *seq* operator for phrase matching inside the *same+* operator – where *strict* stands for all the words appearing in sequence in the textual content (ignoring the stop list words) of the same XML node.

Flexible Sequence Matching Runs. We implemented a relaxed sequence search based only on the *same+* operator. These runs rank as best results the XML elements that contain all the researched terms without taking into account their order of occurrence. XML elements that contain part of the research terms are also retrieved and ranked based on the number and the discriminating power of the enclosed terms.

4.1 SIRIUS CAS Runs

CAS queries are topic statements that contain two kinds of structural constraints: where to look (support elements), and what elements to return (target elements) [1]. When implementing a VVCAS strategy, the structural constraints in both the target elements and the support elements are interpreted as vague using the *in+* operator. We submitted 2 official (1. VVCAS_contentWeight08_structureWeight02 and 2. VVCAS_content Weight05_structureWeight05) and 2 additional runs (3. VVCAS_SEQ and 4. VVCAS_ SAMEPLUS) within the CAS ad-hoc task using the VVCAS strategy and automatic query translation .

All the results described in this paper use the inex-1.8 collection, which is the official 2005 collection. However, due to a misunderstanding, the official VVCAS runs (1 & 2) were obtained with the inex-1.6 version of the collection. The first official submission emphasises the importance of the textual content matching score versus the structural matching using the β parameter set to 0.2 in the *in+* operator. The second official submission uses equal weights for merging the structural and content matching scores. Additional run 3 is equivalent with the second official submission but is obtained using the inex-1.8 version of the IEEE collection. For additional run 4 we use a relaxed matching for phrase search based on the *same+* operator, using $\beta=0.5$ and the inex-1.8 collection.

We report here the system-oriented and user-oriented official INEX 2005 evaluation measures: the effort-precision/gain-recall (*ep/gr*) metric, Extended Q and R metric, respectively the normalized extended cumulated gain (*nxCG*) metric for all the submitted VVCAS runs. Details of the evaluation metrics can be found in [2].

Using the Structural Information. The objective of our study was to determine to what extent the structural hints should be taken into account when implementing a VVCAS strategy. For the two official runs (1, 2) we assigned different weights (within the *in+* operator - Section 2.3) to merge the content and structure relevance scores, i.e. β =0.2 and $\beta=0.5$. The coefficients used were not discriminate enough to highlight important differences in the ranking of the final set of results. However, we may observe that the run that equally weighted the content and structural matching

Table 1. SIRIUS VVCAS Runs (1, 2 official runs; 3, 4 additional runs)

		nxCG			ep/gr						Q	R
	@10	@25	@50	MAnxCG@1500	0,01/@15	0,02/@30	0,03/@45	0,1/@150	MAep	iMAep		
					Overlap=off, Quant=strict							
1.	0.1889	0.16	0.1273	0.2496	0.3459	0.3348	0.2885	0.1288	0.0375	0.0364	0.0401	0.0788
2.	0.1889	0.16	0.1273	0.2518	**0.3461**	**0.3349**	**0.2886**	0.1289	0.0376	0.0365	0.0404	0.0788
3.	0.1667	0.1689	0.1339	0.2724	0.327	0.3169	0.2673	0.133	0.0487	0.0475	0.0516	**0.1007**
4.	0.1444	**0.2022**	**0.1889**	**0.304**	0.2235	0.206	0.2013	**0.1389**	**0.0558**	**0.0555**	**0.0643**	0.0947
					Overlap=off, Quant=gen							
1.	0.283	0.2344	0.1826	0.149	0.343	0.2627	0.1813	0.1452	0.0199	0.0283	0.0248	0.0842
2.	0.283	0.2359	0.19	0.1495	**0.3726**	0.2923	0.1863	0.146	0.0203	0.0291	0.0253	0.0842
3.	0.2643	**0.248**	0.2044	0.1634	0.3588	**0.2966**	0.199	**0.1659**	0.025	0.0374	0.0305	0.0941
4.	0.2219	0.2208	**0.2184**	**0.1864**	0.2555	0.2288	**0.2181**	0.1627	**0.0344**	**0.0468**	**0.0454**	**0.1255**

scores (2nd official run) outperform in average the one biased towards content matching (1st official run) (see table 1). This is true for all of the INEX 2005 evaluation
measures (official and additional) and this independently of the quantization function
used. This indicates (usual disclaimers apply) that the structural hints, and jointly, the
modified editing distance on the XML paths raises the system retrieval performances.
To support this hypothesis we conducted experiments in which we completely
ignored the explicit information provided by the users (setting β =0.0). The gain
obtained between the runs using the explicit structural information and the ones that
completely ignored it was of 6.28% for the flexible sequence search strategy and of
8,7% for the strict sequence search strategy on the *MAep* measure calculated with a
strict quantization function.

Sequence Search Strategy. SIRIUS official VVCAS runs have a high effort/pre-
cision for low values of gain/recall (Table 1). This behaviour is due to the fact that the
runs used strict constraints for phrase searching and the topic set was rich (7 among
the 10 assessed topics used sequence search) in this kind of hints. The restrictive
interpretation of the *seq* operator improved the system precision for the first ranked
results. The SIRIUS VVCAS official runs are ranked several times in the first top ten
runs for the first 10-25 retrieved results. This fact is important because these results
are the most probably to be browsed by an end user. In the same time, this behaviour
has penalized the system overall quality performance. One explanation is that the
system stops to return elements when running out of good answers. This has
important implications, as the system is not increasing its information gain until
reaching the limit of 1500 returned answers by returning imprecise/less perfect
results. This hypothesis is also supported by the system behaviour relatively to the
strict and generalized quantization functions. Our runs were better ranked by all the
official evaluation measures when a strict quantization function was used.

We evaluated an additional run (4) allowing a flexible phrase search based only on
the *same+* operator. With this approach , we loose 32% of the system precision for
the first 15 retrieved results versus the strict sequence search strategy, but we obtain
an obviously improved overall effort-precision/gain-recall curve (gain of 14.57% on

the MAep (overlap=off, quant=strict)). We could further improve these results by defining a new operator combining *same+* ranking with *seq* ranking strategies.

VVCAS Task Rankings. The evaluation results are rather encouraging. In particular, the best values reported for nxCG@{10,25,50} (overlap=off, quant=strict) could be ranked unofficially between the first three positions (from 28 submissions). The best overall performance is obtained by the flexible matching sequence strategy with MAep=0.0558 (overlap=off, quant= strict) that is equivalent with a non official 5th place.

4.2 SIRIUS CO, COS Runs

CO.Thorough & COS.Thorough. For these strategies we used a similar approach as for the VVCAS task. The CO topics were automatically translated in SIRIUS query language and the xml elements directly containing terms relevant to the requests were retuned (usually the leafs). We present hereinafter the evaluation results obtained for two different content matching strategies allowing a strict (SEQ) and flexible (SAMEPLUS) phrase search.

Table 2. SIRIUS CO.Thorough Runs

Overlap=off, Quant=strict											
nxCG				ep/gr						Q	R
@10	@25	@50	MAnxCG@1500	0,01/@15	0,02/@30	0,03/@45	0,1/@150	MAep	iMAep		
SAMEPLUS **0.1158**	**0.1027**	0.126	**0.2154**	**0.1548**	**0.1425**	**0.1314**	**0.1117**	**0.0428**	**0.043**	**0.0491**	**0.0567**
SEQ 0.0769	0.0931	**0.1303**	0.2051	0.1292	0.1254	0.1189	0.0875	0.0374	0.0369	0.0421	0.0513
Overlap=off, Quant=gen											
nxCG				ep/gr						Q	R
@10	@25	@50	MAnxCG@1500	0,01/@15	0,02/@30	0,03/@45	0,1/@150	MAep	iMAep		
SAMEPLUS **0.2081**	0.2095	0.1803	**0.1831**	**0.2691**	**0.2385**	**0.2175**	**0.1423**	**0.0298**	**0.0471**	**0.0401**	**0.1169**
SEQ 0.2075	**0.2153**	**0.1822**	0.167	0.264	0.2312	0.2141	0.1327	0.0232	0.0382	0.0321	0.1027

We obtained particularly good results for both the CO.Thorough and COS.Thorough tasks on the ep/gr and nxCG metric with a strict quantization function (i.e. for the CO.Thorough we obtained an unofficial 3rd place for the SAMEPLUS run with *MAep=0.0428*; the results reported (Table 2) for *nxCG@{10, 25, 50}* for the SAMEPLUS run could be ranked in the top 4th places from the 55 submitted runs for the CO.Thorough task).

Table 3. SIRIUS COS.Thorough Runs

Overlap=off, Quant=strict											
nxCG				ep/gr						Q	R
@10	@25	@50	MAnxCG@1500	0,01/@15	0,02/@30	0,03/@45	0,1/@150	MAep	iMAep		
SAMEPLUS **0.0771**	**0.1395**	**0.1507**	**0.2131**	**0.118**	**0.1162**	**0.1277**	**0.1173**	**0.0557**	**0.0553**	**0.0623**	**0.0669**
SEQ 0.0654	0.1225	0.1201	0.1595	0.0925	0.0938	0.1007	0.0925	0.0465	0.0458	0.051	0.0491
Overlap=off, Quant=gen											
nxCG				ep/gr						Q	R
@10	@25	@50	MAnxCG@1500	0,01/@15	0,02/@30	0,03/@45	0,1/@150	MAep	iMAep		
SAMEPLUS 0.1905	**0.2326**	**0.1929**	**0.205**	**0.2408**	**0.2332**	**0.2364**	**0.1749**	**0.0327**	**0.0563**	**0.0431**	**0.1189**
SEQ **0.1919**	0.1942	0.1662	0.1517	0.2335	0.2123	0.2082	0.1312	0.0185	0.0352	0.026	0.0867

For the COS.Thorough runs we used a vague strategy (*in+* operator) for interpreting the structural constrains as for the VVCAS runs. All the result reported (Table 3) for the two runs at *nxCG@{25, 50}* and *MAep* calculated with a strict quantization function could be ranked unofficially on the first and the second place from the 33 submitted runs.

CO.Focussed & COS.Focussed. The aim of the *Focussed* retrieval strategy is to find the most exhaustive and specific element in a path. In other words, the result list should not contain any overlapping elements. In our approach we consider the XML element containing a researched term as the basic and implicitly valid unit of retrieval regardless of its size. This approach implements "naturally" a focused strategy as it returns the most focused elements containing the research terms. However, the highly mixed nature of the INEX ad-hoc collection and the fact that the distribution of elements is heavily skewed towards short elements such as italics [5], may lead to cases where nested/overlapping XML elements could be returned as valid results. For instance, the *p* (paragraph) and the *it* (italicized text) elements of the excerpt from Fig. 5 will be retrieved by a request aiming to extract relevant elements for the "*query*" term.

```
<p align="left" ind="none">
    The  <it>query optimizer</it>, the query engine's central component, determines the best service
    execution plan based on QoWS, service ratings, and matching degrees.
</p>
```

Fig. 5. Mixed XML element content with italicized text (i.e. one of the SIRIUS 'relevant' answer for CAS topic 244)

Our official VVCAS runs (1, 2) have a *set-overlap*[3] ranging between 0.002 – 0.004 for the first 20 retrieved results and 0.014-0.015 at 1500 results. In order to remove the overlapping elements we implemented a two phase process: i) we recalculate the relevance of the elements in the answer list in order to reflect the relevance of their descendants elements (if any); and ii) we select non overlapping elements from the list. The weights are calculated recursively starting at the leafs to the highest non overlapping nodes composing the answer by using two strategies: i) *max* - the max relevance value is propagated recursively to the highest non overlapping elements; ii) and *avg* - the relevance of a node is computed as the arithmetic average of all its descendant relevant nodes including its own relevance. To select the non overlapping elements we compared several strategies: i) *HA* - the highest ancestor from the answer list is selected; ii) *MR* - the most relevant answer is selected recursively from the answer list as long as it not overlaps with an already selected element – i.e. for equally relevant overlapping elements we choose either the descendant (*MRD*) or the ancestor (*MRA*).

---

[3] Set overlap measures the percentage of elements that either contain or are contained by at least one or other element in the set.

We experimented with different settings for computing the elements relevance and selecting the non overlapping answers for the CO.Focussed and COS.Focussed tasks. In outmost all the experiments the runs based on the *same+* operator outperformed the runs based on the *seq* operator, even at low recall values. Therefore, we rapport here the best performing runs based only on the *same+* operator (*SAMEPLUSmaxHA*, *SAMEPLUSmaxMRD* and *SAMEPLUSavgMRD*) for the CO.Focussed (Table 4) and the COS.Focussed (Table 5) tasks. The main experimental observation is that for the generalized quantization, largest XML elements are preferable (*HA*) while the strict quantization function demands for more focussed XML elements (*MRD*),

Table 4. SIRIUS CO.Focussed Runs: Different Strategies for Removing Overlap

	Overlap=on, Quant=strict											
	nxCG				ep/gr						Q	R
	@10	@25	@50	MAnxCG@1500	0,01/@15	0,02/@30	0,03/@45	0,1/@150	MAep	iMAep		
SAMEPLUSavgMRD	**0.1269**	0.1109	0.1579	0.2982	**0.171**	**0.1462**	**0.1342**	**0.1146**	0.0672	0.0674	0.0766	0.0752
SAMEPLUSmaxHA	0.1231	**0.1332**	**0.1668**	**0.3089**	0.1568	0.1397	0.1244	**0.1146**	0.0682	0.0687	0.0779	0.0772
SAMEPLUSmaxMRD	0.1231	**0.1332**	**0.1668**	0.3077	0.1568	0.1397	0.1244	**0.1146**	**0.0684**	**0.0688**	**0.078**	**0.0776**
	Overlap=on, Quant=gen											
	nxCG				ep/gr						Q	R
	@10	@25	@50	MAnxCG@1500	0,01/@15	0,02/@30	0,03/@45	0,1/@150	MAep	iMAep		
SAMEPLUSavgMRD	**0.1924**	0.1826	0.1782	0.3454	0.2548	0.239	**0.2391**	0.1827	0.0744	0.0752	0.1153	0.1607
SAMEPLUSmaxHA	0.1903	**0.2009**	0.1873	**0.3596**	0.2551	0.2431	0.2352	**0.1906**	**0.0783**	**0.0793**	**0.1218**	0.176
SAMEPLUSmaxMRD	0.1903	**0.2009**	0.1873	0.3566	0.2551	0.2431	0.2351	**0.1906**	0.0779	0.0789	0.121	**0.1761**

The system is well ranked for both the strict and generalised quantization functions and in both the CO.Focussed and COS.Focussed tasks. For the CO. Focussed task we obtain *MAep* values (Table 4) equivalent with an unofficial 5th and 8th place (from 44 submissions) for a strict and respectively generalized quantization function. We are better ranked on the COS.Focussed task were we obtain *MAep* values (Table 5) equivalent with a 2nd and 5th place (from 27 submissions) for strict and respectively generalised quantization. Also the values reported for the nxCG@{10, 25, 50} with strict quantisation for both the CO.Focussed and COS.Focussed tasks could be ranked in the top 10 results. These results may be explained by the fact that in the approach taken for the INEX 2005 ad-hoc task we return mostly leaf elements (i.e. paragraphs) which are shown to be effective retrieval units for the focussed strategy [19].

Table 5. SIRIUS COS.Focussed Runs: Different Strategies for Removing Overlap

	Overlap=on, Quant=strict											
	nxCG				ep/gr						Q	R
	@10	@25	@50	MAnxCG@1500	0,01/@15	0,02/@30	0,03/@45	0,1/@150	MAep	iMAep		
SAMEPLUSavgMRD	0.0941	0.1331	0.2005	0.3206	0.1068	0.1049	0.1088	**0.1211**	**0.0897**	**0.0895**	**0.1003**	0.0921
SAMEPLUSmaxHA	**0.1059**	**0.162**	**0.2021**	**0.3211**	**0.1086**	**0.1081**	**0.1121**	0.1197	0.0891	0.0891	0.0997	**0.0923**
SAMEPLUSmaxMRD	**0.1059**	**0.162**	0.1937	0.3198	**0.1086**	0.1067	0.1105	0.1194	0.0895	0.0894	0.1001	0.0921
	Overlap=on, Quant=gen											
	nxCG				ep/gr						Q	R
	@10	@25	@50	MAnxCG@1500	0,01/@15	0,02/@30	0,03/@45	0,1/@150	MAep	iMAep		
SAMEPLUSavgMRD	**0.1847**	0.1961	0.1894	0.3633	0.2168	0.2163	0.2098	0.2015	0.0845	0.0877	0.1253	0.1461
SAMEPLUSmaxHA	0.1841	**0.215**	**0.1981**	**0.3712**	**0.218**	**0.2181**	**0.2126**	**0.2028**	**0.0892**	**0.0927**	**0.1311**	**0.1594**
SAMEPLUSmaxMRD	0.1806	**0.215**	0.1944	0.367	0.2176	0.2179	0.2123	0.2025	0.0886	0.092	0.1301	0.1593

5 Conclusions

We evaluated the retrieval performances of a lightweight XML indexing and approximate search scheme currently implemented in the SIRIUS XML IR system [6, 7, 8]. At INEX 2005, SIRIUS retrieves relevant XML elements by approximate matching both the content and the structure of the XML documents. A modified weighted editing distance on XML paths is used to approximately match the documents structure while strict and fuzzy searching based on the IDF of the researched terms are used for content matching.

Our experiments show that taking into account the structural constraints improves the retrieval performances of the system and jointly shows the effectiveness of the proposed weighted editing distance on XML paths for this task. They also show that the approximate search inside XML elements implemented using our *same+* operator improve the overall performance of the ranking, compared to a more restrictive sequence search (*seq* operator), except for low recall values. The complementarities of the two operators call for the design of a new matching operator based on their combination to further improve the retrieval performance of our system.

While designing our lightweight indexing and XML approximate search system we have put forward the performance and the implementation simplicity. SIRIUS structural match is well adapted for managing mismatches in writing constraints on XML paths involving complex conditions on attributes and attributes values [6]. Unfortunately, this was not experimented in INEX 2005 campaign. SIRIUS was designed to retrieve relevant XML documents by highlighting and maintaining the relevant fragments in the document order (approach explored by the INEX CO.FetchBrowse and COS.FetchBrowse tasks). For this year, at the ad-hoc task we evaluated only a subset of its functionalities and proved its ability of retrieving relevant non overlapping XML elements within the CO.Focussed and COS.Focussed tasks. Even if SIRIUS is not able to compute dynamically the most appropriate size for a returned element, it obtained average and good quality results in the range of the 10-25-50 first ranked answers for all the tasks in which it was evaluated. This is quite encouraging since first ranked elements are the ones end users will most probably browse.

Future research work will include: further evaluations for the *FetchBrowse* strategy using the best performing *Focussed* runs; new experiments and evaluations involving semantic enrichment of the requests (at both xml tag and query term levels), index models better suited for the approximate search scheme, and new matching operators.

Acknowledgements

This work was partially supported by the ACIMD – ReMIX French grant (Reconfigurable Memory for Indexing Huge Amount of Data).

References

1. Lalmas M., INEX 2005 Retrieval Task and Result Submission Specification In INEX 2005 Workshop Pre-Proceedings, Dagstuhl, Germany, November 28–30, 2005, page 385–390, 2005.
2. Kazai, G. and Lalmas, M., INEX 2005 evaluation metrics. In Advances in XML Information Retrieval and Evaluation: Fourth Workshop of the INitiative for the Evaluation of XML Retrieval (INEX 2005), Lecture Notes in Computer Science, Vol 3977, Springer-Verlag, 2006.
3. Trotman A., and Sigurbjörnsson B., Narrowed Extended XPath I (NEXI) In Proceedings of the INEX 2004 Workshop, p. 16-40, (2004)
4. Sigurbjörnsson B., Trotman A., Geva S., Lalmas M., Larsen B., Malik S., INEX 2005 Guidelines for Topic Development. In INEX 2005 Workshop Pre-Proceedings, Dagstuhl, Germany, November 28–30, 2005, page 375–384, 2005.
5. Kamps J., de Rijke M., and Sigurbjörnsson B., The Importance of Length Normalization for XML Retrieval, Information Retrieval, Volume: 8. Issue: 4, p. 631-654, (2005)
6. Ménier G., Marteau P.F., Information retrieval in heterogeneous XML knowledge bases, The 9th International Conference on Information Processing and Magement of Uncertainty in Knowledge-Based Systems, 1-5 July 2002, Annecy, France.
7. Ménier G., Marteau P.F., PARTAGE: Software prototype for dynamic management of documents and data, ICSSEA, 29 Nov.- 1 Dec. 2005, Paris.
8. Popovici E., Marteau P.F., Ménier G., Information Retrieval of Sequential Data in Heterogeneous XML Databases, AMR 2005, 28-29 July 2005, Glasgow, (2005)
9. Tai, K.C, The tree to tree correction problem, J.ACM, 26(3):422-433, (1979)
10. Wang T.L.J, Shapiro B., Shasha D., Zhang K., Currey K.M., An algorithm for finding the largest approximately common substructures of two trees, In J. IEEE Pattern Analysis and Machine Intelligence, vol.20, N°8, August 1998.
11. Levenshtein A., Binary Codes Capable of Correcting Deletions, Insertions and Reversals, Sov.Phy. Dohl. Vol.10, P.707-710, (1966)
12. Wagner R., Fisher M., The String-to-String Correction Problem, Journal of the Association for Computing Machinery, Vol.12, No.1, p.168-173, (1974)
13. Mignet L.,Barbosa D.,Veltri P., The XML Web: A First Study, WWW 2003, May 20-24, Budapest, Hungary, (2003)
14. Carmel D., Maarek Y. S., Mandelbrod M., Mass Y. and Soffer A., Searching XML documents via XML fragments, SIGIR 2003, Toronto, Canada p. 151-158, (2003)
15. Fuhr N., Großjohann K., XIRQL: An XML query language based on information retrieval concepts, (TOIS), v.22 n.2, p.313-356, April 2004
16. Clark J., DeRose S., XML Path Language (XPath) Version 1.0, W3C Recommendation 16 November 1999, http://www.w3.org/TR/xpath.html, (1999)
17. Porter M.F., An algorithm for suffix stripping, Program, 14(3):130-137, (1980)
18. Salton G. and Buckeley C., Term-weighting approaches in automatic text retrieval, Information Processing and Management, 24, p. 513-523, (1988)
19. Mihajlovic V., Ramirez G., Westerveld T., Hiemstra D., Blok H. E., de Vries A., TIJAH Scratches INEX 2005: Vague Element Selection, Overlap, Image Search, Relevance Feedback, and Users', Pre-Proceedings of INEX 2005 Workshop, (2005)

Machine Learning Ranking and INEX'05

Jean-Noël Vittaut and Patrick Gallinari

Laboratoire d'Informatique de Paris 6
8, rue du Capitaine Scott, F-75015 Paris, France
{vittaut, gallinari}@poleia.lip6.fr

Abstract. We present a Machine Learning based ranking model which can automatically learn its parameters using a training set of annotated examples composed of queries and relevance judgments on a subset of the document elements. Our model improves the performance of a baseline Information Retrieval system by optimizing a ranking loss criterion and combining scores computed from doxels and from their local structural context. We analyze the performance of our algorithm on CO-Focussed and CO-Thourough tasks and compare it to the baseline model which is an adaptation of Okapi to Structured Information Retrieval.

1 Introduction

Different studies and developments have been recently carried out on ranking algorithms in the machine learning community. In the field of textual documents, they have been successfully used to combine features or preferences relations in tasks such as meta search [1] [2] [3], passage classification, automatic summarization [4] and recently for the combination of different sources of evidence in Information Retrieval (IR) [5]. One of the challenges of this paradigm is to reduce the complexity of the algorithms which is in the general case quadratic in the number of samples. This is why most real data applications of ranking are based on two-classes problems. Nevertheless, some linear methods has been proposed [3] [4] and under some conditions, fast rates of convergence are achieved with this class of methods [6].

Ranking algorithms work by combining features which characterize the data elements to be ranked. In our case, these features will depend on the doxel itself and on its structural context. Ranking algorithms will learn to combine these different features in an optimal way according to a specific loss function using a set of examples. It is hoped that ranking algorithms may help to improve the performance of existing techniques.

The paper is organized as follows, in section 2 we present the ranking model, in section 3 we show how we adapted it to CO-Focussed and CO-Thorough tasks. In section 4 we comment the results reached by our model and compare it to a baseline Okapi method adapted for Structured Information Retrieval (SIR).

N. Fuhr et al. (Eds.): INEX 2005, LNCS 3977, pp. 336–343, 2006.

2   Ranking Model

We present in this section a general model of ranking which can be adapted to IR or SIR. The idea of the ranking algorithms proposed in the machine learning community is to learn a total order on a set $\mathcal{X}$, which allows to compare any element pair in this set. Given this total order, we are able to order any subset of $\mathcal{X}$ in a ranking list. For instance in IR, $\mathcal{X}$ can be the set of couples (document, query), and the total order is the natural order on the document scores.

As for any machine learning technique, one needs a training set of labeled examples in order to learn how to rank. This training set will consist in ordered pairs of examples. This will provide a partial order on the elements of $\mathcal{X}$. The ranking algorithm will use this information to learn a total order on the elements of $\mathcal{X}$ and after that will allow to rank new elements. For plain IR, the partial ordering may be provided by human assessments on different documents for a given query.

2.1   Notations

Let $\mathcal{X}$ be a set of elements with a partial order $\prec$ defined on it. This means that some of the element pairs in $\mathcal{X}$ may be compared according to the $\prec$ relation. For Structured Information retrieval $\mathcal{X}$ will be the set of couples (doxel, query) for all doxels and queries in the document collection. This set is partially ordered according to the existing relevance judgments for each query.

2.2   Ranking

Let f be a function from $\mathcal{X}$ to the set of real numbers. We can associate a total order $\prec_T$ to f such that:

$$x \prec_T x' \Leftrightarrow f(x) < f(x') . \tag{1}$$

Clearly, learning the f function is the same as learning the total order. In the following, we will extend the partial order $\prec$ to a total order $\prec_T$, so we will use the same notation for both relations.

An element of $\mathcal{X}$ will be represented by a real vector of features:

$$x = (x_1, x_2, ..., x_d).$$

In our case, the features will be local scores computed on different contextual elements of a doxel. In the following, f will be a linear combination of x's features:

$$f_\omega(x) = \sum_{j=1}^{d} \omega_j x_j \tag{2}$$

where $\omega = (\omega_1, \omega_2, ..., \omega_d)$ are the parameters of the combination to be learned.

Ranking loss. f_ω is said to respect $x \prec x'$ if $f_\omega(x) < f_\omega(x')$. In this case, couple (x, x') is said to be well ordered by f_ω. The ranking loss [3] measures how much f_ω respects $\prec$.

By definition, the ranking loss measures the number of mis-ordered couples in $\mathcal{X}^2$:

$$R(\mathcal{X}, \omega) = \sum_{\substack{(x,x') \in \mathcal{X}^2 \\ x \prec x'}} \chi(x, x') \qquad (3)$$

where $\chi(x, x') = 1$ if $f_\omega(x) > f_\omega(x')$ and 0 otherwise.

Ranking aims at learning ω for minimizing (3).

Exponential loss. In practice, this expression is not very useful since χ is not differentiable, ranking algorithms use to optimize another loss criterion called the exponential loss:

$$R_e(\mathcal{X}, \omega) = \sum_{\substack{(x,x') \in \mathcal{X}^2 \\ x \prec x'}} e^{f_\omega(x) - f_\omega(x')}. \qquad (4)$$

If is straightforward that $R(\mathcal{X}, \omega) \leq R_e(\mathcal{X}, \omega)$. (4) is differentiable and convex, and then can be minimized using standard optimization techniques. Minimizing (4) will allow to minimize $R(\mathcal{X}, \omega)$.

We can compute a gradient descent. The components of the gradient of R_e are:

$$\frac{\partial R_e}{\partial \omega_k}(\mathcal{X}, \omega) = \sum_{\substack{(x,x') \in \mathcal{X}^2 \\ x \prec x'}} (x_k - x'_k) e^{f_\omega(x) - f_\omega(x')}. \qquad (5)$$

With no more hypothesis, the computation of (5) is in $O(|\mathcal{X}|^2)$.

3   Application to CO Tasks

3.1   Definitions

Let denote $\mathcal{D}$ is the set of doxels for all the documents in the collection and $\mathcal{Q}$ the set of CO queries. $\mathcal{X} = \mathcal{Q} \times \mathcal{D}$ is the set of elements we want to order.

We suppose that there exists a partial order $\prec$ on $\mathcal{X} = \mathcal{Q} \times \mathcal{D}$, this partial order will reflect for some queries, the evidence we have about preferences between doxels provided via manual assessments. Note that these relevance assessments are only needed for a few queries and doxels in the collection. We consider here the task which consists in producing a ranked list of doxels which answer the query $q \in \mathcal{Q}$. For that, we will train the ranking model to learn a total strict order on $\mathcal{X}$.

3.2   Vector Representation

Each element $x \in \mathcal{X}$ is represented by a vector $(x_1, x_2, ..., x_d)$ were x_i represents some feature which could be useful to order elements of $\mathcal{X}$. Let denote $\mathcal{L}$ the set of doxel types, which are defined according to the DTD of the document collection: article, abstract, sections, paragraphs, lists...

We used the following combination:

$$f_w(x) = w_1^l + w_2^l Okapi(x) + w_3^l Okapi(parent(x)) + w_4^l Okapi(document(x))$$

where l is the node type of x and $Okapi$ is the SIR adapted Okapi model [7] described in [8]. This adaptation consists in using doxels rather than documents for computing the term frequencies, and using as normalization factor for each doxel, the mean size of the doxels with the same node type.

This combination take into account the information provided by the context of the doxel and the structural information given by the node type of the doxel.

This combination leads to the following vector representation:

$$x = \left((x_1^{l_1}, x_2^{l_1}, x_3^{l_1}, x_4^{l_1}), (x_1^{l_2}, x_2^{l_2}, x_3^{l_2}, x_4^{l_2}), ..., (x_1^{l_{|\mathcal{L}|}}, x_2^{l_{|\mathcal{L}|}}, x_3^{l_{|\mathcal{L}|}}, x_4^{l_{|\mathcal{L}|}}) \right)$$

where $|\mathcal{L}|$ is the number of different doxel types in the collection.

In the above expression all vector components of the form $(x_1^{l_i}, x_2^{l_i}, x_3^{l_i}, x_4^{l_i})$ are equal to $(0,0,0,0)$ except for one where l_i is the doxel type of x which is equal to $(1, Okapi(x), Okapi(parent(x)), Okapi(document(x)))$.

3.3   Reduction of Complexity

In this section, we use some properties of SIR in order to decrease the complexity of the computation of (4) and (5).

Queries. Comparing elements from different queries has no sense. We can define a partition $\mathcal{X} = \bigcup_{q \in \mathcal{Q}} \mathcal{X}_q$, where

$$\mathcal{X}_q = \{x = (d, q') \in \mathcal{X} / q' = q\}$$

and we can rewrite (4):

$$R_e(\mathcal{X}, \omega) = \sum_{q \in \mathcal{Q}} \left\{ \sum_{\substack{(x,x') \in \mathcal{X}_q \times \mathcal{X}_q \\ x \prec x'}} e^{f_\omega(x)} e^{-f_\omega(x')} \right\}. \tag{6}$$

Assessments. For each subset $\mathcal{X}_q$, the preferences among doxels are expressed according to a several discrete dimensions. We have:

- an information of exhaustivity, which measures how much a doxel answers the totality of an information need (0 not exhaustive, ..., 3 fully exhaustive)
- an information of specificity, which measures how much a doxel answers only the information need (0 not specific, ..., 3 means fully specific)

There is no preference between doxels sharing the same value of exhaustivity and specificity.

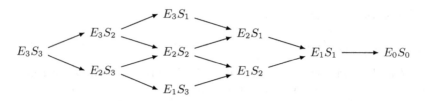

Fig. 1. Graph representing the order between elements for a given query, according to the two dimensional discrete scale of INEX. Doxels labeled E_3S_3 must be the highest ranked, and doxels labeled E_0S_0 the lowest ranked.

An assessment is a couple (exhaustivity, specificity). Let denote $\mathcal{A}$ the set of assessments and $A(x)$ the assessment of element x. We can define a partition $\mathcal{X}_q = \bigcup_{a \in \mathcal{A}} \mathcal{X}_q^a$, where

$$\mathcal{X}_q^a = \{x \in \mathcal{X}_q / A(x) = a\}.$$

We can rewrite (6):

$$R_e(\mathcal{X}, w) = \sum_{q \in \mathcal{Q}} \sum_{a \in \mathcal{A}} \left\{ \left(\sum_{x \in \mathcal{X}_q^a} e^{f_w(x)} \right) \left(\sum_{\substack{b \in \mathcal{A} \\ \mathcal{X}_q^b \prec \mathcal{X}_q^a}} \sum_{x \in \mathcal{X}_q^b} e^{-f_w(x)} \right) \right\}. \qquad (7)$$

where $\mathcal{X}_q^b \prec \mathcal{X}_q^a$ means that the assessments of the elements of $\mathcal{X}_q^a$ are better than those of $\mathcal{X}_q^b$. An possible order between assessments is represented in figure 1.

The complexity for computing this expression is $O(K \cdot |\mathcal{Q}| \cdot |\mathcal{X}|)$ whereas it is $O(|\mathcal{X}|^2)$ for (4) where K is the number of sets in the partition of $\mathcal{X}$. The worst case occurs when $K = \mathcal{X}$.

3.4 Gradient Descent

Since (7) is convex, we can use a gradient descent technique to minimize it. The components of the gradient has the following form:

$$\frac{\partial R_e}{\partial w_k}(\mathcal{X}, w) = \sum_{q \in \mathcal{Q}} \sum_{a \in \mathcal{A}} \left\{ \left(\sum_{x \in \mathcal{X}_q^a} x_k e^{f_w(x)} \right) \left(\sum_{\substack{b \in \mathcal{A} \\ \mathcal{X}_q^b \prec \mathcal{X}_q^a}} \sum_{x \in \mathcal{X}_q^b} e^{-f_w(x)} \right) \right.$$
$$\left. + \left(\sum_{x \in \mathcal{X}_q^a} e^{f_w(x)} \right) \left(\sum_{\substack{b \in \mathcal{A} \\ \mathcal{X}_q^b \prec \mathcal{X}_q^a}} \sum_{x \in \mathcal{X}_q^b} -x_k e^{-f_w(x)} \right) \right\}. \qquad (8)$$

The complexity for computing the gradient is the same $(O(K \cdot |\mathcal{Q}| \cdot |\mathcal{X}|))$ as that of (7).

4   Experiments

4.1   Learning Base

We used the series of topics and assessments from the INEX 2003 and 2004 collections as a learning base. We will comment the results on 2005 collection.

4.2   Filtering

In CO-Focussed task, overlapping doxels were not allowed. In order to suppress all overlapping elements from the lists computed by the ranking algorithm, we used a strategy which consists in removing all elements which are overlapping with an element ranked higher in the list.

As for Okapi model, we used the same strategy exept that biggest doxels like articles or bdy's were not allowed in the final ranking list to reach better performance.

4.3   Results

We comment the results obtained with the ncXG official metric with generalized quantization which is more related to the ranking loss criterion and the different levels of assessment we have used in our model.

CO-Focussed. We have plotted in figure 2 the evaluation of the lists produced by the ranking algorithm and by the modified Okapi when overlap is not authorized. We can see that the ranking algorithm performs better than Okapi. In some parts of the plot, the difference between the two models is not large: this is due to the post filtering of the lists. The ranked lists had not been optimized for non overlapping doxels since there is no notion of overlap in the exponential loss.

The table 1 shows that the ranking model is always better than its baseline Okapi model, and that is quite good to retrieve the most informative doxels in the begining of the list.

Table 1. Rank of Okapi and ranking models among all participant submissions using MAncXG metric for CO-Focussed task

	@1	@2	@3	@4	@5	@10	@15	@25	@50	@100	@500	@1000	@1500
Okapi	21	20	19	19	18	18	19	19	19	18	20	20	20
Ranking	1	1	1	1	2	7	11	13	15	14	10	14	13

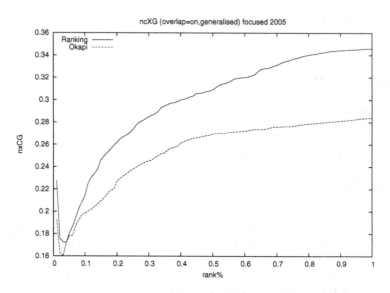

Fig. 2. Performance of ranking and Okapi models for CO-Focussed task evaluated with the cumulated gain based metric ncXG

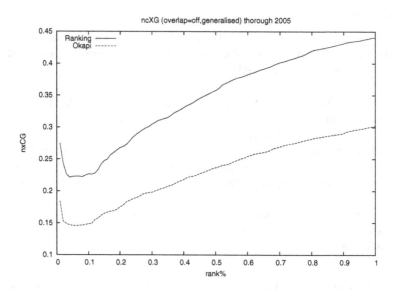

Fig. 3. Performance of ranking and Okapi models for CO-Thorough task evaluated with the cumulated gain based metric ncXG

CO-Thorough. Figure 3 show the evaluation of the lists produced by the ranking algorithm and modified Okapi when overlap is authorized. We can see that the ranking algorithm performs clearly better than Okapi and the difference in performance is superior than in the Focussed task.

Table 2. Rank of Okapi and ranking models among all participant submissions using MAncXG metric for CO-Thorough task

	@1	@2	@3	@4	@5	@10	@15	@25	@50	@100	@500	@1000	@1500
Okapi	26	22	26	26	26	31	34	37	38	38	35	32	32
Ranking	1	1	1	2	2	3	3	4	11	12	5	5	6

The table 2 shows that the ranking model is always better than its baseline Okapi model, and that is quite good to retrieve the most informative doxels in the begining of the list. This can be explained by the expression of the ranking loss which penalize more a irrelevant doxel when it is located in the begining of the list.

5 Conclusion

We have described a new model for CO tasks which relies on a combination of scores from the Okapi model and takes into account the document structure. This score combination is learned from a training set by a ranking algorithm.

For both tasks, the ranking algorithm has been able to increase by a large amount the performance of the baseline Okapi. Ranking methods thus appear as a promising direction for improving SIR search engine performance. It remains to perform tests with additional features (for example the scores of additional IR systems).

References

1. Cohen, W.W., Schapire, R.E., Singer, Y.: Learning to order things. In Jordan, M.I., Kearns, M.J., Solla, S.A., eds.: Advances in Neural Information Processing Systems. Volume 10., The MIT Press (1998)
2. Bartell, B.T., Cottrell, G.W., Belew, R.K.: Automatic combination of multiple ranked retrieval systems. In: Research and Development in Information Retrieval. (1994) 173–181
3. Freund, Y., Iyer, R., Schapire, R.E., Singer, Y.: An efficient boosting algorithm for combining preferences. In: Proceedings of ICML-98, 15th International Conference on Machine Learning. (1998)
4. Amini, M.R., Usunier, N., Gallinari, P.: Automatic text summarization based on word-clusters and ranking algorithms. In: ECIR. (2005) 142–156
5. Craswell, N., Robertson, S., Zaragoza, H., Taylor, M.: Relevance weighting for query independent evidence. In: SIGIR '05: Proceedings of the 28th annual international ACM SIGIR conference. (2005)
6. Clémençon, S., Lugosi, G., Vayatis, N.: Ranking and scoring using empirical risk minimization. In Auer, P., Meir, R., eds.: COLT. Volume 3559 of Lecture Notes in Computer Science., Springer (2005) 1–15
7. Robertson, S.E., Walker, S., Hancock-Beaulieu, M., Gull, A., Lau, M.: Okapi at TREC. In: Text REtrieval Conference. (1992) 21–30
8. Vittaut, J.N., Piwowarski, B., Gallinari, P.: An algebra for structured queries in bayesian networks. In: Advances in XML Information Retrieval. Third Workshop of the INitiative for the Evaluation of XML Retrieval. (2004)

Relevance Feedback for Structural Query Expansion

Ralf Schenkel and Martin Theobald

Max-Planck-Institut für Informatik, Saarbrücken, Germany
{schenkel, mtb}@mpi-inf.mpg.de

Abstract. Keyword-based queries are an important means to retrieve information from XML collections with unknown or complex schemas. Relevance Feedback integrates relevance information provided by a user to enhance retrieval quality. For keyword-based XML queries, feedback engines usually generate an expanded keyword query from the content of elements marked as relevant or nonrelevant. This approach that is inspired by text-based IR completely ignores the semistructured nature of XML. This paper makes the important step from pure content-based to structural feedback. It presents two independent approaches that include structural dimensions in a feedback-driven query evaluation: The first approach reranks the result list of a keyword-based search engine, using structural features derived from results with known relevance. The second approach expands a keyword query into a full-fledged content-and-structure query with weighted conditions.

1   Introduction and Motivation

XML has seen increasing importance recently to represent large amounts of semistructured or textual information in digital libraries, intranets, or the Web, so information retrieval on XML data is growing more and more important. XML search engines employ the ranked retrieval paradigm for producing relevance-ordered result lists rather than merely using XPath or XQuery for Boolean retrieval. An important subset of XML search engines uses keyword-based queries [2, 7, 30], which is especially important for collections of documents with unknown or highly heterogeneous schemas. However, simple keyword queries cannot exploit the often rich annotations available in XML, so the results of an initial query are often not very satisfying.

Relevance Feedback is an important way to enhance retrieval quality by integrating relevance information provided by a user. In XML retrieval, existing feedback engines usually generate an expanded keyword query from the content of elements marked as relevant or nonrelevant. This approach that is inspired by text-based IR completely ignores the semistructured nature of XML.

This paper makes the important step from content-based to structural feedback. We present two independent approaches to exploit the structure of XML with relevance feedback:

N. Fuhr et al. (Eds.): INEX 2005, LNCS 3977, pp. 344–357, 2006.

1. Using the feedback approach by Rocchio [20], we create new content and structural features that are used to rerank the results of a keyword-based engine, enabling structural feedback for engines that support only keyword-based queries.
2. We extend the feedback approach by Robertson and Sparck-Jones [19] to expand a keyword-based query into a possibly complex content-and-structure query that specifies new constraints on the structure of results, in addition to "standard" content-based query expansion. The resulting expanded query has weighted structural and content constraints and can be fed into a full-fledged XML search engine like our own TopX [26] Search Engine.

2   Related Work

Relevance feedback has already been considered for document retrieval for a long time, starting with Rocchio's query expansion algorithm [20]. Ruthven and Lalmas [21] give an extensive overview about relevance feedback for unstructured data, including the assessment of relevance feedback algorithms.

Relevance feedback in XML IR is not yet that popular. Of the few papers that have considered it, most concentrate on query expansion based on the content of elements with known relevance [4, 13, 25, 29]. Some of these focus on blind ("pseudo") feedback, others on feedback provided by users. Pan et al. [15] apply user feedback to recompute similarities in the ontology used for query evaluation.

Even fewer papers have considered structural query expansion [8, 9, 14, 16, 17]. Mihajloviè et al. [14, 16, 17] proposed deriving the relevance of an element from its tag name, but could not show any significant gain in retrieval effectiveness. Additionally, they considered hand-tuned structural features specific for the INEX benchmark (e.g., the name of the journal to which an element's document belongs), but again without a significant positive effect. In a follow-up to this work, Ramírez et al. [17] could show significant improvements with journal names. In contrast, our general approach for exploiting feedback can be applied with the INEX data, but does not rely on any INEX-specific things.

Hlaoua and Boughanem [8] consider common prefixes of relevant element's paths as additional query constraints, but don't provide any experimental evaluation of their approach.

Gonçalvez et al. [5] use relevance feedback to construct a restricted class of structured queries (namely field-term pairs) on structured bibliographic data, using a Bayesian network for query evaluation. While they did not consider XML, their overall approach is somewhat similar to our reranking framework presented in Section 4.

The work of Hsu et al. [9] is closest to our approach. They use blind feedback to expand a keyword-based query with structural constraints derived from a neighborhood of elements that contain the keywords in the original query. In contrast, our approach considers the whole document instead of only a fragment, can generate constraints with negative weight, and integrates also content-based constraints.

3   Formal Model and Notation

3.1   Data Model

We consider a fixed corpus of D XML documents with their elements. For such an element e, $t(e)$ denotes its tag name and $d(e)$ the document to which it belongs.

The *content* $c(e)$ of an element e is the set of all terms (after stopword removal and optional stemming) in the textual content of the element itself and all its descendants. For each term t and element e, we maintain a weight $w_e(t)$. This can be a binary weight ($w_e(t) = 1$ if the term occurs in e's content and 0 otherwise), a tf-idf style [12] or a BM25-based [1, 28] weight that captures the importance of t in e's content. The *content* $c(d)$ of a document d is defined as the content $c(r)$ of its root element r.

We maintain a number of statistics about the occurrence of terms in documents and elements: The *document frequency* df_t of a term t is the number of documents in which the term appears in the content. Analogously, the *element frequency* ef_t of a term t is the number of elements in which the term appears in the content.

3.2   Queries and Relevance of Results

We use an extended version of INEX's query language NEXI [27]. NEXI basically corresponds to XPath restricted to the `descendants-or-self` and `self` axis and extended by an IR-style `about` predicate to specify conditions that relevant elements should fulfil. The wildcard symbol '*' matches any tag and can be used to formulate keyword queries in NEXI. We extend NEXI with additional weights for each content constraint. A typical extended NEXI query looks like the following:

`//article[about(.,"0.8*XML")//*[about(.//p,"0.4*IR -0.2*index")]`

The result granularity of such a query are elements. We currently assume that the relevance of an element with respect to a query is measured with the strict quantization, i.e., an element is either relevant or nonrelevant.

3.3   Feedback Model

We consider a keyword query $q = \{q_1, \ldots, q_p\}$ with a set $E = \{e_1, \ldots, e_l\}$ of results with known relevance. i.e., elements for which a user has assigned an exhaustivness value $e(e)$ and a specificity value $s(e)$. Using the strict quantization, we say that an element e is *relevant* for the query if both $e(e)$ and $s(e)$ are maximal, yielding a set $E^+ = \{e_1^+, \ldots, e_R^+\}$ of relevant elements and a set $E^- = \{e_1^-, \ldots, e_N^-\}$ of nonrelevant elements.

Note that even though we consider only binary relevance, it is possible to extend the mechanism presented here to approaches where relevance is measured with a probability-like number between 0 and 1, for example by representing E^+ and E^- as probabilistic sets.

4   Reranking Results of Keyword-Only Runs

Our first approach aims at identifying documents that contain relevant elements and paths of relevant elements, in addition to standard content-based query expansion. We first compute the results for a keyword query with an existing keyword-based engine and ask a user for relevance feedback. Based on the user input, we compute certain classes of *features* from elements with relevance feedback and select those that best discriminate relevant from nonrelevant results. Using these features, we compute additional scores for element-feature-matches for all remaining elements and rerank them by their combined score. This approach allows to evaluate certain classes of structural constraints with engines that support only keyword-based queries.

For space restrictions we can only informally present our approach here; a more detailed and formal description can be found in [23].

4.1   Features Used for Reranking

We derive the following classes of candidates for query expansion from an element with known relevance:

- all terms of the element's content together with their score (C features),
- tag-term pairs within the element's document (D features), and
- features derived from the path of the element (P features).

The system can be extended with additional classes of features.

Content Features. Content-based feedback is widely used in standard IR and has also made its way into XML retrieval [13, 25]. It expands the original query with new, weighted keywords that are derived from the content of elements with known relevance. As an example, consider the keyword query "multimedia information" retrieval (this is topic 178 from the INEX topic collection). From the feedback of a user, we may derive that elements that contain the terms 'brightness', 'annotation', or 'rgb' are likely to be relevant, whereas elements with 'hypermedia' or 'authoring' are often irrelevant.

Document Features. Unlike standard text retrieval where the unit of retrieval are whole documents, XML retrieval focuses on retrieving parts of documents, namely elements. Information in other parts of a document with a relevant element can help to characterize documents in which relevant elements occur. A natural kind of such information is the content of other elements in such documents.

As an example, consider again INEX topic 178 ("multimedia information" retrieval). We may derive from user feedback that documents with the terms 'pattern, analysis, machine, intelligence' in the journal title (i.e., those from the 'IEEE Transactions on Pattern Analysis and Machine Learing') are likely to contain relevant elements. The same may hold for documents that cite papers by Gorkani and Huang (who are co-authors of the central paper about the

QBIC system), whereas documents that cite papers with the term 'interface' in their title probably don't contain relevant elements (as they probably deal with interface issues in multimedia applications).

Other possible structural features include twigs, occurence of elements with certain names in a document, or combination of path fragments with terms. Further exploration of this diversity is subject to future work.

Path Features. Elements with certain tag names are more likely to be relevant than elements with other tag names. As an example, a keyword query may return entries from the index of a book or journal with high scores as they often contain exactly the requested keywords, but such elements are usually not relevant. Additionally, queries may prefer either large elements (such as whole articles) or small elements (such as single paragraphs), but rarely both. However, experiments show that tag names alone do not bear enough information to enhance retrieval quality, but the whole path of a result element plays an important role. As an example, the relevance of a paragraph may depend on whether it is in the body of an article (with a path like `/article/bdy/sec/p` from the root element), in the description of the vitae of the authors (with a path like `/article/bm/vt/p`), or in the copyright statement of the journal (with a path like `/article/fm/cr/p`).

As element tag names are too limited, but complete paths may be too strict, we consider the following six classes of *path fragments*, with complete paths and tag names being special cases:

- P_1: prefixes of paths, e.g., `article/#`,`/article/fm/#`
- P_2: infixes of paths, e.g., `#/fm/#`
- P_3: subpaths of length 2, e.g., `#/sec/p/#`
- P_4: paths with wildcards, e.g, `#/bm/#/p/#`
- P_5: suffixes of paths, e.g., `#/fig`, `#/article`
- P_6: full paths, e.g, `/article/bdy/sec`

Mihajlovià et al. [14] used a variant of P_5, namely tag names of result elements, but did not see any improvement. In fact, only a combination of fragments from several classes leads to enhancements in result quality. Experiments in [23] show that the best results are yielded with a combination of P1, P3 and P4, whereas using P5 or P6 alone actually reduced the quality of results below the baseline without feedback.

4.2   Feature Weights and Selection

We compute the weight for all features using the standard Rocchio weight [20]. We tried several variations, including binary and weighted Rocchio weights, and have yet to explore the whole space of solutions.

Among the (usually many) possible features, we choose the n_c content features and n_s document features with highest absolute weights. If there are too many with the same weight, we use the mutual information of the feature's score

distribution among the elements with known relevance and the relevance distribution as a tie breaker. If there are no positive examples and mutual information
is zero for all features, we use the feature's document frequency (the number of
documents in which this feature occurs) for tie breaking then, preferring features
that occur infrequently.

4.3   Reranking Results

For each element that occurs in the baseline run, we compute an additional
score for each feature class. The score for each feature class is computed in a
separate vector space where each dimension corresponds to a feature that occurs
in at least one element. The score of the element for this class is then computed
as the cosine of the vector with the selected features for this dimension and
the element's feature vector. Each of the scores is normalized to the interval
$[-1.0, 1.0]$. The overall score of the element is then the sum of its score from the
baseline run and its additional scores.

This scoring model can easily integrate new dimensions for feedback beyond
content, path and document features, even if they use a completely different
model (like a probabilistic model). It only requires that the relevance of an
element to a new feedback dimension can be measured with a score between -1
and 1. It is simple to map typical score functions to this interval by normalization
and transformation. As an example, the transformation rule for a probability p,
$0 \leq p \leq 1$, is $2 \cdot p - 1$.

5   Generating Structural Queries from Feedback

Keyword-based queries are the best way to pose queries without knowledge of
the underlying schema of the data, but they cannot exploit the structure of
documents. As an example, consider the keyword query (query 230 from the
INEX benchmark [11]) `+brain research +"differential geometry"`, asking
for applications of differential geometry in brain research. In relevant results,
"brain research" is usually the topic of the whole article, while "differential
geometry" is typically the topic of a section. A query with constraints on both
content and structure would probably yield a lot more relevant results, but it
is impossible to formulate a query like the following without knowledge of the
underlying schema:

`//article[about(.,brain research)]//sec[about(.,differential geometry)]`

We studied the content-and-structure queries from INEX to find patterns that
are regularily used in such queries to describe relevant elements, in addition to
content conditions on the result element. A canonical example for such a query
is the following:

`//article[about(.,"RDF") and about(//bib,"W3C")]//sec[about(.,"query")`
`and about(//par,"performance")]`

This is a content-and-structure version of the simpler keyword query "RDF
W3C query performane". In contrast to the keyword query, the structured query

specifies a tag (or, more generally, a set of tags) that relevant elements should have ("I am interested in sections about 'query'"). Additionally, this query contains constraints on the content of descendants of relevant elements ("sections with a paragraph about 'performance'"), the content of ancestors ("sections in articles about 'RDF'"), and the content of descendants of ancestors ("sections in articles that cite a paper from the 'W3C'").

As such a content-and-structure query specifies much more precisely the conditions that relevant elements must satisfy, we can expect that a search engine will return more relevant results for a content-and-structure query than for the keyword query, provided that the content-and-structure query correctly captures the same information need as the keyword query. Our feedback framework aims at generating a content-and-structure query from a keyword query, exploiting relevance feedback provided by a user for some results of the keyword query.

For space restrictions we can only informally present our approach here; a more detailed and formal description can be found in [24].

5.1 Candidates for Query Expansion

Following the discussion in the beginning of this section, we derive the following classes of candidates for query expansion from an element with known relevance:

- all terms of the element's content together with their score (C candidates),
- all tag-term pairs of descendants of the element in its document, together with their score (D candidates),
- all tag-term pairs of ancestors of the element in its document, together with their score (A candidates), and
- all tag-term pairs of descendants of ancestors of the element in its document, together with their score and the ancestor's tag (AD candidates).

The system can be extended with additional classes of candidates like tags, twigs, or paths, which is subject to future work.

The candidate set of an element is the set of all possible candidates for this element. We extend the notion of frequencies from terms to candidates as follows: the element frequency of a candidate is the number of elements where the candidate appears in the candidate set, and its document frequency is the number of documents with at least one element with the candidate in their candidate set.

5.2 Candidate Weights and Selection

To weight the different candidates, we apply an extension of the well-known Robertson-Sparck-Jones weight [19] to element-level retrieval in XML, applying it for elements instead of documents:

$$w_{RSJ}(c) = \log \frac{r_c + 0.5}{R - r_c + 0.5} + \log \frac{E - ef_c - R + r_c + 0.5}{ef_c - r_c + 0.5}$$

Here, for a candidate c, r_c denotes the number of relevant elements which contain the candidate c in their candidate set, R denotes the number of relevant elements,

E the number of elements in the collection, and ef_c the element frequency of the candidate.

The set of all possible expansion candidates is usually very large and contains many unimportant and misleading expansions, so we have to select the best b of them for generating the expanded query. This problem already exists for content-based expansion of keyword queries, and several possible weights have been proposed in the literature that go beyond naively ordering terms by their weight. We use the so-called Robertson Selection Values (RSV) proposed by Robertson [18]. For a candidate c, its RSV has the form $RSV(c) = w_{RSJ}(c) \cdot (p - q)$, where $p = r_c/R$ is the estimated probability of the candidate occurring in a relevant element's candidate set and q is the probability that it occurs in a nonrelevant element's set. We ignore candidates that occur only within the documents of elements with known relevance as they have no potential to generate more relevant results outside these documents. We order the union of the remaining candidates by their RSV and choose the top b of them, where b is a configuration parameter of the system. To be able to generate a valid NEXI query in the next step, we have to limit the A and AD candidates chosen to contain the same ancestor tag.

5.3 Generating an Expanded Query

Using the top-b candidates, we generate a content-and-structure query from the original keyword query. This expansion is actually straight-forward, and the generated query has the following general structure:

```
//ancestor-tag[A+AD constraints]//*[keywords+C+D constraints]
```

As an example, if the original query was 'XML' and we selected the A candidate (anc,article,'IR'), the AD candidate (article,bib,'index') and the D candidate (desc,p,'index'), the expanded query would be

```
//article[about(.,'IR') and about(//bib,'index')]//*[about(.,'XML')
and about(//p,'index')]
```

Each of the expansions is weighted, where the weight is the candidate's RSJ weight adjusted by a factor that depends on the candidate's class. C and D candidates help finding new relevant results, so they should get a high weight; we allow for C and D conditions at most the weight of all original keywords (to make sure that the new constraints don't dominate the query's results). As an example, for a query with four keywords and six C and D expansions, the factor for each expansion is $\frac{4}{6}$. On the other hand, A and AD conditions are satisfied by most – if not all – elements of a document, so they generate a huge amount of new result elements, most of which will be nonrelevant. Their weight should therefore be smaller than the weight of C and D conditions. We choose a fraction β of the accumulated weight of existing keyword conditions, with $\beta = 0.2$ in our experiments.

6 Architecture and Implementation

We have implemented the reranking approach from Section 4 and the query expansion approach from Section 5 within an automated system that can import queries and results from INEX and automatically generate feedback for the top-k results, using the existing INEX assessments.

Our Java-based implementation requires that important information about elements is precomputed: unique identifiers for the element (`eid`) and its document (`did`), its pre and post order to facilitate the evaluation of structural query conditions like the XPath axes [6] or any other similar information, its tag, and its terms (after stemming and stopword removal), together with their score. This information is stored in a database table with schema (<u>did</u>,<u>eid</u>,<u>term</u>,tag,pre, post,score) that contains one tuple for each distinct term of an element. Our current prototype reuses the `TagTermFeatures` table of TopX (see [26]) that already provides this information. On the database side, we provide indexes on (`eid`,`did`) to efficiently find $d(e)$ for an element e and on (`did`) to efficiently collect all elements of a document. Inverse element and document frequencies of the different candidate classes are precomputed (e.g., while initially parsing the collection) and stored in database tables, too.

7   Evaluation of Feedback Runs

The evaluation of feedback runs for XML IR is a problem that has not yet been solved in a satisfying way. People have agreed that simply comparing the results of a run with feedback to the baseline run (which we call *plain* later) is unfair as the new run has information about relevant elements and hence is biased. The INEX Relevance Feedback track has used two different measures so far:

- In 2004, a variant of the residual collection technique was proposed [1]. Here, all XML elements with known relevance must be removed from the collection before evaluation of the results with feedback takes place. This means not only each element used or observed in the RF process but also all descendants of that element must be removed from the collection (i.e., the residual collection, against which the feedback query is evaluated, must contain no descendant of that element). All ancestors of that element are retained in the residual collection.
- In 2005, the rank of results with know relevance is frozen, thus assessing only the effect of reranking the results with unknown relevance. We label this approach *freezeTop* as usually the top-k results are used for feedback and hence frozen.

Using the residual collection approach opens up a variety of different evaluation techniques:

- *resColl-result*: only the elements for which feedback is given are removed from the collection,
- *resColl-desc*: the elements for which feedback is given and all their descendants are removed from the collection (this is the technique used in this year's RF track),

---

[1] This is stated on the official homepage of the INEX 2004 RF track [10]. We do not know to which extend it was really used by the participants.

– *resColl-anc*: the elements for which feedback is given and all their ancestors are removed from the collection, and
– *resColl-doc*: for each element for which feedback is given, the whole document is removed from the collection.

We evaluate our approaches with all six evaluation techniques in the following section and try to find out if there are any anomalies.

8 Experimental Results

8.1 Official Runs

We submitted reranking runs for the best CO.Thorough runs of our TopX engine [26] (`MPII_TopX_CO.Thorough_exppred`) and our XXL engine [22] (`XXL++`; `CO.Thorough;andish;noExp`), using 5 C and 5 D features. Additionally, we submitted naive reranking runs that simply boost the score of elements within documents with at least one known relevant element (from the feedback). For the structural query expansion technique, we submitted only a run based on the TopX baseline run (this approach is implemented only on top of TopX), using the best 10 of all expansion candidates. For the official runs, the algorithms were provided with the relevance (exhaustivity and specificity) of the top 20 results of the baseline run. Using the *freeze-top* approach, these results with known relevance are replicated at the top of the newly generated runs. The evaluation measured absolute and relative gain over the corresponding baseline runs for the nxCG[50] and ep/gr metrics with the strict, generalized and generalisedLifted quantizations.

For all evaluations, the reranking runs outperformed the query expansion approach and most (usually all) runs submitted by other participants, with peak relative gains of 335% (for the TopX-based non-naive reranking with ep/gr and strict). The naive reranking runs did surprisingly well, with peak relative gains of 196% for the same metrics and quantization. The query expansion approach consistently gave less improvements than the reranking approaches; our experiments with the old inex_eval metric (see below) yielded the opposite result, so this needs further exploration.

8.2 Additional Runs

For the additional unofficial runs that were created after the official deadline, we used a CO.Thorough run created with an enhanced version of TopX engine for the 2005 CO topics[2]. Table 1 shows the macro-averaged precision for this run for the top-k ranked elements per topic, for different k; this corresponds to the average fraction of relevant results among the elements used for top-k feedback.

---

[2] The main reason for the relatively low MAP value of this run compared to our official run is the result of topic 228 where the new run ranks the only result in rank 2 instead of 1, yielding a MAP difference for this topic of about 0.7.

Table 1. Precision at k for the baseline run

k	10	15	20
prec@k	0.0593	0.0519	0.0500

Note that the average precision is much lower than in previous experiments with the INEX 2003 and 2004 CO topics where TopX yielded an average precision of 0.231 at the top-5 and still 0.174 at the top-20 results. We can effectively use only 10 of the 40 2005 CO topics (those with assessments and with at least one relevant result among the top-20 results) for the experiments, which makes the significance of the experiments at least questionable and at the same time explains the relatively low improvements shown in the following subsections. Table 2 gives some more information on this issue: it shows the number of topics in the baseline run that have a certain number of relevant results among the top k, for varying k. Again, it is evident that most topics do not have any relevant results at all. As an additional problem, there are some topics with only a few relevant results, which makes possible that slight changes in the order of results cause huge differences in the resulting MAP values. We decided therefore to present only our results with top-20 feedback in the following as the other results would not be significant anyway.

Table 2. Number of topics in the baseline run with r relevant results among the top k results

k/r	0	1	2	3	4	5	6
5	23	1	3	0	0	0	-
10	19	5	0	2	0	1	0
15	18	5	0	2	1	0	1
20	17	4	1	3	0	0	2

For each run, we measured the MAP using inex_eval with the strict quantization and the latest set of assessments. We plan to evaluate our results with other metrics in the future.

Results for Reranking Queries. Table 3 shows the MAP values of our experiments with different combinations of features to rerank the initial results, providing relevance feedback for a different number of top elements of the baseline run and selecting the best 5 features of each dimension, for the different evaluation techniques.

The results are surprisingly different from our earlier results in [23]: the absolute improvements are quite small, and the best results are achieved with either only P, only D, or both candidates. We attribute this to the fact that there are at most 10 topics with relevant results in the top-k; the remaining topics provide only negative feedback which seems to be not helpful here. Additionally, it

Table 3. MAP values for top-20 feedback runs with different configurations and different evaluation methods, for the reranking approach

evaluation	baseline	C	P	C+P	D	C+D	D+P	C+D+P
plain	0.0367	0.0465	0.1008	0.0534	0.0911	0.0492	**0.1120**	0.0563
resColl-result	0.0262	0.0343	**0.0581**	0.0216	0.0412	0.0312	0.0579	0.0228
resColl-anc	0.0267	0.0340	0.0581	0.0198	0.0400	0.0297	**0.0589**	0.0219
resColl-desc	0.0330	0.0180	0.0489	0.0142	0.0284	0.0132	**0.0498**	0.0151
resColl-doc	0.0309	0.0140	**0.0480**	0.0114	0.0249	0.0097	0.0468	0.0126
freezeTop	0.0367	0.0367	0.0371	0.0353	**0.0373**	0.0369	0.0362	0.0358

is evident that the different evaluation methods don't agree at all about which combination gives the best results. Other than that, it is interesting that some runs (like the D run which looks like the absolutely best choice with the freeze-Top evaluation) do great with some evaluation techniques, but perform worse than the baseline with others. This is an anomaly that should be investigated further.

Results for Queries with Structural Constraints. Table 4 shows a comparison of MAP values with the different evaluation techniques of our experiments with different combinations of candidate classes for query expansion, providing relevance feedback for the top 20 elements of the baseline run and selecting the best 10 candidates for expansion.

The results are less impressive than we had expected after earlier experiments with the 2003 and 2004 CO topics. The best of our techniques (which consistently is the combination of all candidate classes for all five evaluation techniques, not counting the plain run) yields a performance gain of about 5%–20%, whereas we could show up to 100% in the other experiments (with resColl-desc). We think that there are mainly two reasons for this difference: The 2005 topics are inherently more difficult than the older topics (which is also reflected in the much lower MAP scores for the best runs this year), and there are only 10 topics where our approaches have a chance to enhance the quality (because Robertson-Sparck-Jones weights are not useful without relevant results) with top-20 feedback and

Table 4. MAP values for top-20 feedback runs with different configurations and different evaluation methods, for the query expansion approach

evaluation	baseline	C	D	C+D	A	AD	A+AD	A+C+D+AD
plain	0.0367	0.0419	**0.0707**	0.0406	0.0646	0.0663	0.0654	0.0513
resColl-result	0.0262	0.0294	0.0300	0.0295	0.0309	0.0306	0.0294	**0.0324**
resColl-anc	0.0267	0.0350	0.0356	0.0305	0.0298	0.0294	0.0296	**0.0366**
resColl-desc	0.0330	0.0353	0.0355	0.0355	0.0363	0.353	0.0346	**0.0365**
resColl-doc	0.0309	0.0317	0.0313	0.0314	0.0321	0.0310	0.0315	**0.0325**
freezeTop	0.0367	0.0378	0.0374	0.0375	0.0384	0.0378	0.0380	**0.0387**

even fewer for the other runs. Absolute values are slightly higher than the values achieved with the reranking approach, so choosing the best candidates out of a pool of expansion candidates instead of picking a fixed number from each class seems to perform better.

9   Conclusion and Future Work

This paper has made important steps from content-based to structural feedback in XML retrieval. It presented two independent approaches that exploit structural and content features: reranking an existing list of results and evaluating a structurally expanded query. The methods achieved good results in this year's Relevance Feedback Track and reasonable results for the earlier years.

Our future work will contentrate on more complex structural aspects of documents (like twigs, tags and paths) and extending this work to queries with content and structural constraints.

References

1. G. Amati, C. Carpineto, and G. Romano. Merging XML indices. In *INEX Workshop 2004*, pages 77–81, 2004.
2. A. Balmin et al. A system for keyword proximity search on XML databases. In *VLDB 2003*, pages 1069–1072, 2003.
3. H. Blanken, T. Grabs, H.-J. Schek, R. Schenkel, and G. Weikum, editors. *Intelligent Search on XML Data*, volume 2818 of *LNCS*. Springer, Sept. 2003.
4. C. J. Crouch, A. Mahajan, and A. Bellamkonda. Flexible XML retrieval based on the extended vector model. In *INEX 2004 Workshop*, pages 149–153, 2004.
5. M. A. Gonçalves, E. A. Fox, A. Krowne, P. Calado, A. H. F. Laender, A. S. da Silva, and B. Ribeiro-Neto. The effectiveness of automatically structured queries in digital libraries. In *4th ACM/IEEE-CS joint conference on Digital libraries (JCDL04)*, pages 98–107, 2004.
6. T. Grust. Accelerating XPath location steps. In *SIGMOD 2002*, pages 109–120, 2002.
7. L. Guo et al. XRANK: ranked keyword search over XML documents. In *SIGMOD 2003*, pages 16–27, 2003.
8. L. Hlaoua and M. Boughanem. Towards context and structural relevance feedback in XML retrieval. In *Workshop on Open Source Web Information Retrieval (OSWIR)*, 2005. http://www.emse.fr/OSWIR05/.
9. W. Hsu, M. L. Lee, and X. Wu. Path-augmented keyword search for XML documents. In *ICTAI 2004*, pages 526–530, 2004.
10. INEX relevance feedback track. http://inex.is.informatik.uni-duisburg.de:2004/tracks/rel/.
11. G. Kazai et al. The INEX evaluation initiative. In Blanken et al. [3], pages 279–293.
12. S. Liu, Q. Zou, and W. Chu. Configurable indexing and ranking for XML information retrieval. In *SIGIR 2004*, pages 88–95, 2004.
13. Y. Mass and M. Mandelbrod. Relevance feedback for XML retrieval. In *INEX 2004 Workshop*, pages 154–157, 2004.
14. V. Mihajlovic̀ et al. TIJAH at INEX 2004 modeling phrases and relevance feedback. In *INEX 2004 Workshop*, pages 141–148, 2004.

15. H. Pan, A. Theobald, and R. Schenkel. Query refinement by relevance feedback in an XML retrieval system. In *ER 2004*, pages 854–855, 2004.
16. G. Ramirez, T. Westerveld, and A. de Vries. Structural features in content oriented xml retrieval. Technical Report INS-E0508, CWI,Centre for Mathematics and Computer Science, 2005.
17. G. Ramírez, T. Westerveld, and A. P. de Vries. Structural features in content oriented XML retrieval. In *CIKM 2005*, 2005.
18. S. Robertson. On term selection for query expansion. *Journal of Documentation*, 46:359–364, Dec. 1990.
19. S. Robertson and K. Sparck-Jones. Relevance weighting of search terms. *Journal of the American Society of Information Science*, 27:129–146, May–June 1976.
20. J. Rocchio Jr. Relevance feedback in information retrieval. In G. Salton, editor, *The SMART Retrieval System: Experiments in Automatic Document Processing*, chapter 14, pages 313–323. Prentice Hall, Englewood Cliffs, New Jersey, USA, 1971.
21. I. Ruthven and M. Lalmas. A survey on the use of relevance feedback for information access systems. *Knowledge Engineering Review*, 18(1), 2003.
22. R. Schenkel, A. Theobald, and G. Weikum. Semantic similarity search on semistructured data with the XXL search engine. *Information Retrieval*, 8(4):521–545, December 2005.
23. R. Schenkel and M. Theobald. Feedback-driven structural query expansion for ranked retrieval of XML data. In *10th International Conference on Extending Database Technologies (EDBT 2006)*, Munich, Germany, Mar. 2006.
24. R. Schenkel and M. Theobald. Structural feedback for keyword-based XML retrieval. In *28th European Conference on Information Retrieval (ECIR 2006)*, London, UK, Apr. 2006.
25. B. Sigurbjörnsson, J. Kamps, and M. de Rijke. The University of Amsterdam at INEX 2004. In *INEX 2004 Workshop*, pages 104–109, 2004.
26. M. Theobald, R. Schenkel, and G. Weikum. An efficient and versatile query engine for TopX search. In *VLDB 2005*, pages 625–636, 2005.
27. A. Trotman and B. Sigurbjörnsson. Narrowed Extended XPath I (NEXI). available at http://www.cs.otago.ac.nz/postgrads/andrew/2004-4.pdf, 2004.
28. J.-N. Vittaut, B. Piwowarski, and P. Gallinari. An algebra for structured queries in bayesian networks. In *INEX Workshop 2004*, pages 58–64, 2004.
29. R. Weber. Using relevance feedback in XML retrieval. In Blanken et al. [3], pages 133–143.
30. Y. Xu and Y. Papakonstantinou. Efficient keyword search for smallest LCAs in XML databases. In *SIGMOD 2005*, pages 537–538, 2005.

NLPX at INEX 2005

Alan Woodley and Shlomo Geva

School of Software Engineering and Data Communications, Faculty of Information
Technology, Queensland University of Technology,
GPO Box 2434, Brisbane, Queensland, Australia
ap.woodley@student.qut.edu, s.geva@qut.edu.au

Abstract. XML information retrieval (XML-IR) systems aim to provide users
with highly exhaustive and highly specific results. To interact with XML-IR
systems users must express both their content and structural needs in the form
of a structured query. Historically, these structured queries have been formatted
using formal languages such as XPath or NEXI. Unfortunately, formal query
languages are very complex and too difficult to be used by experienced, let
alone casual, users and are too closely bound to the underlying physical structure of the collection. Hence, recent research has investigated the idea of specifying users' content and structural requirements via natural language queries
(NLQs). The NLP track was established at INEX 2004 to promote research into
this area, and QUT participated with the system NLPX. Here, we discuss
changes we've made to the system since last year, as well as our participation in
INEX 2005.

1 Introduction

Information retrieval (IR) systems respond to user queries with a ranked list of relevant results. Traditionally, these results have been whole documents, but since XML
documents separate content and structure XML-IR systems are able to return highly
specific information to users, lower than the document level. However, to take advantage of this capability XML-IR users require an interface that is powerful enough to
express their content and structural requirements, yet user-friendly enough that they
can express their requirements intuitively.

Historically, XML-IR systems have used two types of interfaces: keyword based
and formal query language based. Keyword based systems are user-friendly, but lack
the sophistication to fully express users' content and structural needs. In comparison,
formal query language-based interfaces are able to express users' content and structural needs, but are too difficult to use, especially for casual users [7,9] and are bound
to the physical structure of the document. Recent investigation has begun into a third
interface option via natural language that will allow users to fully express their content and structural needs in an intuitive manner.

We have previously presented NLPX [10,11] an XML-IR system with a natural
language interface. NLPX accepts natural language queries (NLQs) and translates
them into NEXI queries. NEXI is an XPath-like formal query language that is used as
a frontend to many existing XML-IR systems. NLPX participated in the natural

N. Fuhr et al. (Eds.): INEX 2005, LNCS 3977, pp. 358–372, 2006.

language processing track of the 2004 INitiative for the Evaluation of XML Retrieval Workshop (INEX). INEX's NLP uses the same Content Only (CO) and Content and Structure (CAS) topics as its Ad-hoc track, however, as input systems use the topics' *Description* rather than *Title* element.

Since last year's participation we have made several improvements to NLPX. Here we discuses three major improvements: inclusion of more special connotations, introduction of shallow parsing and inclusion of more templates. We also describe our participation in the INEX 2005 NLP track and present our results.

2 Motivation

We have already outlined the motivations for an XML-IR natural language interface in our previous work [10,11]; however, for completeness we include them here. The motivations stem from the problems with formal XML-IR query languages and are twofold: first, formal query languages are difficult to use, and second, they are too tightly bound to the physical structure of documents.

First, formal query languages are too difficult for many users to correctly express their structural and content information needs. Two very good examples of this have occurred at the 2003 and 2004 INEX Workshops. In 2003 INEX used the XPath [3] formal language to specify structured queries; however, 63% of the proposed queries had major semantic or syntactic errors. Furthermore, the erroneous queries were difficult to fix, requiring 12 rounds of corrections. In response to this problem, O'Keefe and Trotman [7] designed a simplified version of XPath called NEXI, which was used in INEX 2004. When NEXI was used, the error rate dropped to 12%, with the number of topic revision halved [9].While these figures are limited to two formal languages, O'Keefe and Trotman investigated other structured query languages such as HyTime, DSSSL, CSS and XIRQL and concluded that all of them are very complicated and difficult to use. Therefore, if experts in the field of structured information retrieval are unable to correctly use complex query languages, one cannot expect an inexperienced user to do so, a consensus that has been confirmed by participants in INEX's interactive track [13]. However, we feel that users would be able to intuitively express their information need in a natural language.

Secondly, formal query languages are too tightly bound to the physical structure of documents; hence, users require an intimate knowledge of the documents' composition in order to fully express their structural requirements. So, in order for users to retrieve information from abstracts, bodies or bibliographies, they will need to know the actual names of those tags in a collection (for instance: *abs*, *bdy*, and *bib*). While this information may be obtained from a document's DTD or Schema there are situations where the proprietor of the collection does not wish users to have access to those files. Or, in the case of a heterogeneous collection, a single tag can have multiple names (for example: abstract could be named *abs*, *a*, or *abstract*). This is a problem identified by participants in the INEX 2004 heterogenous track [6] who have proposed the use of metatags to map between collections [6] and extensions to NEXI [9] to handle multiple tag names. In contrast, structural requirements in NLQs are expressed at a higher conceptual level, allowing the underlying document's structure to be completely hidden from users.

3 Previous Work by Authors

This paper expands on the previous work of the authors presented in [10,11]. We submitted our system, NLPX, to the 2004 INEX Natural Language Processing Track where it performed very successfully (1st in CAS, 2nd in CO). INEX's NLP track used the same topics and assessments as its Ad-hoc track; however, participating systems used a natural language query as input, rather than a formal language (NEXI) query. Examples of both query types are expressed in Figure 1. Note that the query actually contains two information requests, first, for sections about compression, and second, for articles about information retrieval. However, the user only wants to receive results matching the first request. We refer to the former as returned requests/results and the latter as support requests/results.

NEXI: //article[about(.,'information retrieval')] //sec[about(./, compression)]

NLQ: Find sections of articles about image and text compression in articles about efficient information retrieval

---

Fig. 1. A NEXI and Natural Language Query

We had previously participated in INEX's Ad-hoc track with GPX, a system that accepted NEXI formatted queries. Therefore, we decided to use GPX as a backend system. This allowed us to concentrate on developing a frontend that translated natural language queries to NEXI. Translation involved three steps that derived syntactic and semantic information from the natural language query (NLQ). We refer to these three steps as the NLPX framework and outline them below:

1. First, we tagged words in the NLQ as either a special connotation or by their part of speech. Special connotations are words of implied semantic significance. We differentiated between three types: Structures (such as section, abstract) that specified structural requirements, Boundaries (such as contains, about) that separated structural and content requirements, and Instructions (such as find, retrieve) that indicated if we had a return or support request. Words corresponding to special connotations were hard-coded into the system and matched to query words by a dictionary lookup. Remaining words were tagged by their part of speech (such as noun, verb, conjunction) via a Brill Tagger [2].
2. Second, we matched the tagged NLQs to query templates. The templates were derived from the inspection of previous INEX queries. Since the NLQs occurred in shallow context they required only a few templates, significantly less than if one wished to capture natural language as a whole. Each template corresponded to an information request. Each request had three attributes: Content, a list of terms/phrases expressing content requirements, Structure, a logical XPath expression expressing structural requirements, and an Instruction, "R" for return requests, and "S" otherwise.

3. Finally, the requests were merged together and output in NEXI format. Return requests were output in the form **A[about(.,C)]** where **A** is the request's structural attribute and **C** is the request's content attribute. When all return requests were processed, support requests were inserted. The insert position was located by comparing the structural attributes of return and support requests and by finding their longest shared descendant. The output of support requests had the form **D[about(E,F)]** where **D** is the longest matching string, **E** is the remainder of the support's structural attribute and **F** is the support's content attribute. Note, that while NLPX outputs NEXI queries this step has been modulated so that NLPX could be extended to include any number of formal query languages.

4 Improvements

Since our participation in INEX 2004 we have made several improvements to NLPX, here we outline three major improvements. Our first two improvements were to increase the number of special connotations and templates recognised by NLPX. These improvements correspond to the first two steps of the NLPX framework established in Section 3. These improvements increased the range of queries NLPX could handle, thereby increasing its robustness. The third improvement was to implement a shallow parsing stage between the first two framework steps. The shallow parser grouped together query terms into atomic semantic units before full parsing. This allowed for further lexical analysis to be performed on the units, leading to an overall increase in retrieval performance. Here, we discuss these three improvements in detail.

4.1 Additional Special Connotations

The INEX natural language queries are very diverse in nature, presenting a challenge for all those wishing capture their syntactic and semantic meaning via a natural language inference. In NLPX, we tag query words of semantic importance as special connotations. Previously, NLPX recognised three special connotations: Instructions, Boundaries and Structures. These connotations were able to handle many of the INEX queries, however, they were not able to handle some of the more novel NLQs. Therefore, we have extended the number of conations recognised by NLPX to allow for a broader range of queries to be handled. Here, we describe the special connotations we added to NLPX.

4.1.1 Negations
The first connotation added to NLPX was negation. Negations fulfill the user's information need by explicitly stating the information content that the user does not want to retrieve, rather than the information content that they want to retrieve. Negations are expressed in NEXI by the use of a minus symbol (-), and are expressed in NLQs by the use of words such as no, non or not. An example of a negation occurs in topic number 139.

> **NEXI:** //article[about(.//bb//au//snm, Bertino) or about(.//bb//au//snm , Jajodia)) and about(.//bb//atl, security model) and about(.//bb//atl, -"indexing model" - "object oriented model")]
>
> **NLQ:** We wish to identify papers that cite work by authors Bertino or Jajodia that deal with "security models". Security models should thus be the subject in the title of the cited papers by Bertino or Jajodia. We are interested in any kind of security models that Bertino or Jajodia developed (e.g. authorization models). We are **not** interested in other kind of models (e.g. objet oriented/indexing models).

Fig. 2. Topic Number 139. An example of the use of a negation.

4.1.2 Strengtheners

The second connotation we added to NLPX was strengtheners. Users employ strengthens to add weighting to query terms that are highly important to their information need. Strengthens are expressed in NEXI by the use of the plus (+) symbol, and are expressed in NLQs by the use of terms and phrases such as *particularly* and *major focus*. An example of a strengthener occurs in topic number 137.

> **NEXI:** //*[about(.,application algorithm +clustering +k-means +c-means "vector quantization" "speech compression" "image compression" "video compression"
>
> **NLQ:** Find elements about clustering procedures, particularly k-means, aka c-means, aka Generalized Lloyd algorithm, aka LBG, and their application to image speech and video compression.

Fig. 3. Topic Number 124. An example of the use of a strengthener.

4.1.3 Reverse Boundaries

The third connotation added was reverse boundaries. Previously we had identified a boundary as a query term that separates structural items and content items. NLPX uses boundaries to pair structures with their respective content. Examples of boundaries are query terms such as *talk about* or *contains*. Reverse boundaries have a similar function to ordinary boundaries, since NLPX also uses them to pair together structures and content; however, reverse boundaries occur after the content items rather than before. Often reverse boundaries are past tense versions of ordinary boundaries such as *talked about* or *contained*. An example of a reverse boundary occurs in topic number 160.

> **NEXI:** //article[about(., image retrieval)]//sec[about(., "latent semantic indexing")]
>
> **NLQ:** We are looking for sections in articles where "image retrieval" is **talked about**, that describe "latent semantic indexing".

Fig. 4. Topic Number 160. An example of the use of a reverse boundary.

4.1.4 Anaphoric Topics

The fourth connotation added was an anaphoric topic. An anaphoric topic occurs when some part, usual a content item, of the topic is referred to later on in the topic using a pseudonym. Anaphoric topics are conceptually similar to a noun subsequently been referenced via a pronoun. An example of an anaphoric topic occurs in topic number 161 where the phrase *that topic* refers to the previously mentioned content terms *database access methods for spatial and text data.*

> **NEXI:** //article[about(., database access methods for spatial data and text)]//bm//bb[about(./atl, database access methods)]
>
> **NLQ:** Find bibliography entries about database access methods for spatial and text data from articles related to **that topic**.

Fig. 5. Topic Number 161. An example of the use of anaphoric topic.

4.1.5 Inclusion of Stopwords

The final new special connotation recognised by NLPX was stopwords. Stopwords are words that occur in too frequently to be of any value in IR systems and are often ignored. Our backend system GPX already ignores some stopwords; however, we incorporated also them into NLPX since we wanted NLPX to be a generic interface that could be used by any XML-IR backend system. Rather than use the same stoplist used in GPX that is derived from frequently occurring terms (>50,000 times) in the INEX corpus, we used a standard stop list defined in Fox [4]. Once again we made this decision so that NLPX would be a generic interface.

4.2 Shallow Parsing

The second improvement we made to NLPX was to add an intermediate step of shallow parsing between our lexical tagging and template matching. Shallow parsing, also called text chunking, is the process of dividing sentences into atomic, nonoverlapping segments (called chunks), and then classifying them into grammatical classes. It is usually performed after part of speech tagging, and as demonstrated by Abney [1] it can be used as a precursor to full parsing. Alternatively it can be used in other tasks such as index term generation, information extraction, text summation and bilingual alignment. Initial research into shallow parsing was focused on identifying noun phrases; however, more recent work has extended its reach to include general clause identification.

There are two types of chunks that are systems recognised:

- Explicit Chunks: These are chunks that are explicitly defined by users by adding parenthesises around important phrases in the query. Characters used to signify parenthesises were commas, colons, semi-colons, brackets and quotation marks. Generally, we noted that parenthesises were used to signify important content phrases.
- Implicit Chunks: These are chunks that are not explicitly defined by users, but rather derived by analysing the grammatical properties and/or context of query terms. It is used to group together terms of implied significance in the system. A classic example is to group together adjectives and nouns to form a single noun phrase. In NLPX, we identify four chunks of significance: Instructions, Structures, Boundaries (include Reverse Boundaries) and Content.

We have previously incorporated a shallow parser in our previous work [12]. In that version a process called transformation-based learning (TBL) [2] to learn when to include query terms into a chunk based on both its grammatical properties (the tag of the current term) and its context (the tags of surrounding terms). This process was based upon the work of Ramshaw and Marcus [8] who originally used it to group together noun phrases. We extended their theories to work on structured queries. Unfortunately, we did not have time to retrain our system to recognise the new special connotations introduced earlier, therefore, we based the decision solely on the tag of the current term.

4.3 Additional Templates

The final improvement we made to NLPX was the addition of new templates. These additions were needed to handle both the new special connotations and the grouping of query terms into chunks. Figure 6 presents the templates that NLPX previously recognised:

```
Query: Request+
Request : CO_Request | CAS_Request
CO_Request: NounPhrase+
CAS_Request: SupportRequest | ReturnRequest
SupportRequest: Structure [Bound] Content+
ReturnRequest: Instruction Structure [Bound] Content+
```

Fig. 6. Existing NLPX Query Templates

Note that these templates work only on a word rather than a chunk level. However, it was straightforward to migrate the templates since the set of four single–term terminals (Instruction, Structure, Boundary and Content) had corresponding chunk classes. However, we also added new query templates to the NLPX, which we describe here.

4.3.1 Conjuncting Structures

The first template added to NLPX was used to handle conjucting structures. This occurs when two structures are separated by a conjunction (for example and, or). In this situation it is implied that users wish to search elements that match either of the structures. Figure 7 presents the templates added to the system while Figure 8 presents topic 127, an example of conjuncting structures.

Structure: StructureChunk [OtherStructure+]
OtherStructure : Conjunction StructureChunk

Fig. 7. Conjucting Structures Query Templates

NEXI: //sec//(p| fgc)[about(., Godel Lukasiewicz and other fuzzy implication definitions)]

NLQ： Find **paragraphs or figure-captions** containing the definition of Godel, Lukasiewicz or other fuzzy-logic implications

---

Fig. 8. Topic Number 127. An example of the use of conjucting structure

4.3.2 Reverse Boundaries

The second template added to NLPX was to handle the cases of reverse boundaries. When NLPX encounters a reverse boundary it matches the previously parsed content items with the current structure and then begins a new request. Figure 9 presents the new query templates used to handle reverse boundaries and Figure 10 presents topic 160, which contains an example of a reverse boundary (and previous presented in figure 4).

SupportRequest: Structure [Bound] Content+ |
                     Structure Content+ [ReverseBound]
ReturnRequest: Instruction Structure [Bound] Content+ |
                     Instruction Structure Content+ [ReverseBound]

Fig. 9. Reverse Boundary Query Templates

NEXI: //article[about(., image retrieval)]//sec[about(., "latent semantic indexing")]
NLQ: We are looking for sections in articles where "image retrieval" is **talked about**, that describe "latent semantic indexing".

Fig. 10. Topic Number 160. An example of the use of a reverse boundary

4.3.3 Parenthetical Information Requests

Parenthetical information requests occur when a new information request occurs in the middle of another information request. Usually this occurs when a boundary element occurs after a completed information request, thereby indicating that a instruction or a structure has preceded it. When this occurs, NLPX must fully handle the new information request, before returning to handle the remaining content information. Figure 11 presents the new query templates used to handle parenthetical information requests and Figure 12 presents topic 160, which contains an example of a parenthetical information requests (and previous presented in figure 4).

SupportRequest:	Structure [SupportRequest] Bound Content+ |
ReturnRequest:	Instruction Structure [ReturnRequest] Bound Content+

Fig. 11. Parenthetical Information Request Templates

NEXI: //article[about(.,information retrieval)]//p[about(.,relevance feedback)]
NLQ: We are looking for paragraphs in articles about information retrieval dealing with relevance feedback .

Fig. 12. Topic Number 145. An example of the use of a parenthetical information request

5   System Backend

Once the NLQ was tagged, chunked and matched to templates it was transformed into a NEXI query using the existing NLPX system. This is a two stage process. First we expanded the content of the query, by deriving phrases based on its lexical properties, such as noun phrases that include adjectives participles. Then we formatted a NEXI query based upon its instruction, structure and content values. We passed the NEXI query to our existing GPX system for processing as if they were a standard Ad-hoc query. To produce its results list GPX collects leaf elements from its index and dynamically creates their ancestors. GPX's ranking scheme rewards leaf elements with specific rather than common terms, and that contain phrases. It also rewards ancestors with multiple relevant children rather than a single relevant child. A more comprehensive description of GPX can be found in our accompanying paper as well as earlier work [5].

6   INEX 2005

6.1   INEX 2005 Submissions

For this years' INEX 2005 NLP track was made submissions for the CO+S and CAS topics. This is slightly different to the Ad-hoc track where systems can also make additional submissions based on CO topics, however, since CO topics do not contain any structural constraints, they were not considered for inclusion in the NLP track.

Furthermore, all submissions were made automatically, that is, without human intervention such as query expansion via relevance feedback.

6.2 INEX 2005 Results

This section discusses the results of our submissions. We present results for the CO+S and CAS tasks. Due to length constraints we have not included any graphs, however, we have included tables.

6.2.1 CO+S Results

Tables 1 to 4 present the results for the CO+S tasks. In each of the tables we have compared the results of the NLP submission with the results of a baseline that used

Table 1. The Results of the COS Focused Submissions

Metric	Quant	Score NLPX Focused	Score Base	Ratio (N/B)
nXCG[10]	Strict	0.0555	0.1059	0.5241
	Gen	0.1693	0.2395	0.7069
	GenLifted	0.1924	0.2730	0.7048
nXCG[25]	Strict	0.0555	0.1088	0.5101
	Gen	0.1668	0.1998	0.8348
	GenLifted	0.1835	0.2132	0.8607
nXCG[50]	Strict	0.0618	0.1031	0.5994
	Gen	0.1619	0.1892	0.8557
	GenLifted	0.1767	0.2103	0.8402
ep-gr	Strict	0.0222	0.0193	1.1503
	Gen	0.0697	0.0860	0.8105
	GenLifted	0.0781	0.1053	0.7417

Table 2. The Results of the COS Focused (Leaves) Submissions

Metric	Quant	Score NLPX Leaves	Score Base	Ratio (N/B)
nXCG[10]	Strict	0.1059	0.0824	1.2852
	Gen	0.1697	0.0555	3.0577
	GenLifted	0.1874	0.2351	0.7971
nXCG[25]	Strict	0.1104	0.1849	0.5971
	Gen	0.1698	0.2067	0.8215
	GenLifted	0.1879	0.2240	0.8388
nXCG[50]	Strict	0.1025	0.1662	0.6167
	Gen	0.1819	0.1850	0.9832
	GenLifted	0.1920	0.2047	0.9380
ep-gr	Strict	0.0449	0.0420	1.0690
	Gen	0.0807	0.0934	0.8640
	GenLifted	0.0921	0.1103	0.8350

Table 3. The Results of the COS Thorough Submissions

Metric	Quant	Score NLPX	Score Base	Ratio (N/B)
nXCG[10]	Strict	0.0536	0.0359	1.4930
	Gen	0.1917	0.2557	0.7497
	GenLifted	0.2139	0.2904	0.7366
nXCG[25]	Strict	0.0418	0.0903	0.4629
	Gen	0.1784	0.2541	0.7021
	GenLifted	0.1977	0.2827	0.6993
nXCG[50]	Strict	0.0678	0.1207	0.5617
	Gen	0.1802	0.2537	0.7103
	GenLifted	0.1878	0.2704	0.6945
	Strict	0.0188	0.0189	0.9947
	Gen	0.0666	0.0904	0.7367
ep-gr	GenLifted	0.0568	0.0680	0.8353

Table 4. The Results of the COS FecthBrowse Submissions

Metric	Quant	Score NLPX	Score Base	Ratio (N/B)
	Strict	0.1097	0.1504	0.7294
ep-gr	Gen	0.1362	0.1523	0.8943
	GenLifted	0.1537	0.1724	0.8915

Table 5. The Results of the SSCAS Submissions

Metric	Quant	Score NLPX	Score Base	Ratio (N/B)
nXCG[10]	Strict	0.1250	0.1000	1.2500
	Gen	0.2374	0.2517	0.9432
	GenLifted	0.2385	0.2800	0.8518
nXCG[25]	Strict	0.1378	0.1578	0.8733
	Gen	0.2859	0.2885	0.9910
	GenLifted	0.2882	0.3119	0.9240
nXCG[50]	Strict	0.3738	0.1528	2.4463
	Gen	0.3050	0.3681	0.8286
	GenLifted	0.3131	0.3828	0.8179
	Strict	0.0755	0.0770	0.9805
ep-gr	Gen	0.1087	0.1357	0.8010
	GenLifted	0.0985	0.1184	0.8319

the original NEXI title as input. We present results for the Focused, Thorough and FetchBrowse tasks. For the Focused task, 2 submissions were produced, one that accepted the highest-ranking element on an element path (Focused) and one that accepted leaves.

As the results show NLPX performs comparable to the baseline (usually about 0.8). This is an improvement on 2004 when the system was performed about 0.7 of the baseline.

6.2.2 CAS Submissions

Tables 5 to 8 present the results for each of the CAS tasks. In each of the tables we have compared the results of the NLP submission with the results of a baseline that used the original NEXI title as input. We present results for the Focused, Thorough and FetchBrowse tasks.

Again NLPX performs strongly against the baseline and mostly either outperforms the baseline or achieves a score that is very close to the baseline (>0.9). Again this is a

Table 6. The Results of the SVCAS Submissions

Metric	Quant	Score NLPX	Score Base	Ratio (N/B)
nXCG[10]	Strict	0.0800	0.0400	2.0000
	Gen	0.1100	0.0848	1.2972
	GenLifted	0.1056	0.0966	1.0932
nXCG[25]	Strict	0.0662	0.0662	1.0000
	Gen	0.1100	0.1081	1.0176
	GenLifted	0.1082	0.1163	0.9304
nXCG[50]	Strict	0.0582	0.0662	0.8792
	Gen	0.1150	0.1086	1.0589
	GenLifted	0.1161	0.1142	1.0166
ep-gr	Strict	0.0267	0.0274	0.9745
	Gen	0.0323	0.0282	1.1454
	GenLifted	0.0269	0.0214	1.2570

Table 7. The Results of the VSCAS Submissions

Metric	Quant	Score NLPX	Score Base	Ratio (N/B)
nXCG[10]	Strict	0.1333	0.1167	1.1422
	Gen	0.2423	0.2039	1.1883
	GenLifted	0.2600	0.2371	1.0966
nXCG[25]	Strict	0.1133	0.1267	0.8942
	Gen	0.2446	0.2531	0.9664
	GenLifted	0.2544	0.2782	0.9145
nXCG[50]	Strict	0.1833	0.1200	1.5275
	Gen	0.2491	0.2493	0.9992
	GenLifted	0.2557	0.2618	0.9767
ep-gr	Strict	0.0340	0.0383	0.8877
	Gen	0.0646	0.0620	1.0419
	GenLifted	0.0181	0.0186	0.9731

Table 8. The Results of the VVCAS Submissions

Metric	Quant	Score NLPX	Score Base	Ratio (N/B)
nXCG[10]	Strict	0.1222	0.1222	1.0000
	Gen	0.2197	0.2520	0.8718
	GenLifted	0.2262	0.2824	0.8010
nXCG[25]	Strict	0.1644	0.1257	1.3079
	Gen	0.2136	0.2281	0.9364
	GenLifted	0.2250	0.2531	0.8890
nXCG[50]	Strict	0.2698	0.1142	2.3625
	Gen	0.2110	0.2080	1.0144
	GenLifted	0.2252	0.2356	0.9559
ep-gr	Strict	0.0483	0.0454	1.0639
	Gen	0.0758	0.0708	1.0706
	GenLifted	0.0320	0.0297	1.0774

significant improvement over 2004 attempts and verifies our belief that natural language interfaces have the potential to be a viable alternative to formal languages.

6.3 INEX 2005 Examples

Unfortunately, we do not have the space to list the entire INEX 2005 CO+S and CAS topic sets. Here, we provide examples of a successful and unsuccessful translation.

6.3.1 Successful Translation

For an example of a successful translation we have chosen topic 280 (figure 13). This is an example of a complex query that contains both a user's structural and content needs. The query contains one return request and two support requests all of which are handled successfully by NLPX.

NLQ: find sections about approximate algorithms in works about string matching citing Baeza-Yates.
NLQtoNEXI: //article[about(.,string matching "string matching") AND about(.//bb,Baeza-Yates Yates "Baeza Yates" Baeza)]//sec[about(.,approximate algorithms "approximate algorithms")]
Original NEXI: //article[about(.//bb, Baeza-Yates) and about(.//sec , string matching)]//sec[about(., approximate algorithm)]

Fig. 13. Topic Number 280. A successful NLPX translation

NLQ: We are looking for articles whose body is about operating systems.
NLQtoNEXI: //article[about(.,body body operating systems "operating systems")]
Original NEXI: //article//bdy[about(., operating system)]

Fig. 14. Topic Number 285. A unsuccessful NLPX translation.

6.3.2 Unsuccessful Translation

For an example of an unsuccessful translation we have chosen topic number 285. NLPX fails at translating this example because it is unable to determine that the body element is a descendant of the article element.

7 Conclusion

Here we presented the improvements made to our existing XML-IR NLP interface. Overall three improvements were made: the addition of more special connotations, application of shallow parsing and inclusion of more templates. These improvements have resulted in a performance increase in comparison with our previous system, both in CO and CAS queries, where our backend system using NLPX performed comparably to – and even outperformed – the baseline of our backend system using NEXI input. This validates the claim that natural language is a potential viable alternative to formal query languages in XML-IR.

References

1. Abney, S.: Parsing by Chunks. In: Principle-Based Parsing. Kluwer Academic Publisher (1991)
2. Brill, E.: A Simple Rule-Based Part of Speech Tagger. In: Proceedings of the Third Conference on Applied Computational Linguistics (ACL), Trento, Italy (1992) 152–155
3. Clark J., DeRose, S.: XML Path Language XPath Version 1.0. W3C Recommendation, The World Wide Web Consortium, November 1999 available at http://www.w3.org/TR/xpath.
4. Fox, C: Lexical Analysis and Stoplists. In: Frankes, W.B., Baeza-Yates, R. (eds.): Information Retrieval: Data Structures and Algorithms, Prentice-Hall, Upper Saddle River, New Jersey, United States of America (1992) Chapter 7 102-130.
5. Geva, S.: GPX - Gardens Point XML Information Retrieval INEX 2004. In: Fuhr, N., Lalmas, M., Malik, S., Szlavik Z. (eds.): Advances in XML Information Retrieval: Third International Workshop of the Initiative for the Evaluation of XML Retrieval, INEX 2004, Dagstuhl, Germany, December 6–8, 2004, Revised Selected Papers. Lecture Nodes in Computer Science, Vol 3493. Springer-Verlag, Berlin Heidelberg New York (2005) 221–222
6. Larson, R.: XML Element Retrieval and Heterogenous Retrieval: In Pursuit of the Impossible? In Proceedings of INEX 2005 Workshop on Element Retrieval Methodology, Glasgow, Scotland (2005) 38-41.
7. O'Keefe, R., Trotman, A.: The Simplest Query Language That Could Possibly Work, In: Fuhr N., Malik, S. (eds.): INEX 2003 Workshop Proceedings. Dagstuhl, Germany (2003) 167–174
8. Ramshaw, L. Marcus, M.: Text Chunking Using Transformation-Based Learning, In: Proceedings of the Third Workshop on Very Large Corpora (1995) 82-94.
9. Trotman, A., Sigurbjörnsson, B.: NEXI: Now and Next, In: Fuhr, N., Lalmas, M., Malik, S., Szlavik Z. (eds.): Advances in XML Information Retrieval: Third International Workshop of the Initiative for the Evaluation of XML Retrieval, INEX 2004, Dagstuhl, Germany, December 6–8, 2004, Revised Selected Papers. Lecture Nodes in Computer Science, Vol 3493. Springer-Verlag, Berlin Heidelberg New York (2005) 410–423

10. Woodley, A., Geva, S.: NLPX: An XML-IR System with a Natural Language Interface, In: Bruza, P., Moffat, A., Turpin, A (eds.): Proceedings of the Australasian Document Computing Symposium, Melbourne, Australia (2004) 71–74.
11. Woodley, A., Geva, S.: NLPX at INEX 2004, In: Fuhr, N., Lalmas, M., Malik, S., Szlavik Z. (eds.): Advances in XML Information Retrieval: Third International Workshop of the Initiative for the Evaluation of XML Retrieval, INEX 2004, Dagstuhl, Germany, December 6–8, 2004, Revised Selected Papers. Lecture Nodes in Computer Science, Vol 3493. Springer-Verlag, Berlin Heidelberg New York (2005) 393–406
12. Woodley, A., Geva, S.: Applying Error-Driver Transformation-Based Learning to Structured Natural Language Queries, In: Proceedings of the 2005 International Conference on Cyberworlds. IEEE Computer Society, to appear in 2005.
13. van Zowl, Roelof, Bass, J., van Oostendorp, H., Wiering, F.: Query Formulation for XML Retrieval with Brick. In Fuhr, N., Lamas, M., Trotman, A. (eds.): In Proceedings of INEX 2005 Workshop on Element Retrieval Methodology, Glasgow, Scotland (2005) 75-83.

From Natural Language to NEXI, an Interface for INEX 2005 Queries

Xavier Tannier

École Nationale Supérieure des Mines de Saint-Etienne,
158 Cours Fauriel,
F-42023 Saint-Etienne, France
tannier@emse.fr

Abstract. Offering the possibility to query any XML retrieval system in natural language would be very helpful to a lot of users. In 2005, INEX proposed a framework to participants that wanted to implement a natural language interface for the retrieval of XML documents, independantly of the search engine. This paper describes our contribution to this project and presents some opinions concerning the task.

1 Introduction

1.1 Motivation

Asking a question in everyday language ("natural language") and getting a relevant answer is what the everyday user really miss in the process of information retrieval (IR). Moreover, as natural language is the best way so far to explain our information need, using it should help a system if the query is analysed correctly. However, at present, Natural Language Processing (NLP) techniques are not developed enough to come close to the human perception of language, and actual results are not yet up to what we could expect [1, 2].

In the case of "traditional" IR, where documents are considered as text only (*flat* documents), classical search engines need a query composed of a list of keywords. Writing such a query is quite simple for the casual user, and the value added by NLP approaches is not worth the complexity of these techniques.

On the other hand, many natural language interfaces (NLIs) for querying structured documents (databases) have been developed, most of them transforming natural language into Structured Query Language (SQL) [3, 4, 5]. This is probably because the benefits that can be gained in that case are much higher than in traditional information retrieval. Indeed, SQL (and any structured query language used for XML retrieval as well) is hardly usable by novice and casual users. Moreover such languages impose to know the structure of the database (or of the documents).

But database querying is a strict interrogation. It is not information retrieval. The user knows what kind of data is contained in the database, the information need is precise, and a correct query necessarily leads to a correct answer. This means that the natural language analysis must interpret the query perfectly and

N. Fuhr et al. (Eds.): INEX 2005, LNCS 3977, pp. 373–387, 2006.

Table 1. Some features of flat, semi-structured and structured documents in an information retrieval point of view

	Flat documents	*semi-structured documents (XML)*	*structured documents (DB)*
Content	text only	text + structure	structure + data
Information need	general		precise
Request	text only	content and/or structure	
Query	keywords	**Structured query languages**	
Interpretation	**loose (IR)**		strict

unambiguously, failing which the final answer is incorrect and the user dissatisfied. For this reason notably, natural language interfaces for databases only apply to very restricted domains. Even in these domains, the answer to a query is often *"I did not understand your query"*.

XML retrieval stands between these two domains (see Tab. 1). *Document-oriented* XML files [6], as well as databases, contain some structural information, and the use of a NLI would be justified. But in XML IR, as in traditional IR, the information need is loosely defined and there is no perfect answer to a query. A NLI is then a part of the retrieval process, and thus it can interpret some queries imperfectly, and still return useful results. The problem is then made "easier" to solve... and we can even imagine an interface getting better results than manual queries (which makes no sense in databases). Moreover more general applications can be designed. In return, such an interface has to be very robust, and all queries must be analysed, even imperfectly. It is not conceivable that the system returns no answer because it did not understand the question.

1.2   INEX and Natural Language Tasks

The INitiative for Evaluation of XML Retrieval (INEX) aims at evaluating the effectiveness of information retrieval systems for XML documents. The INEX collection groups a set of 16819 articles from the IEEE Computer Society, represented in XML, with a set of topics and human assessments on these topics.

In 2005 campaign, two different types of topics have been designed [7]:

- *Content Only + Structure* (CO+S) topics, as indicated by their name, refer only on textual content, but the user can nevertheless add some structural hints to help the system.
- *Content And Structure* (CAS) topics allow a user that knows the structure of the documents to formulate constraints on structural elements that he/she wants to be searched for.

We participated to the campaign for both categories, but our approach focuses principally on CAS topics. A simplified example of INEX 2005 topic is given in Fig. 1. The element `castitle` is written in NEXI [8], a formal language for XML retrieval.

```
<inex_topic topic_id="203" query_type="CO+S" ct_no="5">
    <title>code signing verification</title>
    <castitle>//article//sec[about(., code signing verification)]</castitle>
    <description>
        Find documents or document components, most probably sections, that
        describe the approach of code signing and verification.
    </description>
    <narrative>
        I am working in a company that authenticates a wide range of web data
        base applications from different software vendors. [...] To be relevant,
        a document or document component must describe the whole process of
        code signing and verification, which means [...]
    </narrative>
</inex_topic>
```

Fig. 1. Example of INEX 2005 topic. The `title` element is used for Content-Only search, `castitle` for structural hints and CAS representation in NEXI. `description` is used by Natural Language Processing tasks participants, while the `narrative` is reserved for human assessors.

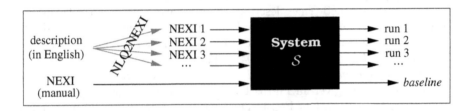

Fig. 2. NLQ2NEXI

NEXI CAS queries have the form $//A[B]//C[D]$ where A and C are paths and B and D are filters. We can read this query as *"Return C descendants of A where A is about B and C is about D"*. B and D correspond to disjunctions or conjunctions of 'about' clauses **about($//E$, F)**, where E is a path and F a list of terms. The `'castitle'` part of Fig. 1 gives a good example of a query formulated in NEXI. More information about NEXI can be found in [8].

In 2005 INEX campaign, two different tasks aimed to involve Natural Language Processing. In the first one, called NLQ (Natural Language Queries), participants had to consider only the `description` part of the topics and to return a set of XML elements (or doxels) corresponding to the request. No matter how they performed their search, or where the NLP was used. The evaluation of NLQ systems was the same as for the *ad-hoc* task.

In the second one, NLQ2NEXI, on which this paper focuses, the aim was to translate natural language queries into `title` (keyword list) and `castitle`

(NEXI) elements from the description. Here the idea is to build a generic interface that could be used by any retrieval system reading NEXI queries. Automatically generated topics have then been run with a search engine S provided by the organizers (Fig. 2). In this case, the evaluation is twofold:

1. a comparison between the effectiveness of each NLQ2NEXI system.
2. a comparison between each system and a baseline obtained by running the system S on initial (manual) topics, in order to quantify the trade-off in performance.

2   Natural Language Query Analysis

In our approach, requests are analysed through several steps:

1. A part-of-speech (POS) tagging is performed on the query. Each word is labeled by its word class (*e.g.*: noun, verb, adjective...). To carry out this task we chose the free tool TreeTagger [9].
2. A POS-dependant semantic representation is attributed to each word. For example the noun *'information'* will be represented by the predicate *information(x)*, or the verb *'identify'* by *evt(e_1, identify)*.
3. Context-free syntactic rules describe the most current grammatical constructions in queries and questions. Low-level semantic actions are combined with each syntactic rule. Two examples of such operations, applied to the description of Topic 130 (INEX 2004: *"We are searching paragraphs dealing with version management in articles containing a paragraph about object databases."*), are given in Fig. 3. The final result is a logical representation shown in the left part of Fig. 4. This representation is totally independent from the queried corpus, it is obtained by general linguistic operations.
4. The semantic representation is then reduced with the help of specific rules:
   - a recognition of some typical constructions of a query (*e.g.*: *Retrieve + object*) or of the corpus (*e.g.*: *"an article written by [...]"* refers to the tag *au – author*);
   - and a distinction between semantic elements mapping on the structure and, respectively, mapping on the content;
   Figure 4 shows the specific rules that apply to the example.
5. A treatment of relations existing between different elements;
6. The construction of a well-formed NEXI query.

Steps 1 to 5 are explained in more details in [10], as well as necessary corpus knowledge and the effect of topic complexity on the analysis. The representation obtained at the end of Step 5 does not depend on any retrieval system or query language. It could be transformed (with more or less information loss) into any existing formal language.

Transformation process from our representation to NEXI is not straightforward. Remember that a NEXI query has the form **//A[B]//C[D]**.

- At content level, linguistic features (like noun_modifier in the example) cannot be kept and must be transformed in an appropriate manner (see Sect. 3).

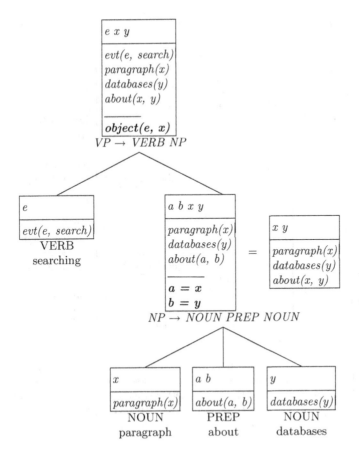

Fig. 3. Example of rule application for the verbal phrase *"searching paragraphs about databases"* (rules *NP → NOUN PREP NOUN* and *VP → VERB NP*). Basic semantic representations are attributed to part-of-speeches (leaf components). When applying syntactic rules, components are merged and semantic actions are added (here identity relations and verbal relation predicate – bold predicates).

– At structural level, a set of several tag identifiers (that can be DTD tag names or wildcards) has to be distributed into parts A, B, C and D, that we respectively call support requests, support elements, return requests and return elements. These four parts A, B, C and D are built from our representation (Fig. 4) in the following way:
  • C is the 'framed' (selected) element name (see Fig. 4 and its caption);
  • D is composed of all C children (relation *contains*) and their textual content (relation *about*);
  • A is the highest element name in the DTD tree, that is not C or one of its children;
  • B is composed of all other elements and their textual content.

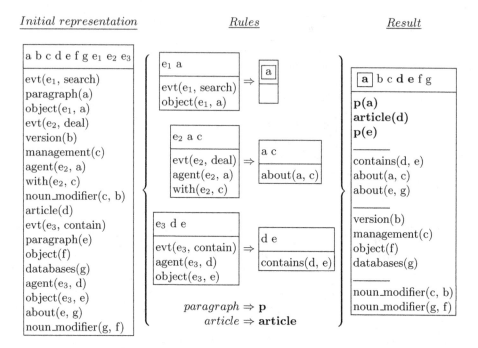

Fig. 4. The semantic analysis of Topic 130 (left), is reduced by some generic rules (center), leading to a new representation (right). Bold predicates emphasize words representing XML tag names and the framed letter stands for the element that should be returned to the user. The first three rules deal with verbal phrases *"to search sth"*, *"to deal with sth"* and *"to contain sth"*.

Wildcard-identified tags of the same part are merged and are considered to be the same element. See an example in Sect. 4.

3   Noun Phrases

Our system generates some linguistic-oriented predicates. The main ones are np_property, noun_modifier and adjective. NEXI format requires the 'about' clauses to contain only textual content. Phrases can be represented with quotation marks. We chose to consider only noun phrases treatment here, because other relations are translated in a straightforward way.

From an IR point of view, noun phrases have the general form [11]:

$$NP \rightarrow det^* \ pre^* \ head \ post^*$$

...Where *det* is a determiner, *pre* (*premodifier*) is an adjective, a noun or a coordinated phrase, *head* is a noun and *post* (*postmodifier*) is a prepositional phrase or a relative clause.

In our representation, relations between premodifiers and head nouns are expressed by predicates `noun_modifier` (if the premodifier is a noun) or `adjective` (if the premodifier is an adjective). Prepositional relations between NPs (*i.e.* the form $NP \rightarrow NP_{head}\ PREP\ NP_{post}$) are represented by `noun_property`.

All forms have been considered when analysing the natural language queries, but we distinguished two specific constructions of NPs to build the formal queries.

3.1   Simple Noun Groups

In English, the simplest noun groups are a succession of adjectives or nouns followed by a head noun:

$$NP \rightarrow (ADJ \mid NOUN) + NOUN \tag{1}$$

These multi-word terms are less ambiguous than simple nouns, and generally refer to a particular domain [12]. They are not subject to many syntactical variations (see next section), and it is quite probable that such terms representing the same concept have the same form in most occurrences of a collection. For all these reasons, these simple NPs are very interesting in information retrieval. Some examples (extracted from INEX 2005 topics) are given in Tab. 2 (with an additional rule for proper names (PNs): $NP \rightarrow PN+$).

When translating to NEXI, all sequences of words obeying to Rule 1 are then transcribed between quotation marks.

Table 2. Examples of simple noun groups (rule 1) in INEX 2005 topics

Topics	Noun phrase
204	"semantic networks" (ADJ NOUN)
231	"graph theory" (NOUN NOUN)
210	"multimedia document models" (NOUN NOUN NOUN)
211	"global positioning systems" (ADJ NOUN NOUN)
204	"Dan Moldovan" (PN PN)

3.2   Complex Noun Phrases

Nouns or noun phrases linked to each other by prepositions are semantically very significant [13, 14]:

$$NP \rightarrow NP\ (PREP\ NP)+ \tag{2}$$

They occur as frequently as constructions made with Rule 1 (see Tab. 3). However it is quite hazardeous to consider them as a unique multi-word term in the same way. In particular, they are subject to many variations in their form. *Fabre and Jacquemin* [15] distinguished five different simple syntactic forms that could represent the same concept in French. For example, even without semantic variation (as synonymy), the NP *"annotation in image retrieval"* found in Topic 220 can be modified with no or little semantic change into *"annotate images for retrieval"*, *"retrieve annotated images"*, *"annotated image retrieval"*, *"retrieval of annotated images"*, *"images have been annotated for retrieval"*, etc.

Table 3. Examples of complex noun phrases (Rule 2) in INEX 2005 topics

Topics	Noun phrase
208	history of Artificial Intelligence
216	the architecture of a multimedia retrieval system
217	user-centered design for web sites
219	the granularity of learning objects
233	development of synthesizers for music creation
276	evaluation measure for clustering

Moreover such a phrase does often not occur at all in a relevant element. In a phrase having the form *"NP_1 PREP NP_2"*, we have noted that one of the sub-NPs represents the *context*, while the other one represents the *subject* of the current sentence. The role of each part depends on the structure of the document.

For example, suppose we look for an element dealing with *"evaluation measure for clustering"* (Topic 276). In an article about *clustering* on the whole, we just need to look for the term *"evaluation measure"* (see Fig. 5). Inversely, an article about *evaluation measures* in general must contain an element treating *"clustering"*.

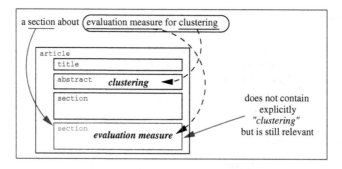

Fig. 5. Contextual search

We have noted, after 2004 campaign, that this issue was an important source of mis-retrieval for search engines. In the case of topic descriptions containing NP_1 PREP NP_2, where NP_2 was the context in most documents, many retrieved doxels contained NP_1 in a bad context, and then were not relevant. For example, a search for *"navigation systems for automobiles"* (Topic 128) returned many doxels about navigation systems in planes or ships in the first ranks.

In this case, to remedy this problem, we would like to perform a *contextual research* (for *"navigation systems"* in the context of a section or an article about *"automobiles"* or inversely), but also a *conditional research* within a single doxel (if a doxel is relevant with *"automobiles"*, then check for *"navigation systems"*).

Unfortunately this kind of features can hardly be represented with a single NEXI query. Even so we tried to simulate such a behaviour. We noticed that the most frequent configuration was "NP_1 in the context of NP_2" when the topic description contained a NP_1 *PREP* NP_2 phrase. We decided to translate such NPs in the following way:

- Contextual search: Addition of NP_2 into a support part concerning the whole article (root element).
- Conditional search: Addition of a sign '+' before NP_2 in the current part.

For example, *"a paragraph about navigation systems for automobiles"* can be translated into:

```
/article[about(., automobiles)]//p[about(.,''navigation systems'')
                            AND about(., +automobiles)]
```

In our tests with INEX 2004 collection, this approach led to a increase in precision of about 10%. But then the support element construction is quite artificial, and this is done to the detriment of strict evaluation metrics (strict quantization and strict interpretation of target and/or support element requirements [16]). By choosing this strategy we admit that we focus principally on vague interpretation and generalised quantization.

4   Example

We give here a significant example, with the analysis of a slightly simplified version of Topic 219 (INEX 2005). Several syntactic parsings could be possible for the same sentence. In practice a "score" is attributed to each rule release, depending on several parameters. In our sample topic only the best scored result is given.

(219) Find sections that discuss the granularity of learning objects.

Figure 6 shows the three major steps of the analysis of this topic. The left frame represents the result of Step 3 (see Sect. 2). Some IR- and corpus-specific reduction rules are then applied and lead to right frame: the term *section* is recognized as tag name **sec** (line 3); the construction *"c2 discusses c4"* is changed into **about(c2, c4)** (lines 4 to 6). The other relations are kept. Translation into NEXI is performed as explained above.

5   Results

We present here our results for both CO+S and CAS INEX 2005 tasks. For CAS task, different evaluations have been performed, depending on the interpretation

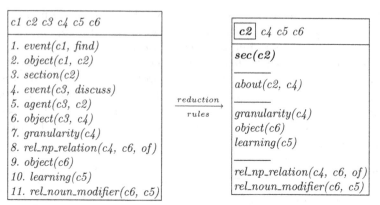

//article[about(., "learning objects")]//sec[about(., granularity) AND
about(., +"learning objects")]

Fig. 6. Semantic representations of Topic 219, and automatic conversion into NEXI

of structural constraints (vague or strict [16]). Different sets of metrics were also used. Tables 4 and 5 present the evaluation with nxCG[25] and ep-gr metrics in generalised quantization [16]. These samples, representative of the entire result set, show the comparison between the baseline and our own best run. We also stress the ratio between our figure and the base score.

Table 4. Results for Content-And-Structure (CAS) submissions

	Baseline	Mines	Ratio		Baseline	Mines	Ratio
SSCAS				**VSCAS**			
nxCG[25]	0.2885	0.2693	0.93	nxCG[25]	0.2531	0.3051	1.21
ep-gr	0.1324	0.1064	0.80	ep-gr	0.0608	0.0682	1.12
SVCAS				**VVCAS**			
nxCG[25]	0.1081	0.1004	0.93	nxCG[25]	0.2281	0.2572	1.13
ep-gr	0.0272	0.0298	1.06	ep-gr	0.0694	0.0799	1.15

These results show a very good performance of our system for CAS task, especially for vague interpretation (as anticipated in Sect. 3.2). Baseline is outperformed in many cases, often widely. This is a strong improvement in comparison with previous year participants results, where the baseline performed about 20% better than natural language systems.

CO+S results are also good, since our system achieves scores that are below, but quite close to the baseline. Results are lower because the interface keeps some meaningless words in the query. This is where our technique needs to be improved.

Anyway it is now proved that an automatic translation can get comparable or better results than a manual process.

Table 5. Results for Content-Only + Structure (CO+S) submissions

	Baseline	Mines	Ratio
COS Thorough			
nxCG[25]	0.2541	0.2146	0.84
ep-gr	0.0904	0.0741	0.82
COS Focussed			
nxCG[25]	0.1998	0.1853	0.92
ep-gr	0.0860	0.0717	0.83

6   Limits

6.1   Limits of the Task

Translation of natural language queries into a formal language like NEXI encounters some limits, mainly due to the fact that the natural language interface cannot give some specific instructions to the retrieval system. The formal language, if not especially designed for this aim, is a pivot preventing from any "communication" between both systems. For example, it is not possible to consider the following features within single NEXI queries[1]:

- NEXI does not allow to perform any conditional search (see Sect. 3.2). The use of '+' sign is not semantically reliable and is often not considered by search engines.
- NEXI cannot either deal with contextual search: A reference to the context occurs preferentially before the retrieved element, in the paragraph preceding it, or in the introduction of the section, etc. Directly refering to the article as a support part of the query (as we did) is too vague.
- NEXI does not bring any proximity operators for terms or structure (but retrieval models can compensate, many systems allow a flexible treatment of phrases [17], and some consider the proximity of doxels [18]).
- It is not possible to represent non-hierarchical relations between elements with NEXI (precedence for example).
- Finally, NEXI is only a query language. It is not designed to deal with any linguistic features. With the linguistic analysis, the interface finds some interesting relations between terms (or elements), as semantic relations (agent, object, etc.), but the translation forces us to give this knowledge up.

On the one hand, formal languages will always stay more precise than natural languages. If sometimes the system with a NLI outperforms the same system with a hand-made NEXI query, this is because the interface found a better, more complete and/or more adequate way to represent the information need in NEXI. On the other hand, for all the reasons above, the use of these formal

---

[1] In addition to this list, NEXI is not designed to deal with many database-oriented constraints, but we are not either interested by this aspect.

languages, if they are not thought with this aim in mind, leads to some loss of information.

If an interface is very interesting because it can be "plugged" to (hopefully) any kind of formal languages, and then be applied to many existing systems, it would also be worthwhile to go further and to build a system with a self-made pivot or without pivot at all.

6.2 Limits of the Evaluation

In the *ad-hoc* task, the input is constant and the retrieval systems are different. To evaluate these systems we look at their output (a ranked list of XML elements). In NLQ2NEXI task, the challenge is precisely to produce the input, and the evaluation is performed indirectly, through the use of a search engine that is common to all participants (different inputs, same system). This way we can make sure that the differences in retrieval performance are really due to the quality of the input, and it becomes possible to compare all NLQ2NEXI systems with each other.

Another way to evaluate interfaces is to compare them with a manual baseline. The same system is run on official NEXI queries[2] (manually written by the author of each topic). In this case, automatic processes are compared with a manual process. Like all human interventions (and IR evaluation is full of them), this introduces a new bias: automatic systems are compared with a query built by a given person at a given time. Probably some different manual translations of the topic description would have led to better results. Moreover, many CO+S topics do not have any NEXI `castitle`[3].

Finally, manual translations from description to NEXI are not always faithful, even if this is much better than it was in 2004 [19]. In particular, many CAS subtopics seem to have a problem with NEXI constraints. Topic 251 is characteristic of this issue:

(251) We are searching paragraphs which are descendant of a section dealing with web information retrieval.

In the official transcription of the description into NEXI, the paragraphs are considered to be dealing with web information retrieval:

`//article//sec//p[about(., web retrieval)]`[4]

Even if this interpretation is syntactically correct, it seems obvious that any human people would understand that the section is concerned by the verbal phrase (*dealing with web information retrieval*):

---

[2] What we call the "official" NEXI title of a topic is the query proposed by the author (see the example of Fig. 1). This NEXI query is used by the INEX *ad-hoc* task participants.

[3] Besides, a study on the performances of automatic NEXI titles compared to CO official titles would probably be very interesting.

[4] By the way we can note that *"web information retrieval"* has been replaced by *"web retrieval"*.

```
//article//sec[about(., web retrieval)]//p
```

But this form is not correct in NEXI (where the returned element must contain an 'about' clause [8]).

The narrative part of this topic confirms the author's NEXI title, but adds to the confusion: *"the paragraphs which are descendants of section describing the topic related to web information retrieval are also regarded as relevant. However, compared with paragraphs described above, these are considered less relevant"*.

6.3   Limits of Our System

The following is a non-exhaustive list of problems encountered by our natural language interface. In our opinion, these issues represent the most important factors that make the system not work well for some topics. We do not broach here the "usual" difficulties that NLP has in traditional information retrieval (spelling mistakes, noise produced by non query terms, anaphoras, pragmatic issues...), but rather those that are specific to structural constraints.

Lexical Ambiguity. Classical lexical problems in IR are semantic relations between different words (synonymy, hyponymy, etc.) and words that have multiple meanings (homographs). Homographs raise a new problem in XML retrieval, where some words can be understood as normal content-based query terms, but also as tag names (or a synonym of a tag name). Using a simple dictionary of synonyms to detect references to tag names is obviously not enough. For example the words *"document"* and *"information"* are, most of the time, used for refering to XML elements (*"Find information/documents about"*). But how to deal with a query about *"multimedia document models"* (Topic 210) or *"incomplete information"* (Topic 224)? What if the query is *"Retrieve information about information retrieval"*? Actually it does not seem so difficult to handle this with specific syntactic features, but we clearly under-estimated this issue so far.

Corpus-dependant Knowledge. Throughout the query analysis, we use several kinds of information about the corpus, among which the DTD (and the terms associated with tag names), but also some specific linguistic constructions. For example, as shown by Fig. 7, a query about *"information by Moldovan"* (Topic 204) implicitly refers to an author (tag 'au' in INEX collection); *"works citing Baeza-Yates"* (Topic 280) introduces a bibliographic element. All these rules are necessary to analyse many queries properly, but are an obstacle to the extension of the tool to general corpora, or to heteregeneous collections[5].

7   Conclusion

INEX 2005 NLQ2NEXI task proves that the help brought by a natural language interface is very effective. NEXI queries that are automatically obtained from a

---

[5] Note that these rules are structure-specific, but not domain-specific (in the case of INEX, this means that no rules have been set up especially for computer science information retrieval).

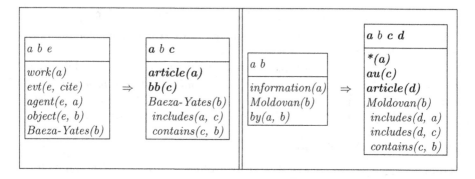

Fig. 7. Examples of corpus-dependant rules, applied on *"works citing Baeza-Yates"* (left, Topic 280) and *"information by Moldovan"* (right, Topic 204)

description in English lead to better results than manual queries, yet written by experts. This is the proof that natural language explanations of an information need are not only easier to formulate, but also more effective. The results also confirm the assumptions made in the introduction: building a natural language interface for XML retrieval is much different than doing it for database querying or traditional IR.

Moreover, techniques used by participants are quite different; While we (Ecole des Mines de Saint-Etienne) obtain the best scores in CAS with a vague interpretation of elements, Queensland University of Technology performs better in strict interpretation and University of Klagenfurt gets its best results in CO task. Teams have a lot to learn from each other, and global results should improve a lot in the future. But each technique produces good scores for a given task to the detriment of another one, and the best way to progress is probably to define a new model taking all what we need into account (like conditional and contextual searches proposed in this article).

References

[1] Strzalkowski, T., Lin, F., Wang, J., Perz-Carballo, J.: Evaluating Natural Language Processing Techniques in Information Retrieval. [20] 113–145
[2] Sparck Jones, K.: What is the role of NLP in text retrieval? [20] 1–24
[3] Androutsopoulos, I., Ritchie, G., Thanisch, P.: Natural Language Interfaces to Databases – An Introduction. Journal of Natural Language Engineering 1 (1995) 29–81
[4] Copestake, A., Jones, K.S.: Natural Language Interfaces to Databases. The Knowledge Engineering Review 5 (1990) 225–249
[5] Perrault, C., Grosz, B.: Natural Language Interfaces. Exploring Articial Intelligence (1988) 133–172
[6] Fuhr, N., Großjohann, K.: XIRQL: A Query Language for Information Retrieval in XML Documents. Proceedings of the 24th ACM SIGIR Conference, New York City, NY, USA (2001) 172–180

[7] Sigurbjörnsson, B., Trotman, A., Geva, S., Lalmas, M., Larsen, B., Malik, S.: INEX 2005 Guidelines for Topic Development (2005)

[8] Trotman, A., Sigurbjrnsson, B.: Narrowed Extended XPath I (NEXI). [21] 16–40

[9] Schmid, H.: Probabilistic Part-of-Speech Tagging Using Decision Trees. In: International Conference on New Methods in Language Processing. (1994)

[10] Tannier, X., Girardot, J.J., Mathieu, M.: Analysing Natural Language Queries at INEX 2004. [21] 395–409

[11] Arampatzis, A., van der Weide, T., Koster, C., van Bommel, P.: Linguistically-motivated Information Retrieval. In Encyclopedia of Library and Information Science. Volume 69. Marcel Dekker, Inc., New York, Basel (2000) 201–222

[12] Moreau, F., Sébillot, P.: Contributions des techniques du traitement automatique des langues la recherche d'information. Technical Report, IRISA, France (2005)

[13] Tzoukermann, E., Klavans, J.L., Jacquemin, C.: Effective use of natural language processing techniques for automatic conflation of multi-word terms: the role of derivational morphology, part of speech tagging, and shallow parsing. In: Proceedings of the 20th ACM SIGIR Conference, Philadelphia, USA (1997) 148–155

[14] Arampatzis, A.T., Tsoris, T., Koster, C.H.A., van der Weide, T.P.: Phrase-based Information Retrieval. Information Processing & Management **34** (1998) 693–707

[15] Fabre, C., Jacquemin, C.: Boosting Variant Recognition with Light Semantics. In: Proceedings of the 18th International Conference on Computational Linguistics, COLING 2000, Saarbrcken (2000) 264–270

[16] Kazai, G., Lalmas, M.: INEX 2005 Evaluation Metrics (2005) http://inex.is. informatik.uni-duisburg.de/2005/inex-2005-metricsv4.pdf.

[17] Geva, S., Leo-Spork, M.: XPath Inverted File for Information Retrieval. Proceedings of the second Workshop of the Initiative for the Evaluation of XML retrieval (INEX), December 15–17, 2003, Schloss Dagstuhl, Germany (2004) 110–117

[18] Sauvagnat, K., Boughanem, M., Chrisment, C.: Searching XML documents using relevance propagation. In: String Processing and Information Retrieval, Padoue, Italy, Springer-Verlag, New York City, NY, USA (2004) 242–254

[19] Woodley, A., Geva, S.: NLPX at INEX 2004. [21] 382–394

[20] Strzalkowski, T., ed.: Natural Language Information Retrieval. Kluwer Academic Publisher, Dordrecht, NL (1999)

[21] Fuhr, N., Lalmas, M., Malik, S., Szlàvik, Z., eds.: Advances in XML Information Retrieval. Third Workshop of the Initiative for the Evaluation of XML retrieval (INEX). Volume 3493 of Lecture Notes in Computer Science. Springer-Verlag, New York City, NY, USA (2005)

Processing Heterogeneous Collections in XML Information Retrieval

Maria Izabel Menezes Azevedo and Klérisson Vinícius Ribeiro Paixão,
and Diego Vinícius Castro Pereira

Department of Computer Science,
State University of Montes Claros, Montes Claros(MG), Brazil
mimaizabel@gmail.com, klerisson@hotmail.com, diegovcastro@yahoo.com.br

Abstract. Our model is based on the observation that the tags used
in XML documents are semantically related to the content that they
delimit. To evaluate the performance of our approach, we participated
in the INEX 2004 heterogeneous track, along with 34 other institutions,
from which only 5 groups, including us, submitted runs. In this paper
we describe how the approach we used in INEX 2004 and 2005 processes
heterogeneous collections without any mapping of DTDs.

1 Introduction

Our model [3] is based on the observation and theorical confirmation [1] that
the tags of an XML [4] document are semantically related to the content that
they delimit. We consider the structure of the XML standard as a new source of
evidence, able to assist in the identification of the information contained in the
documents without being essential to its identification.

According to this premise, formal aspects of XML, such as the DTD, are not
used in our model. Our aim is to associate the XML tags with their content,
based on statistical measures that are similar to those used in the standard
vector space model, which relate the frequency of terms with the information of
the document.

Thus, our model explores the diversity of tags of the XML documents, and its
potential is evaluated in heterogeneous collections, where the structural diversity
allows better linking between the semantics of tags and their content.

In this paper, we show how our model processes heterogeneous collections,
presenting how each one of the subfactors are calculated and how they are placed
in the standard vector space model to explore important aspects of the XML
structure.

The remainder of this paper is organized in as follows. Section 2 presents related work. Section 3 is about the calculation of each subfactor in heterogeneous
collections. Section 4 presents the results and Section 5 concludes the paper.

2 Related Work

In INEX 2004, according to Sauvagnat and Boughanem [12], the idea behind the
heterogeneous track is that the information seeker is interested in semantically

N. Fuhr et al. (Eds.): INEX 2005, LNCS 3977, pp. 388–397, 2006.

meaningful answers irrespective of the structure of documents. Thus, this idea motivated their model which uses the relevance propagation method. This model is based on automatic indexing and introduces an interesting query processing technique that is able to process sub-queries that are logically linked. For this, the first step is to transform NEXI [13] topics into XFIRM queries. Then, this new query is decomposed into sub-queries. After each sub-query has been processed, the result of each one of them is propagated to generate the whole result of the query. However, mapping structural conditions from one DTD onto another was a problem, and to solve it they presented one DTD built manually by comparing the different DTDs.

Another relevant work was presented by [8], which continued to explore the approach of fusion to XML retrieval. This approach, in the heterogeneous track, was used to treat the different collections as separate databases with their own DTD, but these databases can be treated as a single database by the system. Another important work, described by Larson, was the configuration file which could specify subsets of tags to be used with the same meaning, for example //p, //p1, //tf for "paragraphs". We suppose Larson did not have problems with tags without semantic meaning such as Fld001, but he did not mention it.

In [2], an approach for creating a unified heterogeneous structure from heterogeneous data sources was presented. To build this unified conceptual model, first they identified groups of concepts that are semantically similar. To do this, they used an approach called WordNet, developed by Christine Fellbaum [5], which is able to detect similarity between "editor" and "edition", for example. Finally, to treat tags without semantic meaning it is necessary to capture the DTD comments preceding them and searches for the best cluster to put them.

All the participants of the heterogeneous track had difficulties to treat one document that was 217MB in size. To solve this problem, Larson [8] proposed to treat each of the main sub-elements as separate documents. Lehtonen [9] proposed to divide the file into fragments based on size. Although, large documents are problematic at "Het Track", they are not relevant problems of "Het Track" only, but to retrieval systems in general.

3 XML Factor Calculation

In our previous paper [3], we have defined how the standard vector space model [10] [11] was adapted to process an XML document whose relevance is given by:

$$\rho(Q, D) = \sum ti \in Q \cap D \frac{W_q(ti) * W_d(ti) * fxml(ti, e)}{Q * D} \tag{1}$$

where,

- ti is a term in the collection;
- $W_q(ti)$ is the weight of the query;
- $W_d(ti)$ is the weight of the document;
- $fxml(ti,e)$ is the XML factor.

Next, we describe how the factor *fxml* is used to process heterogeneous collections and return elements of different structures without any mapping between those structures.

We consider the following characteristics of the XML standard:

- Its nested structure through the Nesting Factor *(fnh)*;
- The similarity between the query structure and the structure of the document, through the Structure Factor *(fstr)*;
- The semantic relation between terms and tags, through the Co-occurrence Factor *(focr)*.

Then, the factor *fxml* is given by:

$$fxml(ti, e) = fnh(ti, e) * fstr(ti, e) * focr(ti, e) \qquad (2)$$

where,

- *ti* is a term in the collection;
- *e* is an element in the collection.

3.1   The Nesting Factor

The nesting factor expresses the importance of terms considering their positions in the XML tree. As the augmentation factor, this factor reduces the term contribution according to the distance of the elements in XML tree. The factor proposed does not have a defined value. Its value is inversely proportional to the distance between the level of the element that contains the term and its ancestor, whose relevance is calculated. It is given by:

$$fnh(ti, e) = \frac{1}{(1 + nl)} \qquad (3)$$

where,

- *nl* is the number of levels from element *e* to its sub-element that contains the term *ti*.

The nesting factor can vary between the following values:

- *fnh(ti,e)* = *1*, for terms directly in elements *e*;
- *fnh(ti,e)* = *1/nd*, where *nd* is the depth of the XML tree.

In Figure 1, we have *fnh(*computer*,*fm*)* = *1/(1+3)*. This factor reduces the contribution of one term for the relevance of the elements more distant (upwards) in the XML tree. It compensates the high frequency of a term in upwards elements caused by the nesting of the XML structure. Without this consideration the upwards elements tend to occupy the first positions in the ranking showed to the user.

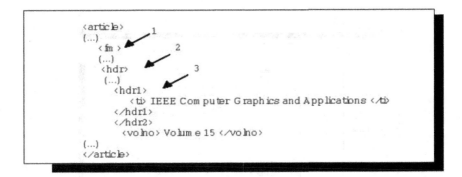

Fig. 1. The Nesting Factor

3.2 The Structure Factor

The Structure Factor expresses how a query with structural constraints (CAS) [7] is satisfied by the context of the determined element. This factor values a context that better satisfies structural constraints present in the query. Mathematically, it is given by the relation between structural constraints in the query and the structure of the element. It is given by:

$$fstr(ti, e) = \frac{(common\_markups + 1)}{(nr\_qmarkups + 1)} \tag{4}$$

where,

- *common_markups* is the number of tags presented in the query structural constraints and also in the context of element *e* that contains *ti*;
- *nr_markups* is the number of tags in the query structural constraints.

It can vary from:

- *fstr(ti,e) = 1/(nr_qmarkups+1)*, when no structural constraints appears in the context of *ti*;
- *fstr(ti,e) = 1*, when all query's structural constraints tags appears in the context of *ti*.

For example, for the NEXI query in Figure 2 processed on the heterogeneous collection, also shown in Figure 2, we obtain the following results:
For the element /artigo/pessoa/nome in the first article:

- *nr_qmarkups = 3;*
- *common_markups = 2;*

and

- *fstr(ti, e) = (2+1)/(3+1) = 3/4.*

For the element /article/person/name in the second article:

- *nr_markups = 3;*
- *common_markups = 0;*

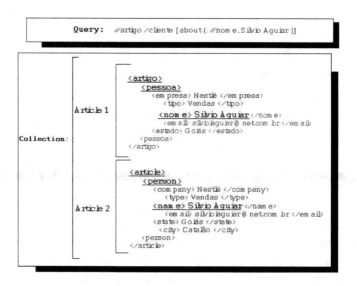

Fig. 2. The Structure Factor

and

$$- fstr(ti,e) = (0+1)/(3+1) = 1/4.$$

This factor gives more value to the element `/artigo/pessoa/nome` in the first article, where *fstr* is equal to *3/4*, and whose context better meets the structural constraints of the query. However, it does allow that the element `/article/person /name` in the second article, where *fstr* is equal to *1/4*, is also returned to the user, demonstrating the model's application on heterogeneous collections.

This is important for CAS queries, where the user specifies the elements that will better fit his or her information need. For CO [7] queries, *fstr* will always be equal to 1 because of the following:

- *nr_qmarkups = 0* (CO queries do not have any structural constraints);
- *common_markups = 0* (there are no common tags between documents and query);

and

$$- fstr\ (ti,e) = 1.$$

Consequentially, in this case the factor *fstr* does not influence the relevance equation.

3.3   The Co-occurrence Factor

The last factor, Co-occurrence Factor, expresses the semantic relation between tags and their contents. To express mathematically this semantic relation, we applied the same principle that is used in standard vector space model to relate terms and documents: the higher the frequency of a term in one document, the greater the semantical relation between them. The value of this semantical relation for a particular query depends on the frequency of terms and tags in the collection, too. This factor is calculated as follows.

$$focr(ti, e) = cf(ti, e) * idf(ti, e) * N * icf(e) \tag{5}$$

where,

- *cf(ti,e)* is the number of times the tag of element *e*, denoted by *m*, delimits a textual content containing term *ti*. In other words, number of co-occurrences of term *ti* and tag *m* in the collection;
- *idf(ti,e)* is the inverse of the number of elements *e* that contain *ti*.

So, $cf(ti, e) * idf(ti, e)$, is the reason between the number of times term *ti* appears with *m* for the number of the elements containing *ti* in the collection.

- *icf(e)* is the inverse of the number of times markup *m* appears in the collection.
- *N* is the total number of elements in the collection;

and

- $icf(e) * N$ express the popularity of tags *m* in the collection.

For example, for the NEXI query of Figure 3 processed on the heterogeneous collection shown in Figure 3, we have the following results:
For the element **/artigo/pessoa/estado** in the first article:

- *cf(Paulo, estado) = 1;*
- *idf(Paulo) = 1/4;*
- *icf(estado) = 1/3;*
- *N = 16;*
- *focr(Paulo, estado) = (1 * 1/4) * (1/3 * 16) = 1.333*

For the element **/artigo/pessoa/nome** in the second article:

- *cf(Paulo, nome) = 2;*
- *idf(Paulo) = 1/4;*
- *icf(nome) = 1/3;*
- *N = 16;*
- *focr(Paulo, nome) = (2 * 1/4) * (1/3 * 16) = 2.666.*

For the element **/article/person/name** in the last article:

- *cf(Paulo, name) = 1;*
- *idf(Paulo) = 1/4;*
- *icf(name) = 1/1;*
- *N = 16;*
- *focr(Paulo, name) = (1 * 1/4) * (1/1 * 16) = 4.0.*

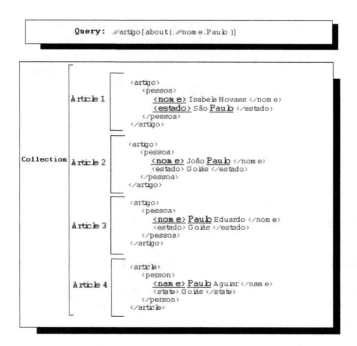

Fig. 3. The Co-occurrence Factor

The fact of /article/person/name and /artigo/pessoa/nome be returned to the user confirms that our model can deal with heterogeneous collections. The element /article/person/name will be presented to the user for having been valued for its rarity within the collection. The element /artigo/pessoa/estado will be presented to the user although it does not meet the query but obtains the lower value of co-occurrence factor.

The co-occurrence factor values the co-occurrence of terms and tags, considering the popularity of tags. With this factor we intend to explore the characteristic of XML originating from its definition: the presence of tags that describe its contents.

For the effectiveness of our model, it is important that it has a narrow semantic relation between terms and tags. This semantic relation will be easier in heterogeneous collections because they present a bigger structure diversity.

To conclude, the XML Factor *(fxml)* explores characteristics of XML by looking for the semantics of terms and information behind words.

4 Results

We submitted runs to the INEX heterogeneous track, but as the assessments were not concluded yet at the time of writing, we have no Recall/Precision curves to show here. It follows an answer to a query containing elements from

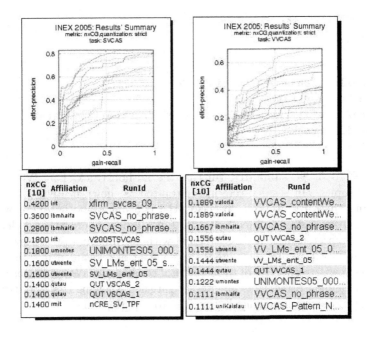

Fig. 4. Adhoc Results for SVCAS and VVCAS sub tasks

many sub-collections, confirming that our model can deal with different DTDs. For query:

$$//\texttt{article[about(.//author,Nivio Ziviani)]}$$

we get the following answer:

```
<topictopic-id=''2''>...
<result>
    <subcollection name=''ieee''/>
    <file>co/2000/ry037</file>
    <path>/article[1]/fm[1]/au[1]</path>
    <rank> 3</rank>
</result>...
<result>
    <subcollection name=''dblp'' />
    <file>dblp</file>
    <path>/dblp[1]/article[177271]/author[4]</path>
    <rank>6</rank>
</result>...
<result>
    <subcollection name=''CompuScience'' />
    <file>exp-dxf1.xml.UTF-8</file>
    <path>/bibliography[1]/article[23]/author[1]</path>
```

```
      <rank> 30</rank>
</result>
...
<result>
      <subcollectionname=''hcibib'' />
      <file>hcibib</file>
      <path>/file[1]/entry[229]/article[1]/author[1]</path>
      <rank>139</rank>
</result>
```

At INEX 2005, we submitted runs to the ad-hoc track. For SVCAS and VVCAS [6] topics, our results were in the top ten as shown in Figure 4.

Analysing these results and observing the concept of both topics, we can conclude that our system worked better for CAS topics, where support elements have been interpreted vaguely. It is coherent with our information retrieval view. We have developed an approach where an element is relevant if it satisfies the information need, irrespective of the structural constraints. We get better results when target element constraints are strictly satisfied, showing that the structure factor (fstr), proposed in our model, can improve performance.

5   Conclusion

In INEX 2005, we get better results than at INEX 2004, showing that our research is going in a correct direction. The ability of our system to deal with a heterogeneous collection and its results when target element constraints are strictly satisfied shown that the structure factor (fstr) proposed in our model can improve performance. For CO queries, specially the CO+S ones, we do get the worst results, demanding further investigation.

For next year, we intend to participate in the heterogeneous track so that we can really evaluate the co-occurrence factor (fcoo) and conclude if tags of XML structure can be used to improve performance of search engines.

References

1. S. Abiteboul, P. Buneman and D. Suciu.: Data on the Web - From Relations to Semistructured Data in XML. Mogan Kaufmann Publishers, San Francisco, California, (2000) 27–50.
2. S. Abiteboul, I. Manolescu, B. Nguyen, N. Preda.: A Test Plataform for the INEX Heterogeneous Track. INEX (2004) LNCS
3. M. Azevedo, L.Pantuza e N. Ziviane.: A Universal Model for XML Information Retrieval. INEX (2004) LNCS 3493 311–321 (2005).
4. T. Bray, J. Paoli, C. M. Sperberg-McQueen and E. Maler.: Extensible Markup Language (XML) 1.0. 2nd ed. http://www.w3.org/TR/REC-xml, Cct 2000. W3C Recommendation 6 October (2000).
5. C. Fellbaum.: *WordNet*: An Electronic Lexical Database. MIT Press. (1998).

6. S. Geva, M. Lalmas, B. Larsen, S. Malink, B. Sigurbjrnsson and A. Trotman.: INEX 2005 Guidelines for Topic Development. In INEX 2005 Workshop Pre-Proceedings,(2005) pp.375.
7. G. Kazai, M. Lalmas and S. Malik.: INEX'03 Guidelines for Topic Development. In INEX 2003 Workshop Proceedings, Duisburg, 2003 pg. 153-154.
8. R. R. Larson.: Cheshire II at INEX '04: Fusion and Feedback for the Adhoc and Heterogeneous Tracks. INEX (2004) LNCS 3493 322–336.
9. M. Lehtonen.: Extirp 2004: Towards Heterogeneity. INEX (2004) LNCS 3493 372–381.
10. B. Ribeiro-Neto e R. Baeza-Yates.: Modern Information Retrieval. Addison Wesley. (1999) pp. 27–30.
11. G. Salton e M. E. Lesk.: Computer evaluation of indexing and text processing. Journal of the ACM. 15(1) (1968) 8–36.
12. K. Sauvagnat, M. Boughanem.: Using a relevance propagation method for Adhoc and Heterogeneus tracks in INEX 2004. INEX (2004) LNCS 3493 337–348.
13. A. Trotman and B. Sigurbjornsson.: Narrowed extended xpath i. In In INEX 2004 Workshop Proceedings,(2004) pp.16.

The Interactive Track at INEX 2005

Birger Larsen[1], Saadia Malik[2], and Anastasios Tombros[3]

[1] Dept. of Information Studies, Royal School of LIS, Copenhagen, Denmark
blar@db.dk
[2] Fak. 5/IIS, Information Systems, University of Duisburg-Essen,
Duisburg, Germany
malik@is.informatik.uni-duisburg.de
[3] Dept. of Computer Science, Queen Mary University of London, London, UK
tassos@dcs.qmul.ac.uk

Abstract. In its second year, the Interactive Track at INEX focused on addressing some fundamental issues of interactive XML retrieval: is element retrieval useful for searchers, what granularity of elements do searchers find more useful, what applications for element retrieval can be viable in interactive environments, etc.. In addition, the track also expanded by offering an alternative document collection, by including two additional tasks, and by attracting more participating groups: A total of 11 research groups and 119 test persons participated in the three different tasks that were included in the track. In this paper, we describe the main issues that the Interactive Track at INEX 2005 attempts to address and the methodology and tasks that were used in the track.

1 Introduction

The overall motivation for the Interactive Track at INEX is twofold. First, to investigate the behaviour of users when interacting with components of XML documents, and secondly to investigate and develop approaches for XML retrieval which are effective in user-based environments.

One of the major outcomes of the Interactive Track in 2004 was the need to investigate methods that can be supportive during the search process based on features extracted from the XML formatting [1, 2]. Problems that might be solved using such methods include overlapping components, and the presentation of retrieved elements in the hit list.

In the system that was offered by the track in 2005 these two issues were addressed. This offered us the opportunity to study how overall user search behaviour was affected by these changes when compared to the behaviour observed in 2004.

In addition, the following aims were addressed in 2005 following the recommendations of the INEX Methodology Workshop at the Glasgow IR Festival[1]:

- To elicit user perceptions of what is needed from an XML retrieval system. The aim is to see whether element retrieval is what users need: Does element retrieval make sense at all to users, do users prefer longer components, shorter components or whole documents, would they rather have passages than elements, etc.

---

[1] See http://www.cs.otago.ac.nz/inexmw/ for the proceedings and presentation slides.

N. Fuhr et al. (Eds.): INEX 2005, LNCS 3977, pp. 398–410, 2006.

- To identify an application for element retrieval. This year, a mixture of topics that were simulated work tasks [3] (based on topics from the ad hoc track) and information needs formulated by the test persons themselves. The aim of including the latter was to enable studies of what characterises the tasks users formulate, and to see what kinds of applications users might need an element retrieval system for. A total of 121 such topics derived from the test persons were collected for further analysis.
- To introduce an alternative document collection with the Lonely Planet collection as an optional task in order to broaden the scope of INEX and to allow test persons with different backgrounds (e.g. educational) to participate.

The format of the Interactive Track in 2005 was deliberately of an exploratory nature, and has relatively broad aims rather than addressing very specific research questions. Element retrieval is still in its infancy and many basic questions remain unanswered as shown by the discussions at the IR Festival. Aside from the automatic and detailed logging of test persons as used last year, more emphasis was placed on producing qualitative results. Many of the aims stated above were therefore dealt with through careful interviewing and detailed questionnaires. A total of three tasks were available to the track participants: one compulsory task that all participants had to fulfil with a minimum number of test persons, and two optional tasks. These tasks combined several element retrieval systems, topic types and XML collections. By providing a multitude of different perspectives it is our hope that the Interactive Track can aid in illuminating some of the core issues in element retrieval.

The remainder of the paper is organised as follows: The three tasks are described briefly in Section 2, followed by details of the participating groups in Section 3. In depth descriptions of Task A and Task C are given in Sections 4 and 5 respectively, whereas Task B is only described briefly in Section 2. Concluding remarks are given in Section 6.

2 Tasks in the INEX 2005 Interactive Track

2.1 Task A - Common Baseline System with IEEE Collection

In this task each test person searched three topics in the IEEE collection: Two simulated work tasks provided by the organisers, and one formulated by the test person herself in relation to an information need of her own. The baseline system used by all participants was a java-based element retrieval system built within the Daffodil framework[2], and was provided by the track organisers. It has a number of improvements over last year's baseline system, including handling of overlaps, better element summaries in the hit list, a simpler relevance scale, and various supportive interface functionalities. Task A was compulsory for all participating groups with a minimum of 6 test persons.

2.2 Task B - Participation with Own Element Retrieval System

This task allowed groups who have a working element retrieval system to test their system against a baseline system. Groups participating in Task B were free to choose

---

[2] See http://www.is.informatik.uni-duisburg.de/projects/daffodil/index.html.en

between the IEEE collection or the Lonely Planet collection, and had a large degree of freedom in setting up the experiment to fit the issues they wanted to investigate in relation to their own system. If the IEEE collection was used Daffodil was offered as baseline system. For the Lonely Planet collection a baseline system was kindly provided by the Contentlab at Utrecht University[3]. The recommended experimental setup was very close to that of Task A, with the main difference that simulated work tasks should be assigned to test persons rather than freely chosen. This in order to allow for direct comparisons between the baseline system and the local system.

Task B was optional for those groups who had access to their own element retrieval system, and was separate from task A. Thus additional test persons needed to be engaged for task B. See [7] for an example of an experimental setup used in Task B.

2.3 Task C - Searching the Lonely Planet Collection

This task allowed interested groups to carry out experiments with the Lonely Planet collection. Each test person searched four topics which were simulated work tasks provided by the organisers. The system (B^3–SDR) provided by Utrecht University was used in this task. The system is a fully functional element retrieval system that supports several query modes. Task C was optional for those groups who wished to do experiments with the new collection, and was separate from task A and B. Thus additional test persons needed to be engaged for task C. Note that the Lonely Planet collection allows for test persons that do not have a computer science background (in contrast to the IEEE CS collection used in Task A).

Detailed experimental procedures including questionnaires and interview guides for all three tasks were provided to the participants. In addition, a specification of a minimum logging format was provided for local systems in Task B [8]. As for last year, minimum participation in the INEX Interactive Track did not require a large amount of work as the baseline system for Task A was provided by the track. The bulk of the time needed for participating groups was spent on running the experiments; approximately 2 hours per test person.

3 Participating Groups

A total of 12 research groups signed up for participation in the Interactive Track and 11 completed the minimum number of required test persons. Their affiliations and distribution on tasks are given in Table 1 below. All 11 groups participated in Task A with a total of 76 test persons searching on 228 tasks. Only one group, University of Amsterdam, participated in Task B with 14 test persons searching on 42 tasks. Four groups participated in Task C with 29 test persons searching 114 tasks. A total of 119 test persons from the 11 active participants took part in the Interactive Track. In comparison, in 2004, 10 groups took part with 88 test persons.

---

[3] See http://contentlab.cs.uu.nl/

Table 1. Research groups participating in the Interactive Track at INEX2005

Research Group	Task A Test Persons (Topics)	Task B Test Persons (Topics)	Task C Test Persons (Topics)
CWI, University of Twente, The Netherlands	6 (18)	-	-
Kyungpook National University, Korea	12 (36)	-	-
Oslo University College, Norway	8 (24)	-	-
Queen Mary University of London, England	6 (18)	-	-
RMIT University, Australia	6 (18)	-	12 (48)
Royal School of LIS, Denmark	6 (18)	-	6 (24)
Rutgers University, USA	6 (18)	-	4 (16)
University of Amsterdam, The Netherlands	6 (18)	14 (42)	-
University of Duisburg-Essen, Germany	6 (18)	-	-
University of Tampere, Finland	8 (24)	-	-
Utrecht University, The Netherlands	6 (18)	-	7 (26)
Total	76 (228)	14 (42)	29 (114)

4 Task A

4.1 Document Corpus

The document corpus used in Task A was the 764 MB corpus of articles from the IEEE Computer Society's journals covering articles from 1995-2004 (version 1.8, merged new & old collection).

4.2 Relevance Assessments

The intention was that each viewed element should be assessed with regard to its relevance to the topic by the test person. This was, however, not enforced by the system as we believe that it may be regarded as intrusive by the test persons [4]. In addition, concerns have been raised that last year's composite two dimensional scale was far too complex for the test persons to comprehend [5, 6]. Therefore it was chosen to simplify the relevance scale, also in order to ease the cognitive load on the test persons. The scale used was a simple 3-point scale measuring the usefulness (or pertinence) of the element in relation to the test person's perception of the task:

> 2 – Relevant
> 1 – Partially Relevant
> 0 – Not Relevant

Please note that in contrast to the assessments made for the ad hoc track, there was no requirement on the test persons to view each retrieved element as independent from other viewed components. We have chosen not to enforce any rules in order to allow the test persons to behave as close as possible to what they would normally do.

For Task C we experimented with a slightly more complex relevance scale (see Section 6.2 below).

4.3 System

The baseline system used in Task A was a Java-based element retrieval system built within the Daffodil framework. The HyREX retrieval engine[4] was used as backend in the baseline system.

Fig. 1 shows the query and results list interface of the baseline system. After entering a query and pressing "Search" a search progress indicator informed the test person about the number documents found. A related term list also appeared, suggesting alternative search terms (not shown). The results were presented as documents and in some cases, the system indicated which elements that might be most closely related to the query.

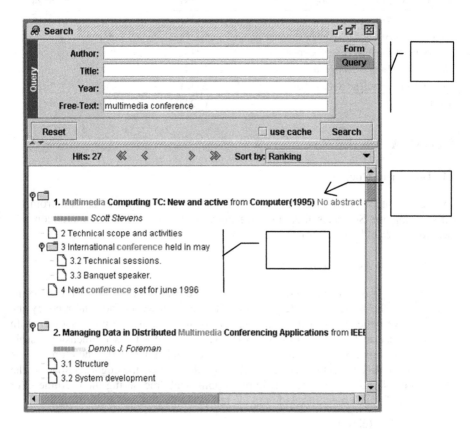

Fig. 1. Query box and result list display in the baseline system used in Task A

Double-clicking a document or an element opened this in a new window as shown in Fig. 2 below. This was split in two panes: one with a Table of Contents of the whole document, and one with the full text of the selected element. The selected

---

[4] http://www.is.informatik.uni-duisburg.de/projects/hyrex/

element was displayed on the right. On the left, the Table of Contents indicated the currently viewed element, other retrieved elements, viewed and assessed elements. The relevance scale was implemented as simple icons to be clicked:

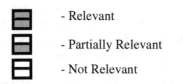

- Relevant

- Partially Relevant

- Not Relevant

The logging in the baseline system was saved to a database for greater flexibility and stability. The log data comprises of one session for each topic the test person searches. The log for each session recorded the events in the session, both the actions performed by the test person and the responses from the system.

4.4 Tasks/Topics

In order to study the questions outlined in Section 1 above related to the needs for element retrieval systems and possible applications of such systems, both real and simulated information needs were used in Task A.

The test persons were asked to supply examples of own information needs. As it may be hard for the test persons to formulate topics that are covered by the collection, the test persons emailed two topics they would like to search for 48 hours before the experiment. The experimenters then did a preliminary search of the collection to determine which topic had the best coverage in the collection. The topics supplied by the test persons were not all well-suited to an element retrieval system, but they all had a valuable function as triggers for the structured interview where it was attempted to elicit user perceptions of what they need from an element retrieval system, and to identify possible applications for element retrieval. They may also be valuable for the formulation of topics for next year's track. Therefore, both topics were recorded and submitted as part of the results.

The simulated work tasks were derived from the CO+S and CAS INEX 2005 ad-hoc topics, ignoring any structural constraints. In order to make the topics comprehensible by other than the topic author, it was required that the ad hoc topics not only detail *what* is being sought for, but also *why* this is wanted, and in what *context* the information need has arisen. This information was exploited for creating simulated work task situations for Task A that, on the one hand will allow the test persons to engage in realistic searching behaviour, and on the other provide a certain level of experimental control by being common across test persons[5].

For Task A, six topics were selected and modified into simulated work tasks. In last year's track we attempted to identify tasks of different types and to study the difference between them, but without great success. This year a simple partition has been made into two categories:

---

[5] See the work of Borlund for more information on simulated work tasks, e.g. Borlund, 2003 (http://informationr.net/ir/8-3/paper152.html).

- General tasks (G category), and
- Challenging tasks (C category), which are more complex and may be less easy to complete.

In addition to their own information need, each test person chose one task from each category. This allows the topic to be more "relevant" and interesting to the test person. A maximum time limit of 20 minutes applied for each task. Sessions could finish before this if the test person felt they have completed the task.

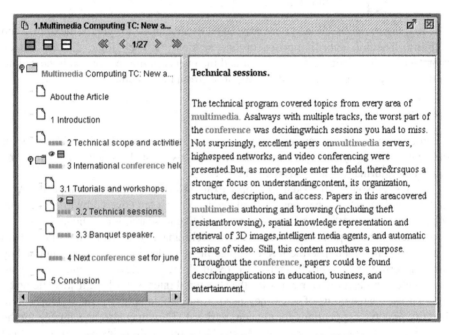

Fig. 2. Full text result in the baseline system used in Task A

4.5 Experimental Design

4.5.1 Experimental Matrix
A minimum of 6 test persons from each participating site were used. Each test person searched on one simulated work task from each category (chosen by the test person) as well as one of their own topics. The order in which task categories were performed by searchers was permuted in order to neutralise learning effects. This means that one complete round of the experiment requires 6 searchers.

The basic experimental matrix looked as follows:

Rotation 1:   OT, STG, STC
Rotation 2:   STC, OT, STG
Rotation 3:   STG, STC, OT
Rotation 4:   STG, OT, STC
Rotation 5:   STC, STG, OT
Rotation 6:   OT, STC, STG

Where OT = Own task, and STG, STC are the two 2 simulated work task categories. As can be seen from Table 1 above some groups did more than 6 test persons. It was attempted to coordinate the permutation rotations across these groups to arrive at an equal distribution of across the track.

4.5.2 Experimental Procedure
The experimental procedure for each test person is outlined below.

1. Experimenter briefed the searcher, and explained the format of the study
2. Tutorial of the system was given with a training task, and experimenter answered any questions
3. 'Instructions to searchers' handed out
4. Any questions answered by the experimenter
5. Entry questionnaire handed out
6. Task description for the first category handed out, and a task selected
7. Pre-task questionnaire handed out
8. Task began, and experimenter logged in. Max. duration 20 minutes. Experimenter logged out.
9. Post-task questionnaire handed out
10. Steps 7-10 were repeated for the two other tasks
11. Post-experiment questionnaire handed out
12. Interview

The system training, the three tasks and completion of questionnaires and interview were performed in one, continuous session. An 'Instructions to searchers' document gave information to the searchers about the experiment and their role in it, including basic information about system information, an outline of the experimental procedure, and how to assess elements for relevance. A number of questionnaires and guidelines for post-experiment interviews were provided by the track organisers. The purpose of the semi-structured interview was to attempt to elicit user perceptions of what they need from an element retrieval system, and to identify possible applications for element retrieval.

5 Task C

Task C was optional for those groups who wished to experiment with the Lonely Planet collection, and was separate from Task A and B. Thus additional test persons needed to be engaged for Task C. Task C was meant as an exploratory task to initiate interactive experiments with the LP collection.

5.1 Document Corpus

The document corpus used in Task C was the Lonely Planet collection. The Lonely Planet collection consists of 462 XML documents with information about destinations, which is particularly useful for travellers that want to find interesting details for their next holiday or business trip. The collection is called the "WorldGuide" and has been provided by the publishers of the Lonely Planet guidebooks. The collection not only contains useful information about countries, but also includes information about interesting regions and major cities. For each destination an introduction is available, complemented with information about transport, culture, major events, facts, and an image gallery that gives an impression of the local scenery.

5.2   Relevance Assessments in Task C

A slightly more complex approach was taken for the collection of relevance assessments in Tack C. The two-dimensional relevance scale was a modified version of a scale proposed at the INEX Methodology Workshop at the Glasgow IR Festival [6]. The relevance assessments were explained to the test persons as follows:

Two different dimensions are used to assess the relevance of an XML document component. The first determines the extent to which a document component *contains relevant information* for the search task. It can take one of the following three values: **highly relevant**, **somewhat relevant**, and **not relevant**. A document component is **highly relevant** if it covers aspects of the search task *without containing* too much non-relevant information. A document component is **somewhat relevant** if it covers aspects of the search task and at the same time *contains* much non-relevant information. A document component is **not relevant** if it *does not cover* any aspect of the search task.

The second relevance dimension determines the extent to which a document component *needs the context* of its containing XML document to make full sense as an answer. It can take one of the following three values: **just right**, **too large**, and **too small**. A document component is **just right** if it is reasonably *self-contained* and it needs *little* of the context of its containing XML document to make full sense as an answer. Alternatively, the document component can be either **too large** or **too small**. A document component is **too large** if it *does not need* the context of its containing XML document to make full sense as an answer. A document component is **too small** if it can only make full sense within the context of its containing XML document.

Given the above relevance values, the final assessment score of a document component can take one of the following *five* values:

- **Not Relevant (NR)** – if the document component does not cover any aspect of the search task;
- **Partial Answer (PA)** – if the document component is *somewhat relevant* (i.e. covers only some aspects of the search task) and *just right* (i.e. it is reasonably self-contained but still needs some of the context of its containing XML document to make full sense);
- **Exact Answer (EA)** – if the document component is *highly relevant* (i.e. covers all, or nearly all, aspects of the search task without containing too much non-relevant information) and *just right;*
- **Broad Answer (BA)** – if the document component is either *highly* or *somewhat relevant* and *too large* (i.e. it is reasonably self-contained and does not really need the context of its containing XML document to make full sense); and
- **Narrow Answer (NA)** - if the document component is either *highly* or *somewhat relevant* and *too small* (i.e. it is not self-contained and can only make full sense in the context of its containing XML document).

The test persons could select one of these values from a T-shaped relevance assessment box as shown in Fig. 4 and Fig. 5.

5.3 System

An interactive system for Task C was provided by Utrecht University. It is a fully functional element retrieval system which has been configured to suit Task C. There were two versions of the system: One which presented the results in context of the full text (i.e., highlighted), and an alternative version which presented the results in isolation. Fig. 3 shows the query ad result list interface common to both system versions. Fig. 4 and 5 shows the interface for the versions which showed results in context and isolated respectively.

5.4 Tasks/Topics

Eight topics that have previously been used for experiments with the Lonely Planet WorldGuide were selected and modified into short simulated work tasks for Task C. The tasks were arbitrarily split into 2 categories, and each test person searched two tasks from each category.

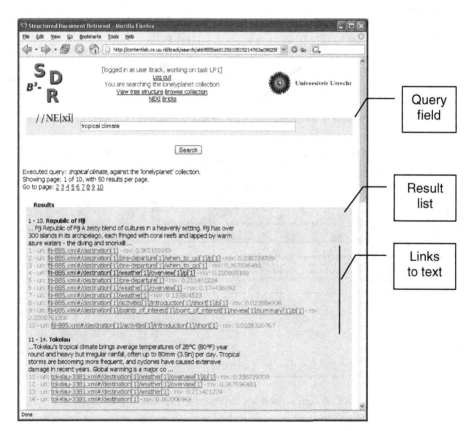

Fig. 3. Query box and result list display used in Task C

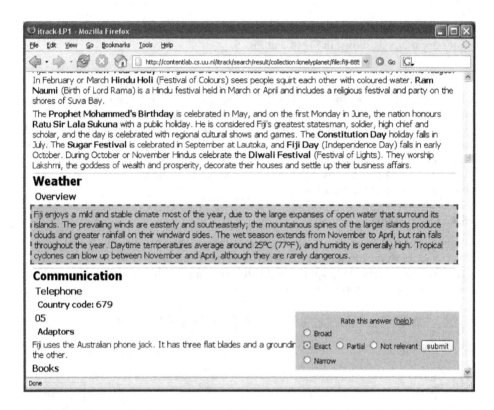

Fig. 4. Task C system version which presented the results highlighted in context of the full text

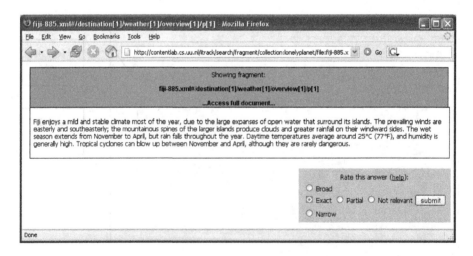

Fig. 5. Task C system version which presented the results in isolation

5.5 Experimental Design

A minimum of 4 test persons from each participating group were used in Task C. Each test person searched two simulated work tasks (chosen by the test person) from each of the two categories – a total of four per test person. The order in which task categories were performed was permuted in order to neutralise learning effects. This means that one complete round of the experiment required 4 searchers.

The basic experimental matrix looks as follows:

Rotation 1:   Iso-C1, Cxt-C2
Rotation 2:   Iso-C2, Cxt-C1
Rotation 3:   Cxt-C1, Iso-C2
Rotation 4:   Cxt-C2, Iso-C1

Where Iso = system with isolated results, and Cxt = system with results in context. C1 and C2 were the two simulated work task categories. The experimental procedure was very similar to the one used in Task A. However, no interview was conducted at the end of the experiment. A number of questionnaires were provided by the track organisers.

6 Concluding Remarks

In its second year, the Interactive Track at INEX looked into some fundamental questions surrounding interactive XML retrieval: does element retrieval make sense at all, do searchers prefer full-text to element retrieval, what applications could exist for interactive XML retrieval? In addition, the track also expanded by including two additional tasks and by attracting more participating groups. A total of 11 research groups and 119 test persons participated in the three different tasks that were included in the track.

In this paper, we have described the main issues that the Interactive Track at INEX 2005 attempts to address and the methodology and tasks that were used in the track. The data has now been released and it is the task of the participating groups to analyse and publish results from the track.

Acknowledgments

As track organisers we would like to thank the participating research groups for their work and input concerning the format of the track. In addition, we would like to thank Pia Borlund from the Royal School of Library and Information Science for help on constructing simulated work tasks, Claus-Peter Klas from University of Duisburg-Essen for help in running Daffodil, Roelof van Zwol, Sandor Spruit and Jeroen Baas, Utrecht University, for making their system available for Task C, and finally Jovan Pehcevski and co-workers for developing their relevance scale for use in the interactive track. Finally, we would like to thank Lonely Planets Publications Pty Ltd and the IEEE Computer Society for access to their data.

References

1. Tombros, A., Larsen, B. and Malik, S. (2005): The Interactive Track at INEX 2004. In: Fuhr, N., Lalmas, M., Malik, S. and Szlávik, Z. eds. *Advances in XML Information Retrieval: Third International Workshop of the Initiative for the Evaluation of XML Retrieval, INEX 2004, Dagstuhl Castle, Germany, December 6-8, 2004, Revised Selected Papers.* Berlin: Springer, p. 410-423. (Lecture Notes in Computer Science; 3493)
2. Larsen, B., Tombros, A., and Malik, S. (2004): *Interactive Track Workshop Report.* Slides presented at the INEX Workshop, December 2004 [http://inex.is.informatik.uni-duisburg.de:2004/workshop.html#Reports]
3. Borlund, P. (2003): The IIR evaluation model: a framework for evaluation of interactive information retrieval. In: *Information Research, vol. 8, no. 3, paper no. 152.* [Available at: http://informationr.net/ir/8-3/paper152.html]
4. Larsen, B., Tombros, A. and Malik, S. (2005): Obtrusiveness and relevance assessment in interactive XML IR experiments. In: Trotman, A., Lalmas, M. and Fuhr, N. eds. *Proceedings of the INEX 2005 Workshop on Element Retrieval Methodology, held at the University of Glasgow, 30 July 2005. Second Edition.* Dunedin (New Zealand): Department of Computer Science, University of Otago, p. 39-42. [http://www.cs.otago. ac.nz/inexmw/Proceedings.pdf, visited 15-12-2005]
5. Pharo, N. and Nordlie, R. (2005): Context matters: an analysis of assessments of XML documents. In: Crestani, F. and Ruthven, I. eds. *Context: Nature, Impact, and Role : 5th International Conference on Conceptions of Library and Information Science, CoLIS 2005, Glasgow, UK, June 2005, Proceedings.* Berlin: Springer, p. 238-248. (Lecture Notes in Computer Science; 3507)
6. Pehcevski, J., Thom, J. A. and Vercoustre, A.-M. (2005): Users and assessors in the context of INEX: Are relevance dimensions relevant? In: Trotman, A., Lalmas, M. and Fuhr, N. eds. *Proceedings of the INEX 2005 Workshop on Element Retrieval Methodology, held at the University of Glasgow, 30 July 2005. Second Edition.* Dunedin (New Zealand): Department of Computer Science, University of Otago, p. 47-62. [http://www.cs.otago.ac. nz/inexmw/Proceedings.pdf, visited 15-12-2005]
7. Kamps, J., de Rijke, M. and Sigurbjörnsson, B. (2005): What do Users Think of an XML Element Retrieval System?. In: *This volume.*
8. Klas, C.P., Albrechtsen, H., Fuhr, N., Hansen, P., Jacob, E., Kapidakis, S., Kovacs, L., Kriewel, S., Micsik, A., Papatheodorou, C., Tsakonas, G. (2006).: *An Experimental Framework for Comparative Digital Library Evaluation: The Logging Scheme.* (Submitted for publication).

What Do Users Think of an XML Element Retrieval System?

Jaap Kamps[1,2] and Börkur Sigurbjörnsson[2]

[1] Archives and Information Science, Faculty of Humanities, University of Amsterdam
[2] ISLA, Faculty of Science, University of Amsterdam

Abstract. We describe the University of Amsterdam's participation in the INEX 2005 Interactive Track, mainly focusing on a comparative experiment, in which the baseline system Daffodil/HyREX is compared to a home-grown XML element retrieval system (xmlfind). The xmlfind system provides an interface for an XML information retrieval search engine, using an index that contains all the individual XML elements in the IEEE collection. Our main findings are the following. First, test persons show appreciation for both systems, but xmlfind receives higher scores than Daffodil. Second, the interface seems to take the structural dependencies between retrieved elements into account in an appropriate way: although retrieved elements may be overlapping in whole or in part, none of the test persons regarded this as problematic. Third, the general opinion of the test persons on the usefulness of XML retrieval systems was unequivocally positive, and their responses highlight many of the hoped advantages of an XML retrieval system.

1 Introduction

In this paper we document the University of Amsterdam's participation in the INEX 2005 Interactive Track. We conducted two experiments. First, we took part in the concerted effort of Task A, in which a common baseline system, Daffodil/-HyREX, is used to study test-persons searching the IEEE collection. Second, as part of the Interactive Track's Task B, we conducted a comparative experiment, in which the baseline retrieval system, Daffodil/HyREX, is contrasted with our home-grown XML element retrieval system, xmlfind.

The rest of the paper is organized as follows. Next, Section 2 documents the XML retrieval systems used in the experiment. Then, in Section 3, we detail the setup of the experiments. The results of the experiments are reported in Section 4, where we focus almost exclusively on the comparative experiment. Finally, in Section 5, we discuss our findings and draw some initial conclusions.

2 XML Retrieval Systems

2.1 Baseline System: Daffodil

The Daffodil system is developed to support the information seeking process in Digital Libraries [1]. As a back-end, the HyREX XML retrieval system was used [2]. For details, see [3].

N. Fuhr et al. (Eds.): INEX 2005, LNCS 3977, pp. 411–421, 2006.

Table 1. Experimental matrix for the comparative experiment

#	Rotation	Task 1 Task	Task 1 System	Task 2 Task	Task 2 System	Task 3 Task	Task 3 System
1	1	G-1	Daffodil	C-1	xmlfind	Own	choice
2	2	C-1	Daffodil	G-1	xmlfind	Own	choice
3	3	G-1	xmlfind	C-1	Daffodil	Own	choice
4	4	C-1	xmlfind	G-1	Daffodil	Own	choice
5	1	G-2	Daffodil	C-2	xmlfind	Own	choice
6	2	C-2	Daffodil	G-2	xmlfind	Own	choice
7	3	G-2	xmlfind	C-2	Daffodil	Own	choice
8	4	C-2	xmlfind	G-2	Daffodil	Own	choice
9	1	G-3	Daffodil	C-3	xmlfind	Own	choice
10	2	C-3	Daffodil	G-3	xmlfind	Own	choice
11	3	G-3	xmlfind	C-3	Daffodil	Own	choice
12	4	C-3	xmlfind	G-3	Daffodil	Own	choice
13	1	G-1	Daffodil	C-1	xmlfind	Own	choice
14	2	C-1	Daffodil	G-1	xmlfind	Own	choice

2.2 Home-Grown System: xmlfind

The xmlfind system provides an interface for an XML information retrieval search engine [4]. It runs on top of a Lucene search engine [5]. The underlying index contains all the individual XML elements in the IEEE collection [6].

Figure 1(top) shows the search box and the result list. The results are grouped per article, where (potentially) relevant elements are shown. A partial view of the document tree, linking retrieved elements to the article root element, is shown. Small text excerpts, or text snippets or teasers, containing query words are generated to give a preview of the XML element's content. Clicking on any of the elements will open a new window displaying the result. Figure 1(bottom) shows the full article with the focus on the selected element. The results display window has three planes. On the left plane, there is a Table of Contents of the whole article. On the right plane, the article is displayed with the selected part of the document in view. On the top plane, the article's title, author, etc. are displayed, as well as a menu for assessing the relevance of the result (added specifically for the Interactive experiments reported in this paper).

3 Experimental Setup

The whole experiment was run in a single session where test persons for both Task A and Task B worked in parallel. The test persons were first year Computer Science students.

3.1 Task A: Community Experiment

Task A is the orchestrated experiment in which all teams participating in the Interactive Track take part [3]. We participated in Task A with six test persons, who searched the IEEE Collection with theDaffodil/HyREX baseline system.

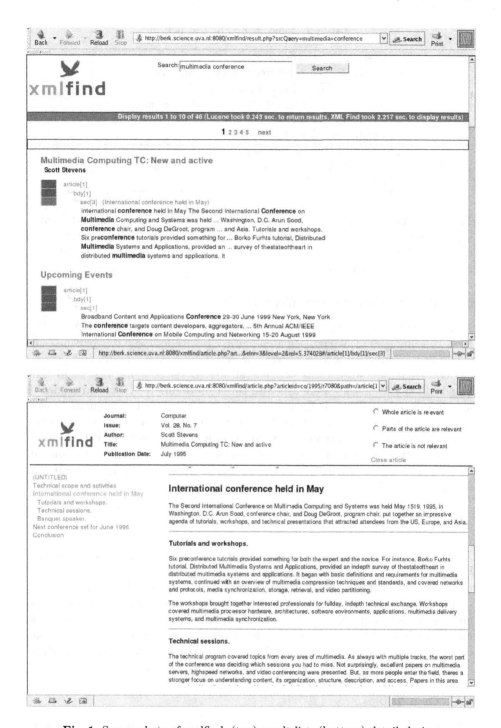

Fig. 1. Screen shots of xmlfind: (top) result list, (bottom) detailed view

Table 2. Topic created by test person

A. *What are you looking for?*   Who build the first computer and what did it look like?
B. *What is the motivation of the topic?*   I would like to know how the history of the computer began and what the first computer looked like, was it very big or very small, did it have a monitor?
C. *What would an ideal answer look like?*   The name of the inventor and a picture of how the first computer looked.

There were three tasks: two simulated work tasks (a 'general' task and a 'challenging' task) and the test person's were asked to think up a search topic of their own. The experiment was conducted in accordance with the guidelines, for further details we refer to [3].

3.2 Task B: Comparative Experiment

Task B is a comparison of the home-grown xmlfind system with the Daffodil/Hy-REX baseline system. We participated in Task B with fourteen test persons. The experimental setup largely resembles the setup of Task A. Again, test persons did two simulated work tasks (a 'general' and a 'challenging' task) and they searched for a topic they were asked to think up themselves. The experimental matrix is shown in Table 1. Every test person searched for two simulated tasks, each one with a different system, following a standard two treatment matrix. Next, the test persons searched for their own topic with a system of their choice.

Due to the number of test persons involved, we were unable to conduct individual exit interviews. Instead, we used an extended post-experiment questionnaire.

4   Results

A large amount of data was collected during the experiments. Each test person searched with four different accounts, one for each task, plus one or two additional accounts for training. This generated in total 94 search logs (24 for Task A and 70 for Task B). In additional, each person filled in questionnaires before and after each task, and before and after the experiment, resulting in, in total, 160 questionnaires (48 for Task A and 112 for Task B). For a discussion of the results of Task A, we refer to the INEX 2005 Interactive track overview paper [3]. Here, we will focus on the results for the comparative evaluation in Task B.

4.1   Own Topics

As part of the experiments, test persons were asked to think up a search topic of their own interest, based on a short description of the IEEE collection's content.

Some topics created by test persons were excellent. Table 2 shows an example of a topic being (i) within the collection's coverage, (ii) reflecting a focused information need, and (iii) even containing potential structural retrieval cues. However, most topic were not so perfect. Even though test persons were asked to think up two different topics, almost half of the test persons (9 out of 20) did not create a very suitable topic. At least six topics addressed very practical advice on computer components or software, typically the sort of computer science related issues that users may search for on the web (targeting product reviews, FAQs or discussion boards). Examples of such created topics are *Latest video cards for best performance gaming* or *How to integrate .net applications in corporate environments*. Evidently, the IEEE Computer Society journals are not the most likely place to find relevant information for these topics. At least three topics were clearly outside the scope of the collection. Examples are *How many flights go from New York to Los Angeles a day?* and *How much energy does a rocket use to orbit?* Again, it is unlikely to find relevant information for these topics in the collection at hand. Perhaps more positively, the vast majority of the topics developed by our test persons were focused, asking for very specific information that could, in principle, be contained in a relatively short piece of text.

4.2   Information Seeking Behavior

During search, we logged the behavior of the test persons. Here, we will report on data from the xmlfind logs. In total, we have 24 sessions with xmlfind (see the experimental matrix in Table 1). In these 24 sessions, the test persons issued 91 queries in total, leading to an average of 3.8 queries per task. In the result list, a total of 172 elements were selected for further inspection. Note that this is, on average, only 1.9 per query, indicating that test-persons consulted only information from a very small number of articles. If we break down this number by the entry point into the article, we see that in 77 cases (44.8%) a test person selected an element, and in 95 cases (55.2%) an article was selected. That is, the test persons do use the option to deep-link particular XML elements in the articles. Finally, we asked the test persons, only once per viewed article, to give their assessment of its usefulness. We gathered 141 assessments in this way, which is 92.8% of all articles which were read in whole or in part. If we break down these judgments, we see that in 54 cases (38.3%) the article was regarded as not relevant, in 22 cases (15.6%) the whole article was regarded as relevant, and in the remaining 65 cases (46.1%) only parts of the article were regarded as relevant. Especially the last category, where relevant information is retrieved from an off-topic article, clearly demonstrates the potential of focused XML element retrieval techniques.

4.3   Appreciation of the Searching Experience

After each completed task, test persons filled in a questionnaire. There were a number of questions on the testperson's satisfaction:

Table 3. Responses on user satisfaction: mean scores and standard deviations (in brackets). Answers were on a 5-point scale, ranging from 1 ("Not at all") to 5 ("Extremely").

	Q3.1	Q3.2	Q3.3	Q3.4	Q3.5
All tasks	3.4 (1.1)	3.0 (1.4)	3.1 (2.2)	3.2 (2.0)	3.6 (0.7)
First task	3.4 (1.2)	3.1 (1.1)	3.0 (2.5)	3.3 (1.9)	3.6 (0.4)
Second task	3.3 (1.5)	2.9 (1.5)	3.2 (1.6)	3.3 (1.3)	3.6 (0.4)
First two tasks	3.4 (1.1)	3.0 (1.1)	3.2 (2.1)	3.3 (1.6)	3.6 (0.4)
General task	3.4 (1.2)	2.9 (1.1)	3.1 (2.2)	3.1 (2.1)	3.9 (0.4)
Challenging task	3.4 (1.2)	3.1 (1.2)	3.3 (2.1)	3.5 (1.2)	3.4 (0.3)
Own task	3.4 (1.2)	3.0 (2.0)	3.1 (2.7)	3.1 (2.8)	3.5 (1.3)
Daffodil (task C and G)	3.1 (0.7)	2.7 (0.5)	3.1 (2.1)	3.1 (1.8)	3.6 (0.3)
xmlfind (task C and G)	3.6 (1.5)	3.4 (1.6)	3.3 (2.2)	3.5 (1.5)	3.7 (0.5)
Daffodil (first task)	3.0 (0.6)	3.0 (0.6)	3.3 (3.1)	3.4 (2.6)	3.8 (0.2)
Daffodil (second task)	3.2 (1.0)	2.3 (0.3)	2.8 (1.0)	2.8 (1.0)	3.3 (0.3)
xmlfind (first task)	4.0 (0.8)	3.5 (1.1)	3.0 (2.8)	3.3 (1.9)	3.5 (0.7)
xmlfind (second task)	3.4 (2.0)	3.3 (2.2)	3.5 (2.0)	3.6 (1.4)	3.9 (0.4)

Q3.1 *Was it easy to get started on this search?*
Q3.2 *Was it easy to do the search on the given task?*
Q3.3 *Are you satisfied with your search results?*
Q3.4 *Do you feel that the task has been fulfilled?*
Q3.5 *Do you feel that the search task was clear?*

Table 3 shows the responses of the test persons. First, we look at the responses over all sessions. The test persons are fairly positive with average results in the range 3.0 to 3.6. Second, we look at responses for the different tasks. Here we see that the reponses for the first and second task are comparable, and in sync with the overall responses. The third task was always the Own task. When we look at the responses for the different task types, General, Challenging, or Own, we see a similar pattern as for the two simulated work tasks. Interestingly, the General task is regarded as clearer (Q3.5), but the search results for the Challenging task are valued higher (Q3.3 and Q3.4). The responses for Own task are surprizing: although formulated by the test person herself, they are not regarded as clearer (Q3.5). The responses for the Own task are, on average, similar to the simulated work tasks. The standard deviation, however, is much larger. The reason for this seems to be the inability of a large fraction of test persons to come up with a topic that is suitable for the collection at hand. Third, we look at the responses for the different search engines, focusing on the simulated work tasks where a proper matrix was used. Over all sessions with the search engines, xmlfind was regarded as easier to use (Q3.1 and Q3.2), and more effective (Q3.3 and Q3.4) than Daffodil. We also look at whether earlier experience with the other search engine did influence the responses. We see that responses for the first task, either using Daffodil or using xmlfind, are much closer; Daffodil gets higher scores on effectiveness (although the standard deviation is large). However, we see that test persons that used

Table 4. Responses on searching experience: mean scores and standard deviations (in brackets). Answers were on a 5-point scale, ranging from 1 ("Not at all") to 5 ("Extremely").

	Q3.9	Q3.10	Q3.11	Q3.12	Q3.13
All tasks	3.2 (1.4)	3.0 (1.3)	3.3 (1.0)	3.4 (1.4)	3.4 (1.3)
First task	3.1 (1.8)	3.0 (1.4)	3.2 (1.3)	3.4 (1.6)	3.6 (1.6)
Second task	3.0 (1.4)	3.0 (0.8)	3.4 (0.9)	3.3 (1.0)	3.5 (0.7)
First two tasks	3.1 (1.5)	3.0 (1.0)	3.2 (0.9)	3.4 (1.3)	3.4 (1.3)
General task	2.8 (1.6)	2.6 (1.0)	3.2 (1.1)	3.1 (1.6)	3.4 (1.5)
Challenging task	3.4 (1.3)	3.4 (0.7)	3.2 (0.8)	3.6 (1.0)	3.4 (1.2)
Own task	3.5 (1.3)	3.0 (2.0)	3.5 (1.2)	3.5 (1.5)	3.2 (1.3)
Daffodil (task C and G)	2.9 (1.5)	2.8 (1.1)	3.2 (0.8)	3.4 (1.5)	3.3 (1.8)
xmlfind (task C and G)	3.2 (1.6)	3.2 (1.0)	3.2 (1.1)	3.3 (1.3)	3.6 (0.9)
Daffodil (first task)	3.1 (1.6)	2.9 (1.3)	3.3 (0.8)	3.6 (2.3)	3.4 (2.6)
Daffodil (second task)	2.7 (1.5)	2.7 (1.1)	3.2 (1.0)	3.2 (0.6)	3.2 (1.0)
xmlfind (first task)	3.2 (2.2)	3.2 (1.8)	2.8 (1.4)	3.2 (1.4)	3.3 (1.5)
xmlfind (second task)	3.3 (1.4)	3.3 (0.5)	3.5 (0.9)	3.4 (1.4)	3.8 (0.5)

Daffodil for the first task, were more positive than those that used Daffodil for the second task (after searching with xmlfind for the first task). Conversely, the test persons that used xmlfind for the second task (after using Daffodil for the first task), were more positive than those that used xmlfind for the first task.[1]

The questionnaire also contained a number of questions on the search experience of the test persons:

Q3.9 How well did the system support you in this task?
Q3.10 On average, how relevant to the search task was the information presented to you?
Q3.11 Did you in general find the presentation in the result list useful?
Q3.12 Did you find the parts of the documents in the result list useful?
Q3.13 Did you find the Table of Contents in the Full Text view useful?

Table 4 shows the responses, using a similar breakdown as before. First, we look at responses over all sessions. The test persons are again fairly positive with averages ranging from 3.0 to 3.4. Second, we look at responses for the different tasks. Responses for the first and second simulated work task are very similar to the overall responses. When we look at the three task types, we see that the responses for the General task deviate for system support (Q3.9) and relevance (Q3.10). Perhaps suprizingly the systems are more appreciated

---

[1] Here, we compare the responses of different test persons, and hence it may be the case that test persons starting with Daffodil were simply more positive than those starting with xmlfind. Note, however, that the group starting with Daffodil gave higher scores to xmlfind in the second task, and the group starting with xmlfind gave Daffodil lower scores in the second task.

Table 5. Responses on the system comparison: mean scores and standard deviations (in brackets). Answers were on a 5-point scale, ranging from 1 ("Not at all") to 5 ("Extremely"). Statistical significance is based on a paired t-test (two-tailed).

	Q4.4	Q4.5	Q4.6
Daffodil	3.1 (0.9)	2.9 (1.1)	3.4 (0.6)
xmlfind	4.2 (0.8)	4.2 (0.3)	4.2 (0.3)
Significance	$p < 0.01$	$p < 0.001$	$p < 0.05$

for the Challenging task than for the General task. Responses for the Own task, always searched after the two simulated work tasks, do not differ much from the overall responses. Third, we look at responses for the diffent systems. We see that both systems receive comparable scores on the presentation issues (Q3.11, Q3.12, and Q3.13). There is, however, a marked difference in the responses for support (Q3.9) and relevance (Q3.10), where xmlfind is prefered over Daffodil. When looking at the interaction between the search experience for both systems, we see, again, that earlier exposure to xmlfind leads to lower scores for Daffodil, and earlier exposure to Daffodil leads to higher scores for xmlfind.

4.4 Comparative Evaluation

Test persons in Task B were free to select with which of the two system they searched for the third topic. Out of the 14 test persons, 4 (28.6%) choose to search with the Daffodil/HyREX system, the other 10 (71.4%) choose to search with the xmlfind system.

In the post-experiment questionnaire, each test person was asked a number of questions about the two systems that they used:

Q4.4 *How easy was it to learn to use the system?*
Q4.5 *How easy was it to use the system?*
Q4.6 *How well did you understand how to use the system?*

Table 5 shows the responses of the test persons. We see that the test persons give a significantly higher score to xmlfind with respect to the easiness to learn (Q4.4), the easiness to use (Q4.5), and the understandability of the system (Q4.6).

4.5 General Views

As part of the extended post-experiment questionnaire, test persons in Task B were asked a number of questions about their opinions on the concept of an XML retrieval engine. Table 6 lists the responses to two of the questions, where each row represents the same test person. The responses where unequivocally positive, and the responses highlight many of the hoped advantages of an XML retrieval system.

Table 6. Responses on the usefulness of focused retrieval

13. *Did you like the idea that the search engine takes into account the structure of the documents? Why?*	14. *Do you find it useful to be pointed to relevant parts of long articles? Why?*
Yes, you will have a good overview of the total article/document.	Yes, because you are able to see which articles are worth reading and which are not.
Yes, for specific information this is very useful.	Yes, gives the user an idea about the article in question.
Yes, easier to see how long the article is.	You don't need to see other parts.
Yes, its easier to see the contents of the document, better navigation.	Yes, you don't have to dig into the article yourself.
Yes, it didn't bother me.	Yes, it's more easy to find what you're looking for.
Yes, less reading time, clear overview.	Yes, saves time.
Yes, it shortens search time.	Yes, because if scan-read long articles, you easily miss some relevant parts.
Yes, saves work.	Yes, works faster.
Yes, because its much faster.	Yes, its faster.
Yes, this way of finding information takes less time.	Yes, now you don't have to read the whole article. You can get straight to the part where the information is.
Yes, its easier to see where relevant information is located.	Yes, it takes less time to find the relevant parts.
Yes, it makes it easier to find specific paragraphs.	Yes, if programmed right it can save time.
Yes, it makes it a lot easier to find what you are looking for.	Yes, it is lots more easier.
Yes, because makes me have to search less.	Yes, to search less.

5   Discussion and Conclusions

This paper documents the University of Amsterdam's participation in the INEX 2005 Interactive Track. We participated in two tasks. First, we participated in the concerted effort of Task A, in which a common baseline system, Daffodil/-HyREX, was used by six test-persons to search the IEEE collection. Second, we conducted a comparative experiment in Task B, in which fourteen test persons searched alternately with the baseline retrieval system, Daffodil/HyREX, and our home-grown XML element retrieval system, xmlfind.

We detailed the experimental setup of the comparative experiment. Both experiments, involving twenty test persons in total, were conducted in parallel in a single session. This ensured that the experimental conditions for all test persons are very equal. Unplanned external causes, such as the down-time of the Daffodil/HyREX system equally affected all test persons. Due to the large number of test persons present at the same time, we had to minimize the need for experimenter assistance. This was accomplished by generating personalized protocols for all test persons. In these protocols, test persons were guided through the experiment by means of verbose instructions on the transitions between different tasks. Four experimenters were available, if needed, to clarify the instructions or provide other assistance. This worked flawlessly, and allowed us to handle the large numbers of test persons efficiently.

A large amount of data was collected during the experiments, both in questionnaires and in search log files. In this paper we focused mainly on the results of the comparative experiment. As for the comparison between the Daffodil/HyREX system and the xmlfind system, we see that the test persons show appreciation for both systems but that xmlfind receives higher scores than Daffodil. It is difficult to pin-point what's the deciding factor in the system comparison, in the questionnaires the ease of use, the speed and stability, and the quality of the search results are mentioned by test persons.

Over the whole experiment, perhaps the most striking result is that some expected problems did not surface in the questionnaires. Note that the xmlfind system retrieves potentially overlapping elements, and that in the result list even all ascendants of found elements are added. Hence, one might have expected the so-called overlap problem that plagues XML retrieval metrics [7] to rear its head. For example, in the Interactive track at INEX 2004 test persons complained about encountering partly overlapping results scattered through the ranked list of elements [8, 9]. Clustering found elements from the same article seems to be an effective way for an interface to deal with the structural dependencies between retrieved elements.

The general opinion on the XML retrieval systems was unequivocally positive. Departing from earlier systems that return ranked lists of XML elements, both the Daffodil/HyREX and xmlfind group the found XML elements per article (similar to the Fetch & Browse task in the Ad hoc Track). Test persons seem to conceive the resulting system as an article retrieval engines with some additional features—yet with great appreciation for the bells and whistles!

Acknowledgments

This research was supported by the Netherlands Organization for Scientific Research (NWO) under project numbers 017.001.190, 220-80-001, 264-70-050, 354-20-005, 612-13-001, 612.000.106, 612.000.207, 612.066.302, 612.069.006, 640.-001.501, and 640.002.501.

References

1. Daffodil: Distributed Agents for User-Friendly Access of Digital Libraries (2006) http://www.is.informatik.uni-duisburg.de/projects/daffodil/.
2. HyREX: Hyper-media   Retrieval   Engine   for   XML   (2006) http://www.is.informatik.uni-duisburg.de/projects/hyrex/.
3. Larsen, B., Malik, S., Tombros, T.: The interactive track at INEX 2005. In: This Volume. (2006)

4. Bakker, T., Bedeker, M., van den Berg, S., van Blokland, P., de Lau, J., Kiszer, O., Reus, S., Salomon, J.: Evaluating XML retrieval interfaces: xmlfind. Technical report, University of Amsterdam (2005)
5. Lucene: The Lucene search engine (2006) http://lucene.apache.org/.
6. Sigurbjörnsson, B., Kamps, J., de Rijke, M.: An Element-Based Approch to XML Retrieval. In: INEX 2003 Workshop Proceedings. (2004) 19–26
7. Kazai, G., Lalmas, M., de Vries, A.P.: The overlap problem in content-oriented XML retrieval evaluation. In: Proceedings of the 27th Annual International ACM SIGIR Conference, ACM Press, New York NY, USA (2004) 72–79
8. Tombros, A., Larsen, B., Malik, S.: The interactive track at INEX 2004. In: Advances in XML Information Retrieval. Third Workshop of the INitiative for the Evaluation of XML Retrieval, INEX 2004. Volume 3493 of Lecture Notes in Computer Science., Springer Verlag, Heidelberg (2005) 410–423
9. Tombros, A., Larsen, B., Malik, S.: Report on the INEX 2004 interactive track. SIGIR Forum **39** (2005) 43–49

Users Interaction with the Hierarchically Structured Presentation in XML Document Retrieval

Heesop Kim[1] and Heejung Son[2]

[1] Department of Library & Information Science, Kyungpook National University,
Daegu, 702-701, Korea
heesop@mail.knu.ac.kr
[2] CIMERR, POSTECH, Pohang, Kyungbuk, 790-784, Korea
sonhjung@postech.ac.kr

Abstract. Some changes were made in the interface design of this year's XML documents retrieval system according to the outcomes of the Interactive track in INEX 2004. One of the major changes was the hierarchical structure of the presentation in the search results. The main purpose of our study was to investigate how the hierarchical presentation of interface influences the searchers' behavior in XML document retrieval. To achieve this objective we analyzed the transaction logs from this year's experiment and compared the results to those of last year's experiment. The subjects' comments on the experiment and the system were also examined. The Daffodil XML retrieval system was used and 12 test persons participated in the experiment. SPSS for Windows 12.0 was used for statistical analysis.

1 Introduction

In the study of 2004 we provided a fundamental data on users' search behavior when they interacted with the structured XML document retrieval system and found some issues needed to be investigated in the interface design [7]. Overlapping elements in the result list was one of those issues. Although overlapping can be considered as one of the benefits of the element retrieval, the overlapping elements in the search results can be an obstruction to effective searching by users. Along this line this year's Interactive Track made some changes in interface design for the experimental retrieval system. Those changes include: (1) a hierarchically structured presentation of the search results was adopted to address the overlapping problem, (2) a search window with more advanced query fields, and (3) a small eye symbol for indicating already viewed elements.

The main purpose of our study was to investigate how the hierarchical presentation of interface influences the searchers' behavior in XML document retrieval. In this paper we report on our study focused on how newly designed interface affects the users' overall search behavior by comparing the subjects' search characteristics of 2005 with those of 2004. In addition we examined the influence of the hierarchically structured presentation of the search results through the statistical analysis of the transaction logs.

N. Fuhr et al. (Eds.): INEX 2005, LNCS 3977, pp. 422–431, 2006.

The experimental method employed in our experiment is presented in Section 2. The subjects' overall search behavior and their satisfaction with the XML retrieval system are shown in Section 3. The results of comparison between the two years and the effect of the hierarchically structured presentation of the retrieval results are also provided in the same section. Finally, our conclusions are presented in Section 4.

2 Experiment

For the experiment we used the Daffodil XML retrieval system which was customized for the INEX Interactive Track and conducted the experiment according to the procedure given by the track organizers [6]. The Daffodil has a number of improvements

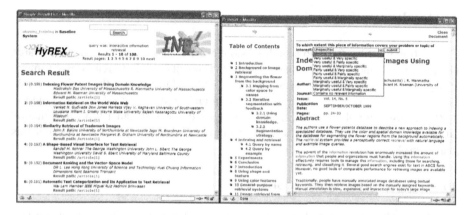

Fig. 1. HyREX Interface for the Ranked List and the Detailed Page (2004)

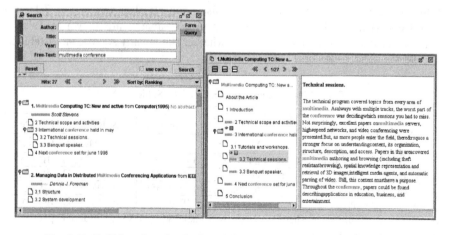

Fig. 2. Daffodil Interface for the Search Results and the Detailed Page (2005)

over last year's HyREX system, for example, a hierarchically structured presentation of the search results, a simpler relevance assessment scale, and various supportive interface functionalities like a small eye symbol for indicating already viewed elements and more advanced query form.

Figure 1 and Figure 2 show an example of the HyREX interface and the Daffordil interface, respectively.

We conducted our experiment using the baseline system, Daffodil, and followed the guidelines from the Track organizers. Particularly, a search session of the subject's own task was newly introduced in this year. See Larsen, Malik, Tombros [8] for more details.

For this year's experiment 12 test persons were volunteered from Kyungpook National University.

3 Results

Transaction log files from 36 search sessions were analyzed for the subjects' search characteristics and then compared with the results of last year's experiment. Responses from 96 questionnaires were also analyzed to find out the subjects' satisfaction with the experimental retrieval system and its interface. SPSS for Windows 12.0 was used for the statistical analysis. Chi-square test and t-test were mainly adopted to identify the significant differences between last year's results and this year's results.

3.1 Subjects' Demographic Information

All of the subjects answered 'Korean' as their first language. The average age was 26.8 years old at that time of the experiment which was almost the same as last year's (i.e., 27.1). It was reported that our subjects have an average of 7.3 years of on-line searching experiences which was also similar to last year's (i.e., 7.1). The various experiences with searching of each year's subjects are shown in Table 1. With the results of t-test we can interpret whether statistically significant differences are exist.

Table 1. Searching Experiences of the Subjects (Year)[1]

Searching experience	2004	2005	t-test for Equality of Means
	M (SD)	M (SD)	t, p, Mean Difference[2]
Computerized library catalogues	3.25 (1.28)	3.42 (0.90)	t=-.34, p=.74, MD=-.17
Digital libraries of scientific articles	3.00 (0.93)	2.83 (1.03)	t=.37, p=.72, MD=.17
WWW search engines	4.63 (0.52)	4.33 (0.65)	t=1.06, p=.30, MD=.30
IEEE journals and magazines	2.00 (1.07)	1.92 (0.90)	t=.19, p=.85, MD=.08

[1] Based upon a 5 points scale where '1= No,' '3= Somewhat,' '5= A great deal of experience.'
[2] Mean Difference= 2004-2005.

As demonstrated in above table, there were no significant differences between 2004 and 2005 for the subjects' searching experiences. The subjects' familiarity with WWW search engines was the highest whereas they had the least experience with IEEE journals and magazines. The average frequency of performing a search on any kind of system were 4.88 (SD: 0.35) in 2004 and 4.25 (SD: 1.06) in 2005 based on a 5 points scale where '1= Never,' '3= Once or twice a month,' and '5= One or more times a day.' There was no significant difference between these two years (t=1.9, p=.08, MD=.63).

3.2 Subjects' Overall Search Behavior

The same as last year we regarded that the subjects are engaged in the three activities (i.e., querying, browsing, and evaluating) during their searching process. Therefore, all of these three activities were taken into account when investigating the subjects' search behavior toward the XML element retrieval.

In order to look into the subjects' behavior in querying, browsing, and evaluating, the transaction log files of 36 search sessions were analyzed. Among them we extracted the seven factors which we thought these are closely related with the subjects' behavior in querying and browsing activities.

The seven factors are as follows: (1) the total number of the queries issued by the subject per each search session (Query iterations), (2) the total number of the query terms used per each session (Query terms used), (3) the number of the unique query terms used per each session (Unique query terms), (4) the number of the unique query terms derived from the description of the task (Unique query terms

Table 2. Overall Search Characteristics

	2004 (8 subjects, 16 sessions)				2005 (12 subjects, 36 sessions)				t-test for Equality of Means
	Min.	Max.	Mean	SD	Min.	Max.	Mean	SD	t, p, Mean Difference[3]
Query iterations	1	8	**5.06**	2.35	1	20	**5.31**	4.03	t=-.22, p=.82, MD=-.25
Query terms used	3	33	**15.88**	9.98	1	67	**12.39**	12.17	t=1.00, p=.32, MD=3.49
Uniq. query terms	3	18	**7.81**	3.83	1	18	**5.06**	3.86	t=2.38, p=.02, MD=2.75
Uniq. query terms in task	3	17	**7.44**	3.46	1	12	**4.00**	2.88	t=3.73, p=.00, MD=3.44
Doc./elem. viewed	2	56	**17.06**	12.16	3	39	**14.33**	8.27	t=.95, p=.35, MD=2.73
Doc./elem. assessed	1	20	**7.06**	5.00	1	25	**6.22**	4.84	t=.57, p=.57, MD=.84
Time spent (mm:ss)	07:10	32:23	**23:15**	07:07	04:35	29:44	**16:40**	06:17	t=3.34, p=.00, MD=06:35

[3] Mean Difference= 2004-2005.

in task), (5) the number of the documents/elements viewed (Documents/elements viewed), (6) the number of the documents/elements assessed (Documents/elements assessed), and (7) the time spent for each search session (Time spent).

Table 2 shows the overall search characteristics with these seven factors. For simple comparison with the results of 2004, the descriptive statistics including the mean values are presented.

We analyzed the mean value for each factor to compare the results of this year's experiment with those of last year's and examined the significant differences of each mean value using the t-test.

The subjects' activities seemed decreased a little in this year than last year. For example, the query terms used, the numbers of the documents/elements viewed and assessed, and the time spent per each search session showed lower than previous year's. However, only the number of the query iterations per each session was a little higher than last year's. There are significant differences in the unique query terms used, the unique query terms in task, and the time spent between 2004 and 2005 in $p<0.05$.

Some additional analysis was done for the subjects' browsing behavior of each year's experiment and Table 3 and 4 show the results. As shown in the tables, most of the subjects accessed and viewed documents/elements using 'Table of Contents (ToC)' (2004: 43.6%, 2005: 62.2%) or 'Result list (or Ranked list)' (2004: 54.9%, 2005: 37.2%). But only a few of them used 'Next or Previous buttons (Next/Prev.)' (2004: 1.5%, 2005: 0.6%). Also 'ToC' (62.2%) was recognized as the most frequently used access mode in this year's experiment.

Table 3. Viewed and Assessed Documents/Elements from Each Access Mode (2004)

		Ranked list	ToC	Next/Prev.	Total
Documents/ Elements Viewed	Document	59 (21.6%)	0 (0%)	0 (0%)	59 (21.6%)
	Section	59 (21.6%)	95 (34.8%)	2 (0.7%)	156 (57.1%)
	Subsection	32 (11.7%)	24 (8.8%)	2 (0.7%)	58 (21.2%)
	Total	150 (54.9%)	119 (43.6%)	4 (1.5%)	273 (100%)
Documents/ Elements Assessed	Document	30 (26.5%)	0 (0%)	0 (0%)	30 (26.5%)
	Section	26 (23.0%)	35 (31.0%)	0 (0%)	61 (53.9%)
	Subsection	13 (11.5%)	9 (7.9%)	0 (0%)	22 (19.5%)
	Total	69 (61.1%)	44 (38.9%)	0 (0%)	113 (100%)

Table 4. Viewed and Assessed Documents/Elements from Each Access Mode (2005)

		Result list	ToC	Next/Prev.	Total
Documents/ Elements Viewed	Document	138 (26.7%)	32 (6.2%)	1 (0.2%)	171 (33.1%)
	Section	22 (4.3%)	165 (32%)	1 (0.2%)	188 (36.5%)
	Subsection	32 (6.2%)	107 (20.7%)	0 (0%)	139 (26.9%)
	Front matter	0 (0%)	17 (3.3%)	1 (0.2%)	18 (3.5%)
	Total	192 (37.2%)	321 (62.2%)	3 (0.6%)	516 (100%)
Documents/ Elements Assessed	Document	36 (16.1%)	11 (4.9%)	1 (0.4%)	48 (21.4%)
	Section	15 (6.7%)	82 (36.6%)	0 (0%)	97 (43.3%)
	Subsection	20 (8.9%)	52 (23.2%)	0 (0%)	72 (32.1%)
	Front matter	0 (0%)	7 (3.2%)	0 (0%)	7 (3.2%)
	Total	71 (31.7%)	152 (67.9%)	1 (0.4%)	224 (100%)

It is interesting to observe that the total viewed proportion through 'ToC' increased in 18.6% points whereas 'Result list' decreased in 17.7% points in this year. There seemed not much deviation in this year's results of the way of the documents/element viewed among 'Document' (33.1%), 'Section' (36.5%), and 'Subsection' (26.9%) compared to last year results which were 'Document' (21.6%), 'Section' (57.1%), and 'Subsection' (21.2%). The proportion of access to 'Document' using 'Result list' was 26.7% which means 5.1% points increase than last year's. But the proportion of access to 'Section' (4.3%) and that of 'Subsection' (6.2%) from 'Result list' were decreased by 17.3% points and 5.5% points, respectively.

As shown in Table 4, 'Section' (43.3%) was found as the most popular way of access and followed by 'Subsection' (32.1%) and 'Document' (21.4%) in this year's experiment.

We also examined the score of the relevance assessment for each documents/elements and it ranked as follows: 'Section' (1.320), 'Subsection' (1.292) and 'Document' (1.188)[4]. The 'Section' is not only the most viewed and assessed element but also the highest scored element for the relevance assessment. However, a direct comparison between two years' seems not possible since the 2 dimensions of relevance assessment were adopted in 2004.

---

[4] Based on a 3 points scale in which '0= Not relevant', '1= Partially relevant,' '2= Relevant.'

3.2 Interaction with Hierarchically Structured Presentation

We investigated how a specific change of interface design, especially in a presentation of the search results, can affect the searcher's browsing behavior. To achieve this objective, we analyzed the transaction logs from the two different experiments: (1) one (2004) provides a search results in an unstructured ranked list and (2) the other (2005) provides a hierarchically structured list. The results are presented inTable 5.

Table 5. Firstly Viewed Documents/Elements after Each Query Issuing

		2004 (Unstructured)	2005 (Structured)	Total
Result list (Ranked list)	Document	27 (43.5%)	60 (74.1%)	87 (60.8%)
	Section	21 (33.9%)	7 (8.6%)	28 (19.6%)
	Subsection	14 (22.6%)	14 (17.3%)	28 (19.6%)
	Total	62 (100%)	81 (100%)	143 (100%)

We used the number of firstly viewed documents/elements after each query issuing as the measure and conducted Chi-square to test the results is statistically different. The results indicated that there is a significant difference between two years' results (Pearson $\chi^2=17.298$, p<0.001). It found that the subjects firstly viewed 'Document' after issuing queries in the experiment of 2005, although 'Section' was the most frequently viewed and assessed element. In contrast, the results from the experiment of 2004 showed a more even distribution over all elements. Overall, based on these two results, we could infer that the subjects tend to access 'Document' initially when the search results are presented in hierarchically structured in XML document retrieval system.

3.3 Subjects' Comments About the Experiment and the System

After all the search sessions closed the subjects were asked to answer the 'Post-experiment questionnaire' which was intended to take the subjects' opinions on the search tasks (i.e., Q4-2: How understandable were the tasks? and Q4-3: To what extent did you find the tasks similar to other searching tasks that you typically perform?) and the system interface (i.e., Q4-4: How easy was it to learn to use the system?, Q4-5: How easy was it to use the system? and Q4-6: How well did you understand how to use the system?).

The results are presented in Table 6. For a quick and easy comparison with last year's results, we analyzed the mean value and the standard deviation of the responses to each question. The results from a t-test showed that the subjects' score for the understandability of tasks and the similarity to the other tasks were significantly increased over last year's in p<0.05.

Table 6. Selected Questions from the Post-experiment Questionnaire[5]

	2004	2005	t-test for Equality of Means
	M (SD)	M (SD)	t, p, Mean Difference[6]
Q4-2 (Understandability of tasks)	3.25 (0.71)	3.50 (0.80)	t=-.72, p=.48, MD=-.25
Q4-3 (Similarity to other tasks)	2.13 (0.84)	2.91 (0.54)	t=-2.49, p=.02, MD=-.78
Q4-4 (Ease of learning to use the system)	3.75 (0.71)	3.42 (1.00)	t=.82, p=.43, MD=.33
Q4-5 (Ease of using the system)	3.88 (0.84)	3.42 (0.90)	t=1.15, p=.27, MD=.46
Q4-6 (Understandability of using the system)	3.63 (0.92)	3.17 (0.94)	t=1.08, p=.29, MD=.46

[5] Based upon a 5 point scale where '1= Not at all', '3= Somewhat,' '5= Extremely.'
[6] Mean Difference= 2004-2005.

The increase of the similarity to other tasks may be resulted from using 'Own' category of tasks which newly adopted this year's experiment. But more detailed analysis seems to be needed to identify an accurate relationship between the responses of Q4-3 and using 'Own' tasks.

The subjects' likes and dislikes about the search system and its interface are listed in Table 7.

Table 7. Subjects' Likes and Dislikes about the Search System and Interface (2005)

Q4-7 (Likes about the search system and interface)	– 'ToC' in the detailed page (6) – Related terms list (4) – Display of the 'Parts of the document' in the result list (3) – Keyword highlighting (2) – Simple interface of the search window (1) – Indication of already viewed ones in the detailed page (1) – Ranked list (1) – Direct links to each relevant element in the result list (1)
Q4-8 (Dislikes about the search system and interface)	–Limited search functions (e.g., 'phrase search', 'search within the results', 'Boolean operators', 'search term weighting') (5) –No indication for the already viewed or assessed documents/elements in the result list (Inconsistency of representing the viewed ones between the result list and the detailed page) (4) –Too slow of the response time (4) –Broken images and numerical formulas (4) –Limited usefulness of 'Related terms list' (2) –Too many windows (1)

(N): Number of subjects

Subjects were pleased with the table of contents ('ToC') and the newly adopted 'Related terms list' in the detailed page as well as the structured presentation of the search results. Some problems such as overlapping elements or limited information in the result list that arose in last year's experiment were not reported from this year. However, many subjects pointed out the following issues: the insufficiency and inconsistency of the indicator for the viewed documents/elements, the broken images and formulas in the detailed page, the delay of the response time, and the limited search functions.

4 Conclusions

Some changes were made to the interface design of 2005 Interactive Track retrieval system according to the outcomes of last year's experiments. The major changes are: (1) a hierarchically structured presentation of documents/elements in the result list, (2) the adoption of a more advanced search window, and (3) the application of an indication symbol for already viewed elements.

At the INEX 2005 Interactive Track, we aimed to investigate how the changes of the interface design, especially in the presentation of the search results, influenced the searchers' browsing behavior when they are interacting with an XML document retrieval system. To achieve this objective, we analyzed the users' search characteristics from the transaction logs and compared these to those of last year's experiment.

A Java-based element retrieval system, the Daffodil, was used in the experiment and 12 test persons took part in it. The transaction log files from 36 search sessions and the responses from 96 questionnaires were collected and analyzed.

From the analysis we found that (1) the subjects' overall searching activities were decreased a little in this year than last year, (2) the subjects are tend to view 'Document' prior to other elements in a hierarchically structured result list, (3) the subjects are tend to access and view the documents/elements through the table of contents (ToC)' (2004: 43.6%, 2005: 62.2%), and (4) the 'Section' is not only the most viewed and assessed element but also the highest scored element for the relevance assessment.

Future experiments will examine how subject's demographic variables effect in their searching with XML documents. Also it is hoped that more detailed investigations will be followed using last two years' experimental data which we already gathered.

Acknowledgement

We would like to thank the anonymous reviewer who gave many constructive comments on our draft and the students from Kyungpook National University who kindly participated in this experiment.

References

1. Belkin, N. J., Cool, C., Kelly, D., Kim, G., Kim, J. Y., Lee, H. J., Muresan, G., Tang, M. C., Yuan, X. J.: "Query Length in Interactive Information Retrieval." In: *Proceedings of the 26th Annual International ACM SIGIR Conference on Research and Development in Information Retrieval*. ACM, New York (2003) 205-212.

2. Borgman, C. L.: "The Study of User Behavior on Information Retrieval Systems." *ACM SIGCUE Outlook*. Vol. 19, No. 3-4. ACM, New York (1987) 35-48.
3. Clarke, Charles L. A.: "Controlling Overlap in Content-Oriented XML Retrieval." In: Marchionini, G., Moffat, Al, Tait, J., Baeza-Yates, R., Ziviani, N. (eds.). *Proceedings of the 28th Annual International ACM SIGIR Conference on Research and Development in Information Retrieval*. ACM, New York (2005) 314-321.
4. Crestani, F., Vegas, J., de la Fuente, P.: "A Graphical User Interface for the Retrieval of Hierarchically Structured Documents." *Information Processing and Management*. 40 (2004) 269-289.
5. Gançarski, A. L., Henriques, P. R.: "Interactive Information Retrieval from XML Documents Represented by Attribute Grammars." In: *Proceedings of the 2003 ACM Symposium on Document Engineering*. ACM, New York (2003) 171-174.
6. "Interactive Track." In: Fuhr, N., Lalmas, M., Malik, S., Kazai, G. (eds.). *INEX 2005 Workshop Pre-Proceedings*. (2005) 418-446.
7. Kim, H., Son, H.: "Interactive Searching Behavior with Structured XML Documents." In: Fuhr, N. et al.(eds.). *INEX 2004. Lecture Notes in Computer Science*, Vol. 3493. Springer-Verlag, Berlin Heidelberg (2005) 424-436.
8. Larsen, B., Malik, S., Tombros, A.: "The Interactive Track at INEX 2005." In: Fuhr, N., Lalmas, M., Malik, S., Kazai, G. (eds.). *INEX 2005 Workshop Pre-Proceedings*. (2005) 313-326.

XML Documents Clustering by Structures

Richi Nayak and Sumei Xu

School of Information Systems, Queensland University of Technology,
Brisbane, Australia
r.nayak@qut.edu.au

Abstract. XCLS is a novel clustering algorithm to assemble heterogeneous
XML documents by measuring their level similarity with a *global* criterion
function. XCLS does not require the pair wise similarity to be computed
between two individual documents, rather it measures the similarity at
clustering level utilising the structural information of XML documents. Quality
of the clustering solution depends on the calculation of the level similarity, and
whether the level similarity can represent the documents' structural similarity
correctly. In this paper, we present the performance of XCLS for clustering the
structural descriptions (ordered labeled trees) of XML documents. We have
reported 5 sub-tasks corresponding to 5 corpuses as provided by the INEX 2005
document mining track.

1 Introduction

The widespread adoption of XML as the main standard for both data and meta-data
representation has led to the massive amounts of collection of XML documents.
Several database tools have been developed to deliver, store, integrate and query the
XML data [2, 4, 10]. However they do require efficient data management techniques
such as indexing based on the structural similarity to support an effective document
storage and retrieval. The data mining (DM) techniques such as clustering can
facilitate these applications [5, 15].

DM techniques have been around for many years for exploration of interesting
knowledge from a large amount of (unstructured and text) data. Mining of XML data
(that is semi-structured and hierarchal) significantly differs from data mining and text
mining. The XML data mining process is more complex [9] due to the nature of the
XML data. Firstly, XML allows the embedding of the semantic and structural aspects
in document contents. This results in XML data capturing the values of individual
elements as well as the relationships between them. The XML mining algorithms
should handle these relationships in the process as well along with values. Secondly,
everyone can design their own XML document with great flexibility and few
restrictions, in both structure and semantics. The heterogeneity in XML documents
presents many challenges to the mining process.

Several XML data clustering [1, 3, 6, 7] methods have been suggested, but there
remains some problems. The major problem is scalability. The majority of these
methods rely on the notion of tree edit distance developed in the combinational pattern
matching methods [14] to find common structures in tree collections. (A document is
usually represented as a tree structure.) These methods are built on pair-wise similarity

N. Fuhr et al. (Eds.): INEX 2005, LNCS 3977, pp. 432–442, 2006.

between data. The pair-wise similarity is measured using the local functions between each pair of objects to maximize the intra-cluster similarity and to minimize the inter-cluster similarity. The similarity value between each pair of trees is mapped into a similarity matrix. This matrix becomes the input to the clustering process using either a hierarchical agglomerative clustering algorithm or a k-means algorithm [5]. They are generally computationally expensive when the data sources are large due to the need for pair wise similarity matching among diverse documents.

Clustering methods, that use global metrics [12, 13] and also consider the hierarchical structure, can overcome the scalability problem. The clustering criterion function (or a global similarity measure) is defined on the cluster level to optimize the cluster parameters. Each new object is compared against the existing clusters instead of comparing against the individual objects. Since the computations of these global metrics are much faster than that of pair-wise, global approaches are very efficient.

We have developed the XML Clustering with Level Similarity (XCLS) algorithm using a global similarity measure [8]. This algorithm is shown to be very time efficient. We participated in INEX 2005 document mining track for clustering the given INEX 2005 XML corpus data with XCLS. We first present the algorithm detailing its working. We then present the experimental analysis of XCLS on 5 sub-tasks corresponding to 5 corpuses as provided by the first document mining track.

2   XML Documents Clustering with LevelSim (XCLS)

The XCLS method (as shown in figure 1) first represents the XML documents in the Level structure format. Progressively, the clustering process groups two objects (document to cluster or cluster to cluster) according to the LevelSim measures. This *global* criterion function measures similarity at the clustering level considering the hierarchical structures of the XML documents. It compares the new document to the existing clusters, thus ignoring the need to compute the similarity between each pair of documents.

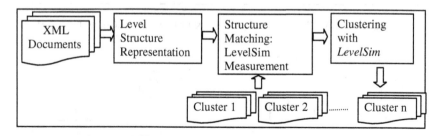

Fig. 1. A high-level view of the XCLS method

2.1   Level Structure: Inferring of XML Documents Structure

To be applicable to general Web documents and any type of XML documents (well-formed, valid and ill-formed) the XCLS algorithms starts by inferring the structural information within the document that is represented as the ordered labelled tree.

When inferring the structure, the focus is on the paths of elements with content values (i.e. leaves in a document tree), without considering attributes in a XML document. The inferred structure preserves the hierarchy and the context of the document. The multiple instances of values are ignored for an element. As this is redundant information for the presentation of a structure and, moreover, the occurrence of elements is not important for clustering in most cases. Additionally, XCLS does not consider the order of sibling when computing the similarity, as the order of sibling is not important for the clustering.

Figures 2 shows a XML document (X_Movie) and its corresponding structural tree (T_Movie). In order to enhance the clustering speed, the name of each element is denoted by a distinct integer.

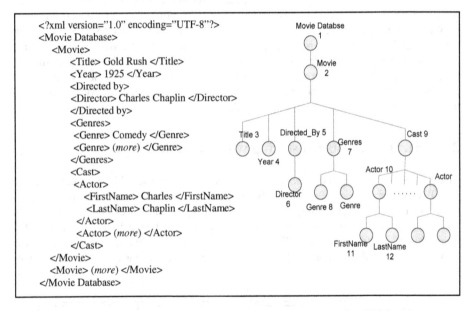

Fig. 2. An XML Document (X_Movie) & its tree representation (T_Movie)

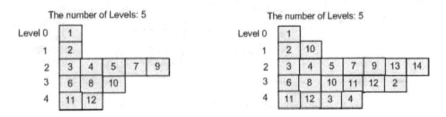

Fig. 3. Level structure for T_Movie   **Fig. 4.** Level structure of a cluster

XCLS uses the concept of the **level structure** to show the levels and the elements in each level of a tree structure. The Figure 3 shows the level structure for T_Movie. The level structure contains the information such as element values and their occurrences and the levels in the hierarchy. Clusters are also represented as the level structure. Each level of a cluster contains a collection of elements of the same level for all documents within the cluster. The figure 5 shows a tree structure of a document on Actor information and its corresponding level structure. The Figure 4 shows the level structure of a cluster containing both the Movie and Actor documents.

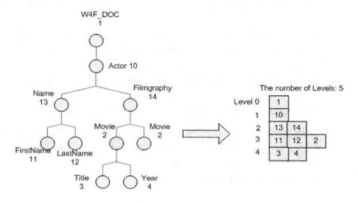

Fig. 5. T_Actor and its level structure

2.2 Clustering *Global* Criterion Function with Level Similarity (LevelSim)

The global criterion function called Level Similarity (LevelSim) measures the structural similarity between two XML objects (tree to cluster) by considering the level information and the elements' relationships/context of the XML data. The *LevelSim* emphasizes a different importance of elements in different level positions by allocating different weights to them. The higher level (e.g. root) has more weight than lower level (e.g. leaf). This is due to the assumption that the documents with different root nodes have higher chance of being assigned in different clusters. The hierarchical relationships of elements are also considered by counting occurrences of common elements sharing common ancestors.

The criterion function LevelSim is defined as follows for matching two objects, a tree and a cluster. Let us say that the tree is the object 1 and the cluster is the object 2. The order of matching between two objects is important due to the structural information present in an XML document. A cluster can contain only one tree as well.

$$LevelSim_{1 \to 2} = \frac{0.5 \times ComWeight_1 + 0.5 \times ComWeight_2}{TreeWeight \times Z}$$

$$= \frac{0.5 \times \sum_{i=0}^{L-1} CN_1^i \times (r)^{L-i-1} + 0.5 \times \sum_{j=0}^{L-1} CN_2^j \times (r)^{L-j-1}}{(\sum_{k=0}^{L-1} N^k \times (r)^{L-k-1}) \times Z}$$

Where:

ComWeight₁	Total weight of the common elements in all levels considering the level information of the object 1.

ComWeight₁ Total weight of the common elements in all levels considering the level information of the object 1.

ComWeight₂ Total weight of the common elements in all levels considering the level information of the object 2.

TreeWeight Total weight of all items in each level of the tree (i.e. the object 1).

Z Size of the cluster in terms of the number of trees within the cluster.

CN_1^i Sum of the occurrences of every common element in the level i of the object 1.

CN_2^j Sum of the occurrences of every common element in the level j of the object 2.

N^k Number of elements in level k of the tree

r Base Weight: the increasing factor of weight. This is usually larger than 1 to indicate that the higher level elements have more importance than the lower level elements.

L Number of levels in the tree.

LevelSim yields the values between 0 and 1; where 0 indicates completely different objects and 1 indicates homogenous objects.

2.3 The Process of Structure Matching Between Two Objects

The steps to match the elements of a tree (object 1) to the elements of a cluster (object 2) are as follows:

1. Start with searching common elements in the 1st level of both objects. If at least one common element is found, mark the number of common elements with the level number in object 1 (N_1^0) and the number of common elements with the level number in object 2 (N_2^0), then go to step 2. Otherwise, go to step 3.
2. Move both objects to next level (level i++, level j++) and search common elements in these new levels; If at least one common element is found, mark the number of common elements with the level number in object 1 (N_1^i) and the number of common elements with the level number in object 2 (N_2^j), then go to step 2. Otherwise, go to step 3.
3. Only move object 2 to next level (level j), then search common elements in the original level (i) of object 1 and the new level (j) of object 2. If at least one common element is found, mark the number of common elements with the level number in object 1 (N_1^i) and the number of common elements with the level number in object 2 (N_2^j), then go to step 2. Otherwise, go to step 3.
4. Repeat the process until all levels in either object have been matched.

After completion of structure matching the Level Similarity (LevelSim) is computed.

Figure 6 shows two different cases of the matching object 1 to object 2. In the first case, object 1 is the T_Movie tree (as shown in figure 5) and the object 2 is the cluster only containing the T_Actor tree (as shown in figure 4). In the second case, object 1 is the same, but the object 2 is the cluster containing both T_Actor and T_Movie (as shown in figure 3).

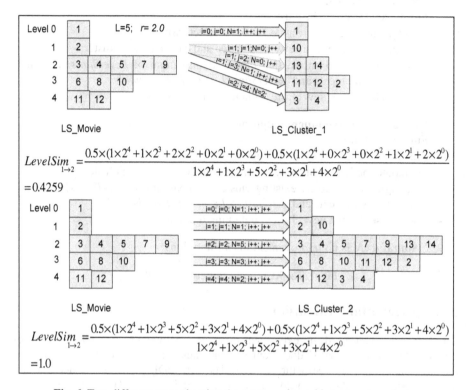

Fig. 6. Two different cases showing the process of matching a tree to a cluster

We have mentioned earlier that the order of matching between two objects is important. This is due to another reason that the operation *LevelSim* is not transitive. As a result, the level similarity between two objects is computed, $LevelSim_{1\to2}$ and $LevelSim_{2\to1}$, and the larger value between these two is chosen:

$$LevelSim = LevelSim_{1\to2} > LevelSim_{2\to1} ? LevelSim_{1\to2} : LevelSim_{2\to1}.$$

2.4 Clustering with Level Similarity

The next task is to group each XML document within the XML sources into a new cluster or to an existing cluster that have the maximum level similarity (*LevelSim*) with the given document. The figure 7 outlines the algorithm that includes two phases of allocation and reassignment. In the allocation phase, clusters are progressively formed driven by *LevelSim*. In the reassignment phase, as the name suggests, the derived clustering solution is refined by optimizing the *LevelSim* between the new document and existing clusters. The XCLS algorithm uses a user-defined threshold *LevelSim_Threshold* below that the cohesion between two objects is not considered i.e., LevelSim < *LevelSim_Threshold*.

/***Phase 1 – Allocation***/
For all XML trees to be clustered
- read the next tree (represented as level structure);
- compute the LevelSim between the tree and each existing cluster;
- assign the tree to an existing cluster if maximum of *LevelSim(s)* is found between two objects and *LevelSim > LevelSim_Threshold*;
- otherwise, form a new cluster containing the tree.

/***Phase 2 – Reassignment** (adjustment) */
For all XML trees
- read the next tree (i.e. level structure);
- compute the LevelSim between the tree and each existing cluster;
- reassign the tree to an existing cluster if maximum of *LevelSim(s)* is found between two objects and *LevelSim > LevelSim_Threshold*;
- otherwise, form a new cluster containing the tree.

/***Stop** if there is no improvement in two iterations*/

Fig. 7. The XCLS core clustering algorithm

3   Experimental Evaluation

Dataset: The data used in experiments are the MovieDB and INEX corpuses provided by the INEX 2005 document mining track. The MovieDB corpus has 11 thematic and 11 possible structure classes. The MovieDB collection is derived into many versions (m-db-s-0, m-db-s-1, m-db-s-2 and m-db-s-3) after a series of transformation to add the complexity in clustering process. The INEX corpus has 6 thematic (Computer, Graphics, Hardware, Artificial Intelligence, Internet, Parallel) and 2 structural classes (Transaction journals vs Others). Some documents could not be parsed and therefore are not valid documents. These documents are excluded during the clustering process. The table 1 shows some characteristics of the data set.

Table 1. Features of the data sets

Dataset	Bad trees (ill-formed)	Trees to be Clustered	Distinct Labels
m-db-s-0-test	5	4811	195
m-db-s-1-test	4	4814	197
m-db-s-2-test	9	4809	197
m-db-s-3-test	9	4809	194
inex-s-test	0	6053	173

Evaluation Criteria: XCLS was evaluated on the given data set with the criteria of purity (micro and macro), entropy (micro and macro) and mutual information. These criteria were set by the INEX 2005 document mining track.

Experimental set-up: All the experiments were done on the machine with 2.8GHZ Intel Celeron CPU and 1G of RAM. We submitted two runs for each data set to the INEX 2005 document mining track. The first run (denoted as run 1) has the parameter for maximum number of clusters set as 1000. It means that XCLS automatically groups the documents into clusters without a prior knowledge. The second experimental run (denoted as run 2) has the parameter for maximum number of clusters set as the required (known) clusters. It means XCLS is guided about when to stop, overriding its natural stopping methods.

Results: Table 2 reports the performance of XCLS on these data sets for the purity, entropy and mutual information measurements. It is interesting to see that XCLS performed similarly in the entire movie corpuses, even though, the transformations on the MovieDB collection have been defined so that each series should be more difficult to cluster than the preceding. E.g., the second MovieDB data set classes have a higher overlap than for the first one to make the clustering more difficult. This shows the strength of the clustering criteria and the approach that XCLS adapts for clustering.

XCLS by its nature does not need to inform about the required number of clusters. In other words, the information of number of clusters does not help the clustering process at all. The results in the tables 2 confirm this. There is no significant difference in quality of the clustering solution in both runs. In the run 1 type experiments where information on the set number of clusters is not provided, the number of clusters are usually large (>100) depending on the similarity threshold in the allocation phase of the clustering algorithm. However, in the following iterations, the number of clusters decreases automatically due to the clustering controlled by the level similarity between the tree and the original cluster or other clusters, rather than the set level threshold. We conclude from this that the XCLS performs independent of the prior information about the number of clusters.

XCLS does better in several movie corpuses in comparison to the INEX corpus (Table 2). The INEX result shows the extreme high entropy indicating that the various classes of documents are incorrectly distributed within clusters. However, the relatively higher purity in the INEX results shows that each cluster contains documents primarily from its corresponding class. The contingency matrix shows that XCLS has clustered majority of documents in cluster 1 (6044 out of 6053), however, XCLS has been successful in allocating relevant classes to cluster 1 (3933/3937).

The contingency matrix for all the data sets shows that XCLS can group most documents belonging to the same class into one cluster; it seldom puts them into separate clusters. However, it sometimes groups documents from several classes into one cluster because of their higher level similarity.

There may be considered many reasons behind this. Firstly, this version of XCLS does not take many semantic similarities such as synonyms, hyponyms, hypernyms between two terms (or tags) into account when converting a tag name into unique

Table 2. The XCLS performance for various measurements

Dataset	Run	Micro-purity	Macro-purity	Micro-entropy	Macro-entropy	Mutual Information
m-db-s-0-test	1	0.604	0.794	0.325	0.171	1.53
	2	0.589	0.786	0.334	0.174	1.51
m-db-s-1-test	1	0.603	0.682	0.331	0.268	1.51
	2	0.596	0.769	0.335	0.203	1.51
m-db-s-2-test	1	0.590	0.720	0.335	0.249	1.51
	2	0.592	0.728	0.335	0.241	1.51
m-db-s-3-test	1	0.592	0.756	0.340	0.197	1.49
	2	0.589	0.707	0.340	0.224	1.49
inex-s-test	1	0.651	0.603	0.934	0.962	0.0
	2	0.651	0.603	0.934	0.962	0.0

integer for better processing. Secondly, due to the nature of XCLS, documents are not compared against each other, but, each document is compared against the existing clusters. Additionally, XCLS does not only consider the parent-child relationship to measure the structural similarity, but also include the ancestor relationships of the data. This makes it more appropriate for clustering the heterogeneous data. Therefore, the full extent of XCLS has not been tested and reflected in the homogenous environment data such as the INEX corpus.

There are also many issues that might have negative effects on the clustering result of XCLS. The dataset given in this challenge is a set of ordered trees. However, XCLS assumes that the order of siblings is not important for clustering. It does not

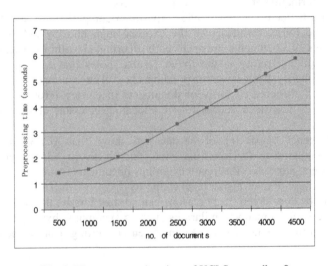

Fig. 8. The preprocessing time of XCLS on m-db-s-0

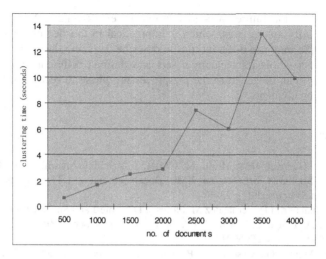

Fig. 9. The clustering time of XCLS on m-db-s-0

consider the order of sibling when computing the similarity. Additionally, XCLS can not efficiently handle the overlapped similar structures due to its level structure representation of cluster structures in which it stores only the elements, their levels and occurrences. It does not store the information about the trees in which they come from for efficiency purpose. Therefore, if trees have complex overlapped structures, the calculation of level similarity between a tree and a cluster is not accurate. E.g., if Tree1 has structures ABC, Tree2 has structures ACD, Tree3 has structures ABCD, in most cases they will be group together by XCLS.

Figure 8 shows the pre-processing time performance of XCLS on m-db-s-0 that includes the generation of level structure for all documents. Figure 9 shows the clustering time performance that includes the time to group the represented level structures in clusters using LevelSim. These figures show that the time cost of XCLS is linear to the number of documents.

4 Conclusions and Future Work

We apply the XCLS algorithm based on the intuitive idea of the *LevelSim* global criterion function to effectively cluster the movie and INEX data by their structures. XCLS measures the structural similarity in clustering level instead of the document level, thus it does not need to calculate the pair-to-pair distance between each pair of documents. The derivation of level structure from a tree is straightforward; and the computation of *LevelSim* is quite effective for documents with varied structures.

The results show that XCLS can cluster a large number of documents belonging to different domains and having a large number of distinct labels. It does it so with the time complexity linear to the number of documents, and without knowing the information on the number of clusters. Although there remains some inaccuracy in solution, but, the main purpose of XCLS is the time effectiveness to cluster the massive amount of documents in heterogeneous environment with good accuracy.

XCLS needs some future work to improve its effectiveness. XCLS ignored the semantic similarity among tags, which is impractical in the flexible environment on web since people may use different tags to describe the same thing. As WordNet can organize English words into synonym sets and defined different relations link the synonym sets, it can be added to the pre-processing phase to recognize the semantic similarity among elements.

References

1. Bertino, E., Guerrini, G. & Mesiti, M. (2004). A Matching Algorithm for Measuring the Structural Similarity between an XML Document and a DTD and its applications. Information Systems, 29(1): 23-46.
2. Boag S. Chamberlin D, Fernández M, Florescu D, Robie J and Siméon J. "XQuery 1.0: An XML Query Language" W3C Working Draft, September, 2005. http://www.w3.org/TR/2005/WD-xquery-20050915/
3. Flesca, S., Manco, G., Masciari, E., Pontieri, L., & Pugliese, A. (2005). *Fast Detection of XML Structural Similarities*. IEEE Transaction on Knowledge and Data Engineering, Vol 7 (2), pp 160-175.
4. Guardalben, G. (2004), *Integrating XML and Relational Database Technologies: A Position Paper*, HiT Software Inc, retrieved May 1st ,2005, from http://www.hitsw.com/products_services/whitepapers/integrating_xml_rdb/integrating_xml_white_paper.pdf.
5. Jain, A. K., Murty, M. N., & Flynn, P. J. (1999). Data Clustering: A Review. *ACM Computing Surveys (CSUR), 31*(3), 264-323.
6. Leung, H.-p., Chung, F.-l., & Chan, S. C.-f. (2005). On the use of hierarchical information in sequential mining-based XML document similarity computation. *Knowledge and Information Systems, 7*(4),pp 476-498.
7. Nayak R and Iryadi W (2006). XMine: A methodology for mining XML structure. *The Eighth Asia Pacific Web Conference*. January 2006, China.
8. Nayak R & Xu S. (2006). "XCLS: A Fast and Effective Clustering Algorithm for Heterogeneous XML Documents, The *10th* Pacific-Asia Conference on Knowledge Discovery and Data Mining (PAKDD), April, Singapore
9. Automatic integration of heterogenous XML-schemas", *Proceedings of the International Conferences on Information Integration and Web-based Applications & Services*. pp. 427-437.
10. Nayak, R., Witt, R., and Tonev, A. (2002) Data Mining and XML documents, International Conference on Internet Computing, USA.
11. Xylem L. (2001). Xylem: A dynamic Warehouse for XML data of the Web," IDEAS'01, pp3-7, 2001.
12. Yergeau, F, Bray T, Paoli *J,* Sperberg-McQueen, C M and Maler E. (2004). Extensible Markup Language (XML) 1.0 (Third Edition) W3C Recommendation, February 2004, http://www.w3.org/TR/2004/REC-XML-20040204/
13. Ying Y, Guan X and You J. (2002), CLOPE: A Fast and effective clustering algorithm for transactional data,
14. Wang, K., Xu, C. (1999), *Clustering Transactions Using Large Items*, in the proceedings of ACM CIKM-99, Kansas, Missouri.
15. Zhang, K., & Shasha, D. (1989). Simple Fast Algorithms for the Editing Distance Between Trees and Related Problems. SIAM Journal Computing, 18(6), 1245-1262.
16. Zhao, Y., & Karypis, G. (2002). Evaluation of Hierarchical Clustering Algorithms for Document Datasets. The 2002 ACM CIKM, USA.

A Flexible Structured-Based Representation for XML Document Mining

Anne-Marie Vercoustre, Mounir Fegas,
Saba Gul, and Yves Lechevallier

INRIA, Rocquencourt, France
Firstname.Lastname@inria.fr
http://www.inria.fr/index.en

Abstract. This paper reports on the INRIA group's approach to XML mining while participating in the INEX XML Mining track 2005. We use a flexible representation of XML documents that allows taking into account the structure only or both the structure and content. Our approach consists of representing XML documents by a set of their sub-paths, defined according to some criteria (length, root beginning, leaf ending). By considering those sub-paths as words, we can use standard methods for vocabulary reduction, and simple clustering methods such as k-means. We use an implementation of the clustering algorithm known as *dynamic clouds* that can work with distinct groups of independent modalities put in separate variables. This is useful in our model since embedded sub-paths are not independent: we split potentially dependant paths into separate variables, resulting in each of them containing independant paths. Experiments with the INEX collections show good results for the structure-only collections, but our approach could not scale well for large structure-and-content collections.

1 Introduction

XML documents are becoming ubiquitous because of their rich and flexible format that can be used for a variety of applications. Standard methods have been used to classify XML documents, reducing them to their textual parts [10]. These approaches do not take advantage of the structure of XML documents that also carries important information.

Recently much attention has been drawn towards using the structure of XML documents to improve information retrieval, classification and clustering, and more generally information mining [4, 5, 7, 13, 22]. In the last four years, the INEX (Initiative for the Evaluation of XML retrieval) has focused on system performance in retrieving elements of documents rather than full documents and evaluated the benefits for end users. Other researches have focussed on clustering large collections of documents using representations of documents that involve both the structure and the content of documents, or the structure only [8, 24, 26]. One motivation for structured-based clustering is to organise XML collections into smaller collections with a specific schema that supports optimisation of the query processing.

N. Fuhr et al. (Eds.): INEX 2005, LNCS 3977, pp. 443–457, 2006.

Approaches for combining structure and text range from adding a flat representation of the structure to the classical vector space model [10] or combining different classifiers for different tags or media [9], to defining a more complex structured vector models [25], possibly involving attributes and links [15].

When using the structure only, the objective is generally to organize large and heterogeneous collections of documents into smaller collections (clusters) that can be stored and searched more effectively. Part of the objective is to identify substructures that characterize the documents in a cluster and to build a representative of the cluster [11], possibly a schema or a DTD.

Since XML documents are represented as trees, the problem of clustering XML documents can be seen as the same as clustering trees. One can identify two main approaches: 1) identify frequent common sub-patterns between trees and group together documents that share the same patterns [22, 27, 11]; 2) define a similarity measure between trees that can be used with a standard clustering algorithm. A possible distance is calculated by associating a cost function to the edit distance between two trees [12, 20, 5]. However, it is well known that edit distance algorithms have complexity issues. Therefore some models replace the original trees by structural summaries [6] or s-graphs [17] that retain only the intrinsic structure of the tree: for example, reducing a list of elements to a single element, flattening recursive structures, etc.

A common drawback of the two approaches above is that they reduce documents to their intrinsic patterns (sub-patterns, or summaries) and do not take into account an important characteristic of XML documents: the notion of list of elements and more precisely the number of elements in those lists. While it may be fine for clustering heterogeneous collection, suppressing lists of elements may result in losing document properties that could be interesting for other types of XML mining.

Our idea is therefore to use a document representation that takes into account the frequency of structure within the documents, while not be as costly as the edit distance.

In this paper we propose a generic model for clustering documents that involves either their structure or both their structure and content. We represent documents by flattening their trees into their sets of sub-paths of length between n and m, two *a priori* given values. We retain the frequency of paths and we consider sub-paths as words. Therefore we can apply standard clustering methods usually used for text. When considering document content as well as structure, sub-paths are extended with the individual words of the text contained in the terminal node of each path. For specific values of m and n, our model is equivalent to models that have been proposed before, so we offer a more general framework.

We evaluate our model using the collections proposed in the INEX XML mining track, while being aware that our approach may not be appropriate for some of the proposed collections, in particular those where the order of elements is significant for clustering.

In Sect. 2, we present our document model for clustering and compare it, in Sect. 3, to previous models for specific values of m and n. Sect. 4 describes our clustering method and some additional feature selection. Sect. 5 details the evaluation metrics we use, while Sect. 6 and 7 present our experiments and the results. In Sect. 8 we propose our conclusions.

2   Our Model for Document Representation

XML documents are usually represented as trees where each node corresponds to an XML tag. The hierarchy of the nodes reflects the embedding of the tags, and leaf nodes have associated text. Attributes can be represented the same way as sub-elements, i.e. as additional descendants of the node they are attached to.

```
<article>
    <fm>
        <au>
            <fnm>werner</fnm>
            <snm>buchholz</snm>
            <role>editor</role>
        </au>
        <abs>This department offers an opportunity to
        comment on previously published articles...
        </abs>
    </fm>
    <bdy>
        <sec sno="01">
            <st>the stored program concept: a reprise</st>
            <p>for historians interested in establishing ... </p>
            <p>when a small number of us under the leadership...</p>
            <bibl>
                <h>additional material on the subject in annal</h>
                <bb>
                    <au>n. metropoli</au>
                    <au>j. worlton</au>
                    <atl>a trilogy of errors in the history of computing</atl>
                </bb>
            </bibl>
        </sec>
    </bdy>
</article>
```

Fig. 1. An example of XML document

Fig. 1 gives an example of an XML document, extracted from the IEEE collection, that we will use throughout the paper.

Our model is based on a tree linearization that represents a document as its set of paths. The precise definition of paths to consider is defined below and correspond, in fact, to a family of possible representations that take into account the structure, the text, or both. By regarding paths as simple words we can use the vector model to represent documents from their structure.

The motivation for a flexible choice of paths or sub-paths in the document is that some analysis or clustering tasks may be interested in the top part of the tree, the lower parts of the tree, or possibly parts in the middle. An example would be clustering very heterogeneous collections based on the structure, where the partition can be done by looking at the top level elements only. On the contrary, if one wants to cluster documents based mostly on the text, it could be appropriate to add some limited context just above the text.

Before presenting our structured document representations, we introduce some definitions:

Definition 1. *The path of a node n is the sequence of nodes from the root to this node, when traversing the tree from child to child. We note it p(n). It is also called a root-beginning path[1], or root path for short.*

Definition 2. *The length of a path is the number of nodes in the path.*

Definition 3. *A sub-path s of length l on a path p is a sequence of l consecutive nodes along the path p. (i.e. a sub-path does not necessarily start at the root). We note |s| the length of the sub-path s.*

Table 1 shows examples of paths and sub-paths of length 3.

To take into account the text of the documents, we introduce "text paths" defined as follow:

Definition 4. *A text sub-path is a sub-path that ends with a word contained in the text associated with the last node in the sub-path. When the last node is not a leaf, the words are those associated with its descendants.*

Table 1. Paths and sub-paths of length 3; the character @ marks an attribute

Paths	Tf
article.bdy.sec	1
article.fm.au	1
bdy.sec.p	2
bdy.bb.au	2
bdy.sec.sno@	1

Table 2. Textual paths of length 4 and 3

Paths	Tf
article.fm.abs. "offer"	1
bdy.sec.p. "historian"	1
bdy.sec.sno@. "01"	1
article.fm.au. "werner"	1
bdy.sec. "historian"	1

Table 2 shows some text paths or sub-paths of length 4 and 3 corresponding to the example in Fig. 1. The last two paths are non terminal paths extended with words that are not directly associated with their final node but with one of their descendants.

We can now define a family of representations for a XML document tree d as:

$$R(d) = \sum_i w_i p_i \tag{1}$$

for all sub-paths p_i in d, where $m \leq |p_i| \leq n, 1 \leq m \leq n$, w_i is the frequency of sub-paths p_i.

---

[1] We use the terminology used in Liu and *al.* [18] for complete paths, root-beginning paths, leaf-ending paths.

The actual representations are defined by a few parameters:

- m and n are two *a priori* fixed integers. The value "n" can be replaced with the symbol "*", meaning that, for each sub-path, the maximum value would be the length of its supporting path.
- when the parameter **root** is set on, only the sub-paths starting from the root (root-beginning paths) are generated.
- when the parameter **leaf** is set on, only the sub-paths ending at leaf nodes (leaf-ending path) are generated.
- with the parameter **text** set on, only "text paths" are generated.
- with the parameter **text-and-node** set on, both text sub-paths and node sub-paths are generated.
- with the parameter **attribute** set on, attributes, as well as nodes, are considered for path generation.

By setting different parameter values, we can use a variety of document representations for different clustering tasks. Before presenting our clustering approach, we are going to interpret the models for some specific values of the parameters, and compare them with other existing models.

3 Comparison with Other Models for Structured Documents

Our document model integrates various representations that have been proposed in other works:

- Case $min = 1$, $max = 1$, $text = true$;
  This case corresponds to representing a document by its text only (standard vector model)
- Case $min = 1$, $max = 1$, $text = false$, $[attribute = (false|true)]$;
  Corresponds to representing a document by the list of its tags. This is the model used, with or without attributes, in Doucet and *al.* [10], for the case "Tag feature only", based on the vector model. It is also used in Flesca and *al.* [11] where both elements and attribute names are considered. Moreover if node-and-text is set to true, we get the "Tag and text features" used in Doucet and *al.* [10].
- Case $min = 1$, $max = *$, $root = true$, $leaf = true$, $[text = (false|true)]$;
  In this case XML documents are represented by the set of their paths from the root to the leaves. In Yoon and *al.* [26] they use a bitmap matrix where lines represent the documents and columns represent the different terminal paths in the collection. The frequency is not used. They also extend their bitmap model by adding quadruplets (document, path, term, b) where b is true if the path contains the term, which corresponds in our case with text set to true. When $text = true$, it is also the representation used in Yi and Sundaresan [25] for the "flat with structured tag" experiments, where each term (document word) is replaced by its *text path* in a flat vector.

- Case $min = 1$, $max = *$, $root = true$, $leaf = false$, $text = true$;
  A document is represented by the set of all the root text paths (of any length) in the document, where a term will belong to its parent node and all the embedding nodes. This model is equivalent to the Structure Vector Model proposed in Yi and Sundaresan [25], where a document is represented by all its paths of length between 1 and the height h of the document tree. The frequency of terms associated with a path is relative to the subtree associated with that path.
- Case $min = 1$, $max = L$, $root = false$, $leaf = false$, $text = false$;
  One of the representation proposed in Liu and $al.$ [18] is based on paths of length smaller than L, although they can also fix the level in the tree where the paths must start. In our case paths will start at the root or at any level in the tree.
- Case $min = n$, $max = n$, $root = false$, $leaf = true$, $text = true$;
  This case corresponds to representing documents by leaf-ending sub-paths of length n, and therefore providing a limited context to the terms in the documents. One of the representations developed in Liu and $al.$ [18] includes the definitions of leaf-ending paths as well root-beginning paths, of length less than L. They seem to use text as well, but this is not clearly described.

Our representation of XML documents using sub-paths is therefore flexible enough to subsume many of the representations used in the above works.

Other representations for XML trees for clustering have recently been proposed. Nayak and Xu [19] represents an XML document by its level structure: each level is represented by the list of labels (tags) that occur at this level; multiple instances are ignored and the order of the labels is not preserved. The clustering algorithm is based on a similarity measure between levels. Candillier and $al.$ [1] transforms the XML trees into sets of attribute-values in order to apply various existing methods on such data. Considered attributes include the set of parent-child relations, the set of next-sibling relations, the set of distinct root paths, etc. Thoses attributes results in a number of features whose values, for a given document, are their number of occurences of this feature in the document. For clustering or classification, they use an adaptation of SSC [2], a *subspace clustering algorithm* that has the advantage of providing an interpretable representation of the resulting clusters, as a decision tree on the discriminent features.

4   Clustering Approach

Since we represent XML documents as a set of paths seen as words, we can use traditional clustering methods for flat texts. However we have to deal with two issues: first, reducing the number of paths in case they are too many; secondly, the possible dependency of paths. Before presenting the clustering approach we address these two issues.

4.1   Further Feature Selection

Algorithms for clustering such as the k-means are linearly dependent on the size of the data, that is, the number of words that represent the documents. In our case the document will be represented not only by the different words in the text but possibly by their contextual paths (i.e. generating as many different occurrences of a word as the different contexts in which it occurs). Moreover they may be extra "words" corresponding to any sub-path in the document trees (node paths) [2]. It is therefore necessary to limit the number of paths that represent the documents to reduce the clustering time.

We apply two levels of feature selection in the path generation: structure level and text level. Then we reduce the number of paths by applying standard selection on words using their relative frequency (TF/IDF).

Structure level. Usually we reduce the number of generated paths by regrouping some tags in more semantic categories, using our knowledge of the DTD or the collections. For example we replace tags for different sections ($ss1$, $ss2$, sec), by a single tag "sec", and ignore presentation tags. Since the INEX collections were specially preprocessed for the XML mining track, we did not have to take care of these semantic groupings.

Text level. For the textual content of the document, we use standard reduction methods:

- stop list word for suppressing insignificant word
- suppression of terms shorter than 4 characters
- pseudo stemming using the Porter stemmer [21].

Frequency of paths. As said before, the documents are represented by a set of paths that depends on the chosen parameters. First, the frequency of a path is calculated and normalized using the TF/IDF formula (number of path occurrences in the document over their number in the whole collection). Paths that are too frequent or too rare will be suppressed. In particular paths that occur only once in the collection will be suppressed since it will not affect the clustering process. Similarly paths that occur in every document will not contribute to partitioning documents.

For the remaining paths, we calculate their normalised weight in the document by dividing the number of occurrences of the path by the number of the paths in the document (standard vector normalization to take into account the length of the documents).

4.2   Word Dependency

Clustering algorithms based on the vector model rely on the independence of the various dimensions (words) for calculating the distance between the vectors. Although this is not always verified in practice with words in texts, it usually works

---

[2] Obviously there will be much more leaf-ending paths than root-paths since trees are expending from the root to the leaves.

fine. In our case, where words are sub-paths in the document tree, there is an obvious dependency between embedded sub-paths. For example, the two paths *bdy.sec* and *bdy.sec.st* are not independent since the second can exist only if the first one exists, the first one being embedded in the second one. However, two overlapping paths, such as *bdy.sec* and *sec.st* would not be regarded as dependent. We only consider structural dependency here, not dependency that would derive from the DTD itself, for example if two siblings are mandatory according to the DTD definition. This later dependency would not affect the clustering results since the two paths would then be present in all the documents and therefore eliminated as very frequent.

To deal with the first case of dependency, we partition the paths by their length and treat each set of paths as different variables in the clustering algorithm as explained below.

4.3   Clustering Method

Our clustering algorithm is based on the partitioning method proposed by Celeux and *al.* [3], where the distance between clusters is based on the frequency of the words of the selected vocabulary. This approach is equivalent to the k-means algorithm. As for the k-means we represent the clusters by prototypes which summarize the information (paths) of the documents belonging to each of them.

More precisely, if the vocabulary counts p words, each document s is represented by the vector $x_s = (x_s^1, ..., x_s^j, ..., x_s^p)$ where x_s^j is the number of occurrences of word x_j in the document s, then the prototype g for a class U_i is represented by $g_i = (g_i^1, ..., g_i^j, ..., g_i^p)$ with $g_i^j = \sum_{s \in U_i} x_s^j$.

Finally, the prototype of each class been fixed, every element is assigned to a class according to its proximity to the prototype. The proximity is measured by a classical distance between distributions (e.g. Euclidean distance):

$$d(x, y) = \sqrt{\sum_{j=1}^{m} (x_j - y_j)^2}, \ m \text{ is the number of modalities.}$$

When there are dependencies between paths[3], we replace the above formula by the following:

$$d(x, y) = \sqrt{\sum_{k=1}^{p} \sum_{j=1}^{m_k} (x_j^k - y_j^k)^2}$$

where p is the number of variables, and m_k is the number of modalities for the variable k.

---

[3] For complete paths (option root=true and leaf=true), there are no embedded paths so (1) can be used.

5   Evaluation and Metrics

Clustering evaluation is always a bit difficult, since, unlike classification, clustering is supposed to discover significant clusters whose number is not known in advance. However standard evaluation can be made on well known collection were some existing classification can be used as a reference. Since training sets are provided for the XML tracks we are able to evaluate our clustering approaches using them. We used different standard measures and compared their behavior when increasing the number of clusters and using different path lengths. We recall below the definition of the four metrics we use: F-measure, entropy, purity and corrected rand.

- The **F-measure** proposed by Larsen and Aone [16] combines the precision and recall measures from information retrieval and treats each cluster as if it were the result of a query and each class as if it were the desired answer to that query. It is the *harmonic mean* between precision and recall.
- The **Corrected Rand Index** has been proposed by Hubert and Arabie [14] to compare two partitions. This measure can be used to compare the resulting clusters with an existing partition, or to compare two partitions resulting of different automatic clustering.
- **Entropy:** It measures the class distribution of each cluster. The smaller the entropy value, the better the clustering solution. A perfect clustering solution would be the one that leads to clusters that contain documents from only a single class, in which case the entropy will be zero [28].
- **Purity:** It measures the percentage of documents in a cluster that belong to the largest class of documents in this cluster. In general the larger the value of purity, the better the clustering solution [28].

6   Experiments with the INEX Collections

The INEX XML mining track provides a number of collections for evaluating clustering methods. Some of them consist only of document tree structures (structure-only collections), while the others correspond to XML documents with textual content (structure and content collections). The training sets consist of a subset of the documents in each collection, together with the class they belong to. As a consequence the expected number of clusters for each collection is known in advance. Below we give a short summary of the test collections we use for our experiments. Unfortunately we were not able to carry out all the experiments before the workshop, in particular because of the size of the structure and content collections.

6.1   The IEEE Collections

From the standard IEEE collection used in the INEX ad-hoc retrieval experiments, the XML mining track's organisers have derived two collections for XML mining, namely INEX-s (structure only) and INEX-cs (content and structure).

They preprocessed both collections in order to eliminate useless tags, as well as to remove information (the name of the Journal) that would identify obviously the class the document belongs to. For INEX-s, the clustering task is to identify the two classes that correspond, first to *Transactions* Journals, second to other Journals. It is expected that the two types of Journals use different parts of the IEEE DTD and that articles could be easily partitioned into the two classes.

For INEX-cs, the clustering task, using both the structure and the content of the articles, is to identify the six classes proposed in Denoyer [7] and built from the 18 existing Journals.

Table 3. Results for Inex-s (training collection) for path length 3 and 4, and cluster number set to 2 or 4

Path length	Root	Leaf	No. of Clusters	Fmeasure	Corr.Rand	Entropy	Purity
3	T	F	2	0.662	0.098	0.755	0.663
3	F	T	2	0.667	0.105	0.745	0.667
3	**T**	**F**	**4**	**0.661**	**0.423**	**0.185**	**0.963**
3	F	T	4	0.549	0.005	0.728	0.682
4	T	F	2	0.625	-0.044	0.871	0.650
4	F	T	2	0.655	0.087	0.757	0.655
4	T	F	4	0.542	0.208	0.457	0.857
4	F	T	4	0.545	-0.001	0.737	0.675

6.2 The Movie Database Collections

The MovieDB corpus is a set of XML documents describing movies. It was built using the IMDB database. It contains 9643 XML documents. Each document is labelled by one thematic category which represents the genre of the movie in the original collection and one structure category. There are 11 thematic categories and 11 possible structure categories which correspond to transformations of the original data structures. There are four resulting test collections for clustering based only on structure, and two test collections for clustering using both content and structure.

7 Results

Since training sets were provided, we use them to evaluate our approach before getting from the track organisers the official results on the test collections.

7.1 IEEE Structure Collection

We first test our approach with different path lengths either starting at the root or ending at the leaves. We present only a few results in Table 3: The best values (especially entropy and purity) are obtained for documents represented by the set of paths of length 3 starting from the root. It must be noticed that it happens

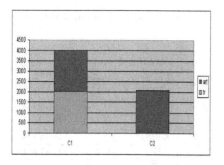

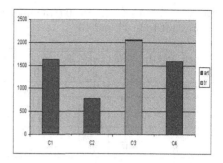

Fig. 2. The repartition of classes *Articles* and *Transactions* on two clusters

Fig. 3. The repartition of classes *Articles* and *Transactions* on four clusters

for four clusters, not the two that were expected. There is nothing wrong with this result since there is no intrinsic reason why some articles would not have an overall structure more dissimilar to other articles than to *Transactions*.

Fig. 2 and Fig. 3 shows the repartition of the two (resp. four) clusters on the two expected classes. We can see that in the case of four clusters, one class (Transaction) maps quite closely to cluster 3, while the other three clusters contain mostly articles. We have not tried to analyse more deeply what could be the similarities between articles within these three clusters.

Then we sent two runs to the XML document mining track. The parameters we used and the official results are shown in Table 4.

Table 4. Official Results for inex-s (test collection) for two runs

Run	Path-length	Root	Leaf	No. of Clusters	Micro Entropy	Macro Entropy	Micro Purity	Macro Purity
Run 1	3	F	T	2	0.744	0.627	0.663	0.627
Run 2	4	T	F	4	0.109	0.137	0.984	0.878

These results confirm the results with the training set that clustering in four clusters give better results than clustering in two clusters.

7.2 MovieDB Structure Collections

We did the same type of experiments for the four structured collections built from the Movie databases. For each of the four collections we set the path length alternatively to 3 and 4, with either root paths or leaf-ending paths. We cluster the documents into 9, 11 or 13 clusters respectively, the expected number of classes being 11.

Table 5 shows the measure values when clustering the training collection m-db-s0. The results are always better when using leaf-ending paths over root paths, unless they are identical when the path length is set to 4. The best value for the purity is obtained when clustering into 11 clusters, but the differences for

Table 5. Results for m-db-s0 (training collection) for path length 3 and 4, and cluster number set to 9, 11 and 13

Path length	Root	Leaf	No. of Clusters	Fmeasure	Corr.Rand	Entropy	Purity
3	T	F	9	0.541	0.370	0.286	0.632
3	F	T	9	0.708	0.575	0.154	0.819
3	T	F	11	0.509	0.357	0.285	0.640
3	**F**	**T**	**11**	**0.642**	**0.506**	**0.151**	**0.820**
3	T	F	13	0.465	0.328	0.284	0.640
3	F	T	13	0.595	0.473	0.151	0.819
4	T	F	9	0.714	0.576	0.158	0.813
4	F	T	9	0.714	0.576	0.158	0.813
4	**T**	**F**	**11**	**0.663**	**0.532**	**0.157**	**0.821**
4	**F**	**T**	**11**	**0.663**	**0.532**	**0.157**	**0.827**
4	T	F	13	0.648	0.519	0.155	0.820
4	F	T	13	0.648	0.519	0.155	0.820

other measures may not be all significant. We carried out similar experiments with the other collections, but there are not shown here for lack of space.

Table 6 shows the official results for the four MovieDB collections for 11 clusters. As we can see, the quality of the results decreases with the increasing difficulty from m-db-0 to m-db-3.

Table 6. Official Results for Movie-DB (test collections) for two runs

Coll.	Run	Path-lgth	Root	Leaf	Micro Entropy	Macro Entropy	Micro Purity	Macro Purity	Mutual Info
m-db-0	Run 1	3	F	T	0.732	0.841	0.203	0.136	1.823
	Run 2	4	T	F	0.732	0.841	0.203	0.136	1.823
m-db-1	Run 1	3	F	T	0.688	0.804	0.326	0.226	1.528
	Run 2	4	T	F	0.707	0.835	0.256	0.144	1.690
m-db-2	Run 1	3	F	T	0.688	0.758	0.296	0.209	1.592
	Run 2	4	T	F	0.458	0.501	0.487	0.446	1.139
m-db-3	Run 1	3	F	T	0.623	0.714	0.316	0.238	1.545
	Run 2	4	T	F	0.553	0.636	0.527	0.438	1.044

We also include in Fig. 4, the comparisons of our results with the runs submitted by other participants. Our approach scores in the top-middle range of the four who have submitted results for the four collections. Although Candillier [1] and Hagenbuchner [23] submitted results only for Movie-db-s-0, their results are very promising.

7.3   Structure and Content Collection

In Vercoustre and *al.* [24] we had experimented the structure and content approach with two collections, including a small percentage of the INEX collection. However we were not able to run our approach on the full Inex-cs collection, due

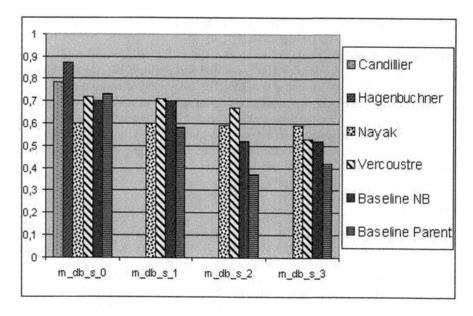

Fig. 4. Comparison of clustering results for the Movie-db-s runs submitted to INEX 2005

to the large number of generated textual paths. We did not experiment with m-db-cs collection but we expect that the same problem would occur.

Table 7 shows the number of different textual paths generated for different parameters, for 10% of the collection.

Table 7. Number of generated textual paths for 10% of the inex-cs collection

type	path-lgth	Root	Leaf	No. of distinct paths
text	1	F	T	313078
text+ tags	1	F	F	340043
leaf path	2	F	T	1271289
root path	3	T	F	367082
root path	4	T	F	387484

The number of paths increases with the length of paths, and, for a fix path length, they are far more numerous for ending paths than for root paths since the tree is larger at the leaves than at the root. Generating leaf paths is more costly and even overflows the generating program when the collection is too large.

8   Conclusion

In this paper we proposed to represent XML documents by a set of their paths generated according to a range of parameters. We evaluated our approach on some of the collections proposed by the INEX XML Mining track and we were relatively successful on the structure-only collections.

However, we have not managed to cluster the full structure-and-content collections, due to the large size of the generated vocabulary. We are thinking of reducing the vocabulary by using the TF/IDF frequency of terms in each specific path, rather than the frequency of textual paths in a document and the collection respectively.

In both cases, structure and structure-and-content, it could also be beneficial to reduce the space dimension before clustering, for example by using Principal Component Analysis like in Liu and al. [18].

References

1. L. Candillier, I. Tellier, and F. Torre. Transforming XML trees for efficient classification and clustering. INEX 2005 Workshop on Mining XML documents, November 2005.
2. L. Candillier, I. Tellier, F. Torre, and O. Bousquet. SSC : Statistical Subspace Clustering. In P. Perner and A. Imiya, editors, *4th International Conference on Machine Learning and Data Mining in Pattern Recognition (MLDM'2005)*, volume LNAI 3587 of *LNCS*, pages 100–109, Leipzig, Germany, July 2005. Springer Verlag.
3. G. Celeux, E. Diday, G. Govaert, Y. Lechevallier, and H. Ralambondrainy. *Classification Automatique des Données, Environnement statistique et informatique*. Dunod informatique, Bordas, Paris, FRANCE, 1989.
4. G. Costa, G. Manco, R. Ortale, and A. Tagarelli. A Tree-Based Approach to Clustering XML Documents by Structure. In *PKDD*, pages 137–148, 2004.
5. T. Dalamagas, T. Cheng, K.-J. Winkel, and T. K. Sellis. Clustering XML Documents by Structure. In *SETN*, pages 112–121, 2004.
6. T. Dalamagas, T. Cheng, K.-J. Winkel, and T. K. Sellis. Clustering XML Documents Using Structural Summaries. In *EDBT Workshops*, pages 547–556, 2004.
7. L. Denoyer. *Apprentissage et inférence statistique dans les bases de documents structurés : Application aux corpus de documents textuels*. PhD thesis, Université de Paris 6, December 2004.
8. L. Denoyer and P. Gallinari. Categorization and Clustering of XML documents using Structure and Content Information. In *INEX 2005 Preproceedings*, Dagstuhl, Germany, November 2005.
9. L. Denoyer, J.-N. Vittaut, P. Gallinari, S. Brunesseaux, and S. Brunesseaux. Structured Multimedia Document Classification. In *ACM Document Engeneering*, pages 153–160, Grenoble, November 2003.
10. A. Doucet and H. Ahonen-Myka. Naïve Clustering of a large XML Document Collection. In *INEX Workshop*, pages 81–87, 2002.
11. S. Flesca, G. Manco, E. Masciari, L. Pontieri, and A. Pugliese. Detecting Structural Similarities between XML Documents. In *WebDB*, pages 55–60, Madison, Wisconsin, USA, June 2002.
12. F. D. Francesca, G. Gordano, R. Ortale, and A. Tagarelli. Distance-based Clustering of XML Documents. In L. De Raedt and T. Washio, editors, *MGTS-2003 : Proceedings of the First International Workshop on Mining Graphs, Trees and Sequences*, pages 75–78. ECML/PKDD'03 workshop proceedings, September 2003.
13. D. Guillaume and F. Murtagh. Clustering of XML documents. *Computer Physics Communications*, 127(2-3):215–227, 2000.

14. L. Hubert and P. Arabie. Comparing Partitions. *Journal of Classification*, 2:193–218, 1985.
15. Y. Jianwu and C. Xiaoou. A semi-structured document model for text mining. *J. Comput. Sci. Technol.*, 17(5):603–610, 2002.
16. B. Larsen and C. Aone. Fast and effective text mining using linear-time document clustering. In *KDD'99: Proceedings of the fifth ACM SIGKDD International Conference on Knowledge Discovery and Data Mining*, pages 16–22, New York, NY, USA, 1999. ACM Press.
17. W. Lian, D. W.-L. Cheung, N. Mamoulis, and S.-M. Yiu. An Efficient and Scalable Algorithm for Clustering XML Documents by Structure. *IEEE Transaction on Knowledge and Data Engineering*, 16(1):82–96, 2004.
18. J. Liu, J. T. L. Wang, W. Hsu, and K. G. Herbert. XML Clustering by Principal Component Analysis. In *ICTAI*, pages 658–662, 2004.
19. R. Nayak and S. Xu. XML documents clustering by structures with XCLS. INEX 2005 Workshop on Mining XML documents, November 2005.
20. A. Nierman and H. V. Jagadish. Evaluating Structural Similarity in XML Documents. In *WebDB*, pages 61–66, Madison, Wisconsin, USA, June 2002.
21. M. F. Porter. An algorithm for suffix stripping. In *Readings in information retrieval*, pages 313–316, San Francisco, CA, USA, 1997. Morgan Kaufmann Publishers Inc.
22. A. Termier, M.-C. Rousset, and M. Sebag. TreeFinder: a First Step towards XML Data Mining. In *ICDM '02: Proceedings of the 2002 IEEE International Conference on Data Mining (ICDM'02)*, page 450, Washington, DC, USA, 2002. IEEE Computer Society.
23. F. Trentini, M. Hagenbuchner, A. Sperduti, A. Tsoi, F. Scarselli, and M. Gori. Clustering XML Documents using Self-Organizing Maps for Structures. INEX 2005 Workshop on Mining XML documents, November 2005.
24. A.-M. Vercoustre, M. Fegas, Y. Lechevallier, and T. Despeyroux. Classification de documents XML à partir d'une représentation linéaire des arbres de ces documents. In *Actes des 6ème journées Extraction et Gestion des Connaissances (EGC 2006), Revue des Nouvelles Technologies de l'Information (RNTI-E-6)*, pages 433–444, Lille, France, January 2006.
25. J. Yi and N. Sundaresan. A classifier for semi-structured documents. In *KDD '00: Proceedings of the sixth ACM SIGKDD international conference on Knowledge discovery and data mining*, pages 340–344, New York, NY, USA, 2000. ACM Press.
26. J. P. Yoon, V. Raghavan, V. Chakilam, and L. Kerschberg. BitCube: A Three-Dimensional Bitmap Indexing for XML Documents. *Journal of Intelligent Information Systems*, 17(2-3):241–254, 2001.
27. M. J. Zaki and C. C. Aggarwal. XRules: an effective structural classifier for XML data. In *KDD '03: Proceedings of the ninth ACM SIGKDD international conference on Knowledge discovery and data mining*, pages 316–325, New York, NY, USA, 2003. ACM Press.
28. Y. Zhao and G. Karypis. Criterion functions for document clustering: Experiments and analysis. Technical Report 01–40, Department of Computer Science, University of Minnesota, Minneapolis, MN, 2001.

Sequential Pattern Mining for Structure-Based XML Document Classification

Calin Garboni[1,2], Florent Masseglia[2], and Brigitte Trousse[2,*]

[1] West University of Timisoara, Romania
[2] INRIA Sophia Antipolis, AxIS Research Team 2004,
route des Lucioles, BP93,
F-06902 Sophia Antiplis Cedex, France
Surname.Name@inria.fr
http://www-sop.inria.fr/axis/

Abstract. This article presents an original supervised classification technique for XML documents which is based on structure only. Each XML document is viewed as an ordered labeled tree, represented by his tags only. Our method has three steps. After a cleaning step, we characterize each predefined cluster in terms of frequent structural subsequences. Then we classify the XML documents based on the mined patterns of each cluster.

1 Introduction

This work is in the context of the Document Mining track[1] of the Inex[2] Initiative. The objective is to bridge the gap between Machine Learning and Information Retrieval. The Document Mining challenge focused on classification and clustering of XML documents using only their structure or using both their structure and their content. In our work, we use only the structure information of the XML documents. Our goal is to show the relevance of using only the structure information in order to detect different "structural families of documents". Each XML document has a single label corresponding to the structural source of the document. Our work consists of characterising each predefined cluster in terms of frequent "structural" patterns and then classifying ordered labeled trees.

Section 2 introduces the used basic theoretical concepts of sequential pattern mining. Section 3 describes how to characterize each cluster of XML documents in terms of frequent structural subsequences. After presenting some related works, we present our approach in Section 4. Section 5 describes some experiments and results. Finally some conclusions and perspectives are presented.

---

* The authors want to thank Sergiu Chelcea for his useful support in the experiments.
[1] URL: http://xmlmining.lip6.fr/Home
[2] Inex: INitiative for the Evaluation of XML Retrieval URL:http://inex.is.informatik.uni-duisburg.de/2005/

N. Fuhr et al. (Eds.): INEX 2005, LNCS 3977, pp. 458–468, 2006.

2   Mining Sequential Patterns

In this section we define the sequential pattern mining problem in large databases and give an illustration. The sequential pattern mining definitions are those given by [1] and [10].

In [1], the association rules mining problem is defined as follows:

Definition 1. Let $I = \{i_1, i_2, ..., i_m\}$, be a set of m literals (*items*). Let $D = \{t_1, t_2, ...t_n\}$, be a set of n transactions ; Associated with each transaction is a unique identifier called its TID and an *itemset* I. I is a k-*itemset* where k is the number of items in I. We say that a transaction T *contains* X, a set of some items in I, if $X \subseteq T$. The *support* of an itemset I is the fraction of transactions in D containing I: $supp(I) = \|\{t \in D \mid I \subseteq t\}\|/\|\{t \in D\}\|$. An *association rule* is an implication of the form $I_1 \Rightarrow I_2$, where $I_1, I_2 \subset I$ and $I_1 \cap I_2 = \emptyset$. The rule $I_1 \Rightarrow I_2$ holds in the transaction set D with confidence c if $c\%$ of transactions in D that contain I_1 also contain I_2. The rule $r : I_1 \Rightarrow I_2$ has *support* s in the transaction set D if $s\%$ of transactions in D contain $I_1 \cup I_2$ (i.e. $supp(r) = supp(I_1 \cup I_2)$).

Given two parameters specified by the user, *minsupp* and *minconfidence*, the problem of association rule mining in a database D aims at providing the set of frequent itemsets in D, i.e. all the itemsets having support greater or equal to *minsupp*. Association rules with confidence greater than *minconfidence* are thus generated.

As this definition does not take time into consideration, the sequential patterns are defined in [10]:

Definition 2. A *sequence* is an ordered list of itemsets denoted by $< s_1 s_2 \ldots s_n >$ where s_j is an itemset. The *data-sequence* of a customer c is the sequence in D corresponding to customer c. A sequence $< a_1 a_2 \ldots a_n >$ is a *subsequence* of another sequence $< b_1 b_2 \ldots b_m >$ if there exist integers $i_1 < i_2 < \ldots < i_n$ such that $a_1 \subseteq b_{i_1}, a_2 \subseteq b_{i_2}, \ldots, a_n \subseteq b_{i_n}$.

Example 1. Let C be a client and $S=< (3) (4\ 5) (8) >$, be that client's purchases. S means that "C bought item 3, then he or she bought 4 and 5 at the same moment (i.e. in the same transaction) and finally bought item 8".

Definition 3. The *support* for a sequence s, also called $supp(s)$, is defined as the fraction of total data-sequences that contain s. If $supp(s) \geq minsupp$, with a minimum support value *minsupp* given by the user, s is considered as a *frequent sequential pattern*.

Example 2. Let us consider the data given in table 1. This can be the result of a pre-processing step performed on raw data from a shop meaning that at time $d1$ (for instance) customer 1 bought item 10. The goal is thus, according to definition 3 and by means of a data mining step, to find the sequential patterns in the file that can be considered as frequent. On of the resulting sequences may be, for instance, $< (\ 10\ ) (\ 30\ ) (\ 20\ ) (\ 30\ ) >$ (with the file illustrated in figure 1 and a minimum support given by the user: 100%).

Table 1. File obtained after a pre-processing step

Client	d1	d2	d3	d4	d5
1	10	30	40	20	30
2	10	30	20	60	30
3	10	70	30	20	30

3   Characterizing a Collection of XML Documents by Frequent Structural Subsequences

In this section, we introduce the principles of structure discovery from a set of XML documents. The idea is similar to the method developed in [5]. Our goal is to extract a schema that will be representative of the whole set of documents. In this context, "representative" will be interpreted as "frequent". In fact, we consider that a frequent sub-tree in a collection of XML documents may be considered as a interesting knowledge regarding this collection. This sub-tree can be exploited as a further DTD (see 4) or may stand for a characteristic of the collection (this is the main idea of our approach and will be detailed in section 5).

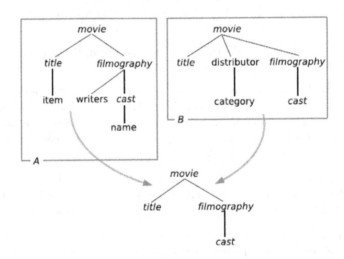

Fig. 1. A frequent sub-tree in a collection of XML documents

Figure 1 gives an illustration of frequent sub-tree mining in a collection of XML documents. Let us consider the documents given in the upper part of figure 1 (respectively labeled "A" and "B"). A frequent sub-tree mining approach is intended to find the sub-tree(s) common to at least $x\%$ (the minimum support) documents of the collection. With the documents labeled "A" and "B" and a minimum support of 100%, the extracted frequent sub-tree is described in the lower part of figure 1. Actually, the tree described by a root node containing "movie" and having two children ("title" and filmography", which is followed by "cast) is embedded in both "A" and "B". Furthermore, there is no larger frequent sub-tree in this collection.

Our method will rely on structure discovery based on sequential pattern mining. For this purpose, we will use a technique intended to transform any XML tree into a sequence. This technique is described below.

In order to perform such a transformation, the nodes of the XML tree first have to be mapped into identifiers. Then each identifier is associated with its depth in the tree. Finally a depth-first exploration of the tree will give the corresponding sequence. We call this last step the "reduction". The transformation is illustrated by figure 2. The original XML document structure (upper left) is first mapped into a new labelled tree. For instance, the node "filmography" becomes "C_2" wich corresponds to the identifier of "filmography" (C) associated with its depth (2) in the tree. The next step (reduction) aims at writing the corresponding sequence after a depth first navigation in the tree.

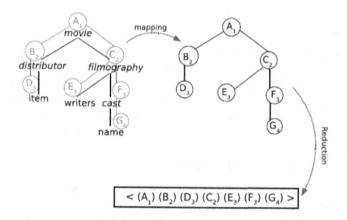

Fig. 2. Transformation of an XML tree into a sequence

Once the whole set of sequences (corresponding to the XML documents of a collection) is obtained, a traditional sequential pattern extraction algorithm is able to extract the frequent sequences. Those sequences, once mapped back into trees, will give the frequent sub-trees embedded in the collection.

4   Related Work

We present here previous works related to our approach. Basically, the studied topics are the following: structure inference from semi-structured data, frequent tree mining, DTD mining and clustering of XML documents.

4.1   Schema Mining

Methods inferring structure from similar semi-structured documents are described in [5]. Efficient approaches for mining regularities are proposed. To improve the candidate generation, some pruning strategies are described in [12]. In [8], the authors propose a method to extract a "reasonably small approximation" for typing a large and irregular data collection.

4.2 Mining DTDs from a Collection of XML Documents

Related to the previously presented topic, mining DTDs is based on the fact that the semi-structured documents are in the XML format. Here is the formal description of the problem:

Let e be an element that appears in the XML documents ($< e > < /e >$) Given a set I of N input sequences nested within element e, compute a concise and precise DTD for e such that every sequence in I is in conformity with the DTD.

Let us cite some systems trying to solve this problem, such as the IBM Alphaworks DDbE tool. XTRACT [4] is a system that automatically extracts DTDs from XML documents. It consists in Generalization / Factorization / MDL modules for inferring DTDs.

4.3 Frequent Tree Mining

Frequent tree mining refers to an important class of data mining tasks, namely patterns extraction. Many algorithms for finding tree-like patterns are developed. Basically, they adopt a straight-forward generate-and-test strategy [7]. TreeFinder [11] does clustering by counting co-occurrences of labelled pairs (in an Apriori manner). It computes the maximal trees. TreeMiner [13] is based on mining frequent subtrees using the "scope-list" data structure.

4.4 Clustering of XML Documents

Grouping XML documents in different classes with non supervised classification method is generally realized in the following manner:

Firstly the XML files are encoded such that each document is represented by an individual. Then, a distance measure is defined in order to group the similar individuals. The main differences between the XML documents clustering algorithms consist in choosing the distance between any pair of clusters (including single document cluster).

In [9], the authors partition the XML collection into smaller classes in order to infer, for each one a DTD. To compare the XML documents, they assign a different cost based on the tree editing operators. In [2] the authors use almost the same tree editing distance and the structural summaries in order to perform the XML clustering. S-GRACE algorithm [6] considers the distance based on s-graph. XRep [3] is designed on three stages: tree matching, merging of trees and pruning of the merge tree.

5   Our XML Document Supervised Classification Method

In this section, we present our supervised method for classifying the XML documents based on their structure. First of all we consider that a set of clusters is

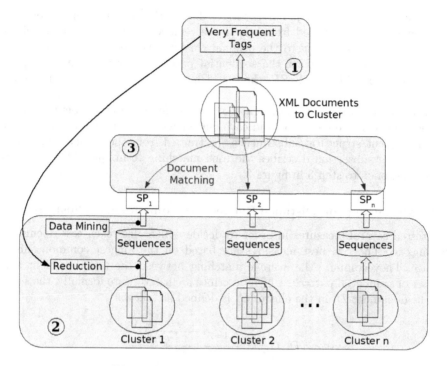

Fig. 3. Overview of the clustering method

provided coming from a previous clustering on a past collection. More formally, let us consider S_1 a first collection of XML documents (the training collection) and $C = \{c_1, c_2, ...c_n\}$ the set of clusters defined for the documents of S_1. Let us now consider S_2 a new collection of XML documents (the test collection). Our goal is to classify the documents of S_2 by taking into account the set of clusters C.

5.1   Overview

To this end, our method will perform as illustrated in figure 3. It is based on the following steps:

1. First of all, we perform a cleaning step: we extract the frequent tags embedded in the collection. This step corresponds to step "1" in figure 3. The main idea is to remove irrelevant tags for clustering operations. A tag which is very frequent in the whole collection may be considered as irrelevant since it will not help in separating a document from another (the tag is not discriminative).

2. Then we perform a data mining step on each cluster from the training collection (namely "C" in the foreword of this section). This step corresponds to step "2" in figure 3. For each cluster, the goal is to transform each XML document into a sequence (according to the techniques

described in section 3). Furthermore, during the mapping operation, the frequent tags extracted from step 1 are removed. Then on each set of sequences corresponding to the original clusters, we perform a data mining step intended to extract the sequential patterns. For each cluster C_i we are thus provided with SP_i the set of frequent sequences that characterizes C_i.

3. Finally the last step of our method relies on a matching between each document of the collection and each cluster which is characterized by a set of frequent structural subsequences (extracted from the second step). The following subsection describes the used matching technique. This last step corresponds to step 3 in figure 3.

5.2   Measuring the Distance Between Documents and Clusters

We tested several measures in order to decide which class each test document belongs to. The two best measures are based on the longest common subsequence. They compute the average matching between the test document and the set of sequential patterns which describes a cluster. More formally, the score for the document D_i in the cluster C_j is defined as follows:

$$score(D_i, C_j) = \frac{\sum_{k=1}^{|C_j|} \frac{|LCS(D_i, sp_{C_j}(k))|}{|sp_{C_j}k|}}{|C_j|}$$

Where $LCS(D_i, sp_{C_j}(k))$ is the longest common subsequence between the document and the kth sequential pattern of C_j.

However, we noticed some particular cases where the scores of a document could be the same for two different clusters. In order to tackle this problem, we provide a modified score measure, which is defined as follows:

$$score2(D_i, C_j) = \frac{\sum_{k=1}^{|C_j|} \frac{i \times |LCS(D_i, sp_{C_j}(k))|}{|sp_{C_j}k|}}{|C_j|}$$

Where i is equal to:

- 0.8 if $sp_{C_j}k$ is a subsequence of D_i (100 % matching) and $sp_{C_j}k$ is "long" ($|sp_{C_j}k| > 0.7 \times (maximum\ length\ of\ a\ sequential\ pattern)$)
- 0.6 if $sp_{C_j}k$ is a subsequence of D_i (100 % matching) and $sp_{C_j}k$ is "short" ($|sp_{C_j}k| < 0.7 \times (maximum\ length\ of\ a\ sequential\ pattern)$)
- 0.4 if $sp_{C_j}k$ only matches D_i at 50 %.
- 0.2 for the remaining cases.

6   Experiments

In order to evaluate and validate our approach, we have exploited the documents provided by one of the INEX'05 tracks on document mining: the MovieDB. The extraction methods are written in C++ on a Pentium PC running a Red-Hat system.

6.1 Data

The MovieDB corpus is a collection of heterogeneous XML documents describing movies. It was built using the IMDB database. It contains 9643 XML documents. There are 11 predefined structure categories which correspond to transformations of the original data structure. Each cluster is characterized in terms of frequent sequential patterns (cf. the step 2). For example, we obtain for the following sequential patterns for cluster 1 and cluster 2:

– Cluster 1:
  - $<$ (0_movie) (1_title) (1_url) (1_Country_of_Production) (2_item) (2_item) (1_filmography) (3_name) $>$
  - $<$ (0_movie) (1_title) (1_url) (1_Country_of_Production) (2_item) (2_item) (2_item) (1_filmography) $>$
  - $<$ (0_movie) (1_title) (1_url) (1_Filmed_In) (2_item) (2_item) (1_filmography) $>$
  - ...

Results for the first score (C.f. 5.2):

	C1	C2	C3	C4	C5	C6	C7	C8	C9	C10	C11
C1	593										
C2		481	4								
C3		41	659								
C4				171	1						
C5				49	387						
C6						199		10			21
C7							256		6		
C8								768			
C9									333		
C10						1		1		384	
C11						426		8			12
Recall	1.0000	0.9215	0.9940	0.7773	0.9974	0.3179	1.0000	0.9759	0.9823	1.0000	0.3636

Results for the second score (C.f. 5.2):

	C1	C2	C3	C4	C5	C6	C7	C8	C9	C10	C11
C1	593										
C2		474	11								
C3		29	671								
C4				171	1						
C5				36	400						
C6						206					24
C7							262				
C8								764			4
C9							1		332		
C10						1				383	2
C11						428					18
Recall	1.0000	0.9423	0.9839	0.8261	0.9975	0.3244	0.9962	1.0000	1.0000	1.0000	0.3750

Fig. 4. Experiments on MovieDB Collection m-db-s-0-test

– Cluster 2:
  - < (0_CL) (2_DC) (2_DC) (2_DC) (2_DC) >
  - < (0_CL) (1_BQ) (2_AX) (3_EH) (3_DT) (3_EH) >
  - < (0_CL) (1_BQ) (3_EH) (3_EH) (3_EH) (3_DT) >
  - < (1_EJ) >
  - ...

MovieDB has been preprocessed using a Porter stemmer. There are four collections, structure only based, with the different degrees of difficulty and overlapping of the classes (files m_db_s 0 to 3). A training collection was provided. The size of this collection was equal to the size of the document collection to be classified. For the structure only track, we use only the tree structure, without any attributes or content of the XML documents.

Results for the first score (C.f. 5.2):

	C1	C2	C3	C4	C5	C6	C7	C8	C9	C10	C11
C1	596										
C2		469	15								
C3		567	132								
C4				163	9						
C5				418	18						
C6						18		1		94	116
C7						255			6		
C8								346		421	
C9									332		
C10						2				378	6
C11								4		179	264
Recall	1.0000	0.4527	0.8980	0.2806	0.6667	0.9000	1.0000	0.9858	0.9822	0.3526	0.6839

Results for the second score (C.f. 5.2):

	C1	C2	C3	C4	C5	C6	C7	C8	C9	C10	C11
C1	596										
C2		437	47								
C3		10	689								
C4				171	1						
C5				36	400						
C6						7				218	4
C7							4		257		
C8								15		752	
C9									332		
C10						3				379	4
C11										447	
Recall	1.0000	0.9776	0.9361	0.8261	0.9975	0.7000	1.0000	1.0000	0.5637	0.2110	0.0000

Fig. 5. Experiments on MovieDB Collection m-db-s-0-test

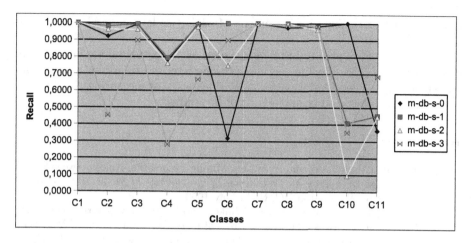

Fig. 6. Experiments on MovieDB Collection

6.2 Results

In this section we will give some results based on our approach. Below is given a part of the table built for the XML documents of the test collection (cf. step 3.).

In figure 4 the classification result is provided for the test file 0 (m-db-s-0-test) with both score functions defined in section 5.2. For each predefined class, the recall is calculated. The scores are quite good, except the 6th and the 11th classes due to the strong similarity of their extracted sequential patterns. Indeed, the candidates are allocated to the most general class, i.e. the class which contains most of the sequential patterns describing another class. Moreover when two scores are equal for a same document, whe arbitrary chose the first class. In figure 5 we report the classification result for the test file 3 (m-db-s-3-test) with both score functions. We can observe that the difference between the functions is clear when the level of noise in the files increases. This can be observed for clusters C2, C4 and C5 for instance, where the second score performs better than the first one.

In Figure 6 the degradation of the results according to the degradation of the four data collections is presented.

Based on the synthesis made by the organisers during the Inex'05 workshop related to the Document Mining track our result is situated in the top 3 ranking (our recall being quite good, between 0.8 and 0.95).

7   Conclusion

In this article we introduced a new supervised classification method for XML documents which is based on a linearization of the structural information of XML documents and on a characterization of each cluster in terms of frequent sequential patterns. Experiments on the MovieDB collection validated the efficiency of our approach.

As perspective we plan to improve our method for better taking into account certain types of XML documents clusters characterised today by a very similar set of frequent sequential patterns. Various ways of measuring the distance between a document and each cluster will be studied.

References

1. R. Agrawal, T. Imielinski, and A. Swami. Mining Association Rules between Sets of Items in Large Databases. In *Proceedings of the 1993 ACM SIGMOD Conference*, pages 207–216, Washington DC, USA, May 1993.
2. Theodore Dalamagas, T. Cheng, K. Winkel, and T. Sellis. Clustering xml documents using structural summarie. In Proc. of ClustWeb - International Workshop on Clustering Information over the Web in conjunction with EDBT 04, Crete, Greece, 2004.
3. F. De Francesca, G. Gordano, R. Ortale, and A. Tagarelli. Distance-based clustering of xml documents. pages 75–78. ECML/PKDD'03 workshop proceedings, September 2003.
4. Minos Garofalakis, Aristides Gionis, Rajeev Rastogi, S. Seshadri, and Kyuseok Shim. XTRACT: a system for extracting document type descriptors from XML documents. pages 165–176, 2000.
5. P.A. Laur, F. Masseglia, and P. Poncelet. Schema mining: Finding structural regularity among semi structured data. Proceedings of the 4th European Conference on Principles and Practice of Knowledge Discovery in Databases (PKDD'2000), Poster session, Lecture Notes in Artificial Intelligence, Springer Verlag, September 2000.
6. Wang Lian, David Wai-Lok Cheung, Nikos Mamoulis, and Siu-Ming Yiu. An efficient and scalable algorithm for clustering xml documents by structure. *IEEE Trans. Knowl. Data Eng*, 16(1), January 2004.
7. Tetsuhiro Miyahara, Takayoshi Shoudai, Tomoyuki Uchida, Kenichi Takahashi, and Hiroaki Ueda. Discovery of frequent tree structured patterns in semistructured web documents. In *PAKDD '01: Proceedings of the 5th Pacific-Asia Conference on Knowledge Discovery and Data Mining*, pages 47–52, London, UK, 2001. Springer-Verlag.
8. Svetlozar Nestorov, Serge Abiteboul, and Rajeev Motwani. Extracting schema from semistructured data. pages 295–306, 1998.
9. Andrew Nierman and H. V. Jagadish. Evaluating structural similarity in XML documents. In *Proceedings of the Fifth International Workshop on the Web and Databases (WebDB 2002)*, Madison, Wisconsin, USA, June 2002.
10. R. Srikant and R. Agrawal. Mining Sequential Patterns: Generalizations and Performance Improvements. In *Proceedings of the 5th International Conference on Extending Database Technology (EDBT'96)*, pages 3–17, Avignon, France, September 1996.
11. A. Termier, M.-C. Rousset, and M. Se'bag. Treefinder: a first step towards xml data mining. In *In International Conference on Data Mining (ICDM 2002), Maebashi City, Japan, 2002*, 2002.
12. Ke Wang and Huiqing Liu. Discovering structural association of semistructured data. *Knowledge and Data Engineering*, 12(2):353–371, 2000.
13. M. Zaki. Efficiently mining frequent trees in a forest, July 2002. In KDD'02.

Transforming XML Trees for Efficient Classification and Clustering

Laurent Candillier[1,2], Isabelle Tellier[1], and Fabien Torre[1]

[1] GRAppA - Charles de Gaulle University - Lille 3
candillier@grappa.univ-lille3.fr
http://www.grappa.univ-lille3.fr
[2] Pertinence - 32 rue des Jeûneurs -75002 Paris
http://www.pertinence.com

Abstract. Most of the existing methods we know to tackle datasets of XML documents directly work on the trees representing these XML documents. We investigate in this paper the use of a different kind of representation for the manipulation of XML documents.

Our idea is to transform the trees into sets of attribute-values, so as to be able to apply various existing methods of classification and clustering on such data, and benefit from their strengths. We apply this strategy both for the classification task and for the clustering task using the structural description of XML documents alone.

For instance, we show that the use of *boosted C5* [1] leads to very good results in the classification task of XML documents transformed in this way. The use of *SSC* [2] in the clustering task benefits from its ability to provide as output an interpretable representation of the clusters found. Finally, we also propose an adaptation of *SSC* for the classification of XML documents, so that the produced classifier is understandable.

1 Introduction

Most of the existing methods we know to tackle datasets of XML documents directly work on the trees representing these XML documents. Some methods are based on the use of metric distances to compare the trees: the *edit distance*, minimum number of mutations required to change a tree into another one [3, 4], or the number of paths they share [5, 6, 7]. Other methods aim at discovering frequent subtrees in the data [8, 9].

We investigate in this paper the use of a different kind of representation for the manipulation of XML documents. We propose to transform the trees into sets of attribute-values. In [10], the authors used such an idea to take into account the structure when classifying XML documents. But the representation they chose for the trees was a simple *bag-of-tags*. We propose to use richer features: the set of parent-child relations, the set of "next-sibling" relations, the set of paths starting from the root and the arity of the nodes.

The use of such representations allows us to apply various existing methods for classifying or clustering sets of XML documents. And we can thus benefit from the strengths of these methods. In particular, our experiments exhibit very good

N. Fuhr et al. (Eds.): INEX 2005, LNCS 3977, pp. 469–480, 2006.

results when applying *boosted C5* [1] on sets of XML documents transformed in this way. The use of *SSC* [2] for clustering tasks on such transformed datasets also benefits from its ability to provide as output an interpretable representation of the clusters found. Moreover, we also propose in this paper an adaptation of *SSC* for the classification of XML documents, so that the produced classifier is understandable.

The remainder of the paper is organized as follows: in section 2, we present our proposed methodology to transform a tree into a set of attribute-values, and how such new dataset can be used for classification tasks; in section 3, we describe the adaptation of the *SSC* algorithm for XML datasets; the results of our experiments, conducted on the datasets provided by the XML mining challenge at INEX [11] on the *structure only tasks*, are then reported in section 4; finally, section 5 concludes the paper and suggests topics for future research.

2   Tree Transformation

There are many possible ways to transform a tree into a set of attribute-values. The first basic possibility is to transform the tree into the set of labels present at its nodes. An XML document would thus be transformed into a simple *bag-of-tags*. If the different sets of documents to be identified use different sets of tags, this representation would be sufficient to distinguish them. However, by doing that, we do not take into account the structure of the XML trees. To go further, we propose to construct the following attributes from a set of available trees:

- the set of parent-child relations (whose domain is the set of pairs of tags labelling the nodes);
- the set of next-sibling relations (whose domain is the set of pairs of tags labelling the nodes);
- the set of distinct paths (including sub-paths), starting from the root (whose domain is the set of finite sequences of tags labelling the nodes).

So, we create as many new attributes as distinct features are encountered in the training set. For each of them, their value for a given document is the number of their occurences in this document. Finally, we also define as many new attributes as there are absolute distinct node positions represented in the trees. The identifier of such a node position can be coded, for example, by a sequence of integers: the root is coded 0, its first child is coded 0.0, its second child 0.1, etc. For every identifier of a node position, the value of the attribute for a document is the arity of the node, that is the number of its child nodes in the document (whose domain is an integer). So the new introduced attributes all take their value into the set of natural numbers. As an intuition, such representation should allow to distinguish, for example:

- two sets of documents that use different tags, or in which the number of some given tags are different;

- one set of documents in which a given relation (parent-child or next-sibling) between some given tags is allowed, from another set that does not allow such a relation;
- or a set of documents in which the number of children of a given node position is different from the one in another set of documents.

Such representation could lead to a high number of generated attributes. So the algorithms used to tackle such new datasets should be able to handle many attributes, and to perform *feature selection* during their learning process. In a classification task, *C5* [1] is for example well suited. In a clustering task, a *subspace clustering* algorithm, that is a clustering algorithm able to characterize every distinct cluster on a limited number of dimensions (eventually distinct for each cluster) could be useful. We describe such a method in the next section.

3   Algorithm SSC

SSC [2] is a *subspace clustering* algorithm based on the use of a probabilistic model under the assumption that the clusters follow independent distributions on each dimension. It uses the well-known *EM algorithm* [12]. *SSC* has been shown to be effective, and it is able to provide as output an interpretable representation of the clusters found, as a set of rules, and a way to visualize them effectively. Moreover, a new step of *hard feature selection* has been added to keep only the best attributes for each cluster, and thus be less sensitive to irrelevant dimensions, and faster.

In the next subsections, we first formalize the different steps of the method. We then present an adaptation for facing datasets of XML documents, and another adaptation for supervised classification. One of the interests of this method is that it provides an output which can be represented by a hierarchy of tests.

3.1   Formalization of the Method

Let us first introduce some notations. We denote by N the number of data points $\vec{X_i}$ of the input dataset D, and by M the number of dimensions on which they are defined. We only present here the case where the dimensions are numerical, but the adaptation for datasets containing also categorical dimensions can be found in [2].

The basis of our model is the classical mixture of probability distributions $\theta = (\theta_1, ..., \theta_K)$ where each θ_k is the vector of parameters associated with the kth cluster to be found, denoted by C_k (we set to K the total number of clusters). In our model, we suppose that the data follow gaussian distributions. So the model has the following parameters θ_k for each cluster C_k: π_k denotes its weight, μ_{kd} its mean and σ_{kd} its standard deviation on dimension d. We then use the *EM algorithm* [12] to find the model parameters that best fit the data.

The E-step consists in computing the membership probability of each data point $\vec{X_i}$ to each cluster C_k with parameters θ_k. In our case, dimensions are supposed to be independent. So the membership probability of a data point to a cluster is the product of membership probabilities on each dimension:

$$P(\vec{X_i}|\theta_k) = \prod_{d=1}^{M} \frac{1}{\sqrt{2\pi}\sigma_{kd}} e^{-\frac{1}{2}\left(\frac{X_{id}-\mu_{kd}}{\sigma_{kd}}\right)^2}$$

$$P(\vec{X_i}|\theta) = \sum_{k=1}^{K} \pi_k \times P(\vec{X_i}|\theta_k) \quad \text{and} \quad P(\theta_k|\vec{X_i}) = \frac{\pi_k \times P(\vec{X_i}|\theta_k)}{P(\vec{X_i}|\theta)}$$

Then the M-step consists in updating the model parameters according to the new class probabilities as follows:

$$\pi_k = \frac{1}{N} \sum_i P(\theta_k|\vec{X_i})$$

$$\mu_{kd} = \frac{\sum_i X_{id} \times P(\theta_k|\vec{X_i})}{\sum_i P(\theta_k|\vec{X_i})} \quad \text{and} \quad \sigma_{kd} = \sqrt{\frac{\sum_i P(\theta_k|\vec{X_i}) \times (X_{id}-\mu_{kd})^2}{\sum_i P(\theta_k|\vec{X_i})}}$$

These two steps iterate until a stopping criterion is reached. Usually, it stops when the *log-likelihood* of the model to the data, $LL(\theta|D) = \sum_i \log P(\vec{X_i}|\theta)$, increases less than a small positive constant δ from one iteration to another. But in order to cope with the problem of slow convergence with the classical EM algorithm, it has been shown in [2] that adding the following *k-means like* stopping criterion is effective: stop whenever the membership of each data point to their most probable cluster does not change from one iteration to another. To do this, we introduce a new view on each cluster C_k, corresponding with the set of data points belonging to it:

$$S_k = \{\vec{X_i}|Argmax_{j=1}^{K} P(\vec{X_i}|\theta_j) = k\}$$

The set of all S_k thus define a partition on the dataset.

And finally, to cope with the problem of sensitivity to the choice of the initial solution, we run the algorithm many times with random initial solutions and keep the model that optimizes the *log-likelihood* of the model to the data $LL(\theta|D)$.

Moreover, a new step of *hard feature selection* has been added to keep only the best attributes for each cluster. This is done by using a user parameter, denoted by nb_ds, that specifies how many attributes to keep for each cluster. Thus, for each cluster, the attributes of highest weights are kept, and the others are ignored. These weights W_{kd} are computed as the ratio between local and global standard deviations:

$$W_{kd} = 1 - \frac{\sigma_{kd}^2}{\sigma_d^2}, \text{ with } \sigma_d^2 = \frac{1}{N} \sum_i (X_{id} - \mu_{kd})^2$$

To make the results as comprehensible as possible, we now introduce a third view on each cluster, corresponding to its description as a rule defined with as few dimensions as possible.

Although we have already selected a subset of dimensions relevant for each cluster, it is still possible to prune some and simplify the clusters representation while keeping the same partition of the data. See figure 1 as an example. In this case, the cluster on the right is dense on both dimensions X and Y. So its true description subspace is $X \times Y$. However, we do not need to consider Y to distinguish it from the other clusters: defining it by high values on X is sufficient. The same reasoning holds for the cluster on the top and the dimension Y.

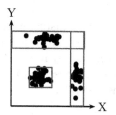

Fig. 1. Example of minimal description

To do this *dimension pruning*, we first create the rule R_k associated with the current cluster C_k. We now only consider the set of dimensions considered as relevant according to the previous selection, and associate with the rule R_k the smallest interval containing all the coordinates of the data points belonging to S_k. We then compute the support of the rule (the set of data points comprised in the rule). This step is necessary since it is possible that some data points belong to the rule but not to the cluster. And then, for all relevant dimensions d presented in ascending order of their weights W_{kd}, we delete the dimension from the rule if the deletion does not modify its support.

3.2   Adaptation for Clustering XML Documents

For ease of interpretation, and to speed up the algorithm for clustering XML documents based on their structure, we propose to adapt SSC so that the dataset is recursively cut into two parts according to a given set of attributes associated with the trees. The output of our clustering method is then a hierarchy in which each node represents a test on various attributes.

Before giving more details on our procedure, let us introduce some notations. A denotes the set of possible attributes associated with the XML documents. As presented in the previous section, A can be partitioned into groups of attributes of increasing complexity:

- we call A_1 the set of tags,
- A_2 is the set of parent-child relations,
- A_3 is the set of next-sibling relations,
- A_4 is the set of node positions,
- and A_5 is the set of paths starting from the root.

A is thus composed of $SA = 5$ classes of attributes. Finally, we denote by $Cut(C_k, A_i)$ the partitionning into two parts of the dataset that is made of the documents included in the cluster C_k, and transformed with the given set of attributes A_i.

The main steps of our new clustering method are presented by algorithm 1. It consists in choosing at each step the cut of highest interest, among all the possible cuts of the current clusters C_k for $k \in [1..K]$ on the possible sets of attributes $A_i \in A$, until the desired number of clusters is reached. The interest of partitionning the elements of the cluster C_k with the attributes of A_i is computed as the ratio between the *log-likelihood* of a partition with two clusters and the *log-likelihood* of a partition with only one cluster, weighted by the number of data points in C_k, to prefer the divisions of clusters containing many data points. The output of the procedure is a hierarchy in which each node corresponds to a membership test to a rule, created as presented in the previous subsection, and defined with as few attributes as possible.

Algorithm 1. SSC for XML

Input: the dataset D of XML documents and the desired number of clusters nb_clus
    - set K, the current number of clusters of the partition, to 1
    - initialize the unique cluster C_1 with all the documents of the dataset D
    - create a new empty hierarchy H
  while $K \neq nb\_clus$ **do**
    for all $k \in [1..K]$ **do**
      for all $i \in [1..SA]$ **do**
        - compute the interest of $Cut(C_k, A_i)$
      end for
    end for
    - select and perform the cut of highest interest
    - compute the associated rule and add it to the hierarchy H
  end while
Output: the hierarchy H, with $nb\_clus - 1$ tests

3.3   Adaptation for Understandable Classification

In order to benefit from the ability of the previously presented method to provide understandable results, we now propose to adapt it for supervised classification. The new method has two main steps: a first step that is *clustering like* but uses the classes, and a second step that is completely guided by the classes.

The first step is described by algorithm 2 and consists in a clustering phase that allows to mix various classes in one cluster but does not allow a class to be splitted into different clusters. At this step, we prefer that a cutting rule is defined on the tags attributes better than on any other set of attributes, because they are *simpler* attributes. In the same way, we prefer to use attributes representing relations between tags (parent-child or next-sibling) than paths information. So more generally, we prefer using A_i than A_j if $i < j$. That's why we perform a cut each time it is possible, rather than comparing the interest on various possible cuts, as is done for clustering. The same reasoning will also holds in the next step.

The second step of our method is described by algorithm 3. It takes as input the output of the previous step and consists in separating the classes that are still

---

Algorithm 2. Step 1

Input: the dataset D of XML documents
   - initialize the unique cluster C_1 with all the documents of the dataset D
   - create a new empty hierarchy H
   - set $CUT = 1$
  while $CUT = 1$ **do**
    - set $CUT = 0$
    for all $k \in [1..K]$ **do**
      - set $CUT_k = 0$ and $i = 1$
      while $CUT_k = 0$ and $i <= SA$ **do**
        if in $Cut(C_k, A_i)$, no class is splitted into different parts **then**
          - perform the partitionning
          - compute the associated rules and update the hierarchy
          - set $CUT_k = 1$ and $CUT = 1$
        else
          - i = i + 1
        end if
      end while
    end for
  end while
Output: the hierarchy H, and the current partition

---

embedded in the same clusters. It is itself composed of two main steps: the first one tries to distinguish the classes using rules, in order to be as understandable as possible, while the second one uses probabilistic models that are richer models, able to fit more complex decision surfaces.

1. If a rule found is able to discriminate one class from the others, then this rule is used as the next test in the hierarchy. As has been motivated earlier, a split is performed as soon as possible.
2. Then, if no rule has been found that is able to discriminate one class from the others in one given cluster, we test the error rates obtained in cross-validation with probabilistic models generated on each possible sets of attributes, and select the one that leads to the lowest error rate as the next test in the hierarchy.

So in the final hierarchy, the tests on the nodes can be of two different natures: they can correspond to membership tests to rules, or to probability tests on probabilistic models. Each of these tests are perfomed on only one set of attributes at a time.

4 Experiments

Our experiments were conducted on the datasets provided by the XML mining challenge at INEX on the *structure only tasks*. The classification method presented in section 2 was applied on all datasets: *inex-s*, *m-db-s-0*, *m-db-s-1*, *m-db-s-2* and *m-db-s-3*. The results are presented in the first subsection. The other

---

Algorithm 3. Step 2

Input: the hierarchy H and the partition from the first step
    for all $k \in [1..K]$ **do**
        while C_k contains different classes **do**
            for all $i \in [1..SA]$ **do**
                for all $class \in C_k$ **do**
                    if a rule is able to distinguish the class from the others **then**
                        - perform the partitionning and update the hierarchy
                    end if
                end for
            end for
            if no split has been done **then**
                for all $i \in [1..SA]$ **do**
                    - compute the classification error rate in cross-validation of the probabilistic
                      model generated on the attributes A_i
                end for
                - choose the model that leads to the lowest error rate and update the hierarchy
            end if
         end while
    end for
Output: the hierarchy H

---

two methods presented in section 3 were only applied on the *m-db-s-0* dataset, due to the lack of time. Their results are presented in the second subsection.

4.1   Boosted C5 on the Transformed Datasets

Table 1 presents the number of new attributes generated by transforming the XML trees into attribute-values for each dataset. We can thus observe that our method creates many new attributes. In particular, the number of attributes representing the paths in the trees is very high.

Table 1. Number of attributes generated for each dataset

dataset	number of tags	number of parent-child relations	number of next-sibling relations	number of node positions	number of paths	total
inex-s	150	1038	827	2475	3674	8164
m-db-s-0	197	2172	419	6575	320	9683
m-db-s-1	197	6477	5617	9159	16772	38222
m-db-s-2	196	8953	7455	9183	25628	51415
m-db-s-3	199	10639	9557	8537	37576	66508

We applied the algorithm C5 [1] boosted 10 times on these datasets. However, as the number of attributes was too high for C5 on the *m-db-s-2* and *m-db-s-3* datasets, we did not use the attributes representing the paths in the trees for these datasets. The error rates obtained in 10-fold cross-validations on all the datasets are provided in table 2, and show that our proposed methodology has reasonable error rates.

Table 2. Error rates of boosted C5 on the datasets transformed into attribute-values

dataset	error rate
inex-s	0.011
m-db-s-0	0.026
m-db-s-1	0.038
m-db-s-2	0.062
m-db-s-3	0.062

Table 3 then reports the *micro-recall* and *macro-recall* computed on the test datasets using this method. Datasets *m-db-s* are all based on the same initial dataset but each succesive dataset contains more noise than the previous one. The results of our method thus shows that it is robust to the presence of noise.

Table 3. Micro-recall and macro-recall of boosted C5 on the test datasets transformed into attribute-values

dataset	micro-recall	macro-recall
inex-s	0.941	0.958
m-db-s-0	0.968	0.960
m-db-s-1	0.966	0.956
m-db-s-2	0.942	0.932
m-db-s-3	0.947	0.935

4.2   Adaptations of SSC

For reasons of time, the algorithms adapted from *SSC* were only experimented on the *m-db-s-0* dataset. The parameter *nb_ds* defined in section 3, and representing the number of most relevant dimensions to be selected for each cluster, was set to 10.

Our clustering method managed to identify correctly the classes number 1 to 5. It mixed classes number 7 and 9 together, and the remaining classes were also mixed together. This clustering thus leads to a *micro purity* of 0.78, a *macro purity* of 0.75, a *micro entropy* of 0.18, a *macro entropy* of 0.21, and a *mutual information* of 1.87 on test data.

The hierarchy formed is presented by figure 2. $R4$, $R10$, $R6$, and $R7$ are conjunctions of 10 tests:

- $R4$ is defined on the attributes representing the next-sibling relations,
- $R10$ concerns the number of children according to the node positions,
- $R6$ is defined on the attributes representing the tags,
- and $R7$ concerns the number of children according to the node positions.

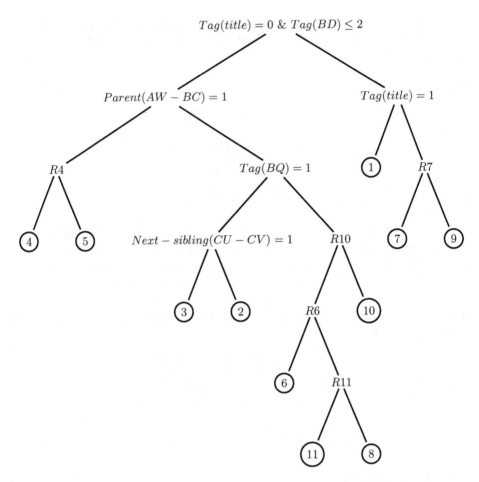

Fig. 2. Tree obtained when clustering dataset m-db-s-0

Finally, $R11$ tests whether the number of paths (BE-AL-AT) is lower or equal to 1, and if there is no path (BE-AL-AT-AR).

The adaptation of our method for supervised learning leads to very interesting results. The hierarchy obtained is presented by figure 3. We can thus observe that the given hierarchy is very understandable.

- $S2$, $S3$, $S4$ and $S5$ represent the probabilities on models based on next-sibling relations, respectively concerning classes 2, 3, 4 and 5.
- $P6$ and $P11$ represent the probabilities on models based on the paths of the trees, concerning classes 6 and 11.
- And $Nb(0.0.0)$ indicates the number of children of the first grand-child of the root.

Thus, for example, the membership to class 1 only depends on the presence of the tag named *movie*. And in the same way, the membership to class 8 only

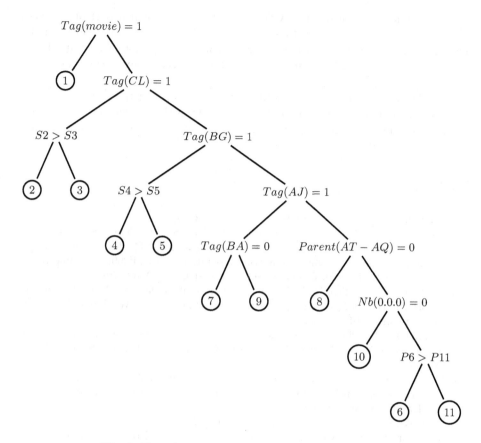

Fig. 3. Tree obtained for classifying dataset m-db-s-0

depends on the absence of the tags *movie, CL, BJ, AJ*, and the presence of the parent-child relation between tags AT and AQ. The error rate of this tree on the train dataset is 0.03. It misclassified very few documents, except those of classes 6 and 11 that were mixed.

The results of this method on test data were also very reasonable, leading to a *micro-recall* of 0.906 and a *micro-recall* of 0.924.

5   Conclusion

We have shown in this paper that transforming XML document trees into sets of attribute-values can lead to very promising results, provided that these attributes are considered as sets of increasing complexity. This representation allows us to benefit from the strengths of existing methods. We have also presented a new original method able to provide an interpretable classifier as an output.

We conjecture it is now possible to go further in the way we transform the trees. For instance, it is possible to consider as new attributes some forks of the trees, of some given height and width, or to identify in which part of the trees the tags or relations between tags are present. But, as has been shown in the experiments part of the paper, we already constructed a lot of new attributes with our method. And by using such attributes, we already obtain very good results.

To take into account such possible differences between trees, a special care should now be taken to find a compromise between the number of new created attributes and the information they carry. This point should be studied in further researchs.

References

1. Quinlan, R.: Data mining tools see5 and c5.0 (2004)
2. Candillier, L., Tellier, I., Torre, F., Bousquet, O.: SSC : Statistical Subspace Clustering. In Perner, P., Imiya, A., eds.: 4th International Conference on Machine Learning and Data Mining in Pattern Recognition (MLDM'2005). Volume LNAI 3587 of LNCS., Leipzig, Germany, Springer Verlag (2005) 100–109
3. Nierman, A., Jagadish, H.V.: Evaluating structural similarity in XML documents. In: 5th International Workshop on the Web and Databases (WebDB 2002), Madison, Wisconsin, USA (2002)
4. Dalamagas, T., Cheng, T., Winkel, K.J., Sellis, T.: Clustering XML documents by structure. In: 3rd Hellenic Conference on Artificial Intelligence, Samos, Greece (May 2004)
5. Flesca, S., Manco, G., Masciari, E., Pontieri, L., Pugliese, A.: Detecting structural similarities between XML documents. In: 5th International Workshop on The Web and Databases (WebDB'02), Madison, Wisconsin (2002)
6. Lian, W., Cheung, D.W., Mamoulis, N., Yiu, S.M.: An efficient and scalable algorithm for clustering XML documents by structure. IEEE transactions on Knowledge and Data Engineering **16** (January 2004) 82–96
7. Costa, G., Manco, G., Ortale, R., Tagarelli, A.: A tree-based approach to clustering XML documents by structure. Technical report, Institute of Italian National Research Council, Rende, Italy (April 2004)
8. Termier, A., Rousset, M.C., Sebag, M.: Treefinder: a first step towards xml data mining. In: IEEE International Conference on Data Mining (ICDM02). (2002) 450–457
9. Zaki, M.J., Aggarwal, C.C.: Xrules: An effective structural classifier for xml data. In: SIGKDD 03, Washington, DC (2003)
10. Doucet, A., Ahonen-Myka, H.: Naïve clustering of a large XML document collection. In: 1st Annual Workshop of the Initiative for the Evaluation of XML retrieval (INEX'02), Schloss Dagstuhl, Germany (2002)
11. Denoyer, L., Gallinari, P., Vercoustre, A.M.: XML Mining Challenge at INEX 2005. Technical report, University of Paris VI, INRIA (2006)
12. Ye, L., Spetsakis, M.: Clustering on unobserved data using mixture of gaussians. Technical report, York University, Toronto, Canada (Oct. 2003)

Clustering XML Documents Using Self-organizing Maps for Structures

M. Hagenbuchner[2], A. Sperduti[3], A.C. Tsoi[4], F. Trentini[1], F. Scarselli[1], and M. Gori[1]

[1] University of Siena, Siena, Italy
[2] University of Wollongong, Wollongong, Australia
[3] University of Padova, Padova, Italy
[4] Monash University, Melbourne, Australia

Abstract. Self-Organizing Maps capable of encoding structured information will be used for the clustering of XML documents. Documents formatted in XML are appropriately represented as graph data structures. It will be shown that the Self-Organizing Maps can be trained in an unsupervised fashion to group XML structured data into clusters, and that this task is scaled in linear time with increasing size of the corpus. It will also be shown that some simple prior knowledge of the data structures is beneficial to the efficient grouping of the XML documents.

1   Introduction

In many scientific and practical situations, there is often a need to visualise, if possible, the relationships, e.g. cluster formation, among high-dimensional data items. Kohonen's [6] self-organizing map (SOM) is one of the most well known methods to help users to achieve this goal. It was developed to help identify clusters in multidimensional, say, p-dimensional datasets. The SOM does this by effectively packing the p-dimensional dataset onto a q-dimensional display plane, where we assume for simplicity $q = 2$ throughout this paper. The SOM consists of a discrete display space with $N \times N$ grid points, each grid point is associated with a p-dimensional vector, often referred to in this paper, as an artificial neuron, or simply a neuron [1]. The contents of these vectors are updated with each presentation of samples from the p-dimensional original data set. The contents of these vectors encode the relationships (distances) among the p-dimensional data. The result is that data items that were "similar" or "close" to each other in the original multidimensional data space are then mapped onto nearby areas of the 2-dimensional display space. Thus SOM is a topology-preserving map as there is a topological structure imposed on the nodes in the network. A topological map is simply a mapping that preserves neighbourhood relations.

Thus, in the SOM, there are $N \times N$ grid points, or neurons, each neuron has an associated p-dimensional vector, often called a codebook vector. This codebook vector m has the same dimension as the i-th input vector x_i. The neurons on the map are bound together by a topology, which is often either hexagonal or rectangular. In general, the SOM is trained on a set of examples in an unsupervised fashion as follows:

---

[1] This is called a neuron for historical reasons.

N. Fuhr et al. (Eds.): INEX 2005, LNCS 3977, pp. 481–496, 2006.

For every x_i in a training set, obtain the best matching codebook by computing:

$$c = \arg\min_j \|x_i - m_j\| \tag{1}$$

where $\| \cdot \|$ denotes the Euclidean norm.

After the best matching unit m_c is found, the codebook vectors are updated. m_c itself as well as its topological neighbours are moved closer to the input vector in the input space i.e. the input vector attracts them. The magnitude of the attraction is governed by a learning rate α and by a neighbourhood function $f(\Delta_{jc})$, where Δ_{jc} is the topological distance between m_c and m_j. As the learning proceeds and new input vectors are given to the map, the learning rate gradually decreases to zero according to a specified learning rate function type. Along with the learning rate, the neighbourhood radius decreases as well. The codebooks on the map are updated as follows:

$$\Delta m_j = \alpha(t) f(\Delta_{jc})(m_j - x_i) \tag{2}$$

where α is a learning coefficient, and $f(.)$ is a neighbourhood function which controls the amount by which the weights of the neighbouring neurons are updated. The neighbourhood function can take the form of a Gaussian function $f(\Delta_{jc}) = \exp\left(-\frac{\|l_j - l_c\|^2}{2\sigma^2}\right)$, where σ is the spread, and l_c and l_j is the location of the winning neuron and the location of the j-th neuron respectively. Other neighbourhood functions are possible.

Equations (1) and (2) are computed for every input vector in the training set, and for a set number of iterations. It is shown in [7] that the strength of the SOM is in its ability to map high dimensional input data onto a low dimensional display space while preserving the topological relationships among the input data. The SOM is trained unsupervised, though some supervised approaches to SOM exist [4, 5, 7].

While there are extensions of the SOM algorithm to allow the processing of data sequences [7], this paper is concerned with more recent developments which extended the capabilities of the SOM towards the processing of graph structured information in a causal manner [1], and a more general approach which is capable of capturing contextual dependencies among the input data [2, 3].

This paper addresses the specific problem of grouping graph structured data into clusters. The task will be executed in an unsupervised fashion (i.e. during network training no knowledge is available about how graphs should be clustered) by using a Self-Organizing Map approach. A collection of XML formatted documents (belonging to the INEX competition dataset) will be used to evaluate the approaches. The performance of these self-organizing methods [2, 3] will be addressed in this paper.

This paper is organized as follows: an introduction to the processing of graphs using a SOM for data structures is given in Section 2. The contextual SOM-SD, capable of encoding more general types of graphs, is given in Section 3. Methods for measuring the performances of SOM-SD based models are defined in Section 4. Results produced when engaging the SOM-SD and the CSOM-SD to the clustering task is presented in Section 5. Finally some conclusions are drawn in Section 6.

2   The SOM for Structured Data

The SOM for Data Structures (SOM-SD) extends the SOM in its ability to encode directed tree structured graphs [1]. This is accomplished by processing individual nodes of a graph one at a time rather than by processing a graph as a whole. The network response to a given node v is a mapping of v on the display space. This mapping is called the *state* of v and contains the coordinates of the winning neuron. An input vector representation is created for every node in a graph G by concatenating a numeric data label l_v which may be attached to a node v with the *state* of each of the node's immediate offsprings such that $x_v = [l_v\ y_{\text{ch}[v]}]$, where ch$[v]$ denotes the children of node v, and $y_{\text{ch}[v]}$ denotes the states or mappings of the children of v. The dimension of x is made constant in size by assuming a maximum dimension for l together with a maximum out-degree of a node. For nodes with less dimensions than the assumed, padding with a suitable value is applied. Since the initialization of x depends on the availability of all the children states, this dictates the processing of nodes in an inverse topological order (i.e. from the leaf nodes towards the root nodes), and hence, this causes information to flow in a strictly causal manner (from the leaf nodes to the root nodes).

A SOM-SD is trained in a similar fashion to the standard SOM with the difference that the vector elements l and y_{ch} need to be weighted so as to control the influence of these components to a similarity measure. Equation (1) is altered to become:

$$c = \arg\min_j(\|(x_v - m_j)\Lambda\|) \tag{3}$$

where x_v is the input vector for vertex v, m_i the i-th codebook, and Λ is a $m \times m$ dimensional diagonal matrix with its diagonal elements $\lambda_{1,1} \cdots \lambda_{p,p}$ set to μ_1, and $\lambda_{p+1,p+1} \cdots \lambda_{m,m}$ set to μ_2. The constants μ_1 and μ_2 control the influence of l_v and $y_{\text{ch}[v]}$ to the Euclidean distance in (3).

The rest of the training algorithm remains the same as that of the standard SOM. The effect of this extension is that the SOM-SD will map a given set of graphs, and all sub-graphs onto the same map. The SOM-SD includes the standard SOM and the SOM for data sequences as special cases.

Since the SOM-SD maintains its ability to cluster input data according to some topology, it is found that leaf nodes (which do not feature any outlinks) are mapped in well distinct areas compared to root nodes. Moreover, since the SOM-SD processes graphs in a causal manner, the root nodes are a representation of the graph as a whole.

The increased encoding capability of a SOM-SD has a drawback. While a single vector is sufficient to represent data in a standard SOM, in a SOM-SD the data is represented by a number of nodes within a graph. Since the SOM-SD maps all nodes, this implies an increased demand in the display space. In general, a SOM-SD requires larger maps in order to perform satisfactorily. This is not a major issue since the algorithm scales linearly in complexity with the size of the map, and the size of the dataset.

This paper will deploy the SOM-SD to cluster XML formatted documents into various clusters. The graphs extracted from the XML documents naturally form trees. Loops or un-rooted structures are not possible. While a SOM-SD is fully capable of encoding such data, this paper also addresses a further extension to the SOM algorithm which is capable of encoding more general types of graphs [2, 3]. This is performed in order to provide an overview of Self-Organizing map methods which can be deployed to the task of clustering XML structured documents. In fact, this is a very recent extension which is applied for the first time to this real world learning problem.

3   The Contextual SOM-SD

With contextual SOM for graphs (CSOM-SD), the network input is formed by additionally concatenating the state of parent nodes and children nodes to an input vector such that $x_v = [l\ y_{\text{ch}[v]}\ y_{\text{pa}[v]}]$, where $y_{\text{pa}[v]}$ are the states of the parent nodes and $y_{\text{ch}[v]}$ are the states of the children nodes. The problem with this definition is that a circular functional dependency is introduced between the connected vertices v and pa$[v]$, and so, neither the state for node v nor the state of its parents pa$[v]$ can be computed. One possibility to compute these states could be to find a joint stable fix point to the equations involving all the vertices of a structure. This could be performed by initializing all the states with random values and then updating these initial states using the above mentioned equations, till a fixed point is reached. Unfortunately, there is no guarantee that such a fixed point would be reached. Moreover, even if sufficient conditions can be given over the initial weights of the map to guarantee stability, i.e. the existence of the fixed point, there is no guarantee that training will remain valid on such sufficient conditions over the weights.

A (partial) solution to this dilemma has been proposed in [2]. The approach is based on an K-step approximation of the dynamics described above: Let

$$y^t = h(x_v^{t-1}), t = 1, \ldots, K \tag{4}$$

where $h(\cdot)$ computes the state of node v by mapping the input x_v^{t-1}, and $x_v^{t-1} = [l_v\ y_{\text{ch}[v]}^{t-1}\ y_{\text{pa}[v]}^{i-1}]$. The algorithm is initialized by setting $y_{\text{ch}[v]}^0 = y_{\text{pa}[v]}^0 = k$, where $k = [-1, -1]$, an impossible winning coordinate. In other words, the approach iteratively re-computes the states of every node in a graph K-times. Then, the network input can be formed by setting $x_v = [l\ y_{\text{ch}[v]}^K\ y_{\text{pa}[v]}^K]$. A suitable value for K could be, for instance, the maximum length of any path between any two nodes in the graph. Although such a choice does not guarantee the full processing of contextual information due to possible latency in the transfer of contextual information from one vertex of the structure to its neighbors vertices, this value for K seems to be a good tradeoff between contextual processing and computational cost.

Training is performed similar to the training of SOM-SD with the difference that Λ is now a $n \times n$ matrix, $n = \dim(x)$ with $\lambda_{m+1,m+1} \cdots \lambda_{n,n}$ set to the constant μ_3. All other elements in Λ are the same as defined before.

Note that this approach is a generalization of a CSOM-SD which operates on un-directed graphs. With un-directed graphs, each node v has a set of neighbors such that the network input would be $x_v = [l\ y_{\text{ne}[v]}^K]$, where ne$[v]$ denotes the state of neighboring nodes. Accordingly, $\mu_2 = \mu_3$ in Λ in Eq. (3).

The training algorithm of the CSOM-SD can be given as follows:

Step 0. Initialize all y with k, where $k = [-1, -1]$ the impossible output coordinate.

Step 1. For every $v \in G_i$ compute $\boldsymbol{y}^t = h(\boldsymbol{x}_v^{t-1})$, where $\boldsymbol{x}_v^{t-1} = [\boldsymbol{l}_v \ \boldsymbol{y}_{\text{ch}[v]}^{t-1} \ \boldsymbol{y}_{\text{pa}[v]}^{t-1}]$. Repeat this step K times, where K is the maximum path length between the two most distant nodes in G_i, and G_i is the i-th graph in the training set. Apply this step to all graphs in the training set.

Step 2. Choose a node v from the training set, initialize $\boldsymbol{x}_v^K = [\boldsymbol{l} \ \boldsymbol{y}_{\text{ch}[v]}^K \ \boldsymbol{y}_{\text{pa}[v]}^K]$, and compute the best matching codebook r by finding the most similar codebook entry $\mathbf{m}_r$. This can be achieved, e.g., by using the Euclidean distance as follows:

$$r = \arg\min_i \|(\mathbf{x}_v^K - \mathbf{m}_i)\boldsymbol{\Lambda}\| \tag{5}$$

Step 3. Update network parameters as follows:

$$\Delta\mathbf{m}_i = \alpha(t)g(\Delta_{ir})(\mathbf{m}_i - \mathbf{x}_v^K) \tag{6}$$

where t is the current training iteration, α is a learning rate which gradually decreases to zero, $g(.)$ is the neighborhood function depending on Δ_{ir} which is the topological distance between neuron i and neuron r. This step is identical to the traditional SOM updating step shown in Eq. (2). Repeat Step 2 and Step 3 for every node in the training set.

The algorithm cycles through Steps 1 to 3 until a given number of training iterations is performed, or when the mapping precision has reached a given prescribed threshold.

Once trained, information can be retrieved efficiently from a CSOM-SD. This is performed by using a set of data in place of the training set, and by executing Step 0 to Step 2 on this dataset. This will compute the mapping of all nodes in a dataset. Given a sample document (represented by a graph) we can now retrieve similar documents by returning graphs which were mapped near the location on which the known document was mapped.

4 Performance Measures

It is evident that a simple quantization error is an insufficient indicator of the performance of a SOM-SD or a CSOM-SD since such an approach neglects to take into account the fact that structural information is being mapped. In fact, there are a number of criteria with which the performance of a SOM-SD or a CSOM-SD can be measured. These are performance indicators on the clustering performance, the mapping precision, and the compression ratio. The clustering performance shows how well data are grouped together on the map, the mapping precision shows how accurately structural information is encoded in the map, and the compression ratio indicates the degree of network utilization. In addition, if target labels are available then the network can also be evaluated on the classification performance, and the retrieval capability.

Retrieval capability (R): This reflects the accuracy of retrieved data from the various SOM models. This can be computed quite simply if for each XML document d_j a target class $y_j \in \{t_1, \ldots, t_q\}$ is given. Since each XML document is represented by a tree, in the following, we will focus our attention just on the root of the tree. Thus, with r_j we will refer to the input vector for SOM,

SOM-SD or CSOM-SD representing the root of the XML document d_j. The R index is computed as follows: the mapping of every node in the dataset is computed; then for every neuron i the set $win(i)$ of root nodes for which it was a winner is computed. Let $win_t(i) = \{r_j | r_j \in win(i) \text{ and } y_j = t\}$, the value $R_i = \max_t \frac{|win_t(i)|}{|win(i)|}$ is computed for neurons with $|win(i)| > 0$ and the index R computed as $R = \frac{1}{W} \sum_{i,|win(i)|>0} R_i$, where $W = \sum_{i,|win(i)|>0} 1$ is the total number of neurons which were activated at least once by a root node.

Classification performance (C): This can be computed as follows:

$$C_j = \begin{cases} 1 \text{ if } y_j = t_r^*, & t_r^* = \arg\max_t |win_t(r)| \\ 0 \text{ else} \end{cases},$$

where r is the index of the best matching codebook for document d_j (typically measured at the root node). Then,

$$C = \frac{1}{N} \sum_{j=0}^{N} C_j,$$

where N is the number of documents (graphs) in the test set. Values of C and R can range within $(0 : 1]$ where values closer to 1 indicate a better performance.

Clustering performance (P): A more sophisticated approach is needed to compute the ability of a SOM-SD or a CSOM-SD to suitably group data on the map. In this paper the following approach is proposed:

1. Compute the quantities R_i as defined above, and let $t_i^* = \arg\max_t |win_t(i)|$.
2. For any activated neuron compute the quantity:

$$P_i = \frac{\sum_{j=1}^{|\mathcal{N}_i|} \frac{|win_{t_i^*}(j)|}{|win(j)|} + \frac{|win_t(i)|}{|win(i)|}}{|\mathcal{N}_i| + 1} = \frac{\sum_{j=1}^{|\mathcal{N}_i|} \frac{|win_{t_i^*}(j)|}{|win(j)|} + R_i}{|\mathcal{N}_i| + 1}$$

   where $\mathcal{N}_i = \{v | v \in ne[i], win(v) \neq \emptyset\}$.
3. The overall neural network performance is then given by:

$$P = \frac{\sum_i P_i}{W}.$$

A performance value close to 1 indicates a perfect grouping, while a value closer to 0 indicates a poor clustering result. Thus, this measure indicates the level of disorder inside a SOM-SD or CSOM-SD.

Structural mapping precision (e and E): These indices measure how well structural (e) and contextual structural (E) information are encoded in the map. A suitable method for computing the structural mapping precision was suggested in [2]. In this case, just the skeleton of the trees is considered, i.e. the information attached to vertices is disregarded, and only the topology of the trees is considered. Notice that these measures do not consider the information about the class to which an XML document (i.e., a tree) belongs. For this reason, all the neurons of a map are now considered, since we are also interested in neurons which are winners for sub-structures. These two measures e and E are respectively computed as follows

$$e = \frac{1}{N} \sum_{i=1, n_i \neq 0}^{N} \frac{m_i}{n_i} \qquad \text{and} \qquad E = \frac{1}{N} \sum_{i=1, n_i \neq 0}^{N} \frac{M_i}{n_i}$$

where n_i is the number of sub-structures mapped at location i, m_i is the greatest number of sub-structures which are identical and are mapped at location i. Similarly, M_i is the greatest number of identical complete trees which are associated with the sub-structure mapped at location i. N is the total number of neurons activated by at least one sub-structure during the mapping process. Hence, e is an indicator of the quality of the mapping of sub-structures, and E indicates the quality of the contextual mapping process. Values of e and E close to 1 indicate a very good mapping (indeed a *perfect* mapping if the value is 1), and values closer to 0 indicate a poor mapping.

Compression ratio: This is the ratio between the total number of root nodes in the training/test set, and the number of neurons actually activated by root nodes in the training/test set. The higher the compression, the fewer the number of neurons are involved in the mapping process. Extremely high or extremely low compression ratios can indicate a poor performance. The compression ratio can vary between 0 and N, where N is the number of root nodes in the training/test set.

5 Clustering Results

The corpus (m-db-s-0) considered consists of $9,640$ XML formatted documents which were made available as part of the INEX Initiative (INitiative for the Evaluation of XML Retrieval), and was obtained via the Web site: *http://xmlmining.lip6.fr*. Each of the XML formatted documents describes an individual movie (e.g. the movie title, list of actors, list of reviewers, etc.). It was built using the IMDB database. Each document is labelled by one thematic category which represents the genre of the movie in the original collection and one structure category. There are 11 thematic categories and 11 possible structure categories which correspond to transformations of the original data structure. Note that the target labels are used solely for testing purposes, and hence, are ignored during network training.

A tree structure was extracted for each of the documents in the dataset by following the general XML structure within the documents. The resulting dataset featured $9,640$ tree structured graphs, one for each XML document in the dataset. The maximum depth of any graph is 3, the maximum outdegree is $6,418$, and the total number of nodes in the dataset is $684,191$. Hence, the dataset consists of shallow tree structures which can be very wide. A three-dimensional data label is attached to every node in the dataset indicating the XML-tag it represents (more on this below). There were a total of 197 different tags in the dataset.

While for the SOM-SD and CSOM-SD there is no specific need to pre-process this set of graphs, we decided to apply a pre-processing step in order to reduce the dimensionality of the dataset. This allows for a reasonable turn around time for the experiments. Dimension reduction was achieved by consolidating XML tags as follows: Repeated sequences of tags within the same level of a structure are consolidated. For example, the structure:

```
<BB>
    <a></a>
    <b></b>                                          <BB>
    <a></a>                                             <a></a>
    <b></b>          is consolidated to                 <b></b>
    <a></a>                                          </BB>
    <b></b>
</BB>
```

A justification for taking this step is inspired by operations in regular expressions. For example, the expression $(ab)^n$ can be simulated by repeatedly presenting ab n-times. Hence, it suffices to process the consolidated structure n times. There were many trees which exhibited such repeated sequences of tags. The consequence of this pre-processing step is that the maximum outdegree is reduced to just 32.

A further dimension reduction is achieved by collapsing sequences into a single node. For example, the sequential structure `<A><b><c></c></b></A>` can be collapsed to `<A><b&c></b&c></A>`, and further to `<A&b&c>`. Since the deepest graph is of depth 3, this implies that the longest sequence that can be collapsed is of length 3. This pre-processing step reduces the total number of nodes in the dataset to $247, 140$.

A unique identifier (ID) is associated with each of the 197 XML tags. In order to account for nodes which represent collapsed sequences, we attach a three dimensional data label to each node. The first element of the data label gives the ID of the XML tag it represents, the second element of the data label is the ID number of the first tag of a collapsed sequence of nodes, and consequently, the third element is the ID of the tag of the leaf node of a collapsed sequence. For nodes which do not represent a collapsed structure, the second and third element in the data label will be set to zero.

The resulting dataset consists of $4, 820$ graphs containing a total of $124, 360$ nodes (training set), and 4,811 graphs containing a total of $122, 780$ nodes (test set). The training set was analysed for its statistical properties, results are illustrated in Figure 1. It is observed that the training set is unbalanced. For example, the table on the left of Figure 1 shows that there are only 172 samples of the pattern instance denoted by "4" but over 700 instances of patterns from the instance denoted by "3". Also, the 3-D plot in Figure 1 shows that the distribution of outdegrees can vary greatly. For example, there is only one instance in the pattern class denoted by "8" which has an outdegree of 10 while there are over 270 instances for the same pattern class with outdegree 5. There are also a number of pattern classes which are similar in features such as class "10" and class "11" which are of similar size and are of similar structure.

There are $2, 872$ unique sub-structures in the training set. This is an important statistical figure since it gives an indication to how much more information is provided to a SOM-SD when compared to the flat vectors used for the SOM. And hence, the larger the number of unique sub-structures in the training set, the greater the potential diversification in the mapping of the data will be. Similarly, there are $96, 107$ unique nodes in different contextual configurations in the training set. This shows that the CSOM-SD is provided with a greater set of diverse features in the training set, and

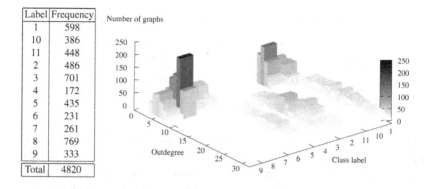

Label	Frequency
1	598
10	386
11	448
2	486
3	701
4	172
5	435
6	231
7	261
8	769
9	333
Total	4820

Fig. 1. Properties of the training set: The table (left) shows the number of graphs in each of the 11 classes. The plot (right) shows the distribution of outdegrees in the dataset. Shown are the number of graphs (z-axis) which have a given outdegree (y-axis) and belong to a given class (x-axis).

hence, may be capable to diversify in the mapping of the data even further. Thus, this dataset provides a challenging learning problem on which various SOM models will be tested.

All SOMs illustrated in this section used a hexagonal topology, and a Gaussian neighborhood function. For the SOM-SD and the CSOM-SD, when generating the input vectors x_i for nodes with less than the maximum outdegree, padding was performed using the impossible coordinate $[-1, -1]$.

The standard SOM is trained on $4,820$ data *vectors*, each one represents an XML document. The i-th element in the data vector represents the frequency of the i-th XML tag within a document. Thus, the input vectors for the SOM are 197 dimensional containing the complete set of information about the XML tags in a document but do not contain any information about the topological structure between the XML tags.

Thus, the SOM is trained on relatively few high-dimensional data vectors while the (C)SOM-SD is being trained on a large number of nodes which are represented by a relatively small size vectors. For the SOM we chose $64 \times 48 = 3,072$ as the size of the network. The total number of network parameters for the SOM is $3,072 \times 197 = 605,184$. Since the codebook dimensions for the SOM-SD is $3 + 32 \times 2 = 67$, this implies that a SOM-SD needs to feature at least $9,033$ codebooks to allow a fair comparison. Accordingly, the CSOM-SD should feature at least $8,771$ neurons. However, since the SOM-SD (and to an even greater extent the CSOM-SD) are to encode a larger feature set which includes causal (contextual) information about the data, this implies that the SOM-SD (CSOM-SD) will potentially diversify the mapping of the data to a greater extent than a SOM would do. Hence, this would justify the choice of even larger networks for the SOM-SD and CSOM-SD respectively for the comparisons. However, we chose to use the network sizes as indicated in Table 1 as these suffice to illustrate the principal properties of the models.

A number of SOMs, SOM-SDs, and CSOM-SDs were trained by varying the training parameters, and initial network conditions. We used the classification measure C as a general benchmark on which to optimize the performance of the various models.

Table 1. Network parameters used for the training procedure

	size	# iterations	$\alpha(0)$	$r(0)$	μ_1	μ_2	μ_3
SOM	64×48	32	1.0	4	1.0	–	–
SOM-SD	110×81	62	1.0	38	0.11	0.89	–
CSOM-SD	110×81	12	0.7	15	0.11	0.88	0.01 [2]

A total of 56 experiments were executed for each of the SOM models, and every experiment was repeated 10 times using a different random initialization of the map as a starting point. The experiments varied the following training parameters: number of training iterations i, initial neighborhood radius $r(0)$, initial learning rate $\alpha(0)$, and the weight values μ (in this order). The set of training parameters which maximised the classification performance of the three models is shown in Table 1. It is observed that the SOM-SD required more training iterations and a larger initial neighborhood radius to achieve optimum classification performance (on the training set). It was also observed that the classification performance of the CSOM-SD improved with smaller values for μ_3 reaching an optimum for $\mu_3 = 0.0$. However, setting μ_3 to zero would reduce the CSOM-SD to a SOM-SD, and hence, would be an unsuitable choice for the comparisons. Further details regarding this observation are given below.

The performances of the three SOM models are illustrated in Table 2. The performance indices are those as defined in Section 4. From Table 2 it can be seen that a standard SOM is able to classify over 90% of patterns in the training set correctly despite of no information about the underlying causal or contextual configuration of XML tags is provided to the training algorithm. However, it was found that the SOM generalizes poorly. In comparison, the SOM-SD improved the classification rate by a noticeable amount, and was able to generalize over unseen data very well. As is seen from the compression ratio Z, the performance increase of the SOM-SD comes despite a doubling of the compression ratio. This is a clear evidence that causal information about the order of XML tags allows to a.) diversify the mapping of nodes to a considerably larger extend, and b.) the diversification in the mappings can result in an overall

Table 2. Best results obtained during the experimentation with maps of size 64×48 (SOM), and for maps of size 110×81 (SOM-SD and CSOM-SD)

	train set						test set					
	C	R	P	e	E	Z	C	R	P	e	E	Z
SOM	90.5%	0.90	0.73	1.0	1.0	2.45	76.5%	0.92	0.73	1.0	1.0	2.45
SOM-SD	92.5%	0.92	0.78	0.77	0.50	5.13	87.3%	0.93	0.79	0.76	0.50	4.9
CSOM-SD	83.9%	0.87	0.73	0.91	0.30	8.53	78.6%	0.88	0.71	0.90	0.37	8.54

improvement of the classification or clustering performances. In contrast, the inclusion of contextual information did not help to improve on the classification performance as it

---

[2] Smallest non-zero value tried. Setting $\mu_3 = 0.0$ resulted in a better classification performance but would reduce the CSOM-SD to a SOM-SD.

is seen from the results obtained from the CSOM-SD. It is found that contextual information helped to diversify the mapping of nodes by almost double when compared to
the SOM-SD. This is indicated by the larger compression ratio. Thus, it is evident that
a correct classification of the graphs in the dataset is independent to contextual information about the XML tags within the original documents. Paired with the greater data
compression which is the result of a greater diversification in the mapping of nodes,
this produced a relative overall reduction in classification performance for the CSOM-
SD, and explains the observation that the performance optimum of the CSOM-SD is at
$\mu_3 = 0$.

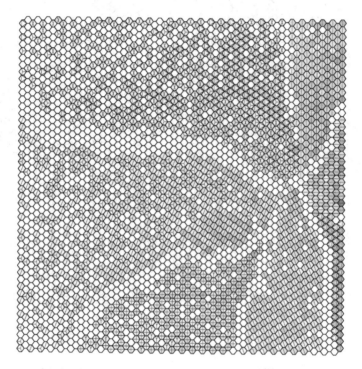

Fig. 2. The mapping of the training vectors on a standard SOM

In addition, it is observed that a CSOM-SD performs worse on the performance
measure E than a SOM-SD. This is a result which arose out of the fact that the experiments were to optimize the classification performance C. It was found that a CSOM-SD
improves on C when using $\mu_3 \rightarrow 0$. However, setting $\mu_3 = 0$ would reduce the CSOM-
SD to a SOM-SD and would have denied us from making a comparison between the
models. Instead, we chose a small value for μ_3 so as to allow such comparisons, and
still produce reasonable classification performances. Using a very small μ_3 reduces the
impact of contextual information to the training algorithm. Paired with the increased
compression ratio in the mapping of root nodes, this resulted in a relative decrease in
the performance on E. Note that the standard SOM performed at $e = E = 1$. This

Fig. 3. The mapping of root nodes (training set) on the SOM-SD

is due to the fact that a SOM handles the simplest type of data structures (viz. single nodes). These render all structures in the dataset identical, resulting in the observed performance values.

A closer look at the mapping of (training) data is made in the standard SOM Figure 2. The hexagons in Figure 2 refer to the neurons on the map. The brightness of the grid intersection represents the number of training data which are assigned to the grid point due to their closeness in the original input space. Thus by examining the brightness in the grid, it is possible to gain an appreciation of the way the given training dataset can be grouped together, according to their closeness in the original input space. Every neuron is also filled in with a pattern indicating the class that most frequently activated the neuron. There are 11 different fill in patterns for the 11 possible classes. Neurons which are not filled in are not activated by any vector in the training set. It can be observed that a number of well distinct clusters

Fig. 4. The mapping of root nodes (training set) on the CSOM-SD

have formed on the map, most of which correspond very nicely with the target label that is associated with the training data. Most clusters are separated from each other by an area of neurons which were not activated. This may indicate a good result since the presence of such border regions should allow for a good generalization performance; a statement which could not be confirmed when evaluating the test set.

In comparison, the mapping of root nodes in the training set on a trained SOM-SD is shown in Figure 3. Neurons which are not filled in are either not activated by a root node, or are activated by a node other than the root node. It can be observed in Figure 3 that large sections of the map are not activated by any root node. This is due to the fact that root nodes are a minority in the dataset. Only $4,824$ nodes out of the total $124,468$ nodes in the training set are root nodes. Hence, only a relatively small portion of the map is activated by root nodes. It is also observed that graphs

Table 3. Confusion table as produced by the best SOM when using the training set

Label	1	10	11	2	3	4	5	6	7	8	9	Perf.
1	598	0	0	0	0	0	0	0	0	0	0	100.0%
10	0	339	33	0	0	0	0	14	0	0	0	87.8%
11	0	69	350	0	0	0	0	29	0	0	0	78.1%
2	0	0	0	362	124	0	0	0	0	0	0	74.4%
3	0	0	0	29	672	0	0	0	0	0	0	95.8%
4	2	0	0	0	0	87	83	0	0	0	0	50.5%
5	0	0	0	0	0	16	419	0	0	0	0	96.3%
6	1	47	12	0	0	0	0	171	0	0	0	74.0%
7	0	0	0	0	0	0	0	0	260	0	1	99.6%
8	0	0	0	0	0	0	0	0	0	769	0	100.0%
9	0	0	0	0	0	0	0	0	0	0	333	100.0%

belonging to different classes form clear clusters some of which are very small in size. This observation confirms the experimental findings which show that the SOM-SD will be able to generalize well.

Table 4. Confusion table as produced by the best SOM-SD when using the training set

Label	1	10	11	2	3	4	5	6	7	8	9	Perf.
1	590	1	0	3	4	0	0	0	0	0	0	98.66%
10	0	384	0	0	0	0	0	0	0	0	2	99.48%
11	0	0	363	0	0	0	0	59	0	25	1	81.03%
2	3	0	0	440	16	8	19	0	0	0	0	90.54%
3	4	0	0	10	686	1	0	0	0	0	0	97.86%
4	1	0	0	86	5	65	15	0	0	0	0	37.79%
5	0	0	0	4	0	2	429	0	0	0	0	98.62%
6	0	0	63	0	0	0	0	150	0	18	0	64.94%
7	0	0	0	0	0	0	0	0	257	4	0	98.47%
8	0	0	5	0	0	0	0	3	0	761	0	98.96%
9	0	0	0	0	0	0	0	0	0	0	333	100.0%

Figure 4 gives the mapping of the root nodes as produced by the CSOM-SD. Again, it is found that the largest portion of the map is filled in by neurons which are either not activated or are activated by nodes other than the labelled root nodes. Clear clusters are formed which are somewhat smaller in size when compared to the SOM-SD case. This illustrates quite nicely that the CSOM-SD is compressing the "root" data considerably more strongly than the SOM-SD since contextual information is also encoded which requires additional room in the map. Nevertheless, the observation confirms that the CSOM-SD will also be able to generalize well even though some of the performance indices may be worse than when compared to a SOM-SD of the same size. This can be expected since the CSOM-SD compresses the "root" data more strongly.

A more detailed look at the classification of the data is made in Table 3, Table 4, and Table 5 which give the confusion matrices as produced by the SOM, SOM-SD, and

Table 5. Confusion table as produced by the best CSOM-SD when using the training set

Label	1	10	11	2	3	4	5	6	7	8	9	Perf.
1	592	1	0	0	5	0	0	0	0	0	0	99.00%
10	0	355	0	0	0	0	0	0	0	0	31	91.97%
11	0	1	274	0	0	0	0	17	0	156	0	61.16%
2	0	0	0	425	17	16	28	0	0	0	0	87.45%
3	15	0	0	7	679	0	0	0	0	0	0	96.86%
4	0	0	0	78	10	68	16	0	0	0	0	39.53%
5	0	0	0	8	3	3	421	0	0	0	0	96.78%
6	0	2	46	0	0	0	0	89	0	94	0	38.53%
7	0	0	0	0	0	0	0	0	261	0	0	100.0%
8	0	0	103	0	0	0	0	2	0	664	0	86.35%
9	0	0	0	0	0	0	0	0	0	0	333	100.0%

the CSOM-SD respectively. It is seen that all three models perform best on classes which are relatively large in size (compare with Figure 1) The poorest classifications are observed for the smallest classes. This is particularly true for the classes labelled 4 and 6, which in addition of being the smallest classes in the dataset, also share features that are similar to the classes 2 and 11. This shows that the performance of all three models is affected by unbalances in the feature space presented in the training set.

The experiments presented in this paper were executed on 2GHz Intel based CPUs. Training times varied from 2 − 12 hours depending on the SOM model and training parameters used. Once trained, data retrieval generally took only a few minutes.

6   Conclusions

The clustering of graphs and sub-graphs can be a hard problem. This paper demonstrated that the clustering task of general types of graphs can be performed in linear time by using a neural network approach based on Self-Organizing Maps. In addition, it was shown that SOM-SD based networks can produce good performances even if the map is considerably smaller than the size of the training set. Using larger maps will generally allow to improve the performance further though this was not illustrated in this paper.

Specifically, it was shown that the given learning problem depends on the availability of causal information about the XML tags within the original document in order to produce a good grouping or classification of the data. The incorporation of contextual information did not help to improve on the results.

The training set used in this paper featured a wide variety of tree structured graphs. We found that most graphs are relatively small in size, only few graphs were either very wide or featured many nodes. This creates imbalances in features represented in a training set which is known to negatively impact the performance of a neural network. Similarly it is true when considering the way we generated data labels for the nodes. An improvement of these aspects (i.e. balancing the features in the training set, using unique labels which are equiv-distant to each other) should help to improve the network performances. An investigation into the effects of these aspects is left as a future task.

Furthermore, it was shown that the (C)SOM-SD models map graph structures onto a finite regular grid in a topology preserving manner. This implies that similar structures are mapped onto nearby areas. As a consequence, these SOM models should be suitable for inexact graph matching tasks. Such applications are considered as a future task.

Acknowledgments

The work presented in this paper received financial support from the Australian Research Council in form of a Linkage International Grant and a Discovery Project grant.

References

1. M. Hagenbuchner, A. Sperduti, and A. Tsoi. A self-organizing map for adaptive processing of structured data. *IEEE Transactions on Neural Networks*, 14(3):491–505, May 2003.
2. M. Hagenbuchner, A. Sperduti, and A. Tsoi. Contextual processing of graphs using self-organizing maps. In *European symposium on Artificial Neural Networks*, Poster track, Bruges, Belgium, 27 - 29 April 2005.
3. M. Hagenbuchner, A. Sperduti, and A. Tsoi. Contextual self-organizing maps for structured domains. In *Relational Machine Learning*, pages pp. 46–55, 2005.
4. M. Hagenbuchner and A. Tsoi. A supervised self-organizing map for structures. In *International Joint Conference on Neural Networks*, volume 3, pages 1923–1928, Budapest, Hungary, 25-29 July 2004.
5. M. Hagenbuchner and A. Tsoi. A supervised training algorithm for self-organizing maps for structures. *Artificial Neural Networks in Pattern Recognition, Special Issue Pattern Recognition Letters*, 26(12):1874–1884, September 2006.
6. T. Kohonen. *Self-Organisation and Associative Memory*. Springer, 3rd edition, 1990.
7. T. Kohonen. *Self-Organizing Maps*, volume 30 of *Springer Series in Information Sciences*. Springer, Berlin, Heidelberg, 1995.

INEX 2005 Multimedia Track

Roelof van Zwol[1], Gabriella Kazai[2], and Mounia Lalmas[2]

[1] Utrecht University, Department of Computer Science, Center for Content and Knowledge Engineering, Utrecht, The Netherlands
roelof@cs.uu.nl
[2] Department of Computer Science, Queen Mary, University of London, London, United Kingdom
{gabs, mounia}@dcs.qmul.ac.uk

Abstract. This paper reports on the activities of the INEX 2005 Multimedia track. The track was successful in realizing its objective to provide a pilot evaluation platform for the evaluation of retrieval strategies for XML-based multimedia documents. In this first exploratory year the focus of the evaluation experiment was to test approaches for the retrieval of XML fragments using a combination of content-based text and image retrieval techniques. The track is set to continue at INEX 2006.

1 Challenge and Objectives

The main objective of the INEX 2005 multimedia track was to provide a pilot evaluation platform for structured document retrieval systems which are not limited to textual content, but combine multiple media types. Many, real-life structured document collections today contain a range of media, such as text, image, speech, and video. Incorporating different media types within the retrieval process and producing meaningful rankings of multimedia documents and components is far from trivial. The goal of the multimedia track at INEX 2005 was to investigate this problem from a new perspective, using the structure of documents as the semantic/logical backbone for the retrieval of multimedia document fragments. In this first year, the track resulted in the construction of a pilot evaluation platform for the retrieval of multimedia structured document fragments. The methodology used in the construction of the test collection was built on established methods used at TREC [1].

The task set for the multimedia track was to retrieve relevant document fragments based on an information need with a structured multimedia character. The challenge for a structured document retrieval system in this case is then to combine the relevance of the different media types into a single (meaningful) ranking that can be presented to the user. The INEX multimedia track differs from other approaches in multimedia information retrieval, like TRECVID [2] and ImageCLEF [3], in the sense that it focuses on the use of document structure to estimate, relate, and combine the relevance of different multimedia fragments. The focus for 2005 was on the combination of text and image retrieval, where a strict interpretation of the structural constraints within the specified information need was adopted.

N. Fuhr et al. (Eds.): INEX 2005, LNCS 3977, pp. 497–510, 2006.
© Springer-Verlag Berlin Heidelberg 2006

1.1 Participants

Eight groups participated in the first year of this track. These are summarised in Table 1.

Table 1. Participants of the multimedia track

ID	Organisation	Created topics	Assessed topics	Submitted runs
utwente	Cirquid Project (CWI and U. of Twente)	6	3	5
qmul	Queen Mary University of London	5	3	1
utrecht	Utrecht University	4	3	5
rmit	RMIT University	3	3	5
qutau	Queensland University of Technology	3	3	5
ugrenoble	University of Grenoble (CLIPS-IMAG)	0	2	0
uberkeley	University of California, Berkeley	0	2	0

1.2 Setting Up the Multimedia Track

A step-by-step outline of the activities involved in setting up the multimedia track is given below.

- **Acquisition of the Lonely Planet WorldGuide XML collection** [4].
  One of the first tasks was to acquire a suitable XML collection that was easily accessible and contained integrated multimedia objects. Such a collection was donated by the Lonely Planet organization in the form of the WorldGuide XML collection.
- **Extension of the NEXI query language.** The original NEXI query language [5] supported only text-based information access. For the multimedia track, it was necessary to allow for searching images as well as text. Therefore, a small extension to NEXI was defined.
- **Baseline system for topic formulation.** Both a text-based and an image-based retrieval system was provided for participants to support the topic creation process.
- **Topic creation procedure and selection.** A topic creation procedure was set up, similar to that used by the INEX ad-hoc track, but extended to address the additional requirements of the multimedia track. For example, in addition to searching for relevant text fragments to a candidate topic, participants were asked to carry out preliminary searches for relevant images. Topic creation resulted in a pool of 25 topics, which now form part of the INEX multimedia test collection. These topics were then used to evaluate the participants' retrieval systems.
- **Assessment procedure.** Binary relevancy judgments and the yellow-marker design for obtaining relevance assessments were employed in the track. Assessments were collected using the XRAI assessment tool [6], which was adapted by Benjamin Piwowarski to fit the track's assessment procedure (which is different from that employed by the ad-hoc track). As a result of the

employed binary relevance, the two-step assessment procedure used in the ad-hoc track was replaced with a single step: Assessors were asked to mark those multimedia fragments relevant that satisfied all requirements of the information need. Based on the SSCAS interpretation of a topic's structural constraints, both support elements, i.e. where to look, and target elements, i.e. what to return, had to be strictly matched by relevant fragments. All eight participants took part in the assessments. Two topics, topic 18 and 20, remained un-assessed.

 - **Evaluation of results.** In total, twenty-five runs were submitted by five participants (qmul, qutau, rmit, utrecht and utwente). Using the TREC evaluation tool, trec_eval [1], the results of several standard measures used in TREC were reported as indications of retrieval performance.

We detail each of the above steps in separate sections in the remainder of this paper.

2   Lonely Planet WorldGuide XML Document Collection

The corpus used for the INEX 2005 multimedia track was based on the Lonely Planet WorldGuide collection, made available by the Lonely Planet organization. The collection consists of 462 XML documents, each providing information about holiday or travel destinations. The most likely users of the collection are hence travelers who are interested in researching the locations of their next holiday or business trip. The collection can be viewed online at: http://www.lonelyplanet.com/worldguide/. The collection contains information about countries, regions and major cities. For each destination an introduction is given, complemented with information about transport, culture, major events, facts, and an image gallery that provides an impression of the local scenery. In Table 2, some additional statistics for the LonelyPlanet document collection are given.

Table 2. Lonely Planet WorldGuide collection statistics

Total number of XML documents	462
Total number of images	2633
Average number of images per file	6.7
Average depth of XML structure	4.73
Maximum depth of XML structure	8
Average number of XML nodes per document	440

3   Topic Creation

We first provide two example topics to introduce the requirements and the chosen approach for combining text and image components within a user request. The main consideration is the inclusion of content-based image retrieval into the specification of an information request using the NEXI query language[1] [5].

In its first year, the multimedia track focused on the use of Content-And-Structure (CAS) topics as these allow for the explicit representation of the multimedia character of an information request. We refer to these as NEXI-CAS queries.

3.1 Examples

Example 1

Information need: *Find images depicting scuba diving for destinations with a tropical climate and with activities that discuss exploring the beautiful underwater nature by diving.*
Information request:

```
//destination[ about(.//weather,tropical climate)
        and about(.//activities, beautiful "underwater nature" diving)]
    //images//image[about(., scuba diving)]
```

The information need of Example 1 contains both textual and image components. E.g. about(.//weather,tropical climate) specifies the condition requesting information about a tropical climate that is to be found within the XML element weather, which is a descendant of a destination element. Furthermore, requested image elements should depict scuba diving scenes.

Although the target elements of the above example are images, so far, simple textual retrieval approaches may have been sufficient to produce the required output, e.g. by searching on image captions. However, a combination of text and image retrieval techniques was encouraged within the track with the aim that these may in fact produce better results. An example of a query that combines both these aspects is shown in Example 2.

Example 2

Information need: *Find images depicting scuba diving, like in BN5970_6.jpg, for destinations with a tropical climate and with activities that discuss exploring the beautiful underwater nature by diving.*
Information request:

```
//destination[about(.//weather,tropical climate)
        and about(.//activities, beautiful "underwater nature" diving)]
    //images//image[about(., scuba diving src:/image/BN5970_6.jpg)]
```

The extension to the information need in Example 2, where a sample image is given by the user, enforces the inclusion of content-based image retrieval techniques into the retrieval process. To specify the corresponding information request in NEXI, a small extension to the query language was required, which is discussed next.

---

[1] NEXI is the XML query language used in INEX, which has been specifically developed to emphasize the content-oriented access to XML documents.

3.2 Multimedia Extension to NEXI

Two possible options were open for extending NEXI with image querying capabilities: 1.) introducing a new `depict` clause that takes an example image as one of its parameters, or 2.) extending the already existing `about` clause for image as well as text querying. The latter approach was chosen. By expressing both the content and image components of the information need within the same `about` clause of NEXI, we are effectively overloading its meaning, leaving it to the retrieval system to decide if a text or image search (or both) is required. The reason for doing so was to emphasize the multimedia nature of the track. By adopting this overloaded `about` clause, we can specify query constraints for a document fragment (which may be pure text, image, or a combination of the two media types) using textual descriptions (e.g. `about(//image, scuba diving)` or `about(//destination, scuba diving))` or using example images (e.g. `about(//image, src:/image/BN5970_6.jpg)` or `about(//destination, src:/image/BN5970_6.jpg))` or any combinations of the above, e.g. as shown in Example 2.

3.3 Topic Format and Topic Development Procedure

Topic Format. The topic format for the multimedia track consists of the following fields: description, castitle, and narrative. The following information is contained in each of these fields:

- <description> A brief description of the information need, specifying any structural, textual, and visual requirements/composition on the content. The description must be precise, concise, and informative. It must contain the same terms and the same structural requirements that appear in the castitle, albeit expressed in natural language.
- <castitle> A valid NEXI expression based on the Lonely Planet document collection that contains at least one `about` clause containing at least one image component. The expression is of the form //A[B] or //A[B]//C[D].
- <narrative> A detailed explanation of the information need and the description of what makes and element relevant or not. The narrative should explain not only what information is being sought, but also the context and motivation of the information need, i.e. why the information is being sought and what purpose it may serve.

Topic Development Guidelines. Each participating group was requested to submit 3 CAS topics following these steps.

Step 1: Initial topic statement. Creation of a one or two sentence description of the information being sought. This had to be a simple description of the information need without regard to retrieval system capabilities or document collection peculiarities. The context and motivation of the information need, i.e. why the information is being sought, also had to be recorded.

Step 2: Exploration phase. In this step the initial topic statement was used to explore the collection and obtain an estimate of the number of relevant elements. This was necessary to evaluate whether a topic can be judged consistently and whether enough but not too many relevant answers exist for it within the collection. For this purpose two search engines were made available to participants: a text and an image retrieval system.

Step 2a: Assess the top 25 text fragments. Participants were asked to judge the relevance of the top 25 retrieved text fragments. Each result had to be judged on its own merits. A search was to be abandoned if there were fewer than 2 or more than 20 relevant text fragments in the top 25 results.

Step 2b: Assess top 25 images. Since most participants did not have an off-the-shelf system available for the multimedia track, we have chosen to carry out a separate scan for the relevance of the image component. Here, participants had to assess the top 25 returned images. As with text, each result had to be judged on its own merits. A minimum of 2 and a maximum of 20 relevant images were required within the top 25 results.

Step 2c: Inspect document matching. To assure that the document collection had a reasonable chance of completely fulfilling the text and image-based constraints of an information need, a check at document level was needed. Participants were asked to count the number of documents that satisfied both the textual and image conditions. A candidate topic was to be rejected if less than 2 documents were found in the top 25 results for both components.

Step 3: Topic formulation. During this step, participants finalised the topic description, castitle, and narrative.

Step 4: Topic submission. Topics were submitted using the on-line Candidate Topic Submission Form on the INEX 2005 website.

Topic Pool. Five of the participating groups submitted a total of 25 topics. Example 3 shows one of these submitted topics. The target elements of this query are `destination` elements, where a relevant fragment needs to fulfill the various conditions formulated using both textual and visual requirements.

Example 3

```
<?xml version="1.0" encoding="ISO-8859-1"?>
<inex_topic topic_id="13" inex_track="MM">
 <castitle>//destination[about(., city river)]//images//image[
           about(., river city) and about(., src:/images/BN6288_22.jpg)]
 </castitle>
 <description>Find images depicting a city with a river, like in
     BN6288_22.jpg</description>
 <narrative>Brisbane is a beautiful city as there is a river flowing
     through the city. We want to find other cities that also have a
     river so that we can create a tour of river cities. </narrative>
</inex_topic>
```

4   Relevance Assessments

The definition of relevance used for the assessments was based on the definition employed in the INEX ad-hoc track with the exception that exhaustivity was measured only on a binary scale. In addition, reflecting the SSCAS task, an XML element was only considered relevant if it strictly matched the structural conditions specified within the query, i.e. only target elements could be relevant and only if they were contained in an XML document that satisfied all the query's containment constraints.

Therefore, a given multimedia fragment was said to be relevant if it discussed (or depicted) the topic of request to any degree and if it strictly adhered to the structural conditions requested by the user. Similarly to the ad-hoc track, the assessment procedure followed the highlighting approach. However, given the binary nature of relevance (exhaustivity), the assessment procedure for the multimedia track consisted only of a single pass. During this single assessment phase,

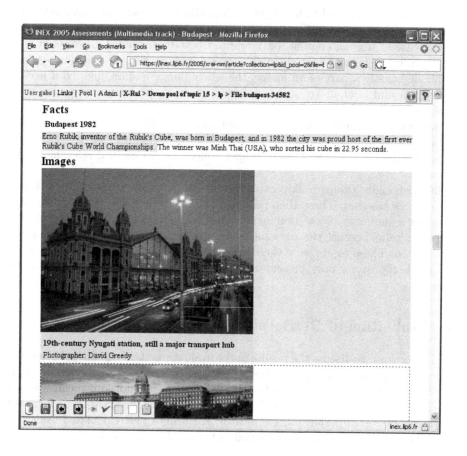

Fig. 1. Snapshot of the XRAI interface

Table 3. Details of the obtained assessments per topic

Topic	Relevant Elements	Topic	Relevant Elements
1	29	14	44
2	75	15	18
3	13	16	40
4	13	17	10
5	4	18	-
6	8	19	20
7	10	20	-
8	*5*	*21*	*25*
9	31	*22*	*21*
10	50	23	4
11	2	*24*	*77*
12	11	25	2
13	64		

assessors were requested to highlight multimedia fragments that contained only relevant content, i.e. contained no (or only minimal) non-relevant information. In the case of textual content, only relevant text fragments, e.g. words or sentences, were to be highlighted. In the case of images, since it was not possible to highlight only a part of an image, the whole image was highlighted if it contained relevant content (regardless of how much of the image may have been non-relevant).

Relevance assessments were carried out using the XRAI assessment tool, developed by Benjamin Piwowarski. Figure 1 shows a snapshot of the interface, where fragments from the Lonely Planet collection are marked relevant (highlighted).

In total, eight groups took part in the assessments. As a result, 23 of the 25 topics were assessed. These then provided the basis for the evaluation. Table 3 provides a summary of the obtained assessments. Topics *8, 21, 22,* and *24* are shown in italic, because the assessments did not match the castitle, and the topic description. These topics were therefore removed from the official evaluation.

In this report we only present results based on the official topic set of 19 topics.

5   Evaluation of Retrieval Performance

In this section, we discuss the results of the evaluation of the submitted runs. We report interpolated recall-precision averages and precision at fixed element cutoff levels for the best scoring run of each participant. In addition, mean average precision (MAP) scores and results of the binary preference (bpref) measure are given as overall performance indicator. All results were calculated using the TREC evaluation scripts, implemented in trec_eval version 7.3.

MAP, Precision@10 and bpref. Table 4 shows results for the best performing run of each participating group (selected based on MAP score). In total 19 topics were used for the official evaluation, however utrecht did not produce a ranking for two topics.

When comparing the number of retrieved elements (Ret.) with the number of relevant elements (Rel.) and the number of relevant and retrieved elements (Rel. & ret.), rmit was particularly successful in retrieving 202 relevant elements out of only 784 retrieved elements. However, the most number of relevant elements were retrieved by qutau: 303 out of a total of 448 relevant elements.

Table 4. MAP, Precision@10 and bpref

Participant	qmul	rmit	qutau	utrecht	utwente
Run	vsm 06	aggr alpha-0.3	text only	annotation	automatic noimg lm 05
Topics	19	19	19	17	19
Ret.	4750	**784**	3366	1112	4750
Rel.	448	448	448	390	448
Rel. & ret.	83	202	**303**	216	282
MAP	0.0412	**0.2779**	0.2711	0.2392	0.2751
Precision@10	0.0368	**0.3105**	0.2842	0.2706	0.2789
bpref	0.2388	0.4455	**0.6516**	0.5113	0.6272

MAP reports the average of the precision values after each retrieved relevant element. Based on the statistics of Table 4, it can be concluded that MAP favors rmit, closely followed by utwente and qutau.

Precision@10 reflects on the ability of a system to retrieve relevant elements in the top 10 positions of the ranking. For this measure, rmit has best performance, followed by qutau and utwente. This suggests that although qutau shows better performance at the top of the ranking, utwente achieves better overall performance.

Bpref has been shown to be a highly stable measure when relevance judgments are sparse [7]. This is therefore especially useful here given the size of the assessment pool. Intuitively, bpref measures the average number of times non-relevant material appears before relevant material. Here the differences between the runs are substantial: qutau and utwente are the only ones with a score of over 60%, while the others follow at some distance. Interestingly, however, bpref leads to a much improved performance score for qmul, compared with MAP and Precision@10.

More detailed information on the overall performances for all other runs submitted by participants can be found in Appendix A, or on the website [8].

Interpolated Recall-Precision Averages. Figure 2 shows the interpolated precision scores calculated at 11 standard recall points for the best performing run of each participating group (selected based on MAP score). Most curves are closely correlated. Two observations may be of interest: 1.) the best rmit run

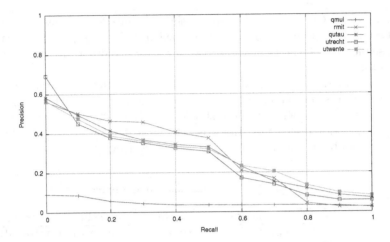

Fig. 2. Interpolated precision-recall averages @ 11 standard recall levels

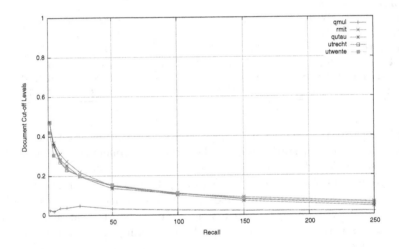

Fig. 3. Precision at element cutoff levels

outperforms all others for mid-recall levels (0.1 – 0.6), and 2.) the best run for utrecht achieves the highest precision of all for low recall levels (<0.1).

Precision at Element Cutoff Levels. Figure 3 plots scores for precision at various element cutoff levels in the range of 1 – 250. Precision at element cutoff is sensitive of the order in which relevant elements are returned. With the exception of the qmul run, all runs show an almost equal performance.

MAP per Topic. The analysis presented here allows us to investigate the performance of the different strategies per topic. In addition, it reveals if there are topics, which could not be answered, or which require specific approaches.

In Figure 4, MAP per topic is plotted for the 19 topics. It shows that retrieval performance is poor for all strategies on topics 1, 9, 12, 15, and 27. Looking at Table 3, it becomes clear that the assessment pools for these topics are relatively small. For example, in the case of topic 25 none of the systems were able to find any of the 2 relevant elements. On the other hand, most systems were more successful on topic 11, which also has only 2 relevant elements. Obviously, topics with sparse relevant elements will have a larger impact on the overall evaluation. It would hence make sense to withdraw such topics from the evaluation.

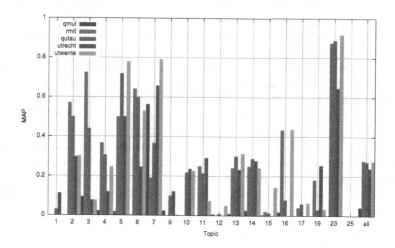

Fig. 4. Mean average precision per topic

Interesting to note that each participant seems to stand out on a number of topics, while performance on the other topics is about average. Furthermore, overall performance for most systems on topics 2 – 7 and 23 seems to be significantly higher than for topics 9 –19. A more detailed analysis on the characteristics of the topics is needed to examine what causes this difference in performance.

6   Discussions at Dagstuhl

At the workshop in Dagstuhl a lively discussion was held, during which the issue was raised that more expertise was needed on image retrieval approaches. It was a common problem that most of the participants did not have an 'off-the-shelf' image retrieval system available and ended up with a poor performing image retrieval strategy. Consequently, their multimedia information retrieval approach suffered, which explains why at current the multimedia-based approaches did not do convincingly better than a plain text-based search.

One of objectives for next year, is to arrange a state-of-the-art image retrieval system that can be used by participants. Ideally, image segmentation and object recognition should be supported by this system.

Another initiative, forthcoming from this discussion is to either extend the Lonely Planet collection with a larger collection of images[2], or to switch to the Wikipedia collection, which is also enriched with a large collection of images. This collection will also be used by the INEX 2006 ad-hoc track [9].

7 Conclusions and Future Work

A detailed analysis of the results for the multimedia track remains to be done. However, at this point we can conclude that, despite the exploratory nature of the first year, many achievements have been realized. We have successfully acquired and exploited the Lonely Planet WorldGuide, which proved to be a very useful starting point to flash out initial problems both in the retrieval approaches and the evaluation methodology. With a minimum extension, we successfully adopted the NEXI query language for *multimedia* structured document retrieval. A topic pool of 23 topics has been created and assessed. Five participating groups succeeded in building a multimedia retrieval system for structured documents and submitted a total of 25 runs for the evaluation.

A solid basis has been created to run the multimedia track again next year. We will have to reconsider many of the choices made, such as for instance the topic creation procedure and the evaluation metrics, which are currently based on the standard TREC methodology (where the retrieval of near-misses is currently not considered).

Acknowledgments

We would like to thank all participants for their efforts in making the first year of the multimedia track a success. In particular, we are grateful for the support we received from Benjamin Piwowarski, who provided the relevance assessments tool. We would like to thank Andrew Trotman, among others, who have helped with the implementation of the NEXI extension. Finally, we would like to express our gratitude towards the Lonely Planet organization for providing us with this interesting XML collection.

References

1. Voorhees, E., Harman, D., eds.: TREC - Experiment and Evaluation in Information Retrieval, MIT Press (2005)
2. Smeaton, A., Kraaij, W., Over, P.:   The TREC Video Retrieval Evaluation (TRECVID): A case study and status report. In: Coupling approaches, coupling media and coupling languages for information retrieval - RIAO 2004, Vaucluse, France (2004) 25 – 37

---

[2] In this case, we will try to obtain access to the stock photography library of the Lonely Planet, which contains a large amount of images associated with a destination. See for more information: `http://www.lonelyplanetimages.com/`.

3. Clough, P., Mueller, H., Sanderson, M.: The CLEF Cross Language Image Retrieval Track (ImageCLEF) 2004. In: Fifth Workshop of the Cross-Language Evaluation Forum (CLEF 2004). Lecture Notes in Computer Science, Springer (2005)

4. Planet, L.: (World guide - http://www.lonelyplanet.com/worldguide/)

5. Trotman, A., Sigurbjornsson, B.: Narrowed Extended XPath I (NEXI). In: Advances in XML Information Retrieval. Volume 3493. Springer, Schloss Dagstuhl, Germany (2005) 16 – 40

6. Lalmas, M., Piwowarski, B.: INEX 2005 relevance assessment guide. In: INEX 2005 Workshop Pre-proceedings. (2005) 391 – 401

7. Buckley, C., Voorhees, E.M.: Retrieval evaluation with incomplete information. In: SIGIR 2004: Proceedings of the 27th annual international ACM SIGIR conference on Research and Development in Information Retrieval, New York, NY, USA, ACM Press (2004) 25 – 32

8. van Zwol, R.: (INEX 2005 Multimedia Track Evaluation Results - http;//contentlab.cs.uu.nl/~roelof/mmtrack/)

9. INEX: (INitiative for the evaluation of XML Retrieval 2006 - http://inex.is.informatik.uni-duisburg.de/2006/)

A   Performance Results

In this appendix the performance of the additional runs that were submitted by participants are reported. Performance results for best runs per group were reported in Section 5.

Table 5. Performance results for rmit

Run	alpha-0.0	alpha-0.1	alpha-0.3	alpha-0.5	alpha-0.9	alpha-1.0
Topics	19	19	19	19	19	19
Ret.	784	784	784	784	784	784
Rel.	448	448	448	448	448	448
Rel. & ret.	202	202	202	202	202	202
MAP	0.2759	0.2771	**0.2779**	0.2764	0.2664	0.2244
Precision@10	0.3053	0.3053	**0.3105**	0.3053	0.2579	0.2105
bpref	0.4455	0.4455	0.4455	0.4455	0.4455	0.4455

Table 6. Performance results for qutau

Run	all Features 5	Fea-all tures 15	Fea-Text Only	all tures 10	Fea-all 15tures 100	Fea-global 3Features 10 100
Topics	19	19	19	19	19	19
Ret.	3767	3793	3366	3882	4009	4132
Rel.	448	448	448	448	448	448
Rel. & ret.	297	297	**303**	300	285	266
MAP	0.1995	0.2064	**0.2711**	0.1844	0.2037	0.2066
Precision@10	0.1947	0.2053	**0.2842**	0.1895	0.2105	0.2053
bpref	0.6507	0.6518	0.6516	**0.6647**	0.6501	0.6319

Table 7. Performance results for utrecht

Run	Text	Annotation	PCA	PCA-cross
Topics	13	17	17	17
Ret.	601	1112	1550	1291
Rel.	188	390	390	390
Rel. & ret.	88	216	216	**220**
MAP	0.2329	**0.24**	0.1769	0.2324
Precision@10	0.2615	0.27	0.2235	**0.2824**
bpref	0.4467	0.51	0.5041	**0.5145**

Table 8. Performance results for utwente

Run	autom. noimg LM 05	manual LM 05	autom. noimg GPX 05	autom. noimg Okapi 15 075	manual GPX 05	manual Okapi 15 075
Topics	19	19	18	19	18	19
Ret.	4750	4750	3142	4750	3826	4750
Rel.	448	448	408	448	408	448
Rel. & ret.	**282**	278	233	216	239	206
MAP	**0.2751**	0.26	0.2567	0.211	0.2627	0.2133
Precision@10	0.2789	0.2579	0.2667	0.2263	**0.2833**	0.2263
bpref	**0.6272**	0.6244	0.5532	0.475	0.5909	0.4853

Integrating Text Retrieval and Image Retrieval in XML Document Searching

D. Tjondronegoro, J. Zhang, J. Gu*, A. Nguyen, and S. Geva

Queensland University of Technology
2 George Street, GPO Box 2434, Brisbane, QLD 4001 Australia
{dian, jinglan.zhang, j2.gu, an.nguyen, s.geva}@qut.edu.au

Abstract. Many XML documents contain a mixture of text and images. Images play an important role in webpage or article presentation. However, popular Information Retrieval systems still largely depend on pure text retrieval as it is believed that text descriptions including body text and the caption of images contain precise information. On the other hand, images are more attractive and easier to understand than pure text. We assume that if the image content is used in addition to the pure text-based retrieval, the retrieval result should be better than text-only or image-only retrieval. We test this hypothesis by doing a series of experiments using the Lonely Planet XML document collection. Two search engines, an XML document search engine using both content and structure based on text, and a content-based image search engine were used at the same time. The results generated by these two search engines were merged together to form a new result. This paper presents our current work, initial results and vision into future work.

1 Introduction

Researchers have studied text retrieval for decades [1]. When text is input into a web browser, the search engine will output something related with the text. However, a traditional query for simple text documents can only return the entire document. In order to improve the functionality and precision of simple text retrieval, the Extensible Markup Language (XML) has been adopted as an industry standard for document formatting by W3C. The XML format contains the document content and metadata. It marks up semantic document elements such as document, paragraph, images, maps, etc. It contains structures and allows exploiting the internal structure in order to find keywords in certain document elements. For example, a traditional document based query can be "return a document that contains an image like this one". An XML document can support the same query. However, it can also support other types of queries requesting more details, e.g. "return the paragraph that contains an image like this one" or "return the images that are similar to the sample image". Structured document searching has attracted intensive research [2-3].

---

* Supported by Jiangsu Government Scholarship of Overseas Studies.

N. Fuhr et al. (Eds.): INEX 2005, LNCS 3977, pp. 511–524, 2006.

A picture is worth a thousand words, and many documents therefore contain a mixture of text and images. For example, almost every webpage contains text and images so that they are more attractive and easier to understand than a page full of text. Images play an important role in webpage or article presentation. However, this information has not been explored sufficiently in traditional Information Retrieval systems, which largely depend on text searching. Many research issues are still open.

Although images can be retrieved using metadata such as captions, authors, date, text description, etc, text-based image retrieval has obvious disadvantages. It is not easy to define a unique set of keywords to one image and when the image database is large it is time consuming to add the keywords. Images can also be retrieved based on its content using features such as colour, texture, and shape extracted from the image and stored in the database. If multiple features are used, the result should be fused to form a single result. Some fuzzy-neural techniques by fusion of texture and colour have been explored in image retrieval [4].

In general, the more information that is used to generate a query, the stricter it is and the more precise the searching results should be. For example, "an excellent IT student" is stricter than "an IT student" which is again stricter than "a student". The text descriptions in an XML document, including the text content or the caption of the image, usually contain more precise information about an image. However, often more information is captured in the image than described in the caption. We assume that if the image content is used in addition to the pure text-based retrieval, the retrieval result should be better than text-only or image-only retrieval in terms of precision/recall. As image specification in the query makes the query stricter than the query without the image, we assume image elements can be treated as if they were text elements containing ordinary keywords.

We propose to use two search engines, an XML document search engine using both content and structure based on text, and a content-based image search engine, at the same time. Multiple tests and image processing algorithms can be implemented. The results generated by these two search engines should be merged together to form a new result. The goal is to include and integrate multiple media types into the retrieval process and to produce a meaningful ranking of documents. This paper presents our current work, initial results, some findings and vision into future work.

The remainder of this paper is organised as follows: Section 2 presents the overall system framework and Section 3 briefly discusses the database management. Section 4 then discusses the XML document searching techniques, while the image processing techniques used are described in Section 5. The result fusion technique used is presented in Section 6, and the implementation and testing is given in Section 7. Finally, Section 8 concludes the paper with a discussion on the evaluation, main lessons learned from the experiments, and vision for future work.

2 System Framework

The diagram shown in Fig. 1 shows the framework and data flow of the prototype system used for the work reported in this paper.

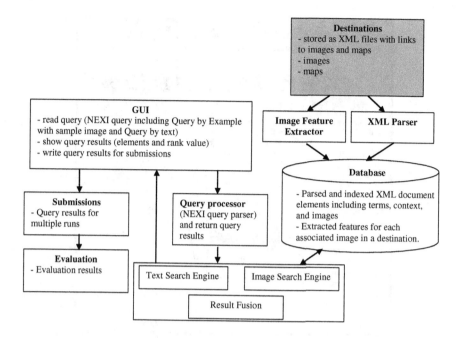

Fig. 1. System Framework

3   Database Management of XML Documents

An existing relational database management system is used to manage the XML documents. XML documents are parsed and document elements are stored and indexed in a database. The structure of the database is shown in Fig. 2. It contains six tables. The **Terms** table is linked to the **List** table through the List_Position field. The document ID in the **Document** table and the context ID in the **Context** table are the foreign keys of the Doc_ID and Context_ID fields in the **List** table respectively. The context ID is also the foreign key of the Context_ID field in the **ImageContext** table. The image file name in the **Images** table is a foreign key of the Term field in the **ImageContext** table.

The text-based searching can start from Term in the **Terms** table, i.e., keywords provided in the query such as mountain, water, etc. Following the links in Fig. 2, we can find where the terms appear, how many times they appear, and retrieve the context of each occurrence. The image-based searching will start from the **Images** table. Given an image name, we can retrieve all its features and calculate the similarity between a sample image and an image in the database. If an image is desirable, we can return the image itself or the context of that image. We assume the same image can appear in multiple documents but within one document, an image just needs to appear once.

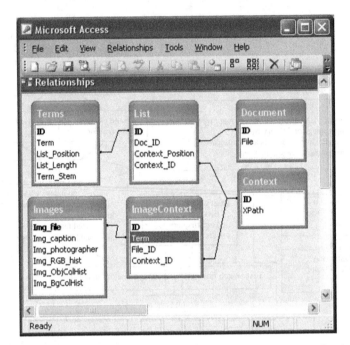

Fig. 2. Database Structure for text- and image-based XML Document Retrieval

4 XML Searching Techniques

4.1 XML File Inversion

In our scheme each term posting in the collection consists of three path elements: the file name, the absolute XPath context, and the ordinal position within the XPath context. The entire collection is inverted and the indexing structure supporting access to the terms inverted lists is stored in a MS Access database (see Fig. 2). Details of the file inversion technique can be found in [5].

4.2 Processing INEX Queries

Processing of complex NEXI expressions is based on parsing of the expression and the incremental construction of a result-tree. The result-tree consists of all the elements in the collection that contains at least one of the keyword in the query (or a synonym or any other term deemed relevant). Each node in the result tree contains the necessary information to allow the computation of a score, using a TF-IDF variant (described in Sect. 3). After the result-tree is constructed, a traversal of the result-tree generates the score for each node, from the leaves to the root node. These results are then organized as a list and sorted by score, with the top N results returned ($N = 250$ for the MM track).

When a NEXI expression contains multiple filters, the system constructs a result-tree for each of the filters. After the score of each node in all trees is determined, the scores of support elements (i.e. elements that satisfy a support filter in the NEXI expression) are used to boost the score of result elements. In this manner, elements with support tend to be ranked higher than elements without support, everything else being equal. More specific details can be found in the paper describing our submission to the ad hoc track, in these proceedings.

4.3 Ranking Scheme

Elements are ranked according to a relevance score. In our scheme, leaf and branch elements need to be treated differently. Data usually occurs at leaf elements, and thus, our inverted list mostly stores information about leaf elements. A leaf element is considered candidate for retrieval if it contains at least one query term. A branch node is candidate for retrieval if it contains a relevant child element. Once an element (either leaf or branch) is deemed to be a candidate for retrieval its relevance score is calculated. A heuristically derived formula (1) is used to calculate the relevance score of leaf elements. The same equation is used for both return and support elements. The score is determined from query terms contained in the element. It penalizes elements with frequently occurring query terms (frequent in the collection), and it rewards elements with more unique query terms within a result element.

Equation 1: Calculation of a Leaf Element's Relevance Judgment Score

$$L = K^{n-1} \sum_{i=1}^{n} \frac{t_i}{f_i} \qquad (1)$$

Here n is the number of unique query terms contained within the leaf element, K is a small integer (we used $K = 5$). The term K^{n-1} scales up the score of elements having multiple distinct query terms. The system is not sensitive to the value of K – we experimented with $K = 5$ to 25 with little difference in results. The sum is over all terms where t_i is the frequency of the ith query term in the leaf element and f_i is the frequency of the ith query term in the collection. This sum rewards the repeat occurrence of query terms with uncommon terms contributing more than common terms.

Once the relevance scores of leaf elements have been calculated, they can be used to calculate the relevance judgment score of branch elements. A naive solution would be to just sum the relevance judgment score of each branch relevant children. However, this would ultimately result in root (i.e. article) elements accumulating at the top of the ranked list, a scenario that offers no advantage over document-level retrieval. Therefore, the relevance score of children elements should be somehow decreased while being propagated up the XML tree. A heuristically derived formula (2) is used to calculate the scores of intermediate branch elements.

Equation 2: Calculation of a Branch Element's Relevance Judgment Score

$$R = D(n)\sum_{i=1}^{n} L_i \qquad (2)$$

Where:

  n = the number of children elements
  $D(n) = 0.49$ if $n = 1$
        0.99 Otherwise
  L_i = the ith return child element

The value of the decay factor D depends on the number of relevant children that the branch has. If the branch has one relevant child then the decay constant is 0.49. A branch with only one relevant child will be ranked lower than its child. If the branch has multiple relevant children the decay factor is 0.99. A branch with many relevant children will be ranked higher than its descendants. Thus, a section with a single relevant paragraph would be judged less relevant than the paragraph itself, but a section with several relevant paragraphs will be ranked higher than any of the paragraphs.

Having computed scores for all results and support elements, the scores of support elements are added to the scores of the corresponding result elements that they support. For instance, consider the query:

$$//A[about(.//B,C)]//X[about(.//Y,Z)]$$

The score of a support element **//A//B** will be added to all result elements **//A//X//Y** where the element **A** is the ancestor of both **B** and **X//Y**.

Finally, the results consist of an entire recall tree for the query where each node is individually scored.

5 Image Processing Techniques

The image features, which have been selected for this experiment are: colour histogram, texture, and detectable-lines. In our database, for each image, we store these features to describe the whole image, the background and the foreground.

5.1 Colour Histogram ($p(r_k)$)

The histogram of a digital image is defined as:

$$h(r_k) = n_k$$

Where r_k is the kth intensity level in the interval $[0, H]$ and n_k is the number of pixels in the image with intensity level equal to r_k. The value of H depends on the image class (i.e. the number of bits used); for example, $H = 255$ when 8 bits are used to define a colour. It is common for the histogram to have N (< 256 for an 8 bit/pixel image) equally spaced bins, each representing a range of data values. The histogram, in this case, would calculate the number of pixels within each range.

A normalized histogram is obtained by dividing all elements of $h(r_k)$ by the total number of pixels in the image, which is denoted by n:

$$p(r_k) = \frac{h(r_k)}{n}$$

Since colour images were used, $p(r_k)$ was computed for each of the red (R), green (G), and blue (B) components. Sixteen bins ($N = 16$) were used such that 48 histogram features were generated.

5.2 Texture ($\Im$)

Texture analysis is frequently based on statistical properties of the intensity histogram. One of the principal approaches for describing the shape of a histogram is by using its *central moments*.

Let r_i be a discrete random variable that indicates intensity levels in an image, and $p(r_i)$ be the corresponding normalized histogram. Given that the range of r_i is 0 to G-1 where G is the number of possible intensity values, a histogram component, $p(r_i)$, is an estimate of the probability of occurrence of intensity value r_i. Thus, central moments can be defined as:

$$\mu_n = \sum_{i=0}^{G-1} (r_i - m)^n \, p(r_i)$$

Where, n is the order of the moment, and m is the mean.

Table 1. Moments used for texture measurement

Moment	Texture Measurement	Equation
Mean	Average intensity	$m = \sum_{i=0}^{G-1} r_i \, p(r_i)$
Standard deviation	Average contrast	$\sigma = \sqrt{\mu_2(r)}$
Smoothness	Relative smoothness of the intensity of a region (0 is for constant intensity and closer to 1 for regions with large excursions in the intensity levels)	$\zeta = 1 - \dfrac{1}{(1+\sigma^2)}$
Third moment	Skewness of histogram (0 is symmetric, negative means skewed to the left whereas positive means skewed to the right)	$\mu_3 = \sum_{i=0}^{G-1} (r_i - m)^3 \, p(r_i)$
Uniformity	Maximum when all gray levels are equal (maximum uniformity) and decreases otherwise	$U = \sum_{i=0}^{G-1} p^2(r_i)$
Entropy	Measurement of randomness	$\Re = \sum_{i=0}^{G-1} p(r_i) \log_2 p(r_i)$

As we are using normalized histograms, the sum of all its components is 1, thus $\mu_0 = 1, \mu_1 = 0$, and:

$$\mu_2 = \sum_{i=0}^{G-1} (r_i - m)^2 p(r_i) ; \text{ and so on.}$$

The higher order moments which can effectively measure texture is described in Table 1. Hence texture is represented by a feature vector of:

$$\Im = [m, \sigma, \zeta, \mu_3, U, \Re].$$

5.3 Detectable Vertical-Horizontal Lines (α)

Hough transform computes projections of an image along specified directions. We can detect straight lines which are formed by strong edges on the edge image (which can be produced by *Sobel* transform).

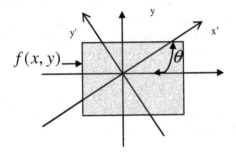

Fig. 3. Geometry of Hough Transform

A projection of a two-dimensional function $f(x, y)$ is a line integral in a certain direction (see Fig. 3). Projections can be computed along any angle θ. The Hough transform of $f(x, y)$ is the line integral of f parallel to the y' axis.

$$H_\theta(x') = \int f(x'\cos\theta - y'\sin\theta, x'\sin\theta + y'\cos\theta) dy'$$

For the purpose of distinguishing images with building(s) as the main object, we have used the statistics of the horizontal and vertical lines. As shown by examples in Fig. 4, images with buildings have stronger detectable horizontal-vertical lines compared to the images with no buildings. It should be noted, nonetheless, that this feature is robust for measuring similarity of other image types, not just for distinguishing buildings. The edge images generated by the process captures the structure of objects and thus the vertical-horizontal line features can be also be used to distinguish between non-building objects.

To capture the characteristics of vertical-horizontal lines of an image, we have used:

$$\alpha = [Vert\{avg, \min, \max, std\}, Horz\{avg, \min, \max, std\}]$$

Where *avg, min, max,* and *std* are the average (mean), minimum, maximum, and standard deviation of the vertical (*Vert*) and horizontal (*Horz*) line's strength. Since the Hough transform returns two vectors containing the strength and the corresponding coordinates along the x'-axis (i.e. the angle), the vertical and horizontal line features are obtained when the angle, $\theta = 180°$ and $90°$ respectively.

Vert{33.40, 0.17, 96.84, 19.17}   *Vert*{34.90, 0.03, 72.03, 20.01}
Horz{33.40, 0.51, 142.78, 37.9359}   *Horz*{34.8966, 0.69, 149.16, 47.76}

Vert{19.46, 0.41, 50.12, 14.60}   *Vert*{13.58, 0.50, 35.14, 8.89}
Horz{19.46, 0.49, 120.15, 33.33}   *Horz*{13.58, 0.07, 156.64, 25.66}

Fig. 4. Vertical-Horizontal Line Features in Images

5.4 Object Extraction

Object(s) can be extracted from an image using the following algorithm:

1. Create a morphological structuring element (*SE*) with a radius of *R* pixels (experimentally set to disk-shaped with *R* = 20).
2. Temporary background (*BG'*) is created by removing objects in original image (*I*) with a radius less than *R* pixels by opening it with the structuring element created in step 1. This operation also estimates the background illumination.
3. Subtract *BG'* from *I* to create the temporary foreground (*FG'*).
4. Binary foreground (FG") is generated by converting FG' into binary by applying *Otsu*'s global image threshold[1].
5. To create the final foreground image (*FG*):
   - For every pixels in FG", if the value = 1, restore the original intensity value of the pixel (based on *I*); Else preset the intensity value to a non-FG value such as black (e.g. R = 0, G = 0, B = 0).
6. To create the final background image (BG):
   - For every pixels in FG", if the value = 0, restore the original intensity value of the pixel (based on *I*); Else preset the intensity value to a non-BG value such as black (e.g. R = 0, G = 0, B = 0).

---

[1] Otsu, N., "A Threshold Selection Method from Gray-Level Histograms," IEEE Transactions on Systems, Man, and Cybernetics, vol. 9, no. 1, 1979, pp. 62-66.

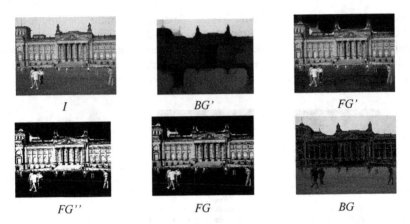

I BG' FG'

FG'' FG BG

Fig. 5. The Process of Object(s) Extraction

The effectiveness of the object extraction algorithm can be demonstrated by the sample scenarios shown in Figs 5 to 8.

5.5 Similarity Calculation and Ranking

Although the physical meanings of different image features are different, they can all be represented by vectors. We used one vector to describe each feature of the image. Thus distance calculation approach can be applied uniformly for different features. We simply use the Euclidean Distance between two vectors, i.e.

$d(v_1, v_2) = \sqrt{\sum_i (v_1(i) - v_2(i))^2}$ for all elements in the two vectors. As all images are

transformed to the same size, the distance calculation is size-invariant and the two vectors are always the same length. All distances are normalized to the range of [0, 1].

6   Result Fusion

The additional complication that is introduced through the addition of image retrieval cues in the NEXI expression is that we need to combine the scores of image elements with the scores of text elements. Rather than re-write much of our code we have decided to treat image elements as if they were text elements containing ordinary keywords. When a NEXI filter specified an image as a retrieval cue we proceeded to generate element scores in two steps. In the first stage, we used image processing techniques to rank the images in the collection for similarity (using features described in Sect. 5). Images were ranked in the range [0, 1]. In the second stage, we heuristically assigned to each image element a pseudo-term frequency, just like we assign a term frequency to every node that contains a given term when we process a textual node. With this, an image node that was ranked first on the basis of image features can be made more dominant by being assigned a pseudo term frequency of say 5, while an image node ranked 250 might be assigned a node frequency of 1. In this

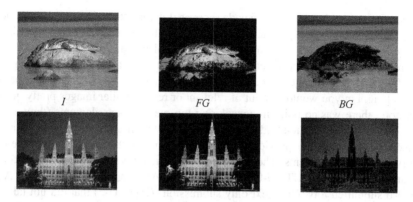

Fig. 6. Images with one dominant object

Fig. 7. Images with multiple objects of interest

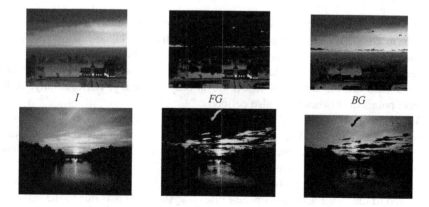

Fig. 8. Images with background as a more dominant feature

manner, we were able to compute a node score as if it consisted of text elements, and we could then seamlessly apply the text ranking scheme that we used for text retrieval.

In our submissions we experimented with several variations over the set of image features used, the length of the candidate images list to be considered, and the pseudo term frequency. The length of candidate images list was varied because the list was always long, but you would run out of relevant or really similar images pretty quickly. Therefore, there was no point in considering too many image elements (though there were only a couple of thousand images in the collection anyway). The pseudo term frequency was varied to provide different weightings between the image elements relative to the text elements. These submissions basically varied in the above parameters and were labelled QUTAU-0, QUTAU-1, QUTAU-3, QUTAU-4, and QUTAU-5. We also submitted a baseline text only submission (QUTAU-2) that did not take into account any image features. The hypothesis is of course that the use of image features would improve precision/recall.

Table 2. Summary results for INEX MM submissions

Measures[†]	QUTAU-0	QUTAU-1	QUTAU-2	QUTAU-3	QUTAU-4	QUTAU-5
topics	19	19	19	19	19	19
Retrieved	3767	3793	3366	3882	4009	4132
Relevant	448	448	448	448	448	448
Rel. ret.	297	297	303	300	285	266
map	0.1995	0.2064	0.2711	0.1844	0.2037	0.2066
R-prec	0.2094	0.2116	0.2641	0.1892	0.1986	0.2181
bpref	0.6507	0.6518	0.6516	0.6647	0.6501	0.6319
Recip_rank	0.4657	0.504	0.5414	0.4561	0.4901	0.5134

[†] *Retrieved* – Total number of document fragments retrieved over all queries; *Relevant* – Total number of relevant document fragments over all queries; *Rel. ret.* – Total number of relevant document fragments retrieved over all queries; *map* – Mean Average Precision; *R-prec* – R-Precision (Precision after R (= number of relevant for topic) document fragments retrieved); *bpref* – Binary Preference (top R judged non-relevant); *recip_rank* – Reciprocal rank of top relevant document.

The assessment of the fusion quality was conducted manually based on statistical (e.g. term frequency) and visual criteria (e.g. image) by human assessors through comparing the retrieval results of different combinations between text and image retrieval with varying weight factors. Along the spectrum of this combination, the two extreme ends are the results of text-retrieval-only and image-retrieval-only. A few discrete points in between were also defined.

An online evaluation tool provided by INEX2005 organizers was used as the evaluation environment. Fig. 9 shows the Interpolated Recall Precision Averages (IRPA), which shows the precision at various recall levels for the different submissions. A summary of the results is tabulated in Table 2.

The text-retrieval-only system can be observed to be superior at all recall levels compared to the fused text- and image-retrieval systems. This is due to the text in the document body and captions of being too well tagged and annotated, and thus high recall performance can be achieved with the text alone. The addition of image

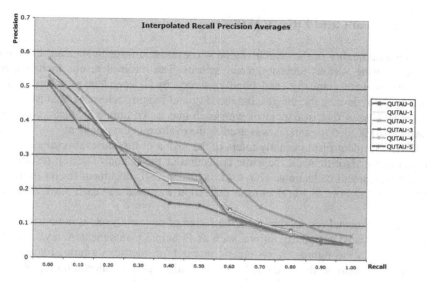

Fig. 9. Recall-Precision results for INEX MM submissions

retrieval results, on the other hand, seems to degrade performance. The difference between the various fused text and image systems are not statistically significant, but in general performed better when a higher text retrieval weighting was used. The results do not imply that image retrieval is not effective nor does it mean that we reject our hypothesis that image features would improve precision/recall; the text was simply too well annotated to allow image features to improve recall. Despite this, image retrieval cues showed potential from their recall performances. This is promising since no semantic or higher level image processing was incorporated into the image retrieval process.

7   Implementation and Testing

The prototype system was implemented on a PC using an existing database management system (Microsoft ACCESS). The C# programming language in the .NET framework was used to implement the text search engine. The image search engine is also implemented using C#, while the image feature extractor is implemented using the MATLAB programming language. Both MATLAB and C# support access to the database.

The test dataset used was a comprehensive database of XML documents containing text- and image- based information on holiday destinations, namely, the Lonely Planet XML document collection. This collection was provided by INEX2005 organizing committee. This database contains a total of 463 XML documents and 1947 images, which contain various types of contents such as landscape, people, and buildings.

8 Conclusion and Future Work

The retrieval quality of the search engine was evaluated through standard evaluation measures using various precision/recall metrics. The retrieval results including text and images were manually (and blindly) scored by independent assessors. This is done through viewing the images and the text, and judging relevance against a stated information need that is associated with each query. An online evaluation tool provided by INEX2005 organizers was used as the evaluation environment.

XML document fusion usually refers to the fusion of the retrieval results of multiple searching algorithms on the same collection or the fusion of search results from multiple document collections. Our work involves XML document fusion in the former case as only one single document collection was used and each XML document was unique.

The experimental results show that the fusion of two result sets is not a trivial task. More complicated fusion algorithms such as Principal Component Analysis need to be explored in the future. A systematic research on metrics (criteria) for assessing fusion quality also needs to be conducted. It is still a great challenge on the objective and automatic assessment of the fusion quality.

In addition, the performance of the system at low recall levels need to be studied, since image similarity is a very limited retrieval cue and a long tail of similar images will unlikely produce improved results. Despite this, the experiments have shown that the image retrieval cues performed relatively well. Higher-level image understanding techniques will likely enhance the retrieval process and is a subject of future investigations.

The current INEX image collection also requires revision since it was not large enough, and secondly, it was too well annotated to allow image features to improve recall. As such no system was able to improve on the text-only alternative. However, it is envisaged that with further investigations on a larger database, the use of image content in addition to pure text-retrieval, should lead to significant improvement in retrieval performance results.

References

1. T. Bray, J. Paoli, and C. Sperberg-McQueen, Extensible Markup Language (XML) 1.0, W3C recommendation, (1998)
2. I. Schlieder and H. Meuss, Querying and ranking XML document. Journal of the American Society for Information Science and Technology, 53(6), (2002), 489-503
3. A. Trotman, Searching structured documents. Journal of Information Processing and Management 40, (2004), 619-632.
4. B. Verma, S.Kulkarni, A fuzzy-neural approach for interpretation and fusion of colour and texture features for CBIR system, Applied Soft Computing 5, (2004), 119-130.
5. S. Geva, GPX-Gardens Point XML Information Retrieval at INEX2004, Advances in XML Information Retrieval – Third International workshop of the Initiative for the Evaluation of XML Retrieval (INEX), (2004), 211-223.

Combining Image and Structured Text Retrieval

D.N.F. Awang Iskandar, Jovan Pehcevski, James A. Thom,
and S.M.M. Tahaghoghi

School of Computer Science and Information Technology, RMIT University
Melbourne, Australia
{dayang, jovanp, jat, saied}@cs.rmit.edu.au

Abstract. Two common approaches in retrieving images from a collection are
retrieval by text keywords and retrieval by visual content. However, it is widely
recognised that it is impossible for keywords alone to fully describe visual content. This paper reports on the participation of the RMIT University group in the
INEX 2005 multimedia track, where we investigated our approach of combining
evidence from a content-oriented XML retrieval system and a content-based image retrieval system using a linear combination of evidence. Our approach yielded
the best overall result for the INEX 2005 Multimedia track using the standard
evaluation measures. We have extended our work by varying the parameter for
the linear combination of evidence, and we have also examined the performance
of runs submitted by participants by using the newly proposed HiXEval evaluation metric. We show that using CBIR in conjunction with text search leads to
better retrieval performance.

1 Introduction

In a large document collection, it is common to find multimedia elements such as
images, audio, and video. Describing these multimedia elements in a standard way
is beneficial as it can assist the retrieval process. The eXtensible Markup Language
(XML) is a standard developed by the World Wide Web Consortium to describe data
in a structured manner, allowing the description of multimedia elements to be represented. The INitiative for the Evaluation of XML Retrieval (INEX) provides a platform
for participants to evaluate the effectiveness of their XML retrieval techniques using
uniform scoring procedures, and a forum to compare results. INEX 2005 comprised
seven tracks. The multimedia track was established with the aim of retrieving relevant
XML document fragments containing various types of multimedia [1], of which only text
and images were used. Besides RMIT University, four other groups participated in the
multimedia track — Queensland University of Technology (QUTAU), Utrecht University (UTRECHT), University of Twente (UTWENTE) and Queen Mary University of
London (QMUL).

The aim of the RMIT University group in participating in the INEX 2005 MM track
was to explore and analyse methods for combining evidence from content-based image retrieval (CBIR) with content-oriented XML retrieval. In this paper, we describe a

---

[1] Multimedia Track @ INEX,
http://inex.is.informatik.uni-duisburg.de:2004/presentations/
INEX-MM-track.pdf

N. Fuhr et al. (Eds.): INEX 2005, LNCS 3977, pp. 525–539, 2006.

```
<?xml version="1.0" encoding="ISO-8859-1"?>
<!DOCTYPE inex_topic SYSTEM "topic.dtd">
<inex_topic topic_id="mm6" inex_track="MM" query_type="CAS" ct_no="14">
<castitle>
//destination[about(., Europe) and about(.//culture//history, king queen)]
//images//image[about(., royal palace residence src:/images/BN7386_10.jpg)]
</castitle>
<description> From all European destinations that were ruled by either
a king or a queen in their cultural history, find images depicting a royal
palace residence. </description>
<narrative>We are a group of historians interested in royal palaces. We
want to visit destinations that contain at least one royal palace. We are
focused on European destinations that were ruled by either a king or a
queen in their cultural history. From these destinations, we want to find
images depicting a royal palace residence.</narrative>
</inex_topic>
```

Fig. 1. Example of a multimedia CAS query with image BN7386_10.jpg, the Royal Palace in Norway (original in colour), in the target element of the query

fusion system that combines evidence and ranks the query results based on text and image similarity. The fusion system consists of two subsystems: the GNU Image Finding Tool (GIFT), and the hybrid XML retrieval system. A technique for linear combination of evidence is used to merge the relevance scores from the two subsystems. Six runs submitted by our group are considered to evaluate the relative importance of image and content-based text components, and these are also compared against the approaches of other participants. The TREC evaluation metric (TRECeval) is used as the official assessment method. We evaluate the performance of our approaches in the INEX 2005 MM track using the standard TRECeval measures: P@1, P@5, P@10, MAP and R-Prec.

We extend our work on the initially submitted runs to further examine the parameter that influences the weighting scheme between the two subsystems. We evaluate the performance of runs submitted by all the INEX 2005 MM track participants using a newlyproposed evaluation metric, namely HiXEval [5]. We also discuss results obtained from the extended work and the HiXEval evaluation in this paper.

The remainder of this paper is organised as follows. In Section 2, we present the multimedia topics and their corresponding relevance judgements. We describe our approach to retrieve the XML document fragments and the associated images based on these multimedia topics in Section 3. In Section 4, we present results obtained from our experiments. Related work on combination of evidence for retrieving image and text are briefly explained in Section 5. We conclude in Section 6 with a discussion of our findings and suggestions for future work.

2   Multimedia Topics and Relevance Judgements

The INEX 2005 multimedia retrieval task focuses on combination of text and images. The *WorldGuide* collection — referred as the Lonely Planet collection in the MM track — was utilised, which was provided by the Lonely Planet organisation[2]. As an initial task, multimedia track participants were asked to propose several topics that might represent typical information needs expressed by users of the collection. As an example, one of the topics proposed by our group is "European destinations ruled by a king or a queen that have a palace". The full specification of this topic and the query image that depicts the royal palace in Norway is shown in Fig. 1.

Two types of queries are explored in INEX using the Narrowed Extended XPath I (NEXI) query: content-only (CO) and content-and-structure (CAS). CO queries are free text queries, while CAS queries contain explicit structural constraints of the desired target and support elements. The multimedia track uses the latter query type to represent a topic. The multimedia query is contained in the `castitle` element which represents the information to be retrieved from the Lonely Planet collection.

The CAS query consists of two elements: target and support. The target element of the query is the last node in the query path, and specifies the element that should be returned as the result. Support elements specify additional structural constraints that should be met. For the topic in Fig. 1, the target element of the query

```
//destination//images//image
```

indicates that the element to be retrieved is an `image` element which contains an image reference in the source (`src`). The support elements of the query are:

```
//destination
//destination//culture//history
//destination//images//image
```

In total, twenty-three multimedia topics that have corresponding relevance judgements were formulated for this collection. These belong to three categories:

1. Topics that contain only text. This topic category does not include any image references in either the target or support elements;
2. Topics that contain a mixture of images and text, where the image reference is explicitly given in the `about` clause of the support elements; and

---

[2] http://www.lonelyplanet.com/

3. Topics that contain a mixture of images and text, except that here the image reference is explicitly stated in the about clause of the target element.

The number of multimedia topics in each category is shown in Table 1. The example given in Fig. 1 belongs to the third topic category.

Relevance judgements for the multimedia topics are divided into two sets: *official* and *extended*. The *official* assessment set includes 19 topics that contain results that match the relevance judgements. The *extended* assessment set has 23 topics, of which the additional four topics contain results that do not match the relevance judgements. These four topics were misinterpreted during the relevance judgements procedure. The *official* assessment set is used for comparing the submitted runs from the INEX 2005 MM track participants.

Table 1. Topic category, number of topics and retrieval systems used, and collection involved

Topic category	1	2	3
Number of *official* topics	8	4	7
Number of *extended* topics	12	4	7
Retrieval system used	Hybrid XML	Hybrid XML and GIFT	Hybrid XML and GIFT
Collection involved	Text only	Text and image	Text and image

3   Our Approach

In this section, we describe our fusion system that consists of two subsystems to obtain the results for the multimedia queries. Since the XML document structure serves as a semantic backbone for retrieval of the multimedia fragments, we use a content-oriented hybrid XML retrieval system [4] to retrieve the relevant document fragments. The GNU Image Finding Tool (GIFT)[3], a content-based image retrieval system, is used to retrieve the results based on the visual features of the images.

We aim to achieve the *chorus effect*. According to Vogt and Cottrell [9], "The chorus effect occurs when several retrieval approaches suggest that an item is relevant to a query ... this tends to be stronger evidence for relevance than a single approach doing so". To achieve this, we use data fusion techniques to combine the evidence from GIFT and the content-oriented hybrid XML retrieval system in three phases [8]:

1. The *collection selection* phase identifies the document collection that is most likely to contain relevant document fragments for the user queries.
2. The *document fragment selection* phase determines the number of relevant document fragments to be retrieved from the document collection.
3. The *merging* (or *fusion*) phase combines the evidence from multiple retrieval systems.

---

[3] http://www.gnu.org/software/gift/

3.1   Phase One: Collection Selection

We view the Lonely Planet collection as having three different groups of information items that are related to one another. The first group contains the XML text documents, the second contains images, and the third contains maps. As illustrated in Table 1, the XML text documents are used to process all the queries, while the image data is used for only the queries in topic categories 2 and 3. The map data was not used, since the topic which specified the map as the target element was not assessed.

3.2   Phase Two: Document Fragment Selection

In this phase, each subsystem retrieves document fragments (text or images) and returns a list of retrieval status values (RSVs) presented in descending order. First 250 top-ranked document fragments are returned from our content-oriented hybrid XML retrieval system. For GIFT, the RSVs of all the images in the collection are returned. The following sections explain how each subsystem is used to generate RSVs for each multimedia query; the lists are later merged in phase three to produce the final results.

Content-Based Image Retrieval. Content-based image retrieval aims to retrieve images on the basis of features automatically extracted from the images themselves. The

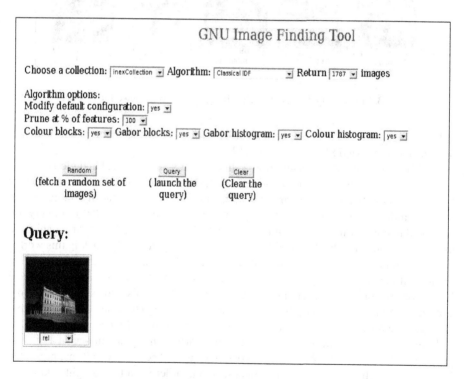

Fig. 2. Querying image BN7386_10.jpg into GIFT (original in colour)

Fig. 3. First twenty results of a GIFT image query (best viewed in colour)

GIFT system indexes an image collection by extracting image features and indexing them using an inverted file data structure [7].

GIFT uses the HSV (Hue-Saturation-Value) colour space for local and global colour features [7]. For extracting the image texture, a bank of circularly symmetric Gabor filters is used. GIFT evaluates and calculates the query image and the target image feature similarity based on the data from the inverted file. The results of a query are presented to the user in the form of a ranked list. GIFT also provides the mechanism to perform relevance feedback. We did not perform any relevance feedback in this work.

For the multimedia topics, we presented the images listed in the source (`src`) element of the multimedia CAS query as the query image to GIFT. We used the default Classical IDF algorithm and set the search pruning option to 100%. This allows us to perform a complete feature evaluation for the query image, even though the query processing time is longer. We retrieved and ranked all the images in the Lonely Planet collection.

Referring to the multimedia topic presented earlier, the query image of Fig. 1 is provided to GIFT and Fig. 2 is a screenshot of the query. The query results are presented in Fig. 3, where the RSVs are ranked in descending order from left to right, and top to bottom.

Table 2. The values for P@n, MAP and R-Prec using TRECeval and HiXEval for each run submitted by INEX 2005 MM track participants

Run	TRECeval					HiXEval				
	P@1	P@5	P@10	MAP	R-Prec	P@1	P@5	P@10	MAP	R-Prec
RMIT										
rmit-0	0.4737	*0.3684*	0.3053	0.2759	*0.3267*	0.3498	0.2668	0.2179	0.1952	*0.2485*
rmit-1	0.4737	*0.3684*	0.3053	0.2771	*0.3267*	0.3491	*0.2669*	0.2177	0.1958	0.2485
rmit-2	0.4737	*0.3684*	*0.3105*	*0.2779*	0.3259	0.3465	0.2664	*0.2216*	*0.1960*	0.2479
rmit-3	0.4737	*0.3684*	0.3053	0.2764	0.3259	0.3488	0.2563	0.2176	0.1953	0.2479
rmit-4	*0.5263*	0.3368	0.2579	0.2664	0.3168	*0.4014*	0.2358	0.1938	0.1930	0.2429
rmit-5	0.4737	0.2737	0.2105	0.2244	0.2525	0.3626	0.2150	0.1671	0.1700	0.1935
QUTAU										
qutau-0	0.4211	0.2737	0.1947	0.1995	0.2094	0.3098	0.1970	0.1457	0.1557	0.1445
qutau-1	*0.4737*	0.2737	0.2053	0.2064	0.2116	0.3135	0.2046	0.1538	0.1582	0.1473
qutau-2	*0.4737*	*0.3579*	*0.2842*	*0.2711*	*0.2641*	0.3161	*0.2602*	*0.2132*	*0.1937*	*0.1871*
qutau-3	0.3684	0.2842	0.1895	0.1844	0.1892	0.2600	0.2037	0.1519	0.1429	0.1360
qutau-4	0.4211	0.3053	0.2105	0.2037	0.1986	0.2575	0.2475	0.1715	0.1532	0.1535
qutau-5	*0.4737*	0.2842	0.2053	0.2066	0.2181	*0.4181*	0.2210	0.1715	0.1744	0.1751
UTRECHT										
utrecht-0	0.4615	0.3385	0.2615	0.2329	*0.2776*	0.3278	0.2007	0.1537	0.1229	0.1627
utrecht-1	*0.5294*	*0.3529*	0.2706	*0.2392*	0.2747	*0.3481*	*0.2497*	*0.1965*	*0.1581*	*0.1974*
utrecht-2	0.3529	0.2941	0.2235	0.1769	0.2073	0.2678	0.2094	0.1487	0.1165	0.1519
utrecht-3	*0.5294*	0.3294	0.2824	0.2324	0.2648	*0.3481*	0.2462	0.1914	0.1477	0.1864
utrecht-4	*0.5294*	0.3294	0.2824	0.2324	0.2648	*0.3481*	0.2462	0.1914	0.1477	0.1864
utrecht-5	0.1579	0.0632	0.0737	0.0554	0.0697	0.1313	0.0524	0.0593	0.0440	0.0567
UTWENTE										
utwente-0	*0.4211*	0.3053	0.2789	*0.2751*	*0.2799*	*0.3559*	*0.2555*	**0.2255**	**0.2208**	*0.2266*
utwente-1	*0.4211*	0.2947	0.2579	0.26	0.2692	*0.3559*	0.2545	0.2246	0.2129	0.2216
utwente-2	0.3889	0.3444	0.2667	0.2567	0.2434	0.2894	0.2346	0.1738	0.1689	0.1681
utwente-3	0.2105	0.2211	0.2263	0.211	0.2227	0.1773	0.1877	0.1739	0.1400	0.1549
utwente-4	0.3889	*0.3556*	*0.2833*	0.2627	0.2458	0.2894	0.2475	0.1896	0.1739	0.1680
utwente-5	0.2105	0.2211	0.2263	0.2133	0.2196	0.1773	0.1877	0.1740	0.1423	0.1518
QMUL										
qmul-0	*0.0526*	*0.0211*	*0.0368*	*0.0412*	*0.0423*	*0.0526*	*0.0211*	*0.0354*	*0.0376*	*0.0409*

Italic values – best performance among runs for each participating group and each measure.
Bold values – best overall performance among all runs for each measure.

Content-Oriented Hybrid XML Retrieval. The second subsystem we used for text retrieval in the INEX 2005 MM track follows a *hybrid* XML retrieval approach [4], combining information retrieval features from Zettair[4] (a full-text search engine) with XML-specific retrieval features from eXist[5] (a native XML database).

Each multimedia topic was first automatically translated into a Zettair query. Terms that appear in the castitle part of the topic (with all structural query constraints and

---

[4] http://www.seg.rmit.edu.au/zettair/
[5] http://exist-db.org/

image references completely removed) were used to formulate the Zettair query. A list of (up to) 250 `destination` elements were presented in a descending order according to their estimated likelihood of relevance. To retrieve *elements* rather than full articles, a second topic translation module was used to formulate a query to eXist. As the support and target parts of each multimedia query were strictly matched, both the terms and the structural query constraints from the topic (without the actual image references) were used to formulate the eXist query. We used the eXist OR query operator to generate the element answer list for a given topic. The answer list contains (up to) 250 matching elements, taken from articles that were highly ranked in the list of articles previously returned by Zettair.

Lastly, a post-processing retrieval module with an XML-specific ranking heuristic (TPF) [6] was used to rank and produce the final list of RSVs.

3.3   Phase Three: Merging Evidence of CBIR and Hybrid XML Retrieval

To fuse the two RSV lists into a single ranked result list R for the multimedia queries, we use a simple linear combination of evidence [1]:

$$R = \alpha \cdot S_I + (1 - \alpha) \cdot S_T$$

Here, α is a weighting parameter (determines the weight of GIFT versus hybrid XML retrieval), S_I represents the image RSV obtained from GIFT, and S_T is the RSV of the same image obtained from the hybrid XML retrieval system.

To investigate the effect of giving certain biases to a system, we vary the α value between 0 to 1. When the value of α is set to 1, only the RSVs from GIFT are used. On the other hand, only the hybrid XML retrieval RSVs are used when the value of α is set to 0. For the INEX 2005 MM track, we submitted six runs with the α value set to 0.0, 0.1, 0.3, 0.5, 0.9 and 1.0, respectively. Results obtained from these runs, which we denote as `rmit-0` to `rmit-5`, are shown in Table 2.

4   Experiments and Results

In this section we provide a description of the evaluation metrics used, and we analyse results obtained from the official INEX 2005 multimedia runs submitted by each participating group, including those obtained from the additional RMIT runs.

4.1   Evaluation Metrics

The TREC evaluation metric was adopted for the multimedia track assessment in INEX 2005. Binary relevance judgements were used to evaluate the runs. We evaluated our results based on the standard recall and precision retrieval performance measures. The following measures were used:

- Precision at cut-off (P@n): Precision after n document fragments have been retrieved.

- Mean Average Precision (MAP): The mean of the average precisions calculated for each topic. Average precision is the average of the precisions calculated at each natural recall level.
- Recall-precision (R-prec): Precision after the total number of relevant document fragments have been retrieved.
- Average interpolated precision at 11 standard recall levels (0%-100%).

In addition to the above evaluation measures, we also report values obtained with HiXE-val, an alternative evaluation metric for XML retrieval that is solely based on the amount of highlighted relevant information [5]. The reported values are: P@n, which measures the proportion of relevant information to all the information retrieved at a rank n; MAP, the mean average precision calculated at natural recall levels; and R-prec, which reflects the measured precision after the total number of relevant document fragments have been retrieved.

4.2 Result Analysis

We present the analysis and evaluation for INEX 2005 multimedia runs and additional RMIT runs based on the 19 topics that belong to the *official* multimedia assessment set.

Official INEX 2005 Multimedia Runs. We analyse the runs submitted by the INEX MM track participants using both TRECeval and HiXEval evaluation met-

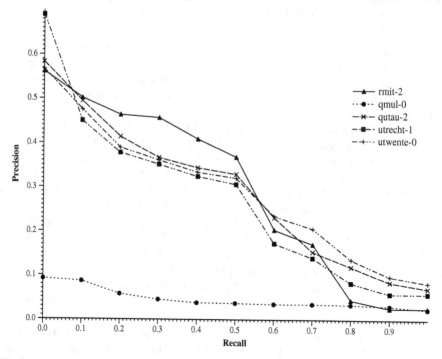

Fig. 4. Interpolated average precision at 11 standard recall levels using TRECeval for the best performing runs submitted by the INEX 2005 MM track participants

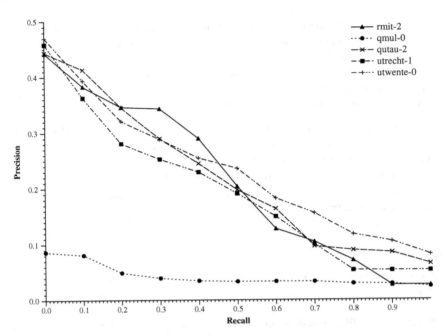

Fig. 5. Interpolated average precision at 11 standard recall levels using HiXEval for the best performing runs submitted by the INEX 2005 MM track participants

rics. As presented in Table 2, we report results obtained with precision at cut-offs 1, 5, 10, and with MAP and R-Prec for both metrics. For each participating group, the best performance under each measure is shown in italics. For each evaluation measure, the best run performance observed among all participants is shown in bold.

Using the TRECeval evaluation metric, UTRECHT performed best for P@1. However, our best run outperformed the others for P@5, P@10, MAP and R-prec. Using HiXEval as an evaluation metric, QUTAU performed best for P@1, our best run again outperformed the others for P@5 and R-Prec, while UTWENTE performed best for P@10 and MAP. The difference in the observed behaviour between the two metrics can be explained by the fact that the two metrics are based on different evaluation methodologies. Indeed, recall under TRECeval is measured as the fraction of relevant *elements* retrieved, whereas HiXEval uses the fraction of relevant *information contained by the elements* retrieved [5]. Arguably, a finer level of evaluation detail is captured by HiXEval which is not captured by TRECeval. This, in turn, suggests that, for the MAP measure of HiXEval, on average the best performing UTWENTE run is indeed capable of retrieving larger quantities of relevant information than our best performing run.

Figure 4 illustrates the performance for the multimedia track participants based on the highest MAP values of the runs using TRECeval. Figure 5 shows the same graph pattern when using HiXEval as the evaluation metric. Both graphs show that, with the exception of QMUL, the observed average performance among the best runs submitted by participants was similar.

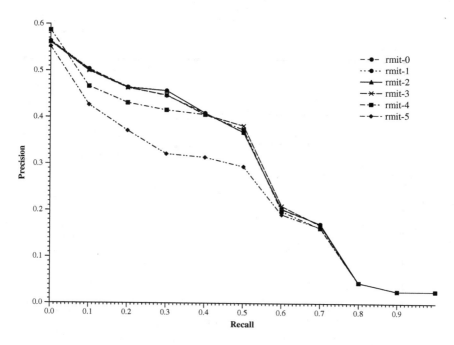

Fig. 6. Interpolated average precision at 11 standard recall levels using TRECeval for the six official RMIT runs submitted to the INEX 2005 MM track

Additional RMIT Runs. As shown in Table 2, at one document fragment retrieved the highest precision among the RMIT runs is observed for run `rmit-4` (with the value for $\alpha = 0.9$). There is no visible difference in precision for all the other runs with `P@1`. With `P@5`, combining evidence from text and image at the same weight ($\alpha = 0.5$) leads to similar performance as when α values of 0.0, 0.1 and 0.3 are used (reflected by the observed performance of runs `rmit-0` to `rmit-3`). The precision values drop as the α value is increased. With `MAP`, the run `rmit-2` ($\alpha = 0.3$) produces the best performance. With `R-prec`, runs `rmit-0` and `rmit-1` perform best and exhibit almost the same performance.

Based on Fig. 6, three RMIT runs (`rmit-0`, `rmit-1` and `rmit-2`) produce the best overall interpolated precision averages. Run `rmit-4` performed best at low recall levels. A constant performance can be seen for all the runs for recall level of 0.8 and above.

To analyse the changes in performance when the parameter α varies between 0 and 1, we performed additional runs at α intervals of 0.05. Figure 7 shows the performance of our runs for twenty different values of the parameter α, as measured by `P@1`, `P@5` and `P@10`. We observe that, to achieve the best performance under `P@1`, values for 0.85 and 0.9 should be used for the parameter α. On the other hand, the best performance under `P@5` and `P@10` is achieved when $\alpha = 0.4$.

The highest `MAP` performance is observed when $\alpha = 0.25$, which can be seen in Fig. 8. On the other hand, the highest `R-prec` performance is obtained when α is less than 0.15. Figure 9 illustrates the `R-Prec` performance when all the 20 α values are used.

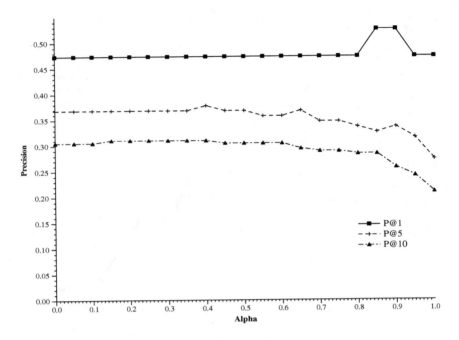

Fig. 7. Precision at cut-off 1, 5 and 10 for α values between 0.0 to 1.0

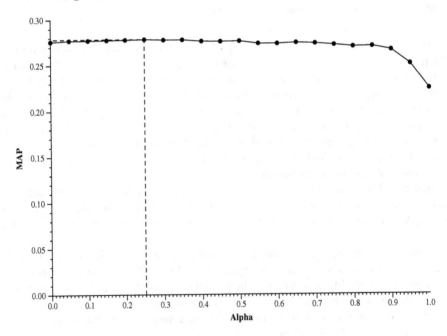

Fig. 8. Mean Average Precision for α values between 0.0 to 1.0

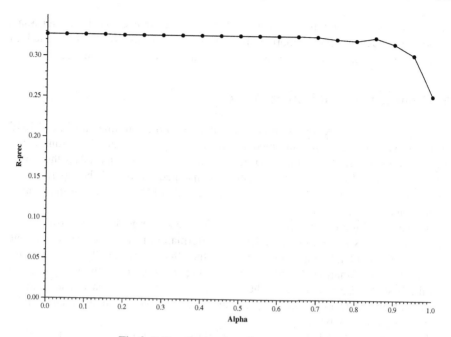

Fig. 9. R-Prec for α values between 0.0 to 1.0

We conclude that the content-oriented XML retrieval system benefits by using some evidence from a CBIR system; indeed, as measured by MAP and R-prec, increasing the weight of the hybrid XML retrieval system component in the fusion system yields better performance than when any of the two subsystems are used in isolation. When only a CBIR system is used to retrieve multimedia document fragments, precision is poor.

5   Related Work

Data fusion, also known as combination of evidence, is a method of merging multiple sources of evidence. In information retrieval, data fusion has been shown to improve the retrieval effectiveness when compared to using a single retrieval strategy [3, 8, 9].

Multimedia retrieval using combination of evidence has been studied by Haque [2], who compared the retrieval performance of using only image and multimedia (combination of text and image). He conducted experiments using three types of combining algorithms: *feature merging, weighted sum of ranking score*, and *weighted sum of inverse rank position*. Haque concluded that using a combination of evidence, multimedia retrieval performs better than image retrieval. The *weighted sum of inverse rank position* algorithm is shown to have the highest eleven point average precision in the multimedia retrieval, while the *weighted sum of ranking score* algorithm performed slightly lower than the *weighted sum of inverse rank position* algorithm.

Aslandogan and Yu [1] have compared the retrieval performance of indexing images of people on the Web using four approaches: text evidence followed by face detection, face detection and recognition, linear combination of evidence, and Dempster-Shafer theory of evidence. They reported that linear combination of evidence and the Dempster-Shafer theory of evidence yielded the same retrieval performance.

6 Conclusions and Future Work

In this paper we have reported on our participation in the multimedia track of INEX 2005. As part of the XML-multimedia retrieval task, we submitted six runs for the official evaluation by the multimedia track organisers. These runs reflect the various relative weights of 0 to 1. Our approach demonstrated the overall best performance for P@5, P@10, MAP and R-Prec in the INEX 2005 MM track using the standard evaluation measures.

We have used the linear combination of evidence to merge the RSVs from two retrieval subsystems for retrieving multimedia information from structured documents. We also carried out additional runs to examine the effect of varying the parameter used for the linear combination of evidence (α). Having $\alpha = 0.25$ leads to the highest MAP, and the best R-prec values are when α is less than 0.15. We have also evaluated the submitted runs from the participants using HiXEval, where we observed a slightly different performance behaviour.

We conclude that a CBIR system needs a substantial support from a text-based system to effectively retrieve the desired images in a collection. Conversely, retrieving images based only on the surrounding text can be achieved without using a CBIR system, but better retrieval performance will be observed if some evidence from a CBIR system is incorporated.

We plan to extend this work by investigating different evidence combination methods for retrieving structured text and multimedia elements.

Acknowledgements

This research was undertaken using facilities supported by the Australian Research Council and an RMIT VRII grant. We acknowledge Lonely Planet for the permission to publish the images, and thank Jonathan Yu for his assistance in proposing and assessing one of the INEX 2005 multimedia topics.

References

1. Y. A. Aslandogan and C. T. Yu. Evaluating Strategies and Systems for Content-Based Indexing of Person Images on the Web. In *MULTIMEDIA 2000: Proceedings of the Eighth ACM International Conference on Multimedia*, pages 313–321, New York, NY, USA, 2000. ACM Press.
2. N. Haque. *Image Ranking for Multimedia Retrieval*. Ph.D. thesis, School of Computer Science and Information Technology, Royal Melbourne Institute of Technology, 2003.
3. J. H. Lee. Analyses of Multiple Evidence Combination. In *SIGIR 1997: Proceedings of the 20th Annual International ACM SIGIR Conference on Research and Development in Information Retrieval*, pages 267–276, New York, NY, USA, 1997. ACM Press.

4. J. Pehcevski, J. A. Thom and A-M. Vercoustre. Hybrid XML Retrieval: Combining Information Retrieval and a Native XML Database. *Information Retrieval*, Volume 8, Number 4, pages 571–600, 2005.
5. Jovan Pehcevski and James A. Thom. HiXEval: Highlighting XML Retrieval Evaluation. In *INEX 2005 Workshop Pre-Proceedings, Dagstuhl, Germany, November 28–30, 2005*, pages 11–24, 2005.
6. Jovan Pehcevski, James A. Thom and S. M. M. Tahaghoghi. RMIT University at INEX 2005. In *INEX 2005 Workshop Pre-Proceedings, Dagstuhl, Germany, November 28–30, 2005*, pages 217–233, 2005.
7. D. M. Squire, W. Müller, H. Müller and T. Pun. Content-based Query of Image Databases: Inspirations from Text Retrieval. *Pattern Recognition Letters*, Volume 21, Number 13–14, pages 1193–1198, 2000. (special edition for SCIA'99).
8. T. Tsikrika and M. Lalmas. Merging Techniques for Performing Data Fusion on the Web. In *CIKM 2004: Proceedings of the Tenth International Conference on Information and Knowledge Management*, pages 127–134, New York, NY, USA, 2001. ACM Press.
9. C. C. Vogt and G. W. Cottrell. Predicting the Performance of Linearly Combined IR Systems. In *SIGIR 1998: Proceedings of the 21st Annual International ACM SIGIR Conference on Research and Development in Information Retrieval*, pages 190–196, New York, NY, USA, 1998. ACM Press.

Multimedia Strategies for B^3-SDR, Based on Principal Component Analysis

Roelof van Zwol

Utrecht University, Department of Computer Science, Center for Content
and Knowledge Engineering, Utrecht, The Netherlands
roelof@cs.uu.nl

Abstract. In this article an XML-driven approach for multimedia information retrieval is presented and evaluated, which uses principal component analysis to derive a composite ranking for a set of XML elements that have a multimedia character. The multimedia strategies that implement the PCA module on top of the B^3-SDR system allow for the integration of image retrieval with the already present text retrieval modules.

Three different strategies are defined. The first strategy implements annotation-based image retrieval, which uses the caption of an image to find related images using a keyword-based search. The second component enables content-based multimedia retrieval by using PCA to derive a composite ranking, which reflects the combined relevance for text and images that are present within an XML element. A simple content-based image retrieval system is build for this purpose, which uses 'query by example'. The last strategy allows for a bidirectional combination of the first two strategies, where the content-based image retrieval component benefits from the additional images retrieved by the annotation-based search, and vice versa.

The multimedia strategies are evaluated within the INEX 2005 multimedia track, where based on the Lonelyplanet Worldguide and a set of related topics the retrieval performance is measured in terms of recall and precision. The outcome of the experiment shows that the multimedia strategies have a positive influence on the retrieval performance when compared to the text-based XML retrieval system. However, the PCA component did not yet fully live up to its expectation, which is probably due to the poor performance of the ad hoc build image retrieval system that is used for the experiment.

1 Introduction

Structured document retrieval allows for the retrieval of document fragments, i.e. XML elements, containing relevant information [1]. The main INEX ad-hoc task focusses on text-based XML element retrieval. Although text is dominantly present in most XML document collections, other types of media can also be found in those collections. Existing research on multimedia information retrieval [2, 3] has already shown that it is far from trivial to determine the combined relevance of a document that contains several multimedia objects. The

N. Fuhr et al. (Eds.): INEX 2005, LNCS 3977, pp. 540–553, 2006.

objective here is to exploit the XML structure that provides a logical level at which multimedia objects are connected, to improve the retrieval performance of an XML-driven multimedia information retrieval system.

To enable XML-driven multimedia retrieval, i.e. to derive a composite ranking that combines the relevance of both text and images that are present with an XML element, principal component analysis (PCA) is used by the B^3-SDR system. PCA [4] is a classical statistical method that has been widely used in data analysis and compression [5]. In short, it provides us the means to transform an N-dimensional data set to a representation in space with a lower dimensionality, while minimizing the error introduced due to the projection. Alternatively, a composite ranking for an XML element can be derived, by using (static) weights for each media object that is present in the collection [6]. However, this can only work, if one assumes that the contribution of the different media types is constant for various information needs. When using PCA, the distribution of these weights varies for the different information requests, and depends on the nature of the individual rankings for each media type. It is therefore expected that this will result in a more natural composite ranking, which better fits the user's information need.

For the integration of image retrieval into the B^3-SDR system, a custom-build image retrieval component is used that allows for:

1. annotation-based search [7] on the caption of images, given an example image or keyword combination.
2. content-based image retrieval[8, 9], where a combination of image features is used to determine the visual relevance of an image to an example image.

The following combinations of text and image retrieval are used to extend the B^3-SDR system:

- Annotation-based image retrieval. Initiated by a keyword search, the captions of images are matched to retrieve relevant images. This component is only activated, whenever an **image** or **map** element is requested.
- PCA-based text and image retrieval. If an **image** or **map** element is requested, two queries are executed. A textual search is executed, using the keywords of the information request, and a content-based image search is performed using the example image provided in the request. PCA is then used to derive a composite ranking of XML elements for both results sets.
- PCA-cross retrieval. This strategy combines the first two approaches. It initiates the annotation-based image retrieval, using both the keywords and the caption of the example image, and extends the content-based image retrieval step with the results found for the annotation-based search. In other words, it uses (bidirectional) query expansion.

The above defined strategies are evaluated in the INEX 2005 Multimedia track [10]. The objective of the track is to retrieve relevant document fragments based on an information need with a structured multimedia character. A structured document retrieval approach in that case should be able to combine the relevances of the different media types into a single (meaningful) ranking that is presented to the user. The INEX multimedia track differs from other approaches in multimedia information retrieval [2, 11, 12], in the sense that it focuses on using the structure of the document to extract, relate, and combine the relevances of different multimedia fragments. The focus for 2005 is on the combination of text and image retrieval, using a strict interpretation of the structural components of the specified information need.

The retrieval strategies are evaluated in a retrieval performance experiment that is coordinated by the INEX 2005 Multimedia track. For the experiment the Lonelyplanet Worldguide is used, which is an XML document collection that uses semantic tagging [13] and contains a combination of text fragments and images discussing useful information about various destinations on our planet. The retrieval performance is measured in terms of recall and precision [14] using a set of 17 topics. More details about the experimental setup can be found in [10].

Organisation

In the remainder of this article an introduction to principal component analysis is given in Section 2. It discusses some theoretical background and presents a step-by-step approach for using PCA in the context of XML-driven multimedia information retrieval. Section 3 discusses the different multimedia strategies that are evaluated in the retrieval performance experiment. The result of the experiment is discussed in Section 4, and finally, the conclusions are presented in Section 5.

2   Introduction to Principal Component Analysis

Principal component analysis (PCA) [4, 5] is a mathematical procedure that transforms a multivariate data set that contains a number of (possibly) correlated variables into a (smaller) number of uncorrelated variables called principal components. The objective of principal component analysis is to reduce the dimensionality (number of variables) of the dataset but retain most of the original variability in the data. The first principal component accounts for as much of the variability in the data as possible, and each succeeding component accounts for as much of the remaining variability as possible.

2.1   Theoretical Background

Analysis of multivariate data plays a key role in data analysis. Multivariate data consists of many different attributes or variables recorded for each observation. If there are N variables in a data set, each variable could be regarded as constituting a different dimension, in a N-dimensional space. Multi-dimensional space is often difficult to visualize, and thus the main objectives of unsupervised learning methods are to reduce dimensionality, scoring all observations based on a composite index and clustering similar observations together based on multi-attributes. In the context of multimedia information retrieval, the objective is to derive a 1-dimensional space, i.e. a ranking, that best describes a composite relevance for each XML fragment, containing 1 or more different multimedia objects.

PCA summarizes the variation in a correlated multi-attribute to a set of un-correlated components, each of which is a particular linear combination of the original variables. The extracted uncorrelated components are called principal components and are estimated from the eigenvectors of the covariance or cor-relation matrix of the original variables. Therefore, the objective of PCA is to achieve parsimony and reduce dimensionality by extracting the smallest number of components that account for most of the variation in the original multivariate data and to summarize the data with little loss of information [4].

In PCA, un-correlated principal components are extracted by linear trans-formations of the original variables so that the first few principal components contain most of the variations in the original data set. These principal compo-nents are extracted in decreasing order of importance so that the first principal component accounts for as much of the variation as possible and each successive component accounts for a little less.

To reproduce the total system variability of the original N variables, we need all N principal components. However, if the first few principal components ac-count for a large proportion of the variability (80-90%), the objective of dimen-sion reduction is successfully achieved. Because the first principal component accounts for the co-variation shared by all attributes, this may be a better es-timate than simple or weighted averages of the original variables. Thus, PCA can be useful when there is a high-degree of correlation is present in the multi-attributes.

2.2   Step-by-Step

To produce a composite ranking for the different media that can be present in an XML fragment, the following PCA procedure is used.

Step 1. Derive a (synchronised) ranking for each media type. First, a ranking is produced for each media type present in the document collection, given a user information need. In the case of the INEX 2005 Multimedia track, a text-based ranking and an image-based ranking of XML elements is produced for each information request. In case of the image-retrieval component, the ranking is based on the distance of an image to the information need, i.e. example image. A low distance score for an image, corresponds with a high relevance score for the (underlying) XML element. If a non-zero relevance score is obtained for an XML element in both rankings, the element apparently contains both textual and visual relevant information. If a relevance score is only contained in one of the rankings, a zero score for that element is added to the other ranking. After this step, both rankings contain the same set of XML elements, over which the PCA will be performed.

Consider the two example rankings T and I of Table 1. T represents a ranking of XML elements based on the textual relevance, while I represents a ranking of XML elements for the image-based component.

Table 1. Example rankings T and I, during various stages of the PCA procedure

Element	T	I	T'	I'	T''	I''
A	10.30	1.50	1.00	0.74	0.51	0.21
B	8.60	1.20	0.79	0.58	0.30	0.05
C	8.40	0.60	0.77	0.26	0.28	-0.27
D	6.70	1.80	0.56	0.89	0.07	0.36
E	6.50	2.00	0.54	1.00	0.05	0.47
F	5.90	0.30	0.46	0.11	-0.03	-0.42
G	4.80	1.00	0.33	0.47	-0.16	-0.06
H	4.70	0.90	0.32	0.42	-0.17	-0.11
I	3.20	1.70	0.13	0.84	-0.36	0.31
J	2.10	0.10	0.00	0.00	-0.49	-0.53
			$T' = 0.49$	$I' = 0.53$		

Step 2. Apply a min-max normalisation to each ranking. A min-max normalisation [15] step is applied to both rankings, such that they both span the $[0,1]$ range. The columns T' and I' contain the normalised rankings of T and I.

Step 3. Subtract the mean for each ranking. The means $\bar{T}$ and $\bar{I}$ are then calculated for both rankings using the formula:

$$\bar{X} = \frac{\sum_{i=1}^{n} X_i}{n} \tag{1}$$

The rankings are balanced around 0 by subtracting the mean relevance score from each of the scores in the ranking. The columns T'' and I'' of Table 1 contain the balanced normalised rankings of T and I. These steps are required to eventually calculate the eigenvectors.

Step 4. Calculate the covariance matrix. The covariance is used to measure the spread of data in a 2-dimensional dataset. If you calculate the covariance between one dimension and itself, you get the variance. The covariance between X and Y is calculated by:

$$cov(X, Y) = \frac{\sum_{i=1}^{n} (X_i - \bar{X})(Y_i - \bar{Y})}{n - 1} \tag{2}$$

The covariance matrix C is defined as:

$$C = (c_{i,j}, c_{i,j} = cov(Dim_i, Dim_j)), \tag{3}$$

where C is a matrix with n rows and n columns, and Dim_x is the xth dimension. Based on the rankings T' and I' the following covariance matrix is constructed:

$$C = \begin{bmatrix} cov(T', T') & cov(T', I') \\ cov(I', T') & cov(I', I') \end{bmatrix} = \begin{bmatrix} 0.095 & 0.028 \\ 0.028 & 0.116 \end{bmatrix}$$

Step 5. Calculate the eigenvalues and eigenvectors of the covariance matrix. Eigenvalues measure the amount of the variation explained by each principal component and will be largest for the first component and smaller for the subsequent components. An eigenvalue greater than 1 indicates that the principal component accounts for more variance than accounted by one of the original variables in the standardised data set [5]. This is commonly used as a cut-off point for which principal components are retained. This property is neglected here, because the outcome should always be a 1-dimensional space. As a consequence, if a low correlation is present, the produced ranking is not as accurate, i.e. reflects the user information need, as desired. Eigenvectors provide the weights to compute the un-correlated principal components, which are the linear combination of the standardized or un-standardized original variables. In this case, the centred standardised original variables (data set) is used. In principle, calculation of the eigenvalues λ and eigenvectors v is based on the property that:

$$Cv = \lambda v \tag{4}$$

Based on the 2×2 covariance matrix C this can be rewritten to:

$$\begin{vmatrix} 0.095 - \lambda & 0.028 \\ 0.028 & 0.116 - \lambda \end{vmatrix} = 0$$

$$\equiv \lambda^2 - 0.211\lambda + 0.01 = 0 \Rightarrow \lambda_1 = 0.135 OR \lambda_2 = 0.076$$

Note that for this example, both eigenvalues are small, which might indicate that the quality of the composite ranking is disputable. With both eigenvalues λ_1 and λ_2 known, the eigenvectors can be derived using:

$$v = \begin{bmatrix} -cov(T,T) \\ cov(T,I) - \lambda \end{bmatrix} \tag{5}$$

Applying this to λ_1 and λ_2 gives the corresponding eigenvectors:

$$v_1 = \begin{bmatrix} -0.095 \\ -0.107 \end{bmatrix} \wedge v_2 = \begin{bmatrix} -0.095 \\ -0.048 \end{bmatrix}$$

Step 6. Choose components and form a feature vector. The principal component is determined by selecting the largest eigenvalue. In this case: λ_1. A feature vector f is used to transform the original data set to the new data set, which has a lower dimension. In this case, the feature vector only consists of the eigenvector for the principal component: v_1. However, using this will not always produce the desired effect. Given the intuitition that an element with maximum score $(1,1)$ should always be ranking first, the feature vector should go through this point. This is visualised in Figure 1, using the normalised rankings T' and I'.

To derive the final composite ranking the follow formula is used:

$$PCA(T,I) = 1 - \left(\begin{bmatrix} T' \\ I' \end{bmatrix} - 1 \right) f, \tag{6}$$

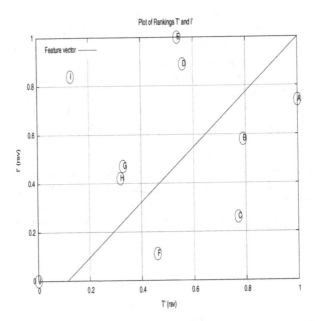

Fig. 1. Normalised rankings T' and I', with feature vector v_1 going through $(1,1)$

Where $\begin{bmatrix} T' \\ I' \end{bmatrix}$ is the matrix filled with the normalised rsv values for the rankings T' and I' and f refers to the feature vector. Applying this to the example gives the composite ranking as presented in Table 2. This ranking would be obtained when using an orthogonal transposition of each point plotted in Figure 1 onto the feature vector.

Step 7. Apply a min-max normalisation to the composite ranking. In the final step, a min-max normalisation step is applied to the PCA ranking to prepare the data for further processing.

3   Multimedia Strategies for B^3-SDR

In this section the four different strategies are described that are evaluated in Section 4. Beside the standard text retrieval module, the multimedia strategies described, allow the B^3-SDRsystem to search for images using image annotations, and to derive a composite ranking for multimedia information retrieval, based on PCA. Furthermore, the strategies can be combined, such that the content-based multimedia information retrieval component based on PCA can benefit from the annotation-based search.

Text-based Retrieval. A simple text-based run is submitted, which only uses the textual component of the information need to retrieve relevant information.

Table 2. The composite ranking derived for the example based on T and I, using PCA

Element	PCA(T,I)
A	0.97184
E	0.95598
D	0.94703
B	0.93525
I	0.90085
C	0.89915
G	0.87996
H	0.87317
F	0.85329
J	0.798

This strategy is intended to function as a base-line, which can be used to see if multimedia information retrieval on an XML-based document collection can lead to a higher retrieval performance in terms of recall and precision. More details on the text-based retrieval strategy can be found in [16].

Annotation-based Retrieval. For each image in the Lonelyplanet Worldguide, a caption, data and the name of the photographer is available. Without using any content-based image retrieval techniques, the captions of images can be used to perform an annotation-based search for relevant images. Given the example image defined in the information request, its caption is used to expand the original query terms of the information request, after which a simple text-based search is performed.

Content-based Multimedia Retrieval Using PCA. The PCA run splits the information request (query) into a text search and an image search, whenever an `image` or `map` element is requested. The results are filtered to match the requested element type, and PCA is used to derive a composite ranking. After having computed the intermediate results for the image/map elements, the additional constraints of the information request are applied.

Content-based Multimedia Retrieval Using PCA and Annotation Enhancement. The PCA-cross run combines the method for content-based information retrieval, based on PCA and the method for annotation-based retrieval. First additional images are retrieved using the image caption of the example image and the already defined keywords of the information request, when the annotation-based search is performed. The result of the annotation-based search is then used to expand the content-based image search with additional images.

4   Results

Evaluation of multimedia retrieval strategies in the Multimedia track is based on the official measures used for TREC. In this section the following is reported: summary table statistics, interpolated recall-precision averages, precision at document cut-off levels and an analysis of the performance per topic.

4.1   Summary Table Statistics

In Table 3 the summary table statistics are presented. For the official evaluation
of the multimedia track 17 topics have been included. The Text-based strategy,
however could not compute a ranking for four topics, due to the multimedia
character of the information need. This is a first indication that if the user has
a (complex) multimedia information need, existing techniques, based on text
retrieval, will not be satisfactory.

Table 3. Summary table statistics

Measures	Text	Annotation	PCA	PCA-cross
Topics	13	17	17	17
Retrieved	601	1112	1550	1291
Relevant	188	390	390	390
Relevant retrieved	88	216	216	**220**
MAP	0.2329	**0.2392**	0.1769	0.2324
Precision@10	0.2615	0.2706	0.2235	**0.2824**
bpref	0.4467	0.5113	0.5041	**0.5145**

In total 390 XML elements are judged relevant for the 17 topics, and the
PCA-cross strategy managed to retrieve the highest number of relevance elements (220). The mean average precision (MAP) indicates that a best overall
performance has been obtained with the Annotation-based strategy, while the
Precision@10 and bpref measures slightly favour the PCA-cross strategy. Unfortunately, the plain PCA run does not lead to an increase in retrieval performance
in terms of precision when compared to the Text-based strategy. However recall
is slightly better for the PCA run.

4.2   Interpolated Recall-Precision Averages

Figure 2 shows the interpolated precision averages at eleven standard recall levels.
From the figure, it can be clearly seen that using the image annotations has a
positive effect on the precision, when inspecting the lower recall levels. It appears
that the Text-based run has higher overall performance than the PCA run. The
PCA-cross run however can compete with the Text-based run and the Annotation-
based run. Note that the results of Figure 2 are distorted, in favor of the Text-based
run. The four missing topics for the Text-based run are not taken into account at
this point. Therefore the Text-based strategy should be ignored here.

4.3   Precision @ Document Cut-Off Levels

Based on the precision at document cut-off levels, it is possible to investigate
the ability of a system to retrieve relevant document at the top of the ranking.
This is plotted in Figure 3 for the four runs. The figure clearly shows that the
Annotation-based, PCA, and PCA-cross strategies, are performing better than
the Text-based strategy, which indicates that it is indeed useful to do XML-based
multimedia information retrieval.

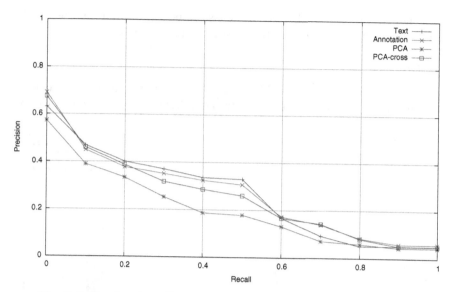

Fig. 2. Interpolated recall-precision averages over 11 standard recall levels

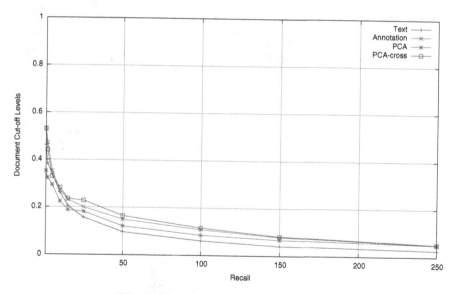

Fig. 3. Precision @ document cut-off levels

Another observation, which can be made based on Figure 3 is that the precision for the PCA-cross strategy exceeds that of the Annotation-based strategy, especially after having seen the top 25 documents. Which is the first real indication that PCA can be useful for multimedia information retrieval, if the correlation of the results between the textual search and the image-based search is high enough. However, no hard conclusions can be drawn from this observation and further research is necessary to investigate this behaviour.

4.4 Topic Analysis

The topic analysis presented in this section is used to gain more insight in the behaviour of the different strategies over the individual topics. Figure 4 shows

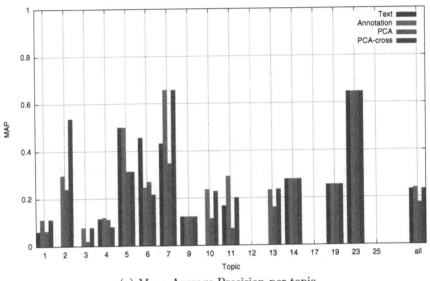

(a) Mean Average Precision per topic.

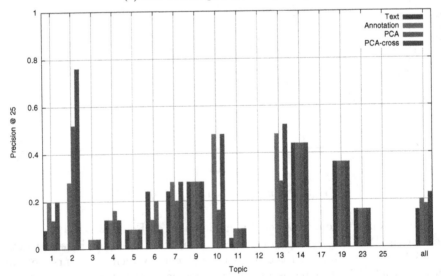

(b) Precision per topic after having seen 25 documents (P@25).

Fig. 4. Topic analysis

two box plots, the first plot presents the result per topic, based on the mean average precision (MAP), while the second plot is used to examine the behaviour of the strategies for the precision@25, which was marked as an interesting point in the previous subsection, due to the performance of the PCA-cross run.

The results of Figure 4.a show that none of the strategies is capable to produce a (relevant) result for topics 12, 17, and 19. This is mainly caused, by the strict and complex nature of the information need. Furthermore, the image retrieval system is performing really poor on the retrieval of maps. According to the system, all maps are equally (ir)relevant. A second observation with respect to the Text-based run is that with a text-based search best performance is achieved for topics 4 and 6, while for topics 2, 3, 10, and 13 text retrieval is not sufficient.

Based on the MAP, the PCA strategy is never the best option, and comparison of the Annotation-based strategy with the PCA-cross strategy show that the PCA-strategy definitely benefits from the use of image annotations. The only positive outlier is found for topic 2, where the PCA-cross strategy outperforms the other strategies.

The results of Figure 4.b show the precision per topic after having seen the top 25 documents of the ranking. At this point, the PCA-cross approach has the best performance over all topics. This is mainly due to performance on topics 2, 4, 7, 10, and 13. Closer examination, reveals that the PCA module has a positive influence on the performance for topics 2, 4, but this is contradicted by the performance for topics 7, 10 and 13. In that case the performance of the PCA-cross strategy seems to depend on the use of annotation-based search. Interesting to see is that the PCA-cross strategy never performs less then the Annotation-based strategy.

5   Conclusions

The increasing amount of multimedia content that is present on the (Semantic) Web and in XML document collections demands for more sophisticated retrieval techniques that enable multimedia information retrieval. In this article an XML-driven approach for multimedia information retrieval is presented and evaluated, which uses principal component analysis to derive a composite ranking for a set of XML elements that have a multimedia character. The multimedia strategies that implement the PCA module on top of the B^3-SDR system allow for the integration of image retrieval with the already present text retrieval modules.

PCA is a proven technique to reduce the dimensionality of a multi-variate point set for various application domains, but has not yet been used in the context of (XML-based) multimedia information retrieval. In this article it is shown how PCA can be used to derive a composite ranking for multimedia document fragments. Theory shows that PCA is especially useful if principal components can be found that have large eigenvalues ($\lambda > 1$). Otherwise there is a strong indication that the correlation between the variables, in this case the textual and image-base ranking, is low.

Various combinations have been tested to validate the ideas for XML-based multimedia information retrieval, using PCA as the combining component. A Text-based strategy has been used to function as a base-line against which is measured if multimedia information retrieval can successfully be performed on an XML document collection. The results are promising, however not that overwhelming. Retrieval performance can be clearly improved with Annotation-based strategy for image retrieval based on the captions of images. Using a plain PCA strategy to combine text retrieval and content-based image retrieval did not lead to better results, however when using the PCA-cross strategy performance did improve, especially when compared to the Annotation-based strategy for the top of the ranking (P@25).

A number of reasons can be identified which might explain the somewhat disappointing results for the PCA-based approaches. One of which will probably be the poor performance of the image retrieval system used. Current state of the art in image retrieval does a better job on efficiently combining different features [9], but also region detection and object recognition [3] in images will definitely help to improve the image retrieval component. Another aspect, which lays beyond the limitations of the system, is that the Lonelyplanet Worldguide has a relatively small image collection. Increasing the size of the image collection is also likely to lead to improved results.

Acknowledgements

The Lonelyplanet organisation provided the Worldguide XML document collection that is used for this research. We are thankful for their co-operation, which allowed us to work with real-data and which has lead to new insights in XML-based multimedia information retrieval.

References

1. Fuhr, N., Lalmas, M., Malik, S., Szlvik, Z., eds.: Advances in XML Information Retrieval. Volume 3493 of Lecture Notes in Computer Science. Springer (2005)
2. Smeaton, A., Kraaij, W., Over, P.: The trec video retrieval evaluation (trecvid): A case study and status report. In: Coupling approaches, coupling media and coupling languages for information retrieval - RIAO 2004, Vaucluse, France (2004) 25 – 37
3. Westerveld, T.: Using generative probabilistic models for multimedia retrieval. PhD thesis, University of Twente, Enschede, The Netherlands (2004)
4. Smith, L.I.: A Tutorial on Principal Component Analysis (2002)
5. Fernandez, G.: Data Mining Using SAS Applications. Taylor & francis CRC Press (2002)
6. Iskandar, D., Pehcevski, J., J.A.Thom, Tahaghoghi, S.: Combining Image and Structured Text Retrieval. In: Advances in XML Information Retrieval. Lecture Notes in Computer Science, Springer (2006)
7. E. Hyvonen, A. Styrman, S.S.: Ontology-Based Image Retrieval. In: Towards the semantic web and web services, Proceedings of XML Finland 2002 Conference. (2002) 15 – 27

8. Flickner, M., Sawhney, H., Niblack, W., Ashley, J., Huang, Q., Dom, B., Gorkani, M., Hafner, J., Lee, D., Petkovic, D., Steele, D., Yanker, P.: Query by image and video content: The qbic system. IEEE Computer **28**(9) (1995) 23 – 32

9. Urban, J., Jose, J.M., van Rijsbergen, C.: An Adaptive Technique for Content-Based Image Retrieval. In: Multimedia Tools and Applications, Kluwer (2005)

10. van Zwol, R., Kazai, G., Lalmas, M.: INEX 2005 Multimedia Track. In: Advances in XML Information Retrieval. Lecture Notes in Computer Science, Springer (2006)

11. Yang, J., Zhuang, Y., Li, Q.: Multi-Modal Retrieval for Multimedia Digital Libraries: Issues, Architecture, and Mechanisms. In: Multimedia Information Systems, Capri, Italy (2001) 81 – 88

12. D., F., Siu, W.C., Zhang, H.J., eds.: Multimedia Information Retrieval and Management: Technological Fundamentals and Applications, Berlin, Germany, Springer (2003)

13. van Zwol, R., Baas, J., van Oostendorp, H., Wiering, F.: Bricks - the Building Blocks to Tackle Query Formulation in Structured Document Retrieval. In: Proceedings of the 28th European Conference on Information Retrieval. Lecture Notes in Computer Science, London, UK, Springer (2006)

14. Baeza-Yates, R.A., Ribeiro-Neto, B.: Modern Information Retrieval. Addison-Wesley Longman Publishing Co., Inc., Boston, MA, USA (1999)

15. Jain, A., Nandakumar, K., Ross, A.: Score normalisation in multimodal biometric systems. Pattern Recognition **38**(12) (2005) 2270–2285

16. van Zwol, R.: B3-SDR and Effective Use of Structural Hints. In: Advances in XML Information Retrieval. Lecture Notes in Computer Science, Springer (2006)

Author Index

Amagasa, Toshiyuki   254
Arvola, Paavo   134
Awang Iskandar, D.N.F.   525
Azevedo, Maria Izabel Menezes   388

Blok, Henk Ernst   72
Bouchachia, Abdelhamid   119
Boughanem, Mohand   88

Callan, Jamie   211
Candillier, Laurent   469
Crouch, Carolyn J.   268

de Vries, Arjen P.   72
Doddapaneni, Nagendra   268
Dopichaj, Philipp   196

Fegas, Mounir   443
Fuhr, Norbert   1
Fujimoto, Kei   254

Gallinari, Patrick   336
Garboni, Calin   458
Geva, Shlomo   240, 358, 511
Gori, M.   481
Gu, J.   511
Gul, Saba   443

Hagenbuchner, M.   481
Hassler, Marcus   119
Hatano, Kenji   254
Hiemstra, Djoerd   72
Hlaoua, Lobna   88
Hubert, Gilles   172

Junkkari, Marko   134

Kamps, Jaap   104, 411
Kazai, Gabriella   1, 16, 497
Kekäläinen, Jaana   134
Khanna, Sudip   268
Kim, Heesop   422
Kinutani, Hiroko   254

Lalmas, Mounia   1, 16, 58, 497
Larsen, Birger   398
Larson, Ray R.   225
Lechevallier, Yves   443
Lehtonen, Miro   296
Lu, Wei   161

MacFarlane, Andrew   161
Malik, Saadia   1, 398
Mandelbrod, Matan   187
Marteau, Pierre-François   321
Mass, Yosi   187
Masseglia, Florent   458
Ménier, Gildas   321
Mihajlović, Vojkan   72

Nayak, Richi   432
Nguyen, A.   511

Ogilvie, Paul   211

Paixão, Klérisson Vinícius Ribeiro   388
Pehcevski, Jovan   43, 306, 525
Pereira, Diego Vinícius Castro   388
Piwowarski, Benjamin   30
Popovici, Eugen   321
Potnis, Poorva   268

Ramírez, Georgina   72
Robertson, Stephen   161

Sauvagnat, Karen   88
Scarselli, F.   481
Schenkel, Ralf   282, 344
Shimizu, Toshiyuki   254
Sigurbjörnsson, Börkur   104, 411
Son, Heejung   422
Sperduti, A.   481
Suzuki, Yu   254

Tahaghoghi, S.M.M.   306, 525
Tannier, Xavier   373
Tellier, Isabelle   469
Terada, Norimasa   254
Theobald, Martin   282, 344
Thom, James A.   43, 306, 525
Tjondronegoro, D.   511

Tombros, Anastasios   398
Torre, Fabien   469
Trentini, F.   481
Trotman, Andrew   58
Trousse, Brigitte   458
Tsoi, A.C.   481

van Zwol, Roelof   146, 497, 540
Vercoustre, Anne-Marie   443
Vittaut, Jean-Noël   336

Weikum, Gerhard   282
Westerveld, Thijs   72
Woodley, Alan   358

Xu, Sumei   432

Yoshikawa, Masatoshi   254

Zhang, J.   511

Lecture Notes in Computer Science

For information about Vols. 1–3942

please contact your bookseller or Springer

Vol. 4053: M. Ikeda, K.D. Ashley, T.-W. Chan (Eds.), Intelligent Tutoring System. XXII, 821 pages. 2006.

Vol. 4044: P. Abrahamsson, M. Marchesi, G. Succi (Eds.), Extreme Programming and Agile Processes in Software Engineering. XII, 230 pages. 2006.

Vol. 4043: A.S. Atzeni, A. Lioy (Eds.), Public Key Infrastructure. XI, 261 pages. 2006.

Vol. 4041: S.-W. Cheng, C.K. Poon (Eds.), Algorithmic Applications in Management. XI, 395 pages. 2006.

Vol. 4040: U. Eckardt, B. Flach, U. Knauer, K. Polthier, R. Reulke (Eds.), Combinatorial Image Analysis. XI, 504 pages. 2006.

Vol. 4039: M. Morisio (Ed.), Reuse of Off-the-Shelf Components. XIII, 444 pages. 2006.

Vol. 4038: P. Ciancarini, H. Wiklicky (Eds.), Coordination Models and Languages. VIII, 299 pages. 2006.

Vol. 4037: R. Gorrieri, H. Wehrheim (Eds.), Formal Methods for Open Object-Based Distributed Systems. XVII, 474 pages. 2006.

Vol. 4034: J. Münch, M. Vierimaa (Eds.), Product-Focused Software Process Improvement. XVII, 474 pages. 2006.

Vol. 4027: H.L. Larsen, G. Pasi, D. Ortiz-Arroyo, T. Andreasen, H. Christiansen (Eds.), Flexible Query Answering Systems. XVIII, 714 pages. 2006. (Sublibrary LNAI).

Vol. 4026: P. Gibbons, T. Abdelzaher, J. Aspnes, R. Rao (Eds.), Distributed Computing in Sensor Systems. XIV, 566 pages. 2006.

Vol. 4025: F. Eliassen, A. Montresor (Eds.), Distributed Applications and Interoperable Systems. XI, 355 pages. 2006.

Vol. 4024: S. Donatelli, P. S. Thiagarajan (Eds.), Petri Nets and Other Models of Concurrency - ICATPN 2006. XI, 441 pages. 2006.

Vol. 4021: E. André, L. Dybkjær, W. Minker, H. Neumann, M. Weber (Eds.), Perception and Interactive Technologies. XI, 217 pages. 2006. (Sublibrary LNAI).

Vol. 4018: V. Wade, H. Ashman, B. Smyth (Eds.), Adaptive Hypermedia and Adaptive Web-Based Systems. XVI, 474 pages. 2006.

Vol. 4016: J.X. Yu, M. Kitsuregawa, H.V. Leong (Eds.), Advances in Web-Age Information Management. XVII, 606 pages. 2006.

Vol. 4013: L. Lamontagne, M. Marchand (Eds.), Advances in Artificial Intelligence. XIII, 564 pages. 2006. (Sublibrary LNAI).

Vol. 4011: Y. Sure, J. Domingue (Eds.), The Semantic Web: Research and Applications. XIX, 726 pages. 2006.

Vol. 4010: S. Dunne, B. Stoddart (Eds.), Unifying Theories of Programming. VIII, 257 pages. 2006.

Vol. 4007: C. Àlvarez, M. Serna (Eds.), Experimental Algorithms. XI, 329 pages. 2006.

Vol. 4006: L.M. Pinho, M. González Harbour (Eds.), Reliable Software Technologies – Ada-Europe 2006. XII, 241 pages. 2006.

Vol. 4004: S. Vaudenay (Ed.), Advances in Cryptology - EUROCRYPT 2006. XIV, 613 pages. 2006.

Vol. 4003: Y. Koucheryavy, J. Harju, V.B. Iversen (Eds.), Next Generation Teletraffic and Wired/Wireless Advanced Networking. XVI, 582 pages. 2006.

Vol. 4001: E. Dubois, K. Pohl (Eds.), Advanced Information Systems Engineering. XVI, 560 pages. 2006.

Vol. 3999: C. Kop, G. Fliedl, H.C. Mayr, E. Métais (Eds.), Natural Language Processing and Information Systems. XIII, 227 pages. 2006.

Vol. 3998: T. Calamoneri, I. Finocchi, G.F. Italiano (Eds.), Algorithms and Complexity. XII, 394 pages. 2006.

Vol. 3997: W. Grieskamp, C. Weise (Eds.), Formal Approaches to Software Testing. XII, 219 pages. 2006.

Vol. 3996: A. Keller, J.-P. Martin-Flatin (Eds.), Self-Managed Networks, Systems, and Services. X, 185 pages. 2006.

Vol. 3995: G. Müller (Ed.), Emerging Trends in Information and Communication Security. XX, 524 pages. 2006.

Vol. 3994: V.N. Alexandrov, G.D. van Albada, P.M.A. Sloot, J. Dongarra (Eds.), Computational Science – ICCS 2006, Part IV. XXXV, 1096 pages. 2006.

Vol. 3993: V.N. Alexandrov, G.D. van Albada, P.M.A. Sloot, J. Dongarra (Eds.), Computational Science – ICCS 2006, Part III. XXXVI, 1136 pages. 2006.

Vol. 3992: V.N. Alexandrov, G.D. van Albada, P.M.A. Sloot, J. Dongarra (Eds.), Computational Science – ICCS 2006, Part II. XXXV, 1122 pages. 2006.

Vol. 3991: V.N. Alexandrov, G.D. van Albada, P.M.A. Sloot, J. Dongarra (Eds.), Computational Science – ICCS 2006, Part I. LXXXI, 1096 pages. 2006.

Vol. 3990: J. C. Beck, B.M. Smith (Eds.), Integration of AI and OR Techniques in Constraint Programming for Combinatorial Optimization Problems. X, 301 pages. 2006.

Vol. 3989: J. Zhou, M. Yung, F. Bao, Applied Cryptography and Network Security. XIV, 488 pages. 2006.

Vol. 3987: M. Hazas, J. Krumm, T. Strang (Eds.), Location- and Context-Awareness. X, 289 pages. 2006.

Vol. 3986: K. Stølen, W.H. Winsborough, F. Martinelli, F. Massacci (Eds.), Trust Management. XIV, 474 pages. 2006.

Vol. 3984: M. Gavrilova, O. Gervasi, V. Kumar, C.J. K. Tan, D. Taniar, A. Laganà, Y. Mun, H. Choo (Eds.), Computational Science and Its Applications - ICCSA 2006, Part V. XXV, 1045 pages. 2006.

Vol. 3983: M. Gavrilova, O. Gervasi, V. Kumar, C.J. K. Tan, D. Taniar, A. Laganà, Y. Mun, H. Choo (Eds.), Computational Science and Its Applications - ICCSA 2006, Part IV. XXVI, 1191 pages. 2006.

Vol. 3982: M. Gavrilova, O. Gervasi, V. Kumar, C.J. K. Tan, D. Taniar, A. Laganà, Y. Mun, H. Choo (Eds.), Computational Science and Its Applications - ICCSA 2006, Part III. XXV, 1243 pages. 2006.

Vol. 3981: M. Gavrilova, O. Gervasi, V. Kumar, C.J. K. Tan, D. Taniar, A. Laganà, Y. Mun, H. Choo (Eds.), Computational Science and Its Applications - ICCSA 2006, Part II. XXVI, 1255 pages. 2006.

Vol. 3980: M. Gavrilova, O. Gervasi, V. Kumar, C.J. K. Tan, D. Taniar, A. Laganà, Y. Mun, H. Choo (Eds.), Computational Science and Its Applications - ICCSA 2006, Part I. LXXV, 1199 pages. 2006.

Vol. 3979: T.S. Huang, N. Sebe, M.S. Lew, V. Pavlović, M. Kölsch, A. Galata, B. Kisačanin (Eds.), Computer Vision in Human-Computer Interaction. XII, 121 pages. 2006.

Vol. 3978: B. Hnich, M. Carlsson, F. Fages, F. Rossi (Eds.), Recent Advances in Constraints. VIII, 179 pages. 2006. (Sublibrary LNAI).

Vol. 3977: N. Fuhr, M. Lalmas, S. Malik, G. Kazai (Eds.), Advances in XML Information Retrieval and Evaluation. XII, 556 pages. 2006.

Vol. 3976: F. Boavida, T. Plagemann, B. Stiller, C. Westphal, E. Monteiro (Eds.), Networking 2006. Networking Technologies, Services, and Protocols; Performance of Computer and Communication Networks; Mobile and Wireless Communications Systems. XXVI, 1276 pages. 2006.

Vol. 3975: S. Mehrotra, D.D. Zeng, H. Chen, B.M. Thuraisingham, F.-Y. Wang (Eds.), Intelligence and Security Informatics. XXII, 772 pages. 2006.

Vol. 3973: J. Wang, Z. Yi, J.M. Zurada, B.-L. Lu, H. Yin (Eds.), Advances in Neural Networks - ISNN 2006, Part III. XXIX, 1402 pages. 2006.

Vol. 3972: J. Wang, Z. Yi, J.M. Zurada, B.-L. Lu, H. Yin (Eds.), Advances in Neural Networks - ISNN 2006, Part II. XXVII, 1444 pages. 2006.

Vol. 3971: J. Wang, Z. Yi, J.M. Zurada, B.-L. Lu, H. Yin (Eds.), Advances in Neural Networks - ISNN 2006, Part I. LXVII, 1442 pages. 2006.

Vol. 3970: T. Braun, G. Carle, S. Fahmy, Y. Koucheryavy (Eds.), Wired/Wireless Internet Communications. XIV, 350 pages. 2006.

Vol. 3968: K.P. Fishkin, B. Schiele, P. Nixon, A. Quigley (Eds.), Pervasive Computing. XV, 402 pages. 2006.

Vol. 3967: D. Grigoriev, J. Harrison, E.A. Hirsch (Eds.), Computer Science – Theory and Applications. XVI, 684 pages. 2006.

Vol. 3966: Q. Wang, D. Pfahl, D.M. Raffo, P. Wernick (Eds.), Software Process Change. XIV, 356 pages. 2006.

Vol. 3965: M. Bernardo, A. Cimatti (Eds.), Formal Methods for Hardware Verification. VII, 243 pages. 2006.

Vol. 3964: M. Ü. Uyar, A.Y. Duale, M.A. Fecko (Eds.), Testing of Communicating Systems. XI, 373 pages. 2006.

Vol. 3963: O. Dikenelli, M.-P. Gleizes, A. Ricci (Eds.), Engineering Societies in the Agents World VI. XII, 303 pages. 2006. (Sublibrary LNAI).

Vol. 3962: W. IJsselsteijn, Y. de Kort, C. Midden, B. Eggen, E. van den Hoven (Eds.), Persuasive Technology. XII, 216 pages. 2006.

Vol. 3960: R. Vieira, P. Quaresma, M.d.G.V. Nunes, N.J. Mamede, C. Oliveira, M.C. Dias (Eds.), Computational Processing of the Portuguese Language. XII, 274 pages. 2006. (Sublibrary LNAI).

Vol. 3959: J.-Y. Cai, S. B. Cooper, A. Li (Eds.), Theory and Applications of Models of Computation. XV, 794 pages. 2006.

Vol. 3958: M. Yung, Y. Dodis, A. Kiayias, T. Malkin (Eds.), Public Key Cryptography - PKC 2006. XIV, 543 pages. 2006.

Vol. 3956: G. Barthe, B. Grégoire, M. Huisman, J.-L. Lanet (Eds.), Construction and Analysis of Safe, Secure, and Interoperable Smart Devices. IX, 175 pages. 2006.

Vol. 3955: G. Antoniou, G. Potamias, C. Spyropoulos, D. Plexousakis (Eds.), Advances in Artificial Intelligence. XVII, 611 pages. 2006. (Sublibrary LNAI).

Vol. 3954: A. Leonardis, H. Bischof, A. Pinz (Eds.), Computer Vision – ECCV 2006, Part IV. XVII, 613 pages. 2006.

Vol. 3953: A. Leonardis, H. Bischof, A. Pinz (Eds.), Computer Vision – ECCV 2006, Part III. XVII, 649 pages. 2006.

Vol. 3952: A. Leonardis, H. Bischof, A. Pinz (Eds.), Computer Vision – ECCV 2006, Part II. XVII, 661 pages. 2006.

Vol. 3951: A. Leonardis, H. Bischof, A. Pinz (Eds.), Computer Vision – ECCV 2006, Part I. XXXV, 639 pages. 2006.

Vol. 3950: J.P. Müller, F. Zambonelli (Eds.), Agent-Oriented Software Engineering VI. XVI, 249 pages. 2006.

Vol. 3948: H.I Christensen, H.-H. Nagel (Eds.), Cognitive Vision Systems. VIII, 367 pages. 2006.

Vol. 3947: Y.-C. Chung, J.E. Moreira (Eds.), Advances in Grid and Pervasive Computing. XXI, 667 pages. 2006.

Vol. 3946: T.R. Roth-Berghofer, S. Schulz, D.B. Leake (Eds.), Modeling and Retrieval of Context. XI, 149 pages. 2006. (Sublibrary LNAI).

Vol. 3945: M. Hagiya, P. Wadler (Eds.), Functional and Logic Programming. X, 295 pages. 2006.

Vol. 3944: J. Quiñonero-Candela, I. Dagan, B. Magnini, F. d'Alché-Buc (Eds.), Machine Learning Challenges. XIII, 462 pages. 2006. (Sublibrary LNAI).

Vol. 3943: N. Guelfi, A. Savidis (Eds.), Rapid Integration of Software Engineering Techniques. X, 289 pages. 2006.